Managing Your
Personal Finances

7e

EDUCATION

CREDIT CARD

TAXES

INSURANCE

VACATION

401K

MORTGAGE

RETIREMENT

Joan S. Ryan

M.B.A., Ph.D., C.M.A.

Clackamas Community College
Oregon City, Oregon

Christie Ryan

MA, LMHC

Institute for Family Development
Vancouver, WA

SOUTH-WESTERN
CENGAGE Learning·

Australia · Brazil · Mexico · Singapore · United Kingdom · United States

SOUTH-WESTERN
CENGAGE Learning·

**Managing Your Personal Finances,
Seventh Edition**
Joan S. Ryan and Christie Ryan

SVP, Global Product Management, Research, School & Professional: Frank Menchaca

General Manager, K-12 School Group: CarolAnn Shindelar

Publishing Director: Eve Lewis

Acquisitions Editor: Jeff Werle

Senior Development Editor: Diane Bowdler

Consulting Editor: Peggy Shelton, LEAP Publishing Services

Editorial Assistant: Deb Roark

Marketing Director: Jeremy Walts

Product Marketing Manager: Kelsey Hagan

Art and Cover Direction, Production Management, and Composition: Lumina Datamatics, Inc.

Media Editor: Tristann Jones

Intellectual Property

   Analyst: Kyle Cooper

   Project Manager: Michelle McKenna

Manufacturing Planner: Kevin Kluck

Cover Image:

RF: Image # 182472506
© Andrew Johnson/Getty Images
description: jigsaw puzzle

Photo Researcher: Darren Wright

For product information and technology assistance, contact us at
Cengage Learning Customer & Sales Support, 1-800-354-9706

For permission to use material from this text or product,
submit all requests online at **www.cengage.com/permissions**
Further permissions questions can be emailed to
permissionrequest@cengage.com

ISBN: 978-1-305-07681-5

Cengage Learning
20 Channel Center Street
Boston, MA 02210
USA

Unless otherwise noted, all items © Cengage Learning.

The Career Clusters icons are being used with permission of the States' Career Clusters Initiative, 2010, **www.careerclusters.org**

Cengage Learning is a leading provider of customized learning solutions with office locations around the globe, including Singapore, the United Kingdom, Australia, Mexico, Brazil, and Japan. Locate your local office at: **www.cengage.com/global**

Cengage Learning products are represented in Canada by Nelson Education, Ltd.

For your course and learning solutions, visit **ngl.cengage.com**

Visit our company website at **www.cengage.com**

Printed in the United States of America
Print Number: 01   Print Year: 2015

Secure Students' Financial Futures

While focusing on the student's role as citizen, student, family member, consumer, and active participant in the business world, *Managing Your Personal Finances 7e* informs readers of their various financial responsibilities. Students will discover new ways to maximize their earning potential, develop strategies for managing resources, explore skills for the wise use of credit, and gain insight into the different ways of investing money. Special features in each chapter focus on current trends and issues that consumers face in the marketplace and help students learn to secure their financial future. The 7th edition provides updated coverage of timely topics including social media, health care, and identity theft, to increase student awareness in these critical areas of personal finance.

- Ensuring that basic personal financial management skills are attained, this content is aligned with the Jump$tart Coalition's national standards for personal financial literacy.

- To prepare students to become knowledgeable and ethical consumers, this content meets the standards for personal financial literacy established by the National Business Education Association (NBEA).

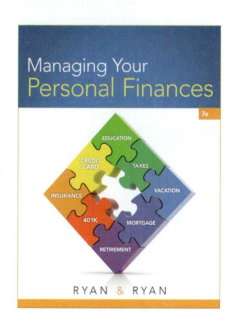

Turn the page to learn more about how to secure students' financial futures with *Managing Your Personal Finances* 7e!

Presenting the
Most Comprehensive

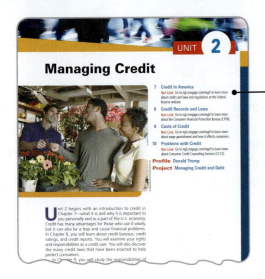

New **Net Links** direct students to the companion website for additional activities related to chapter content.

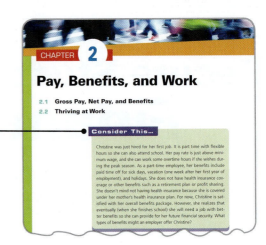

Consider This is a real-world scenario that connects students to the chapter content and gets them engaged.

Lessons make the text easy to use in all classroom environments.

An **Essential Question** frames the main idea that students will explore in the lesson.

Clearly stated **Learning Objectives** preview the concepts and guide students through the lesson.

Personal Finance Program Available!

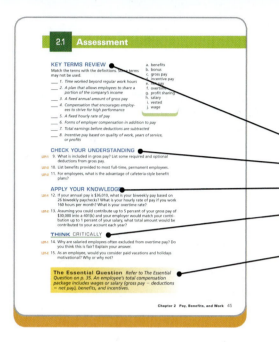

Engaging features within each **Lesson Assessment** give students a chance to check their understanding of the terms and content before advancing to the next lesson.

- Key Terms Review
- Check Your Understanding
- Apply Your Knowledge
- Think Critically

The Essential Question at the beginning of each lesson is answered on the Lesson Assessment page, allowing students to revisit the main points of the lesson and assess their comprehension.

Chapter Assessments give students the opportunity to tie their learning together. The **Summary** is a bulleted list of chapter concepts for quick review. **Apply What You Know, Make Academic Connections, Solve Problems and Explore Issues,** and **Extend Your Learning** challenge students to dig deeper into the issues. New **Chapter Projects** at the end of every chapter allow students to apply their knowledge of the chapters' topics to expanded activities. New **Guided Decision Making** activities lead students through discussion questions designed to encourage critical thinking.

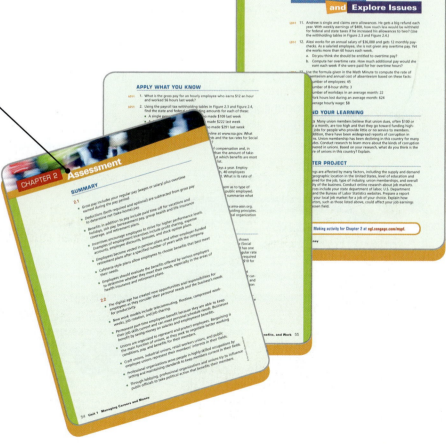

Exceptional Features
Enhance Learning!

Issues in Your World is a full-page feature that enriches students' knowledge by acquainting them with real-world issues.

Planning a Career in... offers robust career information and incorporates the 16 Career Clusters.

Global View

In Australia, "career break schemes" allow an employee to negotiate a fixed period away from work of up to several years for educational study or for family commitments, while maintaining a guaranteed job. Career break schemes frequently involve full-time work for short periods and part-time work for phase-out and phase-in stages. During these stages, pay and benefits are usually available. Career break schemes can reduce the loss of experienced staff. Employers help employees who are on a career break to maintain their skills and knowledge by providing training courses or by ensuring access to current work-related information. These activities make it easier for employees to return to work.

THINK CRITICALLY
How might offering career break schemes lead to greater work satisfaction? Are similar benefits available in the United States? If so, describe them.

Global View feature shows international connections relevant to personal finance.

Communication Connection

When a budget involves two or more persons, it is essential for each person to communicate his or her needs to the other person or persons. Often, *negotiating* is required so that each person's values and priorities are being met. When one person dominates and the other(s) go along even if their needs aren't being met, the budget is not likely to be successful. A *family budget* is one prepared for a group living together, providing for overall needs and sharing of expenses.

If you were living with one or two roommates, how would you go about preparing a budget? What kinds of expenses would you share with others? What kinds of expenses would be each person's solely? How can children contribute to a family's budget? Prepare a summary of what you would do to make sure everyone's needs and priorities are being met in a group or family budget.

Communication Connection offers speaking and writing activities related to the chapter content.

View Points

Downsizing has been defined as the elimination of part of the workforce, especially in business and government, in order to achieve a more efficient and cost-effective organization. Economic downturns and the resulting downsizing can create a tense workplace. Management insists that in order to remain competitive, jobs must be cut. Employees, particularly those with many years of service, believe their work and their loyalty are not important to management anymore.

THINK CRITICALLY
Do you agree with the claims of each side? What point could you make to support each side? How does the state of the economy play a role in this issue?

Viewpoints provide opportunities for students to think critically about issues that have no clear-cut answers.

Math Minute offers a review and practice in basic math skills linked to the chapter topics.

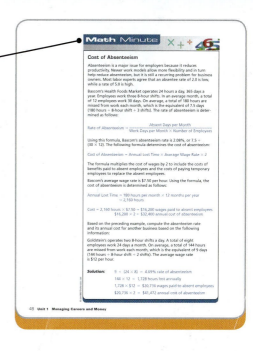

Unit Profiles showcase real people and describe how they applied the skills presented in this text to their own lives.

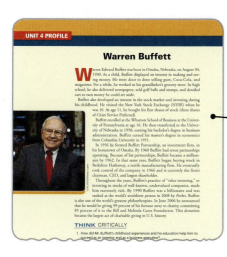

Unit Projects are designed to give students hands-on practice applying and extending what they have learned in the book.

New **Stock Market Simulation** walks students through a realistic stock market experience.

Comprehensive Teaching and Learning Tools

Annotated Instructor's Edition (978-1-305-10784-7)
Find everything you need to create a dynamic learning environment with minimal preparation. Student pages are surrounded by margin notes that provide comprehensive teaching notes and tips.

Student Activity Guide (978-1-305-08135-2)

Cognero IAC (978-1-305-38731-7)

Instructor's Resource CD (978-1-305-38740-9)

- Lesson Plans
- Lesson Outlines
- Instructor's Resource Manual
- PowerPoint Presentations
- English and Spanish Glossaries
- Instructor's Edition of Student Activity Guide

MindTap

MindTap is a personalized, fully online digital learning platform of authoritative content, assignments, and services that engages students with interactivity while also offering instructors choice in the configuration of coursework and enhancement of the curriculum.

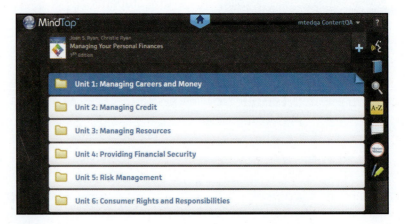

Website

ngl.cengage.com/mypf

Brief Contents

© RHIMAGE/Shutterstock.com

Contents

© wavebreakmedia/Shutterstock.com

© iStock.com/kyalshin

© Syda Productions/Shutterstock.com

© Monkey Business Images/Shutterstock.com

© Stephen Coburn/Shutterstock.com

© artconcept/Shutterstock.com

© Maryna Pleshkun/Shutterstock.com

Reviewers

Amy Bires
Business Education Teacher
Oshkosh West High School
Oshkosh, Wisconsin

Brian Bosch
Business Education Teacher
Fort Atkinson High School
Fort Atkinson, Wisconsin

Katy Catherine M. Brehmer
Business Education Teacher
Hillcrest High School
Simpsonville, South Carolina

Therese Chadowski
Business Instructor/Guidance Counselor
Ashtabula Area City Schools
Ashtabula, Ohio

Justine L. Flora
Business Education Teacher
Bedford High School
Bedford, Massachusetts

Nicholas Haug
Business and Marketing Education
St. Croix Central High School
Hammond, Wisconsin

Donna A. Jones
Business Education Teacher
Northwest Cabarrus Middle School
Concord, North Carolina

Lawrence T. Sakalas
Teacher
Southgate Anderson High School
Southgate, Michigan

Eric Schambers
Finance/Accounting Instructor
Riverview Community High School
Riverview, Michigan

Christine Seher
Business, Computer, and
  Information Technology Teacher
Fort LeBoeuf High School
Waterford, Pennsylvania

Susan Senninger
Business and Technology Instructor
Verona High School
Verona, Missouri

Mike Shady
Business Education and Technology Teacher
Fort LeBoeuf High School
Waterford, Pennsylvania

Michael Vialpando
CTE Department Chair
Teacher, Business Marketing
La Joya Community High School/
  Tolleson Unified School District
Avondale, Arizona

Managing Careers and Money

© iStockphoto.com/kupicoo

© Pan Xunbin/Shutterstock.com

1 Careers in the Digital Age

Net Link Go to ngl.cengage.com/mypf to learn more about career research at the U.S. Department of Labor.

2 Pay, Benefits, and Work

Net Link Go to ngl.cengage.com/mypf to learn more about labor laws protecting workers.

3 Income Tax

Net Link Go to ngl.cengage.com/mypf to learn more about what information and services are available from the IRS website.

4 Budgets and Records

Net Link Go to ngl.cengage.com/mypf to learn more about legal services and fees available through LegalZoom.com.

5 Checking and Banking

Net Link Go to ngl.cengage.com/mypf to learn more about the role of the Federal Reserve System in protecting depositors.

6 Saving for the Future

Net Link Go to ngl.cengage.com/mypf to learn more about the FDIC and how your savings deposits are protected from loss.

Profile Steve Jobs

Project Assessing Your Financial Health

Unit 1 explains how to get started building a plan for financial security. It begins with a look at how careers and privacy are affected in the digital age. Next is an examination of your paycheck and paycheck deductions, which take you from gross pay to net pay. Benefits and incentives in the workplace, the changing work environment, and the role of unions and professional organizations are also discussed.

Next, you will learn how to compute taxes and how to minimize them by understanding tax laws. From there, you will learn about financial planning through the preparation of budgets and other financial records. You will also learn about contracts, both the pros and cons. Finally, you will explore banking services, including effective account management strategies and savings options that can make your money grow.

CHAPTER 1

Careers in the Digital Age

1.1 **Thriving with Technology**

1.2 **The Job Market**

1.3 **Career Management**

Consider This...

"I was looking into a career that I've always thought I'd enjoy," Ashley told her friend Carlos. "But when I researched it, I found that demand is actually declining and that my prospects of getting hired are not good. I would have to get a bachelor's degree, and that degree wouldn't qualify me for other types of work."

"You're right," said Carlos. "My cousin got his degree in social studies. He found a job but learned that he would have to go back to school and get a master's degree in business. His degree just doesn't give him the educational background to get promoted."

"There are so many things to consider," Ashley said. "You know Rachael, right? She got a job she loves, but it doesn't pay enough for her to live on her own. And Jason, he has a job that pays really well, but he doesn't like it. Somehow I have to find a career that I love and one that pays me a solid wage—at the same time! How do I get started?"

The Essential Question *How does technology provide benefits and pose threats, and how can you cope with changes to technology?*

LEARNING OBJECTIVES

> **LO 1-1** Explain how technology affects consumers in their personal lives and careers.
> **LO 1-2** List ways you can protect yourself as change creates benefits and threats.

KEY TERMS

- social media, *4*
- data, *4*
- information, *4*
- data mining, *4*
- rewards card, *4*
- data warehousing, *5*
- lifelong learning, *7*
- upgrading, *7*
- retraining, *7*
- self-assessment inventory, *8*

LO 1-1 Living in the Digital Era

Technology has changed every aspect of our lives—from the way we work and learn to the way we play and communicate. Computers, and specifically the Internet, have helped us leap into the "digital age." We now live in an age where information is instantly and readily available to more people than ever before.

Of course, living in a digital age poses inevitable risks, such as identity theft and other privacy concerns. It's important to consider how living in the digital age affects your life.

The Internet: An Incredible Search Engine

You can look up almost anything on the Internet. You can enter a question or a term in a number of search engines, such as Google, Bing, and Yahoo! Search, and get thousands of possible matches. *Keywords* are used to match your request with websites that provide related information. You can narrow your search by being more specific in your request.

The Internet contains a vast source of information that you can use to help you find and get the job that is right for you. In the past, people read newspapers and circled job openings in the want ads. Today, many jobs are listed on the Internet. Most companies no longer publish their job openings through employment agencies. Instead, they post them on their corporate websites, social networking sites, or employment sites where you can find them and apply electronically. In fact, many businesses now accept online applications only.

Many businesses maintain websites that provide information to customers. You can look up a business's hours of operation or locations. You can also search for and purchase goods from businesses that sell their products online worldwide. Some businesses sell their products exclusively online.

Social Media

Just a few years ago, the Internet was used primarily for e-mail communication and file sharing, both personally and at work. Today, the Internet provides much more in terms of gathering and sharing information. **Social media** refers to forms of electronic communication, such as websites, through which users create online communities to share information. First appearing in 2004, social media sites are very common and popular today. Facebook, Twitter, YouTube, and LinkedIn are some of the most popular social media sites. Other examples include Google Plus, Pinterest, Tumblr, and Instagram. The list of social media sites continues to grow.

Information placed and stored on these sites is collected, packaged, and sold to interested third parties. When you post something, it likely is not private. Whether or not it is factual, this type of information can be used both for and against people. For example, someone can Google you and, based on the information gathered, develop an image of you which may or may not be accurate. Like it or not, when you use these sites, you are allowing them to share the information they receive about you.

Using Technology to Collect Consumer Data

Entire industries are fueled by the analysis and application of information collected about people, both with and without their knowledge and consent. Information gathered about you is often used for your benefit. But it can also be used against you in ways you might never expect.

Data Mining and Warehousing

In the last few years, dramatic advances have been made in the capture, processing, transmission, and storage of data. **Data** refers to facts, numbers, or text that can be processed on a computer. This data is stored in databases where it can be accessed for any number of purposes.

All types of organizations, including government bodies, are collecting vast amounts of data about individuals. **Information** is the arrangement of data into useful patterns or relationships. Businesses convert information into knowledge about historical patterns and projected future trends. *Knowledge* empowers the user to make the right decisions, such as what products will and will not sell and who will and will not buy them. Data mining and data warehousing are business intelligence tools used to turn information into actionable knowledge.

Data Mining The process of gathering and analyzing data from a variety of sources and summarizing it into useful information is known as **data mining**. A *customer loyalty program*, such as a rewards card at your local grocery store, is an example of how companies use data mining. A **rewards card** is a data mining system that gathers and stores information electronically about your purchases and grants points (or rewards) that can be redeemed. When you use a rewards card, you will be sent offers, coupons, and other marketing tools that are specifically targeted to your needs as interpreted by the data mining program. For example, if you buy baby food, you are likely to receive coupons for all types of merchandise needed by new parents. The store or business that uses a customer loyalty program is able to increase sales and profitability by targeting people based on their purchasing habits. Such a program also reduces the business's costs because it can analyze customer profitability and focus efforts on its "best" customers.

Companies also use the Internet to mine data. *Web mining* is the use of data mining techniques to collect information from Internet content. A company can collect data from visitors to its website. It can also collect data you publicly post on blogs and social media sites. For example, a comment you make on a blog about a company's product could be added to that company's database. This kind of information helps businesses identify customers for their products and enables them to market their products directly to those customers.

Data Warehousing The management of data storage and retrieval is known as **data warehousing**. It involves combining data from multiple sources into one comprehensive database, called a *data warehouse*, for easy access. When information is centralized into a data warehouse, it can be used to produce reports that assist in business analysis and decision making. For example, a company can access data specifically related to sales of a certain product. Using reports generated from the data warehouse, the company can answer questions such as, "Which customer bought the largest quantity of this product last year?" The data can be sold to external parties for many purposes, locally, nationally, and even internationally.

Protecting Your Identity

Identity theft is one of the largest and fastest-growing crimes in America. If someone gets enough information about you to assume your identity, he or she can drain your bank account, run up charges on your credit card, and open new accounts. They may even take out mortgages or other loans. In today's age of technology, most identity theft occurs when those to whom you have given your personal information have not protected it from thieves.

You must be careful to whom you give out your personal information such as your name, address, date of birth, and Social Security number. The business in possession of this information stores it in its database. Unless the business takes extreme measures to protect it, your information can be stolen by hackers, dishonest employees, and others who gain access to it. Be wary of a business that wants to make a photocopy of your driver's license or demands your Social Security number. Unless a business is giving you money that must be reported for tax purposes or granting you credit, it does not "need" your Social Security number.

You also must be careful to whom you give debit and credit cards. Information stored on those cards can be used by others to obtain funds from your bank account or charge purchases to your account. Sometimes it's better to use cash or prepaid gift cards. These methods of payment do not contain information related to your identity.

In certain situations, you are required to provide your personal information, such as when applying for a loan or receiving medical treatment. Checking your credit report frequently can help you identify early when someone has stolen your identity.

Why is it important to protect your credit cards, debit cards, and other sources of credit?

In addition, several companies now offer identity theft protection services for a monthly fee. These services include monitoring your credit reports and scanning known criminal websites for the illegal sale of your personal information. Identify theft will be discussed further in later chapters.

Guarding Your Privacy

Privacy is a very important value in America. Some types of information should not be shared with others and should remain private. Information of this nature can hurt your reputation, your employment opportunities, and your credit, and can even impair your ability to get insurance.

As previously mentioned, the Internet is not private. Everything that is posted is stored electronically and can be accessed by virtually anyone. Therefore, be cautious of what you post online about yourself, your lifestyle, and others. Make sure the information posted cannot harm you or others.

There are privacy laws designed to protect you. The Health Information Portability and Accountability Act (HIPAA) and the Family Educational Rights and Privacy Act (FERPA) are two laws that help protect your medical records and your school records. We will discuss these further in a later chapter.

You are the best person to protect your privacy. Be cautious with postings on social media sites; keep them positive and avoid giving out personal information. Use the Internet wisely. Privacy cannot be restored once it is lost.

✔ CHECKPOINT

How is communication changing because of technology?

LO 1-2 Coping with Change

With rapidly advancing technologies, change is certain. You have three options when it comes to change: you can accept it, reject it, or ignore it. If you accept change, you can help shape it. If you reject change, you will be run over by it, because progress cannot be stopped. If you ignore change, you will be left behind. By rejecting or ignoring change, you will end up frustrated, unemployed, or both. By staying informed, becoming a lifelong learner, and taking classes to stay up to date, you can be aware of changes. By completing a self-assessment, you can make an action plan that will enable you to cope with and reduce the stress of uncertainty.

Stay Informed

Staying current with the latest technologies and advances is a long-term commitment. You should stay aware of new and emerging trends, whether or not they will affect you directly. The more you know about what's going on, the more you benefit. For example, as changes to the health care system take effect and records go online nationally, you should understand what this means to you both now and in the future. Although your medical records will be available wherever you are located, enabling you to get better care, your privacy can be compromised more easily, meaning sensitive information about you can be misused by data miners. By being aware of this, you can take steps to help prevent misuse of your data.

A variety of resources report on national and international trends, from general technology to specific industries. You can read newspapers and magazines to keep up with what is going on in the United States and around the world. You can watch the news and pay attention to what's happening with the economy, with job fields, and with businesses. You can also go to shows, expos, and other events that discuss emerging trends and cutting-edge technology. Participate and be active in the changes. Casting your vote and being politically active may help preserve your rights.

Be a Lifelong Learner

Individuals may change jobs seven times or more over a lifetime. Young adults change jobs more frequently as they carve out their career path. The knowledge and skills required in the workplace change over time as well. **Lifelong learning** means actively seeking new knowledge, skills, and experiences that will add to your professional and personal growth throughout your life. You can join professional associations and service organizations that will keep you informed of what's new in specific job areas. You can attend workshops and seminars to learn about current trends. Attending these events will help make you a more knowledgeable and interesting person as well as increase your opportunities to interact with others in your profession. Lifelong learning is essential to your successful career management and can affect your lifetime income.

Take Classes to Stay Current

Sometimes technology brings change that requires new skills—skills you cannot learn by yourself. When this happens, it's time to actively seek new knowledge by taking classes.

Upgrading means advancing to a higher level of skill to increase your usefulness to an employer. Many jobs, especially those affected by technological improvements, will require regular upgrading by employees.

Retraining involves learning new and different skills so that an employee can retain the same level of employability. Community college and vocational training is geared as much to retraining displaced employees as to preparing employees for entry-level positions. There are numerous sources of retraining:

- Many companies offer technical courses to retrain their own employees. Those who volunteer and are eager to learn will position themselves for advancement.
- Training is available through technical schools, vocational centers, job placement services, business colleges, and community colleges. Many employers reimburse employees for the cost of classes related to their jobs.
- Training over the Internet (online learning) is becoming increasingly common. Employer-sponsored training is often free for employees.

Why do employees need to keep their skill level current?

© Blend Images/Shutterstock.com

Complete a Self-Assessment

As you go through life, your needs and values will change. It is important to look inward to define what is important to you and then use this knowledge to plan your future. You should think about what you like doing, what you do well, and what skills and knowledge you want to enhance. For example, you might want to strengthen your understanding of the latest technologies. By learning how to use the newest form of social media, you will be able to communicate with others more effectively. Being more tech-savvy can also help you perform better on the job.

You can find many self-assessment questionnaires at online career sites or by searching with the keyword "self-assessment." A **self-assessment inventory** lists your strong and weak points along with plans for improvement. As you improve your weak points, they become strengths in your inventory.

Figure 1.1 is a self-assessment inventory that lists a typical high school student's strengths and weaknesses, along with a plan of action. Completing a similar inventory based on your personal characteristics can help you determine areas that need work.

You might also ask another person to objectively assess your strengths and weaknesses. A different point of view can sometimes help clarify your self-assessment. Also, many high schools, colleges, and technical training institutes provide assistance with self-assessment inventories.

 CHECKPOINT

What are ways you can cope with change?

FIGURE 1.1	Self-Assessment Inventory

Strengths	Weaknesses	Plan of Action
Education: High school diploma, including business courses	*Education:* Weak in basic math skills; need to learn more software packages such as Excel	Take extra classes in algebra; learn Excel and other software
Experience: Internship in office—part-time summer job as administrative assistant; volunteer at church	*Experience:* Need experience using database programs	Look for part-time job that involves using database applications; take an online course in Access
Aptitudes and Abilities: Good hand-eye coordination; work well with people	*Aptitudes and Abilities:* Poor public speaker	Practice speaking in small groups; lead a class at church; attend more social functions
Appearance: Neat and clean	*Appearance:* Need more professional work clothes	Start buying clothes appropriate for work

Agriculture

Farm workers, farm owners, and those who assist in the production of food face many challenges but can be financially successful by bringing vegetables, fruit, meat, eggs, and milk to your supermarket.

Technology has reduced the demand for many types of jobs in this field. Much of the work is hard physical labor. Agricultural workers feed and care for livestock, operate heavy machinery, and participate in outdoor work.

Urban farming has become a popular trend. This activity involves growing fruits and vegetables and even raising chickens and other small livestock in very limited urban spaces. The popularity and profitability of producing *organic food* items has caused many farmers to enter into this niche market.

Employment Outlook

- A decline in employment (–3%) is expected for farm workers in the next decade.
- An increase in urban farmers and organic farmers is expected in the next decade.

Job Titles

- Farm worker
- Nursery worker
- Equipment operator
- Organic farmer

Needed Skills

- No degree is required; skills are learned on the job.
- Experience is helpful, and specialized work, such as breeding, requires training.

- Self-employment traits and skills are needed to be a farmer.
- Physical ability to tend to outdoor activities, such as crops and animals, is required.

What's it like to work in . . . *Agriculture*

Briana loves working with farm animals. She also likes to grow berries and fruits for sale at the local market. During the spring and summer, she plants, cares for, and harvests her crops. She raises organic products, which means there are no sprays, insecticides, herbicides, or other chemicals on her berries and fruits. She works in her greenhouse and small orchard and cares for the animals year-round.

Briana thinks the demand for organic foods will increase, so she is considering growing a new line of vegetables to sell to the local stores that specialize in organics.

Last year, after paying her expenses, Briana netted roughly $18,000 selling her products. Although she doesn't make a big income from her job, she gets to do what she loves best. And she believes she is contributing to a healthier lifestyle for her customers.

What About You?

Do you like working outdoors with plants and animals? Is fresh food an important part of your lifestyle? Do you think you would enjoy a career in agriculture?

KEY TERMS REVIEW

Match the terms with the definitions. Some terms may not be used.

a. data
b. data mining
c. data warehousing
d. information
e. lifelong learning
f. retraining
g. rewards card
h. self-assessment inventory
i. social media
j. upgrading

____ 1. *Facts, numbers, and text*

____ 2. *Forms of electronic communication through which users create online communities to share information*

____ 3. *A system of gathering information about what you purchase at a store*

____ 4. *Actively seeking new knowledge, skills, and experiences that will add to your professional and personal growth*

____ 5. *Gathering and analyzing data and summarizing it into useful information*

____ 6. *Management of data storage and retrieval*

____ 7. *The arrangement of data into useful patterns or relationships*

____ 8. *Learning new and different skills to retain employability*

CHECK YOUR UNDERSTANDING

LO1-1   9. What is data mining? Why should you care if information is gathered about you?

LO1-1   10. How can you guard your privacy on the Internet?

LO1-2   11. How can you be a lifelong learner?

APPLY YOUR KNOWLEDGE

LO1-1   12. Think about postings you and others have made on the Internet. Did you make any statements that were negative or could affect your or someone else's reputation? Have you read such comments posted by others? What possible effects could result from negative postings?

THINK CRITICALLY

LO1-1   13. Why is it important to protect your Social Security number, date of birth, and other personal information?

LO1-2   14. Why should you do a self-assessment inventory as part of your strategy for coping with change?

The Essential Question *Refer to The Essential Question on p. 3. Technology provides excellent opportunities to communicate and link with others, but information collected can be harmful if misused. Staying informed and current can help you cope with technological changes.*

The Essential Question *How does technology affect demand for careers and the way you learn about and get a job?*

LEARNING OBJECTIVES

› LO 2-1 Discuss how technology affects career planning.
› LO 2-2 Prepare job application tools and describe how to successfully apply for a job.

KEY TERMS

- downsizing, *12*
- job creation, *12*
- service job, *13*
- job application, *14*
- resume, *14*
- references, *16*
- reference letter, *17*
- job interview, *18*
- transcripts, *19*
- follow-up, *19*

LO 2-1   Exploring Career Opportunities

Consumer demand determines which jobs will be needed to produce the products and services people want. To stay in business, companies must offer products and services that meet the diverse and changing needs of customers. Some types of careers will be sustainable far into the future, whereas others will not survive. Rapidly changing technology and an expanding global economy have created new and challenging pathways for career development.

The Effects of Technology and the Economy on Career Choice

No matter what career path you choose, technology and the world economy will affect the way you work. They will also affect your job choices and how you prepare for your future.

Technology

The Internet as well as new technology improvements and innovations have had a dramatic effect on the job market. The Internet has opened worldwide markets and has created global competition for businesses of all sizes. Today's employers look different from past employers, as they explore various ways to meet changing demands. For example, many companies exist only in cyberspace and have no brick-and-mortar buildings. Others specialize in providing companies with services that were traditionally done by inside employees.

Technology has eliminated the need for many jobs. For example, travel agents are no longer needed to make plane and hotel reservations. New technologies

What effect has technology had on the job industry?

To cut costs, many American businesses are hiring firms outside of the United States to handle work that inside employees used to do, from managing customer service call centers to manufacturing the products to be sold. This strategy is known as *outsourcing*. Companies pay for work done in countries close by, such as Canada or Mexico, or far away, such as India or China. Companies argue that they must control costs and provide shareholder value in the form of higher profits. Workers argue that good jobs are being lost to foreign workers and Americans are unable to find jobs to pay the high cost of living in America.

THINK CRITICALLY

Do you agree with the claims of each side? What point could you make to support each side? How does the state of the economy play a role in this issue?

will continue to make some careers obsolete because the work can be done more efficiently with robots, websites, or electronic programming.

But today's technology also opens up many career options. For example, more web designers, web content developers, and others working in computer-related fields are needed to maintain online businesses. Also, people are finding it possible to work from home while interacting with colleagues worldwide. And online job postings allow individuals to easily apply for jobs in other states, or even other countries.

As you consider your career, you may not be able to visualize how it will change over time. You will need to rely on research by others to assess a career's potential.

Economy

Economic factors can also affect jobs. During an economic downturn, jobs and entire industries are downsized. **Downsizing** is an economic event whereby jobs are eliminated because company revenues are falling while costs are rising. People are spending less and, thus, fewer products are needed. Jobs that are downsized often re-emerge with new and different skill sets. Some are never replaced as businesses learn to operate with fewer people and lower costs.

Job creation occurs when the economy is growing (consumer demand is increasing) and new workers are being hired. High demand for new workers affects the supply of labor by reducing the number of available workers. As a result, companies may start offering higher wages to persuade job seekers to work for them. Many of the jobs created may be temporary and/or service jobs. When jobs are being created, it's important to consider whether they will be sustainable over time or will be eliminated in the next economic downturn.

Careers of the Future

Many of today's growing occupations focus on the collection, use, and distribution of information. Computers and the Internet are key tools for gathering, transmitting, and storing data. The skills required to succeed in today's jobs change rapidly.

One of the highest-paying career groups is classified as *professional*, where being knowledgeable is a key job skill. Examples of professionals include

© Vectomart/Shutterstock.com

doctors, lawyers, teachers, and economists. For professionals, much of the job involves creating, processing, storing, retrieving, and transmitting information. As technology continues to evolve, new professional careers will emerge and others will grow. For example, because identity theft is becoming more common, retailers are hiring more information security analysts to ensure their customers' privacy and security.

A **service job** is one in which you perform a task or a service for a person or business. Service jobs are a large and increasing sector of the job market. Over the last 50 years, the nation has shifted from an economy that creates goods to one that provides services. Like the professional sector, service jobs are dominated by technology and information needs. Service employees often use highly sophisticated information storage and retrieval devices, such as point-of-sale computers and optical scanners linked to inventory management and customer databases. Unfortunately, many service jobs do not pay well. Higher-tech service jobs are more likely to provide bigger earnings potential.

Job Titles and Descriptions

General research into careers before choosing your college major is essential. This will help you identify dead-end careers and learn whether the career of your choice will pay you an adequate salary. Several U.S. government publications, available online and in most libraries, provide detailed job descriptions:

- *Dictionary of Occupational Titles (DOT)*, available online as *O*NET* (www.online.onetcenter.org)
- *Occupational Outlook Handbook (OOH)* (www.bls.gov/ooh)
- *Monthly Labor Review* (www.bls.gov/mlr)

*O*NET* is the *DOT* in the form of an online searchable database. It describes occupations in terms of the skills and knowledge required, work tasks performed, and tools and technology used. You can search the database for occupations by entering keywords or by selecting from a list of job families.

The *Occupational Outlook Handbook* provides in-depth job descriptions and information about job opportunities nationwide. The A–Z index arranges careers alphabetically. You can learn whether a career is growing, stagnant, or in decline by reading about the job outlook.

Additional statistics and graphic information are available in the *Monthly Labor Review*. Articles in this publication provide current information about specific occupation clusters (groups of similar occupations) across the nation.

Online career sites such as Monster and CareerBuilder also provide career advice and information about different jobs.

CHECKPOINT

How might consumer demand affect career choices?

- -

LO 2-2 **Applying and Interviewing**

The job-seeking process involves multiple steps. Preparing an application and interviewing for a job are sometimes not easy tasks, yet they are vital steps to landing a job.

The Job Application

Your formal job application process is likely to begin with filling out a **job application**, which is a form that asks questions to be sure you are qualified for a job opening. Many employers today require you to fill out a job application online. When completing a job application, follow these steps:

- Answer every question. When you cannot answer a question, write "N/A" (for "not applicable") or use a line (———) to show that you have not skipped the question.
- Be truthful. Give complete answers. Do not abbreviate if there is any chance the abbreviation could be misread.
- Have with you all information that might be requested on the application form, such as telephone numbers, dates, and addresses.
- Proofread carefully; check every word.

The Resume

You likely will be asked to include a resume with your application. A **resume** describes your work experience, education, abilities, interests, and other information that may be of interest to an employer. It is also known as a personal data sheet, biographical summary, professional profile, or CV (curriculum vitae). The resume tells the employer neatly and concisely who you are, what you can do, and what your special interests are. Always have an up-to-date resume ready for potential employers. Figure 1.2 shows a commonly used resume style. For more examples, go to an online career and employment site, such as Monster, and look for resume samples. Resumes should emphasize your best qualifications and do it in an easy-to-read, attractive, and convincing manner.

Resume Guidelines

There are no set rules for preparing a resume. You should choose the style that best presents you to an employer. However, here are some helpful guidelines:

- Early in your career, keep your resume to one page by carefully arranging the information you choose to include. Employers are busy people. They want a quick overview of you—not a lot of words to read. If you don't have enough information to fill a page, center what you have vertically on the page to make it attractive. After you have more education and work experience to summarize, your resume may extend to a second page. Resumes for professional applicants with extensive work experience may run several pages.
- Include all information pertinent to the job for which you are applying. An employer wants to know that you are interested in the specific job opening. Rather than prepare a "generic" resume to fit all possible openings, use key words from a job posting to show that your skills match that particular job.
- Carefully choose fonts, bold, italic, spacing, and other tools to arrange your information in a way that is attractive yet professional looking and easy to read. Place the most important items in the upper third of the page.

FIGURE 1.2   Resume

Anisa Newkirk
162 NW Marshall Street
Portland, OR 97209-4323
(971) 555-4021
anisan@internet.com

CAREER OBJECTIVE

To assist with animal training for service dog programs in the local area; desire to work with dogs on emergency and trauma response teams.

EDUCATION

Hoover High School, Portland, Oregon (graduate 2015)
   GPA 3.3, Dean's List two years

Relevant Course Work:
Biology
Environmental Science
Public Speaking and Forensics

Relevant Skills:
Work well with animals
American Sign Language (ASL)
MSExcel (spreadsheets)
MSWord (word processing)

Extracurricular Activities:
Volunteer: Red Cross Emergency Response
Debate Team (two years)
Member: National Honor Society (two years)
Athletics: Tennis and volleyball

EXPERIENCE

Volunteer, Noah Animal Hospital, Portland, Oregon (one year)
   Worked with injured animals, gave them food and medication; worked at the all-night emergency room, took data from animal owners; assisted veterinary staff with medical procedures.

Caregiver, County Animal Shelter (two summers)
   Cared for animals; made calls to help find them new homes.

Pet Sitter/Dog Walker (two years)
   Provided care for dogs, cats, rabbits, birds, and snakes while owners were away on vacation; provided daily dog walking services.

REFERENCES

References provided on request.

- Proofread thoroughly. Do not rely solely on your word processor's spell-check. Your resume must have zero errors.

- For hard copies, use a high-resolution printer and good-quality 8½ × 11-inch paper. Avoid bright colors, odd sizes, and stained or discolored paper.

Parts of a Resume

A simple resume should include personal contact information, a career objective (optional), education, experience, additional qualifications or special items of interest (if applicable), and references. You may arrange your resume according to personal preference. However, generally you should show your most favorable section first. For example, if your work experience relates to the open position more closely than your education does, list experience first.

Personal Information This information appears first on the resume and includes your name, address, telephone or cell phone number (with area code), and e-mail address. Do not give information such as age, gender, marital status, number of dependents, or ethnic background.

Career Objective The career objective is optional. As your resume gets fuller, you may wish to omit it. If used, keep it short, indicating your career goal. For example, your goal might be to rise to a particular position. Make the statement forward looking, interesting, and specific. This statement helps the employer see how your plans fit with the company. Avoid weak statements such as "any type of work."

Education List all high school and post-high school institutions you have attended, starting with the most recent. You may include areas of study, grade point average, activities, honors, specific courses that apply to the job opening, or other facts that you think will create a favorable impression. For example, extracurricular activities tell an employer that you are a well-rounded person; offices held in school organizations show that you have leadership skills.

Experience List jobs, paid and unpaid, that you have held, including assisting at school functions, working as a teacher's aide, and any part- or full-time summer or vacation jobs (such as camp counselor). You may write this section in paragraph or outline form. Include information such as name and address of employer, job title, work duties, employment dates or length of time employed, and specific achievements while with this employer. Emphasize tasks you performed that relate to the open position.

Additional Qualifications You may have additional skills to bring to an employer's attention. For example, you may list special equipment you can operate, software you can use, or foreign languages you know. You can also list awards you have received. All of these things give an employer a fuller picture of you.

References Some potential employers will require references. **References** are people who have known you for at least a year and can provide information about your skills, character, and achievements. References should be over age 18 and not related to you. The best types of references include teachers, advisers, current and former employers, counselors, coaches, and adults in business. Be sure to ask permission before listing people on your resume. If you choose not to list references on your resume, state "references provided on request." Then prepare a list of the names, addresses, phone numbers, and e-mail addresses of your references.

Scannable Resumes

Some employers use scanners and special software to search for key words and phrases that match the skills required in their job descriptions. They can scan hard copy as well as electronic resumes. The scan determines which resumes will be considered further and which will not.

A *scannable resume* has been designed for easy reading by a scanner and contains key words from the applicant's career field. To make the scanner's cut, describe your qualifications using key words from your field. For example, a publisher looking for an editor might scan for key words such as "English," "journalism degree," "writing," or "editing." To make your resume easy for the scanner, use a standard font, such as Times Roman; type size of 11 or 12 points for the body of the resume; and headings no larger than 14-point bold or caps. Avoid fancy fonts, italic, underlines, multiple columns, and graphics.

Reference Letter

A **reference letter** is a statement attesting to your character, abilities, and experience, written by someone who can be relied upon to give a sincere report. It is helpful to give those writing a reference letter a copy of your current resume or a short summary of your accomplishments and background. The letter should be on company letterhead. A sample reference letter is shown in Figure 1.3. Note that "To Whom It May Concern" is an acceptable

---

FIGURE 1.3   Reference Letter

FARWEST TRUCK CENTER

402 First Street, NW
Eugene, OR 97402-2143

June 4, 20--

Re: Maribel Boswell

To Whom It May Concern

I have known Maribel for the past three years. She was an employee in our customer service division. Maribel began work here as an intern. She was an excellent employee, so at the end of her internship we hired her on a temporary basis. That temporary job lasted three years until Maribel moved away.

Maribel proved to be energetic and competent. She learned quickly and was a valuable member of our team. She took great pride in her work. She was able to work well independently and as a team member.

Without reservation, I can recommend Maribel to you as a potential employee. I would gladly hire her again if she were to move back to our area.

If you have any further questions, please do not hesitate to call me.

Sincerely

Harry Chen

Harry Chen
Manager

salutation in this case, since copies may be provided to multiple prospective employers.

When you get a reference letter, make copies to give to potential employers along with your resume. Keep the original for your files because you may need to make additional copies for other job applications.

The Job Interview

A **job interview** is a face-to-face meeting with a potential employer to discuss a job opening. During the interview, the employer will have your completed application, resume, and reference letter(s). The interviewer may ask you about information on any of these documents or about any other job-related matters. Thus, you should spend at least as much time preparing for the interview as you did getting the interview.

Preparing for the Interview

Review your resume so that all your qualifications will be fresh in your mind. Prepare a list of likely questions and rehearse how you will answer them. Be prepared to answer *open-ended questions*, which are designed to encourage full, meaningful answers (rather than "yes" or "no"). These questions may include, "Tell me about yourself," "Why do you want to work for us?" or "What would you like to be doing in five years?" Your responses show how well you organize your thoughts, speak, and think under pressure. Emphasize your skills, achievements, and career plans. Avoid speaking negatively about others.

It is also important to learn something about your potential employer prior to the interview. Think of questions you might ask the interviewer about the company and the open position. You want to be able to speak intelligently about the company. Do some *company research* ahead of time, where you find out what the company makes or sells, its history, and what its prospects are for the future. This kind of information can be obtained from a number of sources:

- The company's website tells about its products, history, financial performance, and other data.
- A contact you have with someone who works for the company can provide first-hand knowledge.
- Annual reports (often available on the company website) describe the company and its financial resources.
- Articles in current magazines and newspapers, including online publications, may discuss the company's economic health or plans for expansion.

Making a Good Impression

Because it may affect your whole future, the interview is an important moment in your life. Prepare for it carefully to make a good impression.

- *Arrive on time.* Better yet, arrive ten minutes early so you can check your appearance and compose yourself. Never be late.
- *Dress appropriately.* Be neat and clean. Be conservative in dress, hairstyle, jewelry, perfume, cologne, makeup, and appearance. It is best to err on the side of being overly dressy than overly casual.
- *Go alone.* Don't bring along a friend or relative.

- *Be prepared.* Bring copies of your resume, reference letter(s), and transcripts. **Transcripts** are school records that include a listing of courses you have taken along with the credits and grades you've received for them. Bring a pad of paper, a pen, and any information you may need. Use a briefcase or some type of folder to keep your papers organized.

- *Appear self-confident.* It's normal to be nervous, but don't let your emotions control you. Present the appearance of being relaxed and comfortable by maintaining good eye contact and giving an occasional smile. Don't chew gum or display nervous habits. Allow the interviewer to lead the discussion.

How can you make a good impression in a job interview?

- *Think before you speak.* Take a moment to organize your thoughts before speaking. Don't be afraid of the silent pause; the interviewer will not be put off. Be polite, accurate, and honest. Use proper grammar. Avoid slang and informal speech. Say "yes" rather than "yeah." Speak slowly and clearly.

- *Emphasize your strong points.* Talk about your favorite school subjects, grades, attendance, skills, experience, activities, and goals in a positive manner. Avoid negative comments.

- *Be enthusiastic.* Act interested in the company and the job. Show that you are energetic and ready to work. Let the interviewer know that you are excited about the company, the job, and your future.

- *Look for cues.* Nonverbal cues from the interviewer will tell you when to say less or more. Watch and listen carefully, and then respond appropriately.

When the interview is over, thank the interviewer for his or her time. Say you will check back later. Then do so. Exit with a smile and a positive comment, such as "I look forward to hearing from you."

The Follow-Up

After the interview, the employer will have various candidates to consider. Your follow-up may help you stand out from the crowd. **Follow-up** is contact with the employer after the interview but before hiring occurs. It reminds the employer who you are, which could improve your chance of getting the job.

Thank-You Letter

A thank-you letter is one form of follow-up. The *thank-you letter* shows appreciation to the employer for taking time to speak with you. It also brings you to the forefront of the interviewer's mind, providing a reminder of your qualifications and interest in the company.

When writing a thank-you letter, address the interviewer by name. If more than one person interviewed you during your visit, write a brief letter to each person. Keep it simple and straightforward, and make sure it is error-free. This final opportunity to represent yourself to the potential employer may make the difference that will get you the job.

Figure 1.4 is a sample follow-up thank-you letter. The first paragraph thanks the interviewer. The second paragraph reminds the interviewer of your interest and desire to work for the company. The final paragraph closes with a positive note.

Other Forms of Follow-Up

In addition to a letter, or if time is too short between your interview and the date that selection is made to send a thank-you letter, you may wish to call or stop by and check with the place of business about the status of your application. You can also send an e-mail with the same content as your thank-you letter would include. Remember to keep it short! Such contacts should be courteous and friendly.

✔ CHECKPOINT

How has technology affected the way people apply for jobs?

| **FIGURE 1.4** | **Thank-You Letter** |

1274 Grant Avenue
Portland, OR 97224
becarter@internet.com
July 10, 20--

Mr. Jackson Phillips, Manager
Star Gaze Museum
4484 Grand Avenue
Portland, OR 97201

Dear Mr. Phillips

Thank you for the time you spent with me during our interview yesterday. I enjoyed meeting you and members of your staff.

I am very excited about the prospect of working for your company. The tour guide position is exactly what I was hoping for. As you recall, I have experience and background that make it possible for me to "hit the ground running." I am enclosing another reference who can attest to my ability to learn quickly and fit in well.

If there is any other information I could provide, please feel free to contact me at (971) 555-3344. I look forward to hearing from you.

Sincerely

Brandon Carter

Brandon Carter

Enclosure: Reference

How Can Communication Skills Help You Succeed at Work?

Success on the job depends on good communication skills, whether you are communicating with your employer (supervisor), coworkers, or customers. More than 80 percent of all work activities involve communication in one form or another.

Verbal Communication Skills

Good verbal communication skills involve speaking slowly and clearly, listening carefully to another person's positions and reactions, asking questions to clarify what was said, and responding appropriately. Information must be exchanged clearly in order to solve problems. Communicating in a manner that is respectful and courteous is expected. Saying "please" and "thank you" is always good business etiquette.

To provide good customer service, it is critical to listen, not just hear. *Hearing* is the process of perceiving sound. *Listening* is an active hearing process that requires concentration and effort. Customers are often seeking information about products and services. Sometimes, however, they are stating a complaint about a product or service. In these instances, avoid being defensive. By using *sympathetic listening* (the ability to perceive another person's point of view and sense what he or she is feeling), *critical listening* (the ability to differentiate facts from opinion), and *creative listening* (the ability to listen with an open mind to new ideas), you can help resolve complaints and, in turn, build positive customer relationships. Customers are the business's lifeline; without customers, there is no business.

Nonverbal Communication Skills

Body language, or nonverbal communication, can be just as important as verbal communication in the workplace. Making direct eye contact with coworkers, employers, and customers shows that you are paying attention and listening. Smiling and displaying other pleasant facial expressions expresses friendliness and acceptance. Nodding while the other person is speaking conveys an understanding. The way you dress and the jewelry you wear can also relay a message to others. Even your behavior during a business dinner can make a lasting impression. Proper dining etiquette requires that you keep your elbows off the table, place the napkin in your lap after being seated, use the proper utensils, and maintain good posture (do not bend over food, but bring the food to the mouth).

Digital Communication Skills

Much of communication today is electronic because it is quick and convenient. E-mail messages between supervisors, coworkers, and customers are common. When composing an e-mail, the message should be well written, clear, and concise, providing relevant information. Long e-mails may not be read. Use the subject line to catch the reader's attention. Don't type in all capital letters, which may be interpreted as shouting. Provide accurate details and offer solutions to problems. Check your e-mail inbox at least twice a day and be courteous by responding to e-mails promptly.

THINK CRITICALLY

1. Describe a situation in which you communicated well with a classmate or other person. What verbal and nonverbal skills did you use?

2. Describe a situation in which you observed good or poor customer service skills at a place of business. How could the situation have been improved?

KEY TERMS REVIEW

Match the terms with the definitions. Some terms may not be used.

a. downsizing
b. follow-up
c. job application
d. job creation
e. job interview
f. reference letter
g. references
h. resume
i. service job
j. transcripts

____ 1. A description of your work experience, education, abilities, and interests

____ 2. Contact with an employer after the interview but before hiring occurs

____ 3. The result when the economy is growing and new workers are hired

____ 4. A statement attesting to your character, abilities, and experience

____ 5. School records showing courses taken, number of credits, and grades received

____ 6. An economic event where jobs are eliminated because revenues are falling while costs are rising

____ 7. Performance of a task or service for a person or business

____ 8. A form that asks questions to be sure you are qualified for a job opening

CHECK YOUR UNDERSTANDING

LO2-1 9. What sources are available to help you research job descriptions, job skills, and job outlooks?

LO2-2 10. What kind of information is found on a resume?

APPLY YOUR KNOWLEDGE

LO2-2 11. Find a job opening on an employment site or a company website. What kinds of education and experience is the employer seeking? Prepare a resume that you think would help get you an interview for that job.

THINK CRITICALLY

LO2-1 12. Why are service jobs increasing in this country? How does technology affect service jobs?

LO2-2 13. Why do employers post openings on their websites and require applicants to submit their applications and resumes electronically?

LO2-2 14. Why should you design a resume for each job opening rather than use a generic resume?

The Essential Question *Refer to The Essential Question on p. 11. Technology not only affects job requirements, but it also affects how you will apply, interview, and be successful in getting the job. Technology is the key to successful career paths.*

LEARNING OBJECTIVES

❯ LO 3-1 Describe effective career planning techniques for an employee.

❯ LO 3-2 Discuss the importance of career planning for self-employment.

KEY TERMS

- goal, *24*
- short-term goal, *25*
- intermediate goal, *25*
- long-term goal, *25*
- experience, *26*
- self-employment, *27*
- side business, *27*
- lifestyle business, *27*
- venture business, *28*
- business plan, *28*

LO 3-1 Employee Career Planning

Planning for your future career is an important task. Consider the total time spent working: 8 hours a day, 5 days a week, 50 weeks a year totals 2,000 hours each year, not including any overtime. If you work the average career span of 43 years (from age 22 to age 65), you will spend 86,000 hours or more on the job! Because your work will likely take so much of your time, you will need to plan your career carefully.

Steps in Career Planning

Effective career planning involves careful investigation and analysis—a process that you should start now and revisit throughout your work life. The steps in career planning involve self-analysis, research, a plan of action, and periodic re-evaluation.

Self-Analysis

Using resources available from schools, employment offices, testing services, and the Internet, explore personal factors that relate to your career choice.

1. Determine your wants and needs.
2. Determine your values and desired lifestyle.
3. Assess your aptitudes and interests, and determine how they match job tasks.
4. Analyze your personal qualities and the kinds of job tasks that best suit your personality.

Why is self-analysis a necessary component of career planning?

© Pan Xunbin/Shutterstock.com

© padu_foto/Shutterstock.com

Think of a job you would like to have or a company for which you would like to work in the future. Assume you are going to contact the Human Resources Director for that company and set up an informational interview. An *informational* interview is one in which you are not applying for a specific job but are learning more about the job, the industry, or the company itself. It is a good way to explore careers and can help you achieve career goals. To prepare for your informational interview, compile a list of questions you might ask.

© oculo/Shutterstock.com

Research

Based on a good self-analysis, determine the careers that best suit your interests and aptitudes and will help you meet your lifestyle goals.

1. Seek information in books, magazines, and websites; use resources available from libraries, career counseling centers, and employment offices.
2. Compare your interests, aptitudes, and personal qualities to job descriptions and requirements.
3. Talk to people in the fields of work you find interesting, both in person and online in social networks. These informal discussions reveal positive and negative features of a career that you might not have anticipated.
4. Observe occupations, spend time learning about jobs and companies, and seek part-time work to get direct experience. Sometimes following someone throughout his or her workday will give you real insight into the daily activities and requirements of a career.

Plan of Action

After you have done some job research, develop a plan of action that will eventually bring you to your career goals.

1. Use good job-search techniques. Get organized, make a plan, follow through, and don't give up.
2. Develop necessary skills by taking courses (traditional or online) and gaining exposure to the field in which you want to pursue a career.
3. Seek a part-time or volunteer job to gain experience in your area of choice.
4. Evaluate your choices over time. People change and so do jobs. If you discover you are following the wrong career path, change your direction before you stay on it too long.

Re-Evaluation

Because the world changes rapidly, we all need to prepare ourselves to meet the challenges ahead. You may wish to prepare for career changes to take advantage of new opportunities. About every five years, think about what you will be doing and where you would like to be in the next five years.

The Importance of Goals

A **goal** is a desired end toward which efforts are directed. Goals provide a sense of direction and purpose in life. There are three types of goals: short term, intermediate, and long term.

- A **short-term goal** is one you expect to reach in a few days or weeks. A short-term goal could be to achieve at least a B on next week's math test. You know you must plan time to study soon to meet your goal.
- An **intermediate goal** is something you wish to accomplish in the next few months or years. Some examples are graduation from high school, a vacation trip, or plans for summer employment. These goals take longer to achieve and also require more planning.
- A **long-term goal** is what you wish to achieve in five to ten years or longer. It could involve a college degree, career, marriage, or family. Many people find it helpful to write down long-term goals and then revisit them each year to evaluate their progress.

If goals are to be meaningful, they should be well defined and realistic. They should also be written down to become a part of your life. If you are like most people, your goals will change every few years, either because you have accomplished them or because your values have changed. You may decide to take a different path. Many people find a checklist to be a handy way to help them reach their goals. Figure 1.5 shows a typical goals checklist. Use it as a guide to create your own goals checklist.

The Roles of Experience and Education

In today's highly competitive job market, experience and education both play key roles in protecting and enhancing your employability. For many

FIGURE 1.5   Goals Checklist

GOALS CHECKLIST

Week of _____

	Accomplished
Short-term goals (today/this week):	
1. Buy birthday gift for mom	_____
2. Get haircut (Saturday)	_____
3. See counselor about chemistry class	_____
Intermediate goals (next month/year)	
1. Get a C or better in Chemistry	_____
2. Prepare for SAT (test in May)	_____
3. Finish term report (due December 14)	_____
Long-term goals (future)	
1. Graduate from college	_____
2. Buy a car	_____
3. Get a full-time job	_____

careers, applicants will need a college or technical degree and skills before they will even be considered for employment.

Experience

Experience is the knowledge and skills acquired from working in a career field. As you gain experience in a field, you become more valuable to an employer. Most employers give wage increases that reflect the increased value of an employee's experience. When you change career fields, however, you no longer have the advantage of experience. You may need to accept a lower wage as you work to gain experience in your new career field.

Education

A college degree will make you more attractive to employers. A degree that is focused in the area in which you will work is even more important. A recent study shows that some college degrees will give you a very limited match to jobs available. For example, degrees in anthropology, history, or visual arts may interest you, but when you look at the job market and careers that are in demand and pay well, these degrees do not provide skills that lead to them.

As your level of education increases, your earnings increase with it. Many young people today are delaying entering the workforce to stay in college longer and obtain an advanced degree. An *advanced degree* is a specialized, intensive program (taken after obtaining a bachelor's degree) that prepares students for higher-level work responsibilities with more challenges and higher pay. An advanced degree may include a master's degree, doctorate in a specialized field, or a professional degree.

The Need for Plan B

Many people find it to their advantage to be prepared for the worst while they are hoping for the best. Job security is a thing of the past in many jobs and industries. Thus, workers need to look out for themselves so that they don't end up unemployed and lacking the skills or qualifications needed for other jobs. *Plan B* is the label used to describe what you would do if your job ended. For example, you might to do the following:

- *Get a part-time job.* In addition to your full-time job, take a part-time job where you are able to learn new skills, add value, and do something you really like.
- *Polish a hobby.* Learn how to do something really well—to the point that you could make a living doing it if your full-time job ended.
- *Develop networking contacts.* Networks are informal groups of people with common interests. Keep in touch with people who would know about openings in a field where you are qualified and would like to work.
- *Learn new skills.* In addition to your current job skills, learn new job proficiencies so that you would be qualified for advancement at your current employer or some other employer. These added skills will give you opportunities to change jobs if needed.
- *Be aware.* Know what's happening with your company and your industry. As changes occur, look for ways to be adaptive or to move on.

 **CHECKPOINT**

How can goals motivate you?

Working for yourself is called **self-employment**. A person who takes the risks of being self-employed and owning a business is called an *entrepreneur*. Small businesses contribute billions of dollars to the U.S. economy annually and employ more workers than all of the country's large corporations combined. Owning a business can be challenging, but it can be very rewarding as well.

Advantages of Self-Employment

A major advantage of being the owner is that you get to make the decisions about how the business is run. The owner can say what the business will and will not do. That includes the choice of products and services that will be offered. It also includes the hours of operation, the customer base the business will serve, and the prices it will charge. Small business owners also keep all the profits of the business in a form of income that represents revenues earned by the business minus the expenses of doing business.

Disadvantages of Self-Employment

If the business fails, money invested in the business is lost. Most money invested in a small business comes from the owner and/or the owner's family and friends.

Owning a small business is risky because it can be difficult to get credit. In many cases, the owner must use his or her personal credit, including credit cards, home equity, and loans, in order to get and keep the business running. These types of credit are more expensive; they have higher interest rates than larger businesses must pay because there is more risk to the lenders.

With most small businesses, especially during the first few years, the owner works long hours and does many different tasks to get and keep the business running. Most of the profits are put back into the business rather than the owner's pocket. And because money is tight, the owner cannot always hire others to do the work.

Types of Small Businesses

There are three basic types of small businesses. A **side business** is one where the owner pursues his *avocation*, or secondary occupation, while also working full time for an employer. The side business consumes the owner's personal or spare time. It does not grow into a business that can be sold, and most often it is run from the owner's home. Business activities are conducted "on the side." This means the owner works a full-time job for someone else. His or her avocation may result in a nice "side income."

A **lifestyle business** is one that provides a good income for the owner and allows him or her more freedom to meet personal needs. The business is typically a full-time "job" for the owner, but he or she intends to keep the business small. The business

© Monkey Business Images/Shutterstock.com

Why do you think some people prefer to work for themselves?

exists for the lifetime of the owner and usually has no resale value. For example, a dentist may elect to be a one-dentist office and provide services for her patients. When the dentist retires, the business closes.

Other business owners want their businesses to grow into large companies with unlimited growth potential—this type of business is called a **venture business**. As it continues to grow, it will eventually become a corporation, and many workers are hired. For example, Phil Knight started a business designing athletic shoes in his garage in Eugene, Oregon. When his business grew, it became a publicly held corporation known as Nike. Unlike other types of small business owners, a venture business owner has an "exit plan" so that others can continue operating the business when she or he decides to leave. The business owner simply becomes one of the many stockholders and steps down from total control of the business.

Getting Started in Business

Certain cultures seem to encourage entrepreneurship more than others. Also, people whose parents owned a small business are more likely to start a business than those whose parents worked for someone else. Often, entrepreneurs start out working for other businesses to gain needed knowledge and experience. Many business owners seek formal and/or informal education about how to run a business before they get started.

If you have a desire to run your own business, you should spend time preparing yourself for such an endeavor. A good place to start is to talk with the advisers at a Small Business Development Center (SBDC). These centers are located in cities across the country and are sponsored and funded by the Small Business Administration (SBA). Visit the SBA's website to learn about some of the services it offers. Another good resource is SCORE, which offers free business mentoring services from both active and retired business executives from a wide array of backgrounds.

The Business Plan

Before starting a business, many small business owners will prepare a business plan to attract investors to help with funding. A **business plan** is a formal document that outlines the path a business intends to take to earn and grow revenues. This "living" document generally projects financial data three to five years into the future. It's a living document because it changes and grows as time passes. There are nine basic parts to a business plan:

1. *Executive Summary*. This is a snapshot of the business plan. It touches on the company profile (what it is all about) and goals.
2. *Company Description*. This information explains what you do, what differentiates your business from others, and what markets you will enter to do business.
3. *Market Analysis*. This is an analysis of the industry you are in, the market, and your competitors.
4. *Organization and Management*. This section outlines the structure and organization of your company and introduces the management team.
5. *Service or Product List*. This part describes the products or services you sell, the benefits they provide to customers, and the product life cycle.

6. *Marketing and Sales.* This information describes how you plan to market your business, including your sales strategy.
7. *Funding Request.* This section lists how much money you need to get started and become successful.
8. *Financial Projections.* These are estimates of your company's future financial performance.
9. *Appendix.* This includes additional information, such as resumes, permits, leases, and other documents, that help support statements made in the business plan.

Is Entrepreneurship Right for You?

How can you decide whether being an entrepreneur is the right choice for you? Your answers to the following questions will give you a better idea of whether you should consider self-employment.

1. *Are you self-motivated?* Business owners must do what needs to be done without being told or reminded. They enjoy making their own decisions.
2. *Do you like people?* A friendly disposition goes a long way in winning over customers. You should be able to get along with others.
3. *Are you a leader?* Entrepreneurs are able to get others to follow their lead. They are confident and persuasive.
4. *Do you take responsibility?* Entrepreneurs take charge and follow through.
5. *Are you organized?* Business owners must have a good plan before they get started.
6. *Do you work hard?* To be a successful business owner, you must lead by example. Business owners work long, hard hours. They don't expect others to do what they themselves are unwilling to do.
7. *Do you make decisions easily and quickly?* Decisions sometimes have to be made on the spot without complete or up-to-date information.
8. *Are you trustworthy?* Others must trust you and accept that you are knowledgeable. Long-term relationships are built on honesty.
9. *Are you persistent?* Business owners persevere, even when the going gets tough. They meet goals without giving excuses.
10. *Do you keep good records?* Entrepreneurs must account for their expenses and revenues and pay taxes based on this data. They should understand profitability and cost analyses.

If you have a good business idea, start the process early. Get your thoughts and plans on paper, get advice from those you trust, and work toward your dream of owning your own business. A small business owner is a risk-taker. You have to be willing to take financial and personal risks. It won't be easy, but the payoff can be very rewarding!

Why do entrepreneurs need to keep good records to be successful business owners?

© iStockphoto.com/joel-t

CHECKPOINT

What is the purpose of a business plan?

KEY TERMS REVIEW

Match the terms with the definitions. Some terms may not be used.

____ 1. *What you wish to achieve in five or ten years or longer*

____ 2. *A small business that grows to become a corporation*

____ 3. *Working for yourself*

____ 4. *A business in addition to your full-time job*

____ 5. *A desired end that you work toward*

____ 6. *Knowledge and skills acquired from working in a career field*

____ 7. *A formal document that outlines the path a business intends to take to earn and grow revenues*

____ 8. *What you wish to achieve in the next few months or years*

a. business plan
b. experience
c. goal
d. intermediate goal
e. lifestyle business
f. long-term goal
g. self-employment
h. short-term goal
i. side business
j. venture business

CHECK YOUR UNDERSTANDING

LO3-1 9. What are the three types of goals? Why are they important in career planning?

LO3-1 10. What is meant by Plan B? Why is it important?

LO3-2 11. What are the three types of small businesses? Describe each of them.

APPLY YOUR KNOWLEDGE

LO3-2 12. If you are considering becoming an entrepreneur (owning your own business), what are some steps you would take before you make that commitment? Outline the steps you would take in developing your business idea. Where can you get good advice? Would you want a side business, a lifestyle business, or a venture business? Explain.

THINK CRITICALLY

LO3-1 13. Why is career planning needed if you work for an employer?

LO3-1 14. What is the role of education in keeping your career on track?

LO3-2 15. Why is a business plan considered a "living" document? As an entrepreneur, why would you keep a business plan?

The Essential Question *Refer to The Essential Question on p. 23. To prepare for a career, do career planning, set goals, continue your education, and develop a Plan B. As an entrepreneur, make sure self-employment is right for you; start small and get lots of advice from trusted consultants, such as the SBA.*

SUMMARY

1.1

- *The digital age provides many opportunities and challenges as technology makes new advances.*

- *The Internet is a great resource for finding information by using search engines.*

- *Both data mining and data warehousing are tools that are used to turn information about consumers into actionable knowledge.*

- *You must learn to protect your identity and your privacy when making posts to the Internet. Nothing is private on the Internet.*

- *To cope with change, stay informed, be a lifelong learner, take classes to stay up to date, and complete a self-assessment inventory.*

1.2

- *Technology has had a dramatic effect on the job industry, eliminating the need for many jobs while opening up new options, such as working from home.*

- *Job research can be conducted at a number of U.S. government websites as well as at online career sites.*

- *The job application process has changed because of technology; many job applications are now posted and completed online.*

- *A resume is a concise summary of your work experience, education, abilities, and interests.*

- *The job interview requires preparation. After an interview, a follow-up thank-you letter reminds the interviewer of your qualifications and interest in the job.*

1.3

- *Career planning is needed in today's rapidly changing world. Steps include self-analysis, research, a plan of action, and re-evaluation.*

- *Your personal goals should drive what you seek to do in your career.*

- *Experience and education play key roles in protecting and enhancing employability.*

- *In the event of unemployment, it's always best to be prepared by having a Plan B.*

- *There are three types of entrepreneurial businesses: a side business, a lifestyle business, and a venture business.*

APPLY WHAT YOU KNOW

LO1-1 1. Explain how data mining is both beneficial and potentially harmful.

LO1-2 2. How do upgrading and retraining help you cope with change?

LO2-1 3. How does the economy (demand by consumers) affect jobs that are created or eliminated?

LO2-1 4. How does technology affect careers and income?

LO2-1 5. Name some jobs in the professional sector that are directly related to technology.

LO2-2 6. Name someone who would be a good reference to list on your resume or who would write a reference letter for you. Explain your choice.

LO2-2 7. Why is it important to do company research prior to a job interview?

LO2-2 8. Why would you do follow-up after a job interview? What might it involve?

LO3-1 9. How does a self-analysis help you with career planning?

LO3-1 10. What types of goals are needed to help direct your efforts in career planning? Give examples of each type of goal.

LO3-1 11. Explain how experience and education enhance your ability to get promotions and better job opportunities.

LO3-1 12. List the four major steps in career planning. What are you doing to prepare for a career?

LO3-2 13. Why would a person choose to start a side business rather than a venture business?

LO3-2 14. How would you know if being self-employed is right for you?

MAKE ACADEMIC CONNECTIONS

LO1-1 15. **Technology** Explore two social media sites that are popular with your age group. Explain what each has to offer and why you might choose that site over others. Write a report summarizing your findings and conclude by describing the benefits of social media.

LO2-1 16. **Economics** Identify three countries that are receiving large amounts of outsourced work from the United States. In a one-page report, explain the impact on their economies and standards of living. Then explain the impact on the U.S. economy.

LO2-2 17. **Research** Conduct online job research about three potential careers you might like to pursue. Use the *Occupational Outlook Handbook's* A–Z index. Create a table listing the pros and cons of each potential career choice. Include the median annual wage for each of them as well as any other pertinent information you learn.

LO3-2 18. **History** Prepare a presentation about the SBA, including when and why this agency was created, its role through the years, and its role today. Use visual aids during your presentation, such as charts or electronic slides.

Solve Problems and Explore Issues

LO1-1 19. Explain why privacy is such an important value in America. Conduct Internet research using the keywords "privacy" and "privacy advocates." What can you and others do to guard your privacy on the Internet and in the marketplace?

LO2-1 20. Conduct research on the U.S. economy and the job market. Are businesses hiring, holding steady, or laying off workers? What are the reasons given? What career fields are growing and shrinking? Explain how this type of information will affect your career choices and career planning now and in the future.

LO2-2 21. Your friend Sarah tells you she has a job interview tomorrow. She has never had one before, and she is very nervous. Sarah asks you for advice about the interviewing process. Make a list of ten things Sarah should do before, during, and after the interview.

LO3-1 22. Do you set goals for yourself, both personal and career-related goals? Using Figure 1.5 as a sample, create a list of your short-term, intermediate, and long-term goals.

LO3-2 23. Go online and find a sample business plan. The SBA provides guidelines for preparing a business plan. Explain the various elements contained in the plan and why each one is important.

EXTEND YOUR LEARNING

LO3-2 24. **Ethics** Many people embellish or exaggerate facts on their resumes, leading employers to believe they have skills that they don't really have. The same is true of job applications. Many people who embellish and exaggerate use the excuse that "everybody does it." Does this make it right? Why should you be honest on your resume and employment application?

CHAPTER PROJECT

One American dream is that of owning your own business. Because of the free-market system, anyone in the United States can become an entrepreneur. Some entrepreneurs are successful because they provide a product that meets consumer demand. Others start a business that does not meet consumer demand, and the business ultimately fails. Conduct online research to find entrepreneurs who successfully started a business. Choose one entrepreneur and find out how he or she came up with a business idea. What steps did he or she take to start a business? Prepare a presentation that shows the history of the business and entrepreneur.

Complete the Guided Decision Making activity for Chapter 1 at ngl.cengage.com/mypf.

Pay, Benefits, and Work

Consider This...

Christine was just hired for her first job. It is part time with flexible hours so she can also attend school. Her pay rate is just above minimum wage, and she can work some overtime hours if she wishes during the peak season. As a part-time employee, her benefits include paid time off for sick days, vacation (one week after her first year of employment), and holidays. She does not have health insurance coverage or other benefits such as a retirement plan or profit sharing. She doesn't mind not having health insurance because she is covered under her mother's health insurance plan. For now, Christine is satisfied with her overall benefits package. However, she realizes that eventually (when she finishes school) she will need a job with better benefits so she can provide for her future financial security. What types of benefits might an employer offer Christine?

Gross Pay, Net Pay, and Benefits

The Essential Question *What components make up an employee's total compensation?*

LEARNING OBJECTIVES

› LO 1-1 Compute gross pay and net pay.
› LO 1-2 List and describe employment benefits and incentives.

KEY TERMS

- gross pay, *35*
- wage, *35*
- overtime, *35*
- salary, *36*
- net pay, *37*

- benefits, *40*
- vested, *41*
- incentive pay, *41*
- profit sharing, *41*
- bonus, *43*

LO 1-1 Gross Pay, Deductions, and Net Pay

When you work for an employer, you agree to perform certain tasks in exchange for payment. **Gross pay** is the total amount you earn before deductions are subtracted.

Hourly Wages

A fixed hourly rate earned by employees is a **wage**. Your wage rate is multiplied by the number of hours you worked, and typically those hours are listed on some type of time card or other record.

If you work for $10 an hour and you agree that you will work 30 hours a week, your gross pay from wages would be $300 per week ($10 × 30 hours). The regular rate of pay times the regular hours worked is your gross pay for the week.

Hourly Rate	×	Hours Worked	=	Gross Pay
$10	×	30 hours	=	$300

Overtime

Overtime is time worked beyond your regular hours. When working overtime, you are working more hours than the standard agreed-upon workweek. In most states, working 40 hours in a five-day period is considered a standard workweek, and working more hours beyond that is considered overtime.

Why do people like to work overtime?

© Pan Xunbin/Shutterstock.com

© Alexey Stiop/Shutterstock.com

Chapter 2 Pay, Benefits, and Work 35

The typical wage rate for overtime pay is 1.5 times your regular rate. So if your regular hourly rate is $10 an hour, then your overtime rate is $15 an hour ($10 × 1.5). A person who works 48 hours in a 5-day period would receive 40 hours of regular pay and 8 hours of overtime pay. Gross pay would be computed as follows:

40 hours × $10/hour (regular pay)	$400.00
8 hours × $15/hour (overtime pay)	+120.00
Gross Pay	$520.00

Salary

You may work for a fixed yearly amount rather than an hourly rate. A **salary** is a fixed annual amount of gross pay. Salaried employees often do not receive additional pay for overtime work, unless it is agreed upon between the employee and employer.

A salary stated as a yearly amount is divided into regular pay periods. If you work for $24,000 a year and there are 12 monthly pay periods, you will receive $2,000 per month ($24,000 ÷ 12). Some employers pay biweekly, or every two weeks, so there are 26 pay periods (52 weeks ÷ 2). In this case, you would receive gross pay of $923.08 per paycheck ($24,000 ÷ 26). Another common pay period is semimonthly, or twice a month. Instead of 12 monthly paychecks, you would receive 24 paychecks, and your gross pay would be $1,000 each pay period ($24,000 ÷ 24).

When salaried employees are paid overtime, it is typically based on their hourly rate of pay. If a person is paid $2,000 a month and usually works 160 hours a month (40 hours/week × 4 weeks), the hourly rate would be computed at $12.50 ($2,000 ÷ 160). One and a half times the regular hourly rate of $12.50 equals an overtime rate of $18.75 per hour.

Deductions

Amounts subtracted from gross pay are called *deductions*. Some deductions, such as income tax and Social Security tax, are required by law. *Allowances* are reductions in the amount of tax withheld from your paycheck. The number of allowances is reported on Form W-4, which you will complete when you start a new job. The form includes a simple worksheet to help you calculate your allowances.

Other deductions are optional. For example, you may choose to have your employer deduct a regular amount each pay period to pay for your health insurance premiums or your union dues.

Figure 2.1 is a paycheck that shows an employee's gross pay and deductions. Required deductions include federal income tax, state income tax, Social Security tax, and Medicare tax. For this employee, optional deductions include credit union, health insurance, and union payments. Optional deductions may not be withheld without the employee's written consent, except in the case of a court order. Child support payments or wage garnishments for unpaid debts are examples of optional deductions imposed by a court.

Employers are required to keep detailed records of wages, salaries, hours worked, rates of pay, and deductions. With each paycheck (even if it is deposited electronically), the employee must receive a pay stub, or a detailed list of pay (regular and overtime) and deductions (required and optional).

FIGURE 2.1   **Paycheck with Stub**

Marshall Manufacturing Co.

14 Ault Street, Bates, OR 97817-2341

88-0581 / 1120

PAYROLL CHECK

Co. Code	Department	File No.	Clock No. ID	Social Security No.	TO THE ORDER OF	Pay Date	Check No.
R&T	000108	43329	501 A	999 00 7426	SHARI GREGSON	02 10 —	BELOW

PAY THIS AMOUNT — NET PAY

Two hundred forty-three and 34/100 dollars — $243.34

SHARI GREGSON
1133 ELM STREET,
BATES, OR 97817-1234

BATES BANK
BATES, OREGON

DISBURSING AGENT FOR ABOVE EMPLOYER

Jermaine Davis
AUTHORIZED SIGNATURE

⑈112005812⑈ 010450 001995⑈

Marshall Manufacturing Co.

14 Ault Street, Bates, OR 97817-2341

Co. Code	Department	File No.	Fed. Status	Name		Pay Period Ending		Pay Date
R&T	000108	43329	501 A	GREGSON, SHARI		02 10 —		02 10 —

Hours Units	Rate	Earnings	Type	Deduction	Type	Deduction	Type
4000	800	32000	REG	2500	CR UN		
400	1200	4800	OT	1650	H INS		
				300	UN DUES		

This	Gross	Fed. With. Tax	State With. Tax	Social Security	Medicare	Other Deductions	Net Pay
Pay	368 00	29 00	23 00	22 82	5 34	44 50	243 34
YTD	2,208 00	174 00	138 00	136 92	32 04	267 00	

Net Pay

When all deductions are taken from your gross pay, the amount left is your **net pay**. It is the amount of the paycheck. This is your "take-home pay," and in most cases, it is about 65–70 percent (or less) of your gross pay. So, what's left for you to spend is considerably less than gross pay. Stated mathematically, net pay is calculated as follows:

Regular Pay (Wages or Salary) + Overtime Pay = Gross Pay
Gross Pay − Deductions (Required and Optional) = Net Pay

Figure 2.2 shows an employee withholding sheet. It lists weekly gross pay, deductions, and net pay. The amounts withheld for federal income tax and state income tax are determined from withholding tables. Figure 2.3 shows part of the weekly withholding table for the state of Oregon (the state in which the employee works). Figure 2.4 shows part of the weekly federal withholding tax table. There are different tax tables for different pay periods (weekly, biweekly, and so on). To determine the proper amounts to be withheld for federal and state income taxes, find the range on the left side of the tables that includes the employee's gross pay and the number of allowances across the top.

The Social Security deduction is withheld at the standard rate of 6.2 percent of the first $117,000 for 2014. Medicare tax is withheld at the rate of 1.45 percent of all pay earned. Employers must contribute matching amounts into each employee's Social Security and Medicare accounts.

FIGURE 2.2   Employee Withholding Sheet

EMPLOYEE WITHHOLDING SHEET

Name: <u>Peggy Overton</u>   Social Security Number: <u>123-45-6789</u>

Pay Period: <u>Weekly</u>   Number of Allowances: <u>1</u>

Marital Status: <u>Single</u>   Pay Date: <u>02/06/20--</u>

GROSS PAY:

$19,500 annual pay (52 weeks) $375.00

Overtime: None 0.00

Total $375.00

REQUIRED DEDUCTIONS:

Federal income tax (use tax tables) . . . . $ 30.00

State income tax (use tax tables). 23.00

Social Security tax (6.2% $\times$ gross pay) 23.25

Medicare tax (1.45% $\times$ gross pay) 5.44

OTHER DEDUCTIONS:

Insurance Premiums 30.00

Union Dues 7.50

Retirement Account (401k) 25.00

Charitable Contributions 5.00

Total Deductions 149.19

NET PAY (Automatic Deposit) $225.81

FIGURE 2.3   State Tax Withholding Table—Weekly Payroll

Weekly Payroll Period (Oregon)

Amount of tax to be withheld

Wage		Number of withholding allowances															
		Two or less						Three or more									
At	But less	Single			Married			Single or married									
least	than	0	1	2	0	1	2	3	4	5	6	7	8	9	10	11	12	13	14
0 – 20		4	0	0	4	0	0	0	0	0	0	0	0	0	0	0	0	0	0
20 – 40		4	0	0	4	0	0	0	0	0	0	0	0	0	0	0	0	0	0
40 – 60		4	1	0	4	0	0	0	0	0	0	0	0	0	0	0	0	0	0
60 – 80		5	2	0	4	0	0	0	0	0	0	0	0	0	0	0	0	0	0
80 – 100		6	3	0	4	1	0	0	0	0	0	0	0	0	0	0	0	0	0
100 – 120		7	4	0	5	2	0	0	0	0	0	0	0	0	0	0	0	0	0
120 – 140		8	5	1	6	3	0	0	0	0	0	0	0	0	0	0	0	0	0
140 – 160		9	6	3	7	4	0	0	0	0	0	0	0	0	0	0	0	0	0
160 – 180		11	7	4	8	5	1	0	0	0	0	0	0	0	0	0	0	0	0
180 – 200		12	9	6	9	6	2	0	0	0	0	0	0	0	0	0	0	0	0
200 – 220		13	10	7	10	7	3	0	0	0	0	0	0	0	0	0	0	0	0
220 – 240		15	12	9	11	8	4	1	0	0	0	0	0	0	0	0	0	0	0
240 – 260		16	13	10	12	9	6	2	0	0	0	0	0	0	0	0	0	0	0
260 – 280		18	15	12	14	11	7	4	0	0	0	0	0	0	0	0	0	0	0
280 – 300		19	17	14	15	12	9	5	1	0	0	0	0	0	0	0	0	0	0
300 – 320		21	18	15	16	13	10	6	3	0	0	0	0	0	0	0	0	0	0
320 – 340		22	20	17	17	14	11	8	4	1	0	0	0	0	0	0	0	0	0
340 – 360		24	21	18	19	16	13	9	6	2	0	0	0	0	0	0	0	0	0
360 – 380		25	23	20	20	17	14	11	7	3	0	0	0	0	0	0	0	0	0
380 – 400		27	24	22	21	18	15	12	8	5	1	0	0	0	0	0	0	0	0
400 – 420		28	26	23	22	19	16	13	10	6	3	0	0	0	0	0	0	0	0
420 – 440		30	27	25	24	21	18	15	12	8	5	1	0	0	0	0	0	0	0
440 – 460		31	29	26	26	23	20	17	14	10	6	3	0	0	0	0	0	0	0

Source: http://www.oregon.gov/

FIGURE 2.4 Federal Tax Withholding Table—Weekly Payroll

SINGLE Persons—WEEKLY Payroll Period

(For Wages Paid through December 20--)

And the wages are—		And the number of withholding allowances claimed is—										
At least	But less than	0	1	2	3	4	5	6	7	8	9	10
		The amount of income tax to be withheld is—										
$0	$55	$0	$0	$0	$0	$0	$0	$0	$0	$0	$0	$0
55	60	2	0	0	0	0	0	0	0	0	0	0
60	65	2	0	0	0	0	0	0	0	0	0	0
65	70	3	0	0	0	0	0	0	0	0	0	0
70	75	3	0	0	0	0	0	0	0	0	0	0
75	80	4	0	0	0	0	0	0	0	0	0	0
80	85	4	0	0	0	0	0	0	0	0	0	0
85	90	5	0	0	0	0	0	0	0	0	0	0
90	95	5	0	0	0	0	0	0	0	0	0	0
95	100	6	0	0	0	0	0	0	0	0	0	0
100	105	6	0	0	0	0	0	0	0	0	0	0
105	110	7	0	0	0	0	0	0	0	0	0	0
110	115	7	0	0	0	0	0	0	0	0	0	0
115	120	8	0	0	0	0	0	0	0	0	0	0
120	125	8	1	0	0	0	0	0	0	0	0	0
125	130	9	1	0	0	0	0	0	0	0	0	0
130	135	9	2	0	0	0	0	0	0	0	0	0
135	140	10	2	0	0	0	0	0	0	0	0	0
140	145	10	3	0	0	0	0	0	0	0	0	0
145	150	11	3	0	0	0	0	0	0	0	0	0
150	155	11	4	0	0	0	0	0	0	0	0	0
155	160	12	4	0	0	0	0	0	0	0	0	0
160	165	12	5	0	0	0	0	0	0	0	0	0
165	170	13	5	0	0	0	0	0	0	0	0	0
170	175	13	6	0	0	0	0	0	0	0	0	0
175	180	14	6	0	0	0	0	0	0	0	0	0
180	185	14	7	0	0	0	0	0	0	0	0	0
185	190	15	7	0	0	0	0	0	0	0	0	0
190	195	15	8	0	0	0	0	0	0	0	0	0
195	200	16	8	1	0	0	0	0	0	0	0	0
200	210	16	9	1	0	0	0	0	0	0	0	0
210	220	17	10	2	0	0	0	0	0	0	0	0
220	230	19	11	3	0	0	0	0	0	0	0	0
230	240	20	12	4	0	0	0	0	0	0	0	0
240	250	22	13	5	0	0	0	0	0	0	0	0
250	260	23	14	6	0	0	0	0	0	0	0	0
260	270	25	15	7	0	0	0	0	0	0	0	0
270	280	26	16	8	1	0	0	0	0	0	0	0
280	290	28	17	9	2	0	0	0	0	0	0	0
290	300	29	18	10	3	0	0	0	0	0	0	0
300	310	31	20	11	4	0	0	0	0	0	0	0
310	320	32	21	12	5	0	0	0	0	0	0	0
320	330	34	23	13	6	0	0	0	0	0	0	0
330	340	35	24	14	7	0	0	0	0	0	0	0
340	350	37	26	15	8	0	0	0	0	0	0	0
350	360	38	27	16	9	1	0	0	0	0	0	0
360	370	40	29	17	10	2	0	0	0	0	0	0
370	380	41	30	19	11	3	0	0	0	0	0	0
380	390	43	32	20	12	4	0	0	0	0	0	0
390	400	44	33	22	13	5	0	0	0	0	0	0
400	410	46	35	23	14	6	0	0	0	0	0	0
410	420	47	36	25	15	7	0	0	0	0	0	0

Source: www.irs.gov/pub/irs-pdf/p15.pdf

In addition to required deductions, the employee withholding sheet also lists optional deductions that the employee has authorized. Like the required deductions, the optional deductions are subtracted from gross pay. Common optional deductions are health and life insurance payments, union dues, savings contributions, retirement contributions, and charitable contributions.

✔ CHECKPOINT

What amounts can be found on a pay stub?

Many employers offer **benefits**, which are forms of employer compensation in addition to pay. Common benefits provided wholly or in part by employers include health insurance, retirement savings plans, paid sick leave and vacations, and profit sharing. Some benefits are required by law (such as unemployment compensation, workers' compensation, and matching Social Security and Medicare taxes). Benefits often are offered to full-time, permanent employees only.

Paid Vacations and Holidays

Full-time, permanent employees usually have a set amount of paid vacation time. This means they will be paid as usual while on vacation. *Vacation pay* allows employees to rest and spend time with their families, which helps prevent fatigue and increases employee morale and productivity. Employees commonly receive one week's vacation after one year of employment, two weeks after two years, and three weeks after five years. Employees in stressful occupations (such as firefighting, teaching, and social work) may get more vacation time to help them maintain good mental health.

Full-time employees generally are given paid holidays also (as required by federal and state laws). Paid holidays in the United States typically include Christmas, Thanksgiving, the Fourth of July, Labor Day, and Memorial Day. Other holidays many companies grant to employees include New Year's Day, Veterans Day, Martin Luther King, Jr. Day, and Presidents Day. In many cases, employees who work on holidays are paid at rates that are double, or more than double, the regular rate of pay.

Group Insurance

Employers with more than 50 employees are required by law to offer health insurance. (Group insurance is covered in more detail in Chapter 23.) Most plans today are covered partly by the employer and partly by employee contributions. Typically, employers will pay most, if not all, of the group health insurance premiums for employees, while employees must pay for

Global View

In Australia, "career break schemes" allow an employee to negotiate a fixed period away from work of up to several years for educational study or for family commitments, while maintaining a guaranteed job. Career break schemes frequently involve full-time work for short periods and part-time work for phase-out and phase-in stages. During these stages, pay and benefits are usually available. Career break schemes can reduce the loss of experienced staff. Employers help employees who are on a career break to maintain their skills and knowledge by providing training courses or by ensuring access to current work-related information. These activities make it easier for employees to return to work.

THINK CRITICALLY

How might offering career break schemes lead to greater work satisfaction? Are similar benefits available in the United States? If so, describe them.

©Redshinestudio/Shutterstock.com

coverage for their dependents (spouse and children). Some employers also offer dental and vision insurance.

Group life insurance may also be provided by employers, typically up to the amount of an employee's annual pay. Employees may be able to buy additional life insurance at the group rates. Group insurance rates are often lower than individual policy premiums, especially for older employees. This additional coverage can be paid through payroll deductions. It is important to know that group life insurance may terminate when an employee leaves the company or retires.

Sick Pay and Bereavement Pay

Many businesses also provide a certain allowable number of sick days each year for illness, with pay as usual. It is customary to receive three to ten days a year as "sick days" without deductions from pay. Some employers allow unused sick pay to accumulate and carry over to the next year. This gives an employee more sick days to use if they have a serious injury or illness. Employees with children typically are allowed to use sick leave to stay home when their children are ill.

Bereavement pay is sometimes available to employees who have had a death in their family. Typically, the employee is allowed three or five days to deal with their loss and attend memorial services.

Pension and Retirement Plans

Some employers provide employer-paid *pension plans* for their employees. When the employee retires, he or she receives a monthly check, which is taxable income. The employee becomes **vested** (entitled to the full retirement amount) after a specified period of employment, such as five years. This type of pay is disappearing in today's workplace.

More commonly, companies offer *employer-sponsored retirement savings plans*, such as a 401(k) account for private employers or a 403(b) account for government and nonprofit employees. Money that is voluntarily withheld from employees' earnings goes into these accounts. In some cases, employers match employee contributions, but this is not required. For example, a company may match an employee's contribution up to 10 percent. So, if an employee contributes $200 a month, the employer would contribute $20 a month.

Incentives

Incentive pay is a form of compensation that encourages employees to strive for higher levels of performance. The theory behind incentives is that employees will be more motivated to work for the benefit of the company when they can share in the company's success. This long-term strategy has proven to benefit both the employer and the employee. Companies offer many kinds of incentives to their employees.

Profit Sharing

Profit sharing is a plan that allows employees to share a portion of the company's profits at the end of the corporate year. The more profits the company makes, the more the company shares with its employees. This type of plan may

What are the advantages of using a company credit card for business expenses?

be offered to key executives, management-level and higher-level employees, or in some cases, all employees. Profits can be measured in terms of increases in sales, income, or stock prices.

Leaves of Absence

Some employers allow employees to leave their jobs temporarily (usually without pay) for certain reasons, such as having children, completing their education, or caring for elderly or sick family members. A *sabbatical* is a form of paid or unpaid leave of absence. During a sabbatical, the employee is able to carry out projects, travel, or complete tasks that would not be possible while working full time.

Expense Accounts

An *expense account* typically is provided for management-level employees who must travel or perform out-of-office tasks in the course of their work. They may be given a mileage allowance or, in some cases, a company vehicle to travel to conferences, meetings, or other events. By using a company credit card, they are able to pay for hotel rooms, meals, registration fees, car rentals, and other work-related expenses. These employees typically submit an *expense report* along with receipts and documentation to support the amounts spent.

Some employers allow for *expense reimbursement*. Employees who travel on company business keep track of the expenses they pay for themselves and submit an expense report for reimbursement when they return. Reimbursements of these types of expenses are not taxable income.

Employee Discounts and Extras

Many companies offer "extras" to their employees to improve morale and to encourage them to be customers as well as employees. *Employee discounts* allow employees to buy the company's products or services at a reduced price. Social and recreational programs, free parking, tuition reimbursement, wellness programs, and mental health counseling provide employees with many extras that they value as part of their nontaxable compensation plans.

Child care is a major issue for working parents. Many companies provide on-site child-care facilities. In years to come, federal laws are likely to include more employer child-care incentives for working parents. Some companies are even dog friendly and allow employees to bring their pets to work. Companies such as Amazon, Ben & Jerry's, Google, and even the U.S. Congress allow dogs at the office. A recent study found that employees' stress levels declined throughout the day when dog owners were allowed to bring their pets to work.

Bonuses and Stock Options

Larger corporations and employers often provide bonuses and stock options. A **bonus** is incentive pay based on quality of work done, years of service, or a company's sales and profits. Holiday bonuses often are based on years of service. If a company achieves its target goals for the year, bonuses may be awarded to thank employees for their work. *Stock options* allow employees to buy shares of company stock at reduced prices (lower than market value). This practice gives employees a stake in the long-term success of the company. It is a proven method to motivate employees.

Evaluating Employee Benefits and Incentives

Many of these optional benefits and incentives are of great value to employees. They are not taxable to employees (except bonuses and other benefits paid in cash), yet they provide valuable coverage and advantages. Generally, large companies provide more extensive optional benefits and incentives than smaller companies do.

In recent years, employee benefits have become more flexible to meet the changing needs of the workforce. *Cafeteria-style benefits* are programs that allow employees to select from a range of employer-paid benefits up to a certain value, based on personal needs. Offering flexibility in the selection of benefits is highly valued by employees. For example, a married employee with children might opt for increased life and health insurance, while a single employee may choose a 401(k) contribution.

Benefit packages typically cost about 30 percent or more of payroll costs. So, if an employee is earning $40,000 a year, the value of the benefit package is about $12,000 ($40,000 × 30%). The employer is matching Social Security and Medicare deductions in addition to paying a portion of health insurance premiums, sick pay, vacation pay, profit sharing, and all of the other perks that are used to attract and keep qualified employees. When evaluating benefit packages, you should ask these questions:

Why do cafeteria-style benefits appeal to employees?

- Does the benefit package meet my essential needs for insurance?
- How much of the benefit package is nontaxable?
- What options are available for retirement plans?
- Does the benefit package allow sufficient flexibility so I can care for my family members and myself in the event of illness or major events?

✔ CHECKPOINT

How much value would you place on benefits and incentives provided by your employer?

Graphic Design

Graphic designers create visual concepts, most often using computer software, to communicate ideas that inspire, inform, and captivate customers. They know how to use color, images, and designs to portray an idea or identity to be used in advertising and promotions for products and services.

Graphic designers often work in the publishing, advertising, and public relations industries or related services. They use their creativity and originality to create layouts of printed pages or websites to show how text and images can come together to convey a message about a client's products or services.

Graphic designers must meet with clients to learn about the project needs. They also present designs to clients and advise them on marketing strategies.

Employment Outlook

- An average rate of employment growth is expected through 2020.
- Employment of graphic designers in computer systems design has a higher growth rate.

Job Titles

- Graphic designer
- Graphic artist
- Communication designers

Needed Skills

- A bachelor's degree is required for entry-level work.
- Creativity and originality are essential.
- Additional training is needed for new computer graphics and design software.

What's it like to work in . . . *Graphic Design*

Mike works for a major graphics company that specializes in retail promotions. His annual salary is $45,000. He works both independently and as part of a team. His company allows him to telecommute, so he works from home some days. While in the office, he may attend meetings with the art director and clients.

Today Mike is working on an advertisement for a new client who sells the types of products that he thinks can be displayed very creatively. He's looking forward to developing a design that will captivate the consumers' attention. Although he will incorporate his own ideas into the design, he will also implement any specific requests made by the client regarding colors, logos, and images. As he considers the message the client wants to convey, he starts working on the layout for the advertisement.

What About You?

Are you creative and artistic? Do you like working with technology? What other aspects of this career appeal to you? Are there aspects of this career that you don't like? Do you think a career as a graphic designer might be right for you?

The Career Clusters icons are being used with permission of the: States' Career Clusters Initiative, 2007, www.careerclusters.org

KEY TERMS REVIEW

Match the terms with the definitions. Some terms may not be used.

a. benefits
b. bonus
c. gross pay
d. incentive pay
e. net pay
f. overtime
g. profit sharing
h. salary
i. vested
j. wage

____ 1. Time worked beyond regular work hours

____ 2. A plan that allows employees to share a portion of the company's income

____ 3. A fixed annual amount of gross pay

____ 4. Compensation that encourages employees to strive for high performance

____ 5. A fixed hourly rate of pay

____ 6. Forms of employer compensation in addition to pay

____ 7. Total earnings before deductions are subtracted

____ 8. Incentive pay based on quality of work, years of service, or profits

CHECK YOUR UNDERSTANDING

LO1-1 9. What is included in gross pay? List some required and optional deductions from gross pay.

LO1-2 10. List benefits provided to most full-time, permanent employees.

LO1-2 11. For employees, what is the advantage of cafeteria-style benefit plans?

APPLY YOUR KNOWLEDGE

LO1-1 12. If your annual pay is $36,010, what is your biweekly pay based on 26 biweekly paychecks? What is your hourly rate of pay if you work 160 hours per month? What is your overtime rate?

LO1-2 13. Assuming you could contribute up to 5 percent of your gross pay of $30,000 into a 401(k) and your employer would match your contribution up to 1 percent of your salary, what total amount would be contributed to your account each year?

THINK CRITICALLY

LO1-1 14. Why are salaried employees often excluded from overtime pay? Do you think this is fair? Explain your answer.

LO1-2 15. As an employee, would you consider paid vacations and holidays motivational? Why or why not?

The Essential Question *Refer to The Essential Question on p. 35. An employee's total compensation package includes wages or salary (gross pay − deductions = net pay), benefits, and incentives.*

The Essential Question *How is the work environment changing?*

LEARNING OBJECTIVES

> LO 2-1 Explain the benefit of work models that differ from regular workweeks.
> LO 2-2 Describe the role of unions and professional organizations in the workplace.

KEY TERMS

- telecommuting, *46*
- flextime, *46*
- compressed workweek, *47*
- job rotation, *47*
- job sharing, *47*
- union, *49*
- bargaining, *49*
- seniority, *49*
- lobbying, *51*

LO 2-1 The Changing Work Environment

The digital age has brought new opportunities and challenges for employers and the employees they hire. As needs have evolved, many new work models have been developed to reduce employee costs and burnout, increase safety, and lower costs for employers.

As companies explore new work models for increasing efficiency and effectiveness, they have developed alternative working times and conditions. Many businesses have realized that the standard workweek (eight hours a day, five days a week) no longer meets their needs to provide quality customer service and products. Newer work models allow more flexibility for both the employer and employee.

Telecommuting

Advances in technology have made it possible for many employees to work from home. **Telecommuting** is a work model that allows employees to work off-site and remain in contact with their employers through the use of technology. Often these employees are able to submit work using e-mail and *cloud computing*. Work can be deposited in an Internet cloud site where it can be accessed by both the employer and the remote employee, regardless of where they are located. This technology eliminates the need for storage on a hard drive, desktop, or other location that cannot be accessed remotely.

Many telecommuters travel extensively and require flexibility. Employees who telecommute must be responsible to manage their own schedules and submit work in a timely manner. Companies that allow telecommuting most likely have procedures and policies in place that employees must follow.

Flexible Schedules and Compressed Workweeks

Flextime is a type of work schedule that allows employees to choose their working hours within a defined time limit. While all employees generally are needed during core time periods, such as times of high customer volume, employees on flextime can choose their other work hours to meet their needs. For example, an employee with young children might choose to start work at 10 A.M. after the children are in school instead of at the standard starting time of 9 A.M. Assuming that the core hours are between 10 A.M. and 3 P.M., employees could arrange their work days to arrive and depart outside the peak times.

A **compressed workweek** is a work schedule that fits the normal 40-hour workweek into less than five days. The typical compressed workweek is ten hours a day for four days, followed by three days off. It gives employees larger blocks of time to get their work done. Some types of work are better suited to this type of schedule than others.

Flextime and compressed workweeks are good for business because employees are responsible for working their standard hours regardless of when they arrive on the job or leave from the job. Employees are satisfied and motivated because they are able to fulfill their personal needs, such as going to doctor appointments. Flextime and compressed schedules reduce the stress caused by trying to balance work time and personal time.

Job Rotation

Job rotation is a job design in which employees are trained to do more than one specialized task. They regularly rotate from one task to another. This approach gives employees more variety in what they do each day, which often makes work more satisfying. A major advantage for both employer and employee is that information and ideas are freely exchanged, leading to improved efficiency. When more than one employee is skilled at a particular job, there are others who can keep the work flowing in someone's absence.

Job Sharing

Job sharing is a job design in which two people share one full-time position. They split the salary and benefits according to each person's contributions. Job sharing is very attractive to people who want part-time work while they are raising children or handling other family responsibilities. By allowing employees to meet their personal needs, job sharing reduces absenteeism and lowers fatigue, improving productivity. It also gives the employer more than one person who is skilled in a particular job or task.

Permanent Part Time

Today's labor force is composed of more people who desire to work only part time. Working part time generally means working 16 to 25 hours a week. By hiring part-time employees, companies can save money on salaries and benefits, while reducing absenteeism and fatigue. Part-time employees may receive some employment benefits, but typically they have their health insurance needs met through some other source. The part-time employee has flexibility to meet personal needs while maintaining job security and employment skills. Parents with small children, older employees, and others are finding that permanent part-time work is a good fit for their lifestyles.

 **CHECKPOINT**

How have new technology and work models affected the workplace?

Cost of Absenteeism

Absenteeism is a major issue for employers because it reduces productivity. Newer work models allow more flexibility and in turn help reduce absenteeism, but it is still a recurring problem for business owners. Most labor experts agree that an absentee rate of 2.0 is low, while a rate of 5.0 is high.

Bascom's Health Foods Market operates 24 hours a day, 365 days a year. Employees work three 8-hour shifts. In an average month, a total of 12 employees work 30 days. On average, a total of 180 hours are missed from work each month, which is the equivalent of 7.5 days (180 hours ÷ 8-hour shift ÷ 3 shifts). The rate of absenteeism is determined as follows:

$$\text{Rate of Absenteeism} = \frac{\text{Absent Days per Month}}{\text{Work Days per Month} \times \text{Number of Employees}}$$

Using this formula, Bascom's absenteeism rate is 2.08%, or 7.5 ÷ (30 × 12). The following formula determines the cost of absenteeism:

Cost of Absenteeism = Annual Lost Time × Average Wage Rate × 2

The formula multiplies the cost of wages by 2 to include the costs of benefits paid to absent employees and the costs of paying temporary employees to replace the absent employees.

Bascom's average wage rate is $7.50 per hour. Using the formula, the cost of absenteeism is determined as follows:

Annual Lost Time = 180 hours per month × 12 months per year
         = 2,160 hours

Cost = 2,160 hours × $7.50 = $16,200 wages paid to absent employees
         $16,200 × 2 = $32,400 annual cost of absenteeism

Based on the preceding example, compute the absenteeism rate and its annual cost for another business based on the following information:

Goldstein's operates two 8-hour shifts a day. A total of eight employees work 24 days a month. On average, a total of 144 hours are missed from work each month, which is the equivalent of 9 days (144 hours ÷ 8-hour shift ÷ 2 shifts). The average wage rate is $12 per hour.

Solution: 9 ÷ (24 × 8) = 4.69% rate of absenteeism

         144 × 12 = 1,728 hours lost annually

         1,728 × $12 = $20,736 wages paid to absent employees

         $20,736 × 2 = $41,472 annual cost of absenteeism

© simo988/Shutterstock.com

Many jobs, both in the private and the public sectors, involve union membership and/or participation in professional organizations as requirements of employment. A **union** is a group of people who work in the same or similar occupations, organized for the benefit of the employees in those occupations.

The Purpose of Unions

Unions have four major functions:

- Engage in collective bargaining
- Support political candidates and positions that benefit members
- Provide support services for members
- Recruit new members

Unions support their members by lawfully representing their interests. For example, if a member is treated unfairly by his or her supervisor, the union assists in resolving the issue. The union collects dues from the employees to provide such services.

The main function of unions is collective or group bargaining. **Bargaining** is the process of negotiating an employment contract for union members. Terms of the employment contract set working conditions, wages, overtime rates, hours of work, and benefits. The employment contract also addresses other issues such as how layoffs or downsizing of employees will be handled.

Procedures must be followed so that employees' rights are protected. A *grievance* is a formal complaint brought by an employee (or by the union on behalf of the employee) that states how the employer has violated the employment contract.

Employment contracts often provide for seniority rights. **Seniority** refers to the length of time a person has held a job. It is used to determine promotions, transfers, and vacation time. Generally, more seniority means more job security. If layoffs are necessary, the most recent hires are the first to lose their jobs.

When the union and the employer cannot agree on the terms of a new contract, or when there is a grievance that cannot be resolved, the dispute can be mediated. *Mediation* is the process of using a neutral third party (mediator) to help the two parties reach an agreement. It is voluntary and both parties must fully agree to try to resolve the problem. When mediation fails, the union contract usually provides for arbitration.

© Pressmaster/Shutterstock.com

Why do workers need a union to represent them in contract negotiations?

Downsizing has been defined as the elimination of part of the workforce, especially in business and government, in order to achieve a more efficient and cost-effective organization. Economic downturns and the resulting downsizing can create a tense workplace. Management insists that in order to remain competitive, jobs must be cut. Employees, particularly those with many years of service, believe their work and their loyalty are not important to management anymore.

THINK CRITICALLY

Do you agree with the claims of each side? What point could you make to support each side? How does the state of the economy play a role in this issue?

Arbitration is a formal process whereby an arbitrator (a neutral third party with expertise in legal issues) makes a formal decision that has the same effect as a court order.

Sometimes contract negotiations fail, and the parties cannot reach agreement. When this occurs, the union may decide to *strike*, or refuse to work until an agreement is reached. Before this can happen, strikes require a vote by union members.

Types of Unions

Unions are self-governing organizations. They are organized around employees and their needs for representation. Union leaders work full time in their positions. They often have lawyers on their staffs and hire experts such as economists to advise them on contract issues and economic needs. Dues collected from members are used to pay the salaries of union staff members and to provide the budget to pay for other experts, services, and union activities.

Craft Unions

Membership in a *craft union* is limited to those who practice a specific craft or trade. For example, bricklayers, carpenters, or framers each have their own union and receive work assignments through the union. Major craft unions exist in the building, printing, and maritime trades. Railroad employees also belong to a craft union.

Industrial Unions

Members of an *industrial union* are skilled, semiskilled, or unskilled employees in a particular industry, no matter their skill or trade. This gives workers in the same industry more leverage in bargaining employment contracts. Examples of these unions are the AFL-CIO, Teamsters, and United Auto Workers. Most of this country's basic manufacturing industries (steel, automobiles, rubber, glass, machinery, and mining) are unionized.

Retail Workers and Health Care Industry Workers

Members of a *retail union* include people employed in grocery stores, pharmacies, chain drug stores, and department stores. Health care employees are often represented by *service employee* unions that bargain on their behalf with hospitals, clinics, and other health care providers.

© Vectomart/Shutterstock.com

Public Employee Unions

City, county, state, and federal employees often belong to *public employee unions*. Members include firefighters, police officers, and teachers as well as clerks, office staff, inspectors, and other support positions.

Professional Organizations

A *professional organization* consists of people in a particular occupation who require considerable training and specialized skills. These organizations also collect dues from members and provide support services. Notable professional organizations include the following:

- American Bar Association (for lawyers)
- American Medical Association (for doctors)
- National Education Association (for educators)

In some cases, membership in professional organizations is required to maintain certifications and meet educational requirements. For example, the Institute of Management Accountants (IMA) administers a national exam for the certified management accountant (CMA) certification, but individual state Boards of Accountancy rather than the American Institute of Certified Public Accountants (AICPA) administer the certified public accountant (CPA) exam. Both the IMA and the AICPA provide most other functions of a professional organization, and membership is required.

Professional organizations provide the following types of services for members:

- Establish and maintain professional standards
- Set and enforce ethical practices by members
- Discipline, sanction, and suspend members for unethical or illegal activities
- Supervise and enforce educational updating of skills and certification requirements of members
- Administer exams, accreditations, and admission requirements
- Publish professional journals to keep members up to date
- Maintain contact with members and keep them apprised of current practices, new research, and emerging trends in the field
- Provide pension, retirement, and insurance benefits for members
- Participate in political action activities to promote and protect the interests of their members

Taking political action often involves lobbying. **Lobbying** is an organized activity by *lobbyists* (paid activists) to influence public officials to pass laws and make decisions that benefit a profession. Lobbying efforts can be extensive and have powerful effects on laws that are passed (or rejected) by members of state and federal legislative bodies.

 **CHECKPOINT**

How do unions and professional organizations protect the interests of their members?

What Are Work Ethics?

Work ethics or codes of conduct exist both formally and informally throughout corporate America. Companies are finding that employees, customers, and others are looking at their values, integrity, and sense of fairness in the workplace.

A recent corporate study concluded that outstanding employees want to work for companies whose leadership they trust and values they respect. Many U.S. companies, both large and small, are participating in integrity websites—places for customers and other stakeholders to go and examine values policies, from employee and customer privacy statements to workplace ethics enforcement. To attract and retain customers, stockholders, and financial partners, companies are becoming increasingly aware of the need for values, trust, and commitment.

Many employers are using a work ethics test for pre-employment screening to select the best employees, defined as people who adhere to high ethical principles. Work ethics for employees include giving the employer consistently high-quality work—a full day's work for a full day's pay.

When faced with an ethical dilemma at work, ask yourself these questions before taking action:

- Is it legal?
- Is it morally right?
- Who is affected?
- Would it cause harm?
- Would I be proud or shameful of doing it?
- What does it say about me?

Many ethical issues have no clear-cut right or wrong solution. How you choose to act depends on your values and moral standards. Each person must decide for himself or herself where to draw the line.

THINK CRITICALLY

1. Describe a situation in which you believe a company acted unethically. How would these actions affect your decision to work for the company?
2. Describe a situation in which you faced an ethical dilemma. Are you comfortable with the choice you made?
3. If a company's or an individual's action is legal, does that make it ethical? Explain.

KEY TERMS REVIEW

Match the terms with the definitions. Some terms may not be used.

a. bargaining
b. compressed workweek
c. flextime
d. job rotation
e. job sharing
f. lobbying
g. seniority
h. telecommuting
i. union

____ 1. A work schedule that allows employees to choose their working hours within a defined time limit

____ 2. The length of time one has held a job

____ 3. A work schedule that fits a 40-hour week into less than five days

____ 4. Process of negotiating a work contract

____ 5. Organized activity to influence public officials to pass laws

____ 6. Working offsite and using technology to stay in contact with the employer

____ 7. Group of people working in the same or similar occupations

____ 8. Job design where employees are trained to do more than one specialized task

CHECK YOUR UNDERSTANDING

LO2-1　9. List and describe three work models that offer employees flexibility.

LO2-2　10. What is the main function of unions?

APPLY YOUR KNOWLEDGE

LO2-1　11. Johnson Co. operates 12 hours a day (in a single 12-hour shift). In an average month, 6 employees work 22 days, and a total of 30 hours are missed each month. What is the rate of absenteeism?

LO2-2　12. Visit the website of a labor union or professional organization. What benefits does it offer its members?

THINK CRITICALLY

LO2-1　13. How have newer work models made the workplace more efficient?

LO2-2　14. Unions are diminishing in importance and have fewer members in this country. Why do you think this is the case?

LO2-2　15. Seniority protects employees who have been employed the longest. Younger employees, who are often highly skilled, are the first to lose their jobs during layoffs. Is this a good or bad thing? Explain.

The Essential Question *Refer to The Essential Question on p. 46. The new work environment is creating more flexibility so that employees can work different schedules or work from remote locations. The role of unions has diminished, but it is still an important part of many workplaces, as are professional organizations.*

SUMMARY

2.1

- *Gross pay includes your regular pay (wages or salary) plus overtime earned during the pay period.*

- *Deductions (both required and optional) are subtracted from gross pay to determine net (take-home) pay.*

- *Benefits in addition to pay include paid time off for vacations and holidays, sick pay, bereavement pay, group health and life insurance coverage, and retirement plans.*

- *Incentives encourage employees to strive for higher performance levels. Examples of employment incentives include profit sharing, expense accounts, employee discounts, bonuses, and stock option plans.*

- *Employees become vested in pension plans and other employer-funded retirement plans after a specified number of years with the company.*

- *Cafeteria-style plans allow employees to choose benefits that best meet their needs.*

- *Employees should evaluate the benefits offered by various employers to determine whether they meet their needs, especially in the areas of health insurance and retirement plans.*

2.2

- *The digital age has created new opportunities and responsibilities for employees as they consider their personal needs and the business's needs for productivity.*

- *New work models include telecommuting, flextime, compressed work-weeks, job rotation, and job sharing.*

- *Permanent part-time employees benefit because they are able to keep their job skills current and can meet personal schedule needs. Businesses benefit by saving money on salaries and employment benefits.*

- *Unions are organized to represent and protect employees. Bargaining is the main function of unions, as they seek to negotiate better working conditions, pay, and benefits for their members.*

- *Craft unions, industrial unions, retail workers unions, and public employee unions represent their members' interests in their fields.*

- *Professional organizations serve people in highly skilled occupations by setting and maintaining standards to keep members current in their fields.*

- *Through lobbying, professional organizations and unions try to influence public officials to take political action that benefits their members.*

© Pan Xunbin/Shutterstock.com

APPLY WHAT YOU KNOW

LO1-1   1. What is the gross pay for an hourly employee who earns $12 an hour and worked 56 hours last week?

LO1-1   2. Using the payroll tax withholding tables in Figure 2.3 and Figure 2.4, find the state and federal withholding amounts for each of these:
- A single person, one allowance, who made $109 last week
- A single person, no allowances, who made $222 last week
- A single person, three allowances, who made $291 last week

LO1-1   3. Visit the Social Security Administration online at www.ssa.gov. What are the maximum taxable earnings amounts and the tax rates for Social Security and Medicare for the current year?

LO1-2   4. Employee benefits are an important form of compensation and, in some cases, are more important to workers than the amount of take-home pay. Conduct online research to find out which benefits are most important to employees and create a top-ten list.

LO2-1   5. Miller Company operates 16 hours a day, 280 days a year. Employees work two 8-hour shifts. In an average month, 40 employees work 25 days and a total of 160 hours are missed. What is its rate of absenteeism?

LO2-2   6. List three unions that exist in your area. Classify them as to type of union (craft, industrial, retail, service employee, or public employee). Conduct an online search for one of the unions and summarize what you learn.

LO2-2   7. Visit the American Medical Association online at www.ama-assn.org. Click on the *About AMA* link to view its mission and guiding principles. What are they? How do the members of this professional organization benefit?

MAKE ACADEMIC CONNECTIONS

LO1-1   8. **Math** Prepare an employee withholding sheet like the one shown in Figure 2.2 using the following information: Charlie Suarez (Social Security number 999-00-9962) is paid weekly; he is single and has one allowance. He works in Oregon. He worked 40 hours at his regular rate of $8 per hour plus 6 overtime hours last week. In addition to required deductions, he had $22 for insurance, $12 for union dues, and $10 for charitable contributions withheld.

LO2-2   9. **Research** Visit the National Education Association (NEA) online at www.nea.org. Click on an article on the home page to read about current issues that are the focus of the NEA. Select one of the articles and write a short summary of it. Conclude the summary with your opinion as to why this is an important issue for the NEA.

LO2-2 10. **International Studies** Conduct online research about unions and professional organizations in two other countries (one of which should be in Europe). How do working conditions in these other countries compare with those in the United States?

Solve Problems and Explore Issues

L01-1 11. Andrew is single and claims zero allowances. He gets a big refund each year. With weekly earnings of $400, how much less would be withheld for federal and state taxes if he increased his allowances to two? (Use the withholding tables in Figure 2.3 and Figure 2.4.)

L01-1 12. Alexi works for an annual salary of $36,000 and gets 12 monthly paychecks. As a salaried employee, she is not given any overtime pay. Yet she works more than 60 hours each week.

    a. Do you think she should be entitled to overtime pay?

    b. Compute her overtime rate. How much additional pay would she earn each week if she were paid for her overtime hours?

L02-1 13. Use the formula given in the Math Minute to compute the rate of absenteeism and annual cost of absenteeism based on these facts:

- Number of employees: 45
- Number of 8-hour shifts: 3
- Number of workdays in an average month: 22
- Work hours lost during an average month: 624
- Average hourly wage: $8

EXTEND YOUR LEARNING

L02-2 14. **Ethics** Many union members believe that union dues, often $100 or more a month, are too high and that they go toward funding high-paid jobs for people who provide little or no service to members. In addition, there have been widespread reports of corruption in unions. Union membership has been declining in this country for many decades. Conduct research to learn more about the kinds of corruption uncovered in unions. Based on your research, what do you think is the future of unions in this country? Explain.

CHAPTER PROJECT

Job earnings are affected by many factors, including the supply and demand of labor, geographic location in the United States, level of education and skills required for the job, type of industry, union memberships, and overall profitability of the business. Conduct online research about job markets. Good sources include your state department of labor, U.S. Department of Labor, and the Bureau of Labor Statistics websites. Prepare a report analyzing your local job market for a job of your choice. Explain how various factors, such as those listed above, could affect your job earnings in your chosen field.

Complete the Guided Decision Making activity for Chapter 2 at ngl.cengage.com/mypf.

Income Tax

Consider This...

Jacob worked part time after school last year. He filled out a Form W-4 declaring zero exemptions (withholding allowances). As a result, he had a large amount of taxes withheld from his paycheck, and because he is exempt (does not earn enough to pay income taxes), he is expecting a sizable refund. When Jacob received his Form W-2, listing his taxable income and tax withholdings, he compared it to his pay stubs and verified its accuracy. Now he is ready to prepare his federal and state tax returns. He does so by going to the IRS website and his state Department of Revenue website. He downloads the appropriate tax return forms and files them electronically.

"According to the IRS website, my tax refund should be deposited in my checking account within a couple of weeks," Jacob tells his friend. "That's really quick. I'm going to put most of it in savings. Last year, I blew my whole refund, and now I have nothing to show for it. This year will be different."

The Essential Question *What types of taxes does the government levy against individuals?*

LEARNING OBJECTIVES

> LO 1-1 List the types of taxes and explain the purpose of each.
> LO 1-2 Describe the U.S. tax system and explain how it works.

KEY TERMS

- tax, *58*
- revenue, *58*
- progressive tax, *59*
- regressive tax, *59*
- proportional tax, *59*
- tax bracket, *60*
- voluntary compliance, *61*
- tax evasion, *61*
- audit, *61*

LO 1-1 Types of Taxes

To support the activities of the government in a market economy, taxes are collected from individuals and businesses. A **tax** is defined as a payment imposed on a taxpayer by a governmental unit. Incoming taxes, which are treated as income by the government, are called **revenue**. The government is able to spend revenue collected according to priorities set by Congress, as established by the U.S. Constitution.

The largest source of revenue for government spending is the individual income tax. Other taxes are also levied and provide additional revenue to governmental units, including Social Security and Medicare taxes, unemployment insurance, inheritance and estate taxes, gift taxes, import duties, and payroll taxes.

A commonly accepted principle of tax fairness is that individuals with higher incomes should pay more taxes than those with lower incomes. This theory is called the *ability-to-pay principle*. Some people believe that this principle is unfair because it penalizes those who work hard and rewards those who do not. Others counter that part of the government's role is to redistribute money from those who have much to those who have little. Social responsibility dictates that we care for those who need help.

Do you think the ability-to-pay principle is a fair way to determine how much taxes you owe? Why or why not?

Progressive Taxes

A **progressive tax** takes a larger share of one's income as the amount of income grows. Revenue collected from a progressive tax is based on the ability to pay. The *income tax* is an example of a progressive tax. The more you earn, the more you pay. Federal income tax rates are also progressive. Someone with a low income may pay 15 percent of income as taxes while someone with a higher income might pay 28 percent or more.

Regressive Taxes

A **regressive tax** takes a smaller share of one's income as the amount of income grows. A sales tax is an example of a regressive tax. It is regressive because people with lower incomes pay a higher percentage of their income on sales taxes than do people with higher incomes. Assuming you purchase a $10,000 car and pay 5 percent sales tax ($500), here is how the percentage of income affects low- and high-income earners:

Earnings: $50,000 per year $500 ÷ 50,000 = 1% of income

Earnings: $20,000 per year $500 ÷ 20,000 = 2.5% of income

Thus, a person earning $50,000 spends 1 percent of his income on sales tax, while a person earning $20,000 spends 2.5 percent of his income on sales tax.

Almost all *consumption* or *use taxes* (taxes on goods and services) are regressive. An *excise tax* is another form of consumption tax. It is imposed on specific goods and services, such as gasoline, cigarettes, alcoholic beverages, air travel, and cell phone service.

Proportional Taxes

A **proportional tax**, also known as a *flat tax*, is a tax for which the rate stays the same regardless of one's income. The *real property tax* is an example of a proportional tax. All people who own property worth $100,000 in a community will pay the same tax amount, regardless of income. All people will pay the same rate whether they own property worth $50,000 or $500,000. However, those who own property with a lower value will pay proportionally less in property taxes than those who own property with a higher value.

Property taxes typically fund local education, parks, and police, fire, and health departments. Most of the services provided by property taxes provide for the general welfare of all citizens.

Other Taxes

There are literally thousands of governmental units (federal, state, and local) that have the ability to levy and collect taxes. In addition to income taxes, sales taxes, and property taxes, you will find capital gains taxes, value-added taxes, tariffs, license and registration fees, user fees, and tolls. A *luxury tax* is imposed on certain items, such as yachts and private planes. All of these taxes are collected for the purpose of funding government spending.

 **CHECKPOINT**

Why do governmental units impose and collect taxes?

Our tax system is very complex. Both individuals and businesses pay income taxes and must file income tax returns each year. The basic components that allow the tax system to operate are the Internal Revenue Service (IRS), the country's power to tax income, and each taxpayer's willingness to pay his or her fair share of taxes.

The IRS

The *Internal Revenue Service* is an agency of the U.S. Treasury. It has headquarters in Washington, D.C., and seven regional offices around the country. The main functions of the IRS are to collect income taxes and to enforce tax laws.

The IRS provides services to taxpayers. In local offices, IRS employees assist taxpayers in finding information and forms. The IRS website provides substantial information, instructions, and assistance in understanding tax laws. At the IRS website, you can even file your tax return electronically and have your refund directly deposited to your bank account.

The Power to Tax

The power to levy federal taxes rests with the U.S. Congress. The U.S. Constitution provides that "all bills for raising revenue shall originate in the House of Representatives." Proposals to increase or decrease taxes or tax rates may come from the President, the Department of the Treasury, or a member of Congress representing a geographic area. The House Ways and Means Committee studies the proposals and makes recommendations to the full House. Revenue bills must pass a vote in both the House and the Senate and then be signed into law by the President.

Paying Your Fair Share

The income tax system is progressive. This means that tax rates increase as taxable income increases. A tax rate is applied to an income range, or **tax bracket**. Tax brackets are also called *marginal tax brackets* because they apply to the next dollar you earn. For example, your tax bracket is 10 percent if you earn up to $8,925, but it becomes 15 percent when you earn one dollar more than $8,925. In a recent year, there were seven IRS tax brackets for individuals, as shown in Figure 3.1. The tax brackets are adjusted by the IRS each year.

FIGURE 3.1	IRS Tax Brackets for Individuals

Taxable Income up to. . .	Marginal Tax Rate
$9,075	10%
$36,900	15%
$89,350	25%
$186,350	28%
$405,100	33%
$406,750	35%
Over $406,750	39.6%

Source: www.irs.gov

A significant portion of local public school budgets typically is based on taxes paid by property owners who live within the school districts. Elderly people, who often live on fixed and limited incomes, may feel that they should not have to fund schools since they no longer have school-age children.

© Vectomart/
Shutterstock.com

THINK CRITICALLY

How do you respond to complaints that property taxes on elderly homeowners is unfair? Should elderly property owners be given a tax break or even be exempt from property taxes that fund public school districts?

The U.S. Congress raises taxes when more revenue is needed, such as when there is a large national debt. When the government spends more than it receives in revenue, it has a *national deficit*. An accumulation of deficits makes up the *national debt*. Sometimes Congress approves tax decreases, often when there is a tax surplus (more taxes are collected than money spent). Or if the economy needs stimulating, Congress may approve a tax decrease. Most tax increases and decreases are temporary, until the economy stabilizes.

Our income tax system, both federal and state, is based on **voluntary compliance**, which means all citizens prepare and file tax returns on their own. Responsibility for filing a tax return and paying taxes rests with the individual. Failure to do so can result in a penalty, which usually includes interest on taxes owed plus a fine. Willful failure to pay taxes is called **tax evasion**, which is a serious crime punishable by fine or imprisonment, or both. This is not the same as *tax avoidance*, taking all of the available deductions to reduce taxes.

An IRS Audit

The IRS audits millions of taxpayers each year. An **audit** is an examination of income tax returns. It questions the validity of information on a tax return and requires a response from the taxpayer. Taxpayers can represent themselves or authorize someone else to take their place or attend the audit with them, such as a lawyer, accountant, family member, or *enrolled agent* (someone who is licensed to prepare tax returns). Most audits occur because numbers do not match (the W-2 does not agree with income reported) or there are math errors.

The most common audit is a *correspondence audit*, where the taxpayer receives a letter requesting proof of items reported or deducted. An *office audit* requires the taxpayer to appear in person to answer questions and provide records to justify items on the tax return. A *field audit* is similar to an office audit, except the auditor visits the taxpayer's home or business to examine records or assets and ask specific questions. Once the IRS auditor has made his or her decision regarding taxes owed, errors, and other items of dispute, the taxpayer can appeal that decision to a court of law.

CHECKPOINT

What roles does the IRS play in the U.S. tax system?

How Can You Survive an Audit?

Every year, the IRS audits millions of American taxpayers. You may be one of them if you make math errors on your tax form or report income that does not match the income on your Form W-2. To avoid an audit, here are some helpful tips:

- Check your math. Make sure all your additions and subtractions are correct. Many audits result from simple math errors.

- If you are filling out the form manually, do so neatly. A neat form is easy to read and provokes fewer questions. You may find it easier to file your return online.

- Use a tax software program. Tax software will output a neat form and help prevent math errors. It will also help you take advantage of all the credits and deductions you deserve.

- Keep good records. Keep receipts for all deductions and credits you claim on your tax return.

- File on time. File your tax return by April 15 to avoid penalties and interest.

If you receive an audit notice, remember:

- You have 30 days in which to respond. Get advice and help if needed, and respond to the notice within the time limit.

- You can have a representative such as a CPA, enrolled agent, or attorney with you or in your place.

- Bring all of your receipts, forms, instructions, and other documentation with you to prove your case.

- Learn more about audits and how to prepare for them from Publication 556 (available at www.irs.gov) and from other print and online resources.

- The IRS can make mistakes too. You have rights as a taxpayer (see Publication 1), and in many cases, the Tax Court rules in favor of the taxpayer.

- Don't sign forms that take away your rights. Before you sign anything, be sure to get advice from a tax professional.

- Stay calm and collected. Behave responsibly, return calls, ask questions, give reasonable explanations, and listen carefully.

After the audit is complete, you can appeal the auditor's decision if you feel you have good cause.

THINK CRITICALLY

1. Do you know someone who has been audited by the IRS? Ask that person to share general information about the process. As an alternative, use the Internet to research the audit process. Share what you learn with the class.

2. What can you do to avoid an IRS audit?

KEY TERMS REVIEW

Match the terms with the definitions. Some terms may not be used.

____ 1. A flat tax where the tax rate is the same regardless of income

____ 2. A range of income associated with a tax rate

____ 3. An examination of income tax returns

____ 4. Income to a governmental unit

____ 5. Willful failure to pay one's taxes

____ 6. A payment imposed by a governmental unit

____ 7. A tax that takes a smaller share of income as income grows

____ 8. A tax that takes a larger share of income as income grows

a. audit
b. progressive tax
c. proportional tax
d. regressive tax
e. revenue
f. tax
g. tax bracket
h. tax evasion
i. voluntary compliance

CHECK YOUR UNDERSTANDING

L01-1   9. List three types of taxes levied in the United States. Give examples.

L01-2   10. What is the IRS and what is it empowered to do?

L01-2   11. What is the purpose of an IRS audit?

APPLY YOUR KNOWLEDGE

L01-1   12. List the taxes you and your family pay in a year's time, such as income taxes, sales taxes, gasoline taxes, and so on. Categorize taxes by type—are they progressive, regressive, proportional, or other?

THINK CRITICALLY

L01-1   13. Some people believe there are too many taxes and that tax rates are too high. They refuse to file tax returns or pay taxes because they disagree with how the government spends the money. Do you agree with these arguments? Why or why not?

L01-1   14. Which type of tax (progressive, regressive, or proportional) is considered to be "fairer"? Which type of tax is considered to be less "fair"? Explain.

L01-2   15. The IRS is empowered by the U.S. government to collect taxes from individuals and businesses. Some people feel that the IRS is too powerful and heavy-handed in its practices. Do you agree? Explain. Why do people hire lawyers as a form of protection when dealing with the IRS? Do you think this is necessary?

The Essential Question *Refer to The Essential Question on p. 58. Progressive, regressive, proportional, and other taxes and fees are levied against individuals.*

The Essential Question *What kinds of income and deductions may be reported on a tax return?*

LEARNING OBJECTIVES

> LO 2-1 List and define basic tax terminology.
> LO 2-2 Prepare tax form 1040EZ.

KEY TERMS

- filing status, *64*
- exemption, *65*
- gross income, *65*
- adjusted gross income, *66*
- itemized deductions, *66*
- tax liability, *66*
- taxable income, *67*
- tax credit, *67*
- exempt status, *68*
- estimated tax, *69*

LO 2-1 Tax Terminology

U.S. citizens are expected to file tax returns each year and pay their fair share of taxes. When preparing tax returns, there are many do's and don'ts to follow. It is important that you take full advantage of legally available tax breaks to reduce your tax liability. Let's start with basic tax terms you will need to know.

Filing Status

Filing status describes your tax-filing group, which is based on your marital status as of the last day of the tax year. Single taxpayers and those who are married but filing separately pay higher taxes than others. Married taxpayers can choose to file jointly (with lower tax rates), or they may choose to file separately.

When filing taxes, you must choose one of the following as your filing status:

- Single person (not married)
- Married person filing a joint return (even though only one spouse may have earned income)
- Married person filing a separate return
- Head of household (you may qualify as a head of household whether you are married or single if you provide a home for a dependent)
- Qualifying widow(er)

The IRS website (www.irs.gov) contains a more detailed description of these classifications. You may also get advice about which filing status is right for you from your tax accountant.

Why is marital status important when filing an income tax return?

Buccina Studios/Photodisc/Getty Images

© Pan Xunbin/Shutterstock.com

Exemptions

When computing taxes, an **exemption** is an amount you may subtract from your income for each person who depends on your income to live. Each exemption reduces your taxable income and thus your total tax. As a taxpayer, you are automatically allowed one exemption for yourself unless someone else (such as a parent) claims you as a dependent on his or her return. If you are filing a joint return, you can take an exemption for yourself and for your spouse.

You also are allowed exemptions for dependents. A *dependent* is a person who lives with you and for whom you pay more than half of his or her living expenses. Dependents can include children, a spouse, elderly parents, or disabled relatives living with and dependent on the taxpayer.

Gross Income

Gross income is all of the taxable income you receive during the year. *Earned income* refers to money you earned from working. *Unearned income* refers to money you received from passive activity (other than working). Some forms of income are not subject to income taxes. Examples are shown in Figure 3.2. Scholarships and grants are a form of unearned income. They may be taxable for amounts used for expenses other than tuition and books. Employer-paid tuition is often taxable.

You are also taxed on other forms of income, including winnings from gambling, bartering income, pensions and annuities, Social Security benefits, self-employment income, rental income, royalties, estate and trust income, and income on the sale of property.

Wages, Salaries, and Tips

This category of earnings appears on your *Form W-2*, which is a summary of the income you earned and the taxes withheld by the employer during the year. It contains all income you receive through employment, including bonuses and imputed income. *Imputed income* is added to earnings when you receive a taxable benefit, such as use of a company car. If you receive tips on your job, you must report your tips to your employer. These earnings must be reported as income and are included with your wages on Form W-2.

FIGURE 3.2	Forms of Income	
Earned Income	**Unearned Income**	**Nontaxable Income**
Wages	Interest	Child support
Salaries	Dividends	Gifts
Tips	Alimony	Inheritances
Business income	Social Security	Life insurance benefits
	Unemployment compensation	Veteran's benefits
	Scholarships/Grants	Workers' Compensation benefits
	Prizes/Awards	

Interest Income

Interest income includes all taxable interest from banks, savings and loan associations, credit unions, series HH savings bonds, and so on. You should receive a Form 1099-INT for each investment that earned interest during the year. This form reports the amount of interest you earned from that investment.

Dividend Income

Dividends are money, stock, or other property that corporations pay to stockholders in return for their investment. You will receive a Form 1099-DIV for each stock investment, listing the dividend income. According to the Jobs and Growth Tax Relief Reconciliation Act of 2003, these dividends may be subject to a maximum 15 percent tax rate.

Unemployment Compensation

If you receive any unemployment compensation during the year, you will receive a Form 1099-G, which shows the total you received. You must enter this amount as income on the tax return.

Social Security Benefits

If you receive Social Security payments during the year, as much as 50 to 85 percent of this money is taxable if your total income exceeds $25,000 for single taxpayers and $32,000 for married taxpayers filing jointly. You would receive a Form SSA-1099, listing the total you received for the year.

Alimony and Child Support

Money paid to support a former spouse is called *alimony*. It is taxable for the person receiving it and deductible (from gross income) for the person paying it. Money paid to a former spouse for support of dependent children is called *child support*. This income is not taxable for the person receiving it, nor is it deductible for the person paying it.

Adjusted Gross Income

The law allows you to subtract some types of spending from gross income. You can "adjust" your income by subtracting such things as contributions to individual retirement accounts (IRAs), student loan interest, alimony paid, and tuition and fees. These adjustments are subtracted from gross income to determine adjusted gross income. These adjustments reduce income that is subject to tax. Note that these adjustments are not available on Form 1040EZ. Thus, it may be in your best interest to file a longer form (Form 1040A or Form 1040) if you have these kinds of adjustments to income.

Taxable Income

In Chapter 2, you learned that deductions are amounts subtracted from your gross pay to arrive at your take-home pay. On tax returns, itemized deductions are expenses you can subtract from adjusted gross income to determine your taxable income. Your taxable income determines your tax liability, which is the amount of total tax you owe on a year's income. So anything that reduces taxable income also reduces your tax liability.

To itemize deductions, you must use Schedule A and Form 1040. Common expenses you may deduct are medical and dental expenses beyond a specified percentage of your income, state and local income taxes, property taxes, home mortgage interest, gifts to charity, losses from theft or property damage, and employee business expenses (expenses required but not paid by employers).

If you do not have many deductions, your tax may be less if you take the *standard deduction*. This is a stated amount that you may subtract from adjusted gross income instead of itemizing your deductions. This amount changes each year. After subtracting your standard deduction (or itemized deductions), you need to compute the exemption allowance. The amount for each exemption allowance is stated on the tax form. For example, if the exemption allowance is $3,900 and you are claiming two dependents (including yourself), you would deduct $7,800 on your tax return.

After the standard deduction (or itemized deductions) and exemptions are subtracted from adjusted gross income, you arrive at your **taxable income**, which is the income on which you will pay tax. You can then determine your tax by looking up your taxable income in a tax table.

Tax credits may also be available to you. A **tax credit** is a reduction of taxes owed. Thus, if your tax (from the tax table) is $800 and you have a tax credit of $100, then the amount of taxes you owe would be reduced to $700. Because it directly reduces taxes, a tax credit is better than a deduction. Examples of tax credits are payments for child care, college tuition and expenses, and other special credits created by Congress. It is important to note that you cannot claim tax credits unless you itemize your deductions. (The Math Minute feature on the next page shows the calculations for arriving at income tax.)

 CHECKPOINT

How is gross income different from taxable income?

LO 2-2 Preparing a Tax Return

Once you have gathered your income and expense records, you can start working on your tax return. You can download forms (in PDF format) from the IRS website and enter data directly into them. Then you can submit your tax return electronically or print a hard copy and mail it to the IRS. To file electronically, you can use the IRS e-file program, following the instructions provided on the IRS website. E-filing is free if your income is $57,000 or less. You can even use a debit or credit card to make a payment if you owe taxes. In addition to a federal tax return, you may have to file state and local income tax returns. Save copies of your tax returns, together with all supporting evidence (receipts), Forms W-2, and other tax forms, for six years. In the event you are audited, you are expected to have your records for three previous tax years, or if the IRS believes fraud is involved, six years.

Who Must File and When?

You must file a tax return if you earned enough income to owe taxes. In a recent year, a single person under the age of 65, whose gross income exceeded

Calculating Income Tax

Gross Income
− Adjustments
_____

Adjusted Gross Income
− Standard Deduction (or Itemized Deductions)
− Exemptions
_____

= Taxable Income

(Look up taxable income on the tax table to determine tax liability.)

Tax Liability
− Tax Credits
− Payments (taxes withheld and estimated tax payments)
_____

= Tax Owed or Refund Due

Use the calculations above and the tax table from Figure 3.5 on p. 73 to compute income tax. Assume a single person has gross income of $14,000, has adjustments of $2,200, takes the standard deduction of $6,100, claims one exemption worth $3,900, has zero tax credits, and had federal tax withholdings of $926.

Solution:

$14,000 gross income − $2,200 adjustments = $11,800 adjusted gross income $11,800 − $6,100 standard deduction − $3,900 exemption = $1,800 taxable income. Tax liability from the table (Figure 3.5) = $181 − $0 tax credits − $926 payments made = $745 refund due

$10,000 (allowing for a standard deduction of $6,100 and one exemption of $3,900) likely owed taxes and had to file a return. Because the gross income requirement is adjusted yearly, you can check the IRS website to see if you must file. If you did not earn enough to owe taxes but taxes were withheld from your paychecks, you should file a return to claim a refund.

Exempt status is available to those who know they will not earn enough in one year to owe income tax. To claim exempt status, just write the word "exempt" on your Form W-4 (Employee's Withholding Allowance Certificate). Your employer will still withhold Social Security and Medicare taxes but will not withhold income taxes. If you are exempt, you do not have to file a tax return.

If you must file a tax return, the deadline is April 15 of each year. If that date falls on a weekend or holiday, your tax return is due on the next weekday. Penalties and interest charges are assessed if you file late.

Estimated Tax

If you received income for which taxes were not withheld, you may need to submit estimated tax payments during the tax year. **Estimated tax** is the amount of tax you estimate you will owe on income received without withholdings. For example, if you are in the 15 percent tax bracket and you received $5,000 in income for which no income taxes were withheld, you should send estimated taxes of $750 ($5,000 × 15%) to the IRS so you won't possibly owe interest on that amount.

People who are self-employed, independent contractors, and business owners must pay estimated taxes quarterly (January 15, April 15, June 15, and September 15) based on estimated income for the quarter and for the year. Just like taxes that are withheld, estimated taxes are compared to your tax liability to see if more tax is owed or if a refund is due. Tax forms for paying estimated tax can be found on the IRS website.

Which Form to Use?

All taxpayers must use one of three basic forms (1040, 1040A, or 1040EZ) when filing their individual tax return. There are many other supporting forms that may be required to support line items on the basic form. In all, there are nearly 400 federal tax forms. For your first tax return, you will probably use either Form 1040EZ or Form 1040A. Which form you choose will depend on the type and amount of your income, the amount of your deductions, and your tax situation.

In general, if your deductions add up to more than the standard deduction, your total tax will be lower if you use Form 1040 and itemize your deductions. Taxpayers who earn more than $100,000 in taxable income must use Form 1040. Those with taxable income less than $100,000 may use any of the three forms. If you have no deductions or credits, interest income of $1,500 or less, and no dependents, you should use Form 1040EZ, which is the easiest and shortest form. However, if you qualify for any credits and deductions listed on Form 1040A, use that form. If you have enough deductions to benefit from itemizing, use Form 1040.

Where to Begin?

During the year, save all receipts and proofs of payment for your itemized deductions. You will need these receipts to prove the accuracy of your tax return if you are audited. Save all employee withholding records, such as your pay stubs. By January 31 you should receive a Form W-2 from each of your employers. Compare it with your records to check for accuracy. Any discrepancies between the Form W-2 and your records should be reported immediately to the employer and corrected.

Gather all other necessary information, including tax form instructions and last

Why would a taxpayer choose to use Form 1040?

year's tax return as a model for preparing this year's return. Once you have gathered all your information, prepare both the short and the long form to see if you can save money by itemizing deductions.

Even if you hire a professional *tax preparer*, you are responsible for supplying accurate and complete information. Hiring a tax preparer will not guarantee that you are paying the correct amount. You must check the form before you sign it. If you discover an error after the return has been filed, you may file an amended return (Form 1040X) to make corrections.

Tax Preparation Software

Most professional tax preparers use a tax preparation computer program. You can also use tax preparation software to do your own taxes. Good software provides all of the necessary forms, and it leads you through the process of filling out the forms. Most tax software also provides tips and additional information to help you identify all the deductions and credits you are allowed. Search the Internet to find information about different brands of tax software. Software producers usually provide a feature tour at their website.

Form 1040EZ

You may use Form 1040EZ if you are single or married filing jointly and claim no dependents. Your taxable income must be less than $100,000. Line-by-line instructions for filling out Form 1040EZ are provided at the IRS website. Highlights of the instructions are described in the following paragraphs.

Figure 3.3 shows Form W-2 for Roberto Flores. Figure 3.4 shows his completed Form 1040EZ tax return. Roberto is single and claims one exemption. His wages are found on the W-2. Follow along on Roberto's Form 1040EZ as you read the instructions.

Step 1: Enter Name, Address, and Social Security Number

Fill in your name, address, and Social Security number. You can download the form from the IRS website and fill in this information using your computer or print a copy of the form and fill it in by hand. Check the "Yes" box if you want $3 to go to the Presidential Election Campaign Fund. This is a fund established by Congress so that taxpayers can share in the costs of election campaigns. The $3 contribution will not increase your tax or reduce your refund.

Step 2: Report Income

- First, enter your total wages, salaries, and tips, as shown on your W-2 form(s). On Roberto's Form W-2, you can see that he earned $14,720. He entered this amount on line 1.
- Second, enter interest earned on savings accounts (line 2) and any unemployment compensation you may have received (line 3). Roberto Flores recorded the $234 of interest he earned on his savings. Add these income figures to the earnings shown in line 1. The result is your adjusted gross income, line 4.
- Next, check if you are claimed as a dependent on another person's tax return. If not, you can enter the amount shown on line 5. This is both the standard deduction and your exemption added together ($6,100 + $3,900 = $10,000). Then calculate your taxable income (line 6).

FIGURE 3.3 W-2 for Roberto Flores

22222	**a** Employee's social security number 999-00-3894	OMB No. 1545-0008		
b Employer identification number (EIN) 93-899348488		**1** Wages, tips, other compensation $14,720.00	**2** Federal income tax withheld $1,501.00	
c Employer's name, address, and ZIP code Blanton School District T-31 23855 SW 85th Portland, OR 97215-4562		**3** Social security wages $14,720.00	**4** Social security tax withheld $912.64	
		5 Medicare wages and tips $14,720.00	**6** Medicare tax withheld $213.44	
		7 Social security tips	**8** Allocated tips	
d Control number		**9** Advance EIC payment	**10** Dependent care benefits	
e Employee's first name and initial Last name Suff. Roberto J. Flores 285 SW 28th Street, #8 Portland, OR 97214-4562		**11** Nonqualified plans	**12a**	
		13 Statutory employee ☐ Retirement plan ☐ Third-party sick pay ☐	**12b**	
		14 Other	**12c**	
			12d	
f Employee's address and ZIP code				
15 State OR Employer's state ID number 2384762	**16** State wages, tips, etc. $14,720.00	**17** State income tax $946.00	**18** Local wages, tips, etc. **19** Local income tax	**20** Locality name

Form **W-2** Wage and Tax Statement 20- - Department of the Treasury—Internal Revenue Service

Source: Base art is W-2 from www.irs.gov; fictional copy added

Step 3: Compute Tax

On line 7, enter the total federal tax withheld as shown on the W-2 form(s). This is the amount of tax you have already paid. To figure tax owed, look up your taxable income (line 6) in the tax table that comes with your return. It will look similar to the one in Figure 3.5. In the tax table in Figure 3.5, Roberto found that his taxable income of $4,954 fell within the range of $4,950–$5,000. In that row, he located his total tax liability of $498 in the "Single" column and recorded it on line 10.

Step 4: Calculate Refund or Amount Owed

If the amount of federal taxes withheld (the amount you already paid) is larger than your total tax (from the tax table), you will receive a refund. If you owe more tax than was withheld, you must pay the difference. Write your check to the U.S. Treasury and enclose it with your return. Or if you file electronically, you can use a debit or credit card to pay the tax owed.

When Roberto subtracted his total tax of $498 from his taxes withheld of $1,501, the difference was $1,003, which he recorded on line 11a. He wanted his refund deposited electronically into his checking account, so he entered the routing number (the first nine numbers printed on the bottom of his checks) and account number (the last seven numbers on the bottom of his checks) in the Refund section of his tax form and checked the box for account type: Checking.

Step 5: Sign the Return

Sign and date your tax return. Make sure your W-2 form(s) and check (if you owe taxes) are included with the completed return, and mail them to the regional IRS office designated for your area. Or if you file electronically, be sure to print a hard copy of the return for your files. You can also save the file electronically on your travel or thumb drive.

FIGURE 3.4 1040EZ Tax Return for Roberto Flores

Department of the Treasury—Internal Revenue Service

Form
1040EZ

Income Tax Return for Single and Joint Filers With No Dependents (99)

20--

OMB No. 1545-0074

Your first name and initial	Last name	Your social security number
Roberto J.	Flores	999 00 3894

If a joint return, spouse's first name and initial	Last name	Spouse's social security number

Home address (number and street). If you have a P.O. box, see instructions.
285 SW 28th Street
Apt. no. **8**

▲ Make sure the SSN(s) above are correct.

City, town or post office, state, and ZIP code. If you have a foreign address, also complete spaces below (see instructions).
Portland, OR 97214-4562

Presidential Election Campaign
Check here if you, or your spouse if filing jointly, want $3 to go to this fund. Checking a box below will not change your tax or refund. ☑ You ☐ Spouse

Foreign country name	Foreign province/state/county	Foreign postal code

Income

Attach Form(s) W-2 here.

Enclose, but do not attach, any payment.

1	Wages, salaries, and tips. This should be shown in box 1 of your Form(s) W-2. Attach your Form(s) W-2.	**1**	14,720	00
2	Taxable interest. If the total is over $1,500, you cannot use Form 1040EZ.	**2**	234	00
3	Unemployment compensation and Alaska Permanent Fund dividends (see instructions).	**3**	0	
4	Add lines 1, 2, and 3. This is your **adjusted gross income.**	**4**	14,954	00
5	If someone can claim you (or your spouse if a joint return) as a dependent, check the applicable box(es) below and enter the amount from the worksheet on back. ☐ You ☐ Spouse If no one can claim you (or your spouse if a joint return), enter $10,000 if **single;** $20,000 if **married filing jointly.** See back for explanation.	**5**	10,000	00
6	Subtract line 5 from line 4. If line 5 is larger than line 4, enter -0-. This is your **taxable income.** ▶	**6**	4,954	00

Payments, Credits, and Tax

7	Federal income tax withheld from Form(s) W-2 and 1099.	**7**	1,501	00
8a	**Earned income credit (EIC)** (see instructions).	**8a**	0	
b	Nontaxable combat pay election. 8b			
9	Add lines 7 and 8a. These are your **total payments and credits.** ▶	**9**	1,501	00
10	**Tax.** Use the amount on **line 6 above** to find your tax in the tax table in the instructions. Then, enter the tax from the table on this line.	**10**	498	00

Refund

Have it directly deposited! See instructions and fill in 11b, 11c, and 11d or Form 8888.

11a	If line 9 is larger than line 10, subtract line 10 from line 9. This is your **refund.** If Form 8888 is attached, check here ▶ ☐	**11a**	1,003	00

▶ **b** Routing number 0 0 1 0 7 3 2 6 4 ▶ **c** Type: ☑ Checking ☐ Savings

▶ **d** Account number 4 1 1 2 0 3 6

Amount You Owe

12	If line 10 is larger than line 9, subtract line 9 from line 10. This is the **amount you owe.** For details on how to pay, see instructions. ▶	**12**	

Third Party Designee

Do you want to allow another person to discuss this return with the IRS (see instructions)? ☐ **Yes.** Complete below. ☐ **No**

Designee's name ▶   Phone no. ▶   Personal identification number (PIN) ▶

Sign Here

Under penalties of perjury, I declare that I have examined this return and, to the best of my knowledge and belief, it is true, correct, and accurately lists all amounts and sources of income I received during the tax year. Declaration of preparer (other than the taxpayer) is based on all information of which the preparer has any knowledge.

Joint return? See instructions.

Keep a copy for your records.

Your signature	Date	Your occupation	Daytime phone number
Roberto J. Flores	3/15/20--	mechanic	(503) 555-0052
Spouse's signature. If a joint return, **both** must sign.	Date	Spouse's occupation	If the IRS sent you an Identity Protection PIN, enter it here (see inst.)

Paid Preparer Use Only

Print/Type preparer's name	Preparer's signature	Date	Check ☐ if self-employed	PTIN
Firm's name ▶			Firm's EIN ▶	
Firm's address ▶			Phone no.	

For Disclosure, Privacy Act, and Paperwork Reduction Act Notice, see instructions. Cat. No. 11329W Form **1040EZ** (20--)

Source: Base art is 1040EZ from www.irs.gov; fictional copy added

FIGURE 3.5   Part of 1040EZ Tax Table

20-- Tax Table

Example. Mr. Brown is single. His taxable income on line 6 of Form 1040EZ is $26,250. He follows two easy steps to figure his tax: 1. He finds the $26,250-26,300 taxable income line. 2. He finds the Single filing status column and reads down the column. The tax amount shown where the taxable income line and the filing status line meet is $3,495. He enters this amount on line 10 of Form 1040EZ.

At least	But less than	Single	Married filing jointly
		Your tax is—	
26,200	26,250	3,488	3,041
26,250	26,300	(3,495)	3,049
26,300	26,350	3,503	3,056
26,350	26,400	3,510	3,064

If Form 1040EZ, line 6, is—		And you are—		If Form 1040EZ, line 6, is—		And you are—		If Form 1040EZ, line 6, is—		And you are—		If Form 1040EZ, line 6, is—		And you are—	
At least	But less than	Single	Married filing jointly	At least	But less than	Single	Married filing jointly	At least	But less than	Single	Married filing jointly	At least	But less than	Single	Married filing jointly
		Your tax is—				Your tax is—				Your tax is—				Your tax is—	
0	5	0	0	**1,000**				**2,000**				**3,000**			
5	15	1	1												
15	25	2	2	1,000	1,025	101	101	2,000	2,025	201	201	3,000	3,050	303	303
25	50	4	4	1,025	1,050	104	104	2,025	2,050	204	204	3,050	3,100	308	308
50	75	6	6	1,050	1,075	106	106	2,050	2,075	206	206	3,100	3,150	313	313
75	100	9	9	1,075	1,100	109	109	2,075	2,100	209	209	3,150	3,200	318	318
100	125	11	11	1,100	1,125	111	111	2,100	2,125	211	211	3,200	3,250	323	323
125	150	14	14	1,125	1,150	114	114	2,125	2,150	214	214	3,250	3,300	328	328
150	175	16	16	1,150	1,175	116	116	2,150	2,175	216	216	3,300	3,350	333	333
175	200	19	19	1,175	1,200	119	119	2,175	2,200	219	219	3,350	3,400	338	338
200	225	21	21	1,200	1,225	121	121	2,200	2,225	221	221	3,400	3,450	343	343
225	250	24	24	1,225	1,250	124	124	2,225	2,250	224	224	3,450	3,500	348	348
250	275	26	26	1,250	1,275	126	126	2,250	2,275	226	226	3,500	3,550	353	353
275	300	29	29	1,275	1,300	129	129	2,275	2,300	229	229	3,550	3,600	358	358
300	325	31	31	1,300	1,325	131	131	2,300	2,325	231	231	3,600	3,650	363	363
325	350	34	34	1,325	1,350	134	134	2,325	2,350	234	234	3,650	3,700	368	368
350	375	36	36	1,350	1,375	136	136	2,350	2,375	236	236	3,700	3,750	373	373
375	400	39	39	1,375	1,400	139	139	2,375	2,400	239	239	3,750	3,800	378	378
400	425	41	41	1,400	1,425	141	141	2,400	2,425	241	241	3,800	3,850	383	383
425	450	44	44	1,425	1,450	144	144	2,425	2,450	244	244	3,850	3,900	388	388
450	475	46	46	1,450	1,475	146	146	2,450	2,475	246	246	3,900	3,950	393	393
475	500	49	49	1,475	1,500	149	149	2,475	2,500	249	249	3,950	4,000	398	398
500	525	51	51	1,500	1,525	151	151	2,500	2,525	251	251	**4,000**			
525	550	54	54	1,525	1,550	154	154	2,525	2,550	254	254				
550	575	56	56	1,550	1,575	156	156	2,550	2,575	256	256	4,000	4,050	403	403
575	600	59	59	1,575	1,600	159	159	2,575	2,600	259	259	4,050	4,100	408	408
600	625	61	61	1,600	1,625	161	161	2,600	2,625	261	261	4,100	4,150	413	413
625	650	64	64	1,625	1,650	164	164	2,625	2,650	264	264	4,150	4,200	418	418
650	675	66	66	1,650	1,675	166	166	2,650	2,675	266	266	4,200	4,250	423	423
675	700	69	69	1,675	1,700	169	169	2,675	2,700	269	269	4,250	4,300	428	428
700	725	71	71	1,700	1,725	171	171	2,700	2,725	271	271	4,300	4,350	433	433
725	750	74	74	1,725	1,750	174	174	2,725	2,750	274	274	4,350	4,400	438	438
750	775	76	76	1,750	1,775	176	176	2,750	2,775	276	276	4,400	4,450	443	443
775	800	79	79	1,775	1,800	179	179	2,775	2,800	279	279	4,450	4,500	448	448
800	825	81	81	1,800	1,825	181	181	2,800	2,825	281	281	4,500	4,550	453	453
825	850	84	84	1,825	1,850	184	184	2,825	2,850	284	284	4,550	4,600	458	458
850	875	86	86	1,850	1,875	186	186	2,850	2,875	286	286	4,600	4,650	463	463
875	900	89	89	1,875	1,900	189	189	2,875	2,900	289	289	4,650	4,700	468	468
900	925	91	91	1,900	1,925	191	191	2,900	2,925	291	291	4,700	4,750	473	473
925	950	94	94	1,925	1,950	194	194	2,925	2,950	294	294	4,750	4,800	478	478
950	975	96	96	1,950	1,975	196	196	2,950	2,975	296	296	4,800	4,850	483	483
975	1,000	99	99	1,975	2,000	199	199	2,975	3,000	299	299	4,850	4,900	488	488
												4,900	4,950	493	493
												4,950	5,000	498	498

Source www.irs.gov

CHECKPOINT

Who is eligible to file Form 1040EZ?

Accounting

Accountants prepare and examine financial records and reports, including tax returns. They ensure that financial records are accurate and that taxes are properly paid on time. Accountants also assess financial operations and are part of the management team that oversees the financial success of a company. They may work independently from their home as self-employed accountants or in a public accounting firm.

Accountants complete rigorous education programs and must pass state and national certification tests. As members of the profession, they are also required to meet high ethical and legal standards, whether working for private companies or as external auditors or accountants with public accounting firms.

Employment Outlook

- An average rate of employment growth is expected through 2020.
- Increased globalization of business will lead to a higher demand for accountants.

Job Titles

- Accountant
- Controller
- Auditor

Needed Skills

- A bachelor's degree in accounting is preferred.
- Strong skills in math and logic are required.
- Certifications are preferred, such as certified public accountant (CPA), certified management accountant (CMA), and certified fraud examiner (CFE).
- Strong computer skills (especially with spreadsheets) are helpful.

What's it like to work in . . . *Accounting*

Andrea loves numbers and preparing financial statements and reports. She started as a staff accountant two years ago and is now earning an annual salary of $64,000. She works hard and wants to become the company controller. Andrea is very meticulous about accuracy, and she makes sure that her financial reports are easy to understand and timely for use by the company's decision makers.

Today, Andrea is examining the financial records of her company in preparation for tax day. She will analyze, compare, and interpret facts and figures in order to minimize the company's tax liability while complying with laws and regulations. She will also look for ways that the company's accounting system might operate more efficiently and make recommendations to management.

What About You?

Do you like math and working with numbers? Would you like to have an important supporting position on the management team of a corporation? Could accounting be the career for you?

The Career Clusters icons are being used with permission of the: States' Career Clusters Initiative, 2007, www.careerclusters.org

KEY TERMS REVIEW

Match the terms with the definitions. Some terms may not be used.

_____ 1. *Gross income minus adjustments*

_____ 2. *An amount subtracted from your income for each dependent*

_____ 3. *Tax owed on income for the year*

_____ 4. *Reduction in tax owed deducted directly from your tax liability*

_____ 5. *Your tax filing group based on marital status*

_____ 6. *Condition whereby you will owe no income tax on earnings*

_____ 7. *All taxable income received in a year*

_____ 8. *Amount of tax based on income received without tax withholdings*

a. adjusted gross income
b. estimated tax
c. exempt status
d. exemption
e. filing status
f. gross income
g. itemized deductions
h. tax credit
i. tax liability
j. taxable income

CHECK YOUR UNDERSTANDING

L02-1 9. How is gross income different from taxable income?

L02-1 10. How are deductions different from tax credits?

L02-2 11. What are some advantages of e-filing?

APPLY YOUR KNOWLEDGE

L02-1 12. How does your filing status affect the amount of taxes you owe? Based on the tax table in Figure 3.5, who pays more taxes—someone who is single or married filing jointly?

L02-2 13. Why would a taxpayer choose to use Form 1040 rather than Form 1040EZ?

THINK CRITICALLY

L02-1 14. If you make simple math errors on your tax return, you may be targeted for an audit. What can you do to avoid this?

L02-2 15. It is a good idea to prepare your taxes twice, once using Form 1040EZ and once using Form 1040. Explain your answer.

The Essential Question *Refer to The Essential Question on p. 64. Taxable income includes wages, salaries, and tips and other forms of earned and unearned income. Deductions include mortgage interest, property and state income taxes, medical expenses, and charitable contributions.*

Assessment

SUMMARY

3.1

- *The government collects money, or revenue, from citizens and businesses to spend as specified by Congress.*

- *As income grows, progressive taxes take a larger share of income and regressive taxes take a smaller share.*

- *Proportional taxes, or flat taxes, take the same percentage regardless of income.*

- *The IRS is the government agency in charge of collecting taxes, enforcing tax laws, and supplying information to help taxpayers prepare their tax returns.*

- *The income tax system is progressive. Different tax rates apply to different income ranges, or tax brackets.*

- *Our income tax system is based on voluntary compliance.*

- *Willful failure to pay taxes is called tax evasion and is a serious crime punishable by a fine, imprisonment, or both.*

- *Every year, the IRS audits millions of taxpayers.*

3.2

- *You may claim an exemption for each of your dependents.*

- *Gross income consists of taxable income received from all sources.*

- *Gross income less certain allowable adjustments is called adjusted gross income.*

- *To determine taxable income, subtract adjustments, deductions, and exemptions from gross income.*

- *Tax deductions reduce taxable income, while tax credits are subtracted directly from taxes owed.*

- *You may take a standard deduction or itemize deductions on Schedule A if they will exceed the standard deduction.*

- *File 1040EZ if your income is less than $100,000, you have no dependents or deductions, and you have interest income of no more than $1,500.*

- *If the amount of taxes withheld from your paychecks exceeds your total tax (from the tax table), you will receive a refund. If the amount withheld is less than your total tax, you must pay the difference when you file your tax return.*

© Pan Xunbin/Shutterstock.com

APPLY WHAT YOU KNOW

LO1-1 1. Why are taxes collected from individuals and businesses?

LO1-1 2. Why are regressive taxes considered unfair to lower-income taxpayers?

LO1-2 3. How is tax avoidance different from tax evasion?

LO1-2 4. How do new federal tax laws get passed?

LO2-1 5. How do exemptions affect the amount of tax you will pay?

LO2-1 6. Which of these would reduce tax liability more—a $300 deduction or a $300 tax credit? Explain.

LO2-1 7. What is meant by imputed income? Is it taxable?

LO2-1 8. What types of adjustments can you claim to reduce your adjusted gross income?

LO2-1 9. How is tax liability different from taxable income?

LO2-1 10. What are deductible expenses for taxpayers who itemize?

LO2-2 11. If you are married and want to deduct charitable contributions from your adjusted gross income, which tax form should you use?

LO2-2 12. Under what circumstances is a person required to file a tax return?

LO2-2 13. Why are independent contractors and other self-employed persons required to pay estimated taxes?

LO2-2 14. Why should you keep a copy of your tax return?

MAKE ACADEMIC CONNECTIONS

LO1-1 15. **History** Prepare a report on the history of taxes in this country or in another country. Describe the kinds of taxes, including when they were first introduced and for what purpose.

LO1-1 16. **Government** Compare your state's tax system with that of other states. Which states are considered the worst (in terms of high taxes)? Which states are considered the best (in terms of low taxes)? Create a table or a graphic of your findings.

LO1-2 17. **Research** Visit the IRS website at www.irs.gov and explore the resources available. Learn how the IRS assists taxpayers, the types of assistance available, and the number of forms and instructions available at the site. Write a one-page report describing what you learned.

LO1-2 18. **International Studies** Use the Internet to research taxes assessed in foreign countries, including one country in Europe and one country on another continent. What benefits do taxpayers receive in exchange for their taxes? Compare and contrast your findings with U.S. taxes and benefits.

LO2-1 19. **Economics** Explain how the various forms of earned and unearned income increase the productivity (output) of a nation.

LO1-1 20. Many people are advocates for instituting a flat tax, one that would impose the same tax rate (such as 10 percent) on all income levels, and doing away with most deductions. They feel this would be a fairer way to impose taxes. Search the Internet for a tax calculator. Some calculators figure the income taxes you would pay if our country had a flat tax. Others calculate taxes based on today's system and rates. After entering various amounts of income, summarize what you learned about the tax system and the feasibility and fairness of a flat tax.

LO2-2 21. Download a copy of Form 1040EZ from the IRS website. Using the tax form and Figure 3.5, estimate the tax liability for Erik Wilson and the refund or money he owes. Erik is single and claims only himself as an exemption. He had wages of $11,100 and taxes withheld of $1,116.

LO2-2 22. Download a copy of Form 1040EZ. Prepare a tax return for Tomeka Hunt. Use the tax table in Figure 3.5 and the following information:

Tomeka is a part-time engineer who lives at 54 Center Street, San Francisco, CA 96214-3627. Tomeka's Social Security number is 999-00-9892. She wants $3 to go to the Presidential Election Campaign Fund. She is single and claims only herself as an exemption. Tomeka's salary is $12,880. She earned interest of $155 on her investments. No one else claims her as a dependent, and she had $825 in federal taxes withheld.

EXTEND YOUR LEARNING

LO1-2 23. **Legal Issues** Voluntary compliance is an important part of our tax system. When everyone contributes his or her fair share, the country is able to meet its obligations to its citizens. However, a group of people called *tax protestors* believe that the U.S. Constitution does not require them to pay federal income taxes and that payment of the tax is voluntary. Conduct research on *tax protestors*. Write a paper about tax resisters and those who refuse to pay taxes. Is their argument rational? On what is it based? What is your position on this issue?

CHAPTER PROJECT

When filing taxes, taxpayers may choose from three basic forms—1040EZ, 1040, or 1040A. Based on the steps presented in this chapter, complete Form 1040EZ using the data and forms provided for the Chapter Project in the *Student Activity Guide*. Then using the data and forms also provided in the *Student Activity Guide*, learn how to prepare Form 1040A.

Complete the Guided Decision Making activity for Chapter 3 at ngl.cengage.com/mypf.

Budgets and Records

4.1 **Budgeting and Planning**

4.2 **Agreements and Record Keeping**

Consider This...

Sarah has a part-time job, attends school six hours a day, and participates in two after-school sports. She no longer receives a monthly allowance from her parents. She pays for all of her own clothes, gas, insurance, and entertainment. Last year, she was able to save over $600.

"How do you do it?" asked her friend Ana. "I work more hours than you do, my parents pay for my clothes and most of my expenses, and I still don't have any money left over for entertainment. I didn't save a dime last year!"

"I have a budget," said Sarah. "Every time I get paid, I put aside money for savings. I know how much I spend on everything I buy. Keeping a good record of income and expenses helps me plan better, so I don't run out of money. That doesn't mean I can buy anything I want, but it does mean that I know how much I can spend, which helps me stretch my money to cover as many things as possible."

© Pan Xunbin/Shutterstock.com

The Essential Question *How does budgeting help you achieve your financial goals?*

LEARNING OBJECTIVES

> LO 1-1 Explain the purpose of financial planning and prepare a personal budget.

> LO 1-2 Explain the need for and create a net worth statement and a personal property inventory.

KEY TERMS

- disposable income, *80*
- financial plan, *80*
- budget, *81*
- fixed expenses, *82*
- variable expenses, *82*
- cash surplus, *83*
- cash deficit, *83*
- assets, *85*
- wealth, *85*
- liabilities, *85*
- net worth, *85*

LO 1-1 Financial Planning

Do you have unlimited resources to buy all of the things you want? Some people do, but if you are like most Americans, you will have to plan and work hard to achieve financial success. Planning, budgeting, and keeping good records provide the road map that leads to financial security.

Get Started

We all have to start somewhere. Even if you don't have much income, it will help to make a plan. There are two elements to consider: your income and your expenses. Your gross income is important, but it doesn't represent money over which you have control. Your **disposable income** is the money you have left to spend or save after taxes and other deductions (required and optional) are taken. If you spend all of your income, there won't be money to set aside for the future. To use your income to your best advantage, you need a financial plan.

All of the money you receive is spent, saved, or invested. You may spend it on things you need or want, save it for future needs, or invest it to earn more money. A **financial plan** is a set of goals for spending, saving, and investing the money you receive. Financial planning helps you do the following:

- List and evaluate your choices (what you want to achieve and what's really important to you).
- Assign a dollar amount to your goals.
- Prioritize your choices so your money goes as far as possible.

Why is it important to plan for the future?

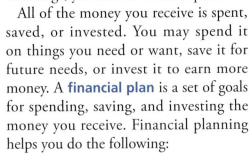

- Avoid careless and wasteful spending.
- Organize your *financial resources* (sources of income) so you can achieve your financial goals.
- Avoid money worries by planning your saving, spending, and borrowing so you can live within your income.

The first step in budgeting (an important part of financial planning) is understanding your *financial resources*—the sources and amounts of money you expect to receive—as well as understanding your obligations. Before you can prepare a budget, you may wish to keep track of money coming in and going out for a month or two. This will give you a clearer idea of what you can expect. Many people keep a journal or log where they record everything they spend. They may keep receipts for cash items. This record forms the basis of understanding what's happening in your current financial picture.

Visualize Your Future

Once you have a good idea of what comes in and how it goes out, you can then start thinking about changes you'd like to make. For many people, just keeping track of what you receive and how you spend it makes a difference. When people can actually see how much they spend on something, they may decide there are other things they'd rather do. Money you spend should reveal your values, choices, and priorities. But taking the next step—actually preparing a budget—will make your financial planning visions a reality.

Prepare a Budget

The next step toward achieving your financial goals is to prepare a budget. A **budget** is a spending and saving plan based on your expected income and expenses. In a budget, money coming in (earnings, gifts, borrowing) must equal money going out (spending and saving). The budget must balance. A budget helps you plan your spending and saving so you won't have to borrow money or use credit to meet your daily needs.

Steps in Preparing a Budget

The steps in preparing a budget are as follows:

1. Estimate your total expected income for a certain time period. Include all money you expect to receive. Use a weekly, biweekly, or monthly budget—whichever best matches how often you expect to receive money.
2. Estimate your expenses, or money you will need for day-to-day purchases—for example, lunches, fees, personal care items, and clothing.
3. Decide how much of your income you want to save, or set aside, for future needs. Most experts advise saving 10 percent of your disposable income each pay period. By saving, you will have money to pay for future needs, both expected and unexpected.
4. Balance your budget. If your expenses plus savings exceed your income, adjust your budget to make them balance. To do this, you may have to delay buying some items you want but don't need. Or you may decide to save a little less this month. If you can't cut your expenses, then you have to increase your income.

FIGURE 4.1   Simple Budget

Austin Albright
Budget for September

Income:

Part-time job (10 hours a week)	$320
Allowance	50
Birthday gift from grandparents	50
Total income	**$420**

Savings and Expenses:

Savings (credit union)	$100
Daily lunches (lunch ticket)	80
Supplies	20
Clothes (new jacket)	40
Entertainment	180
Total savings and expenses	**$420**

Figure 4.1 shows a high school student's budget for one month. This student expects to receive a total of $420 and plans to use the money for certain needs and wants. He also wants to put some money into savings for the future. Notice that total income equals the total of savings plus expenses. A *balanced budget* is one where the total income is equal to total savings and expenses. When you spend no more than what you take in, your budget remains in balance.

Budget Line Items

Some people create a monthly budget by taking an annual budget and dividing it into 12 months. This can be helpful for people who do not have a regular monthly income. *Line items* in a budget represent each item of income and spending that are anticipated during the month or year. Some line items occur only once a year. Other line items may occur monthly, such as rent or insurance.

There are two types of expenses. **Fixed expenses** are costs that do not change from month to month. You are obligated to pay them regardless of income changes. For example, people must pay rent or a house payment, a car loan, and insurance premiums when they are due. Most financial experts recommend that a family have fixed expenses of no more than 50 to 60 percent of take-home, or net, pay. However, this standard is difficult to achieve for young people just starting life on their own. But with time, pay raises, and careful budgeting, a family can achieve that goal.

Variable expenses are costs that vary in amount and type, depending on the choices you make. For example, your grocery bill can be larger or smaller, depending on what you choose to buy. Other examples of variable expenses are costs for eating out, going to movies, and buying clothes.

Figure 4.2 shows a monthly budget for a married couple. Casey and Olive both work and have no children. They estimate their income by adding together the net pay from both of their paychecks. They also expect income from savings and investments.

FIGURE 4.2   Budget for a Couple

Casey and Olive's Budget

Income	Monthly	Yearly
Salary (Casey's take-home pay)	$1,600	$19,200
Salary (Olive's take-home pay)	1,800	21,600
Interest on savings	50	600
Earnings on investments	100	1,200
Total income	$3,550	$42,600
Fixed Expenses		
Rent	$1,000	$12,000
Utilities	150	1,800
Car payment	300	3,600
Car insurance	100	1,200
(Health ins. withheld from paychecks)		
Total fixed expenses	$1,550	$18,600
Variable Expenses		
Cell phone plan	$ 90	$ 1,080
Gasoline	150	1,800
Car repairs and maintenance	60	720
Cable and Internet	120	1,440
Groceries	400	4,800
Personal care items	100	1,200
Insurance deductibles and copays	80	960
Recreation and entertainment	100	1,200
Gifts, donations, miscellaneous	300	3,600
Total variable expenses	$1,400	$16,800
Total fixed and variable expenses	$2,950	$35,400
Cash surplus (income – expenses)	$ 600	$ 7,200
Savings (allocation of cash surplus)		
Emergency fund	$ 100	$ 1,200
Short-term savings	100	1,200
Long-term investing	400	4,800
Total savings	$ 600	$ 7,200
Total expenses plus savings	$3,550	$42,600

Casey and Olive subtract estimated expenses from estimated income, leaving a **cash surplus** (income exceeds expenses). They apply the cash surplus to savings, which is approximately 17 percent of their monthly income ($600 ÷ $3,550). This enables them to set aside money for emergencies, short-term savings, and long-term investing.

When estimated expenses are greater than estimated income, the result is a **cash deficit**. When faced with a cash deficit, you must borrow money, bring in more income (such as by working overtime), or cut your expenses. Managing a budget, or *budgeting*, isn't always easy. It often means making adjustments to variable and fixed expenses so that priorities can be met.

When a budget involves two or more people, it is essential for each person to communicate his or her needs to the other person or persons. Often, *negotiating* is required so that each person's values and priorities are being met. When one person dominates and the other(s) go along even if their needs aren't being met, the budget is not likely to be successful. A *family budget* is one prepared for a group living together, providing for overall needs and sharing of expenses.

If you were living with one or two roommates, how would you go about preparing a budget? What kinds of expenses would you share with others? What kinds of expenses would be each person's solely? How can children contribute to a family's budget? Prepare a summary of what you would do to make sure everyone's needs and priorities are being met in a group or family budget.

Balancing Your Budget

When your budget isn't balanced, there are three basic things you can do. You can cut your expenses, you can borrow money or dip into savings, or you can increase your income. Dipping into savings is not a good thing because it reduces your ability to meet emergency needs in the future. It isn't always easy to increase income either, such as working more overtime or getting another job.

Sometimes balancing your budget is as easy as turning off the lights when you leave home or turning down the thermostat from 70 to 68 degrees. But often, it's more serious than that. Food and gas prices can rise 10 to 15 percent or more, leaving you without enough income to cover rising costs. When this happens, more serious action is required.

Fixed costs are difficult to change in the short run. For example, if you move to a location with lower rent, you will find your costs actually go up for a month or two. You have to pay for moving costs, new deposits, installation and startup fees, and so on. In the long run, however, you can reduce your fixed costs. As another example, you can reduce insurance premiums by shopping around and switching insurance carriers every few years, but to do this, you need a good driving record. When you purchase a car, you should consider not only the payment but also the fuel economy and insurance costs associated with the type of car you purchase.

Variable costs are easier to change in the short run. You can eat out less, spend less on clothing and entertainment, and save on gas by combining trips, avoiding trips, and carpooling. Many variable costs reflect current trends and values. For example, you may spend more on communicating (your cell phone and Internet bills) than you spend on groceries. You might consider less expensive options to save money on these variable costs.

Often, both single people and married couples find that much of their income goes unaccounted for. Or it ends up in miscellaneous expenses. Watching and then avoiding these types of spending will help balance your budget and provide more room for saving and investing.

✔ **CHECKPOINT**

What are three things you can do to balance your budget?

Planning for your future also includes keeping track of your progress. As you achieve goals along the way, you can track what you have accomplished and what remains to be done. This helps you focus on your goals. Keeping good personal records makes long-range planning easier. It also helps when you prepare tax returns, credit applications, and other financial forms. You should keep five types of records: income and expense records, your net worth statement, a personal property inventory, tax records, and other miscellaneous documents.

Income and Expense Records

Your W-2 forms show money earned and deductions from your paycheck. They also reveal taxes withheld, including Social Security and Medicare. You may need these forms to verify your proof of earnings when you want to collect benefits such as Social Security. You should also keep year-end statements from banks and investment companies showing interest and dividend earnings.

Expense items such as receipts for charitable contributions, medical bills, or work-related costs should also be kept. These receipts and statements will serve as proof of income and expenses, as well as help you plan your budget.

Net Worth Statement

A *net worth statement*, such as the one shown in Figure 4.3 on the next page, shows a person's net worth based on his or her assets and liabilities.

Assets are items of value that a person owns. Assets grow over your lifetime as you buy property, make investments, and save money. **Wealth** is the accumulation of assets. Wealth allows you to be financially secure, help others, and achieve your goals.

Liabilities are money or debts owed to others. For example, if you borrow money so you can buy a car, your car loan is a liability, or debt you owe. A responsible person plans to repay debts in the future. *Short-term liabilities* must be paid off soon, usually within a year or less. This might include money borrowed from a family member or a friend. *Long-term liabilities* are paid off over several years, such as a large purchase of furniture.

When you subtract your liabilities from your assets, the difference is called **net worth**. As your net worth increases your wealth is also growing.

Do you have any assets? If so, what are they?

FIGURE 4.3   Net Worth Statement

Net Worth Statement
Alison Jacobs
January 1, 20—

Assets		Liabilities	
Checking account	$ 500	Loan on car	$1,800
Savings account	900	Loan from parents	300
Car value	3,000		
Personal property		Total liabilities	$2,100
(inventory attached)	5,000		
		Net Worth	
		Assets – Liabilities	7,300
Total assets	$9,400	Total	$9,400

Over time your assets are increasing while your liabilities are decreasing because you are paying off your debts. When assets are greater than liabilities you are said to be *solvent*, or in a favorable financial position. When liabilities are greater than assets, a person is said to be *insolvent*, or in a poor financial position. Many people are temporarily insolvent. For example, when you attend college, your expenses are likely to exceed your income and your debts may be greater than your assets.

The net worth statement will provide needed information for applying for credit. The bank or other lender will want to know that you are able to repay your debt. A person who has too much debt is a high risk. Lenders are reluctant to make loans to those who are insolvent or who already have a lot of debt.

The net worth statement also shows how your wealth is growing each year. You should expect to see your assets growing while your liabilities are shrinking. This is a good way to be sure your financial position is improving over time.

Personal Property Inventory

Personal property is anything of value that you own, except real estate. It includes such things as cars, clothing, furniture, appliances, electronic gadgets, and so on. A *personal property inventory* is a list of the valuable items you own, along with their purchase prices and estimated current values.

A personal property inventory is useful in the event of fire, theft, or property damage. The inventory will help you list lost items and their value when you make an insurance claim. As a further safeguard, you can take pictures of the items of value and store them electronically or keep them in a secure place.

A personal property inventory also helps you see what you have to show for the money you have spent. As you buy new items and dispose of others, you should revise the inventory and keep it up to date.

Figure 4.4 is a personal property inventory. The approximate current value is less than the purchase price in most cases (with the possible exception of collectibles). Personal property is a *depreciating asset*, which means it goes down in value over time. Typically, if property is lost or stolen, you will receive the current approximate value, not the current market value.

FIGURE 4.4　　Personal Property Inventory

Personal Property Inventory
Alison Jacobs
January 1, 20—

Item	Purchase Date	Purchase Price	Approximate Current Value
Sphinx HD/3D with 70" screen	2014	$ 2,800	$1,100
Game system with controllers and games	2013	900	300
Furniture (bed, dresser, lamps, clock)	2011	3,000	1,800
Clothing and jewelry	-----	3,000	500
MXZ electric bike	2012	1,000	500
Laptop, digital camera, scanner, printer	2014	2,000	1,000
		$12,700	$5,200

Tax Records

All taxpayers should keep copies of their tax records for at least three years after they file their tax return. *Tax records* include the tax return itself (a copy of the signed form), W-2 forms, and other receipts verifying income and expenses listed on each return. Keep your tax records in a safe place in case of an audit. The IRS has the legal right to audit your tax returns and supporting records for three years from the date of filing (longer if fraud or intentional wrongdoing on your part can be proved).

Other Records

Many consumers keep lists of credit card numbers and phone numbers to call if those cards are lost or stolen. As a part of your financial plan, it is a good idea to reflect on the number of credit accounts you have along with the balances for each, the interest rates charged, and the monthly payments required. It's important to use credit wisely. Overusing your credit can affect your ability to plan for your financial future.

You may choose to keep other records as well, including car titles, insurance policies, birth and marriage certificates, wills, and passports. These documents are sometimes needed for certain financial transactions. The original documents should be placed in a safe place (such as a safe deposit box), and photocopies may be kept for easy reference. If you keep these at home, make sure they are in a secure location that is safe from intrusion, fire, and theft.

✔ **CHECKPOINT**

How can keeping good records help you with financial planning?

How Can You Live Within Your Income?

To be financially responsible, you must recognize that you are accountable for your own financial future.

A balanced personal budget is the first step to financial security. Living within your income means that you spend less than you make and that you plan savings for future as well as current needs.

Setting financial goals is the next step to securing your financial future. You can't achieve future financial goals if you aren't paying your current bills on time.

It is easy to believe advertisements that create demand. Emotional appeals are designed to get you to buy things you don't need in order to be more popular or to keep up with your friends. Ask yourself the following questions:

- Do I need it?
- Why am I buying it?
- How else could I spend the same money?
- How will buying it affect my financial goals?

Many people have a limit on how much money they will spend without a careful analysis and a family decision to spend the money. Whatever your limit, before spending a large sum or accepting a loan that will take a big bite from your future earnings, think through the decision carefully.

Living within your income is an important part of being happy. Regardless of the amount of your income, careful planning and budgeting can enhance your lifestyle and secure your future.

THINK CRITICALLY

1. Make a list of things you'd like to have, along with the purchase price of each. Read this list a week from now. Do you still want the same things? If so, what do you plan to do to buy one or more of them?

2. Do you know people who live within their income? If so, ask one of them to share how he or she does it. Based on the advice you receive, create a list of budgeting tips.

3. Do you know people who live beyond their income? What do you observe about their stress, financial stability, and financial goals?

KEY TERMS REVIEW

Match the terms with the definitions. Some terms may not be used.

a. assets
b. budget
c. cash deficit
d. cash surplus
e. disposable income
f. financial plan
g. fixed expenses
h. liabilities
i. net worth
j. variable expenses
k. wealth

____ 1. Items of value that a person owns

____ 2. A spending and saving plan based on expected income and expenses

____ 3. Assets minus liabilities

____ 4. An accumulation of assets

____ 5. Money you have left to spend or save after taxes and deductions

____ 6. Debts owed to others

____ 7. Costs that do not change from month to month

____ 8. Costs that can vary each month in both amount and type

CHECK YOUR UNDERSTANDING

L01-1 9. What is the first step in budgeting?

L01-1 10. How are fixed expenses different from variable expenses?

L01-2 11. Why would you prepare a net worth statement?

APPLY YOUR KNOWLEDGE

L01-1 12. Using Figure 4.1 as a model, prepare a simple budget for yourself. If your budget does not balance, make adjustments until it does. How much will you set aside for savings? Assume you could set aside this same amount each month. Locate a savings planner tool and calculate your savings after 12 months at 3 percent interest, starting with $0 in savings.

THINK CRITICALLY

L01-1 13. Financial planning should begin early in your life and continue as major life events occur, such as getting married or having children. Explain how a financial plan is based on personal values and choices.

L01-2 14. Why is it important to save personal records, such as receipts and credit card statements? Provide an example of a time when you did not save something and found that you later needed it.

L01-2 15. Why is it important to build wealth?

The Essential Question *Refer to The Essential Question on p. 80. Budgeting is a financial plan by which you can assign dollar amounts to your goals and prioritize them, allowing you to take action.*

The Essential Question *Why are legally enforceable agreements necessary?*

LO 2-1   Legally Binding Agreements

As your finances become more complex, it is likely that you will enter into legally binding agreements. A **contract** is a legally enforceable agreement between two or more people. It spells out your rights and your responsibilities. For example, if you buy a suit and you want it altered, the sales clerk fills out a ticket listing the changes requested and the promised date of completion. The ticket is a contract between you and the store. The store agrees to make the alterations by the stated date and for the stated price, and you agree to pay the price.

Types of Contracts

Common legal agreements are credit accounts, mortgage loans, and rental agreements. When you sign up for a retail credit card, the store agrees to give you products now in exchange for payment on your account later. When you rent an apartment, the landlord agrees to let you live in the apartment, and you agree to pay the rent by a certain day each month. Each of these cases constitutes an *express contract*. Express contracts can be oral or written. What makes them express is that the parties have stated the terms of their agreement in words.

Figure 4.5 shows a credit application from a retail store. A credit application asks you to agree to certain conditions before opening an account. Attached to the application will be an explanation of finance charges and how they are computed. When you sign the application, you are agreeing to pay finance charges if your balance is not paid in full each month. Be sure you have read everything contained in the agreement before you sign it. If something is not clear, ask for an explanation so you understand your rights and responsibilities before you enter into the contract. Many credit applications are available online. What you sign and accept online will also constitute a legal agreement.

© Pan Xunbin/Shutterstock.com

FIGURE 4.5 Credit Application

CREDIT CARD APPLICATION
(Please print. Not valid unless signed below.)

Title (optional): Mr. ☒ Mrs. ☐ Ms. ☐ Other _____

First Name ___Richard___ MI ___J___ Last Name ___Washington___

Street Address _45 Cleveland Avenue_ Apt. # _____

City ___Portland___ State _OR_ Zip + 4 ___97201-1072___

Home Phone _(513)555-0181_ Business Phone _(513)555-9213_ E-Mail _____

Soc. Sec. # _999-00-9384_ Gross Monthly Income $_2,000.00_ # Cards Desired _1_

Former Address _-----_
(if less than 1 year at current address)

City _____ State _____ Zip + 4 _____

Mother's Maiden Name _Hawkins_ Years Employed _3_ Position _Payroll specialist_

Present Housing: Own ☐ Rent ☒ Live with Parents ☐

# of Dependents (exc. self) _1_ Student? Full ☒ Part ☐

> **Note:** An applicant, though married, may apply for a separate Account in his or her own name. If your spouse will use this Account, please indicate his or her name, and social security number for credit reporting purposes.

First Name of Spouse _-----_ MI ____ Last _____ Soc. Sec. # _____

I HAVE READ AND AGREE TO BE BOUND BY THE TERMS OF THIS APPLICATION (INCLUDING THE ADDITIONAL APPLICATION PROVISIONS AND ACCOMPANYING FEDERAL AND STATE NOTICES AND SUMMARY OF CREDIT TERMS PRINTED TO THE RIGHT AND BACK).

I understand and agree that if I am approved for an Account, (i) the Central Credit Bank, N.A., Retail Installment Credit Agreement (the "Agreement") that I will receive with my credit card, will govern my Account, (ii) the Agreement is incorporated by reference into and made a part of the Application, and (iii) THE AGREEMENT INCLUDES AN ARBITRATION PROVISION THAT MAY SUBSTANTIALLY LIMIT MY RIGHTS IN THE EVENT OF A DISPUTE, INCLUDING MY RIGHT TO LITIGATE IN COURT OR HAVE A JURY TRIAL, DISCOVERY AND APPEAL RIGHTS, AND THE RIGHT TO PARTICIPATE AS A REPRESENTATIVE OR MEMBER OF A CLASS IN A CLASS ACTION. I MAY REQUEST THE COMMERCIAL ARBITRATION RULES OF THE AMERICAN ARBITRATION ASSOCIATION, WHICH SERVES AS ARBITRATION ADMINISTRATOR, BY CALLING 1-800-555-0155. I understand and agree that the Bank will first consider this application with respect to the credit card program described in this application. If for any reason, at the Bank's sole discretion, I do not qualify for this program, I request the Bank consider this application with respect to alternative credit card programs. My signature on this Application represents my signature on the Agreement.

NOTICE TO THE APPLICANT: (1) DO NOT SIGN THIS APPLICATION/AGREEMENT BEFORE YOU READ IT OR IF IT CONTAINS ANY BLANK SPACES. (2) YOU ARE ENTITLED TO A COMPLETELY FILLED IN COPY OF THE RETAIL INSTALLMENT CREDIT AGREEMENT

x _Richard J. Washington_ _3/11/--_
Signature of Card Applicant Date

In addition to written agreements, you take part in many unwritten agreements. An *implied contract* is not written but is created by the actions or conduct of the people. For example, suppose you mow your neighbor's lawn and she pays you $25. You continue to mow her lawn, and she continues to pay you $25. This is an implied contract based on the actions of both persons. One person accepts something of value, knowing the other person expects something of value in return. Although the terms of the contract may not have been specifically stated, it would be unfair if the neighbor stops paying you.

Contract Elements

To accomplish its purpose, a contract must be *binding*. That is, all who enter into the contract are legally bound to abide by its terms. A contract is legally binding when it contains these four elements:

- Agreement
- Consideration
- Capacity
- Legality

Agreement

Agreement is reached when a valid offer is made and accepted. An **offer** is an invitation to enter into a contract that is made with serious intent by one person to another person. The offer must be definite and certain so that the offer can be understood. Both the person making the offer and the person accepting it must express a voluntary intent to be bound by the agreement.

Acceptance occurs when a person accepts the terms of the offer. For example, Max may offer to sell his bike to Benji for $75. If Benji accepts, he will get the bike in exchange for $75. When one person makes an offer and another person changes it, the second person is making a counteroffer. The **counteroffer** is a new offer because it changes the original offer. It has to be accepted or rejected by the first person. If Benji offers Max $60 for his bike, Benji has made a counteroffer.

On the Internet, you may click on an "acceptance" of an offer. This click-on acceptance is considered a voluntary intent to be bound. If you do not intend to enter a binding agreement, or if you accidentally hit the wrong button, notify the online seller immediately of your error (and lack of intent to be bound).

It is important that both parties to an agreement genuinely agree to the contract terms. Genuine agreement does not exist when there is a mistake, fraud (an intentional misrepresentation), duress (threats), or undue influence (having free will overcome by a person who has a special interest, such as a parent or guardian).

Consideration

Consideration is something of value exchanged for something else of value. Consideration may be an item of value, money, a promise, or a performed service. If one person is to receive something but gives nothing in return, the contract may not be enforceable. The idea behind consideration is that each party to the agreement receives something of value. When you buy a pair of shoes, you get the shoes and the store gets your money. The shoes and the money are items of consideration.

© Cleve Bryant/PhotoEdit

Have you ever accepted a contractual offer or made a counteroffer? Describe it.

Capacity

Contractual **capacity** refers to the competence (legal ability) of the parties to enter into a contract. Competent parties are people who are legally capable of agreeing to a binding offer. Those who are unable to protect themselves because of mental deficiency or illness, or who are otherwise incapable of understanding the consequences of their actions, cannot be held to contracts. Minors have *limited contractual capacity*, which means that they may legally set aside contractual obligations. This privilege is allowed to protect minors from those who would take advantage of them.

Legality

To be legally enforceable, a contract must have a lawful purpose. A court will not require a person to perform an agreed-upon act if it is illegal. Some contracts must have a special form to be legally enforceable. For example, a contract for sale of real estate would have to contain a specific legal description of the property. A deed to transfer title to property would have to be notarized. When a document is **notarized**, the signature is verified by a notary public, who then applies a notary seal.

Statute of Frauds

Every state has a **statute of frauds**, which requires that some contracts must be in writing to be enforceable. The purpose of this law is to prevent harm due to fraudulent conduct (intentional deceit). Examples include the following:

- Contracts for the sale of real property (homes and land)
- Contracts that cannot be fully performed in less than a year
- Contracts involving the sale of goods for $500 and over
- Contracts in which one person agrees to pay the debts of another
- Contracts in consideration of marriage

These types of agreements must be in writing because they involve special rules. For example, a *prenuptial agreement* is a contract that specifies what will happen if a marriage ends in divorce. Generally, if two parties of unequal wealth enter into a marriage, a prenuptial agreement may be required in which the person without wealth agrees that he or she will receive a set amount as a settlement, rather than half of what the other person owns, if the marriage ends. This type of agreement serves to protect an individual's assets from a spouse who may have entered into the marriage fraudulently for financial gain.

Responsibilities of Agreements

When people enter into contracts, they have several responsibilities. They should do the following:

- Fill in all blank spaces or indicate N/A for items that are not applicable.
- Write all terms clearly. Vague phrases are often not enforceable.
- Enter dates, amounts, and other numbers correctly and clearly.
- Be sure the seller has supplied all relevant information, including rate of interest, total finance charges, cash payment price, and so on.

- Understand all terms contained in the agreement. Do not sign it until you have read it. Your signature acknowledges that you have read and understood the contract.
- Check that no changes have been made after you have signed it. Your initials at the bottom of each page will prevent substitution of pages.
- Keep a copy of the agreement. Put it in a safe place for future use.

Although as a consumer, you are protected by numerous consumer protection laws, you may need legal services occasionally. Your best protection is to arm yourself in advance by understanding the agreements into which you enter.

Negotiable Instruments

In contracts, the word **negotiable** means legally collectible. A *negotiable instrument* is an unconditional written promise to pay a specified sum of money upon demand of the holder. The negotiable instruments most people use are checks (discussed in Chapter 5) and, to a lesser extent, promissory notes.

A *promissory note*, like the one shown in Figure 4.6, is a written promise to pay a certain sum of money to another person or to the holder of the note on a specified date. A promissory note is a legal document, and payment can be enforced by law.

The person who creates and signs the promissory note and agrees to pay it on a certain date is called the *maker*. The person to whom the note is made payable is known as the *payee*. A promissory note is normally used when borrowing a large sum of money from a financial institution.

In some cases, creditors (those extending credit) will require a cosigner with a good credit rating as additional security for repayment of a note. A **cosigner** is a person who promises to pay the debt of another person. The cosigner's signature is also on a note. Young people and others who have not established a credit rating are often asked to provide a cosigner for their first loan. If someone asks you to co-sign a loan, do so only if you are sure the person is

---

FIGURE 4.6   **Promissory Note**

PROMISSORY NOTE

$ __400.00__   __January 15_____ , 20 `- -`

I (we) __Marilyn Huykamp_____ , jointly and severally,
do agree and promise to pay to __Emerald Furniture Co.__
the sum of ____Four hundred and 00/100_____ dollars
with interest at the rate of __9%__ from __January 15, 20- -__ , payable in
monthly installments of $__69.67__ beginning __February 1_____ , 20 `- -`
and on a like day each month until paid in full, the last payment
due __July 1_____ , 20 `- -`. Said payment shall include interest.
In the event of default, the maker hereof agrees to pay attorneys' fees and
court costs in collection of this note.

Marilyn Huykamp
Maker

financially responsible. If that person fails to repay the debt, you will be legally responsible to repay it.

When one person agrees to pay the debts of another person, that agreement must be in writing (signed by the cosigner) to be enforceable.

Warranties

A warranty, also called a *guarantee*, is a statement assuring quality and performance of a product or service. If the product fails, the warranty usually states what remedies are available, such as return of the product for the purchase price or repair of the product at no extra charge. The warranty may be in writing or assumed to exist by the nature of the product. Still, a warranty is not a safeguard against a consumer's poor buying decision.

Specific *written warranties* often guarantee that a product will perform to your satisfaction for a certain period of time. Many written warranties state that you may return a product for repair or replacement if it ceases to work because of a defect. However, warranties will not protect against normal wear and tear of the product. Figure 4.7 illustrates a limited warranty that might accompany home goods. Read it carefully to determine what the manufacturer does and does not guarantee.

All products contain *implied warranties*. For example, all products have the warranty of merchantability. This means that a product will do what

FIGURE 4.7 **Limited Warranty**

Limited Warranty   12 Y 845

This product is guaranteed for one year from the date of purchase to be free of mechanical and electrical defects in material and workmanship. The manufacturer's obligations hereunder are limited to repair of such defects during the warranty period, provided such product is returned to the address below within the warranty period.

This guarantee does not cover normal wear of parts or damages resulting from negligent use or mis-use of the product. In addition, this guarantee is void if the purchaser breaks the seal and disassembles, repairs, or alters the product in any way.

The warranty period begins on the date of purchase. The card below must be received by the manufacturer within 30 days of purchase or receipt of said merchandise. Fill out the card completely and return it to the address shown.

Owner's Name: _____
Address: _____
City, State, Zip: _____
E-Mail Address: _____
Date of Purchase: _____
Store Where Purchased: _____

Return to: ALCOVE ELECTRICAL, INC.
42 West Cabana
Arlington, VA 23445-2909

To register your warranty online, visit our website at www.alcoveelectrical.com.

Serial No.   12 Y 845

it is made to do. You would expect a new tennis ball to bounce. If it does not bounce, you can return the defective ball, even if there is no written warranty.

 **CHECKPOINT**

What makes an agreement legally binding?

LO 2-2 Record Keeping

As you begin to accumulate financial records and legal documents, you should have a good filing system to help organize, store, and retrieve needed information. Many people use a simple paper filing system. An electronic filing system may be a more convenient way to organize some records.

Paper Filing System

A typical home filing system would include folders and labels and a file cabinet. Most households need folders for each category shown in Figure 4.8. You may have additional categories. Name your folders with a descriptive word or short phrase that tells you immediately what records it contains. File your folders alphabetically.

Keep records and receipts in the appropriate folders. For example, in the "automobile" folder, you might want to keep track of oil changes, tune-ups, repairs, and other car expenses. You may also want to keep copies of car titles, car insurance policies, insurance cards, car payment records, and other related information. This way they will be easy to find when you need them.

| FIGURE 4.8 | Home Filing System |

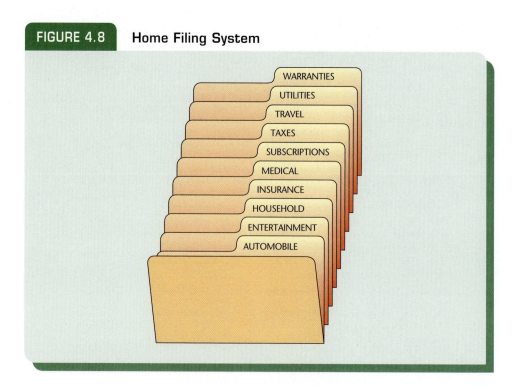

View Points

Information stored on your computer may not be safe. Hackers can get into your computer and steal important information, such as financial records. Antivirus and antispyware programs have not been effective in preventing this type of invasion. Many people advocate for "cloud computing," which allows you to store your information in a virtual place that can be accessed from anywhere. Advocates claim it is safe from unwanted access, uses, and users. Other people believe flash drives and external hard drives are the safest forms of storage. But you have to keep those storage devices in a safe place because they can be vulnerable to thieves. Clearly, important records need to be "backed up," but where is the ideal location?

THINK CRITICALLY

How safe do you consider information that is stored in cyberspace? Do you think flash drives and external hard drives are safer? What will you do to protect yourself and your financial information from unwanted security breaches?

Electronic Records

Many people invest in home computers and software for personal financial planning and record keeping. The advantages of computerized systems include the ease by which information can be updated, stored, and retrieved and the speed by which new computations and comparisons can be made.

Often, people keep financial records on their computer, usually password-protected, or on a travel or flash drive. As with any important files you keep electronically, always keep a current backup of your financial records.

Many software programs can help you keep better records. A **spreadsheet** is a computer program that organizes data in columns and rows and performs calculations using the data. You can use a general-purpose spreadsheet program to maintain a list of your income and expenses. You can enter a formula that will perform math calculations, such as addition. When you enter a new expense, the formula will recalculate the new sum automatically. You can even design your own budget worksheet in a spreadsheet program. Spreadsheet programs, such as Excel (Microsoft), are easy to use and help you keep information up to date.

A *database* is a computer program that organizes data for easy search and retrieval. The program can sort the data in many ways. For example, after entering all of your expenses into a database program, you could ask it to give you a report of only those expenses associated with travel.

A general-purpose database program can be rather sophisticated. However, several available software packages are specially designed for financial planning and record keeping. These programs provide spreadsheet and database forms already set up for personal financial management. For example, Microsoft Money Plus Sunset and QuickBooks are popular financial management programs designed to help you keep track of your income and expenses, keep an electronic checkbook, and create budgets.

✔ CHECKPOINT

What kinds of records should be stored, either manually or electronically?

Law

The legal profession offers a variety of careers, from judges and courtroom workers to lawyers and paralegals. A majority of lawyers work in private law offices. Private corporations also have legal departments that include many staff attorneys who specialize in functions such as contracts, tax, or international business. Some lawyers work in local, state, and federal government positions.

Being a lawyer is a tough and demanding career. Lawyers advise and represent clients, conduct research, interpret laws, present facts, and prepare and file legal documents. Many people assume that they need to seek legal help only under dire circumstances. However, people can hire lawyers for legal advice as a preventative measure to avoid legal problems in business and personal matters.

Employment Outlook

- An average rate of employment growth is expected.
- Competition could be strong because more students graduate from law school each year.

Job Titles

- Lawyer
- Attorney
- Counselor of Record

Needed Skills

- Must have a bachelor's degree plus law degree (JD).
- Must pass bar exam for each state in which law is practiced.

- Excellent communication skills (reading, writing, speaking, and listening).
- Excellent negotiation skills.
- Must maintain high ethical and confidentiality standards.

What's it like to work in . . .
Law

Bryan earned his law degree and passed the bar exam several years ago. He started his career with a large firm, where he works on cases under the supervision of a partner for the firm. His specialty is family law, and he has a dozen cases for which he is directly responsible. His annual salary is $120,000.

Bryan enjoys working with people to help them resolve their disputes. He especially likes putting together property settlement agreements.

Today, Bryan is meeting with a client who is filing for a divorce. He will obtain personal and financial information from his client in order to work out a divorce agreement that is in his client's best interest. To come to a settlement, Bryan will enter negotiations with the other spouse's attorney.

What About You?

Are you prepared for seven years of college? Are you willing to work long and hard hours? Do you like helping people and are you good at negotiating? If so a career in law might be right for you.

The Career Clusters icons are being used with permission of the: States' Career Clusters Initiative, 2007, www.careerclusters.org

KEY TERMS REVIEW

Match the terms with the definitions. Some terms may not be used.

a. acceptance
b. capacity
c. consideration
d. contract
e. cosigner
f. counteroffer
g. negotiable
h. notarized
i. offer
j. spreadsheet
k. statute of frauds
l. warranty

____ 1. An invitation to enter a contract

____ 2. A statement assuring quality and performance of a product or service

____ 3. A person who promises to pay the debt of another person

____ 4. Something of value exchanged for something else of value

____ 5. A computer program that organizes data in columns and rows

____ 6. The competence of a party to enter into a contract

____ 7. A new offer that changes the original offer

____ 8. An instrument that is legally collectible upon demand

CHECK YOUR UNDERSTANDING

LO2-1 9. What are the four elements of a binding contract? How is an express contract different from an implied contract?

LO2-1 10. What is the purpose of the statute of frauds?

LO2-2 11. Describe a paper filing system and an electronic filing system.

APPLY YOUR KNOWLEDGE

LO2-1 12. Using Figure 4.6 as a model, write a promissory note from you to John Doe. The note is payable in one year in the amount of $50 with interest of 11 percent and monthly payments of $4.63. Are you the maker or the payee? What is the total amount you will pay?

THINK CRITICALLY

LO2-1 13. Once you enter into an agreement, you are obligated to perform as agreed. Why might a person who enters into an agreement later refuse to do what she or he agreed to do?

LO2-2 14. Why is it important to keep good financial records? If you fail to keep a backup copy and your house burns down, how will you be able to recreate your records?

The Essential Question *Refer to The Essential Question on p. 90. Legally binding agreements spell out your rights and responsibilities. They also protect you in the event there is a dispute later.*

Assessment

SUMMARY

4.1

- *Disposable income is the money you have left over to spend or save after paying taxes and deductions (required and optional).*

- *A budget is a spending and saving plan based on expected income and expenses.*

- *To prepare a budget, you should estimate your income and expenses and set a savings goal.*

- *If expenses plus savings exceed income, adjust your spending or saving to balance your budget, or find a new source of income.*

- *Fixed expenses are costs that do not change monthly, while variable expenses change depending on choices made.*

- *Four types of personal records to keep include income and expense records, a net worth statement, a personal property inventory, and tax records.*

- *Net worth is the difference between assets (items of value owned) and liabilities (money owed).*

4.2

- *Contracts are legally binding agreements. They can be express (stated in words, either orally or in writing) or implied (created by actions of the parties).*

- *An enforceable contract has agreement (offer and acceptance), consideration (an exchange of something of value), contractual capacity (legal ability), and legality (lawful purpose).*

- *The statute of frauds requires that some agreements must be in writing to be enforceable. This law protects persons from fraudulent conduct (intentional deceit).*

- *It is your responsibility to read contracts carefully, fill in all blanks clearly, confirm that all relevant information is included, and understand your commitments before you sign.*

- *Negotiable instruments, such as checks and promissory notes, are promises to pay a specified sum to the holder.*

- *A warranty guarantees a product's quality and performance. It can be written or implied.*

- *Good filing systems can be paper or electronic. Spreadsheet and database programs can facilitate budgeting and record keeping.*

© Pan Xunbin/Shutterstock.com

APPLY WHAT YOU KNOW

LO1-1   1. What choices do you have if your budget doesn't balance? If you had to reduce your spending to balance your budget, which would you try to reduce first: fixed or variable expenses? Why?

LO1-2   2. Using Figure 4.3 as a model, prepare a net worth statement. List your assets and liabilities and then compute your net worth. How can you use this information?

LO1-2   3. Using Figure 4.4 as a model, prepare a personal property inventory, listing items of personal property in your room at home. Why should you and your family keep a record such as this?

LO1-2   4. Search online for articles or reviews about financial planning software. Write a one-page description of what you could do with the software and what features make one software better than another.

LO2-1   5. The Statute of Frauds requires that some contracts be in writing to be enforceable. Give three examples of contracts that must be in writing in order to be enforceable. Why is a written form necessary?

LO2-1   6. After examining the credit application in Figure 4.5, list the kinds of information requested by a retail store. Why do you think a store wants this type of information?

LO2-1   7. Bring to class a warranty from a product you or your family recently purchased. What does the warranty specifically promise to do? List any restrictions (exceptions) that the manufacturer has placed in the warranty.

LO2-2   8. Prepare a spreadsheet of the personal property inventory that you created in Number 3 above. Explain the advantages of using a spreadsheet to create a personal property inventory.

MAKE ACADEMIC CONNECTIONS

LO1-1   9. **Economics** Use the Internet to search for information regarding the budget of the United States, prepared by the President. List the major categories of proposed revenues and expenditures. What are some important provisions of the budget?

LO2-2   10. **Communication** Write a one-page report on the types of records you are currently keeping. How are they different from records kept by your parents? What kind of record keeping system are you using? Will you need to revise that in the future?

LO1-2   11. **Technology** Use a spreadsheet program to create a budget template that could be used for a monthly and yearly budget. You can use the categories shown in Figure 4.2. Use formulas to calculate totals.

LO2-1   12. **Social Studies** Discuss the role of law in society, such as contract law governing the relationships between people. Explain why laws and rules are important when establishing and enforcing contracts. What remedies are available to people when the other person in a contract breaches that contract?

Solve Problems and Explore Issues

LO1-1 13. Prepare a monthly and yearly budget for Brandy and Ken Harley, using Figure 4.2 as a model. Their monthly income and expenses are as follows: net paychecks, $1,800; interest on savings, $50; rent, $400; utilities, $120; gasoline, $100; insurance, $150; groceries, $200; clothing, $100; car payment, $210; car maintenance, $50; cell phone, $40; entertainment and recreation, $200. Their monthly cash surplus is applied as follows: investment fund, $60; miscellaneous, $120. Calculate the amount remaining for savings.

LO1-1 14. Prepare a monthly and yearly budget for Cathy Kudyrko, using Figure 4.2 as a model. Her monthly income and expenses are as follows: net pay, $1,400; rent, $410; insurance, $60; utilities, $50; gasoline, $60; clothing, $60; entertainment, $100; savings, $120; prepaid cell phone, $15; car payment, $150; car repairs, $20; groceries, $150; miscellaneous, $155.

LO1-2 15. Based on the following information, prepare a net worth statement for Sako Masuta. Follow Figure 4.3. Sako owns a car worth about $3,000 but owes $1,500 on it to the bank. He has $500 in savings and $100 in checking. His personal property totals $3,000, and he also owes $90 to his credit union.

EXTEND YOUR LEARNING

LO2-2 16. **Legal Issues** Fraud is misrepresentation of a material (important) fact with intent to deceive another person or company. People who claim to own assets that they did not purchase and then report them lost or stolen are committing insurance fraud. Or they may claim their vehicle or property was stolen and damaged just to collect insurance. Fraud is a serious crime (felony). Insurance companies investigate claims to be certain that people who file them legitimately owned those items or that the property was actually stolen and/or damaged. Do you know someone who filed a false insurance claim? How can keeping good records, such as a personal property inventory, protect you from being accused of insurance fraud? What other types of records do you think would be helpful in resolving insurance claims?

CHAPTER PROJECT

Your financial plan should be based on your personal values and goals. What do you want to achieve in your lifetime? Prepare a three-page report that outlines your values, your life goals (in priority order), and a proposed timeline to achieve your goals.

Complete the Guided Decision Making activity for Chapter 4 at ngl.cengage.com/mypf.

CHAPTER 5

Checking and Banking

5.1 Checking Accounts

5.2 Banking Services and Fees

Consider This...

Roxanne works part time after school and one weekend per month. She receives a paycheck once a week from her employer.

"I can't cash my paychecks," Roxanne told her friend, "unless my mom goes with me to her bank. The bank teller told me that I need my own account. She recommended a checking account along with a savings account. That way I can transfer the money I don't need each month into savings, where it can earn higher interest."

The bank teller told Roxanne that her mother or another adult has to be a joint account holder with her until she reaches age 18. Then she can have her own private account. But for now, a joint account with her mother will allow Roxanne to deposit her checks into her checking account and manage her own money. Because Roxanne is a minor, the bank won't charge her service fees on either account.

"I definitely don't like cashing my check and having all of the cash with me," Roxanne said. "It's too easy to spend it. Keeping my money in the bank makes me stop and think before I buy something."

The Essential Question *What are some of the responsibilities that go along with having a checking account?*

LO 1-1 Checking Account Basics

Financial institutions such as banks and credit unions offer a number of services. The first service you will likely want is a *checking account*, which allows you to write checks or transfer money electronically to make payments.

Why Use Checks?

A *check* is a written order to a bank to pay the amount stated to the person or business named on it. A checking account is known as a **demand deposit**, because the money may be withdrawn at any time—that is, "on demand." Only you, the depositor, also known as the *maker*, can write checks on the account.

Checks follow a process through the banking system. The *payee* cashes your check. The bank that cashed the check returns it to your bank. Your bank withdraws the money from your account and sends it to the other bank. Your bank then stamps the back of your check, indicating that it has *cleared*, which means it has been processed by the bank. A **canceled check** is a check that has cleared your account. It can be used as proof of payment if a dispute arises. Although banks no longer return checks to depositors, canceled checks can be viewed online and printed.

Many banks no longer send paper checks to other banks for processing. To make processing faster and more efficient, they exchange check information electronically by transmitting an image of the check, called a *substitute check*. A substitute check can be used in the same way as an original check.

A checking account offers several advantages:

- It provides a convenient way to pay your bills.
- Writing a check is often safer than using cash, especially when making major purchases, paying bills, or buying products through the mail.
- It has a built-in record-keeping system that you can use to track expenses and create budgets.

- It gives you access to other bank services, such as loans, online banking, and 24-hour access to your money through automated teller machines (ATMs).

Why do you need to be careful when writing checks?

As an account holder, you should write checks carefully and keep accurate records. You should check the accuracy of the bank statement you receive each month. In the past, canceled checks were returned with the statement. Today, most banks either send copies of canceled checks or simply describe your canceled checks on the statement. Merchants can also use *electronic check conversion* to convert a check into a debit transaction instead of processing the check. With this process, the check may either be destroyed or returned to you immediately after the transaction is processed. It is your responsibility to keep track of all of these entries in your checking account.

You must also maintain enough money in your account to cover all the checks you write. A check written for more money than your account contains is called an **overdraft**. A bank that does not honor a check usually stamps it with the words "not sufficient funds" (NSF) and returns it to the payee's bank. When this occurs, the check has *bounced*. Your bank will charge you a fee of $25 or more for each NSF check processed.

Many people write checks, hoping to deposit money to cover them before they clear. This is called a **check float**. Floating a check is very risky because today's electronic systems allow checks to be processed very quickly. Floating a check is illegal in most states. Intentionally writing bad checks can result in penalties and hurt your credit record.

Opening a Checking Account

To open a checking account, you will sign a signature form, such as the one shown in Figure 5.1 signed by Ardys Johnson. The *signature form* provides an official signature that the bank can compare to the signature you write on your checks. It helps the bank verify your identity. Most banks also require that you have an initial deposit of $50 or more.

Information obtained from the new account holder, such as his or her street address and Social Security number, is entered into the form electronically by the bank's account manager. The form is then signed and becomes an official document. Signature forms look different at various banks, but they contain the same basic information. Ardys also listed her mother's maiden name for use in identification. Someone who tries to forge Ardys's signature is not likely to know her mother's maiden name when questioned by the bank teller.

FIGURE 5.1　Signature Form

First Independent Mutual Savings Bank
Checking Signature Verification

Customer Name　Ardys Johnson

Account No.　08 40 856

Address　4250 West 18th Avenue

City/State/ZIP　Chicago, IL 60601-2180

Social Security No.　999-00-8696

Occupation　Accountant

Employer　Cho and Jackson, Inc.

Contact in case of emergency:　Harold Johnson

Relationship　Father

Mother's Maiden Name or other code word　Williams

Date　4/28/--

Individual　X　Joint

Home Phone　555-8925

Work Phone　555-0100

Birthdate　11/20/90

How long?　2 years

Phone　555-8925

Phone　555-2322

SIGNATURE:　*Ardys Johnson*　　　　Date　4/28/--

(Use second page for joint account holders.)

Parts of a Check

A check consists of the following parts. Look at the lettered elements of the check in Figure 5.2 as you read the following explanations.

A *Check Number.* Checks are numbered sequentially for easy identification.

B *ABA Number.* The American Bankers Association (ABA) number appears as a fraction in the upper right-hand corner of the check. The top half of the fraction identifies the location and district of the bank. The bottom half identifies the specific area and bank for the account.

C *Name and Address of Maker.* The maker, or *drawer*, is the person who wrote the check. Ardys is the maker of this check. The account holder's name, address, and phone number are printed on the check.

D *Date.* Enter the date the check is written. Do not *postdate* a check (write a future date on it). Postdated checks will not be held by the bank to be honored at a later date.

E *Payee.* The *payee* is the person or company to whom the check is payable. Food Mart is the payee in Figure 5.2.

F *Numeric Amount.* Write the amount neatly and clearly close to the dollar sign, with dollars and cents clearly separated.

G *Written Amount.* The written amount shows the amount being paid in words. The word "dollars" is usually printed at the end of the line. Use the word "and" to separate dollar amounts from cents.

H *Signature.* Sign the check on the signature line the same way as your name appears on the signature card.

I *Account and Routing Numbers.* The account number appears in coding at the bottom of the check along with the bank's routing number. These allow for electronic sorting.

FIGURE 5.2   Parts of a Check

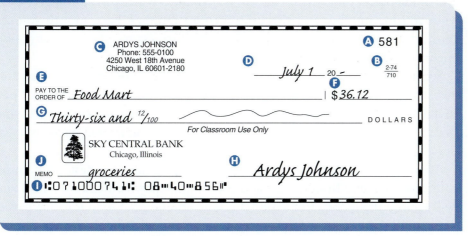

J *Memo.* The memo line appears at the left bottom of the check. There may be identifying information you wish to fill in here.

Banks sell checks to customers. They may provide checks of basic design free to account holders who maintain certain types of accounts. You can also choose to buy checks with special designs or colors, either from your bank or from a check-printing company.

✔ CHECKPOINT

What are some advantages of having a checking account?

LO 1-2   Using Your Checking Account

Checking accounts can help you manage your personal finances, but only if you use them correctly. Careless or improper use of a checking account can result in financial loss. Here are some tips on using a checking account.

Writing Checks

When writing checks, be sure to do the following:

- Always use a pen, preferably one with dark ink that does not skip or blot.
- Write legibly. Keep numbers and letters clear and distinct, without extra space before, between, or after them.
- Sign your name as it appears preprinted on the check and signature card.
- Avoid mistakes. If you make a mistake, write "VOID" across the face of the check to cancel it and then write a new check.
- Be certain you have deposited adequate funds in your account to cover each check you write.

Paying Bills Online

Instead of writing checks to pay bills, you can pay bills online. It is safer than sending checks through the mail and faster because money leaves your account right away. It's also convenient and saves both postage and the cost of checks.

To pay bills online, you have two choices. First, you can register at the website of the business to which you will be making payments. You will give them your routing number and checking account number. Each month you can authorize a payment, or you can allow the business to take automatic payments (deductions) from your account.

Second, you can pay bills from your own bank. To do this, you must first register at your bank's website. During that process, you establish your personal identification number (PIN) or password to gain entry into your account. Screen prompts will lead you to the bank's online bill payment page, such as the one shown in Figure 5.3.

After you set up your list of payees, you can pay bills each month by simply selecting the payee from the list and entering the payment amount. The bank will remove the money from your checking account and send it to the payee's account. Be sure to record these payments in your checkbook register.

Some banks charge a monthly fee for online bill payment privileges. Some limit the number of bills you can pay online each month. Consider the fees and restrictions for online banking when you choose a bank.

Making Deposits

You should complete a *deposit slip* each time you want to deposit money into your account. Figure 5.4 illustrates a deposit slip. To prepare a deposit slip, follow the guidelines listed on the next page.

FIGURE 5.3   Online Bill Payment Page

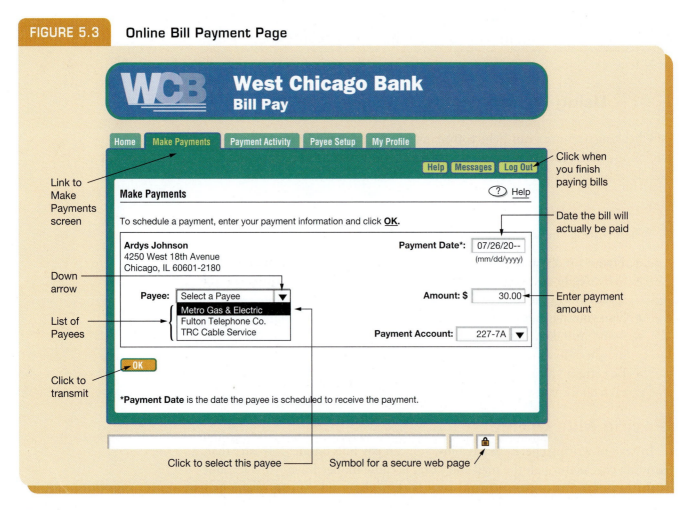

FIGURE 5.4   Deposit Slip

FOR DEPOSIT TO THE ACCOUNT OF

ARDYS JOHNSON
Phone: 555-0100
4250 West 18th Avenue
Chicago, IL 60601-2180

DATE _July 15_____ 20 _

SIGN HERE FOR CASH RECEIVED

🌲 SKY CENTRAL BANK
Chicago, Illinois

⑆07⦂000741⦂ 08⫿40⫿856⫿

CHECKS AND OTHER ITEMS ARE RECEIVED FOR DEPOSIT SUBJECT TO THE TERMS AND CONDITIONS OF THIS INSTITUTION'S COLLECTION AGREEMENT.

	DOLLARS	CENTS
CASH	20	50
CHECKS 585	200	00
SUBTOTAL	220	50
LESS CASH RECEIVED		
NET DEPOSIT	220	50

2-74
710

BE SURE
EACH ITEM
IS PROPERLY
ENDORSED

1. Insert the date of the transaction.
2. In the "Cash" section, write in the amount of currency (paper money) and coins you are depositing.
3. If you are depositing checks, write the amount of each check, together with the check number of each check, in the "Checks" section of the slip.
4. Total the currency, coin, and check amounts. Write this figure on the "Subtotal" line.
5. If you wish to receive some cash at the time of your deposit, fill in the desired amount on the "Less Cash Received" line.
6. If cash is received, subtract it from the subtotal. Write the final amount of the deposit on the "Net Deposit" line.
7. If you will receive cash, enter your signature on the line above the words "Sign here for cash received" (this wording may vary).
8. The teller will give you either a copy of this deposit slip or a receipt. Keep the copy or receipt as proof of your deposit.

You can also make deposits at your ATM. Many banks now make it easy to deposit money using a mobile app that allows you to take a picture of the check being deposited; no deposit slip is needed.

Using a Checkbook Register

A **checkbook register** is a booklet used to record checking account transactions. Figure 5.5 shows a page from the checkbook register of Ardys Johnson. Ardys lists all checks, online payments, fees, interest, and deposits for her account. Follow along in Figure 5.5 as you read the following guidelines for recording transactions in a checkbook register.

1. Record the current amount in your account at the top of the "Balance" column. (When you go to the next page in your register, copy your account balance from the bottom of the previous page to the top of the new page.)
2. As soon as you write a check, use your debit card, make an online payment, or make a deposit, record the transaction in your checkbook register.
3. Write the preprinted check number in the first column. If the transaction is not a check, make up a code to represent the kind of transaction it is, such as DEP for deposit, WD for withdrawal, ON for online transaction, SC for service charge, and INT for interest.

FIGURE 5.5   Checkbook Register

CHECK NO. OR TRANSACTION CODE	DATE	DESCRIPTION OF TRANSACTION	PAYMENT/ DEBIT(–)		FEE (–)	✓	DEPOSIT/ CREDIT (+)		BALANCE $800	00
581	7/1/--	Food Mart	$ 36	12	.20		$		36	32
		Groceries							763	68
DEP	7/15/--	Deposit Paycheck					220	50	220	50
									984	18
WD	7/16/--	ATM Withdrawal	20	00					20	00
									964	18
582	7/20/--	Bellvue Apts.	600	00	.20				600	20
		Rent							363	98
ON	7/22/--	Metro Gas & Electric	32	50					32	50
		Online Payment							331	48
SC	7/31/--	Monthly Account Fee			5.00				5	00
		July							326	48

4. Write the month, day, and year of the transaction in the "Date" column.

5. Enter the name of the payee on the first line of the "Description" section. On the second line, write the purpose of the check or any description of the transaction you find useful.

6. If the transaction will reduce your balance, write the amount in the "Payment/Debit" column. If the transaction will add to your balance, record the amount in the "Deposit/Credit" column.

7. Some banks charge a fee for each check written. In this case, record the fee in the "Fee" column next to the check.

8. Add the amount of the check to the check fee, and record the result in the "Balance" column. For a deposit, simply repeat the amount in the "Balance" column.

9. If the amount is a debit transaction, subtract it from the previous balance. If the amount is a deposit or other credit transaction, add it to the previous balance. Write the new balance on the next line of the "Balance" column.

10. The column headed by a check mark is provided so that you can check off each transaction when it appears on your monthly bank statement. The check mark shows that the transaction was cleared by the bank and is no longer outstanding (unprocessed).

Always keep your checkbook handy so you can write down needed information each time you make a transaction. If you don't record it promptly, you could forget a transaction and accidentally overdraw your account.

Reconciling Your Account

Financial institutions that offer checking accounts provide each customer with a monthly statement. This statement lists checks received and processed by the bank, online payments, and all other withdrawals, deposits, service charges, and interest. While banks no longer return canceled checks with your statement, you can view them online at the bank's website.

The process of matching your checkbook register with the bank statement is known as **bank reconciliation**. The back of the bank statement is usually

FIGURE 5.6 Bank Reconciliation

Bank Statement
SKY CENTRAL BANK

Ardys Johnson
4250 West 18th Avenue
Chicago, IL 60601-2180

Statement Date: July 31, 20—
Opening Balance: $800.00
Ending Balance: $926.68

Checks

Check No.	Date Paid	Amount
581	7/4/—	36.12

Debits and Withdrawals

Date	Amount	Description
7/16/—	20.00	ATM withdrawal
7/22/—	32.50	Online bill payment
7/31/—	.20	Check fee ($0.20 per check)
7/31/—	5.00	Monthly account fee

Deposits

Date	Amount	Description
7/15/—	220.50	Deposit

Account Reconciliation

1. Ending balance shown on the bank statement: 926.68

2. Total of all credits and deposits made but not shown on statement: 0

3. Total lines 1 and 2: 926.68

4. List all checks, withdrawals, and debits made but not shown on statement:

Check No. or Transaction Code	Amount
582	600 00
SC	20

5. Total of outstanding debit transactions: 600.20

6. Subtract line 5 from line 3: (Result should match checkbook balance.) 326.48

printed with a form to aid you in reconciling your account. Bank reconciliation forms are also available online at your bank's website. Figure 5.6 represents both sides of a typical bank statement.

The left side of Figure 5.6 is a statement showing the bank's record of activity on Ardys Johnson's checking account. The statement lists all checks that have cleared as well as all withdrawals, online bill payments, and fees that the bank subtracted from the account. It also shows all deposits added to the balance that month. After subtracting all debit transactions and adding all deposits, the bank arrives at the ending, or current, balance for the account.

The balance your checkbook register shows will not always match the ending balance shown on the bank statement. A check does not appear on the statement until the payee has cashed it and the check completes its route through the banking system. Because you recorded the check and subtracted the amount from your balance when you wrote it, your balance will be lower than the bank's until the check clears and the bank removes the payment from your account. As you can see by comparing Ardys's checkbook register (Figure 5.5) to her bank statement (Figure 5.6), the ending balances do not match. When this occurs, you can check for errors by reconciling your account. Follow along on the right side of Figure 5.6 as Ardys reconciles her account.

1. Write the ending balance shown on the bank statement.
2. From your checkbook register, total any deposits you made that do not appear on the bank statement.
3. Add the outstanding deposits to the ending bank balance.

4. List all debit transactions from your checkbook register that do not appear on the statement. Debit transactions are any transactions that reduce your balance, including checks, online bill payments, withdrawals, and fees. Ardys listed check #582 and its check fee, since these did not appear on her statement.
5. Total all outstanding debit transactions.
6. Subtract the total debits from the previous total. The result should match the balance shown in your checkbook register.

If the balances do not match, check your addition and subtraction in the reconciliation process. Next, make certain that you have deducted service charges from and added any interest earned to your check register balance. For example, Ardys recorded the $5 monthly account fee in her check register. If you still cannot reconcile your account, ask a bank representative for help in discovering where the error lies. Be sure to take your checkbook and bank statement with you.

Complete the reconciliation immediately upon receipt of the bank statement. This will allow you to report any problems to the bank as soon as possible. Occasionally the bank does make an error, which it will correct when you report the mistake. You can also view your current balance and all transactions with online banking and do a "daily" reconciliation with your checkbook.

Endorsing Checks

A check generally cannot be cashed until it is endorsed. When two or more people are named as payees, all must endorse the check if the names are separated by "and." If the names are separated by "or," only one person must endorse it. To endorse a check, the payee named on the check signs the top part of the back of the check in ink. There are three major types of endorsements.

Blank Endorsement

A *blank endorsement* is the signature of the payee written exactly as his or her name appears on the front of the check, as shown below on the left. If Donald's name had been written incorrectly on the face of the check, he would correct the mistake by endorsing the check with the misspelled version first and then with the correct version of his name, as shown below on the right.

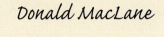

Special Endorsement

A *third-party check* is a check that is signed over to a third person by the original payee. A *special endorsement*, or an endorsement in full, is an endorsement that transfers the right to cash the check to someone else. It consists of the words "Pay to the order of [new payee's name]" and the signature of the original payee. In the following illustration, for example, Donald MacLane uses a check written to him to pay a debt owed to Diane Jones. It can be difficult to cash a third-party check. If you deposit this type of check into your checking account, it may be "held" until the check clears.

> *Pay to the order of*
> *Diane Jones*
> *Donald MacLane*

Restrictive Endorsement

A *restrictive endorsement* restricts or limits the use of a check. For example, a check endorsed with the words "For Deposit Only" above the payee's signature can be deposited only to the account specified. The restrictive endorsement is safer than the blank endorsement for use in mailing deposits, in night deposit systems, or in other circumstances that may result in loss of a check. If a check with a restrictive endorsement is lost, the finder cannot cash it.

> *For Deposit Only*
> *United California Bank*
> *Acct. #8-2011-4*
> *Donald MacLane*

✔ CHECKPOINT

Why is it important to reconcile your bank account(s)?

LO 1-3 Types of Checking Accounts

Financial institutions offer many types of checking accounts. You should carefully study your options, because a wise choice can save you money. Most banks still offer *free checking* (no service fees) accounts. These accounts do not pay interest and may come with certain conditions. For example, you may be required to maintain a certain balance or limit your use of bank teller services. Free checking may also be available to senior citizens, students, nonprofit groups, and to others during special bank promotions.

Joint Accounts

Accounts can be either individual or joint. A **joint account** is opened by two or more people. Such an account is also called a *survivorship account* because any person who signs on the account has the right to the entire amount deposited. If one person using the account dies, the other (the survivor) then becomes the sole owner of the funds in the account.

Special Accounts

Most banks offer a **special account** to customers who have a small amount of activity in their accounts each month. Service fees are charged at a flat rate per month with an additional fee for each check written (for example, $8 per month plus 15 cents for each check cashed). In some instances, banks may charge service fees only when the number of checks written or deposits made in a month exceeds a set limit (such as more than ten checks or three deposits in a given month). If you write only a few checks each month, this type of account might be right for you.

Another type of special account assesses a small (or no) monthly fee, but charges for each teller service. If you make a deposit or withdrawal at a teller station, you will be assessed a fee for the personal service. This type of account is good for people who have their paychecks electronically deposited by their employers and who use ATMs for most of their transactions.

Standard Accounts

A **standard account** usually has a small (or no) monthly service fee and no per-check fee. To avoid a monthly service fee, you are usually required to maintain an average minimum balance in the account. These accounts may or may not pay interest. Many banks offer a package of services for this type of account, such as free traveler's checks, an ATM card, or a free safe deposit box. Some banks offer reduced interest rates on credit card balances to customers who also have checking, savings, and other accounts at their bank.

Money Market Accounts

Most financial institutions offer checking accounts that earn interest. A *money market account* is an interest-bearing checking account that pays a higher rate of interest, but it usually has more restrictions. With a money market account, your account balance usually must not fall below a minimum average set by the bank during any month. The minimum may be $500 or more.

Interest rates rise and fall with economic conditions. When overall interest rates drop, you may receive less than 1 percent. When overall interest rates rise, you might expect a rate that is more competitive with CD rates.

Share Accounts

Most credit unions offer share accounts. A **share account** is a savings account representing ownership interest. A *share draft account* is a checking account with low (or no) average daily balance requirements and, generally, no service fees. If you are eligible for credit union membership, this type of account may be the least expensive and most convenient option. It offers most, if not all, of the services of a checking account in a bank.

 ✔ CHECKPOINT

What are some types of checking accounts?

How Can You Shop for the Right Bank?

A checking account is a personal choice. Some people choose the bank closest to their home or work. Others choose the biggest bank or the one with the most ATMs. While all of these are good reasons, there are many other considerations in choosing your bank. Sometimes the best choice is a credit union where you can have the same services and possibly lower fees.

Finding the right bank can take a lot of time. All banks and services are not the same; they vary a great deal. A good way to start is to make a list of the features that are important to you. Rank them 1 to 10. For example, #1 may be free on-line bill payment; #2 may be a low minimum deposit for a free or interest-bearing account; and #3 may be low or no service fees. Arrange your features into a table, either on paper or in a word processor or spreadsheet. At the top, list the banks that you are considering. Your table might look like this:

	Bank 1	Bank 2	Bank 3
Free online banking	_____	_____	_____
Low/no minimum deposit	_____	_____	_____
Low/no service fee	_____	_____	_____
Low/no fees for other services such as ATM withdrawals	_____	_____	_____
Mobile banking apps available	_____	_____	_____
Low-cost credit card available	_____	_____	_____
Conveniently located ATMs	_____	_____	_____
Fraud account alerts	_____	_____	_____

Fill in your table by inserting information you find out about the different banks. Then compare information to determine which bank overall provides the best services at the lowest costs for you.

THINK CRITICALLY

1. Which is your favorite bank or credit union? Why?

2. What features do you think are the most important when choosing a financial institution for your checking account?

3. What would cause you to switch from one financial institution to another?

KEY TERMS REVIEW

Match the terms with the definitions. Some terms may not be used.

____ 1. Savings type of account available at a credit union

____ 2. Check that has cleared your account

____ 3. Account opened by two or more people with the right of survivorship

____ 4. Check written for more money than is in one's account

____ 5. Matching the checkbook register with the bank statement

____ 6. A booklet used to record checking account transactions

____ 7. A no-fee or low-fee account with a minimum balance requirement

____ 8. Writing a check before a deposit has cleared the account

a. bank reconciliation
b. canceled check
c. check float
d. checkbook register
e. demand deposit
f. joint account
g. overdraft
h. share account
i. special account
j. standard account

CHECK YOUR UNDERSTANDING

LO1-1   9. What does a bank do when you "bounce" a check?

LO1-2   10. What is online banking?

LO1-3   11. How is an individual account different from a joint account?

APPLY YOUR KNOWLEDGE

LO1-1   12. The account number and routing number on checks give counterfeiters the information needed to make false checks. Banks reimburse consumers when this occurs, but pass along the costs to all customers. How can you protect your account from fraud?

THINK CRITICALLY

LO1-2   13. Bank reconciliation allows you to catch errors in your account—your own and the bank's. Many people do not take time to reconcile their accounts. Is this okay? Why or why not?

LO1-3   14. Many people choose to use cash only instead of using a checking account or online banking service. Which viewpoint do you agree with? Why?

The Essential Question *Refer to The Essential Question on p. 104. It's important to fill out checks and deposit slips correctly, keep an accurate checkbook register, reconcile your account, and endorse checks properly.*

The Essential Question *How can you maximize your services and minimize your fees at a bank?*

LEARNING OBJECTIVES

> **LO 2-1** Describe banking services available at most financial institutions.

> **LO 2-2** List and explain fees charged by banks for their services.

KEY TERMS

- certified check, *117*
- cashier's check, *117*
- debit card, *118*
- overdraft protection, *119*
- electronic funds transfer (EFT), *119*
- stop-payment order, *120*
- safe deposit box, *120*
- notary public, *120*
- NSF fee, *121*
- ATM fee, *122*

LO 2-1 | Banking Services

A *full-service bank* is one that offers every possible kind of service, from savings and checking accounts to credit cards, safe deposit boxes, loans, and ATMs. Other services commonly offered are online banking, telephone banking, certified checks, cashier's checks, money orders, and debit cards. Most banks offer FDIC (Federal Deposit Insurance Corporation) insurance, which protects the deposits of customers against loss up to $250,000 per account.

Guaranteed-Payment Checks

A **certified check** is a personal check that the bank guarantees or certifies to be good. Sometimes a payee might want you to get your personal check certified to reduce the risk of accepting your check for payment. For example, if you buy a used car from someone, the owner might want a certified check before allowing you to take the car.

To get a check certified, write your check in the normal manner. Then take it to your bank. A bank officer will immediately deduct the amount from your checking account, stamp the word "certified" on the check, and initial it. In effect, the bank holds in reserve the check amount from your account for specific payment of that check. Most financial institutions charge the account holder for this service. Typically, the fee ranges from $5 to $10 per check.

A **cashier's check**, also called a *bank draft*, is a check written by a bank on its own funds. You can pay for a cashier's check through a withdrawal from your savings or checking account, or in cash. After receiving your

Why would you need a certified or cashier's check?

payment, the teller makes out the cashier's check to your payee, and an officer of the bank signs it.

Cashier's checks are generally used when the payee requires a guaranteed payment but cash is not desirable. A cashier's check also can be used for transactions in which you wish to remain anonymous. The bank is listed as the maker of the check, and your identity need not be revealed. As with certified checks, many banks charge a fee for issuing cashier's checks.

Some financial institutions also provide traveler's checks for their customers. *Traveler's checks* are check forms in specific denominations that are used instead of cash while traveling. Many businesses that will not accept an out-of-state personal check will accept a traveler's check for payment. Because traveler's checks can be easily forged, some businesses will not accept them. When traveler's checks are purchased, money is taken from your bank account to cover them. You sign each check in one place immediately upon purchase. When cashing a traveler's check, you present identification and sign in another place. Traveler's checks are safer than carrying cash because they are payable only upon comparison of the purchaser's endorsement against the original signature on the check.

Money Orders

Some banks sell *money orders* to people who do not wish to use cash or do not have a checking account. A money order is like a check, except that it can never bounce. There is a charge for purchasing a money order. It can cost from 50 cents to $5 or more, depending on the amount of the money order. You also can purchase money orders through the post office and local merchants.

Debit Cards

A **debit card** is a bank card that deducts money from a checking account almost immediately to pay for purchases. The debit card is presented at the time of purchase. When a debit card is used, the amount of the purchase is quickly deducted from the customer's checking account and paid to the merchant. The debit card transaction is similar to writing a check to pay for purchases. The issuing bank may charge an annual fee for the card or a fee for each transaction. A debit card is not the same as a credit card. No credit is extended. Instead, payment occurs instantly because funds are quickly withdrawn from your checking account.

Debit cards can also be used for cash withdrawals at ATMs. Debit cards with a Visa or MasterCard logo can be used for point-of-sale purchases wherever those credit cards are accepted. Usually there is a limit per day on how much can be withdrawn from an account using a debit card. This is to protect consumers from fraud if they lose their card. Be sure to record debit card transactions in your check register to avoid overdrawing your account.

Bank Credit Cards

You can apply to a full-service bank for a bank credit card, such as a Visa or MasterCard. If you meet the requirements and are issued a card, you can use it instead of cash at any business that accepts credit cards. Banks often offer special credit card "perks" to their best customers whose accounts are in good standing. For example, a bank's best customers may be offered lower interest rates and no annual fees on their credit cards.

Women's World Banking (WWB) is a non-profit organization based in New York that is committed to expanding the economic assets, participation, and power of low-income women as entrepreneurs and economic agents. WWB supports a network of financial organizations that provide women with easier access to finance, knowledge, and markets. WWB has more than 23 million end users (women borrowing money) who are low-income borrowers. The network of organizations finances small business loans and health insurance to help increase family incomes, improve nutrition and health, raise education standards, and reduce poverty around the globe.

THINK CRITICALLY

How can WWB help reduce poverty by making small business loans? Do you think more programs like this are needed in the United States? Why or why not?

Banks offering national credit cards usually charge both an annual fee for use of the card and interest on the unpaid account balance. The topics of credit and credit cards will be discussed in more detail in Unit 2.

Overdraft Protection

Overdraft protection allows you to cover checks or withdrawals up to a specified amount, usually between $100 and $1,000, depending on the typical balance in your account. With **overdraft protection**, your checks will be covered even if you have insufficient funds in your checking account. Protection may be offered in the form of an instant "loan" with high interest rates. Other banks may charge a flat fee. With some overdraft-protection agreements, the amount of the overdraft may be pulled from your savings account or charged to your bank credit card. Banks may charge transfer fees for this type of protection.

Automated Teller Machines (ATMs)

Many banks provide ATMs for their customers. At an ATM, you can make cash withdrawals (using your debit card) from your checking or savings account. Using a Visa or MasterCard, you can receive a cash advance electronically. To use 24-hour ATMs, you must have a card that is electronically coded. You also must know your personal identification number (PIN), which usually is some combination of numbers and letters. For safety, do not carry your PIN in written form. Commit it to memory.

Online and Telephone Banking

Most financial institutions offer online and telephone banking services. These services give you the ability to access your accounts from a computer or telephone, transfer money from one account to another, and pay bills by authorizing the bank to disburse money. You can find out your current balance, what checks have cleared, and which deposits have been entered. Online and telephone banking enable you to access your account any time, day or night.

Most banks also allow and encourage electronic transfers of money. An **electronic funds transfer (EFT)** uses a computer-based system that enables you to move money from one account to another without writing a check or exchanging cash. This can be done by telephone, by computer, or in person. Money is available immediately (there is no delay as with waiting for a check to clear). Electronic transfers can also be made between banking institutions, and funds are available immediately.

Stop-Payment Orders

A **stop-payment order** is a request that the bank not honor a specific check. The usual reason for stopping payment is that the check has been lost or stolen. By issuing a stop-payment order, the check writer can safely write a new check, knowing that the original check cannot be cashed if it is found and presented to the bank. Most banks charge a fee (often $20 or more) for stopping payment on a check. The stop-payment order is usually good for only six months. After that, the check may no longer be honored because checks over six months old generally are not valid for cashing or depositing.

Safe Deposit Boxes

Financial institutions offer customers a **safe deposit box** to store valuable items or documents. They charge a yearly fee based on the size of the box. Annual rental fees may range from $50 to $150 or more. The customer is given one key for the box. The bank will also have a key. Both the customer's key and the bank's key must be used to open the box. Documents commonly kept in a safe deposit box are birth certificates, marriage and death certificates, deeds and mortgages, and stocks and bonds. Jewelry, coin collections, and other small valuables also are commonly stored there. Keeping important documents and other items in a safe deposit box ensures that the items won't be stolen, lost, or destroyed. Documents that can be easily replaced with a duplicate need not be stored there.

When you rent a safe deposit box, you will fill out a signature card. Then each time you enter your safe deposit box, you must sign a form so that your signature can be compared to the one on file. This procedure prevents unlawful entry to your box by an unauthorized person.

Loans and Trusts

Financial institutions also make loans to finance the purchase of cars, homes, vacations, home improvements, and other items. Banks can also provide advice for estate planning and trusts. (You'll learn more about estates and trusts in Chapter 20.) In addition, banks can act as trustees of estates for minors and others. A *trustee* is a person or an institution that manages property for the benefit of someone else under a special agreement.

Notary Public Services

A **notary public** verifies a person's identity, witnesses the person's signature on a legal document, and then "notarizes" the signature as valid. Financial institutions typically have at least one person on their staff who is a notary public. This person provides notary services for account holders, usually without charge. For noncustomers, however, there is typically a small fee of $10 or less.

Financial Services

Many banks offer financial services to their depositors, such as purchasing or selling savings bonds and investment brokerage services. You may buy and sell stocks and bonds through the brokerage service. The purchases and sales are "cleared" through your checking or savings accounts with the bank. Brokerage services will be discussed in Chapter 17. Many banks also purchase a block of bonds (debt obligations) that they allow their members and depositors to purchase. Generally there is no additional fee to buy or sell these securities (the fee is included in the purchase price). However, a minimum purchase such as $1,000 is often required.

CHECKPOINT

Why is online banking such an important banking service today?

LO 2-2 Bank Fees

Banks charge fees to their customers to help cover their operating costs. For example, when a bank grants you a loan, it charges you a loan fee. When the bank acts as the trustee of an estate, it charges a fee for this service.

Banks also charge noncustomers for services such as check cashing. If you want to cash a check at a bank where you do not have an account, the bank may charge you a fee or refuse to cash the check. Nondepositors pay for other services that may be free to depositors, such as traveler's checks and notary services.

Under the Truth-in-Savings Act (1993), checking advertised as "free" must carry no hidden charges or conditions. When a customer opens a free-checking account, the bank or savings institution cannot charge regular maintenance or per-check fees or require balance minimums to avoid fees. However, it still may charge for a box of checks and for ATM transactions.

Most banks charge these fees to their customers who have checking accounts:

- Monthly service fees, averaging $5 to $15
- Overdraft fees of $25 to $30 per event
- NSF check charges of $25 to $30 per event
- ATM fees of $1 to $5 per transaction
- Safe deposit box fees of $50 to $150 per year

When you spend more than you have in your account and you don't have overdraft protection, you are assessed an overdraft fee called an **NSF fee**. This is to compensate the bank for having to reprocess your check, withdrawal, or other error. Each and every time you overdraft, you are charged a separate fee.

Why is it important to be aware of the fees your bank charges for its accounts and services?

Banks and other financial institutions have found that customer service is an important part of the success of their business. It is important to have the right mix of products and services to satisfy customers, especially profitable customers. The way banks communicate with their customers can vary based on customer preferences. Some customers like to hear about changes to policies and new products by e-mail. Others prefer to receive a telephone call or a letter by mail. Using the wrong type of communication can seem invasive by some customers. For example, if customers use a post office box for a mailing address as a way to maintain their privacy, they may consider it an invasion of privacy if the bank contacts them by telephone or at their personal residence. Customers may also be offended when banks share personal information about them with third parties without their permission. But as described in their privacy policies, banks have the legal right to share information with their "affiliates," such as investment companies that specialize in retirement planning and advising.

Visit your bank or your parents' bank and request a copy of its privacy policy. You may also be able to obtain the privacy policy online. Read through it, and then in one page, summarize some of the important parts of the policy, using more understandable language.

An **ATM fee** is typically charged by an ATM that does not belong to your own bank. For example, if you do not have an account at Wells Fargo and you use a Wells Fargo ATM, Wells Fargo will charge you a fee. In some cases your own bank will also charge you an ATM fee for using another bank's ATM.

Unless you have a regular checking account, you may also be charged fees for teller services, account balances that fall below the stated minimum, cashier's and certified checks, traveler's checks, notary services, and online bill payment services. In addition, some banks charge a fee to return canceled checks.

The best way to avoid fees is to choose the right kind of account. For example, if you need to write a large number of checks each month, sign up for an account that does not charge a per-check fee. Some accounts charge a fee for using a teller. Only sign up for such an account if you have your paycheck directly deposited by your employer and can do almost all of your transactions online or by ATM. Shop around and find the account that is right for you. Be aware of the rules of your account, so that you don't violate them, resulting in high fees. If your account requires a minimum balance, plan enough cushion so that your balance will not drop below that amount.

One way to avoid service charges is to have more than one account and to link them together. For example, if you have a retirement savings account, it can be "linked" to your checking account. The combined balances of your retirement account and checking account can give you the minimum balance you need to avoid service fees on your checking account.

✓ CHECKPOINT

How can you avoid service fees charged by banks?

- -

Finance

Finance officers and managers are responsible for making sure a business or client has money when it is needed. Almost every firm, government agency, and other type of organization has one or more financial managers. Managers oversee the preparation of financial reports, manage investments, and implement cash management strategies. By doing so, they keep the company on solid financial footing, allowing for growth and expansion.

Financial managers are creative thinkers and problem solvers. They are computer savvy and are very knowledgeable about all aspects of finance, including global issues. They are also very familiar with tax laws and regulations, ensuring that the company is in compliance with them.

Employment Outlook

- A slower than average rate of employment growth is expected.
- Those with a master's degree will have the best opportunities.

Job Titles

- Loan officer
- Finance officer
- Treasurer
- Credit manager

Needed Skills

- A bachelor's degree in finance, accounting, or a related field is required.
- Certifications and advance degrees are preferable.
- Experience and analytical skills are essential.

What's it like to work in . . .
Finance

Rajiv works in an office, right next door to the company president. He reports directly to the president, and they have frequent informal conversations throughout the day. As chief financial officer (CFO), Rajiv has many responsibilities.

Today Rajiv will present his financial analysis to meet the CEO's strategic plan for the next three years. With help from the accounting department, he prepares and revises a forecast of financing options and their costs, along with projected cash management changes. His recommendations include major changes in how the company can operate more efficiently. If his decisions are implemented, many people in the company will have to follow new operating policies to help cut costs and increase profits.

Rajiv started his career in finance earning a salary of 60,000; today he makes around $100,000, close to the median annual wage for financial managers. Plus he receives an annual bonus and incentives.

What About You?

Would you like to be involved in helping a company grow by analyzing its finances and increasing its ability to operate more efficiently? Would you consider a career in finance?

KEY TERMS REVIEW

Match the terms with the definitions. Some terms may not be used.

____ 1. *A request that the bank not honor a specific check*

____ 2. *A bank card that deducts money almost immediately to pay for purchases*

____ 3. *A personal check that the bank guarantees to be good*

____ 4. *A computer-based system that moves money from one account to another*

____ 5. *Check written by a bank on its own funds*

____ 6. *A place to store valuable items at a bank*

____ 7. *Bank service that covers bad checks*

____ 8. *A person who verifies another person's identity and signature*

a. ATM fee
b. cashier's check
c. certified check
d. debit card
e. electronic funds transfer (EFT)
f. notary public
g. NSF fee
h. overdraft protection
i. safe deposit box
j. stop-payment order

CHECK YOUR UNDERSTANDING

LO2-1   9. List five banking services that are found at full-service banks.

LO2-2   10. List bank fees charged to customers and to noncustomers for services provided.

APPLY YOUR KNOWLEDGE

LO2-1   11. Checking accounts have many good features, such as overdraft protection. List banking services that appeal to you and indicate whether each is of high, medium, or low value. Would you be willing to pay a monthly service fee to have the service?

THINK CRITICALLY

LO2-1   12. When customers write too many bad checks, banks may close their accounts, making it difficult to open an account at another bank. Do you agree with the banks' actions? Why or why not?

LO2-2   13. Many people believe that bank fees are too high and that banks pay depositors insufficient interest for the use of their money. Do you agree? Why or why not?

LO2-2   14. When transferring a title (such as when selling a car) many sellers require that buyers use a cashier's check. Why?

The Essential Question *Refer to The Essential Question on p. 117. Choose the right account that has the right features and be aware of all fees that could be imposed, such as ATM fees, so that you can avoid them.*

SUMMARY

5.1

- *A checking account is a demand deposit that provides a safe, convenient way to pay bills.*

- *To open a checking account, fill out a signature form and make a deposit.*

- *As soon as you make a checking transaction, record it in your checkbook register.*

- *A canceled check is one that has been cleared, or processed, by your bank and deducted from your account.*

- *If you float a check, you are risking the possibility of an overdraft on your account because today's electronic systems process checks so quickly.*

- *Reconcile your bank statement with your register each month and correct any errors.*

- *To cash a check, you may endorse it with a blank, special, or restrictive endorsement.*

- *Banks offer individual accounts, joint accounts, special accounts, standard accounts, and money market accounts. Credit unions offer share and share draft accounts.*

5.2

- *Certified checks and cashier's checks are guaranteed by the bank to be paid.*

- *Traveler's checks provide a readily acceptable and safe form of payment for people who are traveling.*

- *You can pay for purchases or make ATM transactions using a debit card, which allows immediate deductions from your checking account.*

- *With overdraft protection, your checks will be covered even if you have insufficient funds in your checking account.*

- *Online and telephone banking enable you to make electronic transfers and access your account 24 hours a day.*

- *A stop-payment order is a request that the bank not honor a specific check.*

- *Financial institutions offer safe deposit boxes for customers to store valuable items or documents.*

- *To avoid high bank fees, choose the type of account that best fits your needs and follow the account rules.*

© Pan Xunbin/Shutterstock.com

APPLY WHAT YOU KNOW

LO1-1

1. Using Figure 5.2 as an example and following the guidelines on pp. 106–107, write these checks: (1) Check No. 12 to Melvin Quigly for $34.44, written today; (2) Check No. 322 to Save-Now Stores for $15.01, written today. The purpose of your check is to buy school supplies; (3) Check No. 484 to M. A. Rosario for $91.10, written today. (Note: Blank checks are available in the *Student Activity Guide*.)

LO1-2

2. Using Figure 5.4 as an example and following the guidelines on p. 109, prepare these deposit slips: (1) Today's date; currency $40.00; coins $1.44; Check No. 1881 for $51.00; no cash received back with the deposit transaction; (2) Today's date; Check No. 4022 for $300.00 and Check No. 2412 for $32.00; $20.00 cash received back with the deposit transaction. (Note: Blank deposit slips are available in the *Student Activity Guide*.)

LO1-2

3. Using Figure 5.6 as an example, determine your ending reconciled checkbook balance when all of the following six conditions exist: (1) Your ending checkbook balance is $311.40 before the monthly account fee (service charge) is deducted. (2) You made a math error, resulting in $30.00 less showing in your account than should be. (3) The monthly account fee is $6.00. (4) The ending bank balance is $402.00. (5) Outstanding deposits total $100.00. (6) Outstanding checks total $166.60.

LO1-3

4. Visit a local bank or go to its website to learn about the different types of checking accounts it offers. Describe some of the features of the bank's special accounts. What features are offered as part of its standard account?

LO2-1

5. Explain the differences among a small state bank, a full-service national bank, and a credit union in terms of services offered and fees charged. Cite local examples.

MAKE ACADEMIC CONNECTIONS

LO1-1

6. **History** Today's banking system has a long history. Use the Internet to research the roots of U.S. banking. Write a report explaining why banks were created. Describe the first banks and discuss any laws that helped lay the foundation for today's banks.

LO2-1

7. **International Studies** Conduct online research to explore banking systems in foreign countries. How are they similar to and different from the U.S. banking system? Do they depend as much on electronic transfers and ATMs? Do customers pay bills on the Internet?

LO2-1

8. **Technology** Visit a bank website that offers online bill payment. Write a summary of how the process works.

LO2-2

9. **Communication** Write a one-page paper discussing bank services and fees. Explain how the banking industry depends on charging fees to its customers to make a profit. Also discuss other ways that banks make money and ways depositors may avoid fees.

Solve Problems
and Explore Issues

LO1-1 10. Find the errors in the following check.

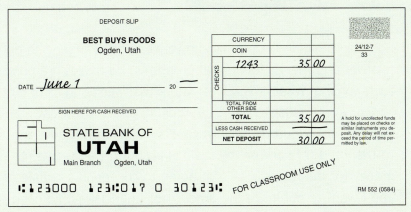

LO1-2 11. The deposit slip shown here was written to deposit the check in Number 10 above. Find the errors on the deposit slip.

LO2-2 12. Debit cards are used widely today. It is legal for merchants to charge an additional fee to customers who use debit cards. Why?

EXTEND YOUR LEARNING

LO1-1 13. **Legal Issues** Many serious crimes involve checks and checking accounts. Depending on the state and the amount of the check, writing bad (NSF) checks can be a felony crime. Forgery is another crime committed with checks. It involves making or altering a check to steal money from another person's account. Research the laws in your state related to these crimes. What are the penalties? How can banks and other businesses help prevent these crimes? What can you do to avoid becoming a victim of forgery?

CHAPTER PROJECT

Complete a checkbook mini practice set for one month. Using the data provided in the *Student Activity Guide*, prepare checks and deposit slips, record transactions in a checkbook register, and reconcile your account. (Note: Directions and working papers for this project are found in the *Student Activity Guide*.)

Complete the Guided Decision Making activity for Chapter 5 at ngl.cengage.com/mypf.

Saving for the Future

Consider This...

Isaac saves regularly from his allowance and the money he gets from relatives and friends for special occasions. He makes it a point to set aside some of what he receives, rather than spending all of it.

"For every dollar I save, Dad adds 10 cents to my savings," Isaac told his best friend. "That gives me a 10 percent return, in addition to the interest I earn on my savings account. Dad wants me to save money for the future. Plus, I'm going to college in a couple of years, and I want to minimize the amount of financial aid I'll need. It may not seem like a lot of money each month, but every year my savings grow. This year, I'll have enough to get a certificate of deposit at the bank. That way, I get a higher interest rate on money deposited. Sure, it's tempting to spend some of my savings on fun stuff, but I have to pay back the 10 percent to my dad on everything I take out. It's kind of like a tax on spending, isn't it?"

The Essential Question *How does saving money add to your financial peace of mind?*

LEARNING OBJECTIVES

> LO 1-1 Discuss why it is important to save money for the future.
> LO 1-2 Explain how money grows through compounding.
> LO 1-3 List the various places where you can save money.

KEY TERMS

- scholarship, *130*
- financial aid, *130*
- subsidized loan, *131*
- unsubsidized loan, *131*
- grant, *131*
- work-study, *131*
- principal, *132*
- interest, *132*
- compound interest, *132*
- annual percentage yield (APY), *133*

LO 1-1 Why You Should Save

The best reason to save money is to provide for future needs, both expected and unexpected. If you set nothing aside for these inevitable needs, you will constantly live on the edge of financial disaster. Saving regularly will help you meet your short-term and long-term needs.

Short-Term Needs

Often you will have *short-term needs*, which are expenses beyond your regular monthly items. Unless you have extra cash income during the month, you will have to pay for these things out of savings. Some short-term needs are predictable; others you can't foresee. Examples of short-term needs include the following:

- *Emergencies*—unemployment, sickness, accident, or a death in the family
- *Vacations*—short weekend trips or longer excursions
- *Social events*—weddings, family gatherings, or other potentially costly special occasions
- *Repairs*—cars, appliances, plumbing, and other items that need routine or unplanned repairs
- *Major purchases*—a car, major appliances, furniture, remodeling, or other items that have limited lives and eventually have to be replaced

Long-Term Needs

While you need savings to meet emergencies and short-term needs, you must also provide for long-term needs. *Long-term needs* are expenses that are costly and require years of planning and saving. These include predictable costs such as home ownership, education, and retirement. Saving money now will enable you to make larger purchases in the future. It will also allow you to invest and accumulate enough money for a secure retirement.

Home Ownership

Many people want to own their own house. At the time of purchase, you will likely have to pay a large sum of cash, or a *down payment*. The amount needed is often 10 to 20 percent of the purchase price. The balance will be paid with a mortgage (home loan) for which you will make monthly payments. The larger the down payment you make, the smaller your monthly mortgage payments will be.

Education

Many young people desire to complete some form of post-secondary education or training. *Education* is a long-term investment that pays off in higher income potential. Many couples begin a savings plan when children are born. When the time comes for college, they have all or some of the money needed for their children's higher education. If there are no savings (or not enough) to pay for a college education, it is usually financed through a variety of other sources, as described below.

Work Students may choose to work part time, full time, summers, or any combination. Working full time while attending college is a *pay-as-you-go* system. Its advantage is that when you finish your education, you have fewer debts. The disadvantage is that it generally takes longer to finish your education. Many students choose a combination of work and other forms of financing to pay for their education.

Scholarships A cash allowance awarded to a student to help pay education costs is called a **scholarship**. Generally, scholarships are paid directly to educational institutions. They often are obtained from donations from private or public sources. For example, professional organizations in a field, such as accounting, may sponsor scholarships for accounting majors. Many scholarships are available based on scholastic achievement, which includes grades earned in high school, high scores on tests, or other qualifying criteria. Scholarships are also awarded for athletic achievement. Other scholarships are based on need, and to qualify, you must show that you do not have other sources to pay for your education (such as parents). The biggest advantage of scholarships is that they do not have to be repaid if you complete your education. But scholarships usually require students to meet certain standards, such as maintaining a certain GPA. Unfortunately, some scholarships become taxable or must be repaid if the student drops out or does not fulfill the requirements.

Financial Aid Students may receive money to help pay for their education in the form of **financial aid**. Forms of financial aid include student loans, grants, and work-study programs.

How do you plan to pay for college?

iStock.com/asiseeit/Steve Debenport

Many people believe that a college education will benefit you throughout your lifetime, such as by giving you much higher earning potential. Others claim that a college degree will help get you an interview, even for a job unrelated to your degree. Because so many people have degrees, competition for jobs is much greater. Some people believe that college isn't for everyone. It's expensive and time-consuming, and often the courses taken have nothing to do with the work that people end up doing. Default rates on student loans show that many people cannot afford to pay back their student loan debt, which may exceed $50,000 for a bachelor's degree.

THINK CRITICALLY

How do you feel about the long-term value of a college education? Do you agree that time spent now getting an education will be rewarded later with higher income over your lifetime? Why or why not? Do you think we should have loan forgiveness for those who cannot get a job in the area that they prepared for with their education? Why or why not?

Student loans are available from the federal government through its FAFSA (Free Application for Federal Student Aid) website or from private lenders, such as banks. Loans may be subsidized or unsubsidized. A **subsidized loan** is a form of federal financial aid for which you pay no interest until after you have completed your education, or are no longer enrolled in school. An **unsubsidized loan** starts accruing interest as soon as you use it to pay for tuition or other education costs. Generally, government loans are subsidized, although some government student loans and loans obtained from private lenders are unsubsidized and have higher interest rates.

Today, student loans are processed through the U.S. Department of Education. Interest rates, which are generally low, are set by the U.S. Congress. The FAFSA program will *consolidate*, or combine, all of your student loans into one monthly loan payment when you complete your education. Although deferring student loan payments while in school is beneficial, it is important to understand the potential consequences. Student loans can lead to a large debt upon graduation that may take several years to repay. So it is important to use student loans responsibly.

A **grant** is a form of educational funding based on financial need that does not have to be repaid. Grants are often funded by the government but are also available through many state programs as a way to encourage residents to go to college.

Students who are eligible for financial aid may also qualify for **work-study** programs, which permit students to work at the campus or other college location to earn money. Generally, the amount of work-study earnings will help offset the need for student loans.

Investing

After you have saved enough to cover daily expenses and emergencies, you can afford to invest your extra savings. Investing in stocks, bonds, mutual funds, real estate, and other investments can make your money grow faster than it would if left in a regular savings account. Because investments are often risky, you should make them in addition to—not instead of—regular savings. Types of investments are described in later chapters.

Retirement

The Social Security system was never designed to provide a comfortable retirement. It is meant to be a supplement to an individual's own savings. To have a financially secure retirement, you must begin to save regularly as early in life as you can.

Peace of Mind

Probably the best reason to save is the peace of mind that comes from knowing that when needs arise, you will have adequate money to pay for them. The amount of money you save will vary according to several factors, including the following:

- The amount of your discretionary or disposable income—what you have left over to spend or save as you wish
- The importance you attach to savings
- Your anticipated needs and wants
- Your willpower, or ability to give up present spending to provide for your future

CHECKPOINT

What short-term and long-term needs can be met by saving?

- -

LO 1-2 How Money Grows

The amount of money you deposit into a savings account is called the **principal**. It is the base on which your savings will grow. For the use of your money, the financial institution pays you money called interest. **Interest** represents earnings on your deposit.

As principal and interest grow, more interest accumulates. This is known as **compound interest**, or interest paid on the original principal plus accumulated interest. Figure 6.1 illustrates how interest is compounded annually. Notice how interest earned each year increases because the saver is earning interest on the previous year's interest as well as on the initial deposit.

The more often interest is compounded, the greater your interest earnings will be. Figure 6.2 illustrates what happens when 6 percent interest is compounded quarterly (every three months) and added to the principal before more interest is calculated. If you compare the ending balances in Figures 6.1 and 6.2, you will notice that you earn more interest with quarterly

FIGURE 6.1	Interest Compounded Annually		
Year	Beginning Balance	Interest Earned (6%)	Ending Balance
1	$100.00	$6.00	$106.00
2	$106.00	$6.36	$112.36
3	$112.36	$6.74	$119.10

FIGURE 6.2   Interest Compounded Quarterly

| | | | Quarterly Compounding Annual Interest Rate = 6% | | | | | |
| | | | Quarterly Interest | | | | | |
Year	Beginning Balance	Rate	1	2	3	4	Ending Balance
1	$100.00	.015	$1.50	$1.52	$1.55	$1.57	$106.14
2	$106.14	.015	$1.59	$1.62	$1.64	$1.66	$112.65
3	$112.65	.015	$1.69	$1.72	$1.74	$1.77	$119.57

compounding than with annual compounding. (Also see the Math Minute feature on the next page to learn more about compounding interest.)

Earnings on savings can be measured by the rate of return or yield. *Yield* is the percentage of increase in the value of your savings due to earned interest. Because financial institutions compound interest in many ways, comparing yields can be difficult. To solve this problem, the law requires all financial institutions to tell consumers the **annual percentage yield (APY)**, which is the actual interest rate an account pays, stated on a yearly basis with the compounding included.

✔ CHECKPOINT

How does compounding cause your money to grow faster?

LO 1-3   Where to Save

Most cities have several commercial banks, savings banks, savings and loan associations, credit unions, and brokerage firms from which you can choose to open an account. Savings accounts are also available through online banks and financial institutions, including credit card companies. Most of these institutions have greatly expanded their services in recent years, so the differences among them are becoming increasingly blurred. Interest rates vary among savings institutions and among the various types of accounts offered. You will have to study your options and determine which type of institution and account is the best deal for you.

What are some of your options if you want to open a savings account?

Computing Interest Compounded Quarterly

Compound interest means earning interest on principal, and then allowing the interest to remain on deposit so you will then earn interest on both your principal and your previous interest. To compute interest compounded quarterly, divide the annual interest rate by 4 to get the quarterly rate. For monthly compounding, divide the annual interest rate by 12. For interest compounded every 6 months (a half year), divide the annual rate by 2.

Suppose you deposit $100 in a savings account that will pay you 6 percent per year, compounded quarterly. This means that for each quarter, you will receive one-fourth of the yearly interest. Six percent divided by 4 is 1.5 percent (or .015) each quarter. At the end of the first quarter, you earn $1.50 in interest, using the following computation:

$$\$100.00 \times .015 = \$1.50$$

At the beginning of the second quarter, you now have $101.50 in your account ($100.00 + $1.50). At the end of the second quarter, you earn interest as follows:

$$\$101.50 \times .015 = \$1.52$$

At the beginning of the third quarter, you have $103.02 ($101.50 + $1.52). At the end of the third quarter, you earn interest as follows:

$$\$103.02 \times .015 = \$1.55$$

At the beginning of the fourth quarter, you have $104.57 ($103.02 + $1.55). At the end of the fourth quarter (the end of the first year), you earn interest as follows:

$$\$104.57 \times .015 = \$1.57$$

Your balance at the end of the first year is $106.14 ($104.57 + $1.57). You earned a total of $6.14 in interest for the year. At the end of Year 3, your balance is $119.57. That's total interest of $19.57 on your original deposit of $100, as shown in Figure 6.2. Based on the previous example, compute your quarterly interest for three years if you deposit $500 at 8 percent, compounded quarterly.

Year	Beginning Balance	Rate	Quarterly Interest 1	2	3	4	Ending Balance
1	$500.00	_____	$_____	$_____	$_____	$_____	$_____
2	$_____	_____	$_____	$_____	$_____	$_____	$_____
3	$_____	_____	$_____	$_____	$_____	$_____	$_____

Solution:

Year	Beginning Balance	Rate	Quarterly Interest 1	2	3	4	Ending Balance
1	$500.00	.02	$10.00	$10.20	$10.40	$10.61	$541.21
2	$541.21	.02	$10.82	$11.04	$11.26	$11.49	$585.82
3	$585.82	.02	$11.72	$11.95	$12.19	$12.43	$634.11

Commercial Banks

Commercial banks, also known *as full-service banks*, provide the widest variety of banking services of any of the financial institutions. Some of these services include safe deposit boxes, 24-hour ATM networks, money transfer services, and loan and investment services. Commercial banks also offer many kinds of savings and checking accounts. Having checking and savings accounts at the same bank makes it easy for people to transfer funds and make deposits and withdrawals. By linking checking and savings accounts, customers can avoid certain service fees. Almost all commercial banks are insured by the Federal Deposit Insurance Corporation (FDIC). This insurance protects depositors from loss due to bank failure, up to $250,000 per account.

Why would you want your checking and savings accounts at the same bank?

Savings Banks

Savings banks are usually referred to as *mutual savings banks*. These financial institutions are few in number—about 500 of them in roughly a dozen states, mostly throughout New England and the Northeast—but substantial in size. Two primary services offered by these institutions are savings accounts and loans on real property, including mortgages and home-improvement loans. Savings banks are insured by the FDIC.

Savings and Loan Associations

Savings and loan associations (S&Ls) are organized primarily to lend money for home mortgages. S&Ls offer many of the services of commercial banks, including interest-bearing checking accounts and special savings plans. You may find a slightly higher interest rate on savings at an S&L. S&Ls are insured by the FDIC.

Credit Unions

Credit unions are not-for-profit organizations established by groups of people, such as employees in similar occupations who pool their money. To use a credit union, you must be a member of the group. Potential members have to meet membership requirements that vary depending on the credit union's objective. For example, a corporation's credit union may accept only employees and their immediate family members. A credit union for teachers, on the other hand, may accept any teacher who works for a certain school district. A few credit unions have more relaxed requirements and may simply request that members live in a certain city or area.

Credit unions are owned by their members, who save their money in the form of "shares," or part ownership in the credit union. From funds accumulated by these shares, the credit union makes loans to its members, generally at lower interest rates. Savings and checking accounts at a credit union are usually called *share accounts*. Credit unions generally offer higher interest rates on savings accounts than commercial banks do. Checking accounts have low (or no) average daily balance requirements and, generally, no service fees. If you are eligible for credit union membership, this type of checking account may be the least expensive and most convenient option.

Credit unions also offer other financial services to members, such as individual retirement accounts (IRAs), certificate of deposits (CDs), and investment planning. Through membership in the National Credit Union Administration (NCUA), depositors' accounts are insured up to $250,000.

Brokerage Firms

Brokerage firms buy and sell different types of securities. *Securities* are stocks and bonds issued by corporations or by the government. *Stocks* represent equity, or ownership. *Bonds* represent debt, or a loan. In other words, when you buy stock, you become an owner of the company. When you buy a bond, you are loaning money to the company or to the government. Investors buy and sell securities through a *stockbroker*, who works for the brokerage firm. As you will learn in a later chapter, you can buy stocks, bonds, and mutual funds directly or through brokerage firms. *Discount brokerage firms* offer broker services for reduced fees. They also offer checking and savings account options. Accounts in brokerage firms are usually not insured.

Why might you choose to have an online savings account?

Online Accounts

Credit card companies and financial services companies offer online accounts that can work in tandem with your credit card. These often are savings accounts that generally pay higher, or market, rates of interest. And as a result of having the online savings account, you can expect to receive a lower rate of interest with your credit card agreement. However, these accounts can be risky. If the account provider is not a financial institution, these accounts are not insured. As a general rule, the higher the amount of interest you can earn, the higher the risk associated with the account.

✔ CHECKPOINT
How are commercial banks different from credit unions?

Education

Teaching careers exist at the pre-school, elementary, secondary (middle and high school), and post-secondary (community college and university) levels. In addition, career and technical schools employ teachers who have specific career-related and technical skills. Qualifications for employment differ by state because public teachers are state employees.

Private industry also has educators that provide corporate training to help workers learn new skills. They impart knowledge and help employees reach their full potential.

Good educators are both proficient in their subject area and also caring, as they provide a supportive learning environment for their students.

Employment Outlook

- An average rate of employment growth is expected for middle school teachers, but a slower growth is expected for high school teachers through 2020.
- Declines in student-to-teacher ratios will result in more jobs.

Job Titles

- Teacher
- Instructor
- Professor

Needed Skills

- A bachelor's degree is required in the subject matter or as required by state law.
- Most K–12 teachers must be certified by their states, which often means passing tests and coursework.
- A master's degree is preferred within several years of beginning employment.
- Excellent communication skills are needed.

What's it like to work in . . . *Education*

Matthew teaches at the middle school level. In addition to teaching social studies classes, Matthew is involved with after-school academic clubs. He enjoys working with young teenagers and helping them learn and succeed. He arrives at work by 7:00 A.M. each morning and usually stays after students are dismissed to grade papers and prepare for the next day or to help students who have questions. Tonight Matthew will participate in parent–teacher conferences to discuss the progress of his students.

As a new teacher, Matthew makes $42,000. Although he does not work during the summers, he is taking classes at a nearby university to earn his master's degree. His pay will increase after he gets his degree.

What About You?

Do you enjoy helping others? Are you ready for the challenges of working with individuals who need extra help and encouragement? If so, a career in education might be right for you.

KEY TERMS REVIEW

Match the terms with the definitions. Some terms may not be used.

____ 1. The amount of money deposited into a savings account

____ 2. Money received to pay for education

____ 3. Earnings on a deposit into savings

____ 4. A form of financial aid based on need that does not have to be repaid

____ 5. Interest earned on principal and interest

____ 6. Cash allowance awarded to a student to help pay education costs

____ 7. A form of financial aid in which no interest accumulates until you finish school

____ 8. A program where students can work on campus or another college location to earn money

a. annual percentage yield (APY)
b. compound interest
c. financial aid
d. grant
e. interest
f. principal
g. scholarship
h. subsidized loan
i. unsubsidized loan
j. work-study

CHECK YOUR UNDERSTANDING

LO1-1 9. Why is it important to start saving early to meet your short-term and long-term needs?

LO1-2 10. Explain the concept of compounding and how your money grows.

LO1-3 11. List the various places where you can have a savings account.

APPLY YOUR KNOWLEDGE

LO1-1 12. Describe the advantages and disadvantages of spending now rather than saving for the future. How can saving improve your financial peace of mind?

THINK CRITICALLY

LO1-1 13. Do you believe that receiving post-secondary training will increase your lifetime earnings? Why or why not?

LO1-2 14. Why is it important to compare the APY on banks' savings accounts?

LO1-3 15. There are many places where you can save money. Some are insured and others are not. The safer your money is (less risk), the lower your rate of return (APY) will be. Are you willing to take more risk to earn more interest on your savings? Explain your answer.

The Essential Question *Refer to The Essential Question on p. 129. Saving provides you money to meet your short-term and long-term needs, thus giving you financial peace of mind.*

The Essential Question *What factors should you consider when choosing among savings options?*

LEARNING OBJECTIVES

> LO 2-1 List the features and explain the purposes of different savings options.
> LO 2-2 Discuss factors that influence selection of a savings plan.
> LO 2-3 Describe ways to save regularly.

KEY TERMS

- liquidity, *139*
- certificate of deposit (CD), *140*
- maturity date, *140*
- early withdrawal penalty, *140*
- maturity amount, *140*
- money market account, *140*
- safety of principal, *141*
- direct deposit, *143*
- automatic deduction, *143*
- payroll savings plan, *143*

LO 2-1 Savings Account Choices

Once you have decided to establish a savings program, you need to know about the different savings options available to you. You may want to deposit money in several types of accounts, because each can contribute to your overall plan in different ways.

Regular Savings Account

A regular savings account has a major advantage—high liquidity. **Liquidity** is a measure of how quickly you can get your cash without loss of value. A regular savings account is very *liquid* because you can withdraw your money at any time without penalty. The trade-off for high liquidity, however, is a lower interest rate. A regular savings account generally pays the least amount of interest of all savings options.

Once you have opened the account, you are free to make withdrawals and deposits. Some financial institutions charge service fees when you make more than a maximum number of withdrawals in a certain period of time. Other institutions charge a monthly fee if your balance falls below a set minimum. In most cases, you will receive a debit or ATM card that goes with the account so

Why is a regular savings account said to be "liquid"?

that you can make withdrawals and deposits at ATMs. If you have a smartphone, you can deposit checks electronically. You can also check your balance and transfer money between your checking and savings accounts online and by phone.

Certificate of Deposit

A **certificate of deposit (CD)**, or *time deposit*, is a deposit that earns a fixed interest rate for a specified length of time—for example, 5 percent for six months. A CD requires a minimum deposit. The interest rate on a CD is usually higher than on a regular savings account because a CD is less liquid.

Unlike a regular savings account, you must leave the money in a CD for a certain period of time. A CD has a set **maturity date**, which is the date on which an investment becomes due for payment. You must leave the money in the CD until the maturity date. If you take out any part of your money early, you will pay an **early withdrawal penalty**. This penalty could be anywhere from 90 days interest to the loss of part of your principal, depending on the terms of your CD.

Typically, within a stated number of days after the maturity date, your certificate will renew automatically. When a CD *renews*, it is extended for another six months or whatever the original time period was. You may prefer to redeem it for cash or purchase a new certificate for a different time period. The **maturity amount** is how much you will receive (principal plus accrued interest from date of deposit) if you choose to redeem your CD. As another option, you may be able to receive a check periodically for the interest earned or have the interest deposited in a separate regular checking or savings account.

Money Market Account

A **money market account** is a type of savings account that offers a more competitive interest rate than a regular savings account. (As described in Chapter 5, it can also function as a checking account.) Brokerage firms as well as banks and other financial institutions offer money market accounts.

There are two different kinds of money market accounts: money market deposit accounts and money market funds. A *money market deposit account* is similar to a regular savings account, but it offers a higher rate of interest in exchange for larger-than-normal deposits. In addition, the interest rate may increase as your balance increases. These accounts are insured by the FDIC.

A *money market fund* is a type of mutual fund that invests in low-risk securities. Money market funds are not FDIC insured, but they are generally considered safe because they invest in short-term government securities. The chance of losing your principal (amount deposited) is very low. On average, money market funds will pay a higher interest rate than money market deposit accounts.

Unlike CDs, there is no penalty for taking money out of money market accounts. As a result, these accounts are quite liquid. However, you usually are limited to a certain number of withdrawals each month. In addition, money market accounts require minimum opening deposits and minimum balances.

CHECKPOINT

What is an advantage and a disadvantage of a certificate of deposit?

In Japan, individuals save a lot of money. Since 1989, Japanese individuals and households have been able to save an average of 11.2 percent of disposable income. This great savings rate is the result of many factors, including the economy's good performance, the economic and financial well-being of the Japanese population, and the good interest rates available on time deposits (CDs). In contrast, U.S. individual and household savings ranged between 4 and 5 percent in this same time period. That trend has somewhat reversed in the United States, with people saving more following the Great Recession (2007–2009). But savings rates still remain far below those of Japan.

THINK CRITICALLY

Why do you suppose people in the United States save more following an economic downturn? Why do you suppose people in Japan save more during an economic boom?

LO 2-2 Selecting a Savings Plan

There are important factors to consider when selecting a savings account and a savings institution. All savings or investment options involve a trade-off between liquidity or safety and yield. The safer or more liquid an investment, the less earning potential it is likely to have. Use the following criteria in judging which savings options best meet your needs: liquidity, safety, convenience, interest-earning potential (yield), and fees and restrictions.

Liquidity

Liquidity is how quickly you can turn savings into cash when you want it. The need for liquidity will vary, based on your age, health, family situation, and overall wealth. For example, if you have little money left over after paying your bills, you may need to keep this money liquid so you can get it quickly, without penalty, if you face some emergency. In this case, a regular savings account or money market account would be best for you. CDs impose a penalty if you withdraw early, so you should choose this option when you don't expect to need the money before the maturity date.

Safety

You want your money to be safe from loss. **Safety of principal** means that you are guaranteed not to lose your savings deposit, even if the bank or other financial institution fails and goes out of business. Most financial institutions are insured by either the FDIC or NCUA. Accounts protected by insurance are safe for up to $250,000. You should be sure the financial institution of your choice has federal insurance to protect your deposit. Deposits in banks, no matter what type, are almost always safer than investments in the stock market.

Convenience

People often choose their financial institution because of convenience of location. Many banks have several branches within a limited geographic area, which makes your banking convenient. Some banks even have locations in

Would convenience be a factor for you when choosing a savings institution?

grocery stores and residential areas. A very large bank may have branches in other states, giving you banking privileges while out of town.

In addition to location, people also choose their financial institution because of the convenient services offered, such as drive-thru windows with expanded hours, number of ATMs nearby, and online and mobile banking.

Because interest rates on various savings accounts and CDs may vary only slightly and service fees can be very similar within a community, selection of a bank may depend on location and types of services offered.

Interest-Earning Potential (Yield)

You want to earn as much interest as you can on your deposit, while maintaining the degree of liquidity, safety, and convenience you want. Shop around for the best APY in your area for the type of account you want. Usually, the more liquid your deposit, the less interest it will earn. A regular savings account usually earns a low rate of interest because you can maintain a low minimum balance and withdraw money as needed. CDs tie up your money for some length of time. In exchange for your commitment to leave this money with the bank for this time period, you will usually earn higher interest.

Fees and Restrictions

Different accounts and institutions have different rules. Before you open an account, be sure to understand the withdrawal restrictions, minimum balances, service charges, fees, and any other requirements. For example, some accounts charge a fee for using a human teller rather than completing transactions through an ATM. CDs may incur a penalty for withdrawing money before maturity. Fees for use of an ATM can vary as well. Some banks may charge nothing to use their ATMs but charge a hefty fee for using another bank's ATM.

 CHECKPOINT

What are five things to consider in selecting a savings plan?

- -

LO 2-3 Saving Regularly

Saving money for future use is important for every individual. It is important not only to save money but also to save it on a regular basis. In addition to meeting all of your financial goals, saving regularly will also give you financial peace of mind. Over time, and with compounding interest, your savings can grow into a substantial sum. Figure 6.3 illustrates the effect of compounding when you make regular deposits and earn interest on interest.

FIGURE 6.3	Compounding with Additional Deposits			
Year	Beginning Balance	Deposits	Interest Earned (5%)	Ending Balance
1	$0.00	$100.00	$5.00	$105.00
2	$105.00	$100.00	$10.25	$215.25
3	$215.25	$100.00	$15.76	$331.01
4	$331.01	$100.00	$21.55	$452.56

Obviously, no savings plan is effective unless you have the willpower to set aside money. There are ways to make regular saving easier. "Pay yourself first" by using direct deposit or automatic deductions and payroll savings plans. Even saving spare coins and cash on a regular basis can add up.

Direct Deposit

Both employers and financial institutions offer direct deposit. With **direct deposit**, your net pay is deposited electronically into your bank account. The advantage of this service is that your money is available in your account faster. You do not have to make a special trip to the bank to deposit your paycheck. Instead, your employer gives you a nonnegotiable copy of your check and stub, notifying you of the amount deposited directly into your account. You can also have your automatic deposit split between accounts, with some going into savings and some going into checking to cover your bills. This way, you are truly paying yourself first. You can earmark the money you set aside for a vacation or some other special purpose.

Automatic Deductions

An **automatic deduction** represents money you have authorized your bank or another organization to move from one account to another at regular intervals. For example, you can automatically have money moved from your checking account to your savings account.

With a **payroll savings plan**, you authorize your employer to make automatic deductions from your paycheck each pay period. For example, this money may be deposited into a savings account, a retirement account, or used to buy government savings bonds.

Collecting Coins and Cash

Some people find it convenient to set aside their spare change and money left over each day or week. They may put it into a piggy bank, a jar, or other storage container. Once a month or several times a year, they take the cash out and have it counted and deposited to their savings accounts. Setting aside small amounts of change on a daily or weekly basis will lead to large sums over time. It's surprising how pennies can add up to make dollars!

 **CHECKPOINT**

How does direct deposit help you save more?

How Does Saving Keep Life Simple?

Saving is often defined as deferred spending. In other words, you set money aside today so you can spend it in the future. But saving money can be more than providing for some future need. Saving itself can be a virtue. Once you start saving money, you'll feel good about what you have achieved. You'll want to save more and be able to experience the peace of mind of knowing that you can take care of yourself and those you care about.

Abraham Lincoln said, "Most people are about as happy as they make up their minds to be." But what is happiness? According to many philosophers, it is enjoying what you have, not wishing for more. Consider what some people learn well into their lives—that the accumulation of possessions does not bring happiness! By keeping your life simple, you don't get used to having more and more and keeping up with what everyone else is doing. This means not continually buying "things" that have to be protected and maintained. Instead, you can enjoy life without having to earn large sums of money to achieve some high standard of consumer spending.

In today's competitive marketplace, people frequently lose their jobs and must retrain and even find a new career. If you keep your life simple, you won't have a lot of payments to make. Then, if you lose your job, you will be less likely to lose your house, car, and other possessions. If you stay liquid, you can more easily move and start a new career and have money on hand to get you through jobless periods.

Many people buy things they don't need, with money they don't have, to impress people they don't like. Those who love and care about you aren't impressed with how much money you spend or all the possessions you own. Wouldn't it be better to put money aside so that you can retire early, enjoy traveling, or live comfortably without the stress of keeping up with the rat race? Remember, even if you win the rat race, you're still a rat!

THINK CRITICALLY

1. Do you sometimes buy things that you later wish you hadn't? If you had the money back, what would you do with it instead?

2. Do you know someone who is "happy" and at peace with his or her life? If so, describe the person's lifestyle.

3. Do you think it's better to "desire less" or "make more money" when faced with the dilemma of keeping your life simple versus having all the things in life you want? Explain.

KEY TERMS REVIEW

Match the terms with the definitions. Some terms may not be used.

____ 1. The date on which an investment becomes due for payment

____ 2. A guarantee that you will not lose your savings deposit

____ 3. A time deposit that earns a fixed rate of interest for a specified length of time

____ 4. Money your employer deposits electronically into an account

____ 5. Measure of how quickly you can get your cash

____ 6. A plan in which you authorize your employer to deduct money from paychecks

____ 7. A type of savings account that offers a more competitive interest rate than a regular savings account

____ 8. The amount of principal plus accrued interest when a CD is redeemed

a. automatic deduction
b. certificate of deposit (CD)
c. direct deposit
d. early withdrawal penalty
e. liquidity
f. maturity amount
g. maturity date
h. money market account
i. payroll savings plan
j. safety of principal

CHECK YOUR UNDERSTANDING

L02-1 9. How is a savings account more liquid than a CD?

L02-2 10. To earn a higher interest rate, what trade-off will you likely have to make? Why?

L02-3 11. What are some ways you can save regularly?

APPLY YOUR KNOWLEDGE

L02-2 12. Why is it important to understand fees and restrictions before choosing a savings option?

THINK CRITICALLY

L02-1 13. If you invest in a one-year CD but need to withdraw it for an emergency, would there be consequences? How could you avoid this?

L02-2 14. Why is safety of principal an important concept, especially for those just getting started with financial planning?

L02-3 15. Do you keep a coin jar where you can stash spare change? What happens when the jar is full?

The Essential Question *Refer to The Essential Question on p. 139. Considerations when choosing among savings options include ways to meet your savings goals and to minimize risk.*

SUMMARY

6.1

- *Savings provide money for short-term and long-term needs.*

- *Examples of short-term needs include emergencies, vacations, social events, repairs, and major purchases (replacement).*

- *Long-term needs are expenses that are costly and require years of planning and saving, such as home ownership, education, and retirement.*

- *The best reason to start saving is to provide for your own future financial peace of mind.*

- *Compounding, or interest earned on principal and previous interest, makes money grow faster.*

- *To compare accounts with different compounding methods, simply compare the stated annual percentage yields (APY).*

- *Commercial banks, savings banks, savings and loan associations (S&Ls), credit unions, brokerage firms, and online companies offer savings accounts.*

6.2

- *Savings account options include regular savings accounts, certificates of deposit (CDs), and money market accounts.*

- *Among the savings options, regular savings accounts usually pay the lowest interest but offer the highest liquidity and safety.*

- *CDs have a set maturity date and are less liquid, but they pay a higher rate of return than regular savings accounts.*

- *Money market accounts pay more interest when economic conditions are good (and growing).*

- *The criteria used in judging which savings options best meet your needs include liquidity, safety of principal, convenience, interest-earning potential (yield), and fees and restrictions.*

- *Most financial institutions offer safety of principal through insurance programs offered by government agencies, such as the FDIC or NCUA.*

- *Saving regularly helps you meet your financial goals more quickly.*

- *Direct deposit, automatic deductions, payroll savings plans, and saving spare change and cash are ways to make regular saving easier.*

APPLY WHAT YOU KNOW

LO1-1   1. In addition to working and saving money for college, what are some other ways to finance your education?

LO1-2   2. Explain the concept of compounding. Select a dollar amount and an interest rate. Set up one table showing the amount compounded annually and another table with the same amount and rate but compounded quarterly. What is the difference in interest earnings?

LO1-2   3. If two savings accounts offered 5 percent interest but one was compounded quarterly and the other was compounded daily, which account would have the higher APY? Why?

LO2-1   4. How is a money market account different from a regular savings account at a commercial bank?

LO2-2   5. What things would you consider when choosing a financial institution for your savings?

LO2-2   6. Define the concept of liquidity, and explain why it is important when choosing a savings account or plan.

LO2-2   7. Why might people choose to save their money in a commercial bank when another type of financial institution offers a higher interest rate?

LO2-3   8. Describe ways to make regular saving easier. What does discretionary income have to do with saving?

MAKE ACADEMIC CONNECTIONS

LO1-2   9. **Technology** Search the Internet for a savings calculator. Plug in different numbers and note the results. For example, enter a savings amount compounded annually, then quarterly, then monthly. Note the differences that occur because of the different compounding methods. Then try different savings amounts using the same compounding method. How does saving just a little more each month affect your total savings in, say, ten years? Then try different interest rates with the same savings amounts and compounding method. Summarize your conclusions.

LO1-3   10. **Research** Use the Internet to research the type of online-only accounts available to consumers. Review websites of credit card companies, insurance companies, brokerage companies, and any other sources you may find that offer consumers online savings accounts. Some may be tied to credit cards or other types of accounts. Prepare a written report of your findings, assessing the safety, liquidity, and return that savers can expect to receive.

LO2-1   11. **Communication** Assume that you and your friend are planning a trip after graduation in two years. You estimate that you will each need $1,000. Write a savings plan for you and your friend to help save the money needed. Consider the different savings options and the characteristics of each one, such as safety, liquidity, and compounding.

Solve Problems and Explore Issues

LO1-2 12. Conduct research to learn more about how APY is calculated? If a bank offers a 4 percent interest rate on its CD, why might the APY be a slightly different rate?

LO1-2 13. Compute the interest and ending balance for Lindsay Dolan, assuming that she deposits $1,000 in a CD with interest compounded every six months at the rate of 8½ percent. The CD matures in three years.

LO1-2 14. Compute the interest compounded quarterly on a deposit of $500 for three years at 8 percent APY.

LO1-3 15. Call a credit union in your area or find one online. Who can be a member of this credit union? What services does the credit union offer its members?

LO1-3 16. Collect advertisements offering various financial services. What factors would you consider before using these services and the financial institutions that offer them?

LO2-1 17. Bianca Arroyo is considering buying a CD with the $500 she has in regular savings. What factors should she consider when choosing a CD?

EXTEND YOUR LEARNING

LO1-1 18. **Ethics** Financial aid is available to those who need assistance to pay for their college education. Rising costs of education require more people than ever to seek student loans. When people fail to repay their student loans, taxpayers are left paying the bill and less money is available for others to use. Some people feel that student loans do not have to be repaid. Nationwide, there is a high student default rate. The U.S. Department of Education releases default rates each year. For those schools that have extremely high default rates (for student loans granted through their institution), their access to future federal student aid funds may be limited. Why should people repay their student loans? If loans aren't repaid, what are the negative effects?

CHAPTER PROJECT

Write out your savings plan, listing one short-term need and one long-term need. Assign a dollar value to each one and a date for meeting your savings goal. On the Internet, locate a savings planner tool and calculate how much you would have to save monthly to meet your short-term and long-term needs, assuming you deposit money in an account paying 3 percent interest compounded annually. Then compare how much more you would have in savings if you started saving now versus if you started saving ten years from now. Prepare a one-page report of your findings. Include charts to help interpret the data.

Complete the Guided Decision Making activity for Chapter 6 at **ngl.cengage.com/mypf**.

Steve Jobs

Steve Jobs was born in San Francisco, California, in 1955. Jobs began working on electronics with his father at an early age. While living in California, he met Steve Wozniak. Wozniak was a computer and electronics whiz kid. After quitting his first job at Atari, Inc., as a video game designer and attending the Homebrew Computer Club with Wozniak, Jobs convinced Wozniak to start a company.

Apple Computer Company was founded as a partnership between Jobs and Wozniak in 1976. Their business began by selling circuit boards. That same year, they invented the Apple I computer. Its successor, the Apple II, was introduced shortly after and became a huge success, turning Apple into an important player in the personal computer industry.

In the early 1980s, times weren't smooth for the creative, but often hard-to-work-with, Jobs. Apple struggled to compete against IBM and Microsoft, and in 1985, Jobs was "fired" from his position at the company. As a "beginner again" he was able to take his creative talent to new and previously unimaginable heights.

In 1986, Jobs bought The Graphics Group (later renamed Pixar) for a tidy sum of $10 million. The first film produced (*Toy Story*) in 1995 paved the way for a long-term relationship with Disney and considerable fame and wealth. Over the next 15 years, the company would produce numerous box-office hits, including *A Bug's Life, Toy Story 2, Toy Story 3, Monsters, Inc., Finding Nemo, The Incredibles, Cars,* and *WALL-E.*

Jobs returned to Apple in 1996 and became its CEO in 1997. Under Jobs's guidance, the company reached new heights and patented the Mac OS system, creating the iMac. The company also branched out into related fields, creating the iPod portable music player and the iPhone, a multitouch display cell phone. The iPad, a tablet computer, also proved to be phenomenally successful.

Throughout his career, Jobs was highly admired and respected for his skills and talent. Steve Jobs died October 5, 2011, at the age of 56.

THINK CRITICALLY

1. Why is Steve Jobs often associated with the beginning of the digital age? How did Jobs cope with change over the years?

2. What kinds of financial records, filing system, and personal records would you imagine someone like Steve Jobs would need? What kind of banking services (including loans) would he need?

Assessing Your Financial Health

Overview

This project is designed to help you begin the financial planning process. Here you will assess your financial health by carefully examining your present financial condition. By taking inventory of where you are now, you can begin to build a plan for the future.

Your Job

Let's begin with your job. The money you earn affects what you are able to purchase and save now, as well as your future prospects for financial stability. Rate your current job in terms of your opportunities for advancement, the company's chances for survival, and job satisfaction. If you feel you are in a dead-end job, working for a weak or financially unstable company, or in an obsolete industry, start looking for a more promising situation. On the other hand, if you like your work, and the future looks good for the company and the industry, then examine your opportunities for advancement. In addition, consider your own mental attitude, skills, and aptitudes for higher-level positions. If you aren't currently working or are in a dead-end job, get started by interviewing a person who has the type of job you'd like to have.

Ryan McVay/Photodisc/Getty Images

Complete Worksheet 1 (Rate Your Job), which is provided in the *Student Activity Guide* and also presented below. Worksheet 1 is designed to help you assess your current job and any potential job you might consider.

A score of 25 points is possible for each section. A score between 20 and 25 for any section indicates good prospects for the future. A score between 15 and 20 indicates that you should examine the characteristics carefully before making long-term commitments. A score between 10 and 15 indicates that you should start looking for a new job soon. A score under 10 indicates that you are in a hopelessly dead-end job that has no future and should be viewed as only temporary.

WORKSHEET 1
Rate Your Job

Directions: Rate each of the following characteristics on a 1- to 5-point scale. A score of 5 means *always;* a score of 4 means *usually;* a score of 3 means *as often as needed;* a score of 2 means *sometimes;* a score of 1 means *never;* and a score of 0 means *not applicable.* If you do not have a job, complete this worksheet after doing research about your desired future job.

Your Score

1. You enjoy the work you do, and you look forward to going to work each day. _____

2. You are willing to get extra training, education, or extra skills in order to be challenged. _____

3. You seek additional responsibility and can do the job well. _____

4. You like the work environment, and others recognize you as someone who will help and be a team player. _____

5. You receive regular pay raises large enough to keep you ahead of inflation and support your desired lifestyle. _____

Your total _____

Job Score

1. The product or service is in demand and prospects look good for the future. _____

2. The industry is growing as a whole, with opportunities for advancement in other companies similar to yours. _____

3. The product or service is economy-resistant (rising prices or economic downturns don't greatly affect sales). _____

4. Turnover among employees is generally low. _____

5. Pay scale and fringe benefits compare well with other companies in the same field. _____

Job total _____

Employer's Score

1. Your boss calls on you to handle tough assignments and gives you credit for your accomplishments. _____

2. The boss regularly solicits your suggestions and follows them. _____

3. The company promotes from within. _____

4. The company has a large number of customers rather than just a few big ones. _____

5. The company is well established and still growing. _____

Employer's total _____

Total of all points _____

Your Income and Outgo (Cash Flow)

Having completed the budgeting exercises in Chapter 4, you recognize the importance of keeping track of dollars that regularly flow through your hands. Complete Worksheet 2 (Cash Flow Statement), which is provided in the *Student Activity Guide* and also presented below. Worksheet 2 helps you identify where your money comes from and where it goes. In addition, it allows you to make projections for future income and outgo on a yearly basis. It's important to pinpoint your spending habits, analyze them, and take steps to improve your financial picture.

Examine your cash flow closely, looking for places where your income may be leaking away. Plugging the small leaks will help you build larger cash reserves and spend money more wisely. For example, think about three things you bought last year and later regretted. What is the total amount of money you could have saved? What other things could you have purchased?

WORKSHEET 2
Cash Flow Statement

Directions: Keep a record of income and expenses for a month (you might want to do this for a year to build a budget base for the following year). In the first column, list each item you receive or spend in a month. In the second column, project your annual income or expense for each item. In the third column, check any items that need attention. In the fourth column, indicate how much (increase or decrease) each item should change monthly. Add a plus sign (increase) or minus sign (decrease) to each entry. In the fifth column, indicate how much additional money you would save or spend annually by making the changes in the fourth column. Use a plus sign (save) or minus sign (spend) for each entry. See the example below.

Example:	THIS MONTH	YEARLY TOTAL	NEED CHANGE	MONTHLY CHANGE	YEARLY EFFECT
Entertainment expense	$38.00	$456.00	✓	+$12.00	−$144.00

ITEM	1 THIS MONTH	2 YEARLY TOTAL	3 NEED CHANGE	4 MONTHLY CHANGE	5 YEARLY EFFECT
Income:					
Take-home pay	_____	_____	_____	_____	_____
Bonuses/gifts	_____	_____	_____	_____	_____
Interest income	_____	_____	_____	_____	_____
Other_____	_____	_____	_____	_____	_____
Totals	_____	_____	_____	_____	_____
Outgo:					
	_____	_____	_____	_____	_____
	_____	_____	_____	_____	_____
	_____	_____	_____	_____	_____
	_____	_____	_____	_____	_____
	_____	_____	_____	_____	_____
	_____	_____	_____	_____	_____
	_____	_____	_____	_____	_____
Savings	_____	_____	_____	_____	_____
Totals	_____	_____	_____	_____	_____

Analysis:
List ways you can cut expenses or increase income (such as by substituting activities, buying cheaper products, or working odd jobs in the summer).

Your Net Worth

An assessment of where you stand begins with what you own and owe at the moment. Complete Worksheet 3 (Net Worth Analysis), which is provided in the *Student Activity Guide* and also presented below. Worksheet 3 is used for listing your assets and liabilities and making projections of where you would like to be at some future date (such as a month, a year, or five years). The purpose of the net worth analysis is threefold: (1) to show you your strong and weak areas, (2) to help you plan for specific short-term changes, and (3) to allow you to project goals into the future based on those decisions.

WORKSHEET 3
Net Worth Analysis

Directions: Fill in the blanks below. In column 1, write in the market value of each item you possess or debt you owe. See Chapter 4 for definitions of terms (assets, liabilities, and net worth). In column 2, write in what each item will be worth in one year. In column 3, indicate the value of each item in five years. You can assume an item will increase it if gains in value over time (through interest or inflation) or if you add to or purchase an item from that category.

ITEM	1 TODAY'S BALANCE	2 ONE-YEAR PROJECTION	3 FIVE-YEAR PROJECTION
Assets:			
_____	$_____	$_____	$_____
_____	_____	_____	_____
_____	_____	_____	_____
_____	_____	_____	_____
_____	_____	_____	_____
_____	_____	_____	_____
_____	_____	_____	_____
_____	_____	_____	_____
_____	_____	_____	_____
_____	_____	_____	_____
_____	_____	_____	_____
_____	_____	_____	_____
Total assets	_____	_____	_____
Liabilities:			
_____	_____	_____	_____
_____	_____	_____	_____
_____	_____	_____	_____
_____	_____	_____	_____
_____	_____	_____	_____
Total liabilities	_____	_____	_____
Net worth	_____	_____	_____

Analysis: List major purchases that you wish to make and how you plan to pay for them.

Your Tax Liability

Based on the income tax returns you prepared in Chapter 3, use Worksheet 4 (Tax Liability) to analyze your total tax and determine whether you can reduce your taxes through careful planning. Worksheet 4 is provided for you in the *Student Activity Guide* and also presented below. Keep copies of your tax returns. Compare total tax by preparing Forms 1040EZ, 1040A, and 1040. Use the form that gives the greatest tax advantage (i.e., the lowest amount of taxes). Then study tax booklets and other information to see where you can benefit from taking more deductions.

WORKSHEET 4
Tax Liability

Directions: To complete this worksheet, first list your gross income, adjusted gross income, taxable income, tax before credits, and total tax for the last three years you have filed tax returns and paid income taxes. If you have not yet filed a tax return, use the projected gross income that you would receive in the entry-level position of your choice (used for Worksheet 1). Compute taxes owed on that amount (see Chapter 3). Then compute how much you could save in income taxes if you made changes as shown. Finally, list some of the tax deductions and credits available on the Form 1040 in the *Student Activity Guide* (or downloaded from www.irs.gov) that you might use to decrease your tax liability.

YEAR	GROSS INCOME	ADJUSTED GROSS INCOME	TAXABLE INCOME	TAX (BEFORE CREDITS)	TOTAL TAX (AFTER CREDITS)
1. _____	_____	_____	_____	_____	_____
2. _____	_____	_____	_____	_____	_____
3. _____	_____	_____	_____	_____	_____

How would each of the above years' tax liabilities have changed *if* you could have had the following changes:

YEAR	CHANGE	TAX DECREASE
1	IRA deduction of $2,000	$_____
2	Child care credit of $500	$_____
3	One more exemption	$_____

Analysis:
Examine Schedule A of Form 1040 (itemized deductions) in the *Student Activity Guide* (or downloaded from www.irs.gov). Identify some deductions you might wish to take advantage of to reduce your tax liability.

Examine Form 1040 in the *Student Activity Guide* (or downloaded from www.irs.gov) and list additional types of income, deductions, and credits that are required and/or permitted when this form is used.

Managing Credit

Profile Donald Trump
Project Managing Credit and Debt

© bikeriderlondon/Shutterstock.com

U nit 2 begins with an introduction to credit in Chapter 7—what it is and why it is important to you personally and as a part of the U.S. economy. Credit has many advantages for those who use it wisely, but it can also be a trap and cause financial problems. In Chapter 8, you will learn about credit bureaus, credit ratings, and credit reports. You will examine your rights and responsibilities as a credit user. You will also discover the many credit laws that have been enacted to help protect consumers.

In Chapter 9, you will study the responsibilities of consumer credit along with the high costs of credit. You will learn how to compute the true cost of credit (APR) and explore ways to minimize costs. Finally, in Chapter 10, you will learn about problems that arise from the use of credit and how to avoid them, both when getting started and as a final resort. In some cases, the best path forward may be bankruptcy and a fresh start.

© Pan Xunbin/Shutterstock.com

Credit in America

7.1   Credit: What and Why

7.2   Credit: Types and Sources

Consider This...

It was two days before the spring festival, and Jasmine still hadn't purchased the supplies she needed to make her costume. She had been saving money for four months and was still $50 short of her goal.

"I'll just have to borrow the rest and pay it back later," she told her friends. "Otherwise, I won't be able to get the costume finished, and I'll let down the team. I really wanted to pay cash and not go into debt, but in this case, it can't be helped. I probably should have used credit a little sooner to get the materials I needed. Now I'll have to work all night to get this costume completed. I learned an important lesson. There's a time and a place for using credit."

© Pan Xunbin/Shutterstock.com

> **The Essential Question** *How has the use of credit changed over time, and what are its advantages and disadvantages today?*

LO 1-1   The Need for Credit

When you borrow money or use a charge account to pay for purchases, you are taking advantage of the most commonly used method of purchase in the United States: credit. **Credit** is the use of someone else's money, borrowed now with the agreement to pay it back later.

The need for credit arose in the United States when the country grew from a bartering and trading society to a currency exchange economy. During the 1800s, the Industrial Revolution started a new economy. Items were manufactured in mass for sale to others. People no longer produced everything exclusively for their own use. With their earnings, they were able to buy the things they previously had to make for themselves. Soon, the need developed for sources of credit to help families meet their financial needs.

Early Forms of Credit

One of the earliest forms of credit in the United States was having a charge account with a local retailer, usually a general store. The account was called a store credit or *book credit*. As the name suggests, the records were kept in a ledger, or book. Wage earners or farmers would pick up supplies and put the amount due "on account." When the borrowers received a paycheck or sold a harvested crop, they would pay their account in full, and the charging process would begin again. The stores rarely charged interest.

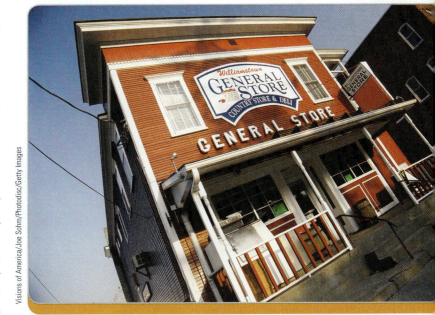

How were some of the earliest forms of credit used?

This early form of credit was a convenience that storeowners provided for customers they knew well and trusted. Because of the more personal nature of the business relationship, repayment schedules tended to vary, according to when the consumer had funds available. During hard times, retailers would often extend credit to help out a trustworthy, longtime customer, even though payments were sporadic. It was one of the advantages of this local, more personal system.

During the 20th century, many different forms of credit developed—most notably the credit card—to meet changing consumer needs and wants. As the use of credit expanded, individual purchasing power also increased. Because credit increased people's ability to buy more goods and services, people bought luxuries as well as necessities and the average American's standard of living rose. Both businesses and consumers benefited from credit.

Credit Today

Today, credit is the American way of life. No longer is credit saved for emergencies. Merchants encourage consumers to use credit to buy all kinds of goods and services. Goods are either *nondurable* (will be used up in less than a year) or *durable* (will last longer than a year). Services include such things as haircuts and cable TV. Together, goods and services are called "products."

Banks, stores, and credit card companies offer credit in the form of cards, loans, and lines of credit. Both short-term and long-term financing is available. Credit cards are the most profitable sector of the American banking system. Everything from airline tickets to cosmetics to groceries can be purchased with a credit card. In fact, some transactions, such as reserving a hotel room, renting a car, or making an online purchase, are difficult to make without a credit card.

Over time, the question of "How can I get credit?" has turned into "How can I wisely manage credit?" Today, millions of Americans are overextended with credit. They have adopted a lifestyle that is dependent on the use of credit to make ends meet. The average American has almost $5,000 in credit card debt, and nearly 40 percent of Americans carry credit card debt from month to month. Some people live beyond their means and abuse credit. They are barely able to make the minimum payment on outstanding debt and resort to tactics such as using one credit card to pay another credit card. In the 1990s, record numbers of people declared bankruptcy, and overuse of credit cards was one of the main reasons.

How is credit being used today?

© iStock.com/PhotoInc

The Use of Credit

A **debtor** is a person who borrows money from others. This money, called *debt*, must be repaid. A **creditor** is a person or business that loans money to others. Creditors charge money for this service in the form of interest and fees. A debtor must be qualified to receive credit.

Qualifying for Credit

To qualify for credit, you must have the ability to repay the loan. Before you apply for credit, consider your income, financial position, and collateral.

Income You need to have a job and earn an income in order to make loan payments. Income can also come from other sources, such as interest, dividends, alimony, royalties, and so on. You should compare your cash inflow (income) to your cash outflow (expenses). When your earnings exceed your expenses, you have the capacity to take on debt.

Financial Position Your financial position is based on capital. **Capital** is the value of property you possess (such as bank accounts, investments, real estate, and other assets) after deducting your debts. Having capital means that you have accumulated assets, which indicates responsibility.

Collateral To borrow large amounts of money, you may need to provide collateral. **Collateral** is property pledged to assure repayment of a loan. For example, when you buy a car on credit, the car serves as collateral. If you do not make your loan payments, the creditor can seize the pledged property, or *repossess* it, and sell it to help repay the loan.

Making Payments

Once you have completed a credit purchase, you owe money to the creditor. The *principal* (amount borrowed) plus interest for the time you have the loan is called the *balance due*. You generally will make monthly payments until you repay the balance due in full. The **finance charge** is the total dollar amount of all interest and fees you pay for the use of credit. It is the price you pay for the privilege of using someone else's money to buy goods and services now.

Credit card or store account statements usually specify a **minimum payment**. This is the least amount you may pay that month under your credit agreement, though you may pay more to reduce your debt further. All credit card payments have a specific due date. Typically, you will be given 10 to 25 days from the date you receive a bill in which to pay. If you do not pay within the time allowed, you are likely to be charged a late fee, which is added to the balance due. Your interest rate may also go up as a result of late payments.

For particularly expensive purchases, you may have to sign a loan agreement in which you agree to make regular payments for a set period of time. At the end of that time, you will have repaid the entire debt. This is a type of *secured loan*, because the goods you purchased with the loan serve as collateral for the money loaned.

 **CHECKPOINT**

How did credit get started in this country?

Traditionally, consumers in Thailand preferred to use cash when purchasing goods and services. This conservative attitude toward cashless transactions hindered consumer credit expansion. In 2002 it was estimated that only 10 percent of the Thai population had a credit card. Major card issuers then began aggressive marketing campaigns and promotional offers to entice new customers. With extensive incentives for consumers and a low minimum income threshold for credit card eligibility, many card issuers witnessed considerable growth in their customer numbers. Today, many consumers in Thailand rely on credit.

THINK CRITICALLY

What consumer benefits as well as problems might result from the boom in credit card use in Thailand? How can consumers avoid the disadvantages of credit as it grows in popularity?

LO 1-2   Advantages and Disadvantages of Credit

Credit can be good when used wisely; however, many people get into trouble each year by not using credit carefully. Like most things in life, there are advantages and disadvantages to using credit.

Advantages of Credit

When used correctly, credit has several advantages:

- *Purchasing Power.* Credit can greatly expand your purchasing power and raise your standard of living. For example, most people are not able to purchase expensive items, such as a car or house, simply by saving money and paying cash. Credit allows you to purchase these items and then pay for them over time. As a result, you can enjoy these items earlier in your life. In addition to things you want, credit also allows you to purchase things in life that you need. For example, the cost of education is continuously rising, and most Americans will need to obtain a loan to pay for college.

- *Security.* Using a credit card is safer than carrying a large amount of cash with you. If you lose cash, there is no way to replace it. If you lose a credit card, you can simply call the company and report your lost or stolen card. The company will freeze your account, and you will not be held responsible for fraudulent charges.

- *Establishing Good Credit.* Having a good credit history is important, not only when applying for credit cards but also when applying for loans, rental housing, and employment. Making payments on time will help you build a good credit history and qualify for loans and lower interest rates.

- *Emergencies.* Credit can also provide emergency funds. A sudden need for cash can be solved by a **line of credit**, which is a pre-established amount that can be borrowed on demand with no collateral. To establish a line of credit, you must go to a lender, such as a bank, and apply for it. The lender examines your income and financial position and approves an amount that it believes you can repay. With a line of credit, money is always available should you need it.

- *Benefits.* Credit customers often get special benefits. Regular charge customers of a department store, for example, receive advance notices of sales and special offers, such as deferred billing, not available to the general public. **Deferred billing** is a service available to charge customers whereby purchases are not billed to the customer until much later than the standard billing time. For example, merchandise purchased in October might not be billed until January, with no payment due until February.
- *Leverage.* Consumers also have more leverage when using credit rather than cash or other methods of purchase. With credit, the money remains to be paid, giving the consumer more power in the event of a dispute. With a debit card, check, or cash, money has already been paid for the purchase, which may make it more difficult to settle a dispute and get a refund.

Disadvantages of Credit

Although credit has several advantages, you should not lose sight of its disadvantages:

- *Fees and Finance Charges.* Merchants must pay fees, which are usually a percentage of credit card sales, to credit card companies. Merchants often pass this cost on to customers in the form of higher prices. In addition, an item purchased on credit and paid for over time costs more because of the finance charge. For example, a finance charge of 18 percent a year is 1½ percent a month. On a $1,000 balance, the finance charge would be $15 a month. The larger your balance and the longer you take to pay it off, the greater the finance charge.
- *Reduction of Future Buying Power.* When you use credit, you tie up future income. You have committed to making payments. Part of everything you earn in the future will go toward what you bought in the past. This may result in funds not being available when you need to purchase other products. This situation can put a strain on your budget.
- *Overspending.* Buying on credit can lead to overspending. Because no cash leaves your bank account, you may not realize how much you are really spending. Using credit too much can result in debts so high that you can never pay them off, which could lead to bankruptcy. Failure to fulfill financial agreements will result in a poor credit record.
- *Identity Theft.* Having a credit card means that you run the risk that your account information could be stolen, allowing someone else to make purchases on your credit card without your knowledge.

How does credit lead to overspending?

 **CHECKPOINT**

How can credit expand your purchasing power?

Loan Processing

Over 85 percent of all loan processors work in banks, savings banks, credit unions, and other financial institutions. Loan processors guide their clients through the process of applying for, qualifying for, and executing loan documents. This process involves meeting with loan applicants to gather personal information and answer any questions they may have, explaining different types of loans and their terms to applicants, and obtaining and verifying financial information, such as credit rating and income level. Loan officers must also be sure that loan applicants are able to meet the requirements of the underwriter—the company that provides the loan funding.

There are various types of loan processors. Most commonly, loan processors specialize in commercial loans (loans to businesses), consumer loans (loans to people), or mortgage loans (loans used to buy real estate).

The form of compensation varies by employer. Some loan processors are paid a salary; others are paid on commission.

Employment Outlook

- An average rate of employment growth is expected.

Job Titles

- Loan officer
- Loan processor
- Loan collection officer
- Mortgage loan specialist

Needed Skills

- A bachelor's degree in finance, economics, or a related field is desirable.
- Training and licensing requirements vary by state.
- Good interpersonal and decision-making skills and high motivation are needed.

What's it like to work in . . . *Loan Processing*

Blake works as a consumer lending specialist for a credit union. He helps customers obtain loans for cars, boats, and major appliances. Blake works with customers to help them obtain the financing option that best meets their needs.

Each day, Blake keeps up with the latest financial market news, such as when interest rates are rising or falling. He knows the best rates he can offer his customers and what it takes to qualify for them.

Today Blake is meeting with a couple who have asked for his assistance in getting a car loan. Blake will walk them through the application process. Based on their credit records, Blake will be able to provide a good estimate of what the loan will cost them and how long it will take to process and close the loan.

What About You?

Would you like to help people obtain financing so that they can meet their goals? Is a career as a loan processor right for you?

KEY TERMS REVIEW

Match the terms with the definitions. Some terms may not be used.

a. capital
b. collateral
c. credit
d. creditor
e. debtor
f. deferred billing
g. finance charge
h. line of credit
i. minimum payment

____ 1. Property pledged to assure repayment of a loan

____ 2. A service whereby purchases are not billed to the customer until much later

____ 3. A person who borrows money

____ 4. The value of property you possess after deducting debts

____ 5. The total dollar amount of interest and fees you pay for the use of credit

____ 6. A person or business that loans money

____ 7. The use of someone else's money, borrowed now with the agreement to pay it back later

____ 8. A pre-established amount that can be borrowed on demand with no collateral

CHECK YOUR UNDERSTANDING

L01-1 9. Compare this country's early use of credit to its use today.

L01-2 10. How can credit affect your future buying power?

APPLY YOUR KNOWLEDGE

L01-2 11. Credit can be very beneficial or it can lead to financial ruin. Describe the advantages of credit in terms of purchasing power. Explain how credit can become a trap and lead to overspending.

THINK CRITICALLY

L01-1 12. Individuals and families must make choices regarding credit—how much credit, when it is appropriate, and so on. How does your family make use of credit? Do you see credit use by your family as a good or bad thing? Explain your answer.

L01-1 13. In the early part of our nation's history, we had no credit. People used coins or paper money to make purchases. Today, we are moving toward a paperless and cashless society. Would it be possible to live without ever using coins, paper money, or even checks? Explain how people might live on credit alone.

The Essential Question *Refer to The Essential Question on p. 157. Credit started slowly, with charge accounts at general stores. Today, credit is available in multiple forms, increasing standards of living and convenience but often leading to overspending and abuse of credit.*

The Essential Question *What kinds of credit are available to consumers, and where can they be found?*

LEARNING OBJECTIVES

> LO 2-1 List and describe the types of credit available to consumers.
> LO 2-2 Describe and compare sources of credit.

KEY TERMS

- open-end credit, *164*
- annual percentage rate (APR), *165*
- grace period, *165*
- closed-end credit, *167*
- service credit, *167*
- finance company, *168*
- usury law, *168*
- loan shark, *169*
- pawnbroker (or pawnshop), *169*

LO 2-1 Types of Credit

You likely will use several forms of credit throughout your life. Different types of credit are designed to meet different consumer needs.

Open-End Credit

Credit card accounts are an open-end form of credit. **Open-end credit** enables a borrower to use credit up to a stated limit. As payments are made, the limit allows for more use of credit. The borrower usually has a choice of repaying the entire balance within 10 to 25 days or repaying it over time while making at least minimum payments. Open-end credit can be used again and again, as long as the balance owed does not exceed the credit limit.

Charge Cards

In a *charge card* agreement, the cardholder is obligated to pay the balance in full by the due date. A 25-day billing period is common. Because charge card balances must be paid in entirety by the due date, you do not incur interest charges and there is no minimum payment. If the bill is not paid on time, late fees and other penalties may apply, depending on the card agreement.

Charge cards are widely accepted nationwide and overseas, usually have high or no credit limits, and provide instant purchasing power. Charge cards also often include rewards or

What are the advantages and disadvantages of a charge card?

© bibiphoto/Shutterstock.com

© Pan Xunbin/Shutterstock.com

rebates based on purchases. These rewards can be a percentage of dollar purchases or gift items of value. American Express and Diners Club are examples of charge cards.

Revolving Accounts

With a *revolving account*, the consumer has the option of paying the balance in full by the due date or making payments at least as high as the stated minimum. The minimum payment is based on the amount of the balance due. If the balance is not paid in full, interest is charged on the balance.

Most all-purpose credit cards, such as Visa, MasterCard, and Discover, as well as store accounts, are revolving credit agreements. Retail store cards, such as department store and gasoline company cards, are also based on revolving credit. Like charge cards, many of these offer rewards or rebate programs. Figure 7.1 shows a credit card statement for a revolving credit account.

Credit Card Agreements

Credit card companies keep a record of transactions made on your account and send you a bill at the end of each billing cycle. If you pay off the balance in full each month, a finance charge likely can be avoided. But remember, a credit card is a form of borrowing and usually involves interest and other charges. Before selecting a credit card, be sure to compare the following terms that will affect the overall cost of the credit you will be using.

- *Annual Percentage Rate.* The **annual percentage rate (APR)** is the cost of credit expressed as a yearly percentage. The Truth in Lending Act requires lenders to include all loan costs in the APR. The APR must be disclosed to you when you open the account and must be noted on each monthly bill you receive. Usually the APR is a variable rate, and it can be very high on credit cards. Sometimes credit cards offer an introductory rate, which is often lower than the actual rate.
- *Grace Period.* The **grace period** is a timeframe within which you may pay your current balance in full and incur no finance charge. The grace period runs from the end of a billing cycle to the next payment due date. Under the Credit CARD Act of 2009, if your credit card balance has a grace period, your statement must be mailed or delivered to you at least 21 days before the finance charge would be added to your balance. If there is no grace period specified, the card issuer will impose a finance charge from the date you use your credit card.
- *Annual Fees.* Many credit card issuers charge an annual fee. The fee can range from $40 to up to $100 or more, and you must pay it whether or not you use the card. The annual fee might be a one-time charge on your credit card during a specific month of the year, or it could be divided and charged to your account monthly. Most cards with an annual fee offer better rewards opportunities than cards without an annual fee.
- *Transaction Fees.* If you use a credit card check (*access check*), pay by phone, or request a balance transfer, you may be charged a transaction fee. These fees may run from 3 to 10 percent of the transaction amount.
- *Penalty Fees.* If you go over your credit limit or make a late payment, you are likely to be charged a penalty fee. Under the Credit CARD Act of

FIGURE 7.1   Credit Card Statement

McAdams

Account Number	Payment Due Date	New Balance	Minimum Payment Due	Indicate Amount Paid
779 19 9171	05/24/--	$244.61	$20.00	

70

0 7 7 3 4 2 7 0 4 2 0 0 0 0 2 4 4 6 1 0 0 0 0 2 0 0 0 4

ADDRESS CHANGE

IhlıhıhlıIhlıhıhlıIIhıııııhlıhlıhıııhlılhıııhll

ADDRESS

CITY/STATE/ZIP

ELIZABETH SANCHEZ
3410 MAIN STREET
VANCOUVER WA 98684-0129

(AREA CODE) PHONE   5008440

Please return this portion
with your payment. Detach here ▼

- -

Account Number	779 19 9171	To avoid additional **FINANCE CHARGES** being applied to your current purchases on next month's statement, pay the new balance on this statement in full by the due date.	Page 1 of 1

Date	Store	Reference	Description	Charges	Payments Or Credits
3/28	021	108475936	SPECIAL CARE TREATMENT COSMETICS	60.00	
4/07	021	108476335	COSMETICS CLEANSERS, TONERS, MOISTURIZERS	80.00	
4/12	311	071070078	PAYMENT-THANK YOU		189.16
4/24	097		FINANCE CHARGE	4.61	

ANNIVERSARY TO DATE PURCHASES $1,853.39
ANNIVERSARY TO DATE DIVIDEND $5.96
YOU WILL EARN A 1% DIVIDEND ON MCADAMS PURCHASES
MADE PRIOR TO YOUR NEXT BILLING.
DIVIDEND WILL BE CREDITED ON YOUR JUNE 19-- STATEMENT.

Previous Balance	+ New Charges	– Payments Or Credits	Average Daily Balance (For Finance Charge Only)	+ FINANCE CHARGE (50¢ Minimum)	+ Late Payment Fee	= New Balance
289.16	140.00	189.16	307.19	4.61		244.61

Billing Date This Month	Payment Due Date	PERIODIC RATE	ANNUAL PERCENTAGE RATE	Credit Line	Amount Past Due	Minimum Payment Due
04/24/--	05/24/--	1.50	18.00	2,000		20.00

McAdams

Payments or credits received after payment due date will appear on next month's statement. For customer service inquiries, please call 1-800-555-6200. **AMOUNTS DUE HEREUNDER MAY BE ASSIGNED.** NOTICE: SEE REVERSE SIDE FOR IMPORTANT INFORMATION.

2009, penalty fees were capped to prevent excessive charges from being passed on to cardholders. Penalty fees are now capped at $25 for most customers—$35 if payments are late more than once within six billing cycles. Also, penalty fees are not permitted to be any bigger than the minimum payment due.

- *Method of Calculating the Finance Charge.* If you pay for purchases over time, it is important to know how the card issuer will calculate your finance charge. The method used can make a difference—sometimes a big difference—in how much finance charge you will pay. Examples of these methods will be shown in Chapter 9.

Closed-End Credit

To pay for very expensive items, such as cars, major appliances, or real estate, consumers often use closed-end credit. **Closed-end credit** is a loan for a specific amount that must be repaid in full, including all finance charges, by a specified due date. Often called *installment credit*, closed-end agreements do not allow continuous borrowing or varying payment amounts. The borrower takes out a closed-end loan for a particular amount and then repays it with fixed payments, or installments, that include principal and interest.

The contract for closed-end credit states, among other things, the amount loaned, the total finance charge, and the amount of each payment. Sometimes a down payment is required. The product purchased with the loan becomes collateral to assure repayment.

Service Credit

Almost everyone uses some type of service credit. **Service credit** involves providing a service for which you will pay later. Your telephone and utility services are provided for a month in advance; then you are billed. Many businesses—including doctors, lawyers, hospitals, dry cleaners, and repair shops—extend service credit. Terms are set by individual businesses. Some of these creditors do not impose finance charges on unpaid account balances, but they do expect regular payments to be made until the bill is paid in full. Others, such as utility and telephone companies, expect payment in full by a specified due date. However, utility companies usually offer a budget plan, which allows you to average your bills to get lower monthly payments.

 **CHECKPOINT**

List some of the fees associated with using credit.

LO 2-2   Sources of Credit

The extension of credit is a service to consumers. It is not free—consumers must pay for it, the same as they would pay for any other purchased service. As with other things you buy, it pays to shop around to get the best deal.

Credit Card Companies

You may receive credit offers directly from credit card issuers, such as Visa, MasterCard, and Discover. You can also get credit cards through your financial institution or other organizations. These companies offer many different types of credit cards, including all-purpose cards and affinity cards.

All-purpose cards are credit cards that are generally accepted nationwide, and even internationally, to pay for just about anything, from clothes at department stores to meals at restaurants. With an all-purpose credit card, you have an automatic line of credit up to the limit set by the card issuer. Some cards even allow you to take a *cash advance*, which is money borrowed against your line of credit. You can access this money at an ATM, at a customer service desk in your bank, or by writing an access check against the credit card account. *Access checks*, which are supplied by the credit card company, look just like regular checks and are treated by the credit card company as a purchase. You must pay back the cash advance in the same way that you pay for credit card purchases. There is often a transaction fee for this service in addition to interest charges, which may or may not be the same interest rate applied to purchases made with the card.

Affinity cards are credit cards associated with specific organizations, such as professional organizations and college alumni associations. Although these cards may show the name of the organization, they are actually issued and serviced by a credit card company. Generally, an affinity credit card is co-sponsored by the organization it is associated with, and the organization receives a percentage of the sales or profits generated by the card. Rates, fees, and benefits of affinity cards vary widely and may make these cards more expensive to use than similar, non-affiliated cards.

Retail Stores

Retail stores sell goods directly to consumers. Examples include department stores, discount stores, and specialty stores. Many retail stores, such as Macy's, Gap, and Walmart, offer their own credit cards. Often, these cards are accepted only at the issuing store. Store credit customers may receive discounts, advance notice of sales, and other privileges not offered to cash customers or to customers using all-purpose credit cards.

Most retail stores also accept credit cards issued by major credit card companies. Accepting credit cards helps retail stores attract customers, because people like to shop where they can buy on credit.

Banks and Credit Unions

In addition to offering credit cards, commercial banks and credit unions make closed-end loans to individuals and companies. They loan money to consumers for specific purchases, such as a home, car, or vacation. Interest on closed-end loans tends to be lower than on credit cards, usually because there is collateral used as security on the loans.

Credit unions make loans to their members only. Interest rates are sometimes lower than those charged by banks because credit unions are nonprofit and are organized for the benefit of members. Credit unions may be more willing to make loans because the members who are borrowing also have a stake in the success of the credit union.

Finance Companies

In many cases, people who are turned down by banks and credit unions can get loans at finance companies. A **finance company** is an organization that makes high-risk consumer loans. These high-risk loans usually are accompanied by high interest rates. The rates depend on whether the state has a usury law. A **usury law** is a state

What types of credit do banks and credit unions offer?

law that sets a maximum interest rate that may be charged for consumer loans. In states where usury laws exist, finance companies charge the maximum rate allowed. Where no usury laws exist, finance companies charge as much as the customer is willing to pay. When an emergency or other extreme need arises, consumers may have to pay these higher rates to get the money they need.

There are two types of finance companies: (1) consumer finance companies and (2) sales finance companies. Both types of finance companies borrow money from banks and lend it to consumers at higher rates.

- A *consumer finance company* makes most of its loans to consumers who are buying durable goods. *Durable goods* are items expected to last several years, such as furniture, appliances, and electronics. Well-known consumer finance companies include HSBC and Wells Fargo Financial.
- A *sales finance company* makes loans to consumers through authorized representatives, such as car dealerships. For example, GM Financial finances General Motors automobile dealers and their customers.

Finance companies are second only to banks in the volume of credit extended. The growth of finance companies is partially the result of efforts to eliminate loan sharks. A **loan shark** is an unlicensed lender who charges illegally high interest rates.

Finance companies take more risks than banks; therefore, they must be more careful to protect their loans. If you do not make your payments when due, you can expect a call from someone at the finance company who will ask for an explanation as to why you haven't made your payment. The company will stay in constant contact with you until you make your payments as agreed. The higher interest rates charged by finance companies serve as a form of protection. The high income earned from interest makes up for the percentage of loans that become uncollectible.

Pawnbrokers

A **pawnbroker** (or **pawnshop**) is a legal business that makes high-interest loans based on the value of personal possessions pledged as collateral. Possessions that are easily salable (such as guns, jewelry, electronics, and tools) are usually acceptable collateral. The customer brings in an item of value to be appraised. The pawnbroker then makes a loan for considerably less than the appraised value of the item. Some pawnshops give only 10 to 25 percent of the value of the article. Most give no more than 50 or 60 percent.

For example, if you have a ring appraised at $500, you could probably borrow between $50 and $300 with the ring as collateral. You would turn the ring over to the pawnbroker and receive a receipt and a specified length of time—from two weeks to six months—to reclaim the ring by paying back the loan plus interest. If the loan is not paid within the specified time period, the pawned item will be offered for sale by the pawnbroker.

What types of possessions do pawnbrokers usually accept as collateral?

Private Lenders

One of the most common sources of cash loans is the private lender. Private lenders might include parents, other relatives, friends, and so on. Private lenders may or may not charge interest or require collateral. Those who loan money to friends and relatives should take special steps to be sure their interests are protected. For example, rather than loaning cash to someone based on oral promises, you should get the agreement in writing with a formally signed note or other document that will serve as evidence of the debt.

Other Sources of Credit

Other sources of credit include the following:

- Life insurance policies
- Borrowing against a deposit
- Borrowing against an asset
- Lines of credit

Life insurance policies that build cash value can be used to borrow money. The loan does not have to be repaid; however, the loan amount will reduce the value of the policy. For example, if you borrow $15,000 from a $100,000 life insurance policy and do not pay it back, then the final payout on your life insurance policy will be $85,000 instead of the original $100,000. If you do decide to pay back the loan, you will have to pay interest on the principal. You will learn more about life insurance policies in Chapter 23.

If you have a certificate of deposit (CD) or retirement account with a financial institution, you might be able to borrow money against it. A loan against this type of account usually has a good interest rate because of the collateral providing safety. In addition, borrowing against such a deposit allows you to avoid the penalties for early withdrawal. However, you should consider the drawbacks to this type of loan. If you do not repay the loan, the bank or other lender can collect the account balance. Also, you are slowing down the growth of your savings plan by withdrawing money from it. Thus, this type of loan should be considered a last resort.

You may also borrow against a personal asset, such as jewelry, collectibles, or your car. For example, if you own a vehicle free and clear (no loan against it), you can take the title to your credit union or bank and ask for a loan. They will use the car title as collateral for the loan. Usually the car must be fairly new—five years old or less—for this type of loan.

If you are a good customer of your bank or financial institution, you may be able to set up a line of credit. With a line of credit, you have a pre-established amount that can be borrowed on demand with no collateral. Sometimes the interest rate is fixed; other times it is a rate that changes with the economy, going up as interest rates in general increase. This form of credit is very convenient because you don't have to arrange a new loan each time you want to borrow money.

 **CHECKPOINT**

Why might it be more advantageous to borrow money from a credit union than to use other sources of credit?

What Are the Signs of a Credit Card Trap?

Credit offers may sound good, but you must read the fine print carefully. There are many traps to avoid. What may appear to be a great deal can be a very expensive lesson that hurts your credit rating. Watch for the following signs that the credit offer is not as good as it sounds:

- *Low Introductory Rate.* Interest rate offers may be as low as 0 percent for six months. The fine print may tell you that if you are late by even one day in making a payment, the rate will rise to 25 to 30 percent or more! This introductory rate may be subject to change without notice.

- *Fixed Percentage Rate.* The offer may say the interest rate is fixed, which should mean that it will not go up. But the fine print may tell you that the fixed rate is subject to change without notice and that it can be "adjusted" (raised) at the option of the creditor.

- *Closed Account Rate.* You may see fine print that says "closed account rate." This is the rate you will be assessed if you close your account. These rates are often very high—25 to 30 percent or more! This tactic is used by credit card issuers to keep you from closing your account when they raise your interest rate. Without this clause, consumers could reject a change in terms regarding interest rates, close the account, and continue making payments based on the original agreement until the balance is paid off.

- *Late Fees.* Most credit card issuers charge a late fee if you do not pay the minimum payment amount by the specified due date. You may also discover that if you are repeatedly late with your payments, the issuer will raise your interest rate. On credit reports, your late payments can make you appear to be a high risk, so other creditors may also raise your interest rates.

- *Over-the-Limit Fees.* Card issuers will charge you a fee for exceeding your credit limit. This fee is added to your balance, meaning it will take even more money to pay the account down (remember, interest charges are increasing your balance daily). Fine print may tell you that if you go over the limit, your interest rate will increase.

- *Transaction Fees.* Some credit card companies allow you to transfer balances from other credit cards. They may also provide you with access checks where you can borrow money without preapproval. There may be very high transaction fees for these types of borrowing, such as 3 to 10 percent of the transaction amount, in addition to flat fees, such as $30.

To avoid being taken advantage of, read the credit offers carefully and compare them to offers by known lenders, such as your credit union or bank. Ask questions and be sure you understand the terms and conditions.

THINK CRITICALLY

1. Look for a credit card offer in your mail. Then read the fine print. Make a list of all the potential "traps" you find.

2. Discuss credit offers with your parents and other adults and ask about their experience with credit offers. Write a paragraph about what you learn.

KEY TERMS REVIEW

Match the terms with the definitions. Some terms may not be used.

____ 1. Providing a service for which you will pay later

____ 2. A timeframe within which you may pay your balance in full and incur no interest charges

____ 3. A legal business that makes high-interest loans based on the value of possessions pledged as collateral

____ 4. A state law that sets a maximum interest rate that may be charged for loans

____ 5. An organization that makes high-risk consumer loans

____ 6. The cost of credit expressed as a yearly percentage

____ 7. An unlicensed lender who charges illegally high interest rates

____ 8. A loan for a specific amount that must be repaid in full by a specified due date

a. annual percentage rate (APR)
b. closed-end credit
c. finance company
d. grace period
e. loan shark
f. open-end credit
g. pawnbroker (or pawnshop)
h. service credit
i. usury law

CHECK YOUR UNDERSTANDING

LO2-1   9. What is a revolving credit account? Give an example.

LO2-2   10. List five sources of credit and give an example of each.

APPLY YOUR KNOWLEDGE

LO2-2   11. How is open-end credit different from closed-end credit? What are the advantages and disadvantages of each?

THINK CRITICALLY

LO2-1   12. Some consumers get "free credit" by taking advantage of the grace period and paying no interest. Is this fair? Explain.

LO2-1   13. One major advantage of credit is that it helps consumers deal with emergencies. How does this relate to service credit?

LO2-2   14. If you were going into business for yourself, you would have to decide whether or not to accept credit cards from customers. Explain the points in favor of both positions.

The Essential Question *Refer to The Essential Question on p. 164. Open-end credit, closed-end credit, and service credit are available from credit card companies, retail stores, banks and credit unions, finance companies, pawnbrokers, private lenders, and utility companies.*

Assessment

SUMMARY

7.1

- *Credit began as the United States grew from a bartering society to a currency exchange economy with mass-manufactured products available to consumers. Today, credit has become a way of life.*

- *The person who borrows money is called the debtor; the person or business that loans money is called the creditor.*

- *Before applying for credit, you should consider your ability to repay debt based on your income, financial position, and collateral.*

- *For the privilege of using credit, you will pay a finance charge, which includes interest and fees.*

- *A line of credit can be pre-established to provide for emergency funds.*

- *Advantages of credit are the ability to buy now and pay later, the safety of not having to carry a large amount of cash, the ability to build a good credit record, a source of emergency funds, deferred billing, and leverage.*

- *Disadvantages of credit are fees and finance charges, the decreased ability to spend in the future, the tendency to overspend, and the risk of identity theft.*

7.2

- *Open-end credit allows you to borrow again and again, up to a set limit.*

- *The annual percentage rate (APR) is the cost of credit expressed as a yearly percentage.*

- *With a grace period, you can avoid a finance charge so long as you pay your balance in full every month by the due date.*

- *Closed-end credit is a loan for a specific amount that must be repaid in full by a specified due date. Lenders generally require fixed payments, or installments.*

- *Many service providers, such as your utility company, provide service credit, allowing you to pay for services a month or more after their use.*

- *Sources of credit include credit card companies, retail stores, banks and credit unions, finance companies, pawnbrokers, and private lenders.*

- *Usury laws in some states protect consumers from unfairly high interest rates.*

- *A loan shark is an unlicensed lender who charges illegally high interest rates.*

APPLY WHAT YOU KNOW

LO1-1 1. Why has the use of credit in the United States grown over the years?

LO1-2 2. Companies and organizations that offer credit cards compete for your credit card business by offering low introductory rates. Search the Internet for offers of a special deal. What is the "low introductory rate"? Read the fine print. What will the rate be after the introductory period? At the regular rate, how much finance charge would you have to pay on a $1,000 balance each month? How does this compare to the introductory rate?

LO2-1 3. Give an example of a situation in which you would use collateral when making a purchase on credit. What would be the advantage to using collateral with a closed-end loan over making the purchase with your credit card?

LO2-2 4. Does your state have a usury law? You can find out by consulting your state's website, a current almanac, or other library resources. Identify the maximum finance rate that your state allows. Then identify the maximum rates allowed by neighboring states.

LO2-2 5. How are consumer finance companies different from sales finance companies? Why do finance companies charge high interest rates?

LO2-2 6. What is the purpose of a pawnshop? What kind of merchandise can you find at a pawnshop?

MAKE ACADEMIC CONNECTIONS

LO1-1 7. **History** Conduct library and/or online research about the Industrial Revolution in this country and how it changed the lives of Americans. How did people adapt? Specifically, explain how people changed their buying and spending habits.

LO1-1 8. **Economics** When people save money, their deposits provide money that can be loaned to others. This increases the supply of money (or credit opportunities) and lowers its cost to borrowers. Research the economic concepts of average propensity to save (APS) and marginal propensity to save (MPS). Explain what these concepts are, how they are computed, and why they are important to the economy as a whole.

LO1-1 9. **International Studies** Choose another nation in the world and research the use of credit in that country. Compare it to the United States. How different is the standard of living enjoyed by its citizens? Prepare a one-page report of your findings.

LO1-2 10. **Communication** Write a one-page paper about credit—the good and the bad of how it has affected you, what it means to your family, and what it means to retailers and other businesses. Explain in a neutral tone how credit is both positive and negative for the economy as a whole.

LO2-1 11. **Technology** Explain how technology makes it possible for consumers to better manage their credit accounts, including loans, credit card accounts, and student loans.

Solve Problems and Explore Issues

L01-1 12. Interview three or four adults about credit. Ask them the following questions: (a) How do you feel about the use of credit? (b) Do you think interest rates charged on credit cards and accounts are reasonable? (c) Do you prefer to make purchases using credit or cash? Why? Prepare a short report from what you learn.

L01-2 13. Suppose that your elderly neighbors have never used credit. When they were young, their families lost their savings during bad economic times. As a result, they don't trust financial institutions and prefer to use only cash. Explain to them what types of problems can result from not using credit. Describe benefits of using credit.

LO 2-1 14. Find three credit card offers. You can find them in junk mail, e-mails (spam), bill enclosures, advertisements, and credit card websites. Analyze and compare the provisions of the offers, such as the introductory rates, regular rates (variable or fixed), grace periods, annual fees, and so on. Prepare a report of your findings.

L02-2 15. A friend of yours wishes to buy a new car but has only enough money to make a down payment. She asks your advice about where she can finance the balance of her loan for $10,000. What will you tell her? Explain.

L02-2 16. Your cousin needs $100 immediately. He has an HD television worth at least $500 and wants to take it to a pawnbroker. Explain to him how much he might be able to borrow against the TV and what can happen when using pawnbroker credit.

EXTEND YOUR LEARNING

L01-1 17. **Ethics** The wide use of credit can lead to abuses. Some people take out more credit than they can repay. Then they refuse to pay back what they have borrowed. When merchants get stuck with unpaid balances, they pass along that cost to other customers in the form of higher prices. Thus, we all pay for people who overuse credit. Is it ethical for people to overextend their credit, knowing or suspecting that they will not be able to repay it? What can we all do to keep the cost of products and services at reasonable levels?

CHAPTER PROJECT

Conduct online research to determine the use of credit by Americans today. Is it being overused? Are Americans using more or less credit? What do the economists and other experts say about the use of credit and how it is affecting the economy? Write a report of your findings and conclusions. Include graphs, charts, or other visuals to enhance your report.

Complete the Guided Decision Making activity for Chapter 7 at ngl.cengage.com/mypf.

CHAPTER 8

Credit Records and Laws

8.1 **Establishing Credit**

8.2 **Evaluating Credit and Credit Laws**

Consider This...

Renae is a full-time student who works part time on weekends and during the summer. By working, she has been able to save a little money. She has just turned 16 and is learning to drive.

"I'd like to buy my own car," she told her friend Bradley. "That way I can drive myself to work. With my own car, I could work after school, too, and I'd have a way to get to more school activities. As it is, I depend on my mom to drive me everywhere. She works full time, so she isn't always available to take me places. To get a car, I'll have to get a loan. My mom says I'll establish credit by getting a loan, but because I don't have any credit already, she'll probably have to cosign for me to get my first car loan."

The Essential Question *Why is your credit history important, and how do you get started with credit?*

LEARNING OBJECTIVES

> LO 1-1 Discuss the purpose of credit records and credit reports.
> LO 1-2 Describe the concept of creditworthiness.
> LO 1-3 Explain how to get started using credit.

KEY TERMS

- credit history, *177*
- credit bureau, *177*
- subscribers, *177*
- credit report, *178*
- credit freeze, *180*
- creditworthy, *181*
- character, *181*
- capacity, *181*

LO 1-1 Credit Records

Before granting you credit, a creditor will check into your past credit performance: Did you pay your bills on time? How much total credit did you receive? How much do you owe now, and how large are your payments? Your **credit history** is the complete record of your borrowing and repayment performance. This record will provide answers to these questions and thus help the creditor determine your ability to pay new debts.

Your Credit File

Every person who uses credit has a credit history on file at a credit bureau. A **credit bureau** is a business that gathers, stores, and sells credit information to other businesses. Maintaining credit files is big business. Credit bureaus assemble and distribute detailed credit information concerning an estimated 200 million consumers.

There are more than 1,000 local and regional credit bureaus around the country. Typically, these smaller local and regional bureaus are affiliated with one of the following three nationwide credit bureaus:

- Equifax (www.equifax.com)
- Experian (www.experian.com)
- TransUnion (www.transunion.com)

Credit bureaus gather information from businesses, called **subscribers**, that pay a monthly fee to the credit bureau for access to this information. Each subscriber supplies information about its customers'

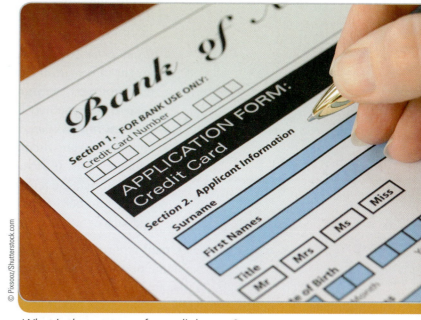

What is the purpose of a credit bureau?

© Pan Xunbin/Shutterstock.com

© Pxsooz/Shutterstock.com

accounts—names, addresses, credit balances, on-time payment record, and so forth—about once a month.

Credit bureaus also gather information from many other sources. For example, public records are searched for information to add to a file. All of the information collected by the credit bureau about a consumer is compiled into a credit report.

Credit Reports

A **credit report** is a written statement of a consumer's credit history. When someone applies to a business for credit, the business (subscriber) asks the credit bureau for the applicant's credit report. Information in the credit report is then used as the basis for granting or denying credit. Usually banks, retail businesses, employers, landlords, and insurance companies have an interest in credit reports. Before entering into a financial agreement with someone, they want evidence that the person is financially responsible.

Reports from different credit bureaus may be arranged differently, but they all contain sections similar to those shown in Figure 8.1.

- *Summary of Information.* This first section is a summary of negative and positive items. It tells the subscribers what to look for as they go through the information that follows. Negative items could harm your ability to get credit. Any negative information stays on your report for seven years (excluding bankruptcy information, which stays on for ten years). Accounts in good standing are favorable to your credit.
- *Public Record Information.* This section lists information found in public records. You would expect to find any lawsuits, judgments, bankruptcy filings, property purchase and sale, marriage, divorce, adoption, and other public information available to anyone who searches public records.
- *Credit Information.* This section lists credit accounts, including those with department stores, credit card companies, and other loans, that have been reported to credit bureaus. It reports details such as each account's high balance since the account was opened and the current payment status.
- *Account Detail.* This section shows the monthly balances of accounts. It also lists the credit limits that have been reported.
- *Requests for Credit History.* This section lists every business that has sought information from your credit file. It includes requests by potential employers, creditors, insurance companies, and others, along with requests that you may have made to inspect your own credit records.
- *Personal Information.* This section lists the personal information that you have given when applying for credit or that is available through public records. It includes your name and previous names, Social Security number, current and previous addresses, date of birth, driver's license number, telephone number, spouse's name, and your employers and salary.

Credit reports may contain errors. For example, a clerical error in entering a name or address, an inaccurate Social Security number, or loan payments that are applied to the wrong account can cause errors. That is why you should review your credit report at least once a year. You are entitled to one free credit report every 12 months from each of the three major credit bureaus. Annual

FIGURE 8.1   Credit Report

PERSONAL CREDIT REPORT

Prepared for	*Report Date*	*Report Number*	**Summary of Information:**	
Jane Smith	June 1, 20--	108881	Potentially negative items:	
			Public records	2
			Accounts with creditors	2
			Accounts in good standing:	3

Public Record Information:

Source	*Date Filed*	*Responsibility*	*Liability Amount*	*Comments*
1. Jess County Courthouse	3/2011	Joint	$5,000	District Court complaint (defendant)
2. U.S. District Court	6/2008	Joint	$85,000	Bankruptcy discharged 11.01

Credit Information:

Source	*Date Opened Last Report*	*Responsibility*	*Type/ Payment*	*High Amount*	*Status*
3. Fidelity Bank (Visa)	6/2007	Individual	Revolv. $100 min.	$5,000	Late 2 payments
4. CC & C Credit	10/2008	Individual	Install. $200/mo.	$8,500	Late charges – 3
5. U.S. Finance Co.	3/2014	Joint	Install. $350/mo.	$18,000	Current

Account Detail:

Source	*Date/Balance*
6. U.S. Finance Co.	3/2014 $0 4/2014 $17,850 5/2014 $17,500 6/2014 $17,150 7/2014 $16,800 8/2014 $16,450
7. Merlo's Dept. Store	5/2013 $0 6/2013 $500 6/2013 $850 7/2013 $700 8/2013 $900 9/2013 $1,000 10/2013 $800 11/2013 $900 12/2013 $1,000 1/2014 $900 2/2014 $700 3/2014 $500 4/2014 $300 5/2014 $100 6/2014 $0

Between 5/2013 and 6/2014 your credit limit was $2,500.

Others Who Have Requested Your Credit History:

11/2011   Bill's Frame Shop (employment check)
2/2012   ABCD Mortgage Co. (related to real estate offer)
8/2014   Art's Motors (car loan application)

Requests Initiated by You:

5/2012   Credit report for denial of credit

Personal Information:

Names: Jane L. Smith   *Social Security Number*: 999-00-9999
          Jane Louise Smith
          J. L. Smith

Residences: 123 Main Street   Single-family house (owned)   4488 West Melody Lane   Condominium (rental)
               Clio, CA 90001   Brighton, NJ 02411

Date of Birth: 9.23.1971   *Driver's License Number*:   CA0948X23
Telephone Numbers: 503.555.3331
                       253.555.4441

Spouse's Name: John B. Smith
Employers: Cranston Bakery (Partner) $48,000 salary, reported 3/2/2012
              4480 West Palm Beach
              Clio, CA 90022

              McGraw School District $37,000 salary, reported 2/1/2007
              42 Maple Wood
              Clinton, NY 00442

Credit Report.com (www.annualcreditreport.com), which was created by the three major credit bureaus, is a centralized service for requesting your free annual credit reports. Although many TV ads, e-mail offers, or online search results

Some people believe that credit bureaus are too powerful and do not adequately safeguard consumer information. Information is gathered and shared without the knowledge or consent of consumers. Credit bureaus sell information about consumers and provide lists of consumers who meet certain criteria. This information is often used by businesses to send out unsolicited credit offers.

Consumer privacy advocates believe that consumers should have more control over their private and personal information contained in credit files. Rather than being allowed to "opt out" of having information supplied at will, they believe that credit bureaus should have to get written permission of consumers (or allow them to opt in) before they can sell and distribute information about them. Credit bureaus disagree and believe that the information is their property and that of their subscribers. They believe they need to have free access to it and be able to share it to generate business profits.

THINK CRITICALLY

With which position do you agree? Why? Would you choose to opt in if this was an option? Explain why or why not.

© Vectomart/Shutterstock.com

---

may tout "free" credit reports, this is the only authorized source for a truly free credit report. When you are denied credit, you can also get a free credit report if you ask within 60 days of being denied. If you need to obtain a credit report at any other time, the credit bureau will charge around $10 or more.

Credit Protection Services

In addition to checking your credit reports regularly, there are other ways to protect your credit files, including credit guard services and credit freezing services.

Credit Guard

Credit guard services are available to consumers who wish to hire a company to monitor their credit files at the three major credit bureaus. With this type of service, you are notified whenever anyone accesses your credit file for any reason. The fee charged for this service ranges from $15 a month to $50 a month, depending on the degree of "protection" provided. For example, you can supply a list of your credit cards, and if one or more is lost or stolen, the service will have it canceled and notify the credit bureaus on your behalf.

Credit Freeze

As a result of increasing credit card fraud and identity theft, many states have passed laws allowing consumers to "freeze" their credit reports and files. A **credit freeze** is a consumer request that requires the credit bureaus to deny all access to a consumer's credit information or files. Thus, new credit applications are blocked and loan solicitation information cannot be given out by the credit bureau. Consumers that choose a credit freeze can unfreeze their credit files when they wish to obtain new credit, and then refreeze them when they are ready. Credit bureaus can charge a fee (such as $15) for each of these activities.

✔ CHECKPOINT

What types of information are in a credit report?

Before potential creditors grant credit to you, they must determine whether you are a good risk—that you are **creditworthy**. To determine this, most lenders utilize some variation of the five "C's" of credit: character, capacity, capital, conditions, and collateral.

Character: Are You Responsible?

Character is a responsible attitude toward honoring obligations, often judged on evidence in the person's credit history. If you have character, you pay your bills on time, and your credit history will show it.

In addition to your credit history, creditors also use stability as a measure of character. For example, a person who has held four different jobs over the past year or has gaps in employment might not be considered a good credit risk.

Capacity: Can You Repay Your Debts?

The financial ability to repay a loan with present income is known as **capacity**. Before lending you money, creditors want to make certain that your current income is sufficient to cover your current expenses each month plus the payments on the new loan. Capacity is often measured as a percentage of take-home pay. For example, as a rule of thumb, payments on your credit card (and other forms of revolving credit) should not exceed 20 percent of your take-home pay. So, if your take-home pay is $2,000 a month, your revolving credit should not exceed $400 a month.

Capital: Do You Have Sufficient Assets?

Capital is the value of financial assets (bank accounts, investments, and property) you possess after deducting your debts. In other words, when you add up all that you own (assets) and subtract all that you owe (liabilities), the difference (net worth or capital) should be sufficient to ensure payment of your debt. Having capital tells creditors that you are in the process of building wealth and providing for your future financial security. Sometimes when your balance sheet is healthy enough, creditors will overlook other requirements. With a lot of financial assets, you are a solid low-risk borrower.

Conditions: What Else Is Going On?

There may be "external" conditions that affect your ability to repay a debt. Conditions refer to the overall economic climate and external environment. For example, if the economy is slowing and many people in your geographic area are losing their jobs, creditors may be less willing to give you a loan. If you lose your job, you may not be able to meet your payments. Therefore, creditors want to know the answers to questions such as the following: How secure is your job? How secure is the firm for which you work? How is the employment situation in your geographic location and in your occupation?

Collateral: Is the Debt Secured?

Collateral is property pledged to assure repayment of a loan, such as the house, car, or furniture being purchased. Collateral protects creditors and

It can be hard getting started with credit. Most credit card companies do not want to take risk on new cardholders. They are looking for responsible people who will take their credit very seriously. Taking responsibility is an important character trait. People who take responsibility for their own actions are able to move forward and make adjustments as needed. They don't blame others for their failures, and they learn from their mistakes. Write a short skit to illustrate how a person might accept responsibility for his or her actions. Describe a situation in which a person demonstrates good character and accountability.

© oculo/Shutterstock.com

lowers their risk, making them more willing to lend to you. If you do not repay your debt as agreed, the creditor can seize the pledged property and sell it to repay the debt. For example, if you stop making your monthly house payments, the creditor can take possession of the home through a process called *foreclosure* and sell it to get back the principal it lent you.

✔ CHECKPOINT

What are the five "C's" of credit?

LO 1-3 Getting Started with Credit

Establishing a good credit record is a slow process. It can take several years of responsible money management to prove your creditworthiness. But everyone has to start somewhere, and here are several good ways to get you going.

Open a Savings Account

Opening a savings account is a good way to start proving your creditworthiness. Start at a financial institution that will not charge you a monthly fee when your savings account balance is small. Credit unions and some banks allow minors to establish accounts with small balances and waive normal fees charged to other depositors. Keep your account growing through regular saving by making a deposit each month or pay period.

Open a Checking Account

As soon as you have enough money in your savings account to allow you a little "cushion," open a checking account, preferably at the same financial institution where you have your savings account. This will provide a convenient method of paying your bills when you have credit accounts and will serve as a record keeping system for your budget. Choose the checking plan that is the least expensive and most convenient for you. Then carefully manage your checking account. Do not write checks or make payments online when your account contains insufficient funds to cover them. Bouncing checks or overdrawing your account will tarnish your creditworthiness. Record all of your transactions immediately in your checkbook register, and balance your checkbook as soon as you receive your statement. If banking online, closely monitor your account balance. This way, you will always know how much is in your account, so that you won't overdraw it accidentally.

Open a Store Credit Account

After opening a checking account and accumulating some money in it, you may look into opening a credit account at a store. Many retail stores will allow you to open a small account with a responsible adult, usually your parent or guardian, as a cosigner. A *cosigner* is someone who promises to pay if the borrower fails to pay. A cosigner has the same responsibilities as the person with the account. As cosigner, the adult is guaranteeing that payments will be made as agreed. If the minor does not make a payment as agreed, the store can demand payment of the account in full, not just the payment owed. This action will affect the creditworthiness of the account holder as well as the creditworthiness of the cosigner.

Make small purchases on your new account and pay the bills promptly, using your checking account. Be sure to make your monthly payments on or before the due date. If you mail your payment, allow sufficient time for it to arrive before the due date. Never pay late!

Get a Small Loan

Another option of proving your creditworthiness is to take out a small loan from the credit union or other financial institution where you have your savings and checking accounts. Use the money to buy something you really need. Then pay back the loan as agreed. Make early payments if possible. Again, you may need to rely on your parents or another adult with a good credit record to cosign your first loan.

Some young people will "piggy back" off their parents' credit. Parents will add the name of their son or daughter to an account or loan or other obligation. This way, the payment is also recorded as part of the minor's credit history.

Apply for a Credit Card

With credit established for a couple of years, a job, and a few credit references, you might now be eligible for a major credit card, such as a Visa or MasterCard. It's often easier and usually safer to apply for a card with your credit union or bank. Because you have a savings and checking account with them, they already know you. Plus, you will be less likely to be hit with high interest rates or fees than if you apply to a credit card company online or respond to an unsolicited credit card offer. Banks may give you a smaller credit limit to get started, but it will be raised over time as long as you manage your account wisely.

Regardless of where you apply for your first credit card, be sure to read the terms and conditions of the card carefully before selecting one. This will tell you about the various fees, charges, interest rates, and benefits of the card. Some credit cards may look like a great deal until you read the fine print.

Once you have your first credit card and you make the payments without fail, you will find it easy to obtain additional credit. It's good to have credit available in case you need it, but don't take out too much credit. Two or three credit cards should be sufficient at any given time.

 **CHECKPOINT**

How can a cosigner help a young person establish credit?

Architecture

Most architects work for architectural firms, or companies that do specialized forms of architecture, such as high-rise buildings, shopping malls, or recreation facilities. These major projects require expert design to be sure they are safe and meet building standards and codes, while at the same time are aesthetically pleasing and designed for durability.

Architects spend most of their time in offices, where they consult with clients to learn the objectives, requirements, and budget of a project; develop construction plans and drawings; and work with other architects and engineers. When a major project has begun, architects also visit construction sites to review the progress of the projects.

Employment Outlook

- Faster than the average rate of employment growth is expected.

Job Titles

- Architect
- Architectural Engineer
- Architectural Designer

Needed Skills

- A five-year professional degree from a school accredited by the National Architectural Accrediting Board (NAAB) is required in most states.
- A passing grade on the Architect Registration Exam is required.

- A training period must be completed by working as an intern at an architectural firm.
- Strong analytical and technical skills, along with high creativity, are required.

What's it like to work in . . . *Architecture*

Adam has worked for a large architectural firm for nearly five years. He began as an intern until he gained enough experience to work jointly on projects. He often works more than 50 hours a week but is well compensated with a yearly salary of $86,000. He has a variety of duties, including consulting with clients, preparing scaled drawings of projects, and preparing contract documents for building contractors.

Adam spends most of his time in his office, which is equipped with computer-aided design and drafting (CADD) and building information modeling (BIM) technology for creating designs and construction drawings. However, as construction proceeds on projects, he also visits building sites to ensure that contractors are following the design, staying on schedule, and meeting work-quality standards.

What About You?

Do you like working independently and on teams? Are you creative? Do you have strong analytical and technical skills? Are you willing to work for five years on a degree plus do an internship? If so, a career in architecture might be right for you.

KEY TERMS REVIEW

Match the terms with the definitions. Some terms may not be used.

a. capacity
b. character
c. credit bureau
d. credit freeze
e. credit history
f. credit report
g. creditworthy
h. subscribers

____ 1. A written statement about a consumer's credit history

____ 2. A person who is a good credit risk

____ 3. A business that gathers, stores, and sells credit information to other businesses

____ 4. A responsible attitude toward honoring one's obligations

____ 5. A consumer request to deny all access to his or her credit information and files

____ 6. The financial ability to repay a loan with present income

____ 7. The complete record of your borrowing and repayment performance

CHECK YOUR UNDERSTANDING

LO1-1   8. How do credit bureaus gather information for your credit file?

LO1-2   9. What does "creditworthiness" mean?

LO1-2   10. How do creditors judge your character?

APPLY YOUR KNOWLEDGE

LO1-3   11. As a teenager, you would like to get started in establishing a good credit history. Based on your personal situation and the stores and banks in your area, prepare a plan that you might follow in getting started using credit.

THINK CRITICALLY

LO1-1   12. As a consumer, you are entitled to one free credit report every 12 months from each of the three major credit bureaus. Why is it important for you to review your credit report at least once a year?

LO1-2   13. How can external conditions affect your ability to repay debt? Why should you be held accountable for things you can't control?

LO1-3   14. How can parents help their child get started with credit? Why would a teenager ask for help from his or her parents?

The Essential Question *Refer to The Essential Question on p. 177. Your credit history helps creditors decide whether to grant credit to you. To get started with credit, begin by opening a savings account. Then after accumulating some savings, open a checking account and and a credit card account.*

The Essential Question *Why are your credit score and credit rating important, and why are consumer protection laws needed?*

LEARNING OBJECTIVES

> LO 2-1 Discuss how credit scores and credit ratings are used to evaluate credit.
> LO 2-2 Discuss major credit laws and their impact on consumers.

KEY TERMS

- point system, *186*
- credit score, *186*
- credit inquiry, *187*
- rate shopping, *187*
- credit rating, *188*
- billing statement, *190*
- discrimination, *190*
- debt collector, *191*

LO 2-1 | Credit Scores and Credit Ratings

Credit bureaus evaluate consumers based on information contained in their credit files and credit reports. This information is used to assign a credit score and credit rating to consumers. Credit scores and credit ratings make it easier to interpret a consumers' credit report.

Credit Scores

Credit bureaus use a point system to compute credit scores for consumers. In a **point system**, the credit bureau assigns points based on factors such as amount of current debt, number of late payments, number and types of open accounts, amount of income, and so on. When your points are added up, they result in a **credit score** that tells potential creditors the likelihood that you will repay debt as agreed. The higher your score, the greater the chance you will be a good credit risk. Business subscribers then use these scores as part of their decision to grant or deny credit.

The most commonly used credit scoring model, used by over 90 percent of creditors, is called FICO (named after its creator, Fair Isaac and Company). Each consumer has three FICO scores—one for each of the three major credit bureaus. Because a consumer's credit report may contain different information at each of the bureaus, FICO scores can vary depending on which bureau provides the score. As information changes, your scores change as well.

Calculating Your FICO Score

To calculate a FICO score, you must have at least one account open for six months or more. FICO scores are calculated from several different pieces of data in your credit report. This data is grouped into the following five categories: payment history, amounts owed, length of credit history, types of credit used, and new credit.

- *Payment history* is rated based on how you pay your debts; the presence of bankruptcy, liens (financial claims against property), or collections; and whether accounts are past due or paid as agreed. This category constitutes 35 percent of your FICO score.
- *Amounts owed* is rated based on how many accounts have balances, the amounts owed on those accounts, and the proportion of the credit line used. This category constitutes 30 percent of your FICO score.
- *Length of credit history* is rated based on the oldest account opened and the average age of all accounts. Accounts that have been open for a long period of time reflect positively on your score. This category constitutes 15 percent of your FICO score.
- *Types of credit used* is rated based on the mix of credit accounts, such as credit cards, retail accounts, installment loans, mortgages, and so on. This category constitutes 10 percent of your FICO score.
- *New credit* is rated based on the number of recently opened accounts and the number of recent credit inquiries (discussed below). This category constitutes 10 percent of your FICO score.

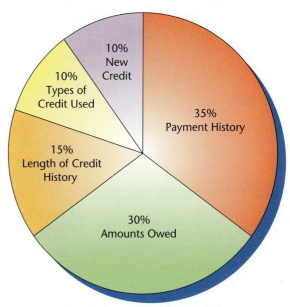

Calculating Your FICO Score

The highest FICO score a person can receive is 850; the lowest is 300. Your FICO score can be accessed for a fee from each of the three major credit bureaus or from the myFICO website (www.myfico.com).

Credit Inquiries

A **credit inquiry** is a request by a business with a "permissible purpose" to check your credit. Businesses can make an inquiry without your permission or knowledge, but usually these requests don't count toward your credit score. For example, before a credit card company sends you a preapproved credit offer, it will pull your credit information. A *personal credit inquiry* made by you to obtain your credit report also does not affect your score.

When you apply for a loan or other credit, you authorize the lender to check your credit. These inquiries, which are prompted by your own actions, will affect your FICO score. One exception occurs when you are rate shopping for an auto or mortgage loan. **Rate shopping** involves looking around for the best interest rate on an auto or mortgage loan. This may cause multiple lenders to request your credit report. To compensate for this, your FICO score does not include inquiries made within a short period of time—usually 30 days. Therefore, if you find an auto or mortgage loan within the 30-day period, the inquiries will have little or no effect on your score while you are rate shopping.

The impact from credit inquiries varies based on a person's credit history. In general, they have a small impact on your FICO score. However, if you have few accounts or a short credit history, inquiries could cause your FICO score to drop. Too many inquiries could mean that you're taking on too much debt.

Improving Your FICO Score

Raising your FICO score takes time and patience. There is no quick way to fix a credit score, but following the tips below can help:

- *Pay your bills on time.* Delinquent payments, even if only a few days late, can have a negative impact on your FICO score.
- *Improve your payment history.* If you have missed payments, get current and stay current. The longer you pay your bills on time after being late, the more your FICO score will increase.
- *Keep balances low on credit cards and revolving credit.* High outstanding debt can negatively affect a credit score.
- *Pay off your debt rather than move it around.* If you pay off one credit card bill by using another credit card, you are simply moving your debt, not reducing it.
- *Open accounts slowly—not several at a time.* Some experts suggest that too many open accounts, even unused, can hurt your credit score because of the potential for obtaining more available credit than you are able to handle.

Credit Ratings

A **credit rating** is another measure of creditworthiness often identified by a letter grade (A, B, C, D). Credit reporting agencies typically base the grades on the consumer's credit score. Credit ratings allow financial institutions to determine how likely an individual will pay back money borrowed or charged. FICO assigns letter grades to credit score numbers as shown in Figure 8.2.

Someone who has an *excellent credit rating*, or an *A-rating*, doesn't miss payments and pays off debts early. Someone who has a *good credit rating*, or a *B-rating*, pays bills on time and often pays more than the minimum payment due. *A fair credit rating* is earned by a customer who usually pays all bills within the grace period, but occasionally takes longer. (When a bill is paid within ten days of its due date, this is considered an *automatic grace period*.) People with a *poor credit rating* are usually denied credit because they miss some monthly payments, have failed to pay back a debt in its entirety, have filed for bankruptcy, or have otherwise shown that they are not a good credit risk.

Credit ratings affect loan terms, such as the interest rate, that you will be offered. For example, if you have an excellent credit rating, you may be offered a loan at a low interest rate, which means your monthly payments would be lower. However, if your credit rating is only fair, you may be offered the same loan at a higher interest rate, meaning your monthly payments would be higher. The difference may not seem like much in the short term, but when you add up the difference between the payment amounts over the life of the loan, you could be paying thousands of dollars more!

CHECKPOINT

What factors determine your credit score?

- -

FIGURE 8.2 Credit Scores and Ratings

Credit Score	Credit Rating	Explanation
720–850	A	Excellent. Has used credit wisely; has considerable capital but low revolving debt. Pays off credit monthly; rarely carries credit balances other than home mortgage loan.
650–719	B	Good. Has good credit payment record; good, solid income and the ability to repay debts. Pays monthly credit obligations on time and pays more than the minimum.
575–649	C	Fair. Has considerable debt and is meeting obligations within the grace period; makes minimum payments; income is adequate; may have some small credit discrepancies.
Below 575	D	Poor. Not able to take on much debt; some credit history but not well established; income may be questionable; has had some credit problems in the past; may have filed bankruptcy.

LO 2-2 Credit Laws

The government has passed a number of laws to protect consumers from unfair credit practices. Together, these laws set a standard for how individuals are to be treated in their daily credit dealings. Several of these laws are summarized on the following pages.

Consumer Credit Protection Act

The *Consumer Credit Protection Act*, also known as the *Truth in Lending Act*, requires lenders to fully inform consumers about all costs of a credit purchase before an agreement is signed. Lenders must disclose the finance charge, which is the total dollar amount of all costs of the credit, including interest, service fees, and any other costs. Lenders must also state the annual percentage rate (APR), which is the yearly percentage of interest charges that must be calculated the same way by all lenders. In addition, the law requires a grace period of three business days in which purchasers can change their mind about a credit agreement. The law also limits the consumer's liability to $50 after the consumer reports a credit card lost or stolen. There is no liability if the card is reported lost prior to its fraudulent use.

Fair Credit Reporting Act

The *Fair Credit Reporting Act* regulates the collection, dissemination, and use of consumer credit information. This act gives you the right to know what is in your credit report and entitles you to a free copy every 12 months from each of the three major credit bureaus. The act also gives you the right to know who has received your credit report in the last year (or two years for employment purposes). A credit bureau may not provide your credit report to an employer unless you give that employer written permission to request your credit report. You may see your credit report from the credit bureau used by the creditor at no charge within 60 days of a credit denial. In addition, the act gives you the right to dispute inaccurate or incomplete information in your report. The credit bureau must correct or delete any inaccurate or incomplete information in your report within 30 days. If potentially damaging information in the file is essentially correct, you can write a statement giving your side of the story and your statement must be added to the file.

Fair Credit Billing Act

Under the *Fair Credit Billing Act*, creditors must resolve billing errors within a specified period of time. A **billing statement** is an itemized bill showing charges, credits, and payments posted to your account during the billing period. Suppose your monthly statement showed a purchase you did not make. Perhaps you were billed for merchandise you ordered but did not receive. Creditors are required to have a written policy for correcting such errors.

If you believe your statement contains an error, write a letter to the creditor giving a complete explanation of why you believe there is an error. Be specific about the amount in dispute and provide any details relevant to the disputed amount. Include your account number and contact information. Figure 8.3 shows an example of what you might say.

Your complaint must be mailed within 60 days after you receive the statement. The creditor must acknowledge the complaint within 30 days. The creditor must either correct the error or show why the bill is correct within 90 days. You are not liable for the amount in dispute while the error is being investigated. However, you must still make payments on all other amounts. Figure 8.4 on p. 192 is an example of a written policy for handling billing errors.

Equal Credit Opportunity Act

The *Equal Credit Opportunity Act* was designed to prevent discrimination in the evaluation of creditworthiness. **Discrimination** is the act of treating people differently based on prejudice rather than individual merit. There are many legitimate reasons for denying an applicant credit. Some reasons, however, are considered discriminatory. The act specifies the following:

- Credit may not be denied solely because you are a woman, single, married, divorced, separated, or widowed.
- Credit may not be denied specifically because of religion, national origin, race, color, or age (except as age may affect your ability to perform or your ability to enter into contracts; for example, minors cannot be held liable for their contracts because they are not considered competent parties).
- Credit may not be denied because you receive public assistance (welfare), unemployment, Social Security, or retirement benefits.
- Credit applications may be oral or written. However, a creditor is prohibited from asking certain questions, such as: Do you plan to have children? What is your ethnic origin? What church do you attend?
- A creditor may not discourage you, in writing or orally, from applying for credit for any reason prohibited by the act (such as being divorced).

FIGURE 8.3   Letter Reporting Billing Error

P.O. Box 4848
Milwaukee, WI 40412-4848
April 10, 20--

Melon Visa Bank
Customer Service Center
24 Chambers Street
New York, NY 02040-3112

RE: ACCOUNT # 4902 3818 4783 1783
      Disputed Amount: $289.00 Melvin's, 3/21/--

As stated in my telephone conversation with Melanie at your 800 number on
April 9, 20--, I am hereby disputing the above charge.

Copies of the invoice and other documentation for the purchase I made on
March 21 at Melvin's Auto Repair are enclosed. I am disputing the amount listed
because the service provided was unsatisfactory. I was charged $589, but within
a week, the same operational problem occurred. I asked Melvin's to correct the
problem, but the manager said it was not the company's responsibility and that
I would be charged an additional $200 in parts and labor. As you can see, I then
went to Barlow's and had the defective part fixed for $300. Therefore, I believe
that of the $589, which is the fair market value of the product, I should not have
to pay more than $289 to Melvin's.

You can reach me at (201) 555-2372 on weekdays. My e-mail address is listed
below. Please let me know if you need any further information.

Thank you,

Jackie B. Chen

JACKIE B. CHEN
Jackiebc@starnet.com

Enclosure

In addition to these prohibitions, the act states that creditors must notify
you whether your credit application is accepted or rejected within 30 days of
submission. If you are denied credit, the denial must be in writing and must
list a specific reason for the denial.

The act also requires that companies reporting to credit bureaus must make
their reports in the names of both the husband and wife if both use an account
or are responsible for repaying the debt. In this way, both spouses establish
their own credit histories.

Fair Debt Collection Practices Act

The *Fair Debt Collection Practices Act* was designed to eliminate abusive
collection practices by debt collectors. A **debt collector** is a person or company hired by a creditor to collect the overdue balance on an account. The fee

FIGURE 8.4   Error-Correction Policy

IN CASE OF ERRORS OR INQUIRIES ABOUT YOUR BILL:

The Fair Credit Billing Act requires prompt resolution of errors. To preserve your rights, follow these steps:

1. Do not write on the bill. On a separate piece of paper, write a description as shown below. A telephone call will not preserve your rights.

   a. Your name and account number.
   b. Description of the error and your explanation of why you believe there is an error. Send copies of any receipts or supporting evidence you may have; do not send originals.
   c. The dollar amount of the suspected error.
   d. Other information that might be helpful in resolving the disputed amount.

2. Mail your letter as soon as possible. It must reach us within 60 days after you receive your bill.

3. We will acknowledge your letter within 30 days. Within 90 days of receiving your letter, we will correct the error or explain why we believe the bill is correct.

4. You will receive no collection letters or collection action regarding the amount in dispute; nor will it be reported to any credit bureau or collection agency.

5. You are still responsible for all other items on the bill and for the balance less the disputed amount.

6. You will not be charged a finance charge against the disputed amount, unless it is determined that there is not an error in the bill. In this event, you will be given the normal 25 days to pay your bill from the date the bill is determined to be correct.

charged by debt collectors is often half of the amount collected. The law prohibits use of threats, obscenities, and false and misleading statements to intimidate the consumer into paying. It also restricts the time and frequency of collection practices, such as telephone calls, and restricts contacts at places of employment. Debt collectors are required to verify the accuracy of the bill and give the consumer the opportunity to clarify and dispute it.

Credit Card Accountability Responsibility and Disclosure Act

The *Credit Card Accountability Responsibility and Disclosure Act (Credit CARD Act)* was enacted to provide more consumer credit protections. The act provides many new provisions regarding interest rates. Credit card issuers are now required to give a 45-day written notice of any interest rate increase. In addition, credit card issuers cannot raise the interest rate on a new account during the first year that the account is open except for promotional rates, which must remain in effect for at least six months.

The act also places new provisions on fees. Credit card issuers can no longer charge you a late fee greater than your minimum payment. Cardholders will also no longer face any fees if they go over their credit limit, unless they have given the creditor permission to authorize over-the-limit transactions.

There are also new disclosures that must be provided to consumers. Your monthly credit card bill must now include information on how long it will take you to pay off your balance if you make only minimum payments. The act also requires consistency in payment dates and times. Credit card issuers

Why do you think the Credit CARD Act has special credit provisions for those under the age of 21?

are now required to mail your statement at least 21 days before your payment is due, and your monthly due date must be the same date each month. The act also prohibits *double-cycle billing*, also known as *two-cycle billing*, or the practice of applying a finance charge on both the current balance and the previous month's balance.

Young consumers receive additional protection under the act. Credit card issuers must now verify proof of income or otherwise require a cosigner before issuing a credit card to someone under the age of 21. Also, credit card issuers cannot raise the credit limit for cardholders under the age of 21 who have a cosigner, unless the cosigner has given written permission to do so.

Dodd-Frank Wall Street Reform and Consumer Protection Act

The *Dodd-Frank Wall Street Reform and Consumer Protection Act*, commonly called the *Dodd-Frank Act*, created the Consumer Financial Protection Bureau. The bureau's stated mission is "to make markets for consumer financial products and services work for Americans, whether they are applying for a mortgage, choosing among credit cards, or using any number of other consumer financial products." At the bureau's website, you can file complaints if you have issues with financial products or services, get questions answered, and access information to make comparisons among credit products and providers. This agency was designed to help consumers navigate complicated credit and financial markets and to ensure fair practices among all consumers.

 **CHECKPOINT**

What are two ways in which credit card billing statements are affected by credit laws?

Issues **IN YOUR WORLD**

How Did the Great Recession Affect Credit?

When the Great Recession hit in 2007, many people were caught off guard with a lot of debt. They had mortgaged their homes to the limit, taking out second mortgages in order to cash out their equity. Credit accounts and balances were at an all-time high as consumers bought goods and services to enjoy life's luxuries. For many families, a second or third job became a reality to pay the high bills that went along with living the dream.

With the economic downturn, many jobs were lost and people with lots of debt were unable to pay their bills. Credit card companies felt the squeeze as collections dropped while delinquencies rose. To increase profitability and reduce risk, they took immediate and harsh actions. Unfortunately, their actions resulted in further hardships for many Americans.

Citibank closed millions of consumer credit accounts. These included both new (those less than two years old) and long-standing accounts. Regardless of payment records or how well consumers had managed their accounts, they were closed. Visa, MasterCard, and American Express all lowered credit limits and closed accounts as well. Fixed interest rates became variable and were raised substantially with a 30-day written notice. Consumers had no choice but to accept the higher rates or face having their account closed if they opted out.

Other creditors raised minimum payment requirements. If they had formerly required 1 percent of the balance to be paid monthly, that became 2 to 5 percent. Thus, a minimum payment of $100 a month became $300 or more a month. With lower wages and lost jobs, it was impossible for many Americans to make these higher payments. As a result of all of these actions, credit scores and ratings dropped significantly for many Americans.

Many people found the practices of credit card companies to be both unethical and illogical. As a result, many Americans turned away from credit and started using debit cards instead. With the passage of the Credit CARD Act of 2009, the government is trying to tame some of the abusive and deceptive tactics used by credit card companies. However, credit card companies are already coming up with new ways to increase their profitability. Today, credit card use is on the rise again, but hopefully, consumers will be better prepared during the next economic downturn.

THINK CRITICALLY

1. What do you think of the credit card companies' actions during the Great Recession? What were the long-term consequences for credit card customers?
2. How can you protect yourself from the tactics credit card companies use to increase their profitability?

KEY TERMS REVIEW

Match the terms with the definitions. Some terms may not be used.

a. billing statement
b. credit inquiry
c. credit rating
d. credit score
e. debt collector
f. discrimination
g. point system
h. rate shopping

____ 1. The total number of assigned points that tells potential creditors the likelihood that you will repay debt as agreed

____ 2. Treating people differently based on prejudice rather than individual merit

____ 3. A method of evaluation in which points are assigned by a credit bureau on factors such as amount of current debt and amount of income

____ 4. An itemized bill showing all charges, credits, and payments posted to your account

____ 5. A letter grade based on a consumer's credit score that indicates his or her creditworthiness

____ 6. A person or company hired by a creditor to collect the overdue balance on an account

____ 7. A request by a business with a "permissible purpose" to check your credit

CHECK YOUR UNDERSTANDING

LO2-1 8. What are some things you can do to improve your FICO score?

LO2-1 9. What is the purpose of rate shopping?

LO2-2 10. Choose one of the credit laws discussed in this chapter and explain how it protects consumers.

APPLY YOUR KNOWLEDGE

LO2-1 11. Explain the purpose of credit scores and credit ratings. Who uses them and why?

THINK CRITICALLY

LO2-1 12. How is an excellent credit rating different from a fair credit rating? Why is having an excellent credit rating so important?

LO2-2 13. Do you think it is fair that young consumers must now either have a job or have a cosigner to get credit? Explain your answer.

LO2-2 14. How do consumers benefit from the creation of the Consumer Financial Protection Bureau?

The Essential Question *Refer to The Essential Question on p. 186. Your credit score and credit rating play a huge role in determining whether creditors grant or deny you credit. Credit laws help protect consumers from unfair credit practices.*

SUMMARY

8.1

- *Your credit history is a complete record of your experience with credit.*

- *Credit bureaus collect information about consumers and prepare credit reports based on the information they collect.*

- *Credit reports provide information about individual consumers, including public record information, credit information, account details, and personal information. Creditors use a consumer's credit report to decide whether to grant credit.*

- *Creditors judge your creditworthiness based on the five "C's" of credit: character, capacity, capital, conditions, and collateral.*

- *To start building a good credit history, follow these steps: open a savings account, open a checking account, open a store credit account, get a small loan, and apply for a credit card.*

- *You may need a cosigner to get started with credit. A cosigner guarantees that payments will be made as agreed.*

8.2

- *Many credit bureaus rate consumers' creditworthiness on a point system, assigning points based on debt, payment history, income, and other factors. Assigned points are totaled to determine your credit score.*

- *A credit rating is a letter grade (A, B, C, D) often assigned by credit bureaus based on a consumer's credit score.*

- *The Consumer Credit Protection Act (Truth in Lending Act) requires full disclosure of all costs of credit, including the finance charge and APR.*

- *The Fair Credit Reporting Act gives you the right to view your credit report and to dispute inaccurate or incomplete information.*

- *The Fair Credit Billing Act requires creditors to resolve billing errors within a specified period of time.*

- *The Equal Credit Opportunity Act prohibits discrimination in judgment of creditworthiness.*

- *The Fair Debt Collection Practices Act prohibits abusive collection practices by debt collectors.*

- *The Credit Card Accountability Responsibility and Disclosure Act (Credit CARD Act) was enacted to provide more consumer credit protections.*

- *The Dodd-Frank Act created the Consumer Financial Protection Bureau.*

APPLY WHAT YOU KNOW

L01-1 1. Visit the website of one of the three major credit bureaus. In no more than one page, summarize what the bureau includes in its credit reports and outline the procedure you would have to follow to get a copy of your own report.

L01-1 2. Are credit guard companies a good deal for consumers? Why or why not? Why would a person choose to freeze his or her credit?

L01-1 3. What reasons would a business have to request a credit report?

L01-2 4. What kinds of credit do you think you will be using in five years? How will you establish a good credit score to be eligible for increasing credit limits and privileges?

L02-2 5. Describe what you must do if you believe a billing statement you receive from a creditor contains an error. Describe the process for error correction, including your responsibilities and time limits and the responsibilities and time limits of your creditor.

L02-2 6. Assume you have a well-established credit history and have filled out an application for credit at a local department store. The store has notified you that it cannot give you credit because you have a poor credit rating. You have not missed any payments or made any late payments, and you have paid off previous debts as agreed. What are your rights, and what are some things you should do? What responsibilities does the credit bureau have to you?

MAKE ACADEMIC CONNECTIONS

L01-1 7. **History** Conduct library and online research about credit bureaus—what they are, when they began, how they are regulated, and the opposition to their practices by consumer privacy advocates. Cite your sources and give direct quotes where possible. Give a historical perspective on the need for credit bureaus.

L02-1 8. **Communication** Write a two-page paper about credit reports, credit scores, and credit ratings. Explain what they are, how they work, and how everyone is affected by them. Give both favorable and unfavorable analyses of how consumer information is gathered and used.

L02-2 9. **Research** Using online sources, find out how your personal information can be revealed through a procedure called *pretexting*. Explain how it works. Countering pretexting are organizations such as the Electronic Privacy Information Center. Explain what it does.

L02-2 10. **Careers** Explore what it would be like to work in the Consumer Protection Division of a state attorney general's office or for a federal agency such as the Federal Trade Commission. How are consumers able to make/file complaints? What does the government agency do to help them? What would be your role as a government employee?

Solve Problems and Explore Issues

LO1-2 11. Evaluate your creditworthiness based on the five "C's" of credit: character, capacity, capital, conditions, and collateral. What do you conclude?

LO1-3 12. Your friend Kamal has just been turned down for credit. He works part time and would like to obtain a credit card from a local department store. The department store stated lack of credit history as the reason for credit denial. What can Kamal do to create a credit history?

LO1-3 13. Obtain a credit application from a local merchant or national credit card company. On a separate piece of paper, create two columns. List each question on the form in the left column. In the right column, indicate whether each question is (a) a personal question, (b) a payment record question, (c) an employment stability question, or (d) an income question.

LO2-2 14. Obtain a written error policy supplied by a credit card company or other creditor. Compare the policy statement with Figure 8.4 and describe the similarities and differences.

EXTEND YOUR LEARNING

LO2-2 15. **Legal Issues** Your neighbor recently purchased a refrigerator on credit but was unable to continue making payments because he lost his job. In the last week, he has received abusive telephone calls at home from a debt collector. Your neighbor has volunteered to return the refrigerator, but the debt collector refuses and threatens him with public humiliation. The collector has now come to your house looking for him and has made false and degrading comments about the neighbor's character. Are the debt collector's actions legal? Why or why not? What advice would you give?

CHAPTER PROJECT

Research one of the consumer credit laws discussed in this chapter (see pp. 189–193). Print and read the full narrative of the law. Write a report detailing the year the law was passed, why it was deemed necessary at that time in history, who was involved in writing the law, who was President at that time, and any other information you can find pertinent to that law. Conclude your report with your opinion on whether the law is still needed today. Explain why or why not.

Complete the Guided Decision Making activity for Chapter 8 at ngl.cengage.com/mypf.

CHAPTER 9

Costs of Credit

9.1   **Using Credit Wisely**

9.2   **Computing the Costs of Credit**

Consider This...

Mike was well on his way to managing credit and taking the next steps, such as buying a house and making a commitment to long-term payments.

"I learned the hard way that all credit isn't created equal," he thought. "Some credit cards have annual fees, and others charge very high interest rates. I switched from credit accounts that didn't meet my needs. Now I have a group of cards and accounts that have no annual fees, low interest rates, and the kinds of rewards and rebates that benefit me. I keep my accounts paid off and use the cards mainly for emergencies and convenience. It wasn't always so easy, though. When I wasn't careful, I ended up spending a lot of money impulsively—money that I could have used later to buy something I wanted more—and I paid much more interest than I needed to. I've learned how to avoid those high interest rates and fees. That gives me more to invest and use for my future."

© Pan Xunbin/Shutterstock.com

The Essential Question *What is involved in using credit wisely?*

LEARNING OBJECTIVES

> LO 1-1 Describe the responsibilities of consumer credit.
> LO 1-2 Discuss how to protect your credit accounts from fraud.
> LO 1-3 Explain how you can reduce or avoid credit costs.

KEY TERMS

- comparison shopping, *200*
- impulse buying, *201*
- judgment, *201*
- garnishment, *201*
- opt out, *202*
- encryption, *203*
- phishing, *204*
- unused credit, *205*
- rewards program, *205*
- rebate program, *205*

LO 1-1 Responsibilities of Credit

Once you have established credit, you have the responsibility to manage it carefully. Failure to take this responsibility seriously can result in having your credit limited or, in some cases, withdrawn. Because using credit is important to your financial future, you should be aware of your responsibilities to yourself and to creditors. In return, creditors have responsibilities to you, their customer.

Responsibilities to Yourself

As a credit user, or *debtor*, you have a responsibility to yourself to use credit wisely and not get into debt beyond an amount you can comfortably repay. Never having enough money and always scrambling to make your next payment is a stressful way to live.

You are also responsible for checking out businesses before making credit purchases. Better Business Bureaus and Chambers of Commerce have information about businesses and complaints that have been filed against them. You can also get information about businesses from the Internet by visiting the company's website, reading consumer reviews and complaints about the company and its products or services, or seeking information from government consumer protection agencies. If you aren't familiar with a business, or if it does not have a brick-and-mortar physical location, it's a good idea to check it out thoroughly before doing business with it.

You owe it to yourself to comparison shop. **Comparison shopping** involves checking several

Why should you check out businesses before making credit purchases?

© Gil C/Shutterstock.com

© Pan Xunbin/Shutterstock.com

places to be sure you are getting the best price for equal quality. Comparison shopping also will help you avoid impulse buying. **Impulse buying** occurs when you buy something without thinking about it and making a conscious decision. It's important to take the time to evaluate all options before buying. Be sure you are buying for the right reasons—because you have a need rather than because you want to impress people. Tying up future income should be done with careful planning to maximize your purchasing power and quality of life.

Finally, as a credit user, you should have the right attitude about using credit. Enter into each transaction in good faith and with full expectation of meeting your obligations and upholding your good credit reputation.

Responsibilities to Creditors

When you open an account, you are entering into a relationship with a retail store, bank, or credit card company. You are pledging your honesty and sincerity in the use of credit.

You are responsible for reading and understanding the terms of your credit agreement, including the finance charge, fees, and any other provisions of the agreement. In addition, you have the responsibility to limit your spending to amounts that you can repay according to the terms of the credit agreement. By signing a credit application, you agree to make all payments promptly, on or before the due date. If an emergency prevents you from making a payment, you should contact the creditor to make arrangements to pay at a later date.

If you are unable to make payments as agreed, a creditor can take you to court and win a judgment against you. A **judgment** is a court order that will allow creditors to collect the debts you have agreed to pay. Once a credit card company has a judgment against you, there are several methods by which it can attempt to collect on the judgment. It may take your assets to repay the debt, levy (freeze) your bank account, or take part of your paycheck to pay the debt you owe. **Garnishment** is a legal process that allows part of your paycheck to be withheld for payment of a debt. Your employer sends the amount directly to the creditor. This is something you wish to avoid as it hurts your credit score and will make it very difficult for you to get credit in the future.

It is your responsibility to contact the creditor immediately if you find an error on your billing statement or discover that the merchandise you bought is defective. You generally can dispute charges for unsatisfactory goods or services (including issues about the quality of an item) if you made a good faith effort to resolve the dispute with the seller, if the charge is for more than $50, or if you made the purchase in your home state or within 100 miles of your current billing address.

If your credit card is lost, stolen, or used without your permission, it is your responsibility to report it to your creditor as soon as possible. If a thief uses your card before you report it missing, you may owe up to $50 for any unauthorized charges. If the thief uses your card number, but not your card, you are not responsible for the unauthorized charges.

The Credit CARD Act of 2009 helped to increase consumer credit protection by enacting new provisions on interest rate hikes and fees. But one area that the Act does not address is credit cancellation policies. Credit card issuers can cancel your account without warning if they choose—and it's perfectly legal for them to do so. Even if you have a zero balance in your account and have never been late with a payment, an issuer can cancel your account at any time. The most common reason credit card issuers give for doing this is that you're not using the account often enough.

Many of these customers claim that this practice by credit card issuers is not fair. They feel that because they've been good customers, credit card issuers should not be allowed to close their accounts without any kind of notice. Credit card issuers counter that getting rid of inactive accounts with large, open lines of credit cuts down on the credit risk to the bank and also increases their profits by giving that line of credit to someone who will use the card frequently and incur interest charges.

THINK CRITICALLY

Do you agree with the claims of each side? What point could you make to support each side?

© Vectomart/Shutterstock.com

Creditors' Responsibilities to You

Creditors also have responsibilities to consumers to whom they grant credit. These responsibilities include the following:

- Assisting consumers in making wise purchases by honestly representing goods and services, including all of their advantages and disadvantages.
- Informing customers about all rules and regulations (such as minimum payments and due dates), interest rates, credit policies, and fees. (The Truth in Lending Act requires credit card issuers to disclose this information to consumers prior to entering into a credit agreement.)
- Cooperating with credit bureaus by providing accurate, up-to-date information on account holders.
- Making credit card statements available to customers, promptly acknowledging complaints, and fixing billing errors when they occur.
- Establishing and adhering to sound lending and credit policies that do not overburden or deceive customers. This includes setting reasonable guidelines for credit use to avoid extending additional credit to customers who cannot afford it.
- Using reasonable methods of contacting customers who fail to meet their obligations and assisting them whenever possible with payment schedules and other means for solving credit problems.
- Keeping credit users informed when changes in credit policies occur and giving them the opportunity to **opt out**, or elect not to accept changes to policies, by canceling the account. Opting out is a reasonable action when creditors alter their credit policies significantly, such as by drastically raising their interest rates or raising minimum payments excessively.

✔ CHECKPOINT

What responsibilities do you have to yourself when using credit?

Credit card fraud takes place every day in a variety of ways. The most common type of fraud is the illegal use of a lost or stolen credit card or of credit card information intercepted online or hacked from an unsecure website.

Safeguarding Your Cards

It is your responsibility to help protect your cards and credit accounts from unauthorized use. While the credit card holder's liability is limited to $50, the merchant is not protected from loss. Consequently, merchants often raise their overall prices to cover such losses. Use the following common sense tips to safeguard your card:

- Sign and activate your cards as soon as you receive them.
- Carry only the cards you need.
- Keep a list of your credit card numbers, their expiration dates, and the phone number and address of each card company in a safe place.
- Notify creditors immediately by phone if your card is lost or stolen and follow up with a letter so that you have written evidence of the notification.
- Keep your card in view during transactions and get it back as soon as you can to avoid giving others the opportunity to steal your credit card information either manually or by swiping it on an electronic reader.
- Keep your sales receipts and promptly verify all charges on your credit card statements, using the procedure printed on your statement to question charges that you think are in error.
- Tear up old receipts no longer needed that contain account information.
- Don't lend your card to anyone or leave it lying around your home or office.
- Destroy expired cards by cutting them up.
- Destroy any unwanted credit card offers to prevent others from trying to obtain credit in your name.
- Don't give credit card numbers and expiration dates by phone or online to people or businesses you don't know.

Protecting Your Accounts Online

Making purchases on the Internet has opened up new avenues for criminals to steal credit card information for illegal use. Software makers and online organizations are fighting back by continuously developing new ways to offer secure electronic transmission of customer information. In addition, there are some steps you can take to help protect your credit card and personal information when making online transactions.

- *Deal only with companies online that you know and trust.* If the retailer also has a physical brick-and-mortar store, then it is likely to be safer than an unknown merchant that exists only in cyberspace.
- *Verify website security.* If you're going to shop online, limit yourself to secure websites. You can tell if a site is secure by the URL. A secure website starts with https:// rather than http://. Secure websites will also have a small lock icon in the address bar or somewhere in the window of the browser. Among other security measures, this icon means that the information you enter will be encrypted. **Encryption** is a code that protects your account name,

number, and other information by making it unreadable to others. If you don't see the secure site icon, it isn't safe to enter your information.

■ *Don't always trust watchdog group seals.* Many sites attempt to offer assurance by displaying the seal of a nonprofit watchdog group, such as the Better Business Bureau (BBB) or TRUSTe. Sites that follow the privacy principles set forth by these organizations are allowed to display their seal. However, oversight of these seals is not fully developed yet, so not all merchants displaying these seals are legitimate.

■ *Read the company's privacy policy.* Legitimate online merchants clearly state their *privacy policy*, which explains how they use the information that you provide and how they protect your privacy. Review the policy to make sure you are comfortable with it before dealing with that company.

■ *Don't store your information on the merchant's site.* Many online merchants offer you the ability to save your credit card information on their servers to speed the shopping process for future transactions. Although it's faster to do so, there are some risks to maintaining your personal information elsewhere. For example, if a company that you're shopping with has a data breach, your personal information could be at risk.

■ *Be alert for phishing scams.* **Phishing** (pronounced "fishing") is a scam that uses online pop-up or e-mail messages to deceive you into disclosing personal information. "Phishers" send e-mail messages or direct you to websites that appear to belong to legitimate businesses but which actually are spoofed websites. The messages may ask you to verify private information, such as bank account numbers, passwords, or credit card numbers. The perpetrators then use your private information to commit fraud. Delete any messages that ask you to confirm or provide personal information. Legitimate companies don't ask for this information via e-mail.

✔ CHECKPOINT

What can you do to safeguard your credit cards?

- -

LO 1-3 Avoiding Unnecessary Credit Costs

Credit can be helpful if you use it wisely. Before deciding whether to borrow money, ask yourself these three critical questions: Do I need credit? Can I afford credit? Can I qualify for credit? If you can answer "yes" to these questions, then follow these guidelines to minimize the cost of credit.

■ *Make more than the minimum payment.* Minimum payments will result in maximum cost and will keep you in debt for a long time. For example, if you owe $5,000 on a credit card at 18 percent APR, make no further purchases, and pay only the minimum payment (often 2 percent or less of the balance owed), it will take you 33 years to pay off the debt, and you will end up paying total interest of nearly $12,000 on a loan of $5,000.

■ *Do not increase spending when your income increases.* Instead of spending the income, use it to pay off credit card debt or put it in your savings account.

■ *Accept only the amount of credit you need.* Although having credit available when you need it may be comforting, unused credit can count against you.

Unused credit is the remaining credit available to you on current accounts; it is your credit limit minus the amount you already owe. For example, if the limit on your credit card is $2,000 and you owe $1,200, your unused credit is $800. Other creditors may be reluctant to lend you money because you could at any time access the other $800, thereby increasing your debt and reducing your ability to repay their loan. It is best to keep your credit card usage to less than half of your available credit limit to avoid being categorized as a high-risk borrower.

How is unused credit both a good thing and potentially a bad thing?

- *Keep the number of credit accounts to a minimum.* Most credit counselors recommend carrying no more than two or three credit cards. The more cards you have, the greater the temptation to buy without thinking.

- *Pay off your balances as quickly as you can.* If you have the financial means to do so, pay off your balances in full to avoid interest charges. Carrying balances from month to month can hurt your credit score.

- *Pay cash for small purchases.* For many people, purchases under $25 represent daily commitments. You shouldn't charge these unless you can pay them off at the end of the month. By paying as you go, you'll avoid financing your current expenses. Paying cash will also help you realize how much you are spending. Thus, you may buy less and purchase only those items you really need.

- *Understand the cost of credit and shop around.* Think about the finance charge, the monthly payments, and the length of time you will be committed to paying off loans and credit card debt. Consider how this will affect your lifestyle and your budget for months or even years to come. Before getting a loan, shop around for the best credit terms. If the interest rate on your credit card rises, consider switching to one with a lower interest rate.

- *Take advantage of credit incentive programs.* There are two major types of credit incentive programs: rewards and rebates. With an account that has a **rewards program**, you will earn points, cash back, airline miles, or other special awards that you can redeem at a later date. With a **rebate program**, you get back a portion of what you spent in credit purchases over the year. For example, you may get a 1 percent rebate in the form of a credit to your account balance, a check that you can cash, or a Visa gift card that you can spend. While credit incentive programs offer many perks, they often have annual fees and/or high interest rates on unpaid balances.

 **CHECKPOINT**

How can you avoid unnecessary credit costs?

What Are the Consequences of Maxing Out Your Credit Card?

A credit card is "maxed out" when you have reached your credit limit and there is no room in your account for additional charges. You cannot buy anything else on credit until you pay down the current balance. Maxing out is not a good idea. Here's why:

- When you get really close to the top, it is very easy to "go over." If you have given your creditor permission to authorize purchases that put you over your credit limit, you will be charged an over-the-limit fee. Going over the limit also gives credit card issuers a reason to raise your interest rate. At the creditor's discretion, it may charge a *penalty rate*, which is an interest rate that varies by creditor but which can rise as high as 25 percent or more depending on the balance.

- When your cards are maxed out, you cannot use the card. Having the credit card offers no advantages when you cannot use it for current purchases. You must be careful not to use it until you have created enough room for additional charges.

- Having maxed-out credit cards does not look good on your credit report. It tells potential creditors that you are already overextended and unable to pay down existing debts.

- A significant portion (30 percent) of your credit score is based on how much of your available credit you're using. If you max out your credit card, you can be sure that your credit score will drop.

- People with maxed-out credit can fall prey to *"easy access" credit*, such as pay-day loans, no-credit-check loans, bad credit loans, and pawnshops. These forms of credit have very high rates of interest and put you in a cycle of borrowing beyond your means.

- When you pay down your charges regularly, credit card companies will be more willing to raise your credit limit. But when the card is maxed out, the credit card company will not likely extend additional credit, even if you need it for a major purchase.

- If you repeatedly max out your credit card, some companies will close or put a freeze on your account, requiring you to pay the entire amount in full before you can use the card again.

For all these reasons, avoid the practice of maxing out your cards. Keep a healthy amount of unused credit on hand, just in case you need it.

THINK CRITICALLY

1. How might maxing out your credit card affect your lifestyle?
2. If you were a creditor and someone with maxed-out cards asked you for a loan, would you grant it? Why or why not?

KEY TERMS REVIEW

Match the terms with the definitions. Some terms may not be used.

____ 1. Checking several places to be sure you are getting the best price for equal quality

____ 2. A code that protects private information

____ 3. A credit incentive program in which you get back a portion of what you spent in credit purchases over the year

____ 4. A legal process that allows part of your paycheck to be withheld for payment of a debt

____ 5. The remaining credit available on current accounts

____ 6. Buying something without thinking about it and making a conscious decision

____ 7. The opportunity to elect not to accept changes to policies

____ 8. A court order that allows creditors to collect debts you owe

a. comparison shopping
b. encryption
c. garnishment
d. impulse buying
e. judgment
f. opt out
g. phishing
h. rebate program
i. rewards program
j. unused credit

CHECK YOUR UNDERSTANDING

LO1-1 9. List three responsibilities you have to your creditors.

LO1-2 10. What is phishing? How does it work?

LO1-2 11. Why is it important to keep your credit card in sight at all times?

APPLY YOUR KNOWLEDGE

LO1-3 12. Explain why it is usually not a good idea to use credit to pay for day-to-day expenses, such as meals and groceries. If you do use credit for such purchases, how can you make credit work to your advantage?

THINK CRITICALLY

LO1-1 13. If you want to buy a new HDTV on credit, why is it important to comparison shop first?

LO1-2 14. When shopping online, some people store their credit card information on the retailer's website to make future transactions easier. Do you think this is a good idea? Why or why not?

LO1-3 15. Explain why you might choose a credit card with a high interest rate that has an attractive rewards program. How could you use this card effectively?

The Essential Question *Refer to The Essential Question on p. 200. Using credit wisely involves meeting responsibilities, both to yourself and to your creditor. It also means taking measures to protect your account(s) from fraud and avoiding unnecessary credit costs.*

The Essential Question *Why do credit costs vary, and how can you compute the interest on your credit?*

LEARNING OBJECTIVES

> LO 2-1 Explain why credit costs vary.
> LO 2-2 Compute and explain simple interest and APR.
> LO 2-3 Compare methods of computing the finance charge on revolving credit.

KEY TERMS

- prime rate, *208*
- fixed-rate loan, *208*
- variable-rate loan, *209*
- simple interest, *209*
- principal, *210*
- rate, *210*
- time, *210*
- down payment, *211*

LO 2-1 Why Credit Costs Vary

Several factors determine how much you will pay for the use of credit. One important factor is the method used to compute interest, explained later in the chapter. Other important factors include the following:

- *Source of credit.* Some lenders offer better credit plans than others.
- *Amount financed and length of time.* The more money you borrow and the longer you take to pay it back, the more interest you will pay.
- *Ability to repay debt.* The greater your ability to repay (creditworthiness), the better your chances of getting credit at reasonable rates.
- *Collateral.* Loans backed with collateral, such as a car, are known as *secured loans*. Because collateral offers some security to the lender in case the borrower fails to pay back the loan, secured loans typically have lower interest rates than *unsecured loans*.
- *Interest Rates.* The interest rates charged for the use of credit are usually affected by the prime rate. The **prime rate** is the interest rate that banks offer to their best business customers, such as large corporations. Individuals pay higher rates because the risk is greater to the lender. Generally, consumers will pay as much as 3 percent or more above the prime rate. Businesses are borrowing money to buy assets that will generate revenue to pay off the loan. These *production loans* are considered less risky than consumption (consumer) loans.
- *Economic conditions.* Interest rates are said to be an *economic indicator*. When you see interest rates rising, it's often because the economy is growing. Falling interest rates are an indicator that the economy is slowing. Borrowers pay more for the use of credit during periods of economic growth. When prices are rising (inflation), money is more in demand to buy higher-priced goods and services. So lenders can charge higher interest rates.
- *Type of credit or loan.* A **fixed-rate loan** is a loan for which the interest rate does not change (go up or down) over the life of the loan. For example,

© Pan Xunbin/Shutterstock.com

if you agree to a 3-year car loan with a fixed rate of 6 percent, the interest rate will remain at 6 percent for the life of the loan. With a **variable-rate loan**, the interest rate goes up and down with inflation and other economic conditions. Creditors can raise the rates on variable-rate loans and credit cards. Most borrowers find that rates go up faster during periods of rising prices than they go down during periods of falling prices. Sometimes variable-rate card agreements will state that the interest rate will rise and fall with the prime rate.

- *The business's costs of providing credit.* Businesses pass along their costs for providing credit to consumers in the form of higher finance charges and higher product prices. These costs are related to delinquent accounts (overdue, but still collectible), bad debts (probably uncollectible), and bankruptcy. Other costs of issuing credit include printing and mailing monthly statements, electronic authorization of credit charges, and salaries and facilities for a credit department. When businesses accept Visa, MasterCard, or other all-purpose credit cards, they are charged a fee each time a customer uses the card. In turn, businesses may raise prices as a way to pass along their cost of offering credit to customers.

© iStock.com/OJO_Images

What are the various costs for businesses that provide credit?

 CHECKPOINT

Why would a secured loan have a lower interest rate than an unsecured loan?

LO 2-2 Computing Interest

In Chapter 6, you learned that *interest* is the money paid by a financial institution for the use of your deposit in a savings (or other) account. In the case of a loan, interest is the cost to you of borrowing money. Businesses such as banks make money from debt; for them, debt is an investment.

Determining the cost of credit is easy using the formula for simple interest. The formula for calculating the total cost of installment credit is somewhat more complicated.

Simple Interest Formula

Simple interest is interest computed only on the amount borrowed, without compounding. The simple interest method of calculating interest assumes one payment at the end of the loan period. The cost is based on three elements: principal, rate, and time. The formula for simple interest is:

$$\text{Interest (I)} = \text{Principal (P)} \times \text{Rate (R)} \times \text{Time (T)}$$

Principal

A loan's **principal** is the amount borrowed, or the unpaid portion of the amount borrowed, on which the borrower pays interest. For example, if you borrow $10,000 to buy a car, that $10,000 is the principal, or the amount of the loan. Part of each payment you make goes toward paying down the principal. The rest of the payment is interest. After several payments, the principal on your loan may drop to $8,000, which is the unpaid portion of the amount you borrowed.

Rate

The **rate** is the percentage of interest you will pay on a loan. For example, you may agree to borrow $10,000 at 6 percent. The higher the rate, the higher the cost of the loan is.

Time

Time is the period during which the borrower will repay a loan; it is expressed as a fraction of a year: 12 months, 52 weeks, or 360 days. (In most transactions, the standard practice is to use 360 rather than 365 as the number of days in a year for computing simple interest.) For example, for a 6-month loan, the time is expressed as ½, because 6 months is half a year. If money is borrowed for 3 months, the time is expressed as ¼ (one-quarter of a year). When a loan is for a certain number of days, such as 90, the time is expressed as 90/360, or ¼.

Figure 9.1 contains a simple interest problem showing the dollar cost of borrowing. In this problem, a person has borrowed $500 and will pay interest at the rate of 12 percent a year. The loan will be paid back in 4 months.

The simple interest formula also can be used to find principal, rate, or time when any one of these factors is unknown. As shown in Figures 9.2 and 9.3, you either plug the numbers into the formula or rearrange the formula.

FIGURE 9.1   **Simple Interest**

$I = P \times R \times T$

To multiply by a percent, first change it to a decimal: drop the percent sign, and then move the decimal point two places to the left.

$I = ?$
$P = \$500$
$R = 12\%$
$T = 4 \text{ months}$

$I = \$500 \times .12 \times {}^{4}/_{12}$
$ = \$500 \times .12 \times {}^{1}/_{3}$ (Four months is ${}^{4}/_{12}$ or ${}^{1}/_{3}$ of a year)
$ = \$60 \times .3333$
$ = \$20$

FIGURE 9.2   Simple Interest (Principal)

$I = P \times R \times T$ Or change the formula to read:

$I = \$26$
$P = ?$ $P = \dfrac{I}{R \times T}$
$R = 18\%$
$T = 18 \text{ months}$

$\$26 = P \times .18 \times {}^{18}/_{12}$ $= \dfrac{\$26}{.18 \times 1.50}$
$\quad\quad = P \times .18 \times {}^{3}/_{2} \,(1.50)$
$\quad\quad = P \times .27$

$P = \$26 \div .27$ $= \dfrac{\$26}{.27}$
$\quad = \$96.30$

$\quad\quad\quad\quad\quad\quad\quad\quad = \$96.30$

FIGURE 9.3   Simple Interest (Rate)

$I = P \times R \times T$ Or change the formula to read:

$I = \$18$
$P = \$300$ $R = \dfrac{I}{P \times T}$
$R = ?$
$T = 240 \text{ days}$

$\$18 = \$300 \times R \times {}^{240}/_{360}$ $= \dfrac{\$18}{\$300 \times {}^{2}/_{3}}$
$\quad\quad = \$300 \times {}^{2}/_{3} \times R$
$\quad\quad = \$200 \times R$

$\quad\quad\quad\quad\quad\quad\quad\quad\quad = \dfrac{\$18}{\$200}$

$R = \$18 \div \$200$
$\quad = .09 \text{ or } 9\%$

$\quad\quad\quad\quad\quad\quad\quad\quad = .09 \text{ or } 9\%$

Annual Percentage Rate Formula

Instead of making one payment at the end of the loan period, consumers often use an installment plan in which they repay the loan by making regular payments over time. An installment plan is typically used to pay for a major purchase, such as a boat, a car, or furniture. An installment plan requires a **down payment**, which is part of the purchase price paid in cash up front. For example, when you buy a car, you will probably have to pay at least 10 percent of the purchase price up front in cash. The value of a car you trade in can also act as your down payment. The down payment reduces the amount of the loan.

The *annual percentage rate (APR)* is the true rate of interest you are paying when you make installment loan payments and spread interest over the life of that loan. To determine the APR for installment plans, use the formula in Figure 9.4. Work through the problem in the Math Minute to see how to apply the formula. (You can also determine the APR for installment plans using APR tables, which are more precise than using the formula. These tables can be found online by searching for "annual percentage rate tables" or "APR tables.")

FIGURE 9.4   Annual Percentage Rate

To calculate the finance charge, use the following formula:

$$\text{Finance Charge} = \text{Total Price Paid} - \text{Cash Price}$$

Where:
Total Price Paid = (number of payments × amount of each payment) + down payment
Cash Price = the total price you would have paid if you had paid in cash rather than with a loan

Then use the finance charge in the following formula to calculate the approximate annual percentage rate:

$$\text{APR} = \frac{2 \times n \times f}{P(N + 1)}$$

Where:
n = number of payment periods in one year
f = finance charge
P = principal or amount borrowed
N = total number of payments to pay off amount borrowed

Math Minute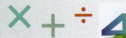

Computing the Finance Charge and APR

The Smiths are buying a new sofa. The cash price is $800. They decide to pay for it with an installment loan rather than with cash. They put $100 down and borrow $700. They will pay off the loan in one year in 12 monthly payments of $66 each. To determine their APR, you must first use the formula in Figure 9.4 to calculate their finance charge:

Total Price Paid = (12 Payments × $66) + $100 Down Payment = $892

Finance Charge = $892 Total Price − $800 Cash Price = $92

Then use the finance charge in the APR formula from Figure 9.4:

$$\text{APR} = \frac{2 \times 12 \text{ payments} \times \$92 \text{ finance charge}}{\$700 \text{ principal}(12 \text{ payments} + 1)} = \frac{\$2{,}208}{\$9{,}100}$$
$$= .2426 = 24.26\%$$

Following the above example, solve for the finance charge and APR in the following case:

Mark and Diane bought a new refrigerator. The cash price was $1,200. They paid $49 down and borrowed $1,151, which they will repay in payments of $49 per month for the next 27 months.

Solution:

Total Price Paid = (27 Payments × $49) + $49 Down Payment = $1,372

Finance Charge = $1,372 Total Price − $1,200 Cash Price = $172

$$\text{APR} = \frac{2 \times 12 \times \$172}{\$1{,}151(27 + 1)} = \frac{\$4{,}128}{\$32{,}228} = .1281 = 12.81\%$$

In the Math Minute, notice that the total price paid is more than the cash price. The total price includes all installment payments plus the down payment. Each *installment payment* includes principal and interest. The difference between the total price paid and the cash price is the finance charge.

 **CHECKPOINT**

How is simple interest different from APR?

LO 2-3 | Credit Card Billing

The cost of using an open-end (revolving) credit account, such as a credit card, varies with the method the creditor uses to compute the finance charge (interest) on the unpaid balance. Most creditors that offer revolving credit give you a *grace period* to pay your balance in full before imposing a finance charge. Creditors must tell you the method they use to calculate the finance charge because it can make a big difference in the size of your credit card bills. They must also tell you the amount of finance charges you will pay if you make only the *minimum payment*. Creditors may calculate the finance charge on open-end credit accounts using the adjusted balance method, the previous balance method, or the average daily balance method.

Adjusted Balance Method

When creditors use the *adjusted balance method*, they apply the finance charge only to the amount owed after you've paid your bill each month. For example, suppose your previous month's balance was $400 and you paid $300. If the creditor uses the adjusted balance method, you will pay additional finance charges only on the unpaid balance ($400 − $300 = $100). As you can see in Figure 9.5, the adjusted balance method results in the lowest finance charge.

FIGURE 9.5 **Three Billing Methods for Computing the Finance Charge**

The adjusted balance method, the previous balance method, and the average daily balance method produce different results. This example is based on an APR of 18% and a billing period of 30 days.

	Adjusted Balance Method	Previous Balance Method	Average Daily Balance Method
Monthly Interest Rate	1.5% (.015)	1.5% (.015)	1.5% (.015)
Previous Balance	$400	$400	$400
Payments	$300	$300	$300 (on the 15th day)
Finance Charge	$1.50	$6.00	$3.75
	($100 × .015)	($400 × .015)	(average balance of $250 × .015)*

---

*To figure average daily balance:

$$\frac{(\$400 \times 15 \text{ days}) + (\$100 \times 15 \text{ days})}{30 \text{ days}} = \$250$$

How does the billing method affect what you ultimately pay for charged purchases?

To calculate the finance charge for this month, first determine the monthly rate by dividing the annual rate (18 percent) by 12 months. In this case, the monthly rate is 1.5 percent (or .015). Then multiply the balance due of $100 by .015 to determine the finance charge of $1.50. Then add the finance charge to the balance to determine the new account balance for the next billing cycle ($101.50).

Previous Balance Method

When creditors use the *previous balance method*, they impose the finance charge on the entire amount owed from the previous month. Payments are not taken into account. As shown in Figure 9.5, this method applies the monthly rate to the entire $400 (the previous month's balance). The finance charge is added to the previous month's balance, and then the payment is deducted to arrive at the new balance ($400 + $6 − $300 = $106), which will be the amount used to calculate the finance charge for the next month. This is the most expensive way to calculate the finance charge for the credit user.

Average Daily Balance Method

Most creditors use the *average daily balance method* for computing finance charges. Using this method, creditors calculate your balance on each day of the billing cycle. Payments made during the billing cycle are applied to determine the daily balance. As shown in Figure 9.5, the credit user starts the 30-day billing cycle with a balance of $400. Then on the 15th day of the billing cycle, the credit user makes a payment of $300, leaving a balance of $100 for the remaining 15 days of the billing cycle. To compute the average daily balance, each day's balance for the billing cycle is totaled [($400 × 15 days = $6,000) + ($100 × 15 days = $1,500)] and then divided by the total number of days in the billing cycle ($7,500 ÷ 30 = $250). The average daily balance is then multiplied by the monthly interest rate to determine the finance charge ($250 × .015 = $3.75). To determine the new account balance for the next billing cycle, add the finance charge to the balance ($100 + $3.75 = $103.75). Because payments made during the period reduce the average daily balance, this method often results in a lower finance charge than does the previous balance method.

✔ **CHECKPOINT**

Which method of computing interest will cost you the most? Why?

- -

Computer Programming

Computer programmers use a variety of computer languages to write code to create software programs. They turn program designs that are created by software developers into instructions that a computer can follow. Programmers must test the programs to make sure that they work correctly. If a program does not work correctly, they must check the code for mistakes and fix them. Therefore, their work often involves trial and error and a lot of patience.

Most computer programmers work for companies in the computer systems design and related services industry. Because writing code can be done anywhere, programmers may have the option to telecommute. Some are self-employed and work for consulting firms that help businesses select and install the right kind of software and other system components that work together.

Employment Outlook

- An average rate of employment growth is expected.

Job Titles

- Programmer
- Systems Engineer
- Systems Technician
- Systems Designer

Needed Skills

- A bachelor's degree in computer science or a related subject is preferred, although an associate degree may be adequate.
- Certification in specific programming languages may be required.
- Strong problem-solving skills, the ability to think logically, and patience are required.

What's it like to work in . . . *Programming*

Juliana works in the Information Technology department for a large marketing firm. She typically works a 40-hour workweek and makes $72,000 a year. Problem solving is a big part of Juliana's job, whether she is working independently or as part of a team.

Today, Juliana is meeting with software developers, who are presenting her with a program design for new marketing research software. Juliana's job is to create the software program using the C++ programming language and to have the program up and running within two months.

Juliana will be responsible for testing the program upon its completion to ensure it produces the desired result the company wants. If problems occur, she will make the appropriate changes to the code and recheck it again until the program is functioning properly.

What About You?

Do you have an aptitude for writing detailed instructions that are logical and systematic? Do you enjoy working with a computer for most of the day? Do you like to solve problems? If so, a career in computer programming might be right for you.

KEY TERMS REVIEW

Match the terms with the definitions. Some terms may not be used.

____ 1. Part of the purchase price that is paid in cash up front

____ 2. The percentage of interest you will pay on a loan

____ 3. A loan with a set rate of interest

____ 4. The period during which the borrower will repay a loan

____ 5. The interest rate that banks offer to their best business customers

____ 6. Interest computed only on the amount borrowed, without compounding

____ 7. A loan where the interest rate goes up and down

a. down payment
b. fixed-rate loan
c. prime rate
d. principal
e. rate
f. simple interest
g. time
h. variable-rate loan

CHECK YOUR UNDERSTANDING

LO2-1 8. Explain how economic conditions affect the cost of credit.

LO2-2 9. What three elements make up the formula for simple interest?

APPLY YOUR KNOWLEDGE ANSWER

LO2-2 10. Use the following information to compute interest using the simple interest formula: (a) principal is $500, rate is 18 percent, and time is 6 months; (b) principal is $1,000, rate is 13.5 percent, and time is 8 months; and (c) principal is $108, rate is 15 percent, and time is 3 months. (Round to the nearest penny.)

THINK CRITICALLY

LO2-1 11. Explain the difference between a fixed-rate loan and a variable-rate loan. Which is better for most purchases? Why?

LO2-2 12. Which would cost you the least amount of interest: A $1,000 loan at 6 percent for 30 days or a $1,000 loan at 5 percent for 90 days?

LO2-3 13. If two credit card offers were identical except for the billing method, which of these would you choose: adjusted balance method, previous balance method, or average daily balance method? Explain.

The Essential Question *Refer to The Essential Question on p. 208. Credit costs vary based on the source of credit, the amount and length of time financed, the interest rate, your creditworthiness, the type of loan, and economic conditions. Interest can be computed by using either the simple interest formula or the APR formula.*

SUMMARY

9.1

- *Credit responsibilities to yourself include not going into debt beyond what you can comfortably repay, checking out businesses before you buy, comparison shopping, avoiding impulse buying, and using credit with the attitude that you will meet your obligations.*

- *Your responsibilities to creditors involve understanding the terms of your credit agreement, limiting your spending to amounts you can repay, and contacting the creditor immediately if you find an error on your billing statement or if your card is lost or stolen.*

- *Creditors are responsible for assisting consumers in making purchases, applying fair credit policies and informing them of the rules, promptly acknowledging any complaints, and dealing fairly with credit problems.*

- *Protect your credit card. Keep account information in a safe place. Notify creditors immediately of a lost or stolen card. Do not lend your card.*

- *To protect your cards online, deal only with companies you trust, enter personal information only on secure websites, read the site's privacy policy, and don't respond to e-mail requests for personal information.*

- *To reduce your credit costs, make more than the minimum payment each month, accept only the amount of credit you need (avoid high amounts of unused credit), have no more than two or three credit cards, pay off your balances as quickly as possible, pay cash for small purchases, and take advantage of credit incentive programs.*

9.2

- *Factors that determine the cost of credit include the source, the amount and length of time financed, your creditworthiness, whether the loan is secured or unsecured, whether the loan is fixed-rate or variable-rate, the prime rate, economic conditions, and the business's costs of providing credit.*

- *The simple interest formula does not involve compounding: Interest (I) = Principal (P) × Rate (R) × Time (T).*

- *The annual percentage rate (APR) formula calculates the costs of installment credit. It includes the down payment and all monthly payments in the total price. The difference between the total price and the cash price is the finance charge.*

- *Most creditors calculate the finance charge by using the adjusted balance method, previous balance method, or average daily balance method. The finance charge varies depending on the method used.*

APPLY WHAT YOU KNOW

LO1-1 1. Explain why it is important for consumers to be responsible with credit. How will they personally benefit?

LO1-2 2. When making online purchases, what can you do to help protect yourself from fraud?

LO1-3 3. How is a rewards program different from a rebate program?

LO2-1 4. Some retailers do not offer their own store credit card to consumers. Instead, they accept major credit cards such as Visa and MasterCard. These retailers pay fees for the charged sales—typically about 2 percent. How might adopting this policy benefit the retailer?

LO2-2 5. Using the simple interest formula, solve for the missing elements, rounding to the nearest penny: (a) interest is $8, rate is 12 percent, and time is 60 days; (b) interest is $54, rate is 18 percent, and time is 18 months; (c) principal is $2,100, interest is $510, and time is 2 years; and (d) principal is $108, interest is $36, and time is 18 months.

LO2-2 6. Using the process illustrated in Figure 9.4 and the Math Minute, determine the APR in the following cases:

    a. A $700 purchase requires a down payment of $60 with the balance to be paid in 12 monthly payments of $60 each.

    b. A $2,000 purchase requires a down payment of $100 and 24 monthly payments of $90 each.

MAKE ACADEMIC CONNECTIONS

LO1-1 7. **Consumerism** Look up a local business at the Better Business Bureau's website (www.bbb.org). Read the Bureau's review of the business and any consumer complaints posted. Prepare a one-page summary of your findings. Would you do business with this company? Why or why not?

LO1-2 8. **Research** Visit an online shopping site and follow links to the company's privacy policy. Write a one-page paper, analyzing the key points of the policy. In what ways does the company safeguard privacy? In what ways will customers give up some privacy if they buy from this company?

LO1-2 9. **Technology** Search the Internet for current articles about Internet security. What ways have hackers and thieves found to take advantage of people who are using the Internet to make purchases? How are these illegal actions being countered by businesses? Write a one-page report on your findings.

LO2-1 10. **Economics** Visit the websites of the Department of Labor (www.dol.gov), the Federal Reserve (www.federalreserve.gov), and *The Economist* magazine (www.economist.com) to learn what is currently happening with the economy and interest rates. Write a summary of your findings, predicting whether interest rates will be rising or falling. Cite expert opinions.

Solve Problems and Explore Issues

LO1-1 11. You are comparison shopping for an important birthday gift. You find the same product that you saw at a local store at an online shopping site for considerably less, so you decide to buy the product online. What will you do to be sure that your online transaction is safe?

LO1-3 12. Your friend Leanna is proud of her ability to have and use credit. She buys lunch every day on credit, and at the end of the month she pays only the minimum balance due. When she reaches the limit on one credit card, she switches to another credit card. She thinks she can just go on charging forever. Do you see any problems with Leanna's actions? Explain your answer.

LO2-1 13. Your cousin is considering whether to buy a new home theater system. She can use installment credit at the store (18 percent APR), or she can put the purchase on her credit card. Her credit card has a variable rate, which is 9.9 percent right now, but it is likely to increase in the next few months. What is your advice?

LO2-2 14. Jason's aunt gave him a loan for $200 and asked him to repay it in 9 months at 5 percent annual interest. How much will Jason owe his aunt 9 months from now?

EXTEND YOUR LEARNING

LO2-1 15. **Ethics** Creditors who make variable-rate loans are quick to raise interest rates when economic conditions change. Many people complain that when the prime rate rises by .25 percent, their loan rates go up by 3 percent or more. Creditors claim they have the legal right to raise rates, because the credit agreements allow for them to do so. Discuss the ethics of variable-rate loans. Why would consumers accept the terms of a variable-rate loan? Should restrictions be placed on creditors?

CHAPTER PROJECT

Compile materials that you will assemble in a folder called *Using Credit Wisely* that can be given to participants in a consumer credit workshop. Use what you've learned in the chapter and conduct online research to create handouts containing ten tips for the following topics: How to protect your credit cards? How to protect yourself when making online purchases? How to reduce the costs of credit? In addition, prepare a sheet describing five popular credit card rewards or rebate programs that consumers might find beneficial. Finally, obtain information describing how two different credit card companies calculate finance charges to include in the folder. Add any other items that you think would help consumers understand how to use credit more wisely.

Complete the Guided Decision Making activity for Chapter 9 at ngl.cengage.com/mypf.

Problems with Credit

Consider This...

Ann Marie has income of $1,500 a month, but when she totals her expenses, she has over $2,100 a month in bills to pay.

"I'm ready for some type of debt relief," Ann Marie told her credit counselor. "My income just doesn't cover my expenses. I didn't overspend, either. Last year, I had to have extensive dental work. I also had to get a new car because my old one was costing too much in repairs each month. And then my dog had to have surgery. The end result is that I'm buried in expenses! What options do I have to improve my debt situation?"

© Pan Xunbin/Shutterstock.com

The Essential Question *What are dangers of credit, and what can you do to avoid them?*

LEARNING OBJECTIVES

> LO 1-1 Discuss good credit management rules and warning signs that you are overextended.
> LO 1-2 List different debt relief options for consumers.
> LO 1-3 Explain how to identify and avoid credit scams.

KEY TERMS

- credit management *221*
- 20/10 Rule, *221*
- credit payment plan, *222*
- credit counseling, *224*
- debt management plan, *224*
- debt settlement program, *225*
- debt consolidation, *225*
- credit repair, *226*

LO 1-1 **Managing Credit**

Many people, from all levels of income and social standing, get into trouble with credit every year. Credit problems often do not happen suddenly. Although emergencies can, and do, occur that cause people to get buried in debt, credit problems typically arise after months and years of poor planning, impulse buying, and careless budgeting. If you recognize early enough that you are falling into excessive debt, you can take steps to fix the problem.

Exercising good **credit management** means following an individual plan for using credit wisely. It involves recognizing your limits and planning your use of credit. There are ways to practice good credit management, including following the 20/10 Rule, being aware of the warning signs that you are overextending your credit, and devising a credit payment plan.

The 20/10 Rule

Credit counselors often suggest use of the **20/10 Rule**—a plan to limit the use of credit to no more than 20 percent of your *yearly* take-home pay, with payments of no more than 10 percent of *monthly* take-home pay (see the Math Minute feature on the next page). Mortgage loans and monthly payment commitments for housing are not included in these limits. However, all other types of borrowing are included in the limits of the 20/10 Rule.

Danger Signs

Another part of credit management is recognizing when you are headed for trouble. Watch for these warning signs that you are overextending your credit.

- You pay for everything with credit.
- You are able to make only minimum payments on your balances.
- You often pay late or at the end of the grace period.
- You often pay one credit card by shifting the balance to another.

Using The 20/10 Rule

Take-home pay is roughly 70 percent of gross pay. If your annual salary is $30,000, then your take-home pay (after taxes) is $21,000 ($30,000 × .70). If your annual salary is paid in 12 equal monthly payments of $2,500, your monthly take-home pay is $1,750 ($2,500 × .70).

Using the 20/10 Rule, your total borrowing should not exceed 20 percent of annual take-home pay:

$21,000 × .20 = $4,200 maximum borrowing

Your monthly credit payments should not exceed 10 percent of monthly take-home pay:

$1,750 × .10 = $175 maximum monthly credit payments

Following the 20/10 Rule can help you keep your debt within your means to repay.

Now, assume you have an annual salary of $42,000. Apply the 20/10 Rule to determine your maximum borrowing and monthly credit payments.

Solution: $42,000 × .70 = $29,400; $29,400 × .20 = $5,880 maximum borrowing

$29,400 ÷ 12 = $2,450; $2,450 × .10 = $245 maximum monthly credit payments

- You use cash advances to pay your balances.
- You worry about how you will be able to pay your bills.
- You recognize that if an emergency arises, you would have inadequate unused credit to take care of it.
- Your credit cards are all at or near the limit.
- The credit card companies are raising the interest rates on your accounts because of late payments and charges that have exceeded your credit limit.
- You must time your payments carefully because otherwise you would not have enough income to pay your bills.
- You skip some payments in order to make other payments.
- Your credit score is falling because you have too much credit.

A Credit Payment Plan

You can also practice good credit management by designing a credit payment plan. A **credit payment plan** is a record of your debts and a strategy for paying them off.

To design a credit payment plan, gather your most recent credit card statements and make a list of all the debts you owe, with enough information to analyze which ones should be paid off first. Generally, accounts with the highest interest rates should be the first priority. Using this method will reduce the total amount of interest you pay on all credit. Focus on paying one off at a time, while making only minimum payments on others. As one card gets paid off, shift your focus to the card with the next highest priority. Once you've listed and analyzed your debt, you can prepare a plan to pay off the balances.

Assume you have the debt listed in Figure 10.1, and you have disposable income of $200 a month with which to pay credit card bills. When you add up the minimum monthly payments in Figure 10.1, it totals $125. This leaves $75 ($200 – $125) to add to the minimum payment of the card having the highest priority. Figure 10.2 illustrates the credit payment plan.

Once Visa #2 is paid off, you can take the $90 you were paying on it and add it to the minimum monthly payment of Visa #1 (the next highest-priority card). You can continue this pattern until all cards are paid off. With this credit payment plan, you will have all of your accounts paid off in 24 months.

FIGURE 10.1 Current Debt Schedule

Credit Card/ Account	Current Balance	Credit Limit	Interest Rate	Minimum Monthly Payment	Priority
1. Visa #1	$ 850	$900	18%	$ 55	2
2. Visa #2	450	500	22.9%	15	1
3. Store #1	300	200	14.9%	10	3
4. Store #2	600	400	11.9%	25	4
5. MasterCard	500	300	9.99%	20	5
Totals	$2,700			$125	

FIGURE 10.2 Credit Payment Plan

Credit Card/ Account	Current Balance	Monthly Payment	No. of Months Required	New Total Minimum Monthly Payment
1. Visa #2	$450	$ 90*	6**	$110***
2. Visa #1	850	145****	7	55
3. Store #1	300	155	3	45
4. Store #2	600	180	4	20
5. MasterCard	500	200	4	0
Total			24	

*$15 (Visa #2 minimum monthly payment) + $75 ($200 − $125) = $90.
**$450 ÷ $90 = 5 months + 1 (additional month to allow for added interest) = 6.
***$125 (total minimum monthly payments) − $15 (Visa #2 minimum monthly payment) = $110.
****$90 (monthly payment that was being paid to Visa #2) + $55 (Visa #1 minimum monthly payment) = $145.

In creating the credit payment plan, you should use the original balances for estimation purposes, because by making minimum payments, balances will go down very slowly as interest continues to accumulate. Also, the number of months required to pay off the debt will not be exact, because you are adding one extra month to allow for accumulating interest charges. Finally, the credit payment plan works best when you are responsible and do not incur new debt.

✔ CHECKPOINT

What is the purpose of a credit payment plan?

LO 1-2 Debt Relief Options

If you find that you cannot pay off your debt by practicing good credit management and you still need help to get back on your feet, there are options available to help you relieve your debt. Some of these options include contacting your creditors yourself or seeking help from a debt relief service.

Contacting Your Creditors

Before contacting a debt relief service, talk with your creditors to try to work out a modified payment plan that reduces your payments to a more manageable level. By explaining your situation, you may be able to negotiate lower interest rates, reduced late fees, a discount on the principal, or even a temporary reduction of your payments.

Using Debt Relief Services

If you are unsuccessful in your efforts to work out a payment plan with your creditors, you may want to consider seeking help from a company that offers debt relief services. There are various types of debt relief services. If you choose this route, your first option may be to get credit counseling.

Credit Counseling

Credit counseling is a service to help consumers manage their debt load and credit more wisely. It is available from nonprofit, government-sponsored, or commercial credit counseling services. Credit counselors are certified and trained in consumer credit, money and debt management, and budgeting.

Counseling sessions can be conducted in person, by phone, or online. During a typical credit counseling session, the counselor discusses your entire financial situation with you, including income, expenses, debt, the reasons for your current financial situation, and your goals. The counselor should also help you develop a personalized budget plan to deal with your money problems.

When your financial situation is serious and needs immediate action, your credit counselor may suggest you enroll in a debt management plan. With a **debt management plan**, you will make a single monthly payment to a credit counseling organization that distributes the funds to creditors based on a payment schedule. The organization uses your money to pay your unsecured debts (such as credit cards) according to the payment plan the counselor develops with you and your creditors. Typically, the creditors have agreed to lower your interest rates and waive fees. These concessions may be available only through a credit counseling organization. Usually, debt management plans take 48 months or longer to complete. You also must agree not to use credit while the plan is underway.

Credit counseling services are typically free, but clients may have to pay a fee for participating in the debt management plan. The majority of the funding for credit counseling organizations comes from creditors who receive money owed to them through the debt management plan.

You can find *consumer credit counseling services* through an online search. Consumer Credit Counseling Services (CCCS) is a nonprofit organization affiliated with the National Foundation for Credit Counseling (NFCC) and the Association of Independent Consumer Credit Counseling Agencies (AICCCA). Their websites will help you find a CCCS office near you. Some churches, private foundations, universities, military bases, credit unions, and state and federal housing authorities provide similar services.

What are the benefits of credit counseling?

Debt Settlement

A debt settlement (also called *debt negotiation*) program is not the same as credit counseling or a debt management plan. In a **debt settlement program**, a company negotiates with your creditors on your behalf to reduce the amount of debt you owe. This type of program is typically offered by a for-profit company, meaning the services are not free. The company usually requires you to make monthly payments into an account administered by a third party. When enough money has accumulated, the company then pays off the negotiated amount of debt to the creditors in one lump sum.

While the thought of having your debt reduced is appealing, there are numerous risks associated with these programs. First, many debt settlement companies charge high fees for their services. Also, many make promises or guarantees they cannot keep (such as reducing your debts by 50 percent or more). In addition, your creditors have no obligation to agree to negotiate a settlement of the amount you owe. Therefore, there is a possibility that the company will not be able to settle some of your debts, even if you set aside the monthly amounts required by the program. Another risk is that these programs often encourage or instruct clients to stop making any monthly payments to their creditors. As a result, you may continue to accumulate late fees and penalties. This will negatively impact your credit report and will harm your ability to get credit in the future. Be sure to check with the Attorney General's office of your state to verify that the debt settlement company is legally in business.

Debt Consolidation

With **debt consolidation**, a finance company loans you money to pay off your debt. They do this by offering you a *debt consolidation loan*, which simply consolidates some or all of your debt into one loan. Rather than making monthly payments to your creditors, the debt consolidation loan requires a lower monthly payment to the finance company until the debt is repaid.

At first glance, it may seem that there is no downside to debt consolidation loans—you have a lower monthly payment and more cash on hand at the end of the month, while your debts still get paid off. However, debt consolidation loans do have some disadvantages. For example, although the monthly amount on a consolidated loan is less than the monthly amount that you would pay your individual creditors, the total amount of your debt doesn't change—you are just taking longer to pay it off. Therefore, depending on the terms of your loan, you may end up paying more in interest over time than if you keep paying your individual creditors. Also, to qualify for a debt consolidation loan, you must have some type of collateral that secures the payment of the debt. Debt consolidation loans can be in the form of a *second mortgage*, with your house acting as the collateral. If you fail to make your monthly payments as agreed, you lose your collateral. In the case of a second mortgage, you would lose your house in a *foreclosure*—a legal process in which property used as collateral is sold to pay off debt.

✔ CHECKPOINT

List three forms of debt relief services.

- -

LO 1-3 Credit Scams

Credit scams are common today. They can drain your finances and hurt your credit, but can be avoided if you keep your guard up. It helps to be aware of some of the most common credit scams. You can find additional information on credit scams (as well as credit advice) at the Federal Trade Commission (FTC) website (www.ftc.gov) and at the MyMoney website (www.mymoney.gov).

Credit Repair Scams

Credit repair is the process of reestablishing a good credit rating. There are numerous companies who run ads in newspapers and on radio, TV, and the Internet that offer assistance to consumers—for a price—to repair their credit. However, you can perform the same services they offer—for free. You can obtain copies of your credit reports, challenge incorrect information, and respond to disputes. Many of the claims these companies make are false. Regardless of what they say, these companies cannot remove negative information from your credit report. Beware of credit repair offers that do the following:

- *Do not tell you your legal rights.* The Credit Repair Organization Act requires that credit repair companies explain your legal rights in a written contract that also details the services they will perform and the total cost.

- *Require you to pay a fee before the company performs any service.* The Credit Repair Organization Act also makes it illegal for credit repair companies to charge you before they have performed their services.
- *Suggest that you create a "new credit identity."* Companies that promise you a "new credit identity" often will provide you with a nine-digit number, called a Credit Profile Number (CPN) that looks like a Social Security number, or they may direct you to apply for an Employer Identification Number (EIN) from the IRS. However, it is illegal to use these numbers to apply for new credit or to default on previous debts.
- *Recommend that you do not contact the credit bureau or creditors yourself.* In many cases, it is recommended that you do contact creditors when you are having problems paying debt to try to work out a payment plan.

Advance-Fee Loans

With an *advance-fee loan*, scammers falsely promise that for an advance payment, even consumers with bad credit histories can get a loan. The payment may range from $100 to several hundred dollars.

There are some red flags to watch for that can tip you off to an advance-fee loan scam. First, legitimate lenders never "guarantee" or say that you are likely to get a loan or a credit card before you apply, especially if you have bad credit. Also, ads that promise loans often feature fee-based "900" phone numbers that consumers must call to find out about the loans. It is illegal for companies doing business by phone in the United States to promise you a loan or credit card and ask you to pay for it before they deliver.

Online Payday Loans

A *payday loan* is a cash advance from your next payroll check. Cash is received on the spot, but steep fees are charged for this service. Although these types of loans are legal, they should be considered as a last resort due to their high interest rates.

Today, many people are finding themselves tempted by ads for online payday loans. However, a large number of the online payday loan companies are nothing but scams. The payday lender asks the consumer to supply personal information along with bank account numbers so it can deposit the borrowed funds electronically. When the borrower's payment is due, the lender will withdraw the amount along with a one-time finance fee. But consumers may find that the lender makes multiple withdrawals and charges a fee each time. By the time the last withdrawal is made, the consumer may have paid two to three times the amount of the original loan. In addition, the lender may use the borrower's information to commit identity theft.

Why should consumers be cautious of online payday loans?

Credit Card Interest Rate Reduction Schemes

Many companies are using prerecorded phone calls, or *robocalls*, to reach out to consumers. Some of these companies claim to have special relationships with credit card issuers that enable them to negotiate significantly lower interest rates with creditors if you pay them an advance fee. They guarantee that the reduced rates they offer will save you thousands of dollars in interest and finance charges, allowing you to pay off your credit card debt up to five times faster. They claim that the lower interest rates are available for a limited time and that you must act now.

According to the FTC, most of these robocalls are scams. FTC investigators found that people who pay for these services don't get the interest rate reductions, don't save the promised amounts, and don't pay off their credit card debt any faster. Many struggle to get their money back from the scammers and also become victims of identity theft.

Gold and Platinum Cards

Be wary of some gold and platinum cards that promise to improve your credit rating. While they may look like all-purpose credit cards, they often permit you to buy only goods from special catalogs. Marketers of these cards often promise that participation in their credit program will lead to future credit offers, larger credit lines, and better credit reports. These claims are usually false. These cards are examples of *easy access credit*.

Most of these credit card companies charge upfront fees of $50 or more for their cards. Additional fees may be added to cover the costs of catalogs and other items. Often, ads promoting gold and platinum cards have fee-based "900" phone numbers. In addition, you may not be allowed to charge the total amount when you buy merchandise from the catalogs; instead, you must pay a cash deposit on each item you charge. For example, if the catalog price for a product is $200, you might be allowed to charge only $150, with the remaining $50 to be paid in cash.

The card offered may be "secured," which means you'll have to open and maintain a savings account as security for your line of credit. Because of the deposit required to open the savings account, this offer is not a true form of credit.

Prescreened Offers

A "prescreened" (or "preapproved") offer of credit is simply the practice of identifying potential customers. These offers are based on information in your credit report that indicates you meet certain criteria, such as a minimum credit score. This is not an offer of credit. It is merely an offer for you to apply for credit. If other criteria are not met when you apply for credit, you will be turned down and this will adversely affect your credit score. You can opt out either temporarily or permanently at www.optoutprescreen.com; this will stop the credit bureaus from selling bits of information to these buyers.

 **CHECKPOINT**

What are some key words to identify credit scams?

Government and Public Administration

Federal, state, and local governments all utilize professionals in the quest to provide consumer protections. Governments employ people in nearly every career field. Careers exist in engineering, law, health, human resources, information technology, and public relations, just to name a few.

All forms of government require qualified people in the management and implementation of public services and programs. This includes public health, safety, finance, human resources, and public relations.

City, county, and state consumer agencies offer a variety of important services. They might mediate complaints, conduct investigations, prosecute offenders of consumer laws, license and regulate professional service providers, provide education materials, and advocate for consumer rights.

Employment Outlook

- A faster than average rate of employment growth (faster than all occupations) is expected.

Job Titles

- Public Worker
- Public Safety Director
- Building Inspector
- Public Relations Specialist
- Benefits Specialist

Needed Skills

- A bachelor's or master's degree in the field of expertise is required.

- Creativity and strong communication, problem-solving, and interpersonal skills are needed.

What's it like to work in . . . Government and Public Administration

Jay works as a public relations officer in the Municipal Building along with other top city officials. He earns $55,000 annually. Jay often is under pressure to meet deadlines and goals. He has to balance the needs of the city and its residents against the funds available in the budget. He has many people that look to him for solutions to their problems.

Jay is a member of several community groups and serves as a liaison to citizen organizations, such as Neighborhood Watch. He meets with these groups regularly and keeps track of their concerns, conveying their messages to others in higher positions of government.

This morning, Jay is meeting with a concerned citizens group about the rising costs of water and waste management in the city. This afternoon, Jay is attending a meeting with the mayor to discuss a new program for low-income families in the city.

What About You?

Are you a problem solver? Can you handle several projects at the same time? Do you like working with a diverse group of people? Are you interested in the public welfare and how to make things better for society as a whole? If so, a career in government and public administration might be for you.

KEY TERMS REVIEW

Match the terms with the definitions. Some terms may not be used.

____ 1. Getting a loan from a finance company to help pay off your debt

____ 2. The process of reestablishing a good credit rating

____ 3. Following an individual plan for using credit wisely

____ 4. Having a company negotiate with creditors on your behalf to reduce the debt you owe

____ 5. A record of your debts and a strategy for paying them off

____ 6. Making a single monthly payment to a credit counseling organization that then distributes the funds to creditors based on a payment schedule

____ 7. A service to help consumers manage their debt load and credit more wisely

a. credit counseling
b. credit management
c. credit payment plan
d. credit repair
e. debt consolidation
f. debt management plan
g. debt settlement program
h. 20/10 Rule

CHECK YOUR UNDERSTANDING

LO1-1 8. Does the 20/10 Rule apply to all types of credit? Explain your answer.

LO1-3 9. What are some warning signs of credit repair scams?

APPLY YOUR KNOWLEDGE

LO1-2 10. If you are unable to pay off your debt by exercising good credit management, what other options do you have (in the order you would pursue them)?

THINK CRITICALLY

LO1-1 11. Explain how the 20/10 Rule can help you manage your use of credit. Why should consumers be concerned with credit management?

LO1-2 12. Why should individuals try to create a credit payment plan before seeking other types of credit advice?

LO1-3 13. Why are gold and platinum cards not always a good deal?

The Essential Question *Refer to The Essential Question on p. 221. Danger signs include using credit for everything, paying late or shifting balances, and having cards at or near the limit. Avoid the dangers of credit by devising your own credit payment plan. You can also contact your creditors to try to work out a modified payment plan or seek help from debt relief services.*

The Essential Question *What are the types, common causes, and advantages and disadvantages of bankruptcy?*

LEARNING OBJECTIVES

› LO 2-1 List and describe types of bankruptcy.
› LO 2-2 Discuss common causes of bankruptcy.
› LO 2-3 Explain advantages and disadvantages of declaring bankruptcy.

KEY TERMS

- bankruptcy, *231*
- voluntary bankruptcy, *232*
- discharged debt, *232*
- involuntary bankruptcy, *232*
- Chapter 7, *232*
- Chapter 13, *232*
- Chapter 11, *233*
- reaffirmation, *233*
- exempted property, *235*

LO 2-1 What Is Bankruptcy?

When a person gets into serious and irreversible debt and cannot pay the bills, the final and most serious step is bankruptcy. **Bankruptcy** is a legal process that relieves debtors of the responsibility of paying their debts or protects them while they try to repay. When you declare bankruptcy, you are said to be *insolvent*. This means you have insufficient income and assets to pay your debts. Bankruptcy is a second chance, but it casts a long, dark shadow over an individual's credit record.

Bankruptcy Laws

Bankruptcy laws in the United States have two goals. The first is to protect debtors by giving them a "fresh start," free from creditors' claims. The second goal is to give fair treatment to creditors competing for debtors' assets.

Bankruptcy laws treat two general classes of debt: secured and unsecured. *Secured debt* is a loan backed by specific assets that the debtor pledged as collateral to assure repayment. If the debtor does not pay, the creditor can take possession of the pledged assets. *Unsecured debt* is a loan not backed by any collateral. If you default, the creditor can obtain a court judgment against you to collect what you owe. Most of the debtor's assets can be used to repay unsecured debt.

What are the two main purposes of bankruptcy laws?

Types of Bankruptcy

Bankruptcy petitions can be voluntary or involuntary. **Voluntary bankruptcy**, the most common kind, occurs when a debtor files a petition with a federal court asking to be declared bankrupt. The court notifies your creditors of the pending bankruptcy. Once notice is given, creditors may file claims. The court decides how much debt you will pay, what assets you can keep, and what debts will be canceled or discharged. **Discharged debt** refers to previous debts erased by the court during bankruptcy proceedings. Creditors can no longer seek payment for these debts. Some debts are not discharged and must still be paid. These include child support, alimony, income taxes and penalties, student loans, and court-ordered damages due to malicious or illegal acts.

Involuntary bankruptcy occurs when creditors file a petition with the court, asking the court to declare the debtor bankrupt. Involuntary bankruptcy petitions do not occur very often because most creditors would prefer to be repaid in full over a period of time rather than settle only for a portion of the debtor's remaining assets.

The bankruptcy process deals with debtors in one of two ways: liquidation or reorganization. Under *liquidation*, the court sells the debtor's assets and uses the proceeds to pay as much of the debt as possible. Usually the value of all of the debtor's assets is not enough to pay off all the debts. The court appoints a trustee to sell the assets and give each creditor a share. Under *reorganization*, debtors may keep their property but must submit a payment plan to the court for repaying a substantial portion of their debts. The types of bankruptcy available to individuals can be distinguished by which of these two methods is used.

Chapter 7 Bankruptcy

Commonly called *straight bankruptcy*, **Chapter 7** is a liquidation form of bankruptcy for individuals. It wipes out most debts in exchange for giving up most assets. Some assets that are considered necessary for survival may be retained.

The advantage of Chapter 7 bankruptcy is immediate debt relief—large debts are wiped out as well as any payments on the debt. As soon as bankruptcy is filed, all collections must stop. Debtors have a clean slate to start over. However, bankruptcy laws passed in 2005 have made it more difficult for a person to qualify for Chapter 7 bankruptcy.

Chapter 13 Bankruptcy

Chapter 13 is a reorganization (payment plan) form of bankruptcy for individuals. It allows debtors to keep most of their property and use their income to pay a portion of their debts over three to five years. Debtors work out a court-enforced repayment plan whereby they make a single monthly payment directly to the court. The court then disburses the funds to the creditors. Under Chapter 13, some debts are totally discharged, while others are paid off as agreed within the payment plan. Chapter 13 may seem like a better option for the debtor in terms of reestablishing credit. However, the blemish on the debtor's credit record caused by any form of bankruptcy is hard to overcome for many years.

Chapter 11 Bankruptcy

Chapter 11 is a reorganization form of bankruptcy for businesses that allows them to continue operating under court supervision as they repay their restructured debts. Chapter 11 bankruptcy is most often associated with corporations, but can be used by small businesses. In rare cases, individuals can file Chapter 11 bankruptcy. Wealthy individuals who have a number of investment properties may have debts that are too high to qualify for Chapter 13 but do qualify for Chapter 11.

Reaffirmation of Debt

Creditors may ask debtors to agree to pay their debts, even after bankruptcy has discharged them. **Reaffirmation** is an agreement to pay debts that have been legally discharged. You may choose to reaffirm a particular debt if a friend or family member cosigned the loan and you don't want to burden this person with the debt. Also, you may choose to reaffirm rather than allow the collateral, such as a car, to be repossessed. Reaffirmation requires a court hearing, and debtors have 60 days to change their minds about promising to repay. A creditor is prohibited from harassing debtors to reaffirm after the court proceedings are over.

Bankruptcy Counseling

If you plan to file for bankruptcy, you must receive credit counseling from a government-approved organization within 180 days before you file. The counseling session should include an evaluation of your personal financial situation, a discussion of alternatives to bankruptcy, and a personal budget plan. You also have to complete a debtor education course before your debts can be discharged. The debtor education course should include information on developing a budget, using credit wisely, and managing money.

A person who is considering filing for bankruptcy should also seek good legal advice. Since the passage of new bankruptcy laws in 2005, the process for filing for bankruptcy has become very complex. A good bankruptcy attorney can assist you in deciding which bankruptcy plan will work best to help you solve your credit problems and also help you navigate through the details and required forms that you must complete.

Why is it best to seek legal advice if you are filing for bankruptcy?

✓ CHECKPOINT

List the types of bankruptcy options for individuals.

Some businesses, such as credit card companies, believe that consumers abuse credit laws and take advantage of creditors. They believe bankruptcy laws are too lenient and make it possible for people to run up debts and then walk away from them. These businesses believe that credit is a privilege and not a right, and people should be held accountable for their decisions.

Others believe that credit laws are designed to protect consumers from unscrupulous businesses that would take advantage of them. Bankruptcy is the ultimate protection to give consumers a new start when they get buried in debt that they can never repay. Those holding this viewpoint believe that creditors use deceptive practices to lure people into buying things they cannot afford. Then they raise interest rates when consumers fall behind on their payments, trapping consumers into a cycle of debt.

THINK CRITICALLY

With which side do you agree? What is your attitude toward credit laws, such as bankruptcy protection for consumers?

© Vectomart/Shutterstock.com

LO 2-2   Common Causes of Bankruptcy

There are many reasons why people are forced or choose to declare bankruptcy. Common causes include job loss, medical expenses, divorce, unexpected disasters, and poor financial planning.

Job Loss

According to Consumers Union, two-thirds of people who have filed bankruptcy have been unemployed for a period of time before the filing. The loss of income from being laid off or terminated from a job can be catastrophic. Those who have debts and are unable to find full-time employment for an extended period of time may not be able to recover from this and be forced to file for bankruptcy. While you cannot control unexpected events in life, such as a layoff, you can plan and save for them. Rather than spend all your income, save a portion each month to help you get through rough financial times.

Medical Expenses

A recent study showed that medical expenses are the biggest cause of bankruptcy. Many people are uninsured or underinsured. Serious illnesses or injuries can easily cost hundreds of thousands of dollars in medical bills. For example, a person hospitalized for a long period of time with a critical illness could easily owe $100,000 a month for medical care, drugs, room charges, and other fees. These bills can wipe out savings and retirement accounts in months. Once these have been exhausted, bankruptcy may be the only option left.

Divorce

Dissolution of marriage creates tremendous financial strain on both partners in the form of legal fees, child support, and/or alimony, as well as the burden of providing for a household on one income. The legal costs alone are enough to force some to file bankruptcy, while wage garnishments to cover back child support or alimony can hinder others of the ability to pay the rest of their bills.

Unexpected Disasters

Loss of property due to theft or casualty, such as a house fire or natural disaster, can be nearly impossible to prepare for. As with medical insurance, many homeowners and renters are uninsured or underinsured. Those without homeowners or renters insurance may find it impossible to recover from debt related to these catastrophes and be forced into bankruptcy.

Poor Financial Planning

Many people who go bankrupt do not have a sound financial plan. They spend their money carelessly or impulsively and do not follow a budget. Credit card bills, large mortgages, and other loan payments eventually spiral out of control. No matter what your financial position, you must keep your spending and borrowing in proportion to your income. Most causes of bankruptcy can be avoided by careful planning and sound decision making, based on good financial judgment, advice, and goals.

CHECKPOINT

What things can lead to bankruptcy?

LO 2-3 Bankruptcy: Friend or Foe?

Bankruptcy has its pluses, but it also comes with its downside. A person considering bankruptcy should carefully weigh the advantages and disadvantages of declaring bankruptcy before making a decision.

Advantages of Bankruptcy

For individuals whose debt situation seems hopeless, bankruptcy offers a solution. While this solution is not without a price, bankruptcy does offer the following advantages:

- *Debts are erased.* The biggest advantage that bankruptcy offers is a fresh start from most debts. It reduces or eliminates overwhelming bills, and the debtors can start over. With good financial planning and counseling, they can avoid future credit problems.
- *An automatic stay is enacted.* Once a bankruptcy petition is filed, an automatic stay is enforced, which stops lawsuits filed against the debtor and temporarily prevents creditor actions such as repossessions, garnishments, foreclosures, utility shutoffs, and in many cases, evictions. Although the automatic stay is temporary, in the case of foreclosure, it allows the debtor more time to find other housing, to work out a payment plan with the lender, or to sell the house before foreclosure.
- *Exempted assets are retained.* While Chapter 7 bankruptcy requires debtors to give up most of their assets to erase their debts, they can keep certain amounts and types of exempted property, or those assets considered necessary for survival. Exempted property includes a limited amount of equity in a residence, interest in a vehicle, personal property and furnishings, clothing, some jewelry, and tools of a trade, including books and equipment. Exempted items allow the debtor to start over and have a base with which to begin.

- *Certain incomes are unaffected.* Bankruptcy will not affect certain types of income a debtor may have, such as Social Security, veterans' benefits, unemployment compensation, alimony, child support, disability payments, and payments from pension, profit-sharing, and annuity plans.

Disadvantages of Bankruptcy

While bankruptcy offers debt relief, it carries serious consequences. Bankruptcy should be considered a last resort. Some of the disadvantages of bankruptcy include the following:

- *Credit is damaged.* Filing bankruptcy can destroy your credit rating. A *bankruptcy judgment* stays on your credit record for seven years (Chapter 13 bankruptcy) or ten years (Chapter 7 bankruptcy). During that time, you could find it very difficult or impossible to obtain credit. If you are able to get credit, it would be at a very high interest rate because you would be considered a high risk. Bankruptcy is a red flag to creditors and others that you were at one time unable or unwilling to meet your financial responsibilities.
- *Property is lost.* Most of your property will be taken and sold to pay your debts. Even if you have an automatic stay, a creditor can file a motion to have it lifted. You may not even be able to keep exempt assets, such as your house. Assume that you own a house worth $120,000 that has a mortgage of $90,000 against it. Your equity is $30,000. While the current bankruptcy code allows you to keep the first $22,975 of equity in your home, you may be required to sell the home. You will be allowed to keep $22,975, and the remaining amount must be used to pay off creditors.

What kind of debts are not erased by bankruptcy?

- *Some debts continue.* Regardless of the type of bankruptcy selected, all debt is not erased. Certain obligations, such as child support and alimony, will remain after bankruptcy. Income taxes and related penalties that are less than three years old, student loans, and other debts at the discretion of the bankruptcy court will also remain. Also, if a lender can prove that there was any type of false representation on the debtor's part in connection with a debt, the debt will not be discharged.
- *Cosigners must pay.* After you have been declared bankrupt under Chapter 7, any cosigners you had must repay the loans they cosigned. Cosigners are likely to be your close friends or family members. Leaving them saddled with the debt can damage your personal relationships.

✔ CHECKPOINT

What are some major advantages and disadvantages of bankruptcy?

When Is Bankruptcy the Best Choice?

Ben and Michelle were married less than two years when she became pregnant with their first child. The pregnancy appeared to be normal until shortly before the expected delivery date. At that time, it was discovered that the baby would be born with serious health problems, including a hole in her heart, birth defects that would leave her deaf, and underdeveloped organs that would require considerable medical attention.

Six months later, Ben and Michelle's baby daughter had survived six weeks in the hospital, three surgeries, and a poor prognosis. She would have to undergo several more surgeries to repair the damage and birth defects. Ben had health insurance, but many procedures were considered "experimental" and the insurance company would not pay for them. Still, the couple wanted their daughter to survive, so they pledged their house and all other assets to secure medical care.

When the baby was a year old, she had her last operation. It both repaired her hearing loss and allowed for the removal of feeding tubes so that she could, for the first time, eat on her own. When the final medical bills came in, the couple found themselves owing more than $500,000 to hospitals, doctors, labs, and surgeons.

Faced with payments that were overwhelming, the couple elected to file for bankruptcy. It was the best choice for several reasons. First, even by spreading out payments over ten years, they would be unable to meet other financial obligations. Second, the debt would prevent them from moving forward with a financial plan for the future of their child as well as their own financial security. Third, bankruptcy allowed them the debt relief they needed to avoid the stress of overwhelming debt.

THINK CRITICALLY

1. Do you agree that filing bankruptcy was the best option for Ben and Michelle? Explain why or why not.

2. Do you know someone who has faced a financial disaster for which bankruptcy was (or might yet be) the best solution? Explain why. As an alternative, describe a situation in which you think bankruptcy would be the best solution.

3. Assume you know someone who is facing bankruptcy because of overspending, careless planning, or greed. What advice would you give this person?

KEY TERMS REVIEW

Match the terms with the definitions. Some terms may not be used.

____ 1. A legal process that relieves debtors of the responsibility of paying their debts or protects them while they try to repay

____ 2. A liquidation form of bankruptcy for individuals

____ 3. A reorganization form of bankruptcy for businesses

____ 4. Bankruptcy that occurs when the debtor files a petition with a federal court

____ 5. Bankruptcy that occurs when creditors file a petition with the court against a debtor

____ 6. Previous debts erased by the court during bankruptcy proceedings

____ 7. Assets considered necessary for survival that a bankrupt debtor is allowed to keep

____ 8. An agreement to pay debts that would otherwise be discharged

a. bankruptcy
b. Chapter 7
c. Chapter 11
d. Chapter 13
e. discharged debt
f. exempted property
g. involuntary bankruptcy
h. reaffirmation
i. voluntary bankruptcy

CHECK YOUR UNDERSTANDING

LO2-1   9. How is involuntary bankruptcy different from voluntary bankruptcy?

LO2-1   10. Why might someone choose to reaffirm a particular debt?

LO2-2   11. How can financial planning help you avoid bankruptcy?

APPLY YOUR KNOWLEDGE

LO2-2   12. List the common causes of bankruptcy for individuals. Next to each one, explain what you could do to avoid bankruptcy caused by these events.

THINK CRITICALLY

LO2-1   13. How is Chapter 7 different from Chapter 13 bankruptcy? Which do you think is the best form for a person with enormous debts? Why?

LO2-3   14. Explain when bankruptcy may be the best option for some consumers.

LO2-3   15. Do you believe the advantages of bankruptcy outweigh the disadvantages? Explain your answer.

The Essential Question *Refer to The Essential Question on p. 231. Bankruptcy can be Chapters 7, 11, or 13. Bankruptcy may result from medical expenses, job loss, divorce, unexpected disasters, and poor financial planning. Although bankruptcy erases most debts, debtors will lose property and damage their credit record.*

SUMMARY

10.1

- *Consumers should have a responsible credit management plan. The 20/10 Rule suggests that your total debt not exceed 20 percent of yearly take-home pay and that your monthly payments not exceed 10 percent of your monthly take-home pay.*

- *Some danger signs that you are overextended include buying everything with credit, paying late, paying off your balance with cash advances, and having inadequate unused credit to meet emergencies.*

- *Consumers should manage their credit with a credit payment plan, which is a strategy to pay off accounts with the highest interest rate first.*

- *If exercising good credit management doesn't pay off your debt, contacting your creditors to try to work out a new payment plan or seeking relief using debt relief services is an option.*

- *Common credit scams include credit repair scams, advance-fee loans, on-line payday loans, credit card interest rate reduction schemes, and gold and platinum credit cards.*

10.2

- *Bankruptcy laws are designed to help people get a "fresh start" and to provide fair treatment to creditors competing for the debtor's assets.*

- *Bankruptcy may be voluntary (filed by the debtor) or involuntary (filed by creditors against the debtor).*

- *Chapter 7 is a liquidation form of bankruptcy for individuals in which debtors must give up most of their assets in exchange for having debts discharged.*

- *Chapter 13 is a reorganization form of bankruptcy for individuals in which debtors may keep most of their property and repay a portion of their debts following a court-enforced repayment plan.*

- *Chapter 11 bankruptcy is a reorganization form of bankruptcy primarily for businesses.*

- *Common causes of bankruptcy are medical expenses, job loss, divorce, unexpected disasters, and poor financial planning.*

- *Advantages of bankruptcy are that debts are erased, an automatic stay is enacted, exempted assets are retained, and certain incomes are unaffected.*

- *Disadvantages of bankruptcy are that credit is damaged, property is lost, some debts continue, and cosigners must still pay.*

APPLY WHAT YOU KNOW

LO1-1   1. Marcos and Elena have the following debts:
- Credit Card #1: $2,000 balance, 18 percent interest, minimum payments of $30 per month
- Credit Card #2: $1,000 balance, 15 percent interest, minimum payments of $20 per month
- Credit Card #3: $3,000 balance, 24.99 percent interest, minimum payments of $50 per month
- Store Account: $800 balance, 21 percent interest, minimum payments of $40 per month.

Prepare a credit payment plan. How many months will it take to pay off their credit cards if they have $200 a month to apply toward credit payments?

LO1-2   2. Search the Yellow Pages, business directories, and the Internet, and list several of the following: (a) nonprofit credit counseling services, (b) finance companies that offer debt settlement programs, (c) attorneys specializing in bankruptcy, (d) classes or other credit counseling services provided in the community, either for a fee or free. Visit the website of one organization of each type and write a brief summary of the kinds of information and services it provides.

LO2-2   3. Jorj and Mandy both have full-time jobs, and Jorj is also taking on a part-time job so he can buy a boat. Neither set aside any of their income in savings. Explain the realities of this type of lifestyle, such as what would happen if the economy went bad or if one of them lost his or her job.

LO2-3   4. Check the classified section of your newspaper for bankruptcy notices every day for one week. Answer these questions: (a) How many total bankruptcies were filed in one week? (b) What were the lowest and highest amounts of debt claimed? (c) What were the lowest and highest amounts of property claimed as exempt?

MAKE ACADEMIC CONNECTIONS

LO1-3   5. **Consumerism** Select one of the credit scams discussed in this chapter, including credit repair scams, advance-fee loans, online payday loans, credit card interest rate reduction schemes, and gold and platinum cards. Conduct online research to find a real-world example of someone who fell victim to this scam. Write a short report describing how it happened and the end result.

LO2-3   6. **Economics** Although bankruptcy is used by consumers to get a "fresh start," it has other effects on businesses and the economy. Research the impacts on our economy and prepare a short report.

LO2-3   7. **International Studies** Choose another nation in the world. Conduct research and prepare a table that compares the bankruptcy law in that country to U.S. bankruptcy law.

Solve Problems and Explore Issues

LO1-1 8. Your friend Al has trouble paying his bills. He has taken a second job in order to make all of his payments, but the long hours and hard work are causing him health problems. What suggestions do you have in helping him manage his credit problems?

LO1-2 9. Ethan and June have decided to get help with their credit problems rather than declare bankruptcy. They are hoping to get lower interest rates, have their late fees waived, and/or extend the time for repaying loans. What options do they have?

LO2-1 10. Betty owns a small store. The store has been losing money for some time. Because she is the sole owner of the business, her personal assets are at risk. Explain to Betty the differences among Chapters 7, 11, and 13 bankruptcies. Which type of bankruptcy would you recommend and why?

LO2-3 11. Dan is considering bankruptcy. He has the following assets: $34,000 equity in home, $5,000 equity in motor vehicle, $500 in personal items and clothing, $2,000 in appliances and furnishings, $2,000 in tools of trade, and $8,000 in jewelry. Search online for the federal bankruptcy exemption amounts for the current year. How much (total) will he be allowed in exempted items?

EXTEND YOUR LEARNING

LO2-1 12. **Legal Issues** Willfully hiding assets (in storage units or other places) so that they cannot be used to pay off debts is called *bankruptcy fraud*. It is a serious federal crime. It is also illegal to transfer title to assets to relatives or friends so that the assets won't be part of the bankruptcy estate. The bankruptcy trustee must be able to access a debtor's full assets to distribute lawful amounts to creditors fairly. Why do people try to hide and transfer assets? How could they get caught? What are the penalties for this type of crime? Do you think the penalties are fair? Why or why not?

CHAPTER PROJECT

Conduct research on federal bankruptcy laws, starting with the original Bankruptcy Act of 1898. As part of your research, learn about other major federal bankruptcy laws throughout history, including the Bankruptcy Abuse Prevention and Consumer Protection Act of 2005. Write a report that summarizes the most important provisions of the laws and explain why they were enacted. To enhance your report, use visuals, such as a timeline, and graphics, such as a chart depicting the rise of bankruptcies over the years.

Complete the Guided Decision Making activity for Chapter 10 at **ngl.cengage.com/mypf**.

Donald Trump

© Christopher Halloran/Shutterstock.com

Real estate entrepreneur and billionaire Donald Trump was born in Queens, New York, on June 14, 1946. While studying at the Wharton School of Business at the University of Pennsylvania, Trump began his business career at his father's real estate development company, Elizabeth Trump & Son. In 1971, he was given control of the organization, which he renamed The Trump Organization, and began taking on larger building projects.

During the 1980s, Trump expanded into the casino gambling business. In 1983, he built Trump Plaza Hotel and Casino. In 1986, Trump purchased a Hilton Hotels casino-hotel in Atlantic City and renamed the $320-million complex Trump Marina. In 1988, Trump acquired the largest hotel-casino in the world, Taj Mahal casino.

Trump's business deals brought him great wealth, but they also led to a mountain of debt. In 1990, the real estate market declined, reducing the value of and income from Trump's empire. Banks and investors with Trump lost hundreds of millions of dollars, and Trump was forced to file for Chapter 11 bankruptcy in 1991 and again in 1992. However, Trump managed to restructure his debt and made a remarkable comeback. The late 1990s saw Trump building the Trump World Tower, a 72-story residential tower in New York City, and Trump Place, a multibuilding development along the Hudson River, among his many projects.

In 2004, it was necessary for Trump to restructure his debt once again. Seeking voluntary bankruptcy to protect his personal interests, Trump was able to re-emerge with much of his business in place. The real estate collapse that began in 2007 led Trump to file for Chapter 11 bankruptcy again in 2009.

As you can see, Trump has had a very up-and-down business career, relying heavily on credit to finance his many large-scale ventures and on U.S. bankruptcy laws to bail him out of debt. Despite declaring bankruptcy four separate times, Trump's personal wealth is estimated at $7 billion.

THINK CRITICALLY

1. Large building projects rely on the use of long-term debt. Comment on Donald Trump's ability to secure financing throughout this life.

2. Trump benefited greatly from bankruptcy laws in the United States. Explain how he was able to preserve his personal wealth.

Managing Credit and Debt

Overview

In the Unit 2 project, you will learn more about managing credit and debt by analyzing your use of credit and assessing your debt load. You will also assess your level of ethics when faced with circumstances involving credit.

Your Use of Credit

Credit will enable you to enjoy a standard of living that otherwise would not be possible. Nearly everyone uses credit. Wise consumers analyze their use of credit, comparing sources, interest rates, minimum payments, and other features (such as rebates). Understanding your current credit and planning future credit purchases is a part of exercising good credit management. To analyze your use of credit, complete Worksheet 1 provided for you in the *Student Activity Guide* and also presented for reference on the next page.

When examining your use of credit, you may want to keep control sheets for tracking your progress in paying off debts. A sample control sheet is shown in Figure U2.1. You can make similar sheets for each credit account and track the monthly payments. At the end of the year, you can total the finance charge.

Keeping credit control sheets will help you see the true cost of your credit card purchases. It will also encourage you as you see the debt going down.

© Goodluz/Shutterstock.com

WORKSHEET 1
Credit Analysis

Directions: List each type of credit you have and its features. Then complete the analysis to determine what action can and should be taken.

	Monthly Payment	No. of Payments Left	Outstanding Balance	APR	Special Features	Ranking
Installment credit:	_____	_____	_____	_____	_____	_____
Personal loans:						
Automobile	_____	_____	_____	_____	_____	_____
Home improvement	_____	_____	_____	_____	_____	_____
Other:_____	_____	_____	_____	_____	_____	_____
_____	_____	_____	_____	_____	_____	_____
Charge accounts:						
1._____	_____		_____	_____	_____	_____
2._____	_____		_____	_____	_____	_____
3._____	_____		_____	_____	_____	_____
Total debt outstanding..			$_____			
Average APR..				_____		

How long will it take to pay off the outstanding debt? (Total outstanding debt divided by total monthly payments)

_____

Which debts do you feel comfortable with? _____

_____

Which debts will you pay off first (those with highest rates/priority ranking)? _____

_____

_____

What are some anticipated future debt needs?_____

_____

_____

Which credit sources will you use for future debt (those with lowest rates)?_____

_____

_____

FIGURE U2.1 Credit Control Sheet

Control Sheet: VISA Account

(1) Date	(2) Previous Balance	(3) Payments (Credits)	(4) New Charges (Debits)	(5) Finance Charge	(6) New Balance (2 − 3 + 4 + 5)
1/1	$280.63	$35.00	$20.00	$7.22	$272.85
2/3	272.85	35.00	0	7.01	244.86
3/2	244.86	35.00	15.00	6.88	231.74
3/4	231.74	35.00	0	6.55	203.29

Comparing Credit Cards Online

As part of good credit management, you should do your homework to determine which credit card is the best deal. The Internet makes this process much easier. Many websites allow you to compare credit card offers. Some websites even rank the best credit cards based on categories, such as best credit card for travelers, small business owners, and college students. The pros and cons of various credit cards are clearly identified, making it easier to determine which card best meets your needs.

Credit card features that are important to most users are listed in Worksheet 2 in the *Student Activity Guide* and also provided below for reference. Find a credit card comparison website and complete this table for two different credit cards.

WORKSHEET 2
Credit Card Comparison Chart

	Credit Card #1	Credit Card #2
Name of credit card		
Type of credit card (charge card or revolving account)		
Annual percentage rate		
Introductory rate		
Annual fee		
Transaction fees (cash advances, balance transfers, etc.)		
Penalty fees (late fees, over-the-limit fees, etc.)		
Grace period		
Rewards program/Rebate plan		
Other features (credit guard, travel accident insurance, extended warranty, etc.)		

Guarding Your Credit

As a consumer and wise financial manager, it is your responsibility to take charge of your own credit, credit history, credit report, and credit score. By monitoring it and following the right steps, credit will be there for you when you need it. At its website, the Federal Reserve System answers questions consumers may have about credit. Visit this site at www.federalreserve.gov and click on the "Consumer Information" link. Review the Fed's advice about guarding your credit and understanding your credit report and credit score.

Use the Federal Reserve System website or other credible sites, such as the Federal Trade Commission website or a national credit bureau (Equifax, Experian, or TransUnion) website, to answer the questions in Worksheet 3, which is provided for you in the *Student Activity Guide* and also presented for reference below. When doing research, look for the latest tips on how to effectively guard and manage your credit. Being educated is an important step to take to protect your credit now and in the future.

WORKSHEET 3
Guarding Your Credit

1. Why is a credit report important to me, both now and in the future?

2. How can I get a free copy of my credit report?

3. Who else can see my credit report?

4. How long does negative information, such as late payments, stay on my credit report? Is there anything I can do to speed up the process?

5. What can cause my credit score to change? What is my role in that process?

6. How can I correct errors on my credit report? What is the cost?

7. What other suggestions about guarding and managing your credit does the website offer?

Your Debt Load

Debt represents future earnings already spent. Unfortunately, many people never assess how much future income they have already committed to debt and whether the types and sources of credit they use are most advantageous to them. You can avoid this trap by periodically making a careful assessment of your debt load throughout your life. A *debt load* is the amount of outstanding debt at a particular time. Whether your debt load is acceptable to you will depend on your ability to meet the regular payments, your ability to pay off the debt quickly if necessary, and your level of comfort with the amount of debt you owe.

Complete your debt-load analysis, using Worksheet 4 provided for you in the *Student Activity Guide* and also presented for reference below. Compute your self-score. Assessing your debt load will help you determine the severity of your debt problem so that you can take corrective action if necessary. In addition, it allows you to make projections for future income and outgo on a yearly basis. It's important to pinpoint your spending habits, analyze them, and take steps to improve your financial picture.

WORKSHEET 4
Your Debt Load

Directions: Answer the following statements with a "Yes" or "No." Then read the information following the statements to make an assessment of your debt load.

1. You pay only the minimum amount due each month on charge and credit accounts.	YES	NO
2. You make so many credit purchases that your debt load (total debts outstanding) never shrinks.	YES	NO
3. You are usually not able to make it until the end of the month and must borrow from savings.	YES	NO
4. You have borrowed from parents or others and do not have plans to repay the debt.	YES	NO
5. You are behind on one or more of your payments.	YES	NO
6. You worry about money often and are discouraged.	YES	NO
7. Money is a source of arguments and disagreements in your family.	YES	NO
8. You often juggle payments, paying one creditor while giving excuses to another.	YES	NO
9. You really don't know how much money you owe.	YES	NO
10. Your savings are slowly disappearing, and you are unable to save regularly.	YES	NO
11. You've taken out loans to pay off debts or have debt consolidation loans.	YES	NO
12. You are at or near the limit of your credit lines on credit and charge accounts.	YES	NO
13. You worry more about the amount of the payment than the amount of interest (interest rate) you are paying on loans.	YES	NO

ASSESSMENT: Total number of "Yes" answers _____

If you answered "Yes" to 8 or more statements, you need to take immediate action to correct your debt load. If you answered "Yes" to 4–7 statements, you should seek to remedy the defects in your debt load soon. If you answered "Yes" to 1–3 statements, you are in pretty good shape and can solve your debt problems. If you answered "No" to all of the statements, congratulations—keep up the good work!

Ethical Decisions

Ethics are principles of morality or rules of conduct. Ethical behavior conforms to these rules; unethical behavior violates them. Ethical behavior becomes a problem when other people get hurt by your actions. You may have many opportunities to take advantage of other people. When these opportunities come your way, stop and think how you might feel if you were victimized.

Worksheet 5 lists some circumstances involving credit. Think about how you might react to each circumstance. To develop skill in analyzing ethical issues, complete the situational analysis using Worksheet 5 provided for you in the *Student Activity Guide* and also presented for reference below.

WORKSHEET 5
Situational Analysis

For each situation described below, explain how you would respond and why. What are the ethical issues involved in each decision?

1. You walk by an ATM in a mall. You see a bank debit card that was left there by a previous user. You look around and there is no one nearby to claim the card. If you leave it there, someone else may find it. What would you do?

2. You make a payment on your credit account at a customer service center. The worker, who is new and in training, accidentally credits your account for more than you paid. For example, you gave her $25 and she credited your account twice, totaling $50. What would you do?

3. Someone you know returns merchandise to a store and gets a credit on his charge account, knowing that he purchased the merchandise elsewhere. What would you do?

4. Your friend frequently buys clothing on credit, wears it to a special event, and returns it to the store before the account is due, claiming the garment is damaged or dirty. She then receives a credit or a refund for the merchandise. What would you do?

5. Your friend Tonya wants to borrow money, but you have none to give her. You have loaned money to her in the past, but she has not repaid it. Your other friend Sally has some extra money from a side job. If you vouch for your friend Tonya, then Sally will lend her the money based on your word. What would you do?

6. Another customer at the credit union where you belong has the same last name as you. Last month, the customer made her car payment of $350, but the credit union accidentally posted her payment to your savings account. It has been a month and nothing has happened; the credit union has not reversed the entry. What would you do?

Managing Resources

© iStock.com/Isaac Koval

Unit 3 begins with personal decision making. You will learn how to make good decisions based on your values, your needs and wants, and your personal goals. Although your goals will change over time, the decision-making process will remain constant and can be used for guidance throughout your life.

When you leave home for the first time, you will face many housing options, such as where to live, whom to live with, and how to divide responsibilities. In addition to learning about these options, you'll also learn about renting or buying a home.

Buying a car, whether new or used, takes thought and preparation. All of the costs, from depreciation to accessories, will be presented. You'll also learn how to maintain your car and preserve its resale value.

Family life is explored in Chapter 15. Marriage, family decision making and compromise, and vacation planning are just a few of the topics discussed.

© Pan Xunbin/Shutterstock.com

Personal Decision Making

11.1   **Making Better Decisions**

11.2   **Spending Habits**

Consider This...

Hector is preparing to go to college in the fall and isn't sure what he'll do with his summer. He can work full time and save more money, or he can go out with his friends and enjoy the break between high school and college.

"Making this decision is really tough," Hector said. "I'd like to have a fun summer with my friends. On the other hand, if I work, I can set aside more money. This would help reduce my student loans and make college less stressful in terms of financing. For me, it's a toss-up. Most of my friends are taking the summer off, and I could join them for one last time. Part of me says that's the right thing to do, but then part of me says it would be more responsible to set aside money for the future."

"That's a good point," said Hector's older brother. "When you're in college, you will have to devote a lot of your time to classes and studying, so you may not have as much time to work. It's probably a good idea to work over the summer and set aside some of your earnings for college expenses."

The Essential Question *How can the decision-making process help you prioritize your wants and needs?*

LEARNING OBJECTIVES

> LO 1-1 Apply the decision-making process to solve consumer problems.
> LO 1-2 Explain economic wants and needs that influence consumer decision making.

KEY TERMS

- sunk cost, *252*
- trade-off, *253*
- opportunity cost, *253*
- basic needs, *254*
- life-enhancing wants, *254*
- values, *254*
- personal preferences, *254*
- collective values, *255*
- innovations, *256*
- public goods, *256*

LO 1-1 The Decision-Making Process

To make better purchase decisions, you should use a rational, step-by-step process to define your needs and evaluate alternatives before making a final choice. This process helps you decide how to use your money in ways that will benefit you most.

Step 1: Define the Problem or Goal

The first step in the decision-making process is to define the problem you want to solve or a goal you wish to achieve. Once it is identified, you can look for ways to resolve it in a manner that fits your financial resources now and in the future.

Defining the problem or goal is not as easy as it sounds. For example, let's say you want to get a laptop computer. First, consider exactly what purpose the computer would fulfill for school, for home, for work, and other reasons. How will it benefit you? Are there special features or programs that the computer must have for you to be proficient in doing your job, doing your homework, and planning your personal schedule? If you can't define the problem or goal (what the laptop would be solving), then perhaps purchasing it would not be a good decision.

Why should you approach purchase decisions with a step-by-step process?

Step 2: Obtain Accurate Information

Once you have defined the problem or goal, gather information on all possible solutions. (How else could you be more proficient—without buying a laptop?) List all alternative solutions and the cost of each. In this example, you might list these possible solutions:

- Use a computer at school (on campus) or at a public library
- Rent a computer at a copy center or technology store
- Buy a used laptop
- Buy a new laptop

Each solution has different costs to consider. To use the computer at school or at a library, you should factor in the time involved and mileage (gas). Most libraries have computers available for public use complete with Internet access at no charge, but you may be charged a lab fee at school. You also could go to a full-service copy center or technology store that rents computers for an hourly fee. To purchase a new computer, you may have to borrow money. Keep a written record of the information you collect about your various choices, as shown in Figure 11.1.

Do not consider sunk costs. A **sunk cost** is an expense that occurred in the past for which money was spent and cannot be recovered. For example, maybe you already have an old computer. It may be slow, not capable of running new programs, or obsolete. Assume you paid $400 for it three years ago. If you added more memory to your old computer, would it solve the problem? The concept of *marginalism* says that if the added benefit will exceed the added cost, you should fix the old computer. Either way, the original price ($400) is a sunk cost and not relevant to the decision.

| FIGURE 11.1 | Comparison Shopping Data |

	Per Month	Per Year
Option 1: Use library/school lab		
Time: 5 hours/weekend	20 hours	240 hours
Gas: 6-mile round trip/weekend	$ 8.00	$ 96.00
Lab fee: $15 per year	1.25	15.00
	$ 9.25	$ 111.00
Option 2: Rent a computer at copy center		
Time: 5 hours/weekend	20 hours	240 hours
Gas: 20-mile round trip/weekend	$ 26.00	$ 312.00
Fee: $8 per hour	160.00	1,920.00
	$186.00	$2,232.00
Option 3: Buy a used laptop		
From private person (one-time cost)		$ 300.00
High-speed/wireless Internet access	$ 45.00	540.00
	$ 45.00	$ 840.00
Option 4: Buy a new laptop		
Cost: $500.00 or $541.56 financed		
Payments on one-year loan at 15%	$ 45.13	$ 541.56
High-speed/wireless Internet access	45.00	540.00
	$ 90.13	$1,081.56

Step 3: Compare Choices

The next step in the decision-making process is to compare each alternative solution based on the information that you have gathered. When you make choices, they often involve making a **trade-off**, or getting something in return for giving up something else. The trade-off results in an **opportunity cost**, which is the value of your next best choice—what you are giving up. For example, in the chapter-opening scenario, Hector's resources (time and money) are limited, so he has to make a trade-off between spending time with his friends and working. Both options have opportunity costs. Suppose Hector could earn $2,000 by working over the summer. If he decides to spend the summer with his friends, the opportunity cost of his choice is the $2,000 income he gives up. If he decides to work, the opportunity cost of that choice is the value to him of the time he could have spent with his friends. Part of comparing choices is considering the value of the options that would be given up.

When comparing choices, convenience should be considered as well. In some cases, convenience may be more important than cost, as long as the cost is reasonable. Using the laptop example, you may decide that the convenience of having your own computer and being able to use it anytime you need it is worth the extra dollar cost. You may also decide that even though the cost of buying a new laptop will be greater, you prefer to avoid the uncertainty of possible repairs if you buy a used laptop.

Step 4: Make a Decision

If you follow the steps outlined in the preceding paragraphs, the decision you make will be based on careful consideration of the problem, a thorough collection of data, and an analysis of that data. The wise decision in any situation is the one that best meets your needs, is within your budget, and gives you the most value for your dollar investment. Take the time you need to carefully evaluate the information you gathered about each choice before you make a decision, especially for expensive or complex products.

Step 5: Take Action

After you make a decision, then take action to implement your chosen solution. Because you have made a thorough analysis of choices for solving your problem, you can be sure that you have made the best decision you could with the available information.

Step 6: Reevaluate Your Choice

After several months have passed, revisit your decision and evaluate whether you "solved" the problem or met the need you identified in Step 1. Are you happy with the choice you made? If not, what could you do differently next time to make a better decision? Should you do something different now? If your needs have changed or your initial decision isn't working out, go through the decision-making process again to decide whether to make a change.

 **CHECKPOINT**

What steps are involved in the decision-making process?

Economic Wants and Needs

Every person has needs and wants. **Basic needs** are the items necessary for maintaining physical life. They include food, water, shelter, clothing, and basic medical care. You might also add safety and security to this list. Until these basic needs are met, there is little need for other enhancements.

Life-enhancing wants are items beyond basic needs that add to your quality of life. Although they may be necessary for your happiness, you do not need them for your physical survival. Life-enhancing wants include, but are not limited to, the following:

- Food, clothing, and shelter beyond what are necessary for biological survival
- Medical care to improve the quality and length of life
- Education to achieve personal goals, both social and economic
- Travel, vacations, and recreation to improve personal enjoyment of life
- Luxury items, such as a jet ski, a big screen TV, or central air conditioning, to make life more fun or comfortable

Individual Wants

Beyond the basics, you decide what you "want" based on factors such as your values, personal preferences, income, and leisure time. Your wants, in turn, drive your buying decisions. The "best" choice is not the same for everyone. These factors vary among individuals and societies. They also change throughout your life.

Values

Each person has his or her own set of values. **Values** are the principles by which a person lives. Different people value things differently. One person may highly value education, whereas someone else may highly value time with family. You make economic choices based on your values. For example, if you highly value education, you will probably decide to save a large portion of your income for college. Someone who highly values time with family may choose to save toward a family vacation. As you move through life, your values may change.

Personal Preferences

Personal preferences or *tastes* are your likes and dislikes. For example, one person may enjoy a weekend of hiking in the mountains, whereas another person may choose a visit to Disneyland. Based on personal preferences, we all make economic choices. We spend money for things consistent with our personal tastes.

© Blend Images/Shutterstock.com

How can your values affect your purchasing decisions?

Prepare a list of the top five "wants" in your life today and briefly describe each one. Place them in order of 1 to 5, assigning 1 to the most important and 5 to the least important item. Then answer these questions: How long have you wanted each of the five items? What is the cost of each choice (including opportunity costs)? Will you need to save or borrow money to purchase them? What benefits will you get from each item? Will the benefits be long-lasting or will they be short-lived? How does each item relate to your values? How might your list be different ten years from now?

Income

The amount you earn will influence the choices you make. As you learned previously, *discretionary income* is the money left over after you have paid your necessary expenses. This is the money you can spend or save as you wish. The more discretionary income you have, the higher the quality and quantity of products you can consider. The ability to afford goods and services to fulfill the wants you consider important will affect your satisfaction with employment, your personal life, your goals, and other personal factors such as self-esteem. For example, if owning many expensive "things" is important to you, then you may want to pursue career goals that will lead to a high-paying job.

Leisure Time

The amount of free time you have and the kinds of activities you enjoy also affect how you choose to spend your discretionary income. *Leisure time* is the time you get to spend doing things you like and enjoy. It allows opportunities for rest, relaxation, and enjoyment of life. You may use it to develop hobbies and an *avocation* (a side career that is meaningful to you). Leisure time gives you the chance to participate in a variety of activities.

Collective Values

Collective values are ideals and values that are important to society as a whole. All citizens share in the costs and benefits related to collective values. Society influences our values, goals, and choices because it demands *social responsibility* from its citizens. For example, owning a vehicle that is fuel-efficient or uses an alternate energy source benefits everyone by reducing air pollution and our dependence on foreign oil.

Legal Protection

In a market economy, it is important to preserve legal and personal rights. *Private property ownership* and the freedom to make individual choices are important American values and part of our legal rights as U.S. citizens. Laws and their enforcement are the result of our desire to have and protect these freedoms. We pay for legal protection through taxes. The U.S. Constitution's Bill of Rights gives us individual freedoms and rights of citizenship.

How does society benefit from the gainful employment of individuals?

Employment

Most people who are able will work because it is expected. It is a way to satisfy needs and life-enhancing wants in this society. Most of us are aware of the subtle, yet very real, pressure to perform in the work arena. Therefore, we strive to do the best we can and to get a job that pays well for the effort we put forth. In this way, we can be personally satisfied with our productivity and, at the same time, satisfy society's demand for citizens who are contributing members.

Progress

The relative state of progress of the country in which you live (its technological advances and perceptions about the importance of those advances) will affect your purchase decisions. The United States is technologically advanced and places a high value on innovations. **Innovations** are new ideas, products, or services that bring about changes in the way we live. Innovations can be fun and entertaining, but they also can add to the quality of life in various ways, such as by saving us time, effort, or money.

Quality of Environment

Natural resources are of great value and concern because they are limited—some cannot be replaced. Because of our collective values, preserving a quality environment for future generations is a priority. Our society supports activities such as recycling and establishing air pollution standards. We also expect manufacturers to minimize the environmental damage caused by the production of their products and services. Environmental quality is important to society as a whole, and individuals respond to this concern by acting and purchasing accordingly.

Public Goods

Our country is organized to be "of the people, by the people, and for the people." We have a highly advanced and intricate system of government made up of the people, performing services for the people, with money contributed (through taxes) by the people. One of the roles of government is to provide its citizens with goods and services, such as police protection, highways, and national defense. These goods and services provided by government to its citizens are known as **public goods**. They are provided by government because private business could not do so efficiently. For example, national defense is necessary to protect our country from those who would do us harm. Each state, family, or business cannot reasonably provide for its own defense.

✔ CHECKPOINT

What factors influence individual wants?

Advertising

Marketing strategy is critical to the financial success of any company. How a product is packaged and sold determines financial success. Advertising executives oversee in-house departments, and in many cases, corporate executives contract with outside professional advertising agencies to provide this crucial service.

Advertising professionals are responsible for creating and expanding markets to sell products and services. They prepare overall promotional campaigns, which include types of media (print, electronic, and new age) and how and when they are used most effectively.

Advertising professionals work in a dynamic, changing, and stressful environment. Putting in more than 40 hours a week is common. This is offset with high earnings, substantial travel, and high visibility.

Employment Outlook

- An average rate of employment growth is expected.

Job Titles

- Advertising manager
- Marketing manager
- Sales manager
- Promotions manager

Needed Skills

- A bachelor's degree with an emphasis in advertising or marketing is required.
- Specialized knowledge in consumer behavior, market research, and sales is needed.

- Creativity and strong analytical, communication, and interpersonal skills are a must.

What's it like to work in . . . *Advertising*

Rich is an advertising manager at his firm. His yearly salary is $89,000. Today Rich is working with a graphic designer to create artistic examples of an advertising campaign for a new technology product. He is also preparing computer simulations to depict uses of the product. The examples and simulations will be used in television infomercials, a key ingredient of the overall marketing plan. Rich is the team leader for the campaign proposal and will work throughout the weekend to finish his presentation for Monday's meeting with team members. At the meeting, the team will go over each part of the presentation and coordinate topics and presenters.

Rich's target audience consists of young adults who typically use hi-tech gadgets and spend top dollar to be the first to get them. The appeal will be emotional by creating a "must-have" image for consumers who want to be on the cutting edge of technology. The promotion will stress how the benefits outweigh the cost of the product. The campaign is expected to result in robust sales.

What About You?

Do you enjoy a creative, changing environment? Are you artistic and intuitive? Would you consider a career in advertising?

KEY TERMS REVIEW

Match the terms with the definitions. Some terms may not be used.

____ 1. Getting something in return for giving up something else

____ 2. The value of your next best choice—what you are giving up

____ 3. Your tastes, or likes and dislikes

____ 4. New ideas, products, or services that bring about changes in the way we live

____ 5. An expense that occurred in the past for which the money cannot be recovered

____ 6. The goods and services provided by government to its citizens

____ 7. Items beyond basic needs that add to your quality of life

____ 8. Items necessary for maintaining physical life

a. basic needs
b. collective values
c. innovations
d. life-enhancing wants
e. opportunity cost
f. personal preferences
g. public goods
h. sunk cost
i. trade-off
j. values

CHECK YOUR UNDERSTANDING

L01-1 9. Besides the dollar cost, what other costs should you consider when comparing alternative solutions to a problem or goal?

L01-2 10. How does discretionary income affect your choices for wants and needs?

APPLY YOUR KNOWLEDGE

L01-1 11. Describe the last time you made a major purchase. Did you go through the six-step decision-making process? Was the decision a good one or would you choose something different today?

THINK CRITICALLY

L01-1 12. Explain how sunk costs and marginalism affect decision making.

L01-2 13. How have you and your family been affected by collective values of our society? List three things your family has done or purchased to meet societal goals and values.

L01-2 14. Explain why public goods cannot be produced by individuals and private businesses. In some cases, they could be done quicker and at less total cost, so why do we leave that role to government?

The Essential Question *Refer to The Essential Question on p. 251. The decision-making process should be based on your needs and wants; as you analyze your purchases, they should also meet your values.*

The Essential Question *How do personal and external factors, including marketing strategies, affect how you plan your major purchases?*

LEARNING OBJECTIVES

> LO 2-1   List and describe factors that influence spending.
> LO 2-2   Explain how to plan for major purchases.
> LO 2-3   Analyze marketing strategies that influence spending.

KEY TERMS

- custom, *260*
- economy, *260*
- product advertising, *263*
- target market, *264*
- company advertising, *264*
- industry advertising, *264*
- odd-number pricing, *265*
- unit pricing, *265*
- loss leader, *265*

LO 2-1   Factors That Influence Spending

Why do you buy the things you do? Consumer purchasing decisions are influenced by personal factors and external factors that encourage or discourage spending. When planning a major purchase, you should examine your motives. You should buy for the right reasons (to meet your needs and wants), instead of being swayed by outside influences that are not in your best interests.

Personal Factors

Personal factors influence your consumer spending choices. They include such things as personal resources; position in life; customs, background, and religion; and values and goals.

Personal Resources

Personal resources include time, money, energy, skills and abilities, and available credit. The more you possess of any one of these factors, the greater your purchasing power. For example, the amount of time you have available to compare prices and options before purchasing a product will affect your ability to make better buying decisions. The job skills you possess will affect the amount of money you can earn and, consequently, your purchasing power.

Position in Life

Your position in life includes such factors as age, marital status, gender, employment status, living arrangements, and lifestyle. These factors have a big influence on an individual's purchasing decisions. For example, spending patterns of single people are different from those of married couples and families. Younger people tend to have different spending priorities than older people. Someone who has a job is more likely to make high-dollar purchases than someone who is unemployed.

© Pan Xunbin/Shutterstock.com

Customs, Background, and Religion

A **custom** is a long-established practice that takes on the force of an unwritten law. Families may be faithful to customs that they have followed for generations. Cultural as well as religious and other groups share common customs. For example, people of a cultural or religious group may observe special holidays that are not observed nationally. The customs of the groups to which you belong are likely to influence your buying patterns.

Values and Goals

Values are the principles by which a person lives. Whereas values are intrinsic and slow to change, goals change often; when you accomplish one goal, you move on to others. Your value system may change as your goals in life are met or not met. Individual and family values and goals are expressed through choices of entertainment, literature, sports, luxuries, and so on. These choices are reflected in many ways, including the purchases you make, the use of your time, and your attitude toward accumulating possessions.

External Factors

Factors outside yourself and your family can affect your spending patterns. These factors include the economy, technological advances, the environment, and social pressures.

The Economy

The **economy** refers to all activities related to the production and distribution of goods and services in a geographic area. The economy goes through stages in the *business cycle*, where it is growing or slowing. *Economists* measure economic activity to describe the financial well-being of the region or the nation. The general condition of the economy affects everyone. When we are concerned about the economy, we cut back and save more. For example, when interest rates on car loans are high, fewer people buy new cars. When the price of fuel skyrockets, people drive less and buy fewer luxury items. When the economy is strong and growing, people are more optimistic, so they travel more, dine out more, and buy more goods and services.

Technological Advances

Americans place a high value on new technological advances. Many people want to have the newest, most convenient, and interesting gadgets, such as 3D TVs or electric-powered cars. As new goods and services are created to raise our standard of living, many consumers willingly purchase them.

© iStock.com/fredrocko

Why is the state of the economy an important factor in our buying decisions?

The Environment

Concern for the environment can affect buying decisions. Citizens are interested in home projects, community activities, and statewide programs that beautify, preserve, recycle, and protect existing resources and the environment. This interest in the environment affects consumers' actions as well as their product preferences. People are buying more products that are ecologically safe, biodegradable, recyclable, and organic.

Social Pressures

Social pressures often persuade consumers to buy goods and services beyond their ability to pay for them. Your friends, family, and coworkers all influence your buying decisions. Through advertising, the media (radio, television, newspapers, the Internet) also act as sources of social pressure for consumers.

✔ CHECKPOINT

What are the personal and external factors that influence consumer purchasing decisions?

LO 2-2 Planning Major Purchases

Major purchases generally tie up future income or take a big bite out of accumulated savings. Before making a major purchase, ask yourself the following questions, take time to reflect on your answers, and then make a final decision based on a rational—not emotional—perspective.

- Why do I want this product?
- How long will this product last?
- What substitutes are available and at what cost?
- By postponing this purchase, is it likely that I will choose not to buy it later?
- What types of additional costs are involved, such as supplies, maintenance, insurance, and financial risks?
- What are the trade-offs and opportunity cost of this purchase?
- What is the total cost of this product (cash price, interest, shipping charges, etc.), and will the cost be higher or lower if the purchase is deferred?

Cash or Credit?

Major purchase decisions involve the choice of whether to pay cash or use credit. Even though you may have the cash available, you should not pay cash for all purchases. If you do, your cash reserves will dwindle.

On the other hand, just because you have unused credit available doesn't mean you should charge a purchase. Examination of your credit choices will lead you to your best options for each type of purchase. For example, you may choose a store financing plan that offers zero percent interest for two years (installment credit) rather than using a credit card that charges 18 percent.

Figure 11.2 shows a comparison of various options available for buying a refrigerator, with positive and negative consequences.

FIGURE 11.2   Cash or Credit

Item	Cash	Credit
New refrigerator		
Price	$800 + $15 delivery charge	$50/month for 18 months + $15 delivery charge
Total cost	$815	$915
Used refrigerator		
Price	$400 + $15 delivery charge	$30/month for 15 months + $15 delivery charge
Total cost	$415	$465
Considerations	Ties up cash; cannot make other purchases. No monthly payments. Reduced savings balance. No interest charges.	Allows for budgeting; ties up future income. Can make other purchases. Establishes credit. Interest charged.

Research Before Buying

Comparison shopping will help you determine whether you are getting the best quality for the best price. The same brand often sells at considerably different prices at different retailers, depending on the sellers' markups. By shopping at various retailers you may be able to save money. In addition, many stores offer sale prices at various times of the year or at regular intervals.

The Internet makes comparison shopping easy. There are numerous comparison shopping sites, such as BizRate and PriceGrabber, that allow individuals to see different prices for specific products. These websites offer the convenience of comparing product prices without ever having to leave your home.

When making a purchase, take advantage of store policies that will refund part of your purchase price if the item you buy goes on sale within the next few weeks or months. This policy, together with a liberal return policy, should affect your choice of merchants. For example, a store that allows you to return a purchase within a reasonable period of time (a month or more) is much better than a store that will not accept returns or give refunds.

Quality and Price

The fact that you are paying a high price does not necessarily mean you are getting the best-quality merchandise. It pays to be aware of what good quality is and what you should expect from the merchandise.

For major purchases, it's important to check reviews in several sources before making your choice. Consumer Reports is an expert, independent, nonprofit organization that tests the quality of many products and compares different brands. It publishes the results in its *Consumer Reports* magazine and on its website.

You can also find product reviews in specialty magazines and websites. For example, *Backpacker* magazine reviews outdoor equipment in its print publication and on its website. Keep in mind that reviews by a for-profit organization can be influenced by the manufacturers that advertise in the organization's magazine or on its website

Sometimes the best reviews of products come from other consumers themselves. Peer reviews of products can be found on a number of websites, such as Epinions.com and Amazon.com.

✔ CHECKPOINT

How can research help you make better buying decisions?

- -

LO 2-3 Marketing Strategies That Influence Spending

Numerous marketing strategies lure us to buy goods and services. Many of these strategies are subtle, and we often are unaware of their impact on our buying patterns.

Advertising

The primary goal of all *advertising* is to motivate consumers to purchase a product or service. Some advertising is informational and valuable; other advertising is false and misleading.

Advertising appears in a variety of media (billboards, television, radio, Internet, newspapers, magazines, flyers), all carefully coordinated to reach specific consumer groups. Marketers help businesses sell products and services by creating colorful and attractive campaigns, often appealing to emotion rather than reason. They hire celebrities, compose catchy jingles, develop slogans, design colorful logos, and choose mascots to identify the business's products. There are three basic types of advertising: product, company, and industry.

Product Advertising

Advertising intended to convince consumers to buy a specific good or service is called **product advertising**. Advertisers often repeat the product name several times during commercials to help consumers remember it. Many ads feature famous athletes, actors, or other celebrities using the

What is the primary goal of advertising?

product. Advertisers hope that your positive feelings for the celebrity will carry over to the product. Giveaways, testimonials from people who have used the product, and other promotional gimmicks are also used to persuade consumers to buy.

Ads are carefully planned to appeal to certain types of consumers. A **target market** is a specific consumer group to which the products are designed to appeal. In planning the advertising campaign, television advertisers consider many factors when placing their product ads, such as the day of the week, time of day, and type of program on which to air the ad. For example, products advertised during football games differ from products advertised during daytime talk shows because the target markets are different.

Company Advertising

Advertising intended to promote the image of a store, company, or retail chain is known as **company advertising**. This type of advertising usually does not mention specific products or prices. Instead, it emphasizes the overall quality and reliability of the company and its products. For example, a company ad might feature company-sponsored community projects. A store ad might talk about the store's friendly employees or wide selection. These ads are designed to promote a favorable attitude toward the company so that you develop a loyalty to the store and shop there frequently.

Industry Advertising

Advertising intended to promote a general product group without regard to where these products are purchased is called **industry advertising**. For example, the dairy industry emphasizes the nutritional value of milk and other dairy products. Consequently, the whole dairy industry benefits when people drink more milk and eat more dairy products. Often, industry ads stress concern about energy conservation or environmental protection. General health and safety ads often are presented as part of industry campaigns, such as ads by the tobacco industry that discourage teen smoking.

View Points

When does advertising "cross the line" and become offensive and inappropriate? Many consumers believe that the First Amendment's protection of free speech is important to our values as a country. They believe that when something is censored or controlled by the government, freedom of speech is in jeopardy. The U.S. Supreme Court has allowed wide latitude in interpreting what individuals and businesses can publish (make known to others). In 2010 the U.S. Supreme Court ruled that corporations have the same First Amendment freedom of speech rights as individuals.

However, many consumers also feel that advertising should be appropriate, both in time and in content. For example, certain advertisements would not be suitable during programs targeting young children. Thus, consumers believe that while businesses have a right to advertise their products, they should be sensitive about how, where, and when those ads appear as well as the possible effects of the ads.

THINK CRITICALLY

Do you believe some television and Internet ads are offensive and inappropriate? Do you think there should be more control over both content and timing in advertising? Why or why not?

© Vectomart/Shutterstock.com

Pricing

The price of merchandise depends on several factors. *Supply and demand* determine what will be produced and the general price range. The cost of raw materials and labor, competitive pressures, and the seller's need to make a profit are some of the factors that determine the price of a product. But there is more to pricing than adding up the production costs and including a profit.

Retailers understand the psychological aspects of selling goods and services and use pricing devices to persuade consumers to buy. For example, if buyers believe they are getting a bargain or think they are paying a lower price than they really are, they are more inclined to buy the product or service. **Odd-number pricing** is the practice of setting prices at uneven amounts rather than whole dollars to make them seem lower. Consumers tend to perceive odd prices as being significantly lower than they actually are. If a price tag reads $5.99 instead of $6.00, consumers tend to round the price down to $5.00, making it more likely they will purchase the product.

Discounts often are available for buying in large quantities. However, you cannot assume that because you are buying the large economy size you are actually paying less per ounce than if you bought a smaller size. Compare unit prices on all sizes. **Unit pricing** tells you how much it costs per ounce or other unit of measure. By using unit pricing, you can compare various sizes of containers. Some member-only stores, such as Sam's Club or Costco, sell only larger quantities of products. While the cost per unit may be lower, you aren't really saving money if you are unable to use all of the product before it spoils.

Sales

Stores advertise end-of-month sales, anniversary sales, clearance sales, inventory sales, holiday sales, pre-season sales, and so on. They may mark down merchandise substantially, slightly, or not at all. To be sure that you are actually saving money by buying sale items, you must practice comparison shopping and know the regular prices. When an ad states that everything in the store is marked down, check carefully—items may only appear to be marked down.

A **loss leader** is an item of merchandise marked down to an unusually low price, sometimes below the store's cost. The store may actually lose money on the sale of this item because the cost of producing it is higher than the sale price. However, the loss leader is used to get customers into the store in the hope that they will buy other products as well. Profits from the sale of other items are expected to make up for the loss incurred on the loss leader. There is nothing illegal or unethical about a loss leader as long as the product advertised is available to the customer on demand.

© iStock.com/kyolshin

How can you be sure you are actually saving money by purchasing "sale" items?

Promotional Techniques

To lure customers into their stores, retailers may use promotional techniques, such as displays, contests and sweepstakes, frequent-buyer cards and customer-loyalty programs, coupons, rebates, packaging, sampling, and micromarketing.

Displays

Retail stores often use in-store displays to entice customers to buy. Variations of in-store displays include *window displays*, which are located in the business's storefront area and show merchandise offered by the store. *Feature displays* are located at the end of aisles to draw attention to a product. Many stores use *point-of-sale displays* located near cash registers to encourage impulse buying. Some stores use *special racks*, where store shelf space is modified to make more space available for new or promoted products or seasonal items. Many displays have themes based on holidays, such as Halloween, Thanksgiving, or Christmas. Color schemes, decorations, music, and special effects often are used to make in-store displays more visually appealing to consumers.

Contests and Sweepstakes

Retail stores and restaurants that depend on repeat customers often use contests and sweepstakes to bring customers into the business. The possibility of winning something or getting something free is appealing. Large and small prizes are offered to get customers to come back and buy more. Careful reading of the rules of the contest or sweepstakes reveals the customer's chances of winning. Usually, the chances of winning a major prize are very small.

Coupons

Manufacturer coupons offer instantly redeemable savings on specific products and may be redeemed wherever the product is sold. *Store coupons* offer discounts on specific products, usually for a short period of time, and only at a specific store. Manufacturer and store coupons can be found inside or on a package, in newspapers or magazines, on a store shelf or an in-store display, and online. Coupons are a form of *mass marketing*—an attempt to reach large numbers of consumers at once.

Rebates

Rebates offer money back to the consumer. They are offered by either the featured product's retailer or manufacturer. The most common types of rebates are mail-in rebates and instant rebates. With a *mail-in rebate*, the consumer typically has to mail a filled-out rebate form, a receipt, and the product's barcode within a specified time period to the retailer or manufacturer. In return, the store or manufacturer will send a check, gift card, or prepaid card for a specific amount to the consumer, usually within 6 to 8 weeks. An *instant rebate* occurs when a product is advertised at a specific price and the discount is applied at the time of purchase. For example, an electronics store may advertise an HDTV for $699.99 with a $100.00 instant rebate. The $100.00 is taken off the total price by the cashier at checkout, and the consumer pays only $599.99 for the television.

Frequent-Buyer Cards and Customer-Loyalty Programs

Merchants continually look for ways to build customer loyalty and repeat business for future purchases. Some stores and restaurants use *frequent-buyer cards* that are punched, stamped, or initialed by clerks with each purchase. Those customers who accumulate enough punches may receive some type of reward, such as a gift certificate or free merchandise.

Customer-loyalty programs offer lower prices, rebates, point-of-sale coupons, or other valued services to enrolled members. Each time the customer makes a purchase at the store, his or her account is accessed. This practice allows the store to track individual purchasing patterns and target advertising accordingly. Customer-loyalty programs often are used by grocery stores and pharmacies.

Packaging

Packages do more than just protect the product. They are also promotional tools. A product's packaging is often what compels consumers to look at a new product. Manufacturers design packaging to appeal to the eye as well as to provide the necessary product information. The visual aspects of the package—color, graphics/pictures, size, and shape—play an important part in attracting consumers' attention. Packaging should also emphasize special features about the product, such as "fat free," "new and improved," and "organic." Manufacturers may also include coupons inside or on the package.

Sampling

Many companies promote their products through sampling. This can reduce consumers' apprehension about buying a new product or introduce them to a product with which they are unfamiliar. Samples are often given out in a store or shopping mall. Sometimes samples of nonperishable items are included in direct marketing mailings to households. Many companies now offer free samples through their websites. This not only encourages consumers to use the product but also allows the company to gather data for marketing purposes.

Micromarketing

Many companies buy marketing data about consumers. *Demographics* include information about a person's age, gender, race, marital status, income, education level, and occupation. *Psychographics* describe consumers' lifestyle, interests, and attitudes. This information is gathered from purchases, customer-loyalty programs, public information, Internet shopping, and other sources provided by the government, postal service, banks, and credit bureaus. *Micromarketing* is a marketing strategy designed to target specific people who are likely to buy certain products. For example, when a couple has a child, they are likely to receive ads, samples, and coupons for baby products because the birth record of the child is public information. These targeted (micromarketing) promotions are efficient. Rather than pay the cost of mailing samples of baby products to everyone, baby product manufacturers can send samples only to consumers with babies.

 **CHECKPOINT**

How do promotional techniques increase sales?

How Does Internet Micromarketing Work?

When you purchase a product from an online retailer, you will likely register with the site and provide some information about yourself. The next time you visit, the site may present you with product recommendations. The products may be companions to your previous purchase or products similar to items you are currently browsing at the site. Even if you don't officially register with the site, you can expect that it has captured information about you with the intent of selling products to you. How does the website know who you are and what you like?

When you visit the website of an online retailer, the site places a cookie, or small data file, on your computer that stores basic information about you. The next time you visit the site, the cookie sends the stored information about you back to the site. This way, the site can recognize a returning customer. It also recognizes your specific computer. As you travel around the site, the cookie keeps track of the product pages you visit. The online retailer is building a database of your preferences. This is micromarketing, Internet-style. The advertising targets you—a target market of one customer. This custom-tailoring service benefits you because the ads you see might interest you. It benefits the retailer by increasing the chances of making another sale to you.

When you provide your e-mail address to an online retailer, you may receive e-mail advertisements in the future. By knowing your product preferences, the retailer can inform you of special offers and discounts on related products.

Internet micromarketing has its dark side—privacy concerns. Many companies that collect customer information online sell their customer databases to other companies. Also, the same technology that allows legitimate retailers to personalize their site for you can be used by criminals to steal information from you. In addition, the cookies placed on your computer can contain *spyware*. This is a program installed on your computer without your knowledge that constantly collects data about you and uses your Internet connection to send that data to advertisers. Although spyware is not illegal, the potential for abuse is cause for concern. Consumers have no control over the data collected or its use. There are many anti-spyware programs on the market that enable you to detect and remove these programs from your computer.

THINK CRITICALLY

1. Suppose you downloaded some songs at an online music store. The next time you visited the website, a list of music from similar artists popped up for your consideration, including some at a special low price. Is this kind of service worth the possible loss of privacy to you? Explain.

2. Do you like to receive e-mail advertising? How is this kind of advertising like or unlike advertising delivered by U.S. mail?

KEY TERMS REVIEW

Match the terms with the definitions. Some terms may not be used.

a. company advertising
b. custom
c. economy
d. industry advertising
e. loss leader
f. odd-number pricing
g. product advertising
h. target market
i. unit pricing

____ 1. Advertising intended to promote the image of a store, company, or retail chain

____ 2. The practice of setting prices at uneven amounts to make them seem lower

____ 3. How much an item costs per ounce or other unit of measure

____ 4. A long-established practice that takes on the force of an unwritten law

____ 5. Advertising intended to convince consumers to buy a specific good or service

____ 6. A specific consumer group to which a product is designed to appeal

____ 7. All activities related to production and distribution of goods and services in a geographic area

____ 8. An item of merchandise marked down to an unusually low price

CHECK YOUR UNDERSTANDING

LO2-1   9. How do social pressures affect your buying habits?

LO2-1 10. Explain what is meant by comparison shopping.

LO2-3 11. Why do companies use micromarketing?

APPLY YOUR KNOWLEDGE

LO2-2 12. You want to make a major purchase that will involve a large amount of cash and/or credit. What questions will you ask yourself before making such a commitment? Why is it important to make rational, rather than emotional, decisions regarding large purchases?

THINK CRITICALLY

LO2-1 13. Does your family have unique customs or cultural values that affect your spending choices? Explain how your values affect decisions.

LO2-3 14. Advertising creates demand. List the types of advertising you experience and explain how they affect your spending choices.

LO2-3 15. What characteristics do you and your peers have that might be targeted by a micromarketer?

The Essential Question *Refer to The Essential Question on p. 259. Your purchasing decisions are influenced by personal and external factors, including marketing strategies. These factors encourage or discourage spending.*

SUMMARY

11.1

- The decision-making process typically involves six steps: (1) define the problem or goal, (2) obtain accurate information, (3) compare choices, (4) make a decision, (5) take action, and (6) reevaluate your choice.

- Giving up one option in exchange for another is called a trade-off. The opportunity cost is the value of what you give up.

- Basic needs include food, water, shelter, clothing, and basic medical care. Life-enhancing wants add to the quality of life.

- Individual wants are shaped by such factors as values, personal preferences, income, and leisure time.

- Collective values include the desire for legal protection, employment, progress (innovations), quality of environment, and public goods.

11.2

- Personal factors that influence individual spending habits include personal resources; position in life; customs, background, and religion; and your values and goals.

- External factors that affect your spending habits include the economy, technological advances, the environment, and social pressures.

- When planning major purchases, make sure you want the product for rational, rather than emotional, reasons. Research and compare before you buy.

- The primary goal of all advertising is to motivate the consumer to purchase goods and services.

- There are three basic types of advertising: product, company, and industry. Product advertising promotes a specific good or service. Company advertising promotes the image of a store, company, or retail chain. Industry advertising promotes a general product group without regard to where these products are purchased.

- Pricing plays a large role in purchasing decisions. Consumers perceive odd-number pricing as being lower than it actually is.

- Retailers use loss leaders to lure customers to the store, hoping they will buy other more profitable products while they are there.

- Promotional techniques to increase spending include displays, contests and sweepstakes, coupons, rebates, frequent-buyer cards, customer-loyalty programs, packaging, sampling, and micromarketing.

© Pan Xunbin/Shutterstock.com

APPLY WHAT YOU KNOW

LO1-1
1. Using the steps in the decision-making process, make a decision that will satisfy your desire for an iPhone, gaming system, or other new technology product you've been wanting. Explain how you completed each step.

LO1-2
2. Interview an adult to find out how his or her individual wants affect spending habits. Ask for examples of how his or her values, income, personal preferences, and leisure time influence wants. How do his or her wants differ from your own? How are they similar?

LO1-2
3. What community and national environmental concerns do you have? What can you do as a concerned citizen to help preserve the quality of the environment?

LO2-1
4. How do your spending patterns differ from those of your parents? What things do you buy that your parents also purchase? Can you trace any of these purchases to a strong family custom, background, or religion?

LO2-2
5. Use a search engine to find and select a price comparison website. Request a price comparison for a product in which you are interested. What is the range of prices for the product? What other features does the site offer to help you research and select products?

LO2-3
6. Spend an evening viewing television. List the jingles, keywords, and slogans used in each commercial. How many commercials can you automatically sing along with? Also list the celebrities you saw in the ads and the products they promoted. Why do you think each celebrity was chosen for that particular product? Explain the emotional appeal behind each advertising slogan or campaign.

MAKE ACADEMIC CONNECTIONS

LO1-1
7. **Communication** Think of a problem that you need to resolve, such as a purchase you want to make or an issue at school or work that you need to resolve. Use the decision-making process to help make a decision. Outline the process in a graphic format. For example, you can create a flow chart that includes each step of the decision-making process and a short description of your actions. Be creative.

LO2-1
8. **Economics** Write a one-page paper about the economy of your geographic region, including the current state of the economy. Explain how the economy affects spending decisions of consumers. How has your family been affected by rising (or falling) prices?

LO2-1
9. **Technology** List three or four new technological advances in the last five years. Explain how they have changed lives. What new technology is expected soon? Explain how it will benefit individuals and society.

LO2-3
10. **Marketing** What advertisements appear on the websites that you visit frequently? Do they seem to target you? Why do you think the companies chose to advertise their products on a specific website? Write a paper reporting your findings.

Solve Problems and Explore Issues

LO1-2 11. Citizens are becoming more concerned about the environment and are making more eco-friendly purchases. Conduct research to learn about a recent eco-friendly product or service being offered by a company. Write a one-page paper on your findings.

LO2-1 12. Consider a purchase you made in the last year. Explain any trade-offs you made and describe what personal and external factors affected your decision. Are you satisfied with your purchase?

LO2-3 13. Browse the Internet and view the different types of online advertising. What kinds of things can advertisers do on the Web that they cannot do in a print magazine? Do you think Internet advertising is as effective as television advertising? Why or why not?

LO2-3 14. List any stores in your area that use one or more of the following promotional techniques: (a) contests and sweepstakes, (b) coupons, (c) frequent-buyer cards or customer-loyalty programs, (d) sampling, and (e) other (be specific). Beside each store name, describe the specific techniques used.

LO2-3 15. Visit a local store in your area. List and describe the types of in-store displays used by the retailer. Describe how the retailer made the displays visually appealing.

EXTEND YOUR LEARNING

LO2-3 16. **Ethics** Since pharmaceutical companies can now advertise prescription drugs to consumers directly via television ads, the sale of expensive drugs has increased dramatically. Sometimes these drugs help consumers, but in many cases, the side effects and long-term health consequences are severe and unpredictable. Many people feel these ads are misleading and emotional, rather than rational. Do you think it's a good idea to present these ads directly to consumers? Do the benefits outweigh the risks? How would you change advertising laws to regulate such ads?

CHAPTER PROJECT

Watch a television program anytime during the day. Determine the program's target audience. Watch the commercials shown during the program and then do the following: (a) List all of the commercials and categorize each as product, company, or industry advertising. (Count public-service and political advertisements as industry advertisements.) (b) Identify the target markets and rate each commercial as good, fair, or poor, depending on how well it is directed to the program's target audience. (c) Explain which ads you think were most effective and why.

Complete the Guided Decision Making activity for Chapter 11 at ngl.cengage.com/mypf.

CHAPTER 12

Renting a Residence

12.1 Housing Choices

12.2 The Renting Process

Consider This...

Anisa is finishing her sophomore year in college, and at age 20, she is ready to make new housing choices. During her first two years, she has lived in university housing, as required by the university.

"We have lots of important decisions to make," she told her roommate, Lydia. "We could stay right here in the dorm, but that may not be our best bet. Living off-campus has advantages, but there are things to consider. For example, we'll have to pay rent and utility bills every month. We'll also need transportation to get to class, and parking is limited on campus. To be able to afford to rent a house, we'd have to take in another roommate. On the other hand, if we rent an apartment or house, we would have much more space. Plus, we would have a lot more privacy, freedom, and independence."

"Yes, there are a lot of advantages to being out on our own, but there are many challenges too," said Lydia. "We would need to make some rules about our living arrangements and responsibilities that everyone agrees on. We don't want our living arrangements to distract us from our main goal—finishing our education. This is all pretty exciting to think about, and I'm looking forward to the change. How do we get started?"

The Essential Question *What are your housing choices, and what is involved in moving to your new residence?*

LEARNING OBJECTIVES

> LO 1-1 List and describe several rental housing options.
> LO 1-2 Discuss potential living arrangements.
> LO 1-3 Explain how to plan a successful move into a rental property.

KEY TERMS

- dormitory, *274*
- co-op, *275*
- studio apartment, *276*
- townhouse, *276*
- duplex, *276*
- condominium, *277*
- security deposit, *278*
- furnished rental, *279*
- unfurnished rental, *279*
- rent-to-own option, *279*
- bundling, *281*

LO 1-1 Housing Alternatives

You will soon have many important choices to make. One is where to live. You may decide to live at home with your parents and commute to college, which is usually less expensive than living on your own. If you do decide to move out while attending college or working, there are numerous housing options to choose from. It is crucial that you weigh your options before you make a final decision.

On-Campus Housing

Many college students prefer to live on campus. Some colleges and universities will not allow freshmen or students under the legal age to live off campus. Living on campus has many benefits, including accessibility to classes and campus resources, such as the library, computer labs, and health center, and more social interaction as part of campus life. The disadvantages to living on campus are little privacy and limited space.

If you live on campus, you will have several housing options: dormitories, apartments, sorority or fraternity housing, or housing cooperatives.

Dormitories

Most students who choose to live on campus will live in a dormitory. A **dormitory** (or residence hall) is an on-campus building that contains many small rooms that are rented to students. The rooms usually come furnished with beds, dressers, and study desks. Some units have their own bathrooms, but most dormitories have communal bathroom facilities. Most rooms are intended for double occupancy.

When you first leave home, what are some housing alternatives open to you at a college campus?

© iStock.com/YinYang

© Pan Xunbin/Shutterstock.com

However, many colleges and universities allow students to have a private room for an extra charge.

Most dormitories have centrally located lounges for watching television and group activities. Most have shared kitchen and laundry areas as well. Meals at the college cafeteria may also be included with the cost of the room (room and board). Although rooms are small, with limited space for living and studying, the cost per school term may be less than the cost of most other housing options.

University-Owned Apartments

In addition to dormitories, many larger colleges and universities have apartments. An *apartment* is a separate living facility that exists among many other similar units. Although some schools permit only graduate students, married students, or students with families to live in the apartments, other colleges and universities allow undergraduate students to live in them as well. The apartments typically come furnished with beds, dressers, study desks, and chairs and include closets, bathrooms, a kitchen, and dining and living room areas.

Sororities and Fraternities

Many colleges have sororities and fraternities that provide housing on or near campus. A *sorority* is a social organization of female students who share a residence, whereas a *fraternity* is a similar organization for male students. Sorority and fraternity houses are often elegant, mansion-type buildings that can comfortably house 20 or more people.

To live in one of these buildings, you have to become a member of the sorority or fraternity in a process called *pledging*. Typically, sororities and fraternities seek new members with goals, abilities, and ideals similar to those of the organization. For example, some require a certain grade point average. Others look for an interest in community service. The cost is usually higher for these facilities; however, you are living with people with similar values and goals to your own.

Housing Cooperatives

Housing cooperatives, known as co-ops, are also available at many larger colleges and universities. When you live in a **co-op**, you get a room similar to one in a dormitory at a lower cost but with added responsibilities. In addition to keeping your room clean and usable, you share in cooking, cleaning, and maintaining the building. In exchange, your monthly cost is less because you help provide services for yourself and the group.

Off-Campus Housing

Some colleges and universities do not provide on-campus housing options. Even if the college you choose to attend does offer housing, you may choose to live off campus. Living off campus has advantages, such as more independence and privacy. Living off campus also helps you be more responsible, because you will be in charge of paying your rent and bills every month, buying groceries, and so on. However, living off campus does not come without its drawbacks. It is more expensive than living on campus. You might also have to drive or use some form of public transportation to get to class.

Would you consider renting an apartment after you finish high school? If so, what kind of apartment building or complex would you find desirable? What features would you want the apartment to have? What amenities would you want available within the apartment complex? Would your ideal apartment be feasible based on your budget after high school?

Keeping your budget in mind, write a one-page report describing the features you desire in an apartment. Explain the advantages and disadvantages of this living arrangement. Would you live by yourself or with a roommate? Describe your plans in detail, assuming you will present them to your parents.

© oculo/Shutterstock.com

When you live off campus, you have several choices, including apartments, duplexes, condominiums, and rental houses.

Apartments

If you choose to live off campus, then you most likely will rent an apartment. An *apartment complex* is a large building or group of buildings that contain many units, often as many as a hundred or more. You can find an apartment in your chosen area in brochures, newspaper ads, online ads, and apartment guides (printed booklets and online).

Apartments come in a variety of floor plans. Typically, the smaller the square footage of the apartment, the less expensive it is. A **studio apartment**, also known as an *efficiency apartment*, has one large room that serves as the living room, dining area, and bedroom. Kitchen facilities may be located either in the central room or in a small separate room, and the bathroom is usually in its own smaller room. Larger apartments with separate living, dining, and sleeping areas are also available. Many apartment units offer two- and three-bedroom apartments with considerably more living space. When two or more roommates are involved, this is often a good option. Typically, a larger apartment is more expensive than a studio apartment but less expensive than a townhouse. A **townhouse** is a living space that has two or more levels. Typically, the kitchen, dining area, and living room are on the ground level, and bedrooms are upstairs.

Apartment amenities may include on-site laundry facilities, a storage area, parking, building security, a swimming pool, tennis courts, a clubhouse, and a fitness center. In addition, all or part of the utilities (heat, water, gas, electric, and garbage service) may be included in the rent. In some cases, you may have a washer and dryer in your apartment.

Apartment living provides independence and flexibility but also requires responsibility and good judgment. Most apartment buildings have rules that make close living more enjoyable for all.

Duplexes and Multiplexes

A **duplex** is a building with two separate living units that share a common central wall. Usually both living areas are the same with separate entrances. Duplexes usually offer more space than apartments and more privacy, with only one close neighbor. They may include a garage or carport, private laundry facilities, and other privileges and responsibilities similar to a house.

A *multiplex* is a building or group of buildings, such as a fourplex (two sets of duplexes) or four units that are together. An eightplex contains eight units that are connected. There are many different types of combinations. For example, a *quad* is a housing choice that has four bedrooms connected to a single kitchen and living room that is shared by the occupants.

Condominiums

A condominium (or *condo*) is an individually owned unit in an apartment-style complex with shared ownership of common areas. Although many owners choose to live in their condos, especially after retirement, many offer them for rent. Because condos are privately owned, the owner often has a larger financial investment in the property. This usually means that the upkeep on the property is better. Also, a condo may offer more stylish and higher-end design elements than found in apartments, such as granite countertops and stainless steel appliances. When renting a condo, you will have the same responsibilities for upkeep as the owner.

Rental Houses

Rental houses offer many attractive features, such as a larger, more private living area, a driveway and garage or carport, a yard, and a patio or deck. Because you are getting many of the comforts of home ownership, the rent is usually more expensive. When renting a house, you are likely to have many of the same restrictions as with other rentals, such as no pets allowed. Also, you may be responsible for upkeep, such as yard maintenance, and utility bills typically will be higher. In addition, because rented houses are investment properties that people buy and sell, the property may be shown to prospective new owners while you are living there. If the property is sold, and the new owner is purchasing it for private use rather than as a rental, you may be asked to move.

✔ CHECKPOINT

What are common forms of on-campus and off-campus housing?

LO 1-2 Living Arrangements

Your living arrangements will depend largely on whether you choose on-campus or off-campus housing. For college students who choose on-campus housing, many of the decisions regarding their living arrangements will be predetermined. Renting in the community involves more planning. You must determine whether you want a roommate, where you want to live, and what items you'll need to furnish your new home.

Who to Live With

To share expenses, you may wish to have a roommate. Choosing a roommate can be difficult. Just because you are friends with someone doesn't mean that you can successfully live together. Your living habits may be very different. Be sure you are compatible with your potential roommate before you move in together. Discuss possible areas of disagreement that may cause trouble if not

The division of responsibilities and financial obligations can leave roommates at odds. Some roommates believe that, because they are now living away from home and enjoying their freedom, they can do anything they want. Other roommates may feel they are being taken advantage of. For example, some people are neat and clean and keep things tidy. It is unsettling for them to see food, clothing, and personal property scattered around. Others are not at all concerned about these things—their definition of clean and presentable may be very different. Some people may be very precise about paying obligations, while others wait until the last minute and are often late or short on money.

THINK CRITICALLY

How would you describe your living habits? How would you feel about having a roommate who has very different living habits? How can roommates avoid these kinds of misunderstandings?

© Vectomart/Shutterstock.com

settled in advance. Some questions that each of you should answer include the following:

- Do you smoke or drink? How do you feel about others who do?
- Do you like a clean living area at all times, or are you easygoing and casual about your environment?
- Do you have steady employment or another source of income to ensure that you can pay your share of expenses?
- What are some of your goals? Do you want to continue your education, work full time, or travel?
- What are your leisure activities? What activities will you share with (or impose on) your roommate?
- What type of transportation do you have? Will you share transportation? If so, what are the costs and how will you divide them?

You might also consider having more than one roommate. The more personalities involved, however, the more difficult it becomes to have problem-free relationships. Matching similar personality types will increase the chances for a successful living arrangement.

Where to Live

Your finances will have a major impact on where you decide to live. You must determine how much rent you can comfortably pay. Then you can begin shopping for the housing option that best meets your needs. There are some additional considerations to think about as you decide where to live.

- *Deposits and fees.* A **security deposit** is a refundable amount paid in advance to protect the owner against damage or nonpayment. If you take care of the property and pay your rent on time, you should get the security deposit back when you move. Utility companies may require you to make a security deposit when you first open an account. You may also have to pay *fees*, which are nonrefundable charges, usually for services provided. For example, the cable company may charge a onetime installation fee.
- *Safety.* You will want to live in a safe area. By researching the crime rates and statistics for various areas, you can learn more about the safety of a neighborhood.

- *Length of time you plan to live in the residence.* If you sign a lease for six months, you have made a commitment to remain for that length of time. You may face penalties if you wish to move sooner. Usually, the shorter your commitment, the higher the monthly rent.
- *Distance from school and work.* Your proximity to the campus and your job and access to public transportation are important considerations, especially if you do not own a vehicle or have to share one.
- *Distance from services.* You will need access to shopping areas, gas stations, and other frequently used services. Your means of transportation can make a difference as to how close you need to live to these services.
- *Repairs and maintenance.* As a renter, you may have responsibilities to maintain the property in minor ways, such as replacing light bulbs, mowing lawns, and repairing damages (such as broken window screens) that you have caused.

What factors might influence your decision of where to live?

What to Take

Rental housing can come furnished or unfurnished. A **furnished rental** means that the basics are provided—bed, dresser, sofa, chairs, lamps, dining table and chairs, and essential appliances. An **unfurnished rental** may or may not include basic kitchen appliances, such as a stove and refrigerator, but little else. Usually the fewer the items furnished, the lower the rent. If you have enough of these furnishings or can acquire the essentials for an unfurnished residence, you can save a considerable amount in rent.

You can buy or rent furnishings. Compare purchase and rental payments carefully before you make a decision. For example, with a **rent-to-own option**, you rent furniture with an option to buy. At the end of the rental period (usually six months or longer), you have the option to buy the furniture at a reduced price. However, rent-to-own options can be more expensive than making payments on furniture you purchase outright with an installment plan. Renting furniture and appliances may be a good idea, however, for those who will be moving long distances in the near future and don't want to take their old furniture with them.

Basic household and personal items necessary for setting up housekeeping include the following:

- Towels, wash cloths, sheets, and cleaning cloths
- Cleaning supplies (mops, brooms, buckets, vacuum cleaner, detergent, and cleansers)
- Personal items (shampoo, cosmetics, soap, and other personal hygiene items)

- Clothing (and clothes hangers), shoes, and other apparel
- Stereo, television, and DVD player
- Kitchen utensils (dishes, silverware, pots, and pans) and a trash can
- Tools (hammer, nails, duct tape), light bulbs, flashlight, extension cords, and batteries
- Lamps, artwork, pictures, and other decorations

You may also need to provide rugs, drapes, shower curtains, and mirrors. You or your roommate(s) may have some of these items, or you may decide to buy them. If you buy some things jointly, it's a good idea to make a list before purchasing them and agree on who will get the joint items if one of you decides to move.

✔ CHECKPOINT

What decisions must a person make regarding living arrangements?

LO 1-3 Planning Your Move

Begin planning your move several months in advance. Others who have experienced a similar move can help you with advice. Here are some ways to prepare:

- *Have savings.* Set aside savings to cover the security deposit, first and last months' rent, fees, and initial expenses. If you have a pet, you may have to pay an additional security deposit or fee.
- *Have income.* Have a reliable source of income to pay monthly rent, utility bills, and expenses. Landlords typically require applicants to earn a specific amount of income on a monthly basis. Because this is your first rental, they may require a large deposit or cosigner on the lease or rental agreement to assume financial responsibility should you become unable to pay your rent or other lease obligations.
- *Have supplies.* Gather what you need to live independently, such as clothing, towels, sheets, pillows, small appliances, and dishes, to minimize the items you need to buy when you move.
- *Consider your goals.* Plan the move with your goals in mind. If your goal is to finish college, then your living plan should help you achieve this goal. For example, if you are planning to go to college in September and live on campus, it would probably not be wise to move out on your own for the three summer months prior to the start of school. The expenses would be significant, and you probably would be better off saving your money to help meet college expenses.

What are some ways you can prepare in advance before moving out on your own?

- *Make reservations.* Make arrangements for transporting furnishings. Professional movers can be expensive, and their services must be reserved in advance. If instead you enlist friends to help you move, you may need to rent a moving truck that you reserve in advance. Also, plan to provide refreshments or a meal for your friends if the move will take several hours.

A good way to organize your preparations is to make a household needs inventory, such as the one shown in Figure 12.1. Decide what you will need and check off each item as you fulfill the need. As you can see, it may take several months to get ready for the move.

Moving Costs

Moving costs include the time and money spent in packing, loading, transporting, unloading, and unpacking. Professional movers typically charge based on the amount you have to move, the distance traveled, and whether or not they do the packing. You can save money by doing your own packing.

You can save even more by renting a truck or trailer and using your own labor for loading, driving, and unloading. If it is just a local move, such as across town, the rental will likely be cheaper if you can return the vehicle to the place where you rented it. However, for a long-distance move, you can rent a truck or trailer one way and return it to the rental agency's branch in the new city.

When you reserve a moving truck or trailer, you may be asked if you would like to purchase additional insurance coverage for your move. This coverage may run up to $40 a day, but it may be well worth it since most truck or trailer rentals are not covered on your auto insurance policy. If you choose not to purchase insurance, you will be held liable for any damage that occurs.

Installation Charges

When you move into a new residence, you will pay some installation charges, such as for telephone, Internet, and cable TV services. You may be able to save money if you can bundle these services. **Bundling** is combining services into one package. For example, one company can provide phone (local and

| FIGURE 12.1 | Household Needs Inventory |

What Is Needed	Date Needed	Cost	Date Completed
1. Dishes/towels	October 1	$100	_____
2. First and last months' rent	October 1	$1,400	_____
3. Security deposit	October 1	$200	_____
4. Moving-in fees	October 1	$250	_____
5. Car (share of expenses)	September 1	$150	_____
6. Job (part-time)	August 1		_____
7. Household budget	September 1		_____
8. Plan with roommates	June 1		_____
9. Plan with parents	May 1		_____

long distance), Internet service, and cable TV for a price that is lower than what you would pay if you used three different companies. Another type of bundling is a family plan for cell phones, whereby you remain a part of your parents' plan to get a greatly reduced rate on your phone services. Be sure to comparison shop when signing up for phone, Internet, and cable TV services for your home. You may be able to find special offers and other types of discount plans.

You must also arrange to turn on the electricity and other utilities. Many utility companies charge new customers a *refundable security deposit*, whereas other companies, such as the telephone company, may charge a onetime nonrefundable fee.

Group Financial Decisions

As previously mentioned, you may decide to live with a roommate (or roommates) to share expenses. All roommates are responsible for meeting the obligations to which they agree. For example, each person must pay his or her share of the rent, so that the total rent is paid on time. You will probably share utilities equally, as well as cable TV, Internet, and group activity expenses. But expenses such as gasoline or groceries might be divided according to percentage of use. Laundry services usually are an individual expense.

Group budgeting allows for the careful allocation of expenses, so that each person pays his or her share. The budget should be prepared and put into writing following a good discussion. Figure 12.2 is an example of a group budget.

To pay group expenses, each person could have a separate account for individual expenses, and the group could have a joint account to pay shared expenses. Each person could make a deposit into the joint account by a certain date each month. Then roommates could take turns writing checks to pay for rent, utilities, and other expenses incurred throughout the month. Another good idea is to have one person in charge of collecting costs from other roommates and submitting them when due.

✔ CHECKPOINT

What is group budgeting, and why is it important?

FIGURE 12.2	Group Budget

Expense	Monthly Cost	Robert's Share	Carlos's Share	Ken's Share
Rent	$900	$300	$300	$300
Utilities (average)	150	50	50	50
Cable TV and Internet access	105	35	35	35
Gasoline/insurance /repairs	120	40	40	40
Groceries	600	200	200	200
Household supplies	90	30	30	30
TOTALS	$1,965	$655	$655	$655

Property Management

When owners of homes, apartments, duplexes, or commercial buildings do not have the time or expertise for the day-to-day management of their real estate properties, they often hire a property manager to take care of the real estate. Some property managers reside on site at the apartment building or housing complex where they work. These managers maintain office hours during which they show rental units to prospective tenants; discuss the lease and explain the terms of occupancy; meet with current tenants to handle requests for repairs or resolve complaints; and inspect the premises to determine if any repairs or maintenance is needed.

Property managers also handle the financial operations, ensuring that rent is collected and that taxes, payroll, and maintenance bills are paid on time. They also keep up-to-date records of income and expenditures and submit regular expense reports to the owner(s).

Managers of large complexes may be supervisors of other office staff and of maintenance personnel. They also must be experts in landlord–tenant laws and make sure that the laws are followed.

Employment Outlook

- An average rate of employment growth is expected.

Job Titles

- Property manager
- Resident manager
- Real estate manager

Needed Skills

- A bachelor's degree in business is preferred.
- Licensure is required for public housing subsidized by the federal government.
- Real estate knowledge and skills are desirable.

What's it like to work in . . . *Property Management*

Kelly works for a property management company that specializes in residential real estate. She earns $52,000 a year. Kelly is responsible for 11 houses and 6 duplexes. She takes calls from renters reporting problems and repair needs. She reviews and signs contracts with plumbers, electricians, and other contractors who provide the repairs and maintenance. She also prepares quarterly reports to owners, itemizing rents collected and expenses incurred. For any expense that is out of the ordinary, she must contact the owner for prior approval, as per their agreement.

Kelly works a normal 40-hour workweek, except under unusual circumstances, such as severe weather. She must make sure that her tenants are safe and that any damages are promptly addressed.

What About You?

Would you like managing property for others, collecting rent, and overseeing maintenance? Would you consider a career in property management?

The Career Clusters icons are being used with permission of the: States' Career Clusters Initiative, 2007, www.careerclusters.org

KEY TERMS REVIEW

Match the terms with the definitions. Some terms may not be used.

a. bundling
b. condominium
c. co-op
d. dormitory
e. duplex
f. furnished rental
g. rent-to-own option
h. security deposit
i. studio apartment
j. townhouse
k. unfurnished rental

____ 1. A refundable amount a renter pays in advance to protect the owner against damage or nonpayment

____ 2. A room similar to one in a dormitory at a lower cost but with added responsibilities

____ 3. A building with two separate living units that share a common central wall

____ 4. An apartment with one large room that serves as the living room, dining area, and bedroom

____ 5. Combining services into one package

____ 6. A living space that has two or more levels

____ 7. An on-campus building that contains many small rooms that are rented to students

____ 8. A rental unit in which basic furnishings—bed, dresser, sofa, chairs, lamps, and so on—are provided

CHECK YOUR UNDERSTANDING

LO1-1 9. How do co-ops differ from dormitories?

LO1-2 10. What questions should you and your potential roommate ask each other before deciding to live together?

APPLY YOUR KNOWLEDGE

LO1-1 11. If you were a college freshman and had the choice of living on campus or off campus, which would you choose? Why? Which type of housing option would you choose? Why?

THINK CRITICALLY

LO1-1 12. How are your obligations different if you live in an apartment complex versus if you live in a rental house?

LO1-2 13. Why is it important to know a person well and have an agreement in terms of sharing responsibilities before you become roommates?

LO1-3 14. Give examples of why you need to have considerable savings when planning to move out on your own.

The Essential Question *Refer to The Essential Question on p. 274. Housing choices include on-campus options, apartments, and houses. Moving involves deciding on living arrangements, paying deposits, meeting housing needs, and planning the move itself.*

The Essential Question *When renting a place to live, what factors must be considered?*

LEARNING OBJECTIVES

› LO 2-1 List the advantages and disadvantages of renting a place to live.
› LO 2-2 Describe the elements of the rental application, rental inventory, and lease forms.
› LO 2-3 Discuss landlord and tenant responsibilities.

KEY TERMS

- renting, *285*
- landlord, *285*
- tenant, *285*
- lease, *287*
- lessor, *287*
- lessee, *287*
- rental agreement, *289*
- rental inventory, *289*
- eviction, *291*

LO 2-1 Renting a Place to Live

Most people begin their independent lives as renters. **Renting** is the process of using another person's property for a fee. A **landlord** is the owner, or owner's representative, of rental property. A person who rents property is called a **tenant** or renter.

Renting is a popular choice among young people who are just getting started on their own. There are numerous benefits to renting, but there are also some downsides. As with anything, it's important to weigh the pros and cons of renting an apartment, duplex, condo, or house before doing so. The more you know about the process, the better prepared you will be.

Advantages of Renting

Renting has several advantages over other forms of living choices.

1. *Flexibility.* If you have a short-term or month-to-month lease, you have the flexibility to move if you need to once your lease is up. If you are unsure about whether you will stay in the same location for a long period, then renting a residence is a wise choice.
2. *Lower cost.* Renting is usually cheaper than the cost of buying a house. Sharing expenses with roommates lowers individual costs even more.
3. *Fewer responsibilities.* Renting usually relieves you of many of the responsibilities of home ownership, such as costly repairs and maintenance.
4. *Amenities.* Many landlords provide a number of amenities for their tenants. For example, rental properties often have laundry, fitness, and recreational facilities.
5. *Convenience.* Rental units are often located in close proximity to major shopping areas, public transportation, and area businesses.
6. *Social Life.* Apartments offer the opportunity to meet others and socialize informally, especially where recreational facilities are provided.

© Pan Xunbin/Shutterstock.com

How can neighbors make apartment-living unpleasant?

Disadvantages of Renting

While there are many advantages to renting, there are also disadvantages.

1. *Noise.* Residents usually share common walls with neighbors above, below, and/or beside them. Consequently, music, conversations, and other activities of neighbors can be overheard. This can be irritating, especially if your neighbors keep unusual hours.
2. *Lack of privacy.* Because conversations and other activities can be overheard through common walls, tenants often feel a lack of privacy. Problems associated with shared facilities—laundry and recreation, for example—can also be annoying.
3. *Small living and storage space.* Unless you are renting a house, you will have a smaller living space. The small size also means little cabinet and closet space. A few rental complexes offer additional storage space, but they may charge an extra fee for its use.
4. *Scarcity of parking.* Many rental properties do not provide garages or off-street parking. In complexes that do provide parking lots, parking is often very limited. Parking spaces may also cost extra, especially when they are covered or reserved.
5. *No tax benefits.* While homeowners usually enjoy a tax deduction, your monthly rent payment is not tax deductible; therefore, there are no tax benefits to you as a renter.

✔ CHECKPOINT

What are some advantages and disadvantages of renting?

- -

LO 2-2 Rental Contracts

When you rent a place to live, you will have to fill out a *rental application*. The purpose of the application is to allow the landlord to verify your income, previous rental experience, credit rating, and so on. The landlord does this to assure that you are a good risk—that you likely will pay your rent and be a good tenant. The landlord can refuse to rent you property or require you to have a cosigner because of your past (or lack of) rental history, employment record, or credit rating. Rental may not be denied, however, solely on the basis of race, religion, national origin, sex, or familial status (such as being divorced or having children). Figure 12.3 shows information asked on a typical rental application.

FIGURE 12.3 Rental Application

RENTAL APPLICATION

Date _____

Section 1. Personal Information

Applicant:
Name _____
Current Address _____
_____
Phone _____
Landlord _____
Landlord's Phone _____
Previous Address _____
_____
Previous Landlord _____
Landlord's Phone _____

Co-Applicant:
Name _____
Current Address _____
_____
Phone _____
Landlord _____
Landlord's Phone _____
Previous Address _____
_____
Previous Landlord _____
Landlord's Phone _____

Section 2. Employment

Employer _____
Address _____
_____
Phone _____
Monthly take-home pay $ _____
Years employed at this job _____

Employer _____
Address _____
_____
Phone _____
Monthly take-home pay $ _____
Years employed at this job _____

Section 3. Credit

Bank _____
___ Checking ___ Savings/Investment

Companies through which you have credit
cards or charge accounts:
_____
_____
_____

Bank _____
___ Checking ___ Savings/Investment

Companies through which you have credit
cards or charge accounts:
_____
_____
_____

Section 4. Personal References

Name _____
Phone _____
Relationship to applicant _____

Name _____
Phone _____
Relationship to applicant _____

I hereby swear that the above information is true and complete. I understand that incomplete or inaccurate information on this application may result in denial and/or eviction.

Applicant Signature:
_____ *Date:* _____

Co-Applicant Signature:
_____ *Date:* _____

Leases and Month-to-Month Agreements

Basically, there are two types of rental contracts: leases and rental agreements. A **lease** is a written agreement that allows a tenant to use property for a set period of time at a set rent payment. The landlord is called the **lessor**, or person responsible for the property. The tenant is called the **lessee**, or person who takes possession of the property. Figure 12.4 is an example of a lease agreement.

FIGURE 12.4 Lease

RESIDENTIAL LEASE AGREEMENT
AND SECURITY DEPOSIT RECEIPT

THIS INDENTURE, made this __29th__ day of __October__, 20 __--__ , between

__Brendan Martin__ , hereinafter designated the Lessor

or Landlord, and __Teresa Thomas__ , hereinafter designated the Lessee,

WITNESSETH: That the said Lessor/Landlord does by these presents lease and demise the residence

situated at __614 Dundas Street__ in __Cincinnati__ City,

__Hamilton__ County, __Ohio__ State,

of which the real estate is described as follows:

614 Dundas Street, Cincinnati, Ohio,

upon the following terms and conditions:

1. **Term:** The premises are leased for a term of __one (1)__ year(s), commencing the __1st__ day of __November__, 20 __--__ , and terminating the __31st__ day of __October__, 20 __--__ .

2. **Rent:** The Lessee shall pay rent in the amount of $ __600.00__ per month for the above premises on the __1st__ day of each month in advance to Landlord.

3. **Utilities:** Lessee shall pay for service and utilities supplied to the premises, except __None__ which will be furnished by Landlord.

4. **Sublet:** The Lessee agrees not to sublet said premises nor assign this agreement nor any part thereof without the prior written consent of Landlord.

5. **Inspection of Premises:** Lessee agrees that he has made inspection of the premises and accepts the condition of the premises in its present state, and that there are no repairs, changes, or modifications to said premises to be made by the Landlord other than as listed herein.

6. **Lessee Agrees:**
(1) To keep said premises in a clean and sanitary condition;
(2) To properly dispose of rubbish, garbage, and waste in a clean and sanitary manner at reasonable and regular intervals and to assume all costs of extermination and fumigation for infestation caused by Lessee;
(3) To properly use and operate all electrical, gas, heating, plumbing facilities, fixtures, and appliances;
(4) To not intentionally or negligently destroy, deface, damage, impair, or remove any part of the premises, their appurtenances, facilities, equipment, furniture, furnishings, and appliances, nor to permit any member of his family, invitee, licensee, or other person acting under his control to do so;
(5) Not to permit a nuisance or common waste.

7. **Maintenance of Premises:** Lessee agrees to mow and water the grass and lawn, and keep the grass, lawn, flowers, and shrubbery thereon in good order and condition, and to keep the sidewalk surrounding said premises free and clear of all obstructions; to replace in a neat and workmanlike manner all glass and doors broken during occupancy thereof; to use due precaution against freezing of water or waste pipes and stoppage of same in and about said premises and that in case water or waste pipes are frozen or become clogged by reason of neglect of Lessee, the Lessee shall repair the same at his own expense as well as all damage caused thereby.

8. **Alterations:** Lessee agrees not to make alterations or do or cause to be done any painting or wallpapering to said premises without the prior written consent of Landlord.

9. **Use of Premises:** Lessee shall not use said premises for any purpose other than that of a residence and shall not use said premises or any part thereof for any illegal purpose. Lessee agrees to conform to municipal, county and state codes, statutes, ordinances, and regulations concerning the use and occupation of said premises.

10. **Pets and Animals:** Lessee shall not maintain any pets or animals upon the premises without the prior written consent of Landlord.

11. **Access:** Landlord shall have the right to place and maintain "for rent" signs in a conspicuous place on said premises for thirty days prior to the vacation of said premises. Landlord reserves the right of access to the premises for the purpose of:
(a) Inspection;
(b) Repairs, alterations, or improvements;
(c) To supply services; or
(d) To exhibit or display the premises to prospective or actual purchasers, mortgagees, tenants, workmen, or contractors. Access shall be at reasonable times except in case of emergency or abandonment.

12. **Surrender of Premises:** In the event of default in payment of any installation of rent or at the expiration of said term of this lease, Lessee will quit and surrender the said premises to Landlord.

13. **Security Deposit:** The Lessee has deposited the sum of $ __600.00__ , receipt of which is hereby acknowledged, which sum shall be deposited by Landlord in a trust account with __Citizens__ bank; savings and loan association, or licensed escrow, __Cincinnati__ branch, whose address is __201 Main Street, Cincinnati, Ohio__

All or a portion of such deposit may be retained by Landlord and a refund of any portion of such deposit is conditioned as follows:
(1) Lessee shall fully perform obligations hereunder and those pursuant to Chapter 207, Laws of 1973, 1st Ex Session or as may be subsequently amended.
(2) Lessee shall occupy said premises for __one (1)__ month(s) or longer from date hereof.
(3) Lessee shall clean and restore said residence and return the same to Landlord in its initial condition, except for reasonable wear and tear, upon the termination of this tenancy and vacation of apartment.
(4) Lessee shall have remedied or repaired any damage to apartment premises;
(5) Lessee shall surrender to Landlord the keys to premises;

Any refund from security deposit, as by itemized statement shown to be due to Lessee, shall be returned to Lessee within fourteen (14) days after termination of this tenancy and vacation of the premises.

IN WITNESS WHEREOF, the Lessee has hereunto set his hand and seal the day and year first above written.

/s/ *Brendan Martin*   /s/ *Teresa Thomas*
LANDLORD   LESSEE
614 Dundas Street

Cincinnati, Ohio

ADDRESS

(Acknowledgment)

You may sign a lease for six months, a year, or longer. During this time, rent remains constant. Before the lease expires, the landlord must inform you of any rent increases. If you do not wish to stay beyond the lease period, you can notify the landlord as specified in the lease. Often leases require 30 days' written notice of rent increases and tenant departures.

A **rental agreement**, also called a *month-to-month agreement*, is a written contract that allows you to leave any time as long as you give the required notice. These are called month-to-month agreements because the agreement does not bind you to pay rent for a period of time longer than a month, as a lease does. However, since renting by the month does not establish the rent amount for more than one month, the landlord can raise the rent at any time or ask you to leave at any time. Still, the ease of moving in and out is an advantage of renting month to month. If your plans are uncertain and you need maximum flexibility, then month-to-month rental may be a good option for you.

Both a lease and a rental agreement include provisions for security deposits, termination of rental, rent payments, tenant and landlord responsibilities, and various other matters. Both a lease and a month-to-month rental agreement are legally binding when signed. Therefore, if you do not understand any part of the lease or rental agreement, ask the landlord to explain. If the answer is unsatisfactory and you still do not understand, do not sign the agreement.

Rental Inventory

When you move out of a rental property, it is expected to be in the same condition as when you moved in. Although normal wear and tear is expected and accepted, anything broken or damaged is not acceptable. To ensure that you are not accused of such acts as breaking, damaging, or taking furnishings, prepare an inventory of the premises at the time you move in.

The **rental inventory** is a detailed list of current property conditions. Noted are such things as missing window screens, holes in walls, torn or stained carpeting, and so on. Figure 12.5 shows an inventory and condition report that can be used in a variety of rental situations.

You and your landlord should tour the property together to take the inventory before you move any of your belongings in. Once the inventory is complete, you and your landlord should sign it to indicate that you both agree on its contents. Then you or the landlord should make a copy for each of you. When you move out, you and your landlord should once again take an inventory. The comparison between this inventory and the initial one will often determine if you get your security deposit back.

If your landlord does not do or require a rental inventory, it is advisable to do one anyway. Videotape or take photos of the conditions of the property when you move in as supporting evidence. Make sure the videos and/or photos are date-stamped. Provide a copy of the inventory and any supporting evidence to the landlord, even if the landlord does not ask for it. Keep your copy of the rental inventory and supporting documents in a safe place to prevent damage.

CHECKPOINT

How are leases different from rental agreements?

- -

FIGURE 12.5   Rental Inventory

INVENTORY AND CONDITION REPORT

Use this report to record the contents and condition of your unit when you move in and before moving out. If you mark anything as being either dirty or damaged, describe it fully on an additional sheet. Use the blank before each item to indicate how many there are. Ask the landlord to sign your copy.

			Dirty Yes* No		Damaged Yes* No	
Living Room						
___	Couch	1	☐ ☐		☐ ☐	
___	Chair	2	☐ ☐		☐ ☐	
___	End table	3	☐ ☐		☐ ☐	
___	Easy chair	4	☐ ☐		☐ ☐	
___	Floor lamp	5	☐ ☐		☐ ☐	
___	Table lamp	6	☐ ☐		☐ ☐	
___	Coffee table	7	☐ ☐		☐ ☐	
___	Light fixture	8	☐ ☐		☐ ☐	
___	Rug or carpet	9	☐ ☐		☐ ☐	
___	Floor	10	☐ ☐		☐ ☐	
___	Walls	11	☐ ☐		☐ ☐	
___	Ceiling	12	☐ ☐		☐ ☐	
Bedroom (1)						
___	Bed frame(s)	13	☐ ☐		☐ ☐	
___	Headboard(s)	14	☐ ☐		☐ ☐	
___	Mattress	15	☐ ☐		☐ ☐	
___	Mattress cover	16	☐ ☐		☐ ☐	
___	Bedsprings	17	☐ ☐		☐ ☐	
___	Dresser	18	☐ ☐		☐ ☐	
___	Nightstand	19	☐ ☐		☐ ☐	
___	Drapes or curtains	20	☐ ☐		☐ ☐	
___	Mirror	21	☐ ☐		☐ ☐	
___	Light fixture	22	☐ ☐		☐ ☐	
___	Rug or carpet	23	☐ ☐		☐ ☐	
___	Floor	24	☐ ☐		☐ ☐	
___	Walls	25	☐ ☐		☐ ☐	
___	Ceiling	26	☐ ☐		☐ ☐	
Bedroom (2)						
___	Bed frame(s)	27	☐ ☐		☐ ☐	
___	Headboard(s)	28	☐ ☐		☐ ☐	
___	Mattress	29	☐ ☐		☐ ☐	
___	Mattress cover	30	☐ ☐		☐ ☐	
___	Bedsprings	31	☐ ☐		☐ ☐	
___	Dresser	32	☐ ☐		☐ ☐	
___	Nightstand	33	☐ ☐		☐ ☐	
___	Drapes or curtains	34	☐ ☐		☐ ☐	
___	Mirror	35	☐ ☐		☐ ☐	
___	Light fixture	36	☐ ☐		☐ ☐	
___	Rug or carpet	37	☐ ☐		☐ ☐	
___	Floor	38	☐ ☐		☐ ☐	
___	Walls	39	☐ ☐		☐ ☐	
___	Ceiling	40	☐ ☐		☐ ☐	
Kitchen						
___	Working stove	41	☐ ☐		☐ ☐	
___	Working oven	42	☐ ☐		☐ ☐	

			Dirty Yes* No		Damaged Yes* No	
___	Oven racks	43	☐ ☐		☐ ☐	
___	Broiler pan	44	☐ ☐		☐ ☐	
___	Working refrigerator	45	☐ ☐		☐ ☐	
___	Ice trays	46	☐ ☐		☐ ☐	
___	Working sink	47	☐ ☐		☐ ☐	
___	Working garbage disposal	48	☐ ☐		☐ ☐	
___	Countertops	49	☐ ☐		☐ ☐	
___	Range hood w/working fan	50	☐ ☐		☐ ☐	
___	Working dishwasher	51	☐ ☐		☐ ☐	
___	Hot and cold running water	52	☐ ☐		☐ ☐	
___	Drawers	53	☐ ☐		☐ ☐	
___	Dinette table	54	☐ ☐		☐ ☐	
___	Dinette chairs	55	☐ ☐		☐ ☐	
___	Light fixture	56	☐ ☐		☐ ☐	
___	Floor	57	☐ ☐		☐ ☐	
___	Walls	58	☐ ☐		☐ ☐	
___	Ceiling	59	☐ ☐		☐ ☐	
Bathroom						
___	Towel racks	60	☐ ☐		☐ ☐	
___	Tissue holder	61	☐ ☐		☐ ☐	
___	Mirror	62	☐ ☐		☐ ☐	
___	Medicine cabinet	63	☐ ☐		☐ ☐	
___	Countertop	64	☐ ☐		☐ ☐	
___	Working sink	65	☐ ☐		☐ ☐	
___	Working tub	66	☐ ☐		☐ ☐	
___	Working shower	67	☐ ☐		☐ ☐	
___	Working toilet	68	☐ ☐		☐ ☐	
___	Toilet seat	69	☐ ☐		☐ ☐	
___	Shower curtain	70	☐ ☐		☐ ☐	
___	Cabinet	71	☐ ☐		☐ ☐	
___	Light fixture	72	☐ ☐		☐ ☐	
___	Hot and cold running water	73	☐ ☐		☐ ☐	
___	Floor	74	☐ ☐		☐ ☐	
___	Walls	75	☐ ☐		☐ ☐	
___	Ceiling	76	☐ ☐		☐ ☐	
Miscellaneous						
___	Door key	77	☐ ☐		☐ ☐	
___	Windows	78	☐ ☐		☐ ☐	
___	Window screens	79	☐ ☐		☐ ☐	
___	Mailbox	80	☐ ☐		☐ ☐	
___	Mailbox key	81	☐ ☐		☐ ☐	
___	Thermostat	82	☐ ☐		☐ ☐	
___	Other	83	☐ ☐		☐ ☐	
___		84	☐ ☐		☐ ☐	

Do all the windows work?_____

Does the heat work properly? _____

_____ Tenant

_____ Witness

_____ Date

_____ Landlord

_____ Date

*Describe fully on an additional sheet.

Landlord and Tenant Responsibilities

Most states have passed landlord–tenant laws that detail the legal rights and obligations of both landlords and tenants. A successful landlord–tenant relationship depends heavily on both landlords and tenants knowing and complying with these laws.

Landlord Obligations

Housing laws in most states require that landlords provide a dwelling that is habitable (livable) at all times. A dwelling is considered habitable if:

- The exterior (including roof, walls, doors, and windows) is weatherproof and waterproof.
- Floors, walls, ceilings, stairs, and railings are in good repair.
- Elevators, halls, stairwells, and exits meet fire and safety regulations. Smoke detectors are required in each unit in most states. (Tenants are responsible for testing the alarms, replacing batteries, and reporting any defects.)
- Adequate locks are provided for all outside doors and working latches are provided for all windows.
- Plumbing facilities comply with local and state sanitation laws and are in good working condition.
- Water supply provided is safe and adequate.
- Lighting, wiring, heating, air-conditioning, and appliances are in good condition and comply with local and state building and safety codes.
- Buildings and grounds are clean and sanitary; garbage receptacles are adequate. (Tenants may be responsible for garbage removal charges.)

Tenant Obligations

Tenants have numerous responsibilities not only to landlords but also to other tenants. These obligations are usually stated specifically in the lease or rental agreement. Even when not stated, tenants have the obligation to:

- Read, understand, and abide by the terms of the rental contract.
- Pay the rent on or before the due date. Failure to make a rent payment as stated in the rental contract may result in late fees, termination of the contract, or eviction. **Eviction** is the legal process of removing a tenant from rental property. If the eviction goes to court and the judge rules in favor of the landlord, it will be reported to credit bureaus. This reflects poorly on the tenant's credit score and makes it difficult for the tenant to rent property in the future.
- Give at least 30 days' written notice of intent to move. This notice will prevent the loss of the security deposit and allow the landlord time to find another renter before you leave.
- Keep the premises in good, clean condition to prevent unnecessary wear and tear or damage to the unit.
- Use a rental unit only for the purpose for which it is intended. For example, if the tenant plans to rent a place to use for a business, the tenant must discuss that with the landlord.
- Allow the landlord access to the living unit to make repairs or improvements.
- Obey the rules specified in the rental contract for the residents of the rental community, covering such things as quiet hours, use of recreational facilities, use of laundry facilities, and parking regulations.

 **CHECKPOINT**

What are a tenant's obligations when renting property?

Why Should You Read a Rental Lease Carefully Before Signing It?

Many owners of rental property would rather lease space to you than rent it to you on a month-to-month basis. A lease gives both the lessor (the landlord) and the lessee (the tenant) the security of knowing the property is committed for a fixed period of time. But the lease can be a trap if you don't understand its provisions before you sign.

For example, many lessors offer "specials" to those who sign leases for a year or more. These specials may include reduced monthly rent, reduced deposits and fees, and other concessions. But in most cases, if you need to terminate the lease before the agreed-upon time, there can be enormous consequences.

In a typical "special" lease offer, the lessor states that regular monthly rent is $800. If the lessee signs a one-year lease, the rent is reduced to $750 and the move-in fee is also reduced from $300 to $200. The savings are significant. But the lease also states that if the lessee terminates the agreement prior to one year, he or she must repay the entire rent reduction and the balance of the reduced fee.

Suppose you are the lessee and you must move out early, say at the beginning of the eighth month. If your lease agreement prohibits *subleasing*, which allows you to find another tenant to take over the rest of your lease, you would have to pay back seven months' worth of reduced rent ($50 × 7) plus the additional $100 move-in fee, for a total of $450. In addition, you are still obligated to pay the remaining five months' rent (at the regular rate of $800) until the lessor can find another tenant to take your place. While the lessor has to make every "reasonable" effort to re-rent your place, he or she has no incentive to try to lease yours first if there are other units available. As you can see, this type of "deal" can be very, very expensive.

Before you sign the lease, be sure to read it carefully and understand your commitments. You may be able to negotiate better terms at the beginning, before you sign the lease.

THINK CRITICALLY

1. Check online or your newspaper for listings of rental housing in your area. Do you see any lease specials? Describe them.

2. Do you know someone who is leasing property? Ask to see the person's lease agreement. What potentially expensive provisions does it contain? Does the contract prohibit subleasing?

KEY TERMS REVIEW

Match the terms with the definitions. Some terms may not be used.

a. eviction
b. landlord
c. lease
d. lessee
e. lessor
f. rental agreement
g. rental inventory
h. renting
i. tenant

___ 1. The landlord, or person responsible for the property

___ 2. A person who rents property

___ 3. The process of using another person's property for a fee

___ 4. The legal process of removing a tenant from a property

___ 5. The owner, or owner's representative, of rental property

___ 6. A month-to-month agreement between landlord and tenant

___ 7. A detailed list of current property conditions

___ 8. A written agreement that allows a tenant to use property for a set period of time at a set rent payment

CHECK YOUR UNDERSTANDING

LO2-1 9. Why do some people choose to rent living space instead of buying a house?

LO2-3 10. What obligations does a landlord have to his or her tenants?

APPLY YOUR KNOWLEDGE

LO2-1 11. Explain the purpose of a preparing a rental inventory when you first move into rental property and when you move out?

THINK CRITICALLY

LO2-2 12. The rental application asks many private and personal questions, and a potential landlord is likely to run your credit report. Why is this lengthy application process necessary?

LO2-2 13. How does a lease give a tenant more protection than a month-to-month rental agreement?

LO2-3 14. Some landlords keep renters' security deposits without proper justification. What can you do to help protect yourself from this practice?

The Essential Question *Refer to The Essential Question on p. 285. When renting a place to live, factors to consider include the advantages and disadvantages of renting, the rental application process, the type of rental contract desired, and the obligations of both the landlord and tenant.*

SUMMARY

12.1

- *On-campus housing options include dormitories, apartments, fraternity or sorority houses, and housing cooperatives.*

- *Off-campus housing options include apartments, duplexes and multiplexes, condominiums, and rental houses.*

- *To live together successfully, roommates must have compatible living habits and work out responsibilities in advance.*

- *When deciding where to live, consider required security deposits and fees, safety of the area, length of time you plan to live there, distance from school and work, and distance from services.*

- *Prepare to move by saving money and having a steady income, accumulating needed items, and making moving truck reservations in advance.*

- *When you move in, you will have to pay fees to have utilities installed or turned on. The bundling of some services may save you money.*

12.2

- *Advantages of renting include flexibility, lower cost, fewer responsibilities, amenities, and convenience.*

- *Disadvantages of renting include noise, lack of privacy, small living and storage space, scarcity of parking, and no tax benefits.*

- *Landlords use the rental application to determine if you are a good risk as a tenant.*

- *If you lease, you (the lessee) agree to rent the space for a set period of time at a set rent payment. During this time, the landlord (the lessor) cannot raise the rent, but there are penalties if you leave early.*

- *If you enter a rental agreement, you can leave at any time with proper notice, but the landlord can also raise the rent or ask you to leave at any time.*

- *To protect yourself from being held responsible for preexisting problems, complete a rental inventory when you move in.*

- *Landlords are responsible for providing a safe and habitable place for tenants to live.*

- *Tenant responsibilities include paying rent on time, obeying the rules, and taking reasonable care of the property. Failure to meet obligations could result in eviction.*

APPLY WHAT YOU KNOW

LO1-1   1. List the advantages and disadvantages of both on-campus and off-campus housing.

LO1-1   2. What are the pros and cons of living in a rental house?

LO1-2   3. Ask two people separately to answer the questions in the "Living Arrangements" section on p. 278. Based on the answers, would the three of you make a compatible living group? List the problems you would have to work out to live together successfully. Then get together and role play a discussion in which you work out these problems. Record your agreements in writing.

LO1-2   4. What possessions have you accumulated that you would need in order to set up housekeeping in an apartment?

LO1-2   5. What basics would you have to acquire to live independently? Which of these would you have to buy and which could you borrow to save money? Would you consider having a roommate with whom to share ownership of these items? Why or why not?

LO1-3   6. Make a list of things you should do before moving out on your own.

LO1-3   7. To move your possessions from your present home to a new residence, what types of transportation are available to you? What is the best and least expensive option for you?

LO2-3   8. What are the negative effects of being evicted from an apartment?

MAKE ACADEMIC CONNECTIONS

LO1-1   9. **Research** Conduct research of the rental housing market in your area. Compare today's prices to those of ten years earlier. Write a report explaining how rentals have changed: How many new rental properties are in the area? Are there more or fewer houses for rent? What types of rental properties are available around local universities?

LO1-1   10. **International Studies** Conduct online research about renting in other countries. Choose a country that interests you and find the types of rental properties that are available, their features, and their prices. How do they compare to most rentals in the United States? Convert foreign currency into U.S. dollars for comparison purposes. How do tenant and landlord responsibilities differ?

LO2-1   11. **Economics** Conduct research to find out if the housing market is a leading, lagging, or coincidental indicator of the state of the economy. For example, what do rental prices and availability say about the housing market and the current state of the economy? Write a one-page report to explain your findings.

LO2-2   12. **Communication** Create a rental application for a house that you or your parents own. What would you be looking for in a tenant? What rules would you set in terms of income?

Solve Problems and Explore Issues

LO1-1 13. Prepare a table or chart comparing the rental prices and availability of similar-sized apartments, duplexes, condominiums, and houses in your area. Also, note how many are presently available in each category, the high and low prices, and the average rental prices.

LO1-1 14. Your friend has decided to move from his apartment to a condo that is available for rent. The condo is in a large building; most of the owners are retired or mid-life professionals. Explain how a condo is different from an apartment and how expectations will change.

LO1-2 15. Renee, Julie, and Brittany just graduated from high school and are planning to attend the same college. They want to get an apartment and be roommates. What advice will you give them so that their experience will be successful?

LO1-3 16. Using the community resources in your area, find out the installation fees and security deposits required for the following services: (a) electricity, (b) cable or satellite TV, and (c) water. Are any of these fees and deposits refundable? If so, under what conditions? Can you bundle any services to save money? Explain how.

EXTEND YOUR LEARNING

LO2-3 17. **Legal Issues** Landlord–tenant laws require that landlords provide a written explanation for any deposits that are withheld from renters when they move out. Deposits cannot be withheld without proof of damages and repairs that were made. Many tenants believe they have been charged for damage they did not cause. How can they prevent this from happening? If landlords keep deposits but do not provide explanations within a reasonable time period (usually 30 days), what legal recourse do tenants have?

CHAPTER PROJECT

Select a large city in another state in which you might like to attend college. Search the Internet for rental properties in that city, both on campus and off campus. Create a table outlining three of your rental options. Include columns for the cost of rent and security deposit, amenities available, and the pros and cons of each property. Based on the city you selected, estimate your moving costs by determining the mileage and the cost of renting a truck or paying a moving company. Make a list of the furnishings and other household and personal items you will take. If you need to purchase any furniture, research and list the costs. Finally, assume you will have one roommate and prepare a group budget as shown in Figure 12.2 on p. 282. Compile your findings in a folder that you will keep to help prepare for your move to college.

Complete the Guided Decision Making activity for Chapter 12 at ngl.cengage.com/mypf.

Buying a Home

Consider This...

Scott and Trisha have been married for five years, and they have managed to save money toward buying their own home.

"I think we have enough money saved to put a down payment on a four-bedroom home, though we really need only two bedrooms right now," Scott said to his wife.

"I'm not sure we have as large a down payment as you think," Trisha replied. "We'll have to pay other costs as well, such as closing costs and moving expenses."

"Okay," Scott agreed. "Let's start out with a smaller house that meets our needs and has potential for improvement. We can sell and move to another house when we start our family. By then, we'll have built up some equity. Now how do we go about finding the right home?"

The Essential Question *Why should you consider buying a home, given the costs and responsibilities of home ownership?*

LEARNING OBJECTIVES

> LO 1-1 Discuss the advantages of home ownership.
> LO 1-2 Describe the costs and responsibilities of buying and owning a home.

KEY TERMS

- market value, *298*
- appraised value, *298*
- assessed value, *298*
- equity, *298*
- tax shelter, *299*
- mortgage, *301*
- escrow account, *301*
- loan origination fee, *301*
- closing costs, *302*
- CC&Rs, *303*

LO 1-1 Advantages of Home Ownership

There are numerous advantages to owning your own home. Home ownership builds equity, increases your quality of life, and helps you save on your income taxes.

Value and Equity

There are four valuation methods commonly used in real estate:

1. *Market value.* The **market value** of a home is the highest price that the property will bring on the market. It generally means what a ready and willing buyer and seller would agree upon as the price.
2. *Appraised value.* Real estate appraisers can prepare an **appraised value** by examining the structure, size, features, and quality as compared to similar homes in the same geographic area. The recent selling price of a similar home in your area is a good estimate of the current value of your home.
3. *Assessed value.* For purposes of computing property taxes owed against your home, the city or county in which you live annually sets an **assessed value**. Assessed value is based on the cost and quality of the construction, the cost of improvements, and the cost of similar properties. It is usually a percentage of the market value. Computer programs, rather than visual inspection, are often used to determine assessed value.
4. *Estimated value.* Real estate agents also estimate the value of homes to help sellers establish a list price. To do this, they compare your house and its features to those of comparable properties, or *comps*, that have recently sold in a close geographic area. Using these comps gives a general idea of a property's value and establishes a point at which to begin negotiations.

The value of most homes *appreciates*, or increases in market value, over time. For example, if you buy a home for $150,000 and two years later you can sell it for $160,000, then your property has appreciated by $10,000. Appreciation is one way that the equity in your home increases. **Equity** is the difference between the market value of property and the amount owed on it.

© Pan Xunbin/Shutterstock.com

Equity also increases because each loan payment you make decreases your debt. Equity turns to cash when you sell your home. For example, if you purchase a home valued at $150,000 and have a loan of $120,000, your initial equity is $30,000. Suppose that when you decide to sell, the market value has increased to $170,000 and your loan debt is down to $100,000. Your equity would be $70,000 (the $170,000 market value minus the $100,000 owed).

What kinds of quality-of-life advantages do homeowners enjoy?

Quality of Life

Owning a home offers many benefits that enhance a person's quality of life. Homeowners generally have more privacy and larger living and storage space than renters have. Homeowners also have more personal freedom. In your own home, you are able to redecorate or remodel to accommodate your own needs and personal style. Knowing that the home is yours to do with as you wish can be very satisfying. Owning a home also provides a feeling of security, stability, and independence. No one can raise your rent or tell you that you have to leave. You also get a sense of belonging. Because you have "put down roots," you become part of a neighborhood.

Although neighborhood living involves responsibilities to surrounding neighbors, the homeowner can have a voice in helping to set the tone of the neighborhood. *Neighborhood associations* are groups of homeowners in geographic areas that voluntarily meet and work to set quality-of-life standards for the area.

Tax Savings

Tax savings result when you can deduct money paid for certain expenses from your tax liability. Renters cannot deduct any part of their rent payments from their income taxes. However, the interest you pay on your home loan and the property taxes you pay are tax deductible. These tax deductions lower the cost of home ownership. Because of these tax savings, owning real estate is a **tax shelter** (a legal write-off that reduces tax liability).

Even though the equity in your home may increase each year, you do not pay tax on the equity until you sell your home. Even then, if the property was your primary residence, you do not have to pay taxes if the gains from the sale are below $250,000 ($500,000 for married couples filing joint taxes).

✔ CHECKPOINT

What is equity? How does equity increase?

Math Minute

Computing Equity in a Home

Suppose you bought a home for $200,000. Your lender required a 20 percent down payment. Therefore, your down payment was:

$$\$200,000 \times .20 = \$40,000$$

Your initial loan amount (ignoring other costs) was:

$$\$200,000 - \$40,000 = \$160,000$$

Now let's say that you have been making payments on your house for two years, reducing your debt (principal) by $8,000. Therefore, you now owe:

$$\$160,000 - \$8,000 = \$152,000$$

Your house has been appreciating at 5 percent per year for two years. As a result, the current market value is:

$$\$200,000 \times 1.05 = \$210,000 \text{ after year 1}$$

$$\$210,000 \times 1.05 = \$220,500 \text{ after year 2}$$

Your equity is now:

$$\$220,500 \text{ market value} - \$152,000 \text{ remaining debt} = \$68,500$$

Based on the preceding example, compute the amount for the (a) down payment, (b) initial loan, (c) current debt, (d) current market value, and (e) current equity in the following situation:

Martin and Jamie bought a house two years ago for $175,000. They put 15 percent down. Their payments have reduced their debt by $6,000. Houses in their area have been appreciating at 4 percent per year.

Solution:

(a) Down payment = $175,000 $\times$ .15 = $26,250

(b) Initial loan = $175,000 − $26,250 = $148,750

(c) Current debt = $148,750 − $6,000 = $142,750

(d) Current market value = ($175,000 $\times$ 1.04) $\times$ 1.04 = $189,280

(e) Current equity = $189,280 − $142,750 = $46,530

© simo988/Shutterstock.com

LO 1-2 Costs of Home Ownership

Home ownership carries significant costs and responsibilities. Before deciding to buy a home, you should make sure that you are financially able to handle the costs and that you are personally ready to accept the responsibilities.

Down Payment

Mortgage lenders usually require that borrowers pay a certain amount down toward the purchase price of a house. Then they will provide a loan for the balance of the price. A *conventional loan* is a mortgage agreement that does not have government backing and that is offered through a commercial bank or mortgage broker. This type of loan often requires a 10 to 30 percent down payment. For example, if you are purchasing a home for $150,000, you will need from $15,000 (10 percent) to $45,000 (30 percent) for the down payment. To qualify for a conventional loan, a borrower must have a good credit score and his or her monthly mortgage payment and debt load must fall within certain percentages in relation to gross monthly income.

Those who do not qualify for a conventional loan may be able to get an FHA loan. An *FHA loan* is a government-sponsored loan that carries mortgage insurance. In other words, borrowers pay a monthly insurance premium and their loan payments are guaranteed through the FHA (Federal Housing Administration) insurance program, making it less risky for banks to lend the money. FHA loans may require down payments of as little as 3.5 percent. FHA loans are often available for first-time homebuyers and low-income buyers.

There are a few types of loans that may not require a down payment. VA loans, which are government-backed, are available for military veterans. Also government-backed is the USDA Rural Development loan. To qualify, houses must be located in an eligible rural area as defined by the USDA.

Mortgage Payments

A loan to purchase real estate is called a **mortgage**. A *trust deed* is similar to a mortgage; it is a debt security instrument that acts as a financial claim against property. Payments on a mortgage or trust deed are made over an extended period, such as 15 or 30 years.

Monthly loan payments include principal and interest. If the borrower is required to have an escrow account, then the monthly payment will also include property insurance and property taxes. An **escrow account**, also called a *reserve account*, is a fund where money is held by a financial institution to pay amounts that will come due during the year. For example, if your property taxes are estimated to be $2,400 a year, an additional $200 a month will be added to your loan payment. This amount will be held in your escrow account monthly so that the property taxes can be paid when the bill arrives.

Mortgage lenders sometimes allow borrowers to buy *discount points*, which are used to lower the mortgage interest rate. Typically, one point equals 1 percent of the loan amount. For example, 3 points on a $100,000 loan would be $3,000. Points are essentially extra interest that borrowers must pay at *closing* (time of purchase). They increase the cost of the loan. However, lenders usually offer lower interest rates in exchange for higher points. Whether this trade-off is a good deal depends on how long you plan to keep your house. A lower interest rate will result in lower monthly payments. Over many years, the lower payments may make up for the cost of the points and save you money. But since points are paid up front, you could lose money if you keep your house for only a few years. When you compare loan rates, be sure to consider the points. Points paid are tax deductible and, thus, another form of tax shelter.

Points are often charged in addition to a loan origination fee. A **loan origination fee**, also called a *mortgage loan fee*, is the amount charged by a bank or other lender to process the loan papers. This fee compensates the loan officer or broker for the time spent in qualifying buyers, preparing paperwork, and working with loan underwriters.

In 2007 the housing market was severely hurt when the economy slowed down and many people were unable to make their mortgage payments. In the years leading up to 2007, many home loans with zero down payments were made. Borrowers were assured that their equity would grow and that over time they would make money on their investment. Unfortunately, with a market slowdown, borrowers found themselves owing more money than their property was worth. This is called an *upside-down equity position*.

Many of the mortgage agreements also allowed for adjustable interest rates. As interest rates on the loans increased in subsequent years, the required monthly payment also increased significantly. As a result, many people—especially those who lost their jobs during the recession—also lost their homes to foreclosure. Some people think that these borrowers should have known better; they made bad financial decisions. Others believe that lenders took advantage of borrowers with loans that had rapidly increasing interest rates and payments.

THINK CRITICALLY

With which side do you agree? Why? How could making a larger down payment have provided a measure of prevention to the situation in which many borrowers found themselves?

Closing Costs

Closing costs, also referred to as *settlement costs*, are the expenses incurred in transferring ownership from buyer to seller in a real estate transaction. The buyer usually pays a credit report fee, title search fee (to make sure the seller is the legal owner and that no one else has a claim on the property), loan origination fee, loan assumption fee (to take over someone else's mortgage), closing fee (for preparing the paperwork), recording fee, and his or her share (called a *proration*) of taxes and interest currently owed on the property.

Typically, homebuyers pay between 2 and 5 percent of the purchase price of their home in closing costs. For example, if you pay $150,000 for a house, you will pay from $3,000 (2 percent) to $7,500 (5 percent) in closing costs. Lenders are required by law to give you a *good faith estimate* of what the closing costs on your home will be within three days of when you apply for a loan.

Property Taxes

Homeowners pay *real estate property taxes* based on the assessed value of land and buildings. A local taxing authority determines the assessed value of property, usually a percentage of the market value. For example, a home worth $200,000 might have an assessed value of $180,000 (or 90 percent of its market value). If the property tax rate is $15 per thousand of assessed value, you will pay $2,700 (180 × $15) in property taxes per year. Property taxes are tax deductible and also serve as a tax shelter for homeowners.

Property Insurance

A homeowner must have *property insurance* covering the structure. This is usually a requirement of the loan agreement to protect the interests of the mortgage lender as well as the homeowner. Standard homeowners insurance includes both fire and liability protection. A more detailed explanation of homeowners insurance is presented in Chapter 22.

© Vectomart/Shutterstock.com

Utilities

Because most homes are larger than apartments or other rental units, the utility bills are usually higher. The homeowner pays for all utilities and garbage services, whereas a renter may pay for some but not all of these services. Utilities may include water and sewer charges, storm drain (watershed) assessments, lighting fees (for neighborhood light poles), gas, and electricity.

CC&Rs and Zoning Laws

Many housing subdivisions are governed by home-owners' associations (HOAs) that set covenants, conditions, and restrictions, known as **CC&Rs**, which are rules designed to maintain property values and protect the interests of all property owners. CC&Rs include things such as maintaining your lawn, limiting the color(s) you can paint your house, specifying where vehicles can and cannot be parked, controlling the kinds of fences or storage buildings that can and cannot be built, specifying the type of roof that can and cannot be installed, and so on.

As a potential homebuyer, what kinds of CC&Rs and zoning laws might you be expected to follow?

Homeowners also must obey all *zoning laws* and local ordinances. These are laws passed by local governments to preserve the quality of life for all people in the community. They require you to obtain a building permit when you add to or modify your home and adhere to rules regarding the kinds and types of buildings that can be constructed in the area. In addition, you must follow setback requirements that force buildings and improvements to be set back a minimum number of feet from streets and other properties.

Maintenance and Repairs

As a homeowner, you will be responsible for maintenance and repairs inside and outside of your home. *Ongoing maintenance* includes such tasks as painting, mowing, weeding, landscaping, and fixing things that break or wear out from normal use. You will incur not only the costs but also the responsibility for doing these tasks or arranging to have them done.

In addition to ongoing maintenance, you occasionally will have to make very expensive repairs or improvements to your home. These can range from replacing your roof to removing a dead tree from your yard or replacing a major appliance, such as the furnace or water heater. Before you choose to buy, make sure you are willing to spend the time and money needed to keep your home in good condition. This will prolong the life of your home.

 **CHECKPOINT**

What is the difference between a conventional and FHA loan?

Real Estate

Because of the complexity of buying or selling a home or commercial property, people often seek the help of real estate brokers and sales agents. These professionals know the real estate market, real estate laws, and real estate financing.

Real estate listing agreements are used to input data about properties for sale. These listings include details such as location and features of the property. The listings are then made available to all local real estate salespersons, both locally and worldwide. Sales associates show properties to prospective buyers or renters, hold open houses, work with buyers to be sure they are qualified to buy real estate, and present purchase offers to sellers.

Brokers and agents are typically on call to meet the needs of their clients, so they often work evenings and weekends. Sales agents usually work for brokers on a contract basis and earn their income from sales commissions, meaning their income varies.

Employment Outlook

An average rate of employment growth is expected.

Job Titles

- Real estate agent
- Real estate broker
- Real estate closer
- Real estate assistant

Needed Skills

- At the minimum, a high school diploma is required, although a college degree is preferred.
- A license is required in all 50 states. To become licensed, candidates must complete a number of real estate courses and pass a licensing exam.
- Strong business, communication, and interpersonal skills are required.

What's it like to work in . . . *Real Estate*

Adam works for a real estate company in a small Midwestern city. He has had his license for three years and works under the supervision of a real estate broker.

Adam specializes in residential houses located in suburban areas. He also sells condos, duplexes, and other forms of rental residential property. He earns his income based on commissions from sales of these properties. He also does preliminary work for his clients, such as searching for properties on the market that meet buyers' wants and needs.

Today, Adam is meeting with prospective buyers who have been prequalified for a mortgage loan. They will be viewing six properties, and they wish to choose one of them by the end of the day. The buyers are being transferred to the area because of a job promotion.

What About You?

Would you like to help people buy, sell, or rent properties? Would you enjoy the challenge of working for commission-based income? Would you consider a career as a real estate broker or sales agent?

The Career Clusters icons are being used with permission of the: States' Career Clusters Initiative, 2007, www.careerclusters.org

KEY TERMS REVIEW

Match the terms with the definitions. Some terms may not be used.

____ 1. The value of your home for purposes of computing property taxes

____ 2. A legal write-off that reduces tax liability

____ 3. The amount charged by a bank or other lender to process mortgage loan papers

____ 4. A loan to purchase real estate

____ 5. HOA rules designed to maintain property values

____ 6. The difference between the market value of a property and the amount owed on it

____ 7. The highest price a property will bring in the marketplace

____ 8. A fund where money is held by your financial institution to pay amounts that will come due during the year

a. appraised value
b. assessed value
c. CC&Rs
d. closing costs
e. equity
f. escrow account
g. loan origination fee
h. market value
i. mortgage
j. tax shelter

CHECK YOUR UNDERSTANDING

LO1-1 9. Why do people choose to buy a house rather than rent a residence?

LO1-2 10. What responsibilities come with home ownership?

APPLY YOUR KNOWLEDGE

LO1-1 11. If you were trying to decide how much a home was worth for the purpose of making an offer to purchase it, what types of value would you consider? Which valuation method is the best? Why?

THINK CRITICALLY

LO1-1 12. Owning real estate is often described as a tax shelter. What does this mean? Explain the tax advantages of owning real estate.

LO1-2 13. If you don't make a substantial down payment, you may be required to pay into an escrow account from which property taxes and insurance will be paid when due. What are the pros and cons of this?

LO1-2 14. Explain how CC&Rs and zoning laws help ensure the quality of neighborhoods and enhance property values.

The Essential Question *Refer to The Essential Question on p. 298. Buying a home offers many advantages, such as tax savings, privacy, freedom, and quality of life. There are responsibilities however, such as making payments; paying closing costs, property taxes, insurance, and utilities; adhering to CC&Rs and zoning laws; and maintaining your property. Most believe it's all worth it.*

The Essential Question *What steps are involved in the home-buying process?*

LEARNING OBJECTIVES

> LO 2-1 Describe the steps in finding a home to buy and making an offer for it.
> LO 2-2 Explain how to qualify for a real estate loan.
> LO 2-3 Explain how to take title to property.

KEY TERMS

- prequalify, *307*
- earnest money offer, *307*
- contingencies, *307*
- inspection report, *308*
- seller's acceptance, *308*
- seller's counteroffer, *308*
- escrow closer, *310*
- title, *310*
- title insurance, *310*
- deed, *311*

LO 2-1 Finding a Home and Making an Offer

When buying a home, factors to consider include location, accessibility, nearness to employment, type and quality of construction, cost and effort of maintenance, and personal likes and dislikes. Before starting your search, determine the price range you can afford. It's also a good idea to list the features you want your home and neighborhood to have and then prioritize the list according to what features are most important to you.

You can look for a new home by yourself or use the services of a real estate agent. If you choose to do your own search, there are numerous places you can look. You can find homes for sale listed in newspaper classified ads and real estate magazines. You can also find listings of homes for sale, both nationally and locally, at numerous real estate websites. All of these sites contain photos and list the features of each home. In many cases, you can take a "virtual tour" of the house, which shows the house's layout and features. You may also want to check online classified sites, such as Craigslist and eBay, to view properties for sale.

Working with a Real Estate Agent

As a first-time homebuyer, it may be in your best interest to work with a real estate agent. Real estate agents act as an intermediary between sellers and buyers of real estate. They earn *commission income*. The commission is a percentage of the home sale price, usually between 6 and 8 percent. The seller pays the commission, and the agents working for the buyer and seller split it. As the purchaser, you do not pay the agents' commission. If you are buying directly from an owner without the assistance of an agent, you might be able to negotiate a lower price because the seller will not have to pay this fee. However, you should still seek advice from a professional, such as a lawyer, to be sure your interests are protected before signing any contracts.

© Pan Xunbin/Shutterstock.com

There are numerous advantages to working with a real estate agent. Agents know the market and can use their knowledge and expertise to help find the right home for you. They will also assist you with the purchasing, financing, inspection, and closing processes. Agents help protect your interests in a complex, and sometimes confusing, marketplace. Having an agent also gives you access to the multiple listings. The *Multiple Listing Service (MLS)* is a real estate marketing service in which agents from many real estate agencies pool their home listings and agree to share commissions on the sales. Sellers gain wide exposure for their properties. Buyers can sift through the large pool of property descriptions to select those they want to visit.

Why is it a good idea to work with a real estate agent when buying your first home?

One of the first things an agent will have you do is go to a mortgage lender and prequalify for a real estate loan. To **prequalify** you will fill out an application asking about your job, income, and monthly debts to help determine how much money you are qualified to borrow. This will guide you and your real estate agent to look for houses in your price range.

After you have been prequalified for your loan and have narrowed your choices to a small number of homes in your price range that match your criteria, you should visit the homes with your agent. Take notes, both pro and con, on the features of each house and neighborhood. Do not make a decision on the spot. After you have done a careful comparison and are certain you have made your best choice, then take the next step: make an offer.

Making an Offer

To let the homeowner know of your interest in buying the home and the price you are willing to pay, you will sign an agreement called an offer. An *offer* is a serious intent to be bound to an agreement. In real estate, when you make an offer to buy property, it is called an **earnest money offer**. The offer is accompanied by a deposit (usually a check) called the earnest money. It generally is a percentage of the sales price. For example, in an offer to buy a house selling for $200,000, the earnest money deposit could be $2,000 (1 percent) or more. This money is held in escrow until the transaction is completed.

Earnest money protects the seller in case you fail to meet the terms of the agreement. If you and the seller have agreed on the transaction, the seller will take the house off the market until the deal is completed. During that time, the house cannot be sold to anyone else. If you later back out of the deal, you will likely forfeit your earnest money to the seller.

One way to avoid losing your earnest money is to include contingencies in your offer. **Contingencies** are conditions that limit a buyer's liability in case one or more of them are not met. For example, you can make your offer contingent on obtaining financing. That way, if you do not qualify for a mortgage

Communication Connection

Write a one-page paper or prepare an electronic multimedia presentation about your ideal house. What would it look like? In what city? How many bedrooms? Describe your house in terms of type or style, number of square feet, size and shape of lot, and other distinguishing features. Include pictures (from magazines, newspapers, or the Internet) or draw diagrams to help illustrate the features you desire. How is your choice of house different from that of your parents? How will your choice of house likely be different in the future?

© oculo/Shutterstock.com

on the property, you will not have violated the contract and you will get your earnest money back. Another contingency may be dependent on the property passing an inspection. During a home inspection, an independent, certified, licensed inspector checks every surface in the house from the roof to the basement, including appliances, windows, doors, flooring and subflooring, electrical, plumbing, and wall safety (for leakage, substandard materials, dry rot, or insect damage). The inspector then prepares a written **inspection report**, which details the existing conditions of the house and property. If the inspection report brings any problems to light, you can negotiate with the seller on how any necessary repairs will be made and who will pay for them. If the seller refuses to negotiate, you can back out of the deal and keep your earnest money.

The seller may or may not accept your initial offer. When the seller agrees to your offer exactly as stated, you have an acceptance. A **seller's acceptance** is a formal agreement to the terms of the buyer's offer, forming a contract between the parties. You may withdraw your offer before the seller accepts it; however, once accepted, the offer becomes a binding contract.

If the seller wants to change any part of the offer, he or she makes a counteroffer. A **seller's counteroffer** is a rejection of the original offer with a listing of what terms would be acceptable. In effect, it is a new offer made by the seller to the buyer. For example, if you offered to buy a house at a lower price than the seller was willing to accept, the seller may make a counteroffer with a different price. The buyer and seller negotiate until they either agree on mutually acceptable terms or decide not to complete the transaction.

✔ CHECKPOINT

What is an earnest money offer, and why is it important?

- -

LO 2-2 Financing Your Home Purchase

After you have come to an agreement with the seller, you will have to arrange for your loan. To finance your purchase, you must have funds for a down payment, meet certain requirements of your lending institution, and select the type of mortgage you want.

Down Payment Sources

There are various sources available for your down payment. Personal savings is often the first source. However, because the down payment can be very expensive and many first-time homebuyers do not have enough money in savings to cover it, some buyers receive help from their parents or other family members in the form of a monetary gift. If any of your down payment is part of a gift, your lender will require the donor to submit a *gift letter*. This letter will state the loan applicant's relationship to the donor and the amount of the gift. Most importantly, since many lending institutions will not allow mortgage applicants to formally borrow their down payment, the donor will have to state that the gift fund is indeed a gift and not a loan.

If you are unable to come up with the down payment from your savings account or family, your retirement account is another option. First-time homebuyers can withdraw up to $10,000 for the purchase of a home from an individual retirement account (IRA) without having to pay the 10 percent early withdrawal penalty.

Qualifying for a Mortgage

To qualify for a mortgage, you must complete an extensive loan application. The lender will check your credit history, employment history, and references. The lender will also look at the type and amount of your current debts, the amount and source of your income, and your creditworthiness. Based on this information, the lender will judge if you can handle the monthly mortgage payments, which as a general rule, should not exceed 25 to 35 percent of your take-home (net) pay. The lender will also require a *real estate appraisal* by a certified real estate appraiser. This is to assure the lender that the property is worth more than the amount of the loan. If the appraisal comes back less than the offer on the house, the lender will not loan an amount in excess of the appraised value.

The lender works with an *underwriter*, who secures the funding for the loan. The underwriter typically evaluates the same factors as the lender but may have additional qualifications that must be met.

Types of Mortgage Loans

There are two basic types of mortgages: fixed-rate mortgages and adjustable-rate mortgages. A *fixed-rate mortgage* is a mortgage on which the interest rate does not change during the term of the loan. Both your monthly payments and the total amount of interest paid on the loan remain constant throughout the loan. An *adjustable-rate mortgage* (ARM) is a mortgage for which the interest rate changes in response to the movement of interest rates in the economy.

The interest rate for an ARM usually starts lower than the current rates for a fixed-rate mortgage. The lender then adjusts the ARM's rate based on the ups and downs of the economy. For example, at a given time, fixed-rate loans may be offered at 6 percent. This rate would

What kinds of information does a lender review to determine whether you qualify for a mortgage?

remain unchanged for the term of the loan. At the same time, an ARM may be offered at 4 percent. The trade-off for this low initial rate is its variability. The lender may raise the rate over time to 7 or 8 percent as interest rates go up in the economy. Many ARMs specify maximum rate increases (such as 2 or 3 percent a year) and ceilings (such as a high of 12 percent) to which the interest rate can rise.

✔ CHECKPOINT

What are some sources where you can get down payment money for a home?

- -

LO 2-3   Taking Title to Property

After you and the seller have reached an agreement (all contingencies are met and approved) and you have arranged your financing, the next step is to prepare for the closing. During the closing process, you will work with an escrow closer. An **escrow closer** is an independent person who gathers and verifies information, prepares the *closing statement* (which lists what the buyer owes and what credits will be applied to the buyer), and makes sure that **title** (legally established ownership), passes to the buyer.

Before you take ownership, you will want to make sure that the title is clear—that is, free of any liens. A *lien* is a financial claim against property. For example, if the previous owner used the home as collateral for a loan other than the mortgage, then that lender has a financial claim or lien on the property. This claim must be paid before ownership of the property can be transferred.

To ensure that a property has *clear title* (no liens or judgments against it), the escrow closer orders a title search. A *title search* is the process of searching public records to check for ownership and claims to a piece of property.

What does an escrow closer do during the closing process?

When the title insurance company confirms that title is clear and all is as represented, it will issue title insurance. **Title insurance** protects the buyer from any claims arising from a defective title. Most lenders also require title insurance to protect the lender's interests. Buyers and sellers often negotiate who will pay the title insurance fees.

Before the closing, the lending institution prepares the loan papers and sends them to the escrow closer. The escrow closer will then prepare the closing statement, and the buyer and seller will be notified of the *closing date*. Prior to the closing date, it is recommended that you make a final walk-through of the property to ensure that the seller has met certain responsibilities. Be sure that the property's condition hasn't

DreamPictures/VStock/Getty Images

changed since you signed the sales agreement, that any agreed-upon repairs have been made, and that no damage has been done to the property. Also ensure that any items included in the sales agreement are present and in satisfactory condition and that all items excluded in the sales agreement have been removed from the property.

If the final walk-through does not present any issues, then you and the seller will meet at the closing (usually at the title insurance company) to sign the papers and pay all related closing costs, such as those shown in Figure 13.1. If you have a real estate agent, the agent will attend the meeting with you and help you through the process. Once the closing costs are paid, the seller receives his or her money, and the **deed** (the legal document that transfers title of real property) is recorded, the ownership of the home is transferred to you.

CHECKPOINT

What occurs at the closing?

| FIGURE 13.1 | Typical Closing Costs |

REAL ESTATE CLOSING COSTS		
Type of Cost	**Typical Amount**	**Who Pays**
Credit report (on buyer)	$50 to $100	Buyer
Property appraisal fee	$350 to $500	Buyer
Pest/damage inspection	$250 to $500	Buyer
Electrical/plumbing/ water inspection report	$250 to $500	Buyer
Loan origination fee	Varies; often 1% of loan amount	Buyer
Points	Varies; often 1% of loan amount	Buyer
Loan assumption fee	Varies; often $500 to $1,500	Buyer
Escrow closing fee	Depends on selling price of property; usually $750 to $1,500	Buyer and Seller
Notary and filing fees	$50 to $150	Buyer and Seller
Title search and title insurance	Depends on selling price of property; usually $750 to $2,000	Buyer and Seller
Survey	$500 to $1,500	Seller
Home warranty (optional)	Depends on selling price of property; usually $300 to $1,000	Seller
Real estate commission	Percentage of sales price of home; usually between 6% and 8%	Seller
Attorney's fees	Varies; depends on services provided, such as preparing contract	Buyer and Seller
Prorated interest and taxes	Depends on date of possession and when title passes	Buyer and Seller
Transfer taxes and fees	Varies by state	Seller

Should You Get a 15-year or a 30-year Mortgage?

Lenders typically offer mortgages that run for a term of 15 years or 30 years. Before choosing a loan term, consider the differences. A 15-year mortgage has significant advantages.

- Because the loan term is shorter, lenders consider a 15-year mortgage less risky. Thus, 15-year loans have lower interest rates than 30-year loans. For example, if a 30-year fixed-rate mortgage has a rate of 6.375 percent, you could likely get a 15-year fixed-rate mortgage for 5 percent or less. Thus, you will pay much less total interest over the life of the loan.

- You will pay off a 15-year mortgage in half the time of a 30-year mortgage, enabling you to build equity at a much faster rate and enjoy the payment-free status sooner.

A 15-year mortgage also has disadvantages that make a 30-year loan more attractive to many homebuyers.

- Because the loan will be paid off in 15 years rather than 30, the monthly payments will be significantly higher. Many homebuyers do not earn enough income to qualify for a 15-year loan because of the payment size.

- The 15-year loan will often require a much higher down payment. In other words, you must have more cash up front, such as 20 percent or more of the cost of the property.

- The 15-year loan payment may put a strain on your budget, even though you are paying off the house at a faster rate. The payment may take such a large bite out of your paycheck that you would not have enough left over to live comfortably. Some people prefer to get a 30-year loan with a lower monthly payment and then pay off the loan earlier by making extra payments toward the principal. Because the extra payments are optional, there is less strain on the budget.

Whether to get a 15-year or 30-year mortgage is an important decision for homebuyers because your choice will affect your budget in a major way. Things to take into consideration include your age, current financial situation, and long-term financial goals.

THINK CRITICALLY

1. Which mortgage term (15 or 30 years) sounds better to you? How does your choice relate to your current age? For example, would your choice of mortgage differ if you were 25 years old versus 42 years old? Why?

2. Ask someone you know who owns a home whether he or she has a 15-year mortgage or a 30-year mortgage. Why did he or she choose this type of mortgage? As an alternative, use the Internet to research additional advantages and disadvantages of 15-year and 30-year mortgages.

KEY TERMS REVIEW

Match the terms with the definitions. Some terms may not be used.

a. contingencies
b. deed
c. earnest money offer
d. escrow closer
e. inspection report
f. prequalify
g. seller's acceptance
h. seller's counteroffer
i. title
j. title insurance

____ 1. A rejection of the original offer with a listing of what terms would be acceptable

____ 2. Legally established ownership to property

____ 3. An offer to buy property accompanied by a deposit

____ 4. Conditions that limit a buyer's liability in case one or more of them are not met

____ 5. A written report detailing existing conditions of the home and property

____ 6. The legal document that transfers title of real property

____ 7. A formal agreement to the terms of a buyer's offer exactly as stated

____ 8. An independent person who gathers and verifies information, prepares closing documents, and makes sure that title passes to the buyer

CHECK YOUR UNDERSTANDING

LO2-1 9. What are the advantages of the Multiple Listing Service (MLS)?

LO2-2 10. What is the difference between a fixed-rate mortgage and an adjustable-rate mortgage (ARM)?

LO2-3 11. What responsibilities do sellers have before the closing?

APPLY YOUR KNOWLEDGE

LO2-1 12. If you were in the market for a new home, would you look by yourself or use a real estate agent to help you through the process? Explain.

THINK CRITICALLY

LO2-1 13. If you take a virtual tour of a property, why is it still important to do an in-person walk-through before making an offer?

LO2-2 14. Why is it important to make a large down payment when you buy a house?

LO2-3 15. Explain what is meant by a title search. Why is it important? Explain how homeowners as well as mortgage lenders are protected by title insurance.

The Essential Question *Refer to The Essential Question on p. 306. The home-buying process includes prequalifying, finding a home in your price range, and making an earnest money offer. Once accepted, you must finance your purchase by making a down payment and qualifying for a mortgage. At closing, you pay closing costs, pay the seller, and take title to the property.*

Assessment

SUMMARY

13.1

- *There are four valuation methods commonly used in real estate: market value, appraised value, assessed value, and estimated value.*

- *Financial advantages of home ownership include an increase in equity as property values increase and the loan balance is paid down.*

- *Quality-of-life advantages for homeowners, as compared to renters, generally include more privacy, space, and personal freedom; a feeling of security, stability, and independence; a sense of belonging to a community; and a sense of pride and accomplishment.*

- *Real estate is considered a tax shelter because mortgage interest and property taxes on primary residences are tax deductible.*

- *Home ownership carries significant costs and responsibilities, such as a down payment, mortgage payments, closing costs, property taxes, property insurance, utilities, CC&Rs and zoning laws, and maintenance and repairs.*

- *A conventional loan requires a larger down payment; an FHA or other government-backed loan often requires a smaller down payment but also requires the borrower to carry mortgage insurance.*

13.2

- *Before starting your house search, determine the price range you can afford and prioritize a list of the features you want. Search the multiple listings for homes that meet your criteria. Once you have narrowed your choices, visit these homes and note their good and bad points.*

- *Real estate agents' commission is a percentage of the home sales price, paid by the seller.*

- *Once you have selected a home, you will make an earnest money offer to buy it. The seller may accept your offer or make a counteroffer.*

- *Once you have agreed on a price and terms of the sale, the offer becomes a contract.*

- *To finance your purchase, you must have funds for a down payment, fill out a loan application and meet the lender's requirements, and select whether you want a fixed-rate mortgage or an adjustable-rate mortgage.*

- *Prior to closing, you will want to have the title verified as free of any liens. You will also want to conduct a final walk-through of the property.*

- *At the closing, you will sign papers and money will change hands. Then the deed will transfer title to you.*

APPLY WHAT YOU KNOW

LO1-1 1. Go to the library or search online to find out the annual rate that houses are appreciating in your area. If you bought a house for $150,000 now, how much would it be worth five years from now at the current rate of appreciation?

LO1-2 2. In addition to your down payment, you will also have to pay closing costs when you buy a house. What are some of the various closing costs that a buyer must pay in a real estate transaction?

LO1-2 3. What is the purpose of CC&Rs? Who benefits from them?

LO2-1 4. Because of the complexities of real estate transactions, it is often wise to engage the services of a professional real estate agent. Find out through research or an interview with one or more real estate agents at least five services that a professional can provide when you are buying a home.

LO2-1 5. Why is it necessary for a buyer to have an inspection done on property he or she is considering purchasing? What happens if defects and other types of repairs are needed?

LO2-2 6. Obtain the home mortgage rates from a local bank, savings and loan association, credit union, and online lender such as Quicken Loans. Compare the rates and other loan terms such as the down payment, loan costs, points, and loan length. Compare the types of loans offered as well. Report on which lender makes the best financing offer.

LO2-3 7. What is a *lien* and how can it affect a homebuyer?

MAKE ACADEMIC CONNECTIONS

LO1-1 8. **Math** You bought your home last year for $130,000. You made a down payment of 20 percent. Through your mortgage payments, you have reduced your debt by $2,000. The annual appreciation rate for homes in your area has averaged 3 percent. Determine (a) the amount of your down payment, (b) the initial loan amount, (c) the amount you owe now, (d) the current market value of your home, and (e) the amount of equity you have in the home.

LO1-2 9. **Communication** Assume you have been appointed president of your homeowners' association. Create a brochure to be distributed to new homeowners that explains their responsibilities as a homeowner in your neighborhood, including the CC&Rs of the subdivision. Include suggestions on how to be a good neighbor and how to maintain the quality of life and property values in the area.

LO2-1 10. **Technology** Search the Internet for the multiple listings in your area. If you cannot gain access without a subscription, go to the website of a large real estate agency that operates in your area or to a national real estate website, such as Zillow. Create a bulleted list of the types of information supplied in the house listings.

Solve Problems and Explore Issues

LO1-1 11. Your friend is considering buying a house, but she is not sure how to determine the property's value. Explain to her the difference between market value, appraised value, assessed value, and estimated value. Which value should she use when making an offer on real estate?

LO1-2 12. If you buy a house for $225,000, how much down payment will you have to make if the lender requires a down payment of (a) 10 percent, (b) 15 percent, (c) 20 percent, or (d) 25 percent?

LO1-2 13. Suppose you accept a mortgage for $150,000. What finance charge will you have to pay at closing if the lender charges (a) 1 point, (b) 2 points, or (c) 3 points?

LO1-2 14. Suppose your local taxing authority requires you to pay property taxes at the rate of $16 per thousand. Your house is assessed at $210,000 by the county. How much property tax will you owe each year?

LO2-1 15. Use the description of your ideal house that you created in the Communication Connection activity on p. 308. Prioritize your list of features in order of importance to you. Select a moderate price range for homes in your area, and search listings that meet your criteria. Clip or print out the listings for three houses that you would like to tour if you were buying a home. Which of your criteria do these houses meet and which do they not meet?

EXTEND YOUR LEARNING

LO1-2 16. **Ethics** Some people feel that when they own property, they should be able to do with it as they wish. However, many neighborhoods and subdivisions require mandatory membership in homeowners' associations (HOAs) that enforce CC&Rs stating what residents can and cannot do with their property. Who is morally correct? Discuss whose rights are being violated and protected with each extreme. If you agree that HOAs should have the right to create and enforce guidelines, at what point would you draw the line?

CHAPTER PROJECT

With your instructor's permission, arrange to visit a real estate agent at work. Discuss with the agent the process of purchasing a house, including the steps and costs involved. Ask the agent to show you what the multiple listings look like. If possible, ask the agent if you can accompany him or her while showing a house to a prospective buyer. Write a brief paper summarizing what you have learned. As an alternative, conduct research on real estate agent careers and use the Internet to take a virtual tour of a house for sale. Write a report on your findings.

Complete the Guided Decision Making activity for Chapter 13 at ngl.cengage.com/mypf.

Buying and Owning a Vehicle

14.1 **Buying a Vehicle**

14.2 **Maintaining a Vehicle**

Consider This...

Patrick works part time and attends school full time. He lives at home with his parents, and his take-home pay is over $600 a month.

"I'm ready to buy a car," Patrick tells his parents. "This ad says that with just $100 down, I can finance the purchase of a brand-new car. I'd have to make 60 payments of $350 each. I make nearly twice that much each month, so I can afford the car. But I'm not sure I want that particular car. My friend Henri just bought a car from an auto dealer that gave him a good deal on last year's model. So that's something to consider too.

"Something else to think about is whether I might be able to get a better deal if I finance a car through my credit union. I've been a member there for several years now, and I have maintained my accounts well. I've never bounced a check or had an overdraft. They also have a car-buying service at the credit union. Would that be the way to get the best deal?"

© Pan Xunbin/Shutterstock.com

The Essential Question *What steps are involved when you buy a car?*

LO 1-1 The Car-Buying Process

Because it is a large purchase, buying an automobile should involve taking the time to make a good decision—one that you won't regret later. Following a decision-making model, such as the one presented in Chapter 11, may help you make better choices as you get ready to buy a car.

Identify Your Wants and Needs

Buying a car starts with identifying both your wants and your needs. Start by asking yourself some basic questions, such as the following:

- What do I need to do with a car?
- How much will I drive? (Fuel efficiency may be an important consideration.)
- Do I plan to haul a number of people or a lot of gear?
- Will I take the car off-road?
- What features would I like to have on the vehicle?

After you have made your list of wants and needs, decide which ones are most important. *Prioritizing* helps you identify what you must have and what you can give up if necessary to keep the price affordable.

Decide What You Can Afford

Before you start shopping for a car, determine how much you can afford to spend. One general guideline is that you can afford monthly payments of no more than 20 percent of the money you have left after paying all of your regular monthly expenses, such as rent or mortgage payment, utilities, credit card payments, and so on. Also figure into your budget the costs of maintaining your car as well as the costs of fuel and auto insurance. Cars can be expensive when you decide to add special features, such as special wheels and stereo equipment. Sometimes these features can be added on later at a lesser cost than the cost of buying a car that is "fully loaded."

© Pan Xunbin/Shutterstock.com

Identify and Research Your Choices

Select several types of cars that would meet your wants and needs and also your budget. Then research the features for each of your selections. Print and online magazines, such as *Car and Driver* and *Consumer Reports*, offer an abundance of information on different car models. Look for articles about performance, repair records, safety records, fuel economy, and prices.

Compare the features of the models you are considering against your list of wants and needs. Note the pros and cons for each model. Use your list and price range to narrow your choices to a few that best meet your criteria. When comparing prices, be sure to compare models that have the same options.

Decide Whether to Buy New or Used

A primary decision is whether to buy a new car or a used one. Cost is a major factor in this decision. A new car is much more expensive. Also, a new car loses much of its market value the minute you drive it off the lot. In fact, a new car can lose as much as 20 percent or more of its resale value in its first year. However, a new car likely won't need new tires, brakes, or any major repairs during its first few years of ownership.

On the other hand, a used car is likely to need more maintenance and repairs. Even if you have a mechanic check the car's overall condition before you buy it, a used car is still a bit of an unknown. A car dealer may offer a used-car warranty that you would not get from an individual seller, but a dealer will typically charge more for the used car.

Decide How You Will Pay for It

If you plan to take out a loan to pay for a car, you'll need to find out how much money you will be qualified to borrow before visiting car dealers. *Preapproval* is the process of getting a new- or used-car loan prearranged through your bank or credit union. Preapproval separates financing from the process of negotiating the price of the car. It also allows you to compare total costs of buying, including credit rates. You may or may not actually take the preapproved loan, but at least you will know how much you can spend and the interest rate you can get before you shop for a car.

To get preapproved, visit your credit union or bank and fill out a loan application. Based on the information you supply, the loan officer will determine how much the institution would be willing to lend you. The loan officer will then give you a form stating this preapproved amount and rate. Typically, the preapproval expires in 30 or 60 days, after which time you must reapply if you want the loan.

© iStock.com/LDProd

Why is getting preapproved before buying a car so important?

Check Insurance Rates

Check out the insurance rates on your vehicle choices. Car insurance rates can differ widely from one car to another. For example, SUVs and pickup trucks cost less to insure than sports cars. A call to your insurance agent to get this information helps rule out choices that may result in insurance that is too high.

Your choice of car may also be influenced by your driving record. If you have numerous moving violations, including accidents or speeding tickets, you may be deemed as a "risky driver" by the state and qualify only for assigned risk insurance. *Assigned risk pools* are state-run (or regionally run) programs that allow people who can't otherwise get needed insurance to get affordable coverage. Typical coverage is for liability only (to cover damages to the other driver). With a car loan, you will need full coverage (to protect the lender). Thus, if you are in a high-risk pool, your car choices are more limited.

Search for Available Vehicles

Search the Internet for cars available from car dealers and individual sellers in your area. Many websites, such as AutoTrader, Cars.com, and Kelley Blue Book, allow you to search for specific models, both new and used. Many websites will even give you price quotes.

Make a list of the available cars that match your criteria, including their features and prices. These are your finalists—the cars that you think are worth your time to investigate further.

Test Drive Vehicles

Sometimes descriptions are quite different from the actual car. That's why it is important to test drive the cars of interest to you before choosing one. A *test drive* is a simple road test where you drive the car for several miles in typical traffic and road conditions.

Begin the test drive by simply sitting in the car and asking yourself a few questions to help you decide whether the car is a good fit:

- Is it easy to get in and out of the car?
- Is there enough legroom?
- Is the seat comfortable?
- Are the gauges and controls easy to read and use?

Once you begin the test drive, evaluate the ride, steering and handling, acceleration, power, visibility, and braking. Try out the car's features, such as the climate control and stereo, to see how well they work. Once you test the stereo, though, turn it back off so that you can hear the sounds of the car as you drive. Especially when evaluating used cars, listen for noises that might indicate a problem. When you accelerate, look for dark smoke from the exhaust. This is a sign that the car is burning oil, which would require an expensive repair. If you are test driving a used car, look for rust and mismatched paint on the body. This may mean the car has been in an accident.

After the test drive, some salespeople will try to pressure you into buying right away. However, resist that temptation and take your time. You will enhance your bargaining position with patience and knowledge of the car you are planning to buy. If buying a car, be sure to check the dealer's reputation first. Checking with the Better Business Bureau will give you valuable information about any complaints consumers have made about this dealer.

Check the History of a Used Vehicle

If you are considering buying a used car, you should learn about its history. You can do so by looking up the car's **vehicle identification number (VIN)**, which is an alphanumeric number that identifies each vehicle manufactured or sold in the United States. This number is available on vehicle documents and on the dashboard on the driver's side. It is visible through the front windshield.

Get the VIN from the used vehicle(s) you are considering and enter it into the online search tool at the CARFAX website. A detailed history for one vehicle costs approximately $40, or you can get reports on an unlimited number of vehicles for around $55. The full report provides information, such as whether the vehicle has been in a serious accident, how many times the vehicle has been sold, and the mileage readings each time it was sold so that you can check for odometer rollbacks. Cars that have been totaled (wrecked) or used as rental cars will show a *branded title* to alert you to possible condition issues or high mileage.

Get the Vehicle Checked Mechanically

After the used vehicle has passed the VIN check and you've decided you'd like to buy it, have it checked out by an independent mechanic. For around $100 to $150, you can get a general indication of the mechanical condition of the vehicle. The vehicle inspection will let you know whether the engine is in good shape. A **compression test** can tell you whether to expect serious engine trouble ahead, such as head gaskets that are about to go out. You'll also want to be sure that the transmission is okay. If the vehicle passes these two critical tests, then ask for a complete check to see what repairs might need to be made in the near future and how much they might cost. For example, you'll want to know how much longer the brakes will last, whether new tires are needed, and so on. Once the vehicle has been inspected, ask the mechanic for a written report with a cost estimate for all necessary repairs. If you decide to make an offer after considering the results of the inspection, you can use the estimated repair costs to negotiate the price of the vehicle.

Many states require vehicles to pass a **vehicle emission test**, which verifies that a vehicle meets the minimum clean-air standards. If buying a used car, ask the

Why is it important to get a vehicle checked mechanically before purchasing it?

© iStock.com/Blend_Images

What is the difference between the sticker price and invoice price of a vehicle?

seller for the record showing that it passed the most recent vehicle emission test. If the seller cannot produce the record, ask the seller to have the vehicle tested before you buy it.

Determine a Fair Price

Decide what price you feel is fair before you make any offer for a used car. Kelley Blue Book publishes a popular pricing guide for used cars. Published quarterly, the consumer edition of the *Kelley Blue Book Used Car Guide* includes current trade-in values and suggested retail values on more than 10,000 models of used vehicles. You can find the publication in the library or in bookstores, or you can go to Kelley Blue Book's website to look up the model and year of the vehicle you are considering. You can also get a feel for a fair price by checking other ads for cars of the same model and year to see what other sellers are charging.

For a new car, the **sticker price**, or *manufacturer's suggested retail price* (MSRP), is the price shown on the tag in the car's window. A fair price for a new car usually lies somewhere between the sticker price and the price the dealer paid for it, called the **invoice price**. Typically, the MSRP is about 10 to 15 percent higher than the invoice price. Depending on the vehicle's popularity and the number currently on the market, a fair price is likely to be 3 to 6 percent above invoice. Arm yourself with this knowledge before making an offer.

Negotiate the Price

When it comes time to negotiate the price of a vehicle, you have the option of doing it yourself or using a professional to negotiate on your behalf. If you do your own negotiating, there are a few things to keep in mind. First, be relaxed and don't be intimidated. Stick to facts and don't reveal emotions to sellers. For example, don't make statements such as, "This car is just what I want." This type of information can weaken your bargaining position. Also, make your initial offer lower than your top price. In addition, do not be pressured into paying more than you think is fair. Walk away from the deal if you feel you are being pressured or the dealer won't come down to a price you feel is fair.

When negotiating, you should also be aware of common dealer negotiating tactics. For example, the salesperson might initially act positive toward your offer, allowing you to get your heart set on the car. Then the salesperson may tell you that he or she needs approval from the sales manager, leave you for several minutes, and then return to say your offer isn't acceptable. If this occurs, and the new price the dealer offers is still below the maximum you set for yourself as the fair price, then make a counteroffer that is a little higher but still lower than your top price. If the dealer won't come down any, then walk away.

Sometimes you will have a car that you want to trade in when buying a new car. To prevent confusion in determining the true price of the new car, negotiate the price for it separately from the price for your trade-in. After you have settled on a fair price for the new car, ask how much the dealer will give you for your old car. If the dealer does not offer an amount close to the trade-in value quoted for your car by Kelley Blue Book, then plan to sell your old car yourself rather than trade it in. Selling the car yourself can be a hassle, but you will likely get more money for it that way.

If you are uncomfortable negotiating the price of a vehicle, you may wish to use the services of a professional. Through your automobile club, a wholesale club (such as Costco), your credit union, or an online car-buying service, you can get a price based on cost to the dealer. A **car-buying service** allows you to choose the vehicle features you want and have a professional car buyer handle the price negotiation for you. Once you know exactly what car you want, the service will locate the car, negotiate the price, and arrange for its delivery. This service is not free, but it can potentially save you money.

Avoid Dealer Add-Ons

After you have agreed on the price of a car, the dealer may try to increase the purchase price with **dealer add-ons**—high-priced, high-profit dealer services that add little or no value. For example, dealer preparation is nothing more than cleaning the car and checking the air in the tires and the oil in the engine. These services should be provided without extra charge. Other common dealer add-ons include protective wax or polish, pinstriping, rust-proofing, and other services. Rarely are these special services worth the cost. If you are considering adding special features to your car, such as chrome-plated wheels, headlight covers, or window tinting, check with outside companies first. Usually, these features can be added on at a lesser cost by a specialty shop rather than by the car dealership.

CHECKPOINT

Why is it important to check the history of a used vehicle?

LO 1-2 Financing Your Car

After you've narrowed your choices based on your wants, needs, and budget, the next step is to decide how you will pay for the car. While some people opt to pay cash and avoid interest charges, most people cannot afford to make one lump-sum payment. Therefore, the majority of car buyers finance their cars by getting a loan.

Financial Institutions

Banks and credit unions typically offer car loans for 36, 48, 60, or 72 months. Longer terms mean lower monthly payments but higher total interest paid because you are using the money for a longer period of time. In many cases, your local credit union will offer the best deal on a car loan.

Often, a credit union will finance more of your purchase (requiring less of your own cash), have lower interest rates, and require smaller monthly payments.

Car Dealers

Most car dealerships also offer financing. On particular models and at particular times of the year, they may offer you better terms than those available from other sources. These special deals are sponsored by the auto manufacturers, or the manufacturers' financing agencies, to stimulate sales or to promote a particular model. Although you finance through the dealer, you will make your payments to the finance company. GM Financial is an example of a finance company that makes loans on cars through dealerships. Use caution with this type of financing. Don't allow a special promotional loan rate to influence you to buy a more expensive car.

Leasing

Rather than purchasing a new car, you might consider leasing. A *car lease* is similar to an apartment lease. It is a written agreement that allows you to use the property (in this case, a car) for a specified time period and monthly payment. You do not own the car; rather, you are simply renting its use. However, at the end of the lease period, you usually have an option to buy the car for a price specified in the lease agreement. The selling price specified in the lease is based on the expected value of the car at the end of the lease term.

For some people, leasing is an attractive alternative to buying a car. There is no large down payment or trade-in to worry about. Just drive away for a set monthly payment! In addition, consumers can afford to lease a more expensive car than they could buy on credit. On the other hand, after your lease is up, you still won't own the car, even after making all of the payments. Also, you may have to pay penalties if you return the car with excessive wear and tear or too many miles as defined in your lease agreement. Not all auto manufacturers offer leasing. So if interested, you may have to shop around to find a participating auto dealer.

CHECKPOINT

What are your financing options when buying a new car?

LO 1-3 Consumer Protection for Car Buyers

Once you've made your purchase, you need to know what to do if you have any problems with your vehicle. As you learned in Chapter 4, a *warranty* is a written statement about a product or service's qualities or performance that the seller assures are true. A warranty clearly states what the manufacturer will do if the product or service does not perform as it should. A new-car warranty provides a buyer with some assurance of quality. Car warranties vary in the time and mileage of the protection they offer and in the parts they cover. The important aspects of a warranty are the coverage of basic automobile parts against manufacturer defects and the coverage of the power train for the engine, transmission, and drive train. In addition to the basic warranty, there are a number of other ways that new- and used-car buyers are protected.

Extended Warranties

Many car dealers offer their customers extended warranties. For a flat fee, such as $2,500, car buyers can purchase an *extended warranty* to cover the costs of expensive repairs and defects that are not covered by the standard warranty or that occur after the standard warranty expires. However, most extended warranties are nothing more than extended service plans. You are simply paying up front for things that will need repairing or replacing later.

Extended warranties can be purchased either through the dealer or through a third-party provider. Dealer warranties often require you to have the repair made at the dealership. Therefore, if you are on a trip or if you move to another city, you would have to take the car back to the dealer where the extended warranty was purchased to get any repairs done.

Lemon Laws

A **lemon** is a car with substantial defects that the manufacturer has been unable to fix after repeated attempts. You have a lemon if, in the first year of ownership or 12,000 miles, (a) you've taken the car into the dealer for four or more unsuccessful attempts to repair the same substantial defect or (b) your car has been out of service for a total of at least 30 days.

Lemon laws exist in many states and protect consumers from the consequences of buying a defective car. Lemon laws allow you to get a new car or your money back. Unfortunately, this protection is not automatic. You need to have good documentation and be prepared for a long process. A proceeding called *arbitration* and a possible lawsuit may be necessary to enforce your state's law. Figure 14.1 indicates what to do if you buy a lemon.

The FTC Used Car Rule

People who buy a used car must be concerned about whether it has some hidden defects or potentially expensive repairs ahead. The Federal Trade Commission's (FTC's) **Used Car Rule** requires that dealers fully disclose to buyers what is and is not covered under warranty for the used vehicle. This rule also requires used-car dealers to inform consumers prior to purchase about who will be responsible for paying for certain repairs if they occur after the sale.

Do you think lemon laws are necessary? Why or why not?

FIGURE 14.1   What to Do If You Buy a Lemon

Here are some things you can do to protect yourself in the event you end up with a lemon.

1. When you take the car in for repair, give the dealer a written list of problems. Make sure these problems are in the dealer's repair records. Keep copies of each list and the repair receipts you are given.

2. Any time you are returning to have the same item repaired, point it out to the dealer. Make the dealer aware that the problem is continuing and not new. Again, keep copies of all records and attempted repairs.

3. If your car qualifies as a lemon, tell the car dealer. Bring copies of your records. If the dealer is not responsive, contact the manufacturer's zone office. Talk to someone in the consumer relations office, or go all the way to their national headquarters if necessary. Follow up the conversation with a letter and copies of your records. Be sure you keep your own copy of the letter and the original documentation.

4. If the defect is serious and the car is dangerous to drive, file for arbitration immediately. Make sure you fill out all necessary forms. State the problem clearly and, once again, provide copies of your documentation.

5. Demand a quick hearing date. Remind the arbitrators that under Section 703 of the Magnuson-Moss Warranty Act you are entitled to an arbitration decision within 40 days of filing.

6. You are under no obligation to accept a prolonged hearing. You can demand that the arbitration panel meet and make a decision.

7. If you are not satisfied with the arbitrator's decision or the process, you might want to contact a lawyer who specializes in lemon-law cases. The Center for Auto Safety in Washington, D.C., may be able to help you.

The rule requires dealers to place a sticker, called the "Buyer's Guide," on all used cars they offer. Figure 14.2 illustrates this sticker. If the "As Is – No Warranty" box is checked, the buyer must pay all repair costs. If the "Warranty" box is checked, the dealer pays for the items listed for the specified period of time. If the "As Is" box is checked, it is recommended that you have an independent mechanic conduct a pre-purchase vehicle inspection.

Buying Private-Party Cars

Many people prefer to sell their own vehicles, using online listings and local advertising. You may see cars for sale parked along the street, in driveways, or in a consignment lot. A *consignment lot* is a large parking lot where car owners can park and advertise their cars and pay a fee to the owner of the property. The property owner makes no representations as to the value or worthiness of the vehicle.

Private sellers are not covered under the FTC Used Car Rule and, thus, do not have to display the Buyer's Guide sticker. A car purchased from a private

FIGURE 14.2   Buyer's Guide (FTC Used Car Rule)

BUYER'S GUIDE

IMPORTANT: Spoken promises are difficult to enforce. Ask the dealer to put all promises in writing. Keep this form.

Ford	Focus	2012	A0A085C147961
VEHICLE MAKE	MODEL	YEAR	VIN NUMBER

T6204B

DEALER STOCK NUMBER (Optional)

WARRANTIES FOR THIS VEHICLE:

⊠ AS IS – NO WARRANTY

YOU WILL PAY ALL COSTS FOR ANY REPAIRS. The dealer assumes no responsibility for any repairs regardless of any oral statements about the vehicle.

☐ WARRANTY

☐ **FULL** ☐ **LIMITED WARRANTY.** The dealer will pay ___% of the labor and ___% of the parts for the covered systems that fail during the warranty period. Ask the dealer for a copy of the warranty document for a full explanation of warranty coverage, exclusions, and the dealer's repair obligations. Under state law, "implied warranties" may give you even more rights.

SYSTEMS COVERED: **DURATION:**

_____   _____
_____   _____
_____   _____
_____   _____

⊠ **SERVICE CONTRACT.** A service contract is available at an extra charge on this vehicle. Ask for details as to coverage, deductible, price, and exclusions. If you buy a service contract within 90 days of the time of sale, state law "implied warranties" may give you additional rights.

PRE-PURCHASE INSPECTION: ASK THE DEALER IF YOU MAY HAVE THIS VEHICLE INSPECTED BY YOUR MECHANIC EITHER ON OR OFF THE LOT.

SEE THE BACK OF THIS FORM for important additional information, including a list of some major defects that may occur in used motor vehicles.

seller typically will be sold "as is." Be sure to test drive the car. Taking someone along with you who is knowledgeable about cars and who can give you good advice is always a good idea. The best protection you can get is to have the vehicle inspected by an independent mechanic. Used cars are not going to be perfect, but they should be in good running condition so that you will not experience major repairs within the next 30 to 90 days.

If you buy from a private party, be sure to pay for the vehicle and exchange ownership information (title and registration) at your state department of motor vehicles (DMV). This will ensure you that the seller is the true owner and has the right to transfer title to you as the buyer.

✔ **CHECKPOINT**

What does it mean when a vehicle is sold "as is"?

How Do You Sell a Used Car?

If you decide to sell your old car yourself, here are some steps that will help you make a quicker sale:

1. *Give your car "curb appeal."* Wash and polish the outside, vacuum and clean the inside, and shampoo the upholstery. Remove all personal property. Make sure the car is mechanically sound. A car that appears well cared for will bring a higher price.

2. *Set a reasonable price.* Check a Kelley Blue Book publication (in print or online). You can also use the online appraisal tool at Edmunds.com or visit NADAguides to determine the fair market value of your car. Check online classified ads to be sure this price is within the range advertised by other people selling the same model and year as your car.

3. *Advertise your car.* Advertise your vehicle on websites such as AutoTrader, Cars.com, and Craigslist as well as in local newspapers. Putting a "For Sale" sign in the car window can also be an effective way to sell it.

4. *Screen potential buyers.* Use your intuition to evaluate potential buyers. If they seem suspicious, difficult, or pushy, wait for another buyer. If you do not feel comfortable having buyers come to your house to see the car, arrange to show the car at a neutral place, such as the parking lot in a shopping center.

5. *Be truthful.* Present the truth to prospective buyers—what's good about the car as well as its weaknesses. Disclose the last time you had a tune-up, and allow prospective buyers to check maintenance records.

6. *Accompany the potential buyer on the test drive.* Prospective buyers will want to test drive the car. Ride along with them so you can answer any questions about the car's performance.

7. *Be prepared to negotiate.* The buyer's offer may be lower than the price you have advertised, so be prepared to negotiate. Once a price has been agreed upon, always ask for payment in the form of cash or a cashier's check.

8. *Finalize the sale.* Once you have money for the sale, prepare and sign a bill of sale and any other documents your state may require. Make copies of all paperwork. Remove the license plates if they cannot be transferred. Meet the buyer at the department of motor vehicles to transfer title. Never let a new owner drive away with a car that is still in your name.

After you sell the car, remove all registration and other documents that contain your name and address. Also, notify your insurance company immediately to cancel your policy.

THINK CRITICALLY

1. Why should you tell the truth about your car when you are trying to sell it? What consequences might you face if you don't?

2. Why is it best to go along on a potential buyer's test drive?

3. If you were selling your car, what kind of payment would you accept? Explain your answer.

KEY TERMS REVIEW

Match the terms with the definitions. Some terms may not be used.

a. car-buying service
b. compression test
c. dealer add-ons
d. invoice price
e. lemon
f. lemon laws
g. sticker price
h. Used Car Rule
i. vehicle emission test
j. vehicle identification number (VIN)

____ 1. A federal law that requires dealers to fully disclose to buyers what is and is not covered under warranty for the used vehicle

____ 2. An alphanumeric number that identifies each vehicle manufactured or sold in the United States

____ 3. A test to verify that a vehicle meets the minimum clean-air standards

____ 4. A car with substantial defects that the manufacturer has been unable to fix after repeated attempts

____ 5. A test that detects engine trouble in a car

____ 6. The manufacturer's suggested retail price (MSRP) shown on the tag in the car's window

____ 7. High-priced, high-profit dealer services that add little or no value

____ 8. A professional negotiating service that helps consumers buy cars

CHECK YOUR UNDERSTANDING

LO1-1 9. Why should you turn the radio off when you are test driving a car?

LO1-3 10. Why is it important to know the dealer invoice price before making an offer on a new car?

APPLY YOUR KNOWLEDGE

LO1-1 11. Describe the vehicle that would be your first choice, based on your wants and needs. Describe the process you would use to research your choices.

THINK CRITICALLY

LO1-1 12. Being able to negotiate a fair price for your vehicle is an important skill. Explain what makes someone a good negotiator. What are some tactics you must learn to be a better negotiator?

LO1-2 13. What are the advantages of leasing a car instead of buying one?

LO1-3 14. What is a warranty, and why is it important in the car-buying process?

The Essential Question *Refer to The Essential Question on p. 318. Steps in the car-buying process include identifying your wants and needs, deciding what you can afford, researching your choices, searching for cars, test driving vehicles, checking their histories, and arranging the financing.*

The Essential Question *What are the costs of owning a vehicle, and how can you maintain its resale value?*

LEARNING OBJECTIVES

> LO 1-1 Identify the costs of owning and operating a car.
> LO 1-2 Describe methods for extending the life of your car and maintaining its resale value.

KEY TERMS

- hybrid, *330*
- depreciation, *331*
- classic cars, *331*
- appreciation, *331*
- car title, *331*
- car registration, *332*
- oxidize, *335*
- polishing compound, *335*
- car detail, *335*
- paintless dent removal, *335*

LO 2-1 | Costs of Owning a Car

Most people spend more of their income on transportation than on any other item, except housing. Costs of owning a car include the monthly car payment and car insurance (discussed in Chapter 22). Other costs associated with owning and operating your car include fuel, depreciation, registration and title fees, vehicle emission fee, maintenance and repairs, and the cost of accessories.

Fuel

Most engines today are gas powered. Gasoline is a *fossil fuel* that is refined from crude oil taken from the earth. The cost of gas depends on world supplies of crude oil, political conditions, and world energy markets. The amount of gas you consume depends on your car's fuel efficiency, the number of miles you drive, and your driving habits.

Because of environmental concerns and the rising prices of gas, you may want to buy a hybrid or other alternative fuel vehicle. A **hybrid** is a type of vehicle that uses alternate energy sources, such as natural gas or battery power, in addition to gasoline. Hybrids get better gas mileage than cars that use conventional fuel. Car manufacturers are also developing vehicles that use other types of energy, from electricity (with cars that recharge when plugged into your home outlets) to biodiesel and hydrogen. Alternative fuel vehicles not only cut consumers' fuel costs but also cut fossil fuel

Why is fuel efficiency an important factor when shopping for a car?

© tristan tan/Shutterstock.com

© Pan Xunbin/Shutterstock.com

How to Calculate Miles per Gallon (MPG)

Because of rising fuel prices, fuel efficiency is more important than ever. Determining how many miles per gallon your car gets is very useful. You can calculate MPG as follows:

1. Go to the gas station and fill up your tank. It doesn't matter if it's empty or half-full before doing so.

2. Record the mileage on your odometer before leaving the gas station.

3. Drive your normal route until your tank is almost empty.

4. Return to the gas station, record the mileage on your odometer, and fill up your tank again. Look at the pump to see how many gallons of gas were needed to fill up your tank.

5. Subtract the first odometer reading from the last odometer reading. Then divide this number by the number of gallons needed to refill your tank to calculate the MPG.

Suppose you filled up your tank and had an odometer reading of 11,300. After driving your normal route all week, you refill your car, which now has an odometer reading of 11,725. It takes 12 gallons of gas to refill the car. What is your MPG?

Solution: 11,725 − 11,300 = 425 miles ÷ 12 gallons = 35.4 MPG

emissions from cars, thus helping to preserve and enhance air quality. To promote the use of alternative fuels, the federal government and many state governments offer tax incentives to consumers who purchase qualifying vehicles.

Depreciation

As a car ages, the number of miles it has been driven increases, the physical condition begins to deteriorate, and mechanical difficulties arise. Also, styles and consumer tastes change over time. All of these factors lead to **depreciation**, which is a decline in the value of property due to normal wear and tear. However, not all cars depreciate. Rare cars and older vehicles that are kept in excellent condition, called **classic cars**, may experience **appreciation**, or an increase in value, if valued as collectors' items.

Depreciation is the single greatest cost of owning a car. The cost of gasoline comes second. In most cases, the age of a car is the most important factor in determining its resale or trade-in value. Other factors include mileage, mechanical condition, model popularity, size, and color. Cars that maintain a high demand and are low in supply typically have better resale values.

Registration and Title Fees

All states charge fees for title and registration. A **car title** is a legal document that establishes ownership of the vehicle. A car title lists the legal owner (usually the lending institution) and the registered owner (you). You must pay title fees only at the time you buy the car. In addition, you must also pay an annual **car registration** or *license tag* fee. The license plate on your vehicle carries a sticker that shows you have paid the current year's renewal registration fee.

Vehicle Emission Fee

As mentioned earlier in the chapter, many states require vehicles to be tested to make sure they are meeting environmental standards for vehicle emissions. Whether a car needs this testing usually depends on the type and model year of the vehicle and the county in which you reside. Cars that require vehicle emission tests usually must be tested every two years once the car is four or more years old. The fee for the test is usually about $15 to $30.

Maintenance and Repairs

To keep a well-maintained car, you will be required to perform regular maintenance. The owner's manual for the vehicle provides a maintenance schedule that tells you what services are needed and how often. Typically, you can expect to change the oil every 3,000 to 5,000 miles or every three months—whichever comes first; have a major engine tune-up every 20,000 to 30,000 miles; and perform other maintenance, such as rotation of your tires, at scheduled intervals. Car systems that you should monitor and maintain include emissions control, air conditioning, brakes, and transmission.

You should also plan for unscheduled repairs. Such things as broken belts and leaky hoses happen from time to time, and these repairs can add up. Setting aside money for car repairs should be part of your monthly budget. As your car gets older, repair costs will increase. You should expect to replace relatively inexpensive parts, such as fan belts, hoses, the battery, and the muffler, but also plan for occasional expensive repairs, such as replacing the alternator and getting new tires.

Accessories

Many people choose to add certain features to their car to make it safer, more functional and attractive, or more efficient. These items include GPS systems, satellite radio, remote start systems, snow tires, wheel covers, window tinting, pinstriping, alarm systems, and sound systems. In some cases, these accessories will add to the value of the vehicle; in other cases, they will subtract from it. As mentioned earlier in the chapter, many dealers offer these features as

What are some examples of the regular maintenance you will be expected to perform when you own a car?

© iStock.com/andresrimaging

Many states have passed laws making it illegal to use a handheld cell phone while driving. They usually allow a hands-free system, which may include earphones, a Bluetooth, a mounted cell phone, or a cell phone speaker through the sound system. The laws are based on safety. Many of these laws specifically target teenagers. When people are talking or texting on the phone, especially inexperienced drivers, they become distracted, which can be dangerous and cause accidents. Their driving skills are also impaired when they have only one hand available to drive. For example, distracted drivers often fail to signal when changing lanes.

Many motorists believe, however, that a cell phone is no more dangerous than speaking to a passenger, using a GPS, eating, or any other distraction. They advocate that cell phones are a great convenience and help people get where they need to go. When on long trips or in traffic jams, they can save time and allow for multitasking.

THINK CRITICALLY

With which side do you agree? Why? Do you think that vehicles should contain features, such as game systems and televisions? Why or why not? Do you think laws targeting teenagers are discriminatory? Explain your answer.

© Vectomart/Shutterstock.com

add-ons when you purchase a car; however, you can usually get accessories added to your car at a much lower cost by going to a specialty shop.

CHECKPOINT

What are the benefits of owning a hybrid or alternative fuel vehicle?

LO 2-2 Extending the Life of Your Car

Because a car is expensive, you will get your best value (cost versus benefit) if you take care of your investment. By performing routine maintenance, keeping your car in a garage, taking care of the interior and exterior, and practicing good driving habits, you can keep your car running well and looking good.

Perform Routine Maintenance

Performing regular maintenance is vital to keeping your car on the road. For example, you should regularly check and maintain the proper fluid levels for your transmission, power steering, windshield washer, radiator, and brakes. These car functions must have fluid to work properly. Regular maintenance also includes rotating and balancing your tires. Rotating the tires extends their life by making sure all tires are getting equal wear. Tread wear puts you in danger of a blowout. You should also regularly inspect belts, hoses, and spark plugs.

Another important part of routine maintenance is having your oil changed often. Oil lubricates the moving parts of the engine and keeps it running smoothly and efficiently. Oil must be changed to eliminate accumulated dirt and sludge. Your individual driving habits will dictate how often you should change the oil. For example, the frequent starting and stopping of city driving use up oil sooner than long expressway trips. However, as a general rule, most experts advise having your oil changed every 3,000 to 5,000 miles or every three months—whichever comes first. You should also replace the oil filter when you change the oil. The filter helps clean the oil circulating through the engine. The average cost of an oil change (which typically includes the lube, oil, and filter) is $20 to $35, depending on the size and type of engine.

Consult the vehicle maintenance schedule in the owner's manual to determine when these and other preventive maintenance checks and services should be performed. Regular vehicle maintenance can seem like a lot of work, but the time and effort you put into keeping up with scheduled maintenance can save you big money in the long run.

Keep Your Car in a Garage

If possible, keep your vehicle in a garage. Using a garage protects the vehicle from theft and vandalism. It also protects it from weather, which can damage or destroy the vehicle's finish and even affect its mechanical condition. Low temperatures, for example, affect almost every component. The engine is harder to start, and the battery is weaker. Thus, the starter has to work harder, and the charging system is stressed.

Preserve the Interior

The condition of the inside of your vehicle is very important for good resale value. The *upholstery* is the seat-covering material. Generally, cloth upholstery is more durable than vinyl. Although spills and dirt are more difficult to clean on cloth upholstery, vinyl can crack and tear when it gets too hot or cold. Leather upholstery holds up best, but it is more expensive and requires regular cleaning and lubricating to keep it soft and to prevent cracking.

Floor mats will protect the carpeting and are a good investment. You can cover the interior of your trunk with an old blanket to protect it. Avoid eating in the car, especially messy foods, and vacuum frequently to keep your car's interior in good condition. Products are available to rub on vinyl dashboards and plastic interior surfaces to protect them from fading and cracking from exposure to the sun's rays. If you must park your car in the sun for long periods of time, you might consider covering the inside of your windshield and windows with sun shades.

Preserve the Exterior

Proper care of your car's exterior finish is one of the most important ways to extend the life of your car. Your car's body picks up a lot of dust and grime while you are driving. All of that grime slowly chips away at your vehicle's paint, exposing the metal underneath. Once the metal is exposed, rust can occur. Regular car washes to clean off road dust and grime will protect the car's shiny finish.

In addition to regularly washing your car, it is recommended that you wax the paint twice a year—before the cold and rainy/snowy winter and before the hot and dry summer. Applying protective wax can guard your paint from the snow-melting chemicals spread on streets in cold climates and the damaging rays of the sun. If you live near the coast, wax is essential for protecting the car's finish from the salty spray of ocean breezes. Once the paint has begun to **oxidize** (permanently lose its color and shine because of chemical reaction with the air), it is very difficult to restore the original gloss. In most cases, a vehicle with oxidized paint must be repainted to restore its shine. A **polishing compound** is a substance that can smooth out surface scratches, scuffs, and stains. Polishing compounds, often called cleaners or pre-waxes, can be tricky to use. They may contain *abrasives*, which are coarse materials that scour or rub away a surface. Used gently, an abrasive can remove the top layer of paint and expose the shiny paint underneath. But when rubbed too vigorously or too much, an abrasive will strip the paint.

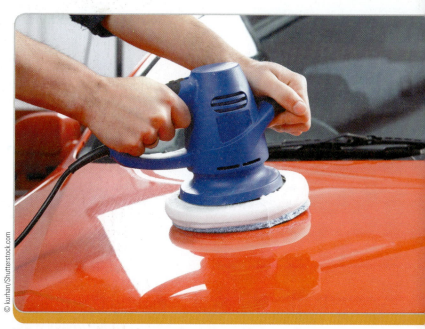

What can you do to preserve the exterior of your vehicle?

Many people choose to have their vehicles detailed. A **car detail** is a service provided by specialists who clean and polish the exterior, along with cleaning and treating the interior. These specialists can provide high-shine polishes that help restore the shine to your vehicle paint job. They can also remove stains in the carpet and even dye carpet to cover damage. Car detailing prices vary depending on what type of package you select and the size of your vehicle. Experts recommend the service twice a year (as seasons change from hot to cold and vice versa).

It is also important to repair paint chips and dents before rust has a chance to take hold. You can get vehicle paint that matches your car's color from a dealer that sells your make of car and, in many cases, auto parts stores. When something nicks your paint, such as a rock that hits your car while you are driving, it's a good idea to touch up the ding. Clean the area with mild soap, dry it, and then apply the touch-up paint in very small amounts. **Paintless dent removal** is a service in which a suction device is attached to your car to remove small dents. The suction pops out the indention but does not require painting or other repair. This service is relatively inexpensive, and it keeps your car looking good. If larger dents are involved, such as scratches or scrapes where the paint is damaged, you should take your car to a body shop and have it professionally repaired.

Follow Wise Driving Habits

Your driving habits have a direct effect on the lifespan of your car. For example, many new vehicles have a recommended *break-in period*, during which you may need to drive differently. Breaking in your car can impact the way it performs. Your owner's manual will most likely include information if your car has a recommended break-in period.

There are several driving tips you should follow during and after your car's break-in period. By practicing good driving habits, you can keep your vehicle running efficiently for years.

When the vehicle is new:

1. Don't drive for long stretches at a constant speed. Vary speed as driving conditions permit.
2. During the first 1,000 miles, drive progressively faster, accelerating gradually.
3. Avoid fast starts, sudden stops, sharp turns, and rapid gear changes to help break in your brakes.
4. Drive at moderate speeds and around town, avoiding long trips, so your tires can get adjusted.

For all vehicles:

1. Don't race a cold engine. Give it 10 to 15 seconds to warm up to allow the oil to start circulating. Then drive off gently as soon as the engine is running smoothly.
2. Keep coolant in the radiator during hot weather and antifreeze in it during very cold weather.
3. Check and maintain all fluid levels. Don't keep driving a car when the "check engine" light is on. Take it in for service right away.
4. Make sure your brakes and tires are in good shape at all times. Having a flat tire can cause more than an inconvenience.
5. When driving a vehicle with a manual transmission, shift deliberately, pausing as you move through the neutral position.
6. Don't shift into a forward gear when your vehicle is rolling backward, or vice versa.
7. When stopped in traffic, hold the vehicle in place with the brakes rather than engaging the clutch to avoid excessive wear on the clutch.
8. Turn the steering wheel only when the vehicle is moving. Turning it when the vehicle is motionless strains the front-end components.
9. Keep the windshield and back window free of ice, using a scraper rather than your wiper blades. Running wipers over a dry or icy surface can scratch the glass and tear the blades.
10. Glance at gauges and warning lights as you drive. When your vehicle signals for you to get something checked, do it right away. When your engine shows it's too hot, turn off the air conditioner and drive slower. If overheating is severe, pull over and stop the engine. Open the hood, but do not unscrew the radiator cap. (Hot steam and fluid will gush out and burn you.)
11. Keep a safe distance from other cars. Adjust your speed with weather conditions. For example, leave more space when it is raining because it will take longer to stop. When you are stopped at a red light, make sure you can see the rear tires of the car in front of you. If you can't see them, you are too close.
12. Keep up with new traffic laws; check the new driver's manual in your state at least every few years.
13. Drive courteously, sharing the road with others, including bicycles, motorcycles, and pedestrians. Yield the right of way even when it's not required.
14. Finally, always wear your seat belt. It can save your life!

✔ CHECKPOINT

How does preserving the interior and exterior of your car affect its resale value?

Transportation, Distribution & Logistics

Automotive Service and Repair

All vehicles require service and maintenance throughout their useful lives. Automotive technicians inspect, maintain, and repair a wide range of vehicles.

Technicians perform basic care and maintenance, such as changing oil and rotating tires. They also test parts to make sure they are working correctly and identify mechanical problems, often by using computerized diagnostic equipment. They follow checklists to ensure all critical parts are examined.

Most newer models of cars have complex computer systems that control various parts, such as steering. Therefore, in addition to traditional mechanical components, today's technicians must be knowledgeable about a growing number of electronic systems.

Technicians who work in large shops often specialize in certain types of repairs, such as air conditioning or brakes. Most technicians work a standard 40-hour workweek, but overtime is often required to meet customer needs.

Employment Outlook

- About as fast as average employment growth is expected.

Job Titles

- Service technician
- Automotive technician
- Automotive mechanic

Needed Skills

- At the minimum, a high school diploma is required, but many employers prefer technicians who have completed a formal training program in a postsecondary institution.
- Automotive Service Excellence (ASE) certification is usually required.
- Being detail-oriented and having troubleshooting skills are required.

What's it like to work in . . . *Automotive Service and Repair*

Janelle works for a large repair shop that services and repairs most models of cars. She works a normal 8-hour shift, plus every other Saturday, and makes about $36,000 a year. She also attends training workshops to obtain certification.

She enjoys working with both older and newer cars. The older cars often require simple mechanical repairs. The newer cars have complex electronic systems, which require a different set of mechanical skills. Regardless of the type of car, she is expected to troubleshoot and fix problems rapidly for customers who often need their car back the same day.

Today, Janelle is waiting for a part to install in the computer module of a new car that has Internet access in the driver's panel. She will test the system before delivering the car to its owner.

What About You?

Do you have mechanical aptitude and like to work on cars? Would you like to work in auto repair?

KEY TERMS REVIEW

Match the terms with the definitions. Some terms may not be used.

a. appreciation
b. car detail
c. car registration
d. car title
e. classic cars
f. depreciation
g. hybrid
h. oxidize
i. paintless dent removal
j. polishing compound

___ 1. A license tag fee that must be renewed annually

___ 2. A service provided by specialists who clean and polish the exterior as well as clean and treat the interior of a car

___ 3. A type of vehicle that uses alternate energy sources in addition to gasoline

___ 4. A substance that can smooth out surface scratches, scuffs, and stains

___ 5. Older vehicles in excellent condition that appreciate if valued as collectors' items

___ 6. A chemical reaction with the air that causes paint to lose its color and shine

___ 7. A decline in the value of property

___ 8. A legal document that establishes ownership of the vehicle

CHECK YOUR UNDERSTANDING

LO2-1   9. Why do vehicles usually depreciate? What might cause a particular vehicle to appreciate?

LO2-2 10. Why should you avoid turning the steering wheel when a car is *motionless*?

APPLY YOUR KNOWLEDGE

LO2-1 11. Considering all of the costs of owning a vehicle, which ones will be the most expensive over time?

THINK CRITICALLY

LO2-1 12. Many items that people add to their cars add resale value, while other items do not. List an accessory that adds value and one that detracts from the value of a vehicle. Explain why.

LO2-2 13. As you observe other drivers, list several habits that are dangerous to the drivers and to others. Give examples of distracted driving.

The Essential Question *Refer to The Essential Question on p. 330. Costs of owning a car include the monthly car payment, car insurance, fuel, depreciation, registration and title fees, vehicle emission fee, and maintenance and repairs. You can maintain your car's resale value by performing routine maintenance, caring for the interior and exterior, and practicing good driving habits.*

Assessment

SUMMARY

14.1

- *The car-buying process begins with identifying and prioritizing your wants and needs. Then determine what you can afford. Identify affordable models that will meet your wants and needs. Research and compare features, and narrow your choices to a few. Decide whether to buy new or used.*

- *If you determine you need to finance part of the cost, obtaining preapproval at your bank or credit union will let you know how much you can borrow and at what rate before you commit to a purchase.*

- *Test drive your top choices. Before buying a used vehicle, check its history by looking up its VIN at the CARFAX website and have a mechanic perform a vehicle inspection.*

- *The fair price for a vehicle is somewhere between the sticker price and invoice price. Make your initial offer below your top price. Then negotiate, but be prepared to walk away if the seller pressures you or will not come down to a fair price. If you are uncomfortable with negotiations, you can hire a car-buying service to negotiate the purchase for you.*

- *Rather than purchasing a new car, you can also lease. Leasing is renting the use of a vehicle, often with an option to buy at the end of the lease term.*

- *All new cars come with warranties to provide the buyer with some assurance of quality. Lemon laws help consumers get a new car or their money back if the car they purchased has substantial, unfixable defects. The FTC's Used Car Rule is designed to protect consumers who buy used cars from dealers.*

14.2

- *Costs of operating a vehicle include the monthly car payment, car insurance, fuel, depreciation, registration and title fees, vehicle emission fees, maintenance and repairs, and the cost of accessories.*

- *Most vehicles depreciate, or decline in value, over time. However, older vehicles in excellent condition (classic cars) may appreciate.*

- *You can extend the life of your car by performing routine maintenance as prescribed in your owner's manual, keeping your car in a garage, preserving the interior and exterior, and following wise driving habits.*

- *A car's interior can be preserved by regularly cleaning upholstery and other interior surfaces. Car paint can oxidize, so it's important to protect the exterior with wax. A polishing compound with abrasives gently applied can restore shine. A car detail service does these tasks for you.*

© Pan Xunbin/Shutterstock.com

APPLY WHAT YOU KNOW

LO1-1 1. Visit the Kelley Blue Book website and look up the trade-in value of your car or your family's car. This is the estimated amount a dealer will give you for your car in trade for a new one. Now look up the used-car retail price for the same car. This is an estimate of a fair price that a buyer can expect to pay for the car. Now subtract the two figures. What is the difference? What does this number represent?

LO1-2 2. Make a list of car dealers in your area. Divide into groups to visit dealerships. Ask about interest rates when purchasing or leasing a vehicle. As a group, report on your findings. What kinds of loans do they offer (interest rate, length of loan)? Is it a better deal to lease or buy? Explain.

LO1-3 3. Visit a car dealership in your area and look at the Buyer's Guide stickers on the cars for sale. Is there a difference in warranties for new versus used cars? If so, why?

LO1-3 4. Conduct online research about the lemon laws in your state. Write a one-page report explaining what qualifies as a lemon, how long you have to file a claim, and what the burden of proof is. Include any additional information in your report that you think is pertinent.

LO2-1 5. Find out the costs of registration, title, and driver's license fees in your county. Also find out whether your county requires vehicle emission testing and what the fees are if required. You can get this information by calling or visiting the website of your state's department of motor vehicles (DMV), or by visiting the DMV's local office.

LO2-2 6. Obtain the owner's manual for your car or a family member's car. Describe the contents of the owner's manual. What kinds of information does it provide for the car owner?

MAKE ACADEMIC CONNECTIONS

LO1-1 7. **Technology** List three or four new technological advances in vehicles in the past three to five years. Explain how they have improved safety, efficiency, and/or comfort for the owners. Then research technological advances that are currently under development. Select two and explain the purposes (benefits) of each one.

LO1-1 8. **Communication** Write a one-page paper describing the car of your dreams, its features, its cost (including payments), and why you would want to own that particular vehicle. Present your choice to the class.

LO2-1 9. **Science** Conduct a study about fossil fuels, including how much is still available and when supplies are expected to run out. Discuss other sources of energy that are more environmentally friendly. What might these alternate sources of energy mean for our future?

LO2-2 10. **International Studies** Conduct online research to learn about speed limits and traffic laws in three other countries. Write a report comparing those laws to similar laws in your state. How are they different? How do auto accident rates compare among all three countries and your state?

Solve Problems and Explore Issues

L01-1 11. Devon is considering buying an older used car. He works part time after school and on weekends. In the summer, he makes good wages but is saving for college. He visits a local dealer who suggests that buying an older car is not a good idea. He points out that the car will likely cost a lot to maintain and wouldn't be dependable. Do you agree? What advice would you give Devon?

L01-1 12. You are buying a new car and are considering whether to trade in your old vehicle. The dealer tells you that you are paying $1,500 less on the new car because of your trade-in. You think that your car is worth more than $1,500 and that you should be able to get a reduction in price without the trade-in. Discuss the pros and cons of trading in your car versus selling it yourself.

L01-2 13. Grace has decided to buy a car. To buy the new car she wants, she needs to finance $20,000. The dealer will finance the loan at 6.5 percent for 60 months. Use an online car loan calculator to determine the (a) monthly payment, (b) total payments, and (c) total interest.

L02-2 14. Ryan just purchased a new car. He plans to drive the car at least 100,000 miles and then sell it to get as much money as he can for it. What advice can you give Ryan about extending the life of the car and improving its resale value?

EXTEND YOUR LEARNING

L02-2 15. **Legal Issues** Most states have traffic laws that require drivers to stay to the right except when passing. Yet some drivers believe that as long as they are driving the speed limit, they have the right to drive in the left lane. Some states will ticket people for staying in the passing lane. Similarly, speed limits are set on interstate highways to enhance traffic flow, promote safety, and keep traffic moving. What are the laws in your state regarding the use of the passing lane and speed limits? Why are they needed?

CHAPTER PROJECT

Research the potential costs that a car owner might face. Ask someone who has owned a car for a long period of time to help you. In computing depreciation, look up the value of an older car of the same model using Kelley Blue Book or an online search. Deduct this from the purchase price of the car and divide by the age (number of years) of the car to determine the total cost of depreciation. Based on your information, create a table that lists the annual costs of operating a vehicle. Then to help you budget, break down the annual costs to determine monthly costs. Also as part of the table, include potential ways to reduce these costs.

Complete the Guided Decision Making activity for Chapter 14 at **ngl.cengage.com/mypf.**

Family Decisions

Consider This...

Aaron and Chloe have announced their engagement and plans to be married. They both have large families and want a formal wedding with all of the trimmings.

"By waiting a year, we'll be able to plan this wedding thoroughly, and we'll both be finished with college," Aaron said to Chloe. "It also gives us time to save money, since we can't expect our parents to pay for all of the costs of such a large wedding."

"You're right," replied Chloe. "There are a million details, and I'd like to enjoy this period of time. I think a year is just the right amount of time between the announcement and the wedding. We also need to plan the honeymoon. Do you want to hike in the mountains or relax on the beach?"

The Essential Question *Why is it important to plan ahead for a wedding or vacation?*

LEARNING OBJECTIVES

› LO 1-1 Describe the steps, costs, and planning involved in getting married.
› LO 1-2 Discuss important family living decisions.
› LO 1-3 Outline the steps needed to plan a successful vacation.

KEY TERMS

- engaged, *343*
- wedding party, *344*
- formal wedding, *345*
- semiformal wedding, *345*
- informal wedding, *345*
- civil ceremony, *346*
- family budget, *347*
- itinerary, *348*
- reservation, *348*
- travel agency, *349*
- overbook, *351*

LO 1-1 Marriage and Commitment

Marriage has changed dramatically in the last half-century. Statistics show that more and more people today are either choosing to remain single or waiting until later in life to get married and start families. For those that do decide to get married, the planning process can be vastly rewarding and surprisingly complex.

Engagement

When a couple decides to commit to a life together, they become **engaged**, or formally pledged to each other. An engagement ring, a symbol of this pledge, can cost anywhere from a few hundred to thousands of dollars. The average engagement period lasts between 12 and 18 months, although some couples opt to have shorter or longer engagements. The engagement period allows the couple time to prepare for the wedding, make plans for the future, and set joint goals.

Premarital Counseling

Assuming that a couple has the maturity and legal capacity (age 18 in most states) to get married, many honest discussions about goals and values should precede the wedding. For example, if one person feels that having children is a vital part of the couple's life together while the other does not want children, this difference could present an insurmountable obstacle. It's also important to discuss issues that may affect family life, such as career goals, political and religious beliefs, roles (such as who pays the bills), hobbies, vacations, and living preferences and habits.

To help prepare for marriage, many couples choose to attend premarital counseling sessions. In fact, some religions require it. *Premarital counseling* helps partners improve their ability to communicate, set realistic

Con Tanasiuk/Design Pics Inc./Alamy

What is the purpose of premarital counseling?

expectations for marriage, and develop conflict-resolution skills. The couple meets with a designated counselor or member of the clergy, together and separately, to discuss issues that will be vital to the success of the marriage. Topics most often discussed include money and budgeting, the meaning of the marriage commitment, beliefs and values, children and parenting, family relationships, and religious aspects of marriage that are unique to each partner's faith.

Ceremony Plans and Costs

Planning for a wedding can be an exciting, yet stressful, undertaking. There will be questions about everything from the wedding cake to the wedding gown to the reception music. There will also be issues about budgets, guest lists, and styles. A number of print magazines and websites offer helpful information for planning a wedding.

Planning for the wedding ceremony should begin at least six months in advance. The bride and groom, along with their parents, usually plan and share in the expenses of the wedding together. Figure 15.1 is a bride's budget worksheet, which shows the many preparations and expenses that planning a wedding can entail. In addition to these expenses, there are also expenses that traditionally have been the responsibility of the groom:

- Bride's ring(s)
- Marriage license
- Wedding gift for the bride
- Gifts for the groom's wedding party
- Bride's bouquet, corsages for mothers and grandmothers, and boutonnieres for the men in the wedding party
- Cleric's or judge's fee
- Bachelor dinner (unless given and paid for by the best man)
- Lodging (if necessary) for out-of-town wedding party members
- Groom's special clothing, including clothing for rehearsal dinner, wedding, and honeymoon
- Delivery of wedding presents to new home

As costs begin to add up, the bride and groom may decide to adjust their preferences to reduce expenses.

The bride and groom and each set of parents should prepare guest lists and then combine them. The number of guests and the size of the wedding party will determine the number of invitations needed, size of the church or facility, cost of the reception, and so on. The **wedding party** consists of the people who are active participants in the wedding ceremony: the bride and groom, best man, maid or matron of honor, bridesmaids, ushers, flower girl, and ring bearer.

FIGURE 15.1 Bride's Worksheet

Engagement Party

Invitations . . . . $_____
Food. . . . . _____
Beverages . . . . _____
Music. . . . . _____
Rental fees . . . . _____
Decorations. . . . . _____
Professional services. . . . _____
Gratuities . . . . _____

Total. . . . . $_____

Stationery

Invitations . . . . $_____
Announcements . . . . _____
At-home cards . . . . _____
Personal stationery . . . . . _____
Stamps . . . . _____

Total. . . . . $_____

Clothing

Wedding dress. . . . . $_____
Headpiece/veil . . . . _____
Shoes. . . . . _____
Accessories. . . . . _____
Personal trousseau . . . . . _____

Total. . . . . $_____

*Denotes expenses usually
shared by both families

Bridesmaids' Luncheon

Invitations and
    place cards . . . . $_____
Food . . . . _____
Beverages . . . . _____
Rental fees . . . . _____
Decorations. . . . . _____
Professional services. . . . _____
*Gratuities . . . . _____

Total . . . . $_____

Photographs

Engagement portrait. . . . $_____
Wedding portrait . . . . . . _____
Formal photos . . . . _____
Reprints . . . . _____

Total . . . . $_____

Wedding Ceremony

Sanctuary rental . . . . $_____
Music. . . . . _____
Decorations. . . . . _____
Flowers for attendants. . . _____
Aisle runner. . . . . _____
Transportation
    to/from ceremony. . . . _____
*Gratuities. . . . . _____
Miscellaneous . . . . _____

Total . . . . $_____

Reception

Hall rental . . . . $_____
Decorations . . . . _____
Music. . . . . _____
Food . . . . _____
Beverages . . . . _____
Wedding cake . . . . _____
Favors . . . . _____
Professional services. . . . _____
*Gratuities . . . . _____

Total. . . . . $_____

Other

Bridal consultant fees . . . $_____
Accommodations for
    out-of-town
    attendants . . . . _____
*Security guard . . . . _____
Sound recording of
    ceremony . . . . _____
*Insurance for
    wedding gifts . . . . . . _____
Bride's blood test
    (if required). . . . . _____
Groom's ring . . . . _____
Gift for groom . . . . _____
Gift for attendants . . . . . _____
Special effects. . . . . _____
Other fees . . . . _____
    _____
    _____
    _____

Total. . . . . $_____

GRAND TOTAL . . . . $_____

Many couples participate in gift registries, whether in-store or online. A *gift registry* is a listing of the couple's choices of dishes, housewares, and other products. Having a gift registry helps prevent duplicate gifts and helps gift givers decide on what to buy.

The size of the wedding, time of day, location, and formality of the bride's dress determine the style of the wedding. A **formal wedding** may be held in the afternoon or in the evening, usually at a church or hotel, and participants as well as guests wear formal attire (long gowns and tuxedos). A **semiformal wedding** is held during the afternoon or early evening, typically at a church, with less formal wear required of guests. While members of the wedding party may still dress as formally or informally as they choose, guests generally wear clothing normally chosen for special occasions. An **informal wedding** is

Arranged marriages are common in the Indian subcontinent (India, Pakistan, and Bangladesh), even among those individuals in the educated middle class. Many people believe that these arranged marriages are more successful than marriages in Europe and the United States. They assert that romantic love does not necessarily lead to a good marriage and that real love comes from a properly arranged union between two individuals and their families.

THINK CRITICALLY

How might family decision making in the Indian subcontinent be different from the way it is in Western societies?

usually held during the afternoon and may take place almost anywhere, such as outside or in a home. No special attire is required for the wedding party or guests. *Destination weddings*, in which the wedding party and the families of the bride and groom gather at a vacation destination for a few days for the wedding festivities, are becoming increasingly popular.

Some couples prefer a **civil ceremony**, which is a wedding performed by a public official, such as a judge or justice of the peace, rather than a member of the clergy. This is a quick, inexpensive ceremony and requires the presence of two witnesses in most states.

The Honeymoon

Immediately following the wedding reception, the newlyweds often take a *honeymoon*. A honeymoon may be a road trip, luxury cruise, or romantic getaway to an all-inclusive resort or exotic island. It generally lasts anywhere from several days to a couple of weeks and costs several thousand dollars. A couple typically plans the honeymoon together months before the wedding date, carefully considering preferences and sharing costs. Many couples who have a destination wedding opt to combine the wedding ceremony with the honeymoon.

CHECKPOINT

What are the various styles of weddings that couples may have?

LO 1-2 Family Living Decisions

When people live together in a committed relationship, they form a new family unit. The family should make major decisions together, based on each person's needs and wants.

Family Goals

Couples should examine their needs and set goals for their future together. *Short-term goals* involve decisions about the near term, such as where to live, whether both partners will work, major purchases to make this year and next, and leisure activities. *Intermediate goals* are those the couple wants to pursue in the next five or so years: whether they want children, where the couple will put down roots, and training or education needs. *Long-term goals* are for the distant future. They include decisions about children's education (savings and investments), job changes, and retirement.

When setting goals, especially financial goals, you should use the "SMART" acronym:

- *Specific*—Clearly state what you want to achieve and how you will do it.
- *Measurable*—Identify how you will measure progress toward your goal.
- *Attainable*—Set goals that are not too far out of reach.
- *Realistic*—Set goals that represent things you are able and willing to do.
- *Timely*—Specify target dates or a timeline for achieving your goals.

For example, a goal of "accumulating $9,000 in a savings account within five years by depositing $150 in it each month" is SMART when compared to a goal of "saving money for the future."

The Family Budget

In Chapter 4, you learned the steps in creating a personal budget. You can follow these same steps in creating a budget for your family. A **family budget** is a plan that allocates spending, saving, borrowing, and investing of the family's pooled resources to meet future goals.

Unlike an individual budget, a family budget must consider the needs and goals of each family member in allocating resources. Joint decisions can be difficult because more people are involved in the decision making. Nevertheless, family budgeting and communicating are essential parts of a successful marriage.

Dividing Responsibilities

Maintaining a household entails sharing responsibilities, both financial and domestic. Successful division of household responsibilities involves communication and compromise.

Many couples choose to have individual checking accounts, with each partner responsible for part of the income and part of the bills. For example, the couple may decide that one will pay the utilities, groceries, and car payment, while the other will pay the mortgage or rent, insurance premiums, and other miscellaneous expenses. Then each partner is responsible for balancing his or her own checking account and meeting his or her part of the budget. Other couples choose to have a joint checking account, whereby all income is deposited into and bills are paid out of one account. If a couple chooses to have a joint checking account, managing the account will be easier if only one person writes the checks. Otherwise, accidental overdrawing can easily occur.

Couples must divide other ongoing household tasks as well. Perhaps one person might take charge of cooking and doing the laundry. The other person might take responsibility for yard maintenance and household repairs. Housecleaning can be less distasteful if partners do the tasks they like best and share equally the tasks that neither likes to do. By agreeing on how to divide up household responsibilities, both partners can do their fair share and avoid any resentment that may result from an unequal division of tasks.

 **CHECKPOINT**

What goes into a family budget?

Vacations are an important part of life. Well-planned vacations maximize the time available for fun, while managing costs and timelines.

Kind of Vacation

Apply the decision-making process from Chapter 11 to help you choose a vacation. First, define the problem or goal: What does your family want most from a vacation—relaxation, excitement, travel, adventure, time with relatives, or a combination of these items? Based on the goals of your vacation and the time and money available, identify your alternatives, as shown in Figure 15.2. Then gather information about each alternative, weigh the pros and cons of each, and make a final decision. A successful vacation depends on selecting the trip that will best satisfy family members, saving for it, and planning it carefully.

Itineraries

If you plan your vacation activities ahead of time, then you can use your vacation time to do them rather than wasting time finding hotels, figuring out transportation, and handling other practical details. To help plan their vacation, many people choose to create an itinerary. An **itinerary** is a detailed schedule of events, times, and places. Figure 15.3 is an example of a vacation itinerary.

When designing your itinerary, list each day's activities. You may want to list the time it takes to do certain activities, distances to and from activities, and methods of transportation. Be sure to leave enough time to do the planned activities in a relaxed way. You may also want to list special notes, such as "bring camera." Take into consideration that bad weather or unexpected problems may require you to change your plans. Leave a copy of your itinerary with a family member or friend in case of emergency.

Travel Arrangements and Reservations

When going on vacation, make travel arrangements and reservations in advance whenever possible. A **reservation** is an advance commitment to receive a service at a specified later date. For example, if you are planning to fly to your vacation destination, you'll need to make airline reservations. Since hotels may be *booked up*, or full, well in advance of your vacation date, you'll want to reserve a hotel room as early as possible. Depending on your method of transportation while on vacation, you may also want to make rental car

---

FIGURE 15.2 Vacation Analysis

VACATION ANALYSIS		
$500 or less	**$500–$1,500**	**More than $1,500**
Camping	Car trip	Car or plane trip
Visiting relatives	Sports (skiing, other adventure)	Tours/group travel
Sports events	Amusement parks	Varied entertainment options
Three days or less	Three to five days	Five days or more

FIGURE 15.3 Itinerary

ITINERARY

Date	Time	Activity
Monday	8:00 A.M.	Arrive at airport (Flight 739 leaves at 9:05 A.M.).
	10:00 A.M.	Arrive at Los Angeles airport. Take hotel shuttle service; arrive at hotel by 10:45 A.M.
	12:00 noon	Lunch at hotel restaurant.
	1:30 P.M.	Disneyland for remainder of day. Dinner at Disneyland.
Tuesday	8:00 A.M.	Breakfast at Howard Johnson's.
	9:00 A.M.	Knott's Berry Farm (20-minute ride by tour bus). Spend day there; eat lunch there.
	7:00 P.M.	Leave Knott's Berry Farm; go to dinner at Outback Steakhouse.
	8:00 P.M.	Return to hotel.
Wednesday	8:00 A.M.	Breakfast at Pancake House.
	9:00 A.M.	Universal Studios. Tour begins at 10:00 A.M., lasts until noon.
	12:00 noon	Lunch at nearby restaurant. Catch tour bus at 1:30 P.M. to return to hotel.

reservations. In addition to your flight, hotel, and rental car, you may also want to make restaurant reservations and purchase advance tickets for any attractions you plan on visiting, such as amusement parks or entertainment.

You can make reservations and purchase tickets online by going to the websites of specific airlines, hotels, car rental agencies, and attractions. Or you may choose to make your airline, hotel, and rental car reservations through a full-service travel site, such as Expedia or Orbitz. With a full-service travel site, you can enter your travel date and preferences and the site presents you with several hotel, flight, and car rental options that meet your search criteria. You can even sort the list by price. Many travel sites offer packaged discounts if you book multiple services together, such as your flight and hotel. If you are signed up for an airline's *frequent-flyer program* that allows you to earn credit toward free tickets, it may affect your choice of airlines. Some frequent-flyer programs even give you credit for staying at participating hotels or renting from participating car rental agencies.

Another option for making travel arrangements and reservations is to use a travel agency. A **travel agency** is a business that arranges transportation, accommodations, and itineraries for customers. The agent can make plane, hotel, and rental car reservations for you and can help you plan the whole trip if you like. This is especially helpful when traveling to unfamiliar places overseas. You most likely will pay a fee to the travel agent for booking flights. Agents earn other fees from the hotels and car rentals they book for you.

Some airlines also assist with car rental and hotel reservations. Some travel destinations, such as Disney, also provide package deals, offering flight, hotel, and amusement park tickets. You can save money by comparing your options.

At-Home Preparations

Before leaving on your vacation, you should take care of a few things at home. Contact your local newspaper delivery person and either stop your paper delivery for the duration of your trip or ask that your papers be held for delivery until your return. Also, fill out a form at the post office to have your mail held there rather than delivered. By stopping these deliveries, you avoid a buildup of mail and newspapers that may tip off burglars that you are away from home. You may also want to consider purchasing an automatic timer for lights in different rooms of your house so that they come on in the evening and go off a few hours later, giving the appearance that you are home. Arrange for someone to keep an eye on things while you are away. This may include feeding your pets if you do not board them, caring for your plants, and mowing the lawn. Contact your credit card company(ies) and inform them of your travel plans. Advise them of possible unusual charges or more frequent spending from various locations so they won't suspect fraud and put a hold on your card(s).

Packing

Before you begin packing for your trip, you should first make a list of everything you will need to take. Creating a packing list not only will ensure that you don't forget to take something important, but it also will help you avoid overpacking.

It is also a good idea to look at your airline's website and read its *baggage policy*. Most airlines permit each traveler to bring one personal item, such as a laptop computer or purse, and one carry-on bag on planes. The carry-on bag must be under a specified size that will fit in the overhead storage bin or under the seat. Any other bag you pack will have to be checked in. Most airlines charge a fee for checked bags. An extra fee is charged for checked bags that are over a certain weight limit.

Be sure to pack enough clothing to last the entire vacation without laundering (unless it is a very long vacation). Put medications and any valuable or essential items in your carry-on baggage in case the airline loses your checked bag(s). Also, any liquid products, such as shampoo, deodorant, and gels, that you pack in your carry-on bag should be placed inside a single, clear, zip-top bag. Otherwise, they may be confiscated by a Transportation Security Administration (TSA) agent when you go through the security checkpoint at the airport. The TSA also prohibits certain items, such as sharp objects, to be brought onto airplanes.

Do not take all of your credit cards with you; only take the ones you need. Take enough cash to pay the expenses that require cash only. Charge other expenses on a credit card. Because of the availability of ATMs, you can obtain cash easily while on vacation.

Last-Minute Details

Before you leave for the airport, be sure to confirm your flight reservations. Flights are often canceled or changed at the last minute. You may also want to check in online and print your boarding pass at home to save time at the airport, especially if you are not checking in any bags. Most airlines allow you to print your boarding pass within 24 hours of the flight. Also, adjust the thermostat in your house to save energy costs while away. Shut down all computers and unplug any electronic devices. Throw away any perishable items from your refrigerator. Take the garbage out. Be sure to lock all doors and windows and close the curtains.

At the Airport

Arrive at the airport at least two hours before a domestic flight and three hours before an international flight. This gives you time to check in and pass through security. You will need a photo ID, such as your driver's license or passport, for the check-in and security processes.

If you do not print your boarding pass at home, the first thing you will need to do when you get to the airport is check in. You can either check in at one of the airline's self-service kiosks or go to the ticket counter and have a customer service representative print your boarding pass.

When you check in, you may find that the flight has been overbooked. Often, airlines **overbook** flights, meaning they sell more reservations than they can fulfill. Airlines overbook flights expecting that some people will not show up for a scheduled flight. If more people show up for a flight than the plane can accommodate, the airline may ask if you would like to give up your seat voluntarily in exchange for a future free ticket and a later flight. Passengers "bumped" (forced to miss a flight involuntarily) are usually entitled to compensation, often in the form of cash, a coupon, or a free flight. By arriving early to check in, you can decrease your risk of being "bumped."

You'll need to check in your baggage if you have any to check. Once your bags are checked, you'll proceed to the security checkpoint. Before entering the checkpoint, you must show a TSA agent your photo ID and boarding pass. At the security checkpoint, any carry-on bags and personal items you are taking onboard the plane will be scanned. You will also be required to pass through a metal detector or full-body scanner.

After passing through security, you are ready to board your flight. You may want to grab a bite to eat if you have time or pick up some snacks and beverages to take on the flight with you. Depending on the airline you are flying with and how long your flight is, there may not be any meals served, and you may be charged for the snacks and beverages that are available during the flight.

© iStock.com/EXTREME-PHOTOGRAPHER

What are some things you'll need to do at the airport when traveling?

✔ CHECKPOINT

Why are reservations a good idea for many vacations?

What Is Online Travel Planning?

Have you ever considered doing all of your travel planning online? The Internet offers a number of travel-planning websites. At some websites, such as CheapTickets, Expedia, Hotwire, Orbitz, and Travelocity, you can do fare searches; check seat availability; and book flights, hotel rooms, rental cars, and vacation packages. While there are some risks of using these sites, the savings can be substantial.

At Priceline.com, travelers can name their price for airline tickets, hotel rooms, car rentals, and vacation packages through its "Name Your Own Price" program. The benefit to using this program is that you can get substantial discounts—sometimes between 40 and 60 percent off the regular price. The downside is that you must be flexible with your travel plans. While you can select a general location and price, you've got to let Priceline take care of everything else, such as the airline, flight times, hotel, and rental car company. After the purchase has gone through, you cannot cancel it.

Another popular travel site is Trivago. It compares prices for over 700,000 hotels from over 200 booking sites. You can search by location as well as the dates and type of room. You can then make the search more specific, using search criteria such as available amenities and other features. Based on your criteria, the website will provide links to all available offers from other external booking sites.

Many sites, such as SkyAuction, offer airline tickets, hotel rooms, and cruises on an auction basis. For example, a cruise line may offer an auction for a seven-night cruise to Jamaica on the site. If you are the highest bidder in the auction, you've won the trip.

Often major attractions, such as theme parks, have their own travel agencies to help guests have a more pleasant stay. These services include hotel and flight reservations, park admission, and car rental arrangements—all of which can usually be taken care of at the attraction's website. Even major credit card companies, such as American Express and Visa, offer travel-related discounts and arrangements through their websites. You can take advantage of special deals, get travel packages and upgrades, and pay for your vacation with a special credit offer.

Conducting online research when planning trips can save you both time and money. Even if you book your tickets by phone, you can still benefit from the information and search-and-compare features of the Internet prior to booking your trip.

THINK CRITICALLY

1. What distant vacation destination appeals to you most? Use the Internet to find the best airfare and hotel rate for this destination. Do travel dates affect the cost?

2. What is the downside of using the Internet to make reservations and pay for flights?

KEY TERMS REVIEW

Match the terms with the definitions. Some terms may not be used.

____ 1. A wedding held outside or in a home with no special attire needed

____ 2. Being formally pledged or in a committed relationship

____ 3. A detailed schedule of events, times, and places to visit

____ 4. Active participants in a wedding ceremony

____ 5. An advance commitment to receive a service at a specified later date

____ 6. A business that arranges transportation, accommodations, and itineraries for customers

____ 7. To sell more reservations than an airline can fulfill

____ 8. A wedding with long gowns and tuxedos worn by both the wedding party and guests

a. civil ceremony
b. engaged
c. family budget
d. formal wedding
e. informal wedding
f. itinerary
g. overbook
h. reservation
i. semiformal wedding
j. travel agency
k. wedding party

CHECK YOUR UNDERSTANDING

LO1-1 9. What purpose does an engagement period serve?

LO1-3 10. What is an advantage of booking your travel arrangements through a full-service travel website?

APPLY YOUR KNOWLEDGE

LO1-1 11. Explain what you might learn through premarital counseling and why it is an important step before getting married.

THINK CRITICALLY

LO1-2 12. Family financial goals differ from individual plans because two people must merge their future plans. Explain the differences, and discuss why the family budget can be both complicated and controversial.

LO1-3 13. Explain how vacation planning changes over time, beginning with a young couple and ending with a retired couple?

LO1-3 14. When traveling by airplane, explain what additional steps to take to avoid frustrations and extra costs?

The Essential Question *Refer to The Essential Question on p. 343 . Both weddings and vacations can be costly but very rewarding experiences. Planning ahead allows you to maximize your money and time to get the most out of both.*

The Essential Question *How can unforeseen events affect your personal finances?*

LEARNING OBJECTIVES

> LO 2-1 Describe the cost and steps involved in a divorce.
> LO 2-2 Explain what to do when a major illness or injury interrupts life unexpectedly.
> LO 2-3 Discuss preparations for death and life's final plans.

KEY TERMS

- dissolution of marriage, *354*
- divorce decree, *355*
- custodial parent, *355*
- child support, *355*
- spousal support, *356*
- property settlement agreement, *356*
- adult foster care, *357*
- employee assistance plan (EAP), *358*
- hospice, *358*
- cremation, *360*

LO 2-1 Divorce

Many marriages end in divorce each year. A divorce, or **dissolution of marriage**, is a legal process in which a judge dissolves the bonds of matrimony between two people. Divorce in the United States is governed by state, rather than federal, law. Although divorce laws vary by state, all 50 U.S. states allow *no-fault divorce*, which means that one partner does not have to prove fault by the other to be granted a divorce. If one partner wants the marriage to be dissolved, it can be done.

Steps in Divorce

Dissolving a marriage is often a lengthy and unpleasant process. The divorce process begins when one party contacts an attorney to file a *Petition for Dissolution of Marriage*. The petition states the grounds for divorce and specifies how the filing party (the *plaintiff* or *petitioner*) proposes to divide property and award custody, amounts desired for any child support, visitation rights, and so on. The attorney prepares the forms and files them with the court. Once the petition is filed, the other party (the *defendant* or *respondent*) is served with copies of the papers and given a short time (usually 20 to 30 days) to file an answer if there is a disagreement with the proposals set forth in the petition. If the defendant does not answer (defaults), then the plaintiff is awarded whatever is asked in the petition. In most cases the defendant does file an answer, and a hearing is set to decide the issues that cannot be settled.

Because it often takes many months, even a year or more, for the case to be heard in court, a *temporary hearing* may be held to establish temporary custody, child support, visitation rights of the noncustodial parent, and other matters. Many of these temporary provisions tend to become permanent. Often both parties agree in writing to property settlement, child custody and visitation, and other matters prior to the court date. When the judge approves the written agreement, it is entered as part of the **divorce decree**, which is a final statement of the dissolution decisions. A decree is final and binding on both parties until modified by the court.

If the parties cannot reach an agreement, the case then goes to court for a judge's decision. There is no jury in divorce cases. Both parties present their cases. In child-custody cases, witnesses may be called to determine which parent would be the better custodial parent. The judge bases the final decision on the evidence presented. Once the decree is entered, the court usually imposes a waiting period (typically 30 to 90 days) before either party may remarry.

What costs are involved in getting a divorce?

Costs of Divorce

Expenses involved in divorce are high. They may include attorneys' fees, court costs and filing fees, child support and spousal support, division of assets, and other settlement costs. The more issues that the divorcing couple can settle out of court, the less the divorce proceedings will cost.

Attorneys' Fees

Most attorneys charge by the hour; however, if the couple has an *uncontested divorce* (one in which both parties are able to come to an agreement without going to court) that doesn't involve spousal support or child-custody issues, it may be possible for an attorney to be hired for a flat fee. The more issues there are to settle, the higher the attorneys' fees will be.

Most attorneys will ask for an advance payment, called a *retainer*, when hired. The retainer is held in a special trust account, and any legal fees and expenses will be deducted from this account as they accrue. In most cases, retainers are not refundable. In some states, parties can fill out and file paperwork without an attorney. This may or may not be in the parties' best interest.

Court Costs and Filing Fees

In addition to attorneys' fees, there is also the additional expense of court costs. Court costs may include a service fee for the delivery of the divorce petition to the defendant, a fee for finalizing the divorce decree, deposition expenses, and so on. Filing for divorce also involves a fee. This fee varies by state, but generally costs from $100 to $400.

Child Support and Spousal Support

When dissolving a marriage, the court can order two kinds of support: child support and spousal support. The **custodial parent**, or the parent with whom the children will live, fulfills most support obligations by taking care of the children every day. In most cases, the parent who is not granted custody will be required to pay **child support**—monthly payments to the custodial parent to help provide food, clothing, and shelter for the children. The amount of the payments will depend on the income of both parents and their ability to pay. Sometimes both parents have *joint custody*, and the children live part of the year with each parent.

Spousal support, also called *alimony*, is money paid by one former spouse to support the other. The money may be paid as one lump sum or monthly payments, usually for a set number of years until the former spouse can become self-supporting. Spousal support is awarded in some cases when one spouse has been dependent on the other for a number of years and has little means of self-support.

Child support and alimony are at the discretion of the court and become binding on the parties under the divorce decree. Amounts of child support and alimony can be modified only by another court order.

Division of Assets

When a couple goes through a divorce, they will have to decide how to divide assets. For example, they will have to decide who will keep the family home, who will keep the furniture and other tangible property, how they will divide retirement benefits, and so on. Often they can agree outside of court and enter into a **property settlement agreement**, which is a document specifying the division of assets agreed to by both parties and entered in court for the judge's approval. If they can't agree on these issues, however, a judge will divide their property for them.

CHECKPOINT

What is the purpose of a temporary hearing during divorce proceedings?

- -

LO 2-2   Major Illness or Injury

Accidents and illnesses happen. Such occurrences will interrupt finances and plans. But there are certain things to know and do that will ease the financial burden on the family.

Absence from Work

If you or a close family member suffers from a major illness or accident, it is often necessary to miss work. You may be able to use your accumulated sick leave or personal leave to miss work without losing pay. If more time is needed, the *Family and Medical Leave Act (FMLA)* provides up to 12 weeks of unpaid time from work in any 12-month period. To qualify, you must meet certain eligibility requirements. If you take FMLA leave, your employer must continue your health insurance as if you were not on leave. However, when a wage earner's salary is lost, the house payment and other expenses continue. Therefore, additional forms of insurance are needed to cover lost wages.

Short-Term Disability

Many employers offer *short-term disability* insurance that provides for replacement of a wage earner's salary, up to a percentage (typically 70 percent or more). This benefit generally lasts between three and six months.

If your employer does not have such a group plan, individual coverage can be provided through private insurance (covered in Chapter 23).

Long-Term Disability

If you are still unable to return to work after your short-term disability runs out, you need *long-term disability* coverage (also covered in Chapter 23). Most long-term disability plans cover 50 to 70 percent of monthly salary. The benefits last until you can go back to work or for the number of years stated in the policy. Should the disability become permanent, long-term disability can bridge the gap between the injury or illness and retirement. As with short-term disability, if your employer does not offer long-term disability insurance, individual coverage can be provided through private insurance.

Long-term disability coverage is also available through the Social Security Administration (SSA). *Social Security Disability Insurance (SSDI)* pays monthly benefits to you if you become disabled before you reach retirement age and aren't able to work. To qualify for SSDI, you must have worked a certain number of years in a job where you paid Social Security taxes and you also must have a medical condition that meets the SSA's definition of "disability." When applying for SSDI, forms and paperwork along with detailed documentation must be provided. It often takes a year or longer to get approved and for monthly payments to begin.

Extended Care Expenses

Some types of insurance policies provide coverage so that people can remain at home and receive nursing care, physical rehabilitation, and other services when needed. When family members are unable to provide adequate care for the injured or ill person, **adult foster care**, which is personal care and services provided for adults in a facility outside of the home, may be required. Sometimes the care is temporary; other times, it is permanent. For example, a person who suffers a stroke may need physical therapy and recovery treatment for six months to a year. After that time, he or she may be recovered well enough to return home to resume life. Other people will not recover and must have ongoing care.

Private or group health insurance will cover some of these expenses, but there are limits, both in dollars and in time. Special kinds of insurance are needed to provide for these expenses (discussed further in Chapter 23). Many people use savings and home equity extensively to pay for costs of treatment and recovery. If all of their money is used up, public assistance may be available to help them.

There are also private and nonprofit groups who seek to help families with certain extended care expenses. For example, the Shriners help uninsured children get adequate eyeglasses and other essential services. St. Jude's Hospital was founded to help poor children receive life-saving care when they have diseases such as cancer. Ronald

Keith Brofsky/Photodisc/Getty Images

Under what circumstances would adult foster care be needed?

McDonald House is a program sponsored by McDonald's to help families of critically ill children. The Make a Wish Foundation also provides support services for very ill children.

Mental Health Services

Sometimes the impact of a major illness or injury within a family creates the need for mental health services. Counseling may also be needed when individuals are having marital problems or dealing with depression, addiction, or dependency issues. An **employee assistance plan (EAP)** is a group benefit that allows employees and their families to seek counseling and other services. Often these plans are limited as to the types of services and number of appointments allowed. Thus, many families must bear the cost of continuing these services if they are needed for an extended period.

Outpatient services are more common and less expensive than inpatient programs. With *outpatient services*, those needing counseling or other services attend meetings on a regular basis (usually weekly) and complete self-directed plans. With *inpatient programs*, people move into residential facilities for a month to six months or longer to recover and make new life plans. Fees for these services, which can be paid by insurance, may range from a few hundred dollars to tens of thousands of dollars.

CHECKPOINT

How is short-term disability different from long-term disability?

LO 2-3 Death: A Final Plan

Death is often an issue many people prefer to avoid discussing or even thinking about. However, death is a part of life. Planning for it makes the process easier for loved ones left behind.

End-of-Life Care

End-of-life planning includes making choices about where you want to spend your final days and what type of care you would like to receive. When asked, most people say they would prefer to die at home; however, that may not be possible, and they may need to receive round-the-clock care at a nursing home or hospital.

For those who are terminally ill and have less than six months to live, an end-of-life-care option is hospice. **Hospice** is a nonprofit program consisting of medical and support services provided by a team of professionals and volunteers for those who are dying and for their families. Hospice care can be provided in the patient's home or an outside facility. The goal of hospice is not to prolong life but rather relieve pain and provide the highest quality of remaining life for the patient. In addition, a hospice also provides counseling and grief recovery programs for those who have lost their loved ones. The hospice team will also help in making final arrangements for transporting the deceased's body when a person dies at home. This relieves the family of dealing with police and other governmental agencies (because it is considered a planned death).

Final Instructions

All adults should prepare for death to help ensure their final wishes are carried out. Many people prepare a *letter of final instruction* that offers guidance for family members. It may include financial details (names and contact information of financial planners and insurance agents, a list of bank and retirement accounts, and so on) and memorial or funeral instructions (what songs should be sung, who should officiate, who should act as pallbearers, etc.), among other things.

Many people also fill out a *Do Not Resuscitate (DNR)* directive. A DNR tells physicians, EMT workers, and other medical providers that once a person has died and has no brain activity (they cannot recover), no extraordinary measures should be taken. This allows people to die with dignity instead of being put on life-support for long periods of time when there is no hope for survival.

By preparing these final instructions in advance, you spare survivors the anguish of making these difficult decisions. It's critical that these last wishes be spoken, written, and made available to persons who will be expected to carry them out. Placing them in a safe deposit box with other important documents may mean that these wishes aren't known until it is too late to fulfill them.

Last Expenses

The costs involved when a person dies can range from a few hundred dollars to thousands of dollars. These expenses include final medical and hospital bills and the cost of the funeral or cremation service.

Medical and Hospital Bills

Typically, the estate of the deceased is liable for unpaid medical and hospital bills, which can be sizable. Any assets the deceased had at the time of death become a part of his or her estate. The estate sells off these assets and uses the proceeds to pay the bills. Collection agencies may try to convince grieving family members that they are responsible for any unpaid medical bills. If this is the case, an attorney may need to be contacted to deal with the collectors.

Funerals

The cost of a funeral can range from $5,000 to $10,000 or more, depending on the type of services provided, the casket, and the burial. Typical funeral charges include moving the body (to the funeral home, church or synagogue, and cemetery), embalming and preparation for public viewing, casket, use of facilities, and funeral staff fees. They may also include the hearse, family limousine, escort to the cemetery, obituary (newspaper death notice), clergy fees, printed memorial folders, memorial book, death certificate, and all necessary permits. The costs of a burial plot and marker (gravestone) are significant additional expenses.

Many funeral homes have *prearranged funeral plans* available at guaranteed costs. Payments are made in advance for the funeral and other arrangements. You should be able to get a full refund if you cancel the plan. It is wise to look over any "preneed" or prepayment plan that you consider. It may lock you into using the services of a particular funeral home at uncertain future prices. If you move away or the funeral home goes out of business, you may have trouble getting your money back.

Cremation

While traditional funerals and burials are popular, cremation is becoming more common. **Cremation** is a process of reducing a body to ashes in a high-temperature oven. The ashes are then placed in an urn. The urn is presented to the family for safekeeping or burial. Cremation is a less expensive alternative to embalming and "cosmetizing" the body for public viewing. When a body is not cremated within a certain time span, usually two days, it must be embalmed or otherwise prepared for burial. Cremation, like immediate burial without a funeral, permits the survivors to hold a memorial service at any time or place, without having the body present. This procedure may be more comfortable for families and other mourners. It also allows family members to choose a more suitable place to bury or place the remains.

Survivors' Benefits

The surviving spouse and children are usually provided with some kind of death benefits. For example, if the deceased had a life insurance policy, survivors (known as *beneficiaries*) may receive a nontaxable, lump-sum payment. Benefits from a life insurance policy can be obtained by mailing a copy of the death certificate, the original life insurance policy, and a claim form to the life insurance company. (Life insurance is described in detail in Chapter 23.)

What types of death benefits are available to survivors?

The Veterans Administration pays a benefit to survivors of armed-service veterans. The benefit may include a grave marker, funeral service, and a small amount of cash. Children of veterans may also be entitled to scholarships and educational grant benefits.

The Social Security Administration also pays a monthly death benefit to surviving family members who are eligible. The more the deceased person earned over his or her lifetime, the larger the payment. An estimated death benefit will appear on your annual Social Security statement. The SSA also pays a one-time death benefit of $255 to the surviving spouse or minor children who qualify.

Many employer group life insurance, pension, and retirement plans also pay lump-sum or monthly benefits to the surviving families. In most cases, the family will have to apply to receive these benefits.

© Feng Yu/Shutterstock.com

✔ **CHECKPOINT**

Why should you plan for the end of life?

- -

ealth Science

Nursing

Nurses have a variety of job duties. They provide and coordinate patient care, educate patients, and provide advice and emotional support to patients and their families. Nurses also record patients' medical histories and symptoms, perform diagnostic tests and analyze results, operate medical equipment, administer patients' treatments and medications, and help with follow-up rehabilitation.

Although most nurses work in hospitals, many also work in home care, nursing care facilities, physicians' offices, and clinics. Because nurses are in contact with individuals who have infectious diseases, they must follow rigid procedures to avoid spreading germs.

Nurses spend considerable time walking, bending, stretching, and standing. They often work long, difficult shifts, including nights, weekends, and even holidays. Many times, they are on call.

Employment Outlook

- A faster-than-average rate of employment growth is expected.

Job Titles

- Registered nurse
- Emergency room nurse
- Surgical nurse
- Radiology nurse

Needed Skills

- Either a bachelor's degree in nursing, an associate's degree in nursing, or a diploma from an approved nursing program is required.

- In all states, registered nurses must have a nursing license.
- Compassion, emotional stability, and physical stamina are required.

What's it like to work in . . . *Nursing*

Henri works in the cancer ward of a large local hospital. He works four 10-hour shifts a week and earns a little over $65,000 a year.

Most of Henri's time is spent in the chemotherapy patient room where he administers chemotherapy treatments to patients as instructed by their doctors. He monitors patients throughout their treatment to ensure no problems arise. Henri also sees patients for follow-up visits. He performs blood tests and then monitors the patients over a period of time to determine whether they are adapting to the treatments. When he's not working in the chemotherapy patient room, Henri works in the radiology unit where he assists patients who need X-rays.

Today, Henri is helping with a patient who has just completed a bone marrow transplant. He will provide close care for the first several hours after surgery, while also providing emotional support and answering any questions the patient's family may have.

What About You?

Do you want to learn and apply lifesaving skills? Would you like to work in nursing?

The Career Clusters icons are being used with permission of the: States' Career Clusters Initiative, 2007, www.careerclusters.org

KEY TERMS REVIEW

Match the terms with the definitions. Some terms may not be used.

____ 1. *Monthly payments to the custodial parent to help provide food, clothing, and shelter for the children*

____ 2. *A group benefit that allows employees and their families to seek counseling and other mental health services*

____ 3. *A legal process in which a judge dissolves the bonds of matrimony between two people*

____ 4. *A document specifying the division of assets agreed to by both parties and entered in court for the judge's approval*

____ 5. *Money paid by one former spouse to support the other*

____ 6. *A final statement of the dissolution decisions*

____ 7. *Personal care and services provided for adults in a facility outside of the home*

____ 8. *A process of reducing a body to ashes in a high-temperature oven*

a. adult foster care
b. child support
c. cremation
d. custodial parent
e. dissolution of marriage
f. divorce decree
g. employee assistance plan (EAP)
h. hospice
i. property settlement agreement
j. spousal support

CHECK YOUR UNDERSTANDING

LO2-1   9. What is a no-fault divorce?

LO2-3 10. List the costs involved with planning and paying for a funeral.

APPLY YOUR KNOWLEDGE

LO2-1 11. Explain why it is better for a couple to reach a property settlement agreement outside of court.

THINK CRITICALLY

LO2-3 12. Why is a waiting period imposed before a divorced person can remarry?

LO2-2 13. An adult foster care home or a nursing home may be needed for a person who requires care beyond what can be provided at home. Why do most individuals and families try to avoid these arrangements?

LO2-3 14. Why do many people choose cremation rather than a traditional burial?

The Essential Question *Refer to The Essential Question on p. 354. Divorce, illness, and death are not things people like to think about, but each comes with costs. If you are not prepared for these events, you could be facing huge bills that may become a financial burden on you and/or your family.*

SUMMARY

15.1

- *When a couple becomes engaged, they are formally pledged to each other. The engagement marks the time to begin planning the wedding ceremony, honeymoon, and living arrangements.*

- *Premarital counseling helps prepare couples for a successful marriage.*

- *Planning the wedding begins with determining the size of the wedding party and number of guests. Weddings can be formal, semiformal, or informal, or you can choose a civil ceremony.*

- *Family financial decisions should be based on common goals, and a family budget should be agreed upon by all family members.*

- *Maintaining a household entails sharing responsibilities, both financial and domestic.*

- *Vacation planning is based on time and money available, along with interests of all family members. Plan your itinerary and make travel arrangements and reservations ahead of time.*

- *You can make reservations and purchase tickets for your vacation online or by phone, or you can use a travel agency.*

15.2

- *Divorce, or dissolution of marriage, is a legal process in which a judge dissolves the bonds of matrimony between two people. All states now allow no-fault divorces.*

- *Divorce is often a lengthy and unpleasant process. It also can be expensive. Divorcing spouses can save on costs by reaching a property settlement agreement and child-custody agreement outside of court.*

- *Steps in getting a divorce include filing a petition, agreeing to a property settlement, attending a court hearing, and obtaining a divorce decree.*

- *Short- and long-term disability insurance can help cover lost wages resulting from injury or illness. If family members are unable to provide adequate care, adult foster care may be required.*

- *Mental health services are sometimes covered by health insurance policies or employee assistance plans (EAPs) but are often limited in scope.*

- *All adults should prepare for their death to ensure their final wishes are carried out and to help make the process easier for their loved ones left behind.*

- *Last expenses include final medical and hospital bills and the cost of the funeral or cremation service.*

APPLY WHAT YOU KNOW

LO1-2 1. As couples set their future goals, they often include short-term, intermediate, and long-term goals. What types of goals might appear in each of these categories? Explain why families as a unit should set goals in addition to individual goals.

LO1-3 2. Design a three-day itinerary for a trip to a resort area within about 1,000 miles of where you live. Include all necessary information. Use the Internet to determine prices and availability of transportation, accommodations, and entertainment tickets.

LO2-1 3. Explain the purpose of child support and spousal support. Should a noncustodial parent be required by a divorce decree to provide child support while adult children obtain a college education? Why or why not?

LO2-2 4. Visit an adult foster care facility or nursing home in your area. Prepare a report on the kinds of services provided, the living conditions for the patients, and how the use of the facility would affect family life and finances.

LO2-2 5. Interview a person whose employer provides an employee assistance plan (EAP). Write a report on the kinds of services provided and any limitations imposed.

MAKE ACADEMIC CONNECTIONS

LO1-1 6. **Psychology** Conduct research to learn about factors that affect the success of a marriage. Use the Internet or interview a counselor or married couples to determine common characteristics that are present in successful relationships. Report your findings in a two-page report.

LO1-1 7. **Communication** After the wedding, it is important that the newly married couple express their appreciation for gifts received and other acts of kindness. Assume you are newly married. Compose a thank-you letter to someone who sent you a wedding gift or to a church member who helped with the preparations and decorations at the church.

LO1-3 8. **Technology** List new security devices and procedures being used in airports, train terminals, sports arenas, and other areas where many people on vacation gather. How do these protect large numbers of people? How much do they cost?

LO2-1 9. **Research** Conduct a research study about current U.S. divorce statistics, including rate of divorce, reasons for divorce, how divorce trends have changed over time, and why they have changed.

LO2-1 10. **International Studies** Perform online research to learn about divorce laws in another country. Compare those laws to dissolution or divorce laws in your state and in the United States. How does religion and culture play a part in the laws? How do the divorce rates in the other country compare to those in the United States?

Solve Problems and Explore Issues

LO1-1 11. Write a report describing different engagement ring options: (a) diamond solitaire with matching bands (compare costs of different diamond sizes), (b) gold and silver bands (compare quality, width, and costs), (c) costs of stones other than diamonds (rubies, emeralds, and sapphires in varying sizes), and (d) financing options.

LO1-2 12. Joshua and Larissa will be married in a month. Both of them work 40 hours a week. They have asked for your opinion on how they should divide household responsibilities. Devise a plan for dividing financial responsibilities as well as domestic duties.

LO1-3 13. You and a friend have decided to take a trip. For each of the following situations, describe a trip you would take and list all of the costs that would be involved in each trip: (a) You each have $100 to spend for a three-day weekend. (b) You each have $500 to spend for a three-to-five-day trip. (c) You each have $1,500 to spend for a seven-to-ten-day trip.

LO2-3 14. Divide into groups. With your instructor's permission, each group should arrange to visit a local funeral home. Ask someone there to walk you through funeral preparations, including the costs and decisions you would have to make. Present an oral report to the class.

EXTEND YOUR LEARNING

LO2-2 15. **Legal Issues** Most states have laws regulating nursing homes, home caregivers, and other services provided to people who cannot care for themselves. Although it is against the law, elder abuse happens frequently. Relatives or others closely associated with an ill or aged person may take advantage of that person by stealing his or her money and other assets. They may abuse or neglect the person and not provide for his or her basic needs. What are some laws in your state regarding elder abuse? How can it be prevented? Are the laws working or are more restrictions needed?

CHAPTER PROJECT

Describe the wedding you would choose for yourself, including the setting, type of ceremony, size of wedding party, total cost, and so on. Use the Internet to help you complete the bride's worksheet shown in Figure 15.1. (The bride's worksheet is also provided in the *Student Activity Guide*.) As an alternative, create and complete a groom's worksheet based on the groom's responsibilities discussed on p. 344. Then think about your honeymoon. Choose three possible destinations and use the Internet to help you do a vacation analysis as shown in Figure 15.2. Based on your preferred destination, create a checklist you can use to help you pack for your honeymoon.

> Complete the Guided Decision Making activity for Chapter 15 at **ngl.cengage.com/mypf**.

Robert (Ted) Turner

Ted Turner was born in Cincinnati, Ohio, in 1938 and moved to Savannah, Georgia, as a child. He attended Brown University, where he majored in economics, was active in debate, and was captain of the sailing team. Ted started his business career at age 24 when he inherited his father's billboard advertising business (Turner Outdoor Advertising). The business was worth approximately $1 million at the time. Today, Turner's empire is worth more than $2 billion.

ALLISON JOYCE/Reuters /Landov

As a businessman, Turner is best known as the founder of CNN (Cable News Network), the first 24-hour cable news channel; WTBS (Turner Broadcasting System), which pioneered the superstation concept in cable television; TNT (Turner Network Television); and TCM (Turner Classic Movies). He has also successfully ventured into sports team ownership (the Atlanta Braves and Atlanta Hawks), environmental initiatives, and restaurant ownership (his Ted's Montana Grill chain), just to mention a few.

Along the way, Turner has also given back. In 1986 he launched the charitable Goodwill Games. In 1989 he created the Turner Tomorrow Fellowship, which offers positive solutions to global problems. As a philanthropist, he is best known for his $1 billion pledge (one-third of his $3 billion worth at the time) to the United Nations. He also serves as chairman of the United Nations Foundation board of directors. In 1991 Turner was named *TIME* magazine's Man of the Year.

Throughout his life, Ted Turner has devoted his assets to a blend of environmentalism and capitalism. Until 2011 he owned more land than any other American, and he currently owns the largest herd of bison in the world. He has taken many risks and grown his business ventures into well-known enterprises. At the same time, he has cared deeply about the environment and social issues.

THINK CRITICALLY

1. Comment on Ted Turner's success in effective decision making. How did he grow his net worth from $1 million to more than $2 billion today?

2. Turner places great value on land and ownership of property. Rather than renting, he believes in owning real estate to protect his privacy and provide him a quality of life. What are the benefits of property ownership?

3. Why do wealthy people often establish foundations and give large sums of money when they have reached their life goals?

Resource Planning and Management

Overview

Unit 3 presented personal decision making (Chapter 11), renting and buying a home (Chapters 12 and 13), owning a car (Chapter 14), and family decisions (Chapter 15). This project will extend your knowledge into related areas.

Personal Decisions: Avoiding Scams

As you get started in life making a good, solid income and accumulating wealth, you will need to exercise caution to protect your assets. Home improvements, car purchases, and other major expenses are common areas in which scam artists take advantage of unsuspecting consumers. Let's look at some situations you may face in the future.

Don't Call Me, I'll Call You

A typical *home-improvement fraud* might work like this: Someone knocks on your door and compliments you on your well-maintained yard. The person notices that your house needs painting. The person assures you that he or she is qualified to perform the work and could do the job more quickly and cheaply than a large company. To get started, he or she will need payment up front to buy materials and cover expenses. After getting your money, the person may never do the work or may do such a poor job that you would have been better off without it. Figure U3.1 lists some tips for handling this type of pitch.

© iStock.com/cabania

When you are solicited at home:

1. *Don't say "yes" today.* Any agreement that is worthwhile can wait until you have time to think about it.

2. *Don't give cash.* When you give a check, you may have the option of stopping payment. But you must act quickly. It is better to avoid giving cash or a check until you have had time to reconsider. Many states have laws (called "cooling-off rules") that allow you three business days after a purchase over $25 with a check or credit card to change your mind and revoke the transaction.

3. *Check it out.* Ask the Better Business Bureau or your state attorney general's office for consumer complaints about the individual or company. Are they authorized to do business in your state? Are there consumer complaints on file against them?

4. *Compare prices.* Compare the prices for labor and materials with other sources. This may take several days but is worth it.

5. *Don't hurry.* If you didn't originate the sale, don't allow others to "create demand" for a product. Don't allow others to talk you in to something you don't want.

6. *When in doubt, don't.* Make this your motto. As the saying goes, "If something seems too good to be true, it probably is." Get all the information you need, and then evaluate it carefully. If you still have doubts, wait.

Promises, Promises

An "unconditional, lifetime, money-back guarantee" is only as good as the person or company that offers it. When the company goes out of business, the guarantee goes with it.

Another common guarantee says, "Good as long as you own this car." The dealer offering this guarantee is counting on the fact that you won't keep the car more than a few years. When things start to go wrong, you will no longer be the owner. Remember: If it sounds too good to be true, it probably is!

All That Glitters

This "investment" scheme capitalizes on the desire to get rich quick, coupled with an attraction to beautiful and rare objects (from gold to diamonds). Thousands of counterfeit Krugerrands (gold coins) circulate across the nation. Investors have no idea they are fake until they try to resell them. By then, the seller has vanished. Gold-painted lead also appears to be the real thing—gold bullion. Investors who pay up front, before verifying true value, get stuck with worthless lead. Junk gems often are passed off as valuable rubies, sapphires, emeralds, and diamonds.

A Deal You Just Can't Beat

Advertisements on television, in print media, and on the Internet offer fabulous "deals" for consumers who are willing to sign up and get started. These deals may promise you a sampling of free products, lots of "valuable" merchandise at a fraction of the cost, and other exciting offers. Often, these ads state that the offer is available only for a limited time to entice consumers to sign up right away. However, once you sign up, your personal information is sold to various "affiliates" who target you with product offers that are mostly worthless. You are shipped junk merchandise and then billed, including shipping and handling. Avoid signing up for these types of offers.

Complete Worksheet 1 (Before You Buy: Rip-offs and Warning Signals) provided for you in the *Student Activity Guide* and also presented for reference below.

WORKSHEET 1
Before You Buy: Rip-offs and Warning Signals

BEFORE YOU BUY. . .

Directions: Analyze the following situations and determine what might be wrong.

Situation 1. You receive an e-mail that says you qualify for a new mortgage. You can get a $300,000 loan for as little as $600 a month. Bad credit is no problem. You can refinance at any time. Just click the link for a free consultation.

Situation 2. You receive a telephone call that offers you free products for answering a few simple questions. All you have to do is give them your name, Social Security number, address, and other personal information, and they will send you free samples of merchandise that you use or would like to try based on your lifestyle.

Situation 3. On a classifieds website, you see an ad posted by someone who is seeking to unload his collection of rare baseball cards and comic books at lower-than-market prices. He needs the money right away and will sell to the highest bidder. You call to get the address, and when you show up, there are several others there who are interested in the merchandise and are bidding on it.

Home Loan Payments

First-time homebuyers need to know the anticipated monthly payment when they purchase a house. The monthly payment will depend on the type of loan: fixed rate or adjustable rate.

Computing Your Payment Amount

The largest cost of home ownership is the house payment. The total payment is based on the (a) loan amount (principal), (b) interest rate, and (c) length of time to repay the loan. As you learned in Chapter 13, the interest rate on a fixed-rate mortgage remains constant over the life of the loan. Under a fixed-rate loan, the payment for a $50,000 loan at 4 percent spread over 15 or 30 years would be:

	30-Year Loan	15-Year Loan
Monthly payment:		
Principal and interest	$238.71	$369.84

Note that the above payment amounts do not include property taxes or insurance premiums, which some mortgage contracts require be included with your monthly payment.

While monthly payments are higher on the 15-year loan, your total interest would be lower over the life of the loan. For example, under the 30-year term, you would repay $85,935.60 ($238.71 × 12 payments per year × 30 years). Under the 15-year term, you would repay $66,571.20 ($369.84 × 12 payments per year × 15 years). This is a savings of $19,364.40!

The interest rate on an adjustable-rate mortgage (ARM) usually starts low but changes over time with changes in the economy. For example, an ARM might be offered at 3 percent, while a fixed-rate mortgage is offered at 5 percent. However, the lender may raise the rate of the ARM over time to 8 or 9 percent as interest rates increase in the economy, whereas the fixed-rate mortgage would remain at 5 percent over the life of the loan. ARMs typically have maximum rate increases and ceilings to which the interest rate can rise.

An ARM is ideal for individuals who plan to move frequently and expect the market value of the house to increase in the short term. They can sell the house and move before it is time for a mortgage rate increase. The profit realized from the increased property value can cover the selling costs and moving expenses.

Loan Fees

When financial institutions loan money to homebuyers, they charge loan fees that pay the costs of setting up the loan. Loan fees may range from $100 to $2,500 or more, depending on the loan. In most cases, if the loan does not go through for some reason, the borrower forfeits the loan fees. Borrowers also may pay points, or finance charges, for a loan. Typically, one point is 1 percent of the loan amount. For example, three points charged for a $50,000 loan would be a 3 percent fee, or $1,500 ($50,000 × 3%).

Mortgage Payment Amount

The chart below provides a simple way to estimate what your mortgage payment amount would be. The higher the interest rate, the higher your monthly payment. To estimate your monthly mortgage payment (for principal and interest only), complete the steps listed at the top of the next page.

Monthly Mortgage Payment Factors (per $1,000 of loan amount)	Loan Rate %	30 Yrs.	25 Yrs.	20 Yrs.	15 Yrs.
	5.0	5.59	6.07	6.86	8.11
	6.0	5.94	6.40	7.16	8.40
	6.5	6.29	6.73	7.46	8.69
	7.0	6.64	7.06	7.76	8.98
	7.5	6.99	7.39	8.06	9.27
	8.0	7.34	7.72	8.36	9.56
	8.5	7.69	8.05	8.68	9.85
	9.0	8.05	8.39	9.00	10.14
	9.5	8.41	8.74	9.32	10.44
	10.0	8.78	9.09	9.65	10.75

1. Find your mortgage interest rate in the first column.

2. Run your finger across that row until you reach the column for the length of your loan. This number is your monthly mortgage payment factor. For example, for a 7 percent, 30-year mortgage, the factor is 6.64.

3. Multiply this factor by the number of thousands in the mortgage principal. For example, in $50,000, there are 50 thousands. Therefore, you would multiply 6.64 times 50. Your monthly payment for a $50,000 loan at 7 percent for 30 years would be $332.

Complete Worksheet 2 (Computing Loan Payments) provided for you in the *Student Activity Guide* and also presented for reference below. Use it to estimate mortgage or loan payments for different rates and amounts.

WORKSHEET 2
Computing Loan Payments

Directions: Compute the following estimated mortgage amounts, using the chart supplied on p. 370.

What is your estimated mortgage payment for:

1. A 30-year mortgage for $50,000 at 8%?

_____

2. A 25-year mortgage for $70,000 at 6%?

_____

3. A 15-year mortgage for $80,000 at 7.5%?

_____

4. A 30-year mortgage for $100,000 at 6%?

_____

5. A 25-year mortgage for $100,000 at 7%?

_____

6. A 15-year mortgage for $100,000 at 8%?

_____

7. A 30-year mortgage for $150,000 at 7.5%?

_____

8. A 25-year mortgage for $150,000 at 9%?

_____

9. A 15-year mortgage for $150,000 at 5%?

_____

Housing Option: Building a Home

If you decide to build a new home, rather than buy an existing one, you will need to hire a builder (often called a *building contractor*). You must choose the land where you want to build your house. Often the builder has lots for sale, and you may select one of these lots. In other cases, you may own a vacant lot or purchase a lot and contract with the builder for only the house itself.

You'll also need to pick a house plan for the size and style of the house you want. Many new homes are built using stock plans from a catalog. The builder may make modifications in room size, window style, or other details at your request. A custom-designed home, on the other hand, is one that is created specifically for the family which will live there. In most cases, custom-designed homes require the services of an architect. Based on your desires and what you can afford, the architect prepares a house plan. The architect will charge a fee, called the *architect's fee*, for drawing up the house plans. The architect's fee typically ranges from $2,500 to $5,000 or more, depending on house size and value. The more complicated the floor plans, the higher the fee.

Once you and the builder agree on the house specifications and price, the builder will have a building contract drawn. It specifies what is to be done, what materials are to be used, and a timetable for completion. You will most likely have to make a large down payment so that the builder can purchase materials. Your purchase loan (mortgage) will generally be approved only after the house is completed. Therefore, the builder may get a temporary *construction loan* that finances construction and is paid off when the house is completed. While you do not pay for the construction loan, the interest costs on the loan are a part of the builder's costs of operation and are included in the price of the house. Any changes in the original plans will increase your costs. Such a change requires a separate agreement to account for the added costs of this construction.

The government requires inspections of new construction at regular intervals for electricity, plumbing, and so on to make sure it meets *building codes*. While the builder is responsible for any required charges related to inspection (as a part of the total price), delays can result when construction must wait for inspectors to arrive.

Once construction is complete and before closing, you and the builder will "walk through" the house to conduct an inspection. This is often referred to as a *presettlement walk-through*. The government will also conduct one final inspection. If the home passes the inspection, you will be issued a *certificate of occupancy* (verifying that your new home is ready for you to move in).

At closing, all *subcontractors* (companies and individuals contracted by the builder to do specific jobs, such as install plumbing or electrical wiring) and all expenses of construction will be paid. Once funds are released to the builder, you can then take possession of your new home.

To get an idea of the type of house you would like to build, complete Worksheet 3 (Building Your Dream Home) provided for you in the *Student Activity Guide* and also presented for reference on the next page.

WORKSHEET 3
Building Your Dream Home

Directions: Answer the following questions and complete the research suggested to specify your dream home. Be sure to list your sources of information.

1. What style of house do you prefer? (two-story, ranch, Victorian, Tudor, and so on)

2. Attach a picture of a house that closely resembles the home of your dreams.

3. Prepare a floor plan that details the rooms and configuration, along with windows, doors, and so on.

4. What is the total square footage of your home?

   How many bedrooms?

   How many bathrooms?

   Describe the bedrooms, bathrooms, kitchen, and living area(s).

   Describe the general layout of the house, starting at the front door and ending at the back door or on the second floor.

5. Describe the lot and landscaping, including lot size and shape.

6. Describe the block—what part of town, city or county, the neighborhood or region.

7. Based on today's costs of building real estate, what would it cost to build this house? (*Hint:* You need to consult newspaper or online ads that describe similar new properties or interview a builder or other reliable source.)

8. Prepare a report of your findings, including a cover page, drawings or exhibits, narrative of information, and list of sources of information.

Auto Repair Rip-Offs

Overcharging and needless repairs cost motorists billions of dollars each year. Some states require repair shops to give written estimates. The final bill cannot be increased by more than 10 percent without your prior authorization. Many states require that the repair shop return replaced parts to you rather than discard them. This practice allows you to examine the part that has been replaced.

You should be wary when allowing others to check your car's engine, tires, belts, fluid levels, and the like. For example, you may go in for an oil change, but the mechanic may tell you that you should replace your water pump, hoses, valve covers, or other part(s). These repairs may or may not be needed. If the mechanic finds a number of problems, or one very expensive problem, be suspicious. Ask for evidence of the problem.

Figure U3.2 shows a list of tips from New York City's Department of Consumer Affairs to help you know what to do when you experience car trouble. Also, to help you practice identifying potential rip-off situations and warning signals when you experience car trouble, complete Worksheet 4 (Rip-offs and Warning Signals for Your Car) provided for you in the *Student Activity Guide* and also presented for reference on the next page.

FIGURE U3.2   **When You Run into Car Trouble**

Tips from New York City's Department of Consumer Affairs

- Look for a reliable mechanic before you are faced with an emergency. Ask friends for references.

- If you suspect your car needs repairs, have it checked before it becomes a big repair.

- For large repairs, get two estimates and compare the charges. Let the shops know you are comparison shopping.

- List all symptoms so you won't forget anything when you are talking to a mechanic. Give a copy of the list to the mechanic and keep a copy for yourself. Make sure all of the symptoms are taken care of before you accept the work for full payment.

- Don't authorize work unless you understand what is being done. Add-on work that does not apply to the reason for your repair should be suspect.

- Don't tell a mechanic to "get this car in good running order." This is a blanket opportunity for him or her to do anything whether or not it is essential.

- Don't sign a repair order unless you understand what is being done to your car. Question each line item.

- Keep itemized bills. Good records will help you in the event work is not satisfactory. Mechanics should stand behind their work. Be able to tell the mechanic, "I had this fuel pump replaced by you two months ago. It should be working." Have the documentation with you to prove it.

- If you suspect you are being overcharged, ask to see the supplier's parts price list.

- Find out which local and state government agencies have jurisdiction over auto repair complaints. Use the agency if necessary to get satisfaction.

WORKSHEET 4
Rip-offs and Warning Signals for Your Car

Directions: Read each of the following statements that could be a potential rip-off. Identify the warning signal (a point that makes you uncomfortable) and what you would do about it.

1. Your car is making pinging noises every time you accelerate to pass another car or go up a hill. You stop by a service station, and while your car is being filled with gas, you casually ask what could be wrong. The attendant replies that he would be happy to take a look at it when he gets off work, and that he could probably fix it in his spare time. Repairs could cost as little as $50 or as much as $250.

2. You are on vacation and driving the family car. You had it tuned up before you left, and your tires are fairly new. Along the way, you stop for gas. While checking the oil, the attendant notices that one of your hoses is loose. He fixes it (no charge) but then sees that you have an oil leak. He offers to make the repair within an hour for $100 plus parts.

3. You take your car in for its regular tune-up and maintenance. You take a list of things that need to be done. An hour later, you receive a telephone call and are asked to authorize extra repairs that total $500. These repairs are not related to the tune-up or regular maintenance. But when the car is up on the rack, the mechanic sees that the work needs to be done.

4. You decide you'd like to add a specialty after-market product to your new car. You visit the dealership, and the salesman quotes you $400 for parts and $200 for labor to install it. You order it and put down a deposit of $200. When you check on the part to see if it has arrived a week later, you are told that the part will now cost $600 (new price list) and labor will cost $400 because installation will be more complicated.

5. You've driven your car less than 500 miles after purchasing it. It has a full manufacturer's warranty. When you make sharp right-hand turns, you can hear a strange scraping noise from that area of the car. You take the car back to the dealership, and the service technician tells you the right wheel bearing needs to be replaced and quotes you $1,000 to fix it. He indicates that this repair isn't covered by the warranty because it isn't part of the drivetrain. The dealer offers to sell you an extended warranty that will cover this repair, but the cost of the extended warranty is $2,500, which must be paid up front.

Final Directions

All adults should prepare for death to help ensure their final wishes are carried out. To ensure their final wishes are carried out, many people create a letter of final instruction. This letter offers points of guidance for family members, such as listing financial details (names and contact information of financial planners and insurance agents, a list of bank and retirement accounts, and so on); listing where important documents are located; and specifying memorial or funeral instructions, among other things. This letter of instruction does not have to be notarized, although some people take this extra precaution to assure that any final wishes will be honored.

A typical letter of final instruction is shown in Figure U3.3. It outlines a person's wishes and helps others to implement them. Read the letter and see if there is anything you might like to add to the list, or something you would remove from the list. Then prepare Worksheet 5 (Letter of Final Instruction) provided for you in the *Student Activity Guide*, or simply prepare a letter of final instruction using a word processing program.

FIGURE U3.3   **Letter of Final Instruction**

Date: _____

To my family,

This is a list of my last wishes and arrangements I have made which I hope will make decisions easier for you.

1. I wish to be cremated. I have prearranged services at the Bennet Funeral Home. These arrangements include the details of announcements, selection of urn, etc. I have prepaid these services, and the receipt is attached to this document.

2. I do not wish to be an organ donor. Please do not sign forms to indicate otherwise.

3. My Last Will and Testament is in my safe-deposit box at First Independent Bank, Main Branch, this city. A copy is also in my attorney's office (Anderson & Anderson, this city).

4. I have the following accounts and policies which should be included in my estate:

   Checking Account ....First Independent Bank
   Savings Account ....First Independent Bank
   Life Insurance Policy ($100,000) ....New York Life
   Mortgage Insurance ....Veterans Services

5. My safe-deposit box contains deeds to property I own, past tax returns, and lists of credit and charge accounts I hold.

_____

J. B. Adams

Providing Financial Security

Unit 4 explores options for investing money to achieve future financial security. In Chapter 16, you will learn about basic investing concepts and the effects of risk, such as inflation, on investment choices.

Chapter 17 discusses stock investments. Understanding how the markets work and how to evaluate potential stock choices will help you get started.

Chapter 18 looks at bond investing and how it can be used to balance your portfolio, acting as a hedge against losses that may occur in more risky markets.

Chapter 19 focuses on mutual funds, which are managed by professionals who make your buy-and-sell decisions. You'll also learn about other investment choices, such as real estate, collectibles, and some other very risky options.

Chapter 20 wraps up the unit with retirement planning. You'll learn about trusts, estates, wills, and other tools to help you manage your assets.

CHAPTER 16

Investing for the Future

16.1 **Basic Concepts of Investing**

16.2 **Making Investment Choices**

Consider This...

Pavel has saved some money that he will use for college expenses in a few years. Right now, it's in a regular savings account, earning 1.5 percent per year.

"My parents say I can do better," Pavel tells his best friend. "If I invest the money, I could get 6 to 8 percent, or maybe even more. So I've been checking my options. You know what I've found so far? That investing is filled with risk, and there are many types of risk. If I'm willing to take a lot of risk, then I may be able to earn more money. But I also stand a chance of losing part or all of my money. As a beginning investor, I'm not willing to lose my principal. So I have to decide what my goals are, weigh the trade-offs, and make the best choice to meet my goals. This is interesting stuff, but it isn't as easy as it sounds."

The Essential Question *What are the stages of investing and what risks are involved?*

LO 1-1 Why Should You Invest?

Investing is the use of long-term savings to earn a financial return. It is a proven and powerful way to strengthen your financial position over time. Investing is an essential part of providing for future needs. It provides a source of income in addition to a paycheck, allowing you to make money on money.

Investing Is a Way to Beat Inflation

Inflation is a rise in the general level of prices. Inflation reduces your purchasing power over time. As prices rise, it takes more money to buy the same goods and services. Thus, investors seek investments that will grow faster than the inflation rate. For example, if the annual inflation rate is 4 percent, you will want your investments to yield a rate of return higher than 4 percent.

Thus, investing will help protect your purchasing power. As prices rise, your investments will keep your net worth rising. Investments allow your net worth to grow at a faster rate than general price levels.

A quick way to evaluate an investment's rate of return is to use the Rule of 72.

How can you protect yourself from the effects of inflation?

The **Rule of 72** is a technique for estimating the number of years required to double your money at a given rate of return. Simply divide the percentage rate of return into 72. For example, if an investment is yielding an average of 6 percent, it will take 12 years to double your money (72 ÷ 6). As shown in the Math Minute feature, you can also use the Rule of 72 to estimate the rate of return needed to double your money in a given number of years.

Investing Increases Wealth

Financial success grows from the assets that you build up over time. Investing helps you accumulate *wealth* faster than if you simply saved your excess cash in a savings account. Because you are participating in helping businesses make and sell new products and services when you invest in stocks and bonds, you will be rewarded with dividends and interest.

Investing Is Fun and Challenging

Investors make choices and hope to pick winners. Once you gain experience, you can have fun choosing investments, buying and selling when the time is right, and using your knowledge to plan for your financial security.

 **CHECKPOINT**

What are three reasons why you should consider investing?

 **Math** Minute

The Rule of 72

The Rule of 72 is a rule of thumb or approximation technique. You can use it to estimate either the number of years or rate of return needed to double your money.

If you want to find the number of years, divide 72 by the rate of return.

Example: You are earning 10 percent on your money. How long will it take to double your money?

Solution: 72 ÷ 10 = 7.2 years

If you want to find the rate of return, divide 72 by the number of years in which you want your money to double.

Example: You have $5,000 and want to double it in six years. What rate must your investment earn to achieve $10,000 in six years?

Solution: 72 ÷ 6 = 12%

At 12 percent, your money will double in six years.

© simo988/Shutterstock.com

Stages of Investing

Before you begin investing, you must consider your budget, including your income, expenses, and savings. Typically, as your income grows and exceeds your expenses, you can progress through stages from temporary savings into different kinds of investing and greater amounts of risk. (See Figure 16.1.)

Stage 1: Put-and-Take Account

When you begin to earn a paycheck, you will put it into an account and take money out as needed to pay your bills. This money is your *emergency fund*, or your *"put-and-take" account*. The purpose of this money is to pay for your short-term needs, with enough left over to cover unexpected expenses. Thus, you should put your money in an account that offers security. Experts recommend that you set aside three to six months' net pay in this fund.

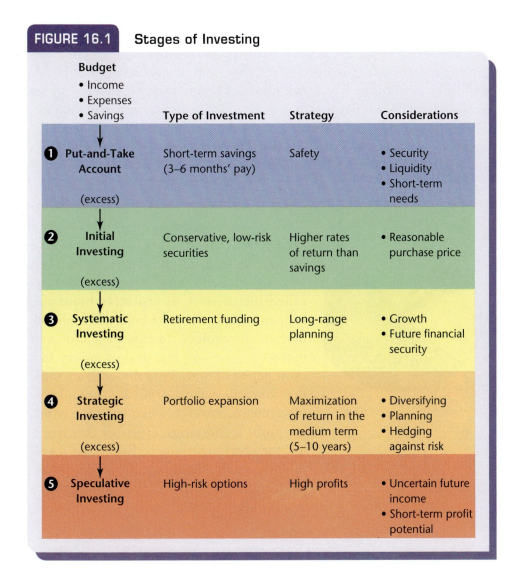

FIGURE 16.1   Stages of Investing

Budget • Income • Expenses • Savings	Type of Investment	Strategy	Considerations
❶ Put-and-Take Account (excess)	Short-term savings (3–6 months' pay)	Safety	• Security • Liquidity • Short-term needs
❷ Initial Investing (excess)	Conservative, low-risk securities	Higher rates of return than savings	• Reasonable purchase price
❸ Systematic Investing (excess)	Retirement funding	Long-range planning	• Growth • Future financial security
❹ Strategic Investing (excess)	Portfolio expansion	Maximization of return in the medium term (5–10 years)	• Diversifying • Planning • Hedging against risk
❺ Speculative Investing	High-risk options	High profits	• Uncertain future income • Short-term profit potential

Stage 2: Initial Investing

Investing really begins when you have "excess" savings beyond what you need for daily expenses and emergencies. Your **initial investing**, which is your first amount set aside for investment purposes only, should be conservative with low risk. At this stage, you don't have much money to invest, so you don't want to risk losing it. Once you have established a safe cushion of investment, you can afford to make riskier (and potentially more profitable) investments.

Stage 3: Systematic Investing

Once you are comfortable with your initial investments, you can then enter a stage called systematic investing. **Systematic investing** involves making investments on a regular and planned basis. Money is set aside regularly for investing each month. As income grows, the amount invested also grows. At this stage, your goals are long range. You are investing for a financially secure future.

Stage 4: Strategic Investing

Once you are able to make investments on a regular basis, you can begin to build a **portfolio**, or collection of investments. **Strategic investing** is the careful management of investment alternatives to maximize growth of your portfolio over the next five to ten years. Many people like to keep their portfolios growing and diversified. In other words, they want to make a variety of investment choices with a variety of risk factors. This minimizes overall risk of the portfolio itself. When the growth prospects for one investment seem to be declining, you can move your money into another investment where the prospects for growth seem greater. You should invest in different types of securities (stocks and bonds) to try to maximize your returns.

Stage 5: Speculative Investing

When you are investing regularly in a broad collection of investments but you still have money available to take bigger risks, then you can choose to move into the final stage, called speculation. **Speculative investing** happens when you make bold and high-risk investment choices. In this stage, you can make—or lose—a great deal of money in a short period of time. Typically, odds are small that you will make a profit in a speculative investment; however, when it does pay off, the profit is enormous. *High-risk investing* is not for everyone, though. Beginning investors, especially, should avoid speculative investments because they cannot afford the loss that is likely to occur.

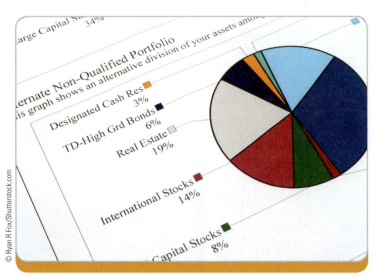

Why is it wise to invest in different types of securities?

CHECKPOINT

What is a "put-and-take" account?

Investing risk is the chance that an investment's value will decrease. All types of investing involve some degree of risk. Short-term investments are generally less risky than long-term investments.

The greater the risk you are willing to take, the greater the potential returns. Some people are willing to take more risks than others. *Risk-takers* (investors who like to take on a great deal of risk) will likely make considerably more in the long run than investors who are *risk averse* (those afraid to make investments in which they might lose some or all of their investment). However, risk-takers can also lose a lot. The best plan for most investors is to plot a moderate course, somewhere between no risk and extreme risk, where they feel comfortable.

Diversification Lowers Risk

One way to minimize risk is through **diversification**, which is the spreading of risk among many types of investments. Rather than buying only one kind of investment, you should choose several types of investments, such as stocks, bonds, and real estate. Also, you should diversify among types of stocks. For example, you might select some low-risk stocks to balance others with greater risk. Diversification reduces overall risk because not all of your choices will perform poorly at the same time. If one choice does not do well, the others will likely make up some or all of the loss.

Types of Risk

There are numerous types of risk that can affect the performance of an investment. These include interest-rate, political, market, nonmarket, and company and industry risks.

Interest-Rate Risk

Interest-rate risk is the chance that inflation will rise faster than the return on your investments. Inflation makes your fixed-rate investments worth less because they are "locked in" at lower rates. The value of a fixed-rate investment decreases when overall interest rates increase. Their value increases when overall interest rates decrease. For example, if you own a security paying a fixed interest rate of 5 percent and interest rates are increasing to a level greater than 5 percent, your investment will be worth less over time.

Political Risk

Political risk refers to actions the government might take that would reduce the value of your investment. Increased taxes and certain regulations, such as costly environmental controls that businesses are required to apply, can make some investments less attractive.

Market Risk

Market risk is caused by the business cycle—periods of economic growth or decline. When the economy is doing well, the financial markets usually follow (and vice versa).

The euro is the official currency of the European Union (EU). When the euro began in 1999, it was merely an electronic currency. Euro cash and currency became a major tender on January 1, 2002. It currently is used in 18 member nations, known collectively as the Eurozone. It is also used in nine other countries around the world that are not members of the EU. All European countries are eligible to join the EU, but not all EU members (such as the United Kingdom) have chosen to adopt the currency. Four other European states (Andorra, Vatican City, Monaco, and San Marino) have adopted the euro, though they haven't joined the EU.

THINK CRITICALLY

Some nations are members of the EU but have chosen not to adopt the euro as their currency. What might be some reasons for this? Why would nations that are not part of the EU adopt the euro as their currency?

©Redshinestudio/Shutterstock.com

Nonmarket Risk

Nonmarket risk is unrelated to market trends. Nonmarket risk is entirely unpredictable and uncontrollable. For example, terrorism threats affect all investments in the short term. Because of the violent and unpredictable nature of such events, people change their behavior and seek ways to protect themselves. This causes markets to suffer as people sell their investments to hold more cash for personal security.

Company and Industry Risk

Company risk is associated with owning one company's stock. Bad management decisions, other internal missteps, or even external situations can have a negative impact on a company's performance and, as a consequence, on the value of your investment in that company.

Industry risk affects groups of businesses. For example, if you invest in the candy industry, a nationwide trend toward dieting or the avoidance of sugar may adversely affect your investment.

CHECKPOINT

What are five types of risk you can face while investing?

LO 1-4   Investment Strategies

Many individuals don't start an investment program because they think they don't have enough money. Others may have the fortune of receiving gifts of money, such as an *inheritance* from a family member. Rather than choosing to spend this extra money on something that may have only limited value, a better choice might be to invest it. Regardless of the amount of money you have, start investing as soon as you can and continue to invest over your lifetime to achieve financial security.

Criteria for Choosing an Investment

When determining whether an investment is appropriate for you, evaluate your choice based on these factors:

- Degree of safety (risk of loss)
- Degree of liquidity (ability to get your money quickly)
- Expected dividends or interest
- Expected growth in value, preferably exceeding the inflation rate
- Reasonable purchase price and fees
- Tax benefits (saving or postponing tax liability)

No investment offers a high degree of all of these. Each investment choice represents a *trade-off*. For example, in exchange for tax benefits, you would likely have to give up a high return and liquidity. You should choose investments that offer the highest degree of safety you can get for the expected return. A *diversified portfolio* of investments achieves a balance among these factors. It would include some safe but low-yield investments as well as some riskier, higher-growth choices and some *tax-deferred investments* that allow investors to pay taxes on income earned from investments at a later date.

Wise Investment Practices

People commonly make investment mistakes. Some mistakes are minor and can be corrected easily; others cause serious financial damage. The suggestions that follow will help you avoid making investment mistakes while at the same time maximize your investing returns.

Define Your Financial Goals

Clearly defined financial goals will help you to identify which investments to purchase. To be useful, investment goals must be specific and measurable. Identify how you plan to use the money and how soon you need to accomplish each goal.

Go Slowly

Before making investments, gather the information you need to make a wise decision. Make temporary investments until you are certain they will meet your needs. **Temporary investments** are investment choices that should be reevaluated within a year or less.

Follow Through

A common mistake is keeping temporary investments too long and not reevaluating them regularly to determine how well they are performing. If they aren't performing as expected, they should be sold and other choices selected. Temporary investments that perform well often end up becoming permanent investments. **Permanent investments** are investment choices that are held for the long run—five or ten years, or longer. These securities will become the "critical mass" of your investment portfolio. They will sustain good solid returns over long periods of time and will grow substantially in principal as well.

Keep Good Records

Good record keeping is an essential part of investing. Keeping good financial records will help you keep a clear view of your progress toward future needs and goals. Pay attention to how your investments are doing. Every year,

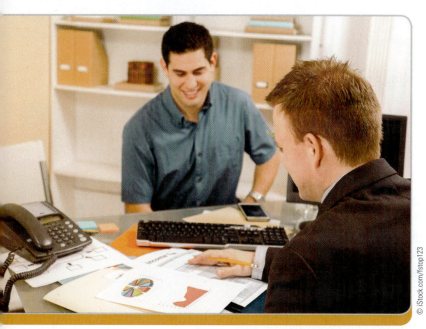

What are some suggestions that can help you make wise investment decisions?

compare your investments' current balances with their previous years' balances. Keep statements to verify your account balances and make transfers when needed. Unless you know where you have been and where you are now, it is difficult to plan where you are going.

Seek Good Investment Advice

Don't be afraid to ask questions. Seek competent advice from a trained professional as you make investment decisions. To get this advice at low cost and without a commitment, consider attending an investment seminar. At an investment seminar, you can learn about products, costs, and risks. Then you can decide what to do in your own home without any pressure. Be wary of those offering investments that deliver higher than usual returns. Avoid get-rich-quick schemes—if they sound too good to be true, they probably are.

Keep Investment Knowledge Current

Be aware of what is new in the financial market, what kinds of investments are currently good prospects, when to sell, and when to buy. It is your responsibility to know when to ask questions and to make the final decisions about your investments. Understanding the economy and how it works will help you make better investment choices. For example, you should expect that stock prices are rising and people are investing during periods of economic growth. But when economic decline begins, stock prices often are falling as people take their money out of the markets.

Know Your Limits

Understand your risk tolerance and the amount of money you can afford to risk, so you can maximize returns within your risk comfort zone. If you are uncomfortable taking large risks, then avoid them. The chance of making huge profits is not worth being stressed out by the risk.

Join an Investment Club

Consider joining an *investment club*. These clubs have regular meetings and talk about investing strategies, how to get started, when it's time to pull back, who you can trust, and so on. They help you develop your own investment skills without having to rely on someone else to tell you when it is time to make a move.

✔ CHECKPOINT

How do temporary investments differ from permanent investments?

How Do Investment Clubs Work?

When you buy the stock of a publicly held company, you actually own a piece of that company. No doubt, you wouldn't mind owning shares in companies that will grow in value over the long term with increasing prices and growing dividends. Procter & Gamble, Coca-Cola, and Disney are just a few examples of large companies that have been in business for decades. Technology firms such as Google, Facebook, and Twitter have been public companies for less than ten years.

An *investment club* is a group effort of like-minded friends, relatives, or acquaintances who share an interest in studying companies. Some clubs have a social aspect to their meetings as well. Members usually pool a monthly amount, such as $25–$50, to purchase and hold stocks in the club's partnership. They share responsibility for researching and presenting possible purchases. While there are several methods of operating investment clubs, the oldest network of investment clubs is BetterInvesting, Inc. Founded in 1951, it follows four guiding principles for making investment decisions:

- Invest a regular amount of money at regular intervals.

- Invest in companies with solid sales and profits in at least the past five years.

- Reinvest the dividends.

- Diversify by buying stocks from different industries and different-size companies (large, medium, and small). You don't want to put all of your eggs in one basket!

BetterInvesting's tool for evaluating stocks is called the Stock Selection Guide (SSG). In the early days of investment clubs, members made manual calculations, plotting a company's ten-year sales and earnings per share (EPS) on a graph. If the lines were up, straight, and parallel, indicating consistent growth, the members would continue to complete the SSG, resulting in the placement of the stock in the buy, hold, or sell zones based on past valuations. The SSG is now available as an online tool and is widely used by investment club members.

Annual and quarterly reports that include the financial history and future plans for products and services can be found on company websites, as well as Yahoo! Finance, Morningstar, and other investor websites. People who enjoy learning about investing through clubs often manage their own investments or, at the very least, are better prepared to work with professional investment advisers. For more information about investment clubs, visit www.betterinvesting.org.

THINK CRITICALLY

1. What are three advantages to joining an investment club?

2. Do an online search for "investment clubs" in or near your town or city. What did you find?

3. If you joined an investment club, which companies would you be interested in researching? Why?

KEY TERMS REVIEW

Match the terms with the definitions. Some terms may not be used.

_____ 1. The first amount you set aside for investment purposes only

_____ 2. The chance that an investment's value will decrease

_____ 3. The use of long-term savings to earn a financial return

_____ 4. A collection of investments

_____ 5. The spreading of risk among many types of investments

_____ 6. Making investments on a regular and planned basis

_____ 7. Making bold and high-risk investments

_____ 8. A rise in the general levels of price

a. diversification
b. inflation
c. initial investing
d. investing
e. investing risk
f. permanent investments
g. portfolio
h. Rule of 72
i. speculative investing
j. strategic investing
k. systematic investing
l. temporary investments

CHECK YOUR UNDERSTANDING

LO1-1 9. How does investing help you beat inflation?

LO1-2 10. Why do you need to establish an emergency fund before investing?

LO1-3 11. What is diversification and what is its purpose?

APPLY YOUR KNOWLEDGE

LO1-4 12. Why is it important to start with temporary investments that lead to permanent investments?

THINK CRITICALLY

LO1-2 13. Describe the five stages of investing. Which stage do you think is most important? Explain why.

LO1-3 14. Why is risk an important consideration when investing? How will your comfort level with risk affect your investment decisions?

LO1-4 15. Explain the connection between keeping good records and making good investment choices.

The Essential Question _Refer to The Essential Question on p. 379. Stages of investing include your "put-and-take" account, or emergency fund; initial investing; systematic investing; strategic investing; and speculative investing. Your goal when investing is to find ways to reduce risk while maximizing your return._

The Essential Question *What are some sources of financial information for investors, and how do investment choices vary by risk?*

LEARNING OBJECTIVES

> LO 2-1 List and describe sources of investing information.
> LO 2-2 Describe investing choices and rate them by risk.

KEY TERMS

- annual report, *391*
- bond, *392*
- stock, *393*
- mutual fund, *393*
- annuity, *394*
- real estate, *394*
- futures, *395*
- option, *395*
- penny stocks, *395*
- collectible, *395*

LO 2-1 Sources of Financial Information

To make good investment choices, you must have good information. Investment information can be found in both print and online sources as well as through other sources to help you evaluate investment options.

Newspapers

Found in your local newspaper, *financial pages* list all types of securities, including stocks and bonds, as well as other information related to investing. Reading these pages daily will help you keep track of financial markets and obtain information needed to make wise investment decisions.

The *Wall Street Journal* is a daily newspaper that provides detailed coverage of the business and financial world. *Barron's* is a weekly newspaper that also provides charts of trends, financial news, and technical analysis of financial data. Both of these publications offer online subscriptions as well as free articles and data at their websites.

Investor Services and Newsletters

Companies called *investor services* provide extensive financial data to clients. Major services include Moody's Investors Service, Standard and Poor's Financial Services, and Value Line. Their publications are found in public libraries and brokerage firms, as well as online. They contain precise current and historical financial data.

What information is found in the financial pages of a newspaper?

Many investors subscribe to weekly or monthly *investment newsletters*. These newsletters provide the latest financial data and information as well as advice and commentary.

Financial Magazines

A number of weekly and monthly magazines specialize in business and financial information. These magazines provide the latest news in the world of business and finance, market analysis, commentary, and other information about finances and investing. Some of the more popular financial magazines include *Business Week*, *Forbes*, *Investor's Business Daily*, *Money*, *Kiplinger's Personal Finance*, and *The Economist*. All of these publications also offer financial news and data at their websites.

Brokers

There are two general categories of brokers: discount and full-service. *Discount brokers* buy and sell securities for clients for a reduced commission but provide little or no investment advice to their clients. Examples of discount brokers include Charles Schwab, E*TRADE, and TD Ameritrade. These brokers are typically used by people who are well informed and know what they want to buy and sell.

Full-service brokers provide analysis and opinions based on their judgments and the opinions of experts at the company they represent. In addition to buying and selling securities for their clients, full-service brokers research various investments and keep clients up to date on market trends and stock performance, while providing them with investment ideas and recommendations. Some well-known full-service brokerage companies are Edward Jones, Morgan Stanley Wealth Management, and Merrill Lynch.

Because of the increasing popularity of inexpensive trading, many full-service brokers also offer discount trading at their websites. Some banks, credit unions, and other financial institutions also assist their customers with buying and selling securities. Money can be transferred in and out of your checking or savings account to pay for securities purchased and sold. You will receive statements showing the current value of your securities.

With most types of brokerage accounts, you can manage them online. You can give buy and sell orders, transfer money among investment accounts, and track the progress of your investments, either with your own software or with a platform supplied by the broker or bank.

Financial Advisers

Professional *financial advisers* are trained to give investment advice and manage your investments. *Certified financial planners (CFPs)* have completed education requirements and have passed CFP Board certification exams. CFPs are required to have a minimum of three years experience in the financial planning process.

Advice given is based on your goals, age, lifestyle, and other factors. The adviser will ask you to supply confidential information about your assets, liabilities, net worth, income, and budget, as well as your financial goals. The adviser usually receives a fee for consulting services, although some also receive a commission when they sell you investment products (such as stocks, bonds, or life insurance policies). Generally, you will get better overall advice when the adviser does not stand to make a profit on the investments you choose to buy.

Annual Reports

An **annual report** is a summary of a corporation's financial results for the year and its prospects for the future. The Securities and Exchange Commission (SEC) requires all public corporations to prepare this report each year and send it to their stockholders. Investors can use the information to evaluate the corporation as an investment prospect.

You can find annual reports online at the SEC's website (www.sec.gov). Corporations often publish their financial performance data in the "Investors" section of their websites. Also, some large libraries keep copies of annual reports of major corporations.

Online Investor Education

In addition to the websites of print publications and brokers, the Internet offers a number of free educational sites for new investors. For example, Teenvestor is a website dedicated to helping teens learn how to invest and manage their money. The Motley Fool website offers a wealth of investing advice, commentary, analysis, and articles. BetterInvesting is a nonprofit site dedicated to investor education. Investopedia contains a wealth of articles and tutorials covering all aspects of finance and investing, in addition to a comprehensive financial dictionary. Investopedia also offers free weekly newsletters and interactive tools such as its stock market simulator, which allows individuals to set up a brokerage account with play money and trade publicly traded stocks on stock exchanges. These are just a few of the many educational sites available to investors online. An online search using a search engine will produce many more.

CHECKPOINT

How does a discount broker differ from a full-service broker?

LO 2-2 Investment Choices

Once you are ready to make investments, it's time to consider all of your investment choices. Investments can be categorized by their degree of risk and expected return. In Chapters 17 through 20, you will explore each type of investment more thoroughly.

Low Risk/Low Return

For your first investments, you will likely want to consider fairly safe investments, even though their returns will be relatively low. Even as you grow as a sophisticated investor, however, you should continue to include some low-risk investments as part of your diversified portfolio.

Corporate and Municipal Bonds

A **bond** is a debt obligation of a corporation (*corporate bond*) or a state or local government (*municipal bond*). When a corporation or government body sells a bond, it is borrowing from an investor. When you invest in a corporate bond, the corporation pays you a fixed amount of money (called interest) at a fixed interval (usually every six months). The corporation also must repay the principal (amount borrowed) at maturity. The *maturity date* of a bond is the date on which the borrowed money must be repaid.

When you loan money to a state or local government unit, such as a city, county, community college district, or utility district, you are also paid interest on your investment. Your principal is repaid when the bond matures. Typically, interest earned on municipal bonds is tax-free, giving the investor a tax advantage. Bonds are explained in detail in Chapter 18.

U.S. Government Savings Bonds

When you buy a savings bond, you are lending money to the U.S. government. *Savings bonds* help pay for the U.S. government's borrowing needs. They are considered one of the safest investments because they are backed by the full faith and credit of the U.S. government. You can buy savings bonds online only at the U.S. Department of Treasury's TreasuryDirect website (www.treasurydirect.gov); paper certificates are no longer issued.

U.S. savings bonds are available in two forms: Series EE and Series I. Both Series EE and Series I savings bonds are sold at face value. For example, you would pay $50 for a $50 bond. They must be held for a minimum of one year and can be held for a maximum of 30 years. Bonds redeemed within five years must pay a three-month interest penalty. The two forms of bonds differ in how they earn their interest. Series EE savings bonds earn a fixed rate of interest. Series I savings bonds earn a fixed rate of interest in combination with a semiannual adjustment for inflation. The interest that both Series EE and Series I savings bonds earn is subject to federal income tax, but not state or local income tax. However, if the bond is used to finance a college education, you may not have to pay federal income tax on your interest.

U.S. Government Treasury Securities

Like savings bonds, U.S. Treasury securities are considered safe investments because they are backed by the U.S. government. They are taxed by the federal government but are exempt from state and local income taxes. You can buy U.S. Treasury securities at the TreasuryDirect website or through a bank or broker. There are three types.

- *Treasury bills.* These bills, called *T-bills*, are available for a minimum purchase of $100. They are issued for terms of 4, 13, 26, and 52 weeks. T-bills are typically sold at a discount rather than face value. For example, you might pay $990 for a $1,000 bill. When the bill matures, you would be paid $1,000. The difference between the purchase price and face value constitutes the earnings on the bill.

- *Treasury notes*. These notes, called *T-notes*, are available for a minimum purchase of $100. They are issued for terms of 2, 3, 5, 7, and 10 years. They earn a fixed rate of interest every six months until maturity.
- *Treasury bonds*. These bonds, called *T-bonds*, are issued for a minimum of $100 with a 30-year maturity. They pay interest every six months until they mature. Interest rates are generally higher than rates for either T-bills or T-notes because of the longer maturity.

Medium Risk/Medium Return

When you feel secure enough to take more risk and you have additional money to invest, you are ready to step up to the medium-risk range to increase your return. Some of these medium-risk options involve investing with companies that manage the investment.

Stocks

Stock is a unit of ownership in a corporation. The owner of stock is called a stockholder. A *stockholder* receives a stock certificate, which is evidence of the ownership. When you are a stockholder, you will share in a corporation's profits, which are paid to you as *dividends*. If the company does well, you also earn returns in the increased value of the stock you own, called *capital gains*.

Stocks generally carry more risk than investment choices with a fixed interest rate because a stockholder's earnings can go up or down, depending on the company's profits. Stocks in well-established companies are reasonably safe, whereas stocks in less-stable companies can be quite risky. However, a diversified portfolio of stocks of various risk levels can achieve a medium overall risk. You will learn more about investing in stocks in Chapter 17.

Mutual Funds

Suppose you have $500, which is not enough to buy a diversified portfolio of stocks. Instead, you can buy shares in a large, professionally managed group of investments called a mutual fund. A mutual fund is the pooling of money from many investors to buy a large selection of securities. Security funds are grouped to meet the fund's stated investment goals. Two major advantages of a mutual fund for investors are professional management and diversification. Because the fund invests in a wide variety of securities, it provides diversification that small investors could not otherwise achieve with their limited resources.

Communication Connection

© oculo/Shutterstock.com

Most families have some type of investment plan. After individuals or couples have been working for several years, they are likely to have company-sponsored investments as well as individual investment choices. These investments allow them to grow in wealth and to beat inflation.

Talk with a relative or friend who has investments. What different types of investments does the person have? How would you describe the investments in terms of degrees of risk and expected returns? Does this person use a financial adviser? What advice about investments can this person offer? Write a one-page summary of your findings.

Although some mutual funds fall in the speculative category and others fall in the low-risk category, such as those that specialize in money market securities, most mutual funds fall somewhere in the broad medium range in terms of risk and return. You can further diversify your portfolio by investing in mutual funds with different objectives. For example, some funds buy securities in riskier small companies, hoping to earn a higher return. Others stick to well-established, safe companies to earn a lower but stable return. By investing money in both funds, you are diversifying your investments. If your riskier fund does not do well, your stable fund will limit your losses. Mutual funds are the fastest-growing segment of the American financial services industry. You will learn more about mutual funds in Chapter 19.

Annuities

An annuity is a contract in which you make a lump-sum payment or series of payments that earn interest in return for regular disbursements, often after retirement. You usually buy an annuity directly from a life insurance company. Generally, you will receive income monthly, with disbursements continuing as long as you live or for a specified number of years. The interest on the principal as well as the interest compounded on that interest builds up free of current income tax. Taxes are deferred until you receive disbursements from your annuity (these are called *tax-deferred annuities*).

The payments from an annuity are normally used to supplement retirement income. An annuity often is described as the opposite of life insurance. It pays while you are alive; life insurance pays when you die.

Real Estate

Many people like to invest in real estate—buildings and land. Your house will be one of your biggest investments. While this type of investment usually represents a large and often nonliquid investment of cash, it generally has proven to be protection against inflation in most parts of the United States. In some areas, market values of homes have increased faster than the inflation rate. During recessionary periods in the economy, however, real estate may lose value. But in the long run, real estate generally is a good investment.

Real estate investments also have tax benefits. Certain costs associated with home ownership are deductible from gross income, thus lowering taxable income. While investing in your own home carries little risk, investment in other types of real estate can be very risky. Investing in real estate is covered in greater depth in Chapter 19.

High Risk/High Return

High-risk/high-return choices involve considerable uncertainty. Returns can be high, but they can also be low or even negative, resulting in a loss of principal (the amount of the original investment). If you are willing to take the risks involved with these choices, you stand to make high returns over time. But you also risk high losses if your investments are poor performers.

Futures

A **futures** contract obligates the buyer to purchase (or the seller to sell) stock or a *commodity* (a product that is mined or grown) for a specified price on a specified date in the future. The investor is betting that the price of the stock or commodity will be higher on that future date than it is at the time of the contract. Thus, trading in futures is very risky speculation. If prices rise, the investor can make a lot of money; if prices fall, the investor loses. This type of investment is not for beginners or for individuals who cannot afford to lose their investment.

Options

An **option** is the right, but not the obligation, to buy or sell stock or a commodity for a specified price within a specified time period. As with futures, the investor is betting that, during the option period, the price of the stock or commodity will rise. If it does, the investor can choose to buy it at the lower option price, resulting in an instant profit. Typically, options are short-term investment devices used by speculators to make a quick profit. They are risky for inexperienced investors.

Penny Stocks

Penny Stocks are low-priced stocks of small companies that have no track record. The stock usually sells below $5 per share. The small companies often have low revenues and few assets to assure future growth. Dot-com (Internet) companies typically begin this way. Many of them fail, making the stock worthless. Occasionally, a penny stock is successful, and the investor makes a large windfall. Generally, penny stocks are highly risky.

Collectibles

A **collectible** is any physical asset that appreciates in value over time because it is rare or desired by many. Collectibles can be things such as coins, art, stamps, ceramics, or other items that are popular from time to time, such as Beanie Babies or baseball cards. If you collect an item that goes up in value rapidly, you can reap large rewards. However, if you don't sell when your item is a hot commodity, it is likely to lose its value just as quickly, making it a risky investment. Collectors must be aware of the market and realize that their collections are subject to changing public tastes and can be difficult to resell.

What are the pros and cons of investing in collectibles?

 **CHECKPOINT**

Give three examples each of low-risk, medium-risk, and high-risk investment choices.

Arts, A/V Technology & Communications

Communications

Communications specialists spend their time creating and maintaining a favorable public image for the organization that they represent. They are involved in verbal as well as written communications, including writing press releases (for the media) and responding to information requests (from the media). They also evaluate advertising and promotion programs to determine their compatibility with their organization's public relations efforts.

Communications specialists know what to say to whom and how to manage what information is shared and how it is shared. When there is a major issue to deal with, such as a product recall, it is important to share information that is both appropriate and accurate. At the same time, it is also important to protect the interests of those who may be vulnerable, such as employees, customers, or clients.

Communications specialists work in many industries, including civic organizations, advertising, government, and health care. Most of their time is spent working in the office; however, they also attend meetings and community events, give speeches, and occasionally travel.

Employment Outlook

- An average rate of employment growth is expected.

Job Titles

- Communications specialist
- Public relations specialist
- Media specialist
- Press secretary

Needed Skills

- A bachelor's degree in public relations, journalism, or related field is usually required.
- Experience in public relations is highly desirable.
- Interpersonal, speaking, and writing skills are needed.

What's it like to work in . . . *Communications*

James works as a public relations specialist for a large consumer goods company, where he makes $50,000 a year. He works closely with the firm's marketing department. As part of his job, he helps maintain the organization's corporate image by writing press releases for the media. He also helps design the advertising campaigns so they will appeal to special target groups. He often organizes media events to help introduce the company's new products to the market.

James is currently working with the marketing department on a new public relations campaign for next quarter. He must help create a campaign that will positively reflect the company's increased focus on environmentally friendly practices. "I think it has great potential for the future growth and image of this company," he told the company president.

What About You?

Are you good at speaking and writing? Do you like helping others discover new ideas? Do you enjoy working with people? Is a career in communications right for you?

The Career Clusters icons are being used with permission of the: States' Career Clusters Initiative, 2007, www.careerclusters.org

KEY TERMS REVIEW

Match the terms with the definitions. Some terms may not be used.

____ 1. A debt obligation of a corporation or a state or local government

____ 2. The right, but not the obligation, to buy or sell stock or a commodity for a specified price within a specified time period

____ 3. Low-priced stocks of small companies that have no track record

____ 4. Buildings and land

____ 5. A unit of ownership in a corporation

____ 6. A summary of a corporation's financial results for the year and its prospects for the future

____ 7. The pooling of money from many investors to buy a large selection of securities

a. annual report
b. annuity
c. bond
d. collectible
e. futures
f. mutual fund
g. option
h. penny stocks
i. real estate
j. stock

CHECK YOUR UNDERSTANDING

LO2-1 8. Why might it be a good idea to use a financial adviser?

LO2-2 9. Why should beginning investors choose low-risk investments?

LO2-2 10. Why is investing in stock more risky than investing in bonds?

APPLY YOUR KNOWLEDGE

LO2-1 11. Visit a library or go online to obtain a copy of a current annual report of a major corporation that does business in your state. Outline the contents of the report. Decide whether this corporation would be a good investment choice. Explain why or why not.

THINK CRITICALLY

LO2-2 12. Explain why it is not possible for one investment to offer both low risk and a high return. Which is most important to you?

LO2-2 13. Compare U.S. government savings bonds to mutual funds and collectibles in terms of risk and potential return. Explain why these investments are categorized as they are.

The Essential Question *Refer to The Essential Question on p. 389. Sources of information include newspapers, investor services and newsletters, financial magazines, brokers, financial advisers, annual reports, and websites. Investment choices can either be low risk, such as bonds; medium risk, such as stocks and mutual funds; or high risk, such as futures and options.*

SUMMARY

16.1

- *Investing helps you beat inflation when your investments give you a return that is higher than the inflation rate.*

- *As your income grows beyond current needs, you can progress through investment stages involving greater amounts of risk.*

- *All investments involve some risk that your investment will lose value. Diversification helps minimize overall risk.*

- *Types of investment risk include interest-rate risk, political risk, market and nonmarket risk, and company and industry risk.*

- *Evaluate investment options for their degree of safety, degree of liquidity, expected dividends or interest, expected growth in value, cost, and tax benefits. All investment choices involve trade-offs among these criteria.*

- *To make wise investments, define your financial goals, go slowly, follow through, keep good records, seek good investment advice, keep your investment knowledge current, know your limits, and consider joining an investment club.*

16.2

- *You can get investment information from newspapers, investor services and newsletters, financial magazines, brokers, financial advisers, and annual reports, as well as from online sources.*

- *Full-service brokers give you advice in buying and selling securities; discount brokers do not give advice, but their cost is lower.*

- *Generally, the more risk you are willing to take, the more you stand to gain or lose from an investment.*

- *Investment choices can be low risk, medium risk, or high risk—depending on the investor's ability and willingness to take risks.*

- *Low-risk/low-return investment options include corporate and municipal bonds, U.S. government savings bonds, and U.S. government Treasury securities.*

- *Medium-risk/medium-return investments include stocks, mutual funds, annuities, and real estate.*

- *Futures, options, penny stocks, and collectibles carry a high risk of loss but also offer large gains if they are successful.*

© Pan Xunbin/Shutterstock.com

APPLY WHAT YOU KNOW

L01-1 1. How do inflation and investing affect purchasing power?

L01-3 2. What is the difference between company risk and industry risk? Provide an example of how each affects investments.

L01-4 3. Identify criteria you can use when choosing an investment. Which of the criteria is most important to you? Why?

L01-4 4. How might you benefit from joining an investment club?

L02-1 5. Using keywords such as "investment," "stock," or some others you can think of, search the Internet for resources to help you make investing choices. List the names and URLs of three websites that you think would help you most. Briefly describe the types of investment information available at those sites.

L02-2 6. Consult a financial newspaper or magazine or search the Internet to find the current rate for each of the following securities: Series EE savings bonds, one-year Treasury bills, two-year Treasury notes, and thirty-year Treasury bonds.

L02-2 7. Conduct online research for information on how the stock market has performed over the last 30 years. What was its high? What was its low? Draw a line graph representing the stock market during this time period.

MAKE ACADEMIC CONNECTIONS

L01-1 8. **Math** Using the Rule of 72, compute how long it would take to double your money at the following annual rates of return: (a) 1 percent, (b) 3 percent, (c) 5 percent, (d) 7 percent, (e) 9 percent, (f) 11 percent, and (g) 13 percent. Assuming the inflation rate is 5.5 percent in a given year, how do these rates of return meet your needs?

L01-4 9. **Research** Conduct research on a famous person (past or present) who has invested wisely over his or her life, resulting in substantial wealth. Consult the person's biography (if available) and other sources, and explain his or her investment strategies. Report on your findings.

L02-1 10. **Careers** Assume you would like to work as a broker some day. Research the qualifications and skills required. What are the educational requirements? Describe the work environment and characteristics of this occupation. What is the average salary? Compile your research into a "career profile" of a broker.

L02-2 11. **Economics** How would your investment choices be affected if the economy is growing? What if the economy is slowing? Consult *The Economist* magazine and find an article about the business cycle. Where is the United States at this point in time (recession, recovery, peak, or trough)? Explain what that means in terms of investing.

L02-2 12. **History** Look up a famous work of art, painting, or sculpture. Where is it located today? What is its approximate value? Why has it gained in value so much over time? What would make a piece of art a good investment?

Solve Problems and Explore Issues

LO1-1 13. Ryan, who is 19 and in college, has just inherited $1,000. He does not need the money for his put-and-take account. What would you tell him to do with it? If Ryan invested the money in a stock that earned, on average, a 10 percent return, how much would his investment be worth in 5 years? Using the Internet, locate a financial planning calculator (or a compound interest calculator) for help.

LO1-1 14. If Ryan invested his $1,000 at a 5 percent average return, how many years would it take for his investment to be worth $2,000?

LO1-2 15. Allison is considering investing $500. Explain to her what factors she should consider when choosing investment alternatives.

LO1-3 16. Diane plans to invest $10,000 that she inherited from her uncle. She would like to have the money for her daughter's college education. Her daughter is now 10 years old and will start college in 8 years. She does not want to take a lot of risk because she cannot afford to lose the $10,000. What course of action would you suggest for Diane?

LO2-1 17. Karmyn would like to invest in XYZ Corporation. You've never heard of it. What kinds of information should she have before she invests in this company? Where can she get that information?

EXTEND YOUR LEARNING

LO2-3 18. **Legal Issues** Insider trading occurs when someone who has inside information about a company makes stock market transactions that create wealth for that individual. Why is insider trading illegal? What are the consequences or penalties? What is the Security and Exchange Commission's (SEC) role in enforcing laws against insider trading?

CHAPTER PROJECT

Choose six of the investment alternatives presented in this chapter. Create a table and rank the choices from high to low on the factors of safety, risk, and liquidity. Assume that 3 is the highest score and 1 is the lowest score for each factor. Based on the results of your review of possible investments, which three alternatives would you select as temporary investments? Are there any you would select as permanent investments? Write a one-page report explaining your investment choices.

Complete the Guided Decision Making activity for Chapter 16 at ngl.cengage.com/mypf.

CHAPTER 17

Investing in Stocks

17.1 Evaluating Stocks

17.2 Buying and Selling Stocks

Consider This...

Ernesto worked during the summer and managed to save $500 to invest. He decided he wanted to buy some stock and see if he could double his money in the next year or two.

"I've been doing research about a medical research company, and I think it's on the verge of something big," he said to a discount broker whom he met through his father. "I've been reading about this company, and I think the stock price is low now because the company isn't paying dividends. Instead, it is using company profits to develop new products. Some of those products are on the cutting edge of research. All of the information I've gathered suggests that the company is solid and growing and will be a leader in its industry. I think this company's stock is worth the risk, so I'd like to buy as many shares as my money will purchase. Do you think this is a good investment?"

© Pan Xunbin/Shutterstock.com

The Essential Question *What are reasons for owning stock, what types of stock are available, and how do you value stock?*

LEARNING OBJECTIVES

> LO 1-1 Describe the features of stock and types of stock.
> LO 1-2 Explain how to value a stock and determine a fair price to pay for a stock purchase.

KEY TERMS

- public corporation, *402*
- dividends, *402*
- common stock, *403*
- proxy, *403*
- preferred stock, *403*
- income stocks, *403*
- growth stocks, *404*
- blue chip stocks, *404*
- par value, *405*
- market value, *405*
- earnings per share (EPS), *406*
- bull market, *406*
- bear market, *406*

LO 1-1 **Owning Stock**

Investing in stock is often viewed as one of the best ways to build up your personal wealth and reach your long-term financial goals. Today, around 50 percent of Americans own stock. When you buy a share of stock, you are buying an ownership interest in a company. A **public corporation** is a company whose stock is traded openly on stock markets.

People who own shares of stock are called *stockholders*, or shareholders, of the corporation. If the corporation does well, stockholders will profit in two ways. One way stockholders make money is through dividends. **Dividends** are money paid to stockholders from the corporation's earnings (profits). For example, if you owned 100 shares and a company declared a $1 dividend (per share), you would receive $100.

The other way that stockholders profit is through *capital gains*. This is an increase in the value of the stock over time. For example, if you bought stock for $5 per share and the corporation thrived, its stock price might go up to $10 per share. If it did, you could sell it for a substantial profit. Part of the risk in owning stock, however, is that the price could also go down below the price initially paid for it, resulting in a *capital loss*. Also, a capital gain becomes profit only when you sell the stock. Until then, it is a profit only "on paper."

Stockholders can also lose all of their investment if the company fails or goes out of business. However, one advantage to owning stock is that stockholders can lose no

Why is owning stock risky?

© Erdal Bayhan/Shutterstock.com

© Pan Xunbin/Shutterstock.com

more than their investment in the stock. The owner of a small business, on the other hand, can also lose personal assets if the business fails.

Stocks are traded in round lots or odd lots. *A round lot* is 100 shares or multiples of 100 shares of a particular stock. An *odd lot* is fewer than 100 shares of a particular stock. Brokerage firms usually charge higher per-share fees for trading in odd lots. Odd lots are usually combined into round lots before they are traded.

Common Stock

Common stock represents a type of stock that pays a variable dividend and gives the holder voting rights. The board of directors, which guides the corporation and decides the amount of dividends to pay each year, is elected by the common stockholders. Common stockholders vote on major policy decisions, such as whether to issue additional stock, sell the company, or change the board of directors. Each share of common stock has the same voting power; therefore, the more shares a stockholder owns, the greater the power to influence corporate policy.

Common stockholders may vote in person at the stockholders' meeting or by proxy. A **proxy** is a stockholder's written authorization to transfer his or her voting rights to someone else, usually a company manager. Most common stockholders vote by proxy.

Preferred Stock

Preferred stock represents a type of stock that pays a fixed dividend but has no voting rights. Preferred stockholders earn the stated dividend, regardless of how the company is doing. Thus, preferred stock is less risky than common stock. In the event the company fails, preferred stockholders are paid before common stockholders. As with most investments, however, the trade-off for less risk is lower return. Dividends on preferred stock may be lower than the dividends common stockholders would earn if the company is thriving.

Categories of Stocks

Investors often classify stocks (common and preferred) into different categories. Categories of stocks include income, growth, blue chip, emerging, cyclical, and defensive. Some stocks may fall into more than one category. Which category is best for you will depend on how much risk you are willing to assume for a chance to earn large returns. Most investors buy stocks in several of these categories to diversify their risk.

Income Stocks

Corporations can use their profits in two ways. They can reinvest the profits in the business to help it grow, or they can distribute the profits to stockholders as dividends. **Income stocks** are stocks in corporations that have a consistent history of paying high dividends to stockholders. Investors choose income stocks in order to receive current income in the form of dividends. Income stocks are ideally suited for investors seeking a relatively safe and regular source of current income from their investment capital. Thus, income stocks are a popular choice for retirees.

Growth Stocks

Growth stocks are stocks in corporations that reinvest their profits into the business so that it can grow. These corporations may pay little or no dividends. Instead of current income, investors buy growth stocks for future capital gains. If the reinvested profits make the business grow, the stock will be worth more in the future, and the investor can sell it to make a profit. Thus, growth stocks are long-term investments. They are often selected by younger people who have more time to let investments grow.

Blue Chip Stocks

Blue chip stocks are stocks of large, well-established corporations with a solid record of profitability. These companies generally sell high-quality, widely known products and services. They include IBM, AT&T, and the Coca-Cola Company. Blue chip stocks are a conservative investment. Investors choose them for relatively safe and stable, but moderate, returns.

Emerging Stocks

Stocks in young, often small, corporations that have higher overall risk than stocks of companies that have been successful for many years are called *emerging stocks*. These young companies may be on their way to becoming highly profitable. Or, they may be among the many small companies that fail every year. Because the future of these companies is so uncertain, their stocks are often inexpensive but risky.

Cyclical Stocks

Cyclical stocks are affected by ups and downs in the economy. Examples include travel-related companies (airlines and resorts), car manufacturers, and housing/construction companies. When the economy is doing well, people can afford to travel, buy new cars, and buy or build new houses. However, during a recession, many people lose their jobs or earn less than they would during good economic times. As a result, these discretionary expenses are some of the first things consumers will cut. This, in turn, causes reduced profits for these companies. In response to poor profit performance, the value of the stocks in these companies will likely decline.

Defensive Stocks

Defensive stocks, or *noncyclical stocks*, are stocks that remain stable and pay dividends during an economic decline. They are not affected as much by the ups and downs of business cycles. Examples include utility, pharmaceutical, health care, and food companies. These companies generally have a history of stable earnings because the demand for these products remains fairly consistent regardless of economic conditions. Therefore, stocks in these industries protect the investor from sharp losses during bad economic times.

 **CHECKPOINT**

What are the different categories of stock available for investment?

Suppose a couple is having difficulty deciding what investments to make and how much money to keep in liquid savings. One of them is a risk-taker and wants to do aggressive, high-risk investing; the other is risk averse and wants to put all of their savings into short-term CDs.

How can these two resolve their investment perspective into one that is compatible for both? What kinds of stock would you suggest they invest in to meet their needs now and in the future? Write a one-page report that outlines your investing advice.

LO 1-2   Valuing Stock

When you purchase stock, you may receive a *stock certificate* or you may have it held electronically. The certificate states the number of shares you own, the name of the company, the type of stock (common or preferred), and the par value. The **par value** is an assigned dollar value given to each share of stock. For preferred stock, par value is used to calculate dividend payments. However, par value is generally meaningless for common stock since it can be issued without a par value (no-par value stock).

Par value has nothing to do with a stock's **market value**, which is the price for which the stock is bought and sold in the marketplace. The market value of a stock reflects the price that investors are willing to pay for the stock. How a company currently is performing, its track record, and how well it is expected to perform in the future determine market value.

Some stocks perform very well, yet their market value seems too low. These "undervalued" stocks are worth more than the price for which they are selling. Stocks that are undervalued make good bargains for investors, while creating a dangerous situation for businesses by leaving them vulnerable to a *takeover* by a large investor or company. Takeovers may be unfavorable for employees but can be very favorable for stockholders, because the market value of the stock is likely to rise. On the other hand, stocks can be "overvalued," which means they are selling at a price that is perceived to be too high. The price of the stock is not justified by its earnings but is based on its superior growth potential in the future. This situation is very risky for the investor, because it is likely that the price of the stock will drop. The wider the price swings, the riskier the stock.

Stock Price

Several factors affect the price you will pay for a share of stock. These factors include the company's financial situation, current interest rates, the market for the company's products or services, the company's earnings per share, and the current condition of the stock market.

The Company

When a company is performing well (paying its current debts and earning a profit), the company's stock is attractive. Investors consider the company's earning power (its ability to continue to make a strong profit) as well as its debt (how much the company owes). If the company seems to be in a good financial position, the stock price will continue rising.

Stock analysts review information about companies, both public news and information from the company's financial statements as found in its annual reports and SEC filings. These analysts prepare ratios and compare a company to its past performance, the performance of other companies, and industry standards. Stocks are rated by analysts as "buy," "hold," or "sell." It is the desire of public corporations to be on the "buy" list, or at worst, to drop to the "hold" list. Stock prices can drop dramatically when analysts tell their customers to sell the stock.

Interest Rates

When interest rates are low, people who would normally put money in savings accounts and CDs look for more profitable places to invest their money. As interest rates rise, however, people tend to move their money to the safer investments. Generally, when interest rates fall below the current rate of inflation, people buy more stock, and stock prices rise.

The Market

The marketplace determines a company's ability to sell its products or services. If the company is in a popular industry and its products or services are selling well, its stock price will rise. For example, when people are buying computers, software, and related items, companies in the technology industry are considered wise investments. If the demand for a particular product or service declines, the price of the stock will decline.

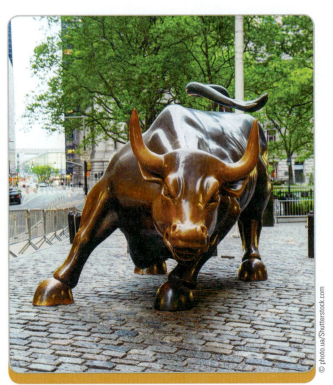

What is the difference between a bull market and a bear market?

© photo.ua/Shutterstock.com

Earnings per Share

Earnings per share (EPS) are a corporation's after-tax earnings (net profit) divided by the number of common stock shares outstanding (shares in the hands of investors). For example, assume that in a given year, XYZ Corporation had after-tax earnings of $1,000,000 and 100,000 shares of common stock outstanding. Therefore, its EPS is $10 ($1,000,000 ÷ 100,000). EPS serves as an indicator of a company's profitability and is the most commonly quoted measure for determining a stock's value.

Stock Market Conditions

The stock market goes through cycles of rising and falling prices. A **bull market** is a prolonged period of rising stock prices and a general feeling of investor optimism. Confidence in the country's economy also serves to drive up stock prices. A **bear market** is a prolonged period of falling stock prices and a general feeling of investor pessimism. It develops when investors become negative about the overall economy and start to sell stocks. In bear markets, stock prices may fall 20 percent or more. Bear markets are usually short and savage. The average bull market often lasts three to four times as long as a bear market. Whether the stock market is bullish or bearish affects your decisions about when to buy stocks, which ones to buy, and how much to pay for them.

Return on Investment

Return on investment (ROI) is used to evaluate the efficiency of an investment. Because you can make money on stocks from dividends and from an increase in the price of the stock (capital gain), you should consider both when computing the return on your investment.

Figure 17.1 shows the formula for computing a stock's ROI. Your profit is the difference between what you paid for the stock and what you sold it for, plus any dividends you earned. To compute the total costs, add any commission you paid to the stockbroker to the purchase price of the stock.

Stock Indexes

A *stock index* is a benchmark that investors use to judge the performance of their investments. The Dow Jones Industrial Average is the oldest and most widely known stock index. Often called simply "the Dow," it is an average of the price movements of 30 major (blue chip) stocks listed on the New York Stock Exchange (NYSE). This average provides a general overview of how stock prices are doing in the stock market as a whole. Investors compare the price fluctuations of their stocks against this average to judge how well their stocks are performing compared to the overall stock market. Indexes for judging the performance of all kinds of stocks are available online and in print publications. Other commonly used indexes are the Standard & Poor's 500 and the NASDAQ Composite Index.

✔ CHECKPOINT

What does a stock's return on investment (ROI) tell you?

FIGURE 17.1   Computing Return on Investment

Computing a Stock's One-Year ROI

$$\frac{\text{Current Profit on Stock}}{\text{Purchase Price} + \text{Commission}} = \text{Return on Investment (ROI)}$$

Example: Selling price (or current stock price): $40/share
Dividends received during the year: $1/share
Purchase price: $38/share
Discount brokerage fee: $19
Number of shares owned: 100

Computations:
Current profit: $40/share − $38/share = $2/share × 100 = $200 + $100 dividends = total profits of $300

$$\frac{\$300}{(100 \times \$38) + \$19} = \frac{\$300}{\$3,819} = 7.86\%$$

Stock Brokerage

Stockbrokers sell securities directly to individual clients, called investors. They provide investing advice based on the client's financial expertise and help their clients buy and sell at the right times to maximize their profits.

Finding clients is a large part of a stockbroker's job. Beginning stockbrokers spend much of their time building a customer base by relying on networking and social contacts. Some join civic organizations and social groups to expand their networks. After stockbrokers are established, they do most of their business through referrals from satisfied clients.

Most stockbrokers work long hours under stressful conditions. They earn commissions each time they buy or sell a security. In addition to commissions, most firms pay stockbrokers a minimum salary.

Employment Outlook

- An average rate of employment growth is expected.

Job Titles

- Securities broker
- Floor broker
- Independent stockbroker
- Commodities sales agent

Needed Skills

- A bachelor's degree in business, finance, accounting, or economics is required for entry-level jobs; a master's degree in business administration (MBA) is often required for higher-level positions.
- Brokers must be licensed and pass a licensure exam.
- Maturity and ability to work independently are critical.

What's it like to work in . . . *Stock Brokerage*

Alysha is a stockbroker who works for a top investment company that has a seat on the New York Stock Exchange. She works in a regional office, has more than two dozen clients, and is responsible for brokerage accounts worth more than $5 million. On average, she earns $72,000 a year.

Alysha works hard to help her clients meet their investment objectives. She advises clients about mutual funds and other investment options to help them attain the risk level and returns they desire. When clients have selected stock in which to invest or sell, Alysha makes the transactions.

Much of Alysha's day is spent on the telephone taking orders from clients or offering help and information on their accounts. Because many of her clients work during the day, she often has to work evenings to accommodate clients' schedules.

What About You?

Would you like working independently and on commission? Do you enjoy social groups, civic organizations, and other networking events? Does a career as a stockbroker interest you? Why or why not?

The Career Clusters icons are being used with permission of the: States' Career Clusters Initiative, 2007, www.careerclusters.org

KEY TERMS REVIEW

Match the terms with the definitions. Some terms may not be used.

____ 1. A type of stock that pays a fixed dividend but has no voting rights

____ 2. The price for which stock is bought and sold in the marketplace

____ 3. Money paid to stockholders from a corporation's earnings

____ 4. Stocks in corporations that have a consistent history of paying high dividends

____ 5. A company whose stock is traded openly on stock markets

____ 6. A prolonged period of rising stock prices and a general feeling of investor optimism

____ 7. Stocks of large, well-established corporations with a solid record of profitability

____ 8. A stockholder's written authorization to transfer his or her voting rights to someone else

a. bear market
b. blue chip stocks
c. bull market
d. common stock
e. dividends
f. earnings per share (EPS)
g. growth stocks
h. income stocks
i. market value
j. par value
k. preferred stock
l. proxy
m. public corporation

CHECK YOUR UNDERSTANDING

L01-1 9. In what two ways can you make money from owning stock?

L01-2 10. Why do stockholders want to know a corporation's EPS?

APPLY YOUR KNOWLEDGE

L01-1 11. Read through the stock listings in the financial pages or online and list several well-known stocks that are considered blue chips, in addition to the ones mentioned in the text.

THINK CRITICALLY

L01-1 12. Why should young people (just starting to plan their long-term investment strategy) invest in growth stocks rather than income stocks?

L01-2 13. If you had money to invest, what stock would you choose? Why? What criteria would you use to evaluate a potential stock purchase?

The Essential Question Refer to The Essential Question on p. 402. Owning stock is a good way to earn income (dividends) and save for the future (capital gains). Income, growth, blue chip, emerging, cyclical, and defensive stocks are available. A stock's market value is based on a combination of the company's financial standing, interest rates, the market, earnings per share, and the current condition of the stock market.

The Essential Question *How is stock bought and sold, and how do you know when to buy or sell?*

LEARNING OBJECTIVES

> LO 2-1 Describe the channels involved in buying and selling stocks.
> LO 2-2 Describe short-term and long-term strategies for buying and selling stocks.
> LO 2-3 Explain how to read the stock listings and stock indexes.

KEY TERMS

- securities exchange, *410*
- auction market, *411*
- leverage, *412*
- short selling, *413*
- stock split, *414*
- dollar-cost averaging, *414*
- direct investment, *414*
- dividend reinvestment, *415*

LO 2-1 The Securities Market

The *securities market* consists of the channels through which you buy and sell *securities* (stocks and bonds). To purchase common or preferred stock, you need a trading agent. Your agent will buy or sell for you in a securities marketplace, which is either a securities exchange or the over-the-counter market.

Securities Exchange

A **securities exchange** is a marketplace where brokers who are representing investors meet to buy and sell securities. The largest organized exchange in the United States is the New York Stock Exchange (NYSE). To have a stock listed with the NYSE, a company must meet a minimum number of public shares and dollar market-value requirements. Securities listed with the NYSE are traded only during official trading hours—9:30 A.M. to 4 P.M. (EST), Monday through Friday (except holidays).

In the NYSE building, the *trading floor* (where stocks are bought and sold) is about two-thirds the size of a football field. Around the edge of the trading floor are booths with computer terminals and room inside for a dozen or more floor brokers. *Floor brokers* buy and sell stocks on the exchange. Brokers must be members of the exchange to do business there.

Spaced at regular intervals around the trading floor are horseshoe-shaped counters, called *trading posts*, each occupying about 100 square feet on the floor. Behind each counter are *specialists*—the brokers to the floor brokers. All buying and selling is done around trading posts. About 90 different stocks are assigned to each post. Post display units above each counter show which stocks are sold in each section, the last price of that stock, and whether that price represents an increase or a decrease from the previous price.

Orders received at a brokerage firm or discount brokerage are phoned or sent by computer to that firm's booth at the exchange. A message is printed

© Pan Xunbin/Shutterstock.com

The Tokyo Stock Exchange (TSE) is the largest stock exchange outside of the United States, as determined by the dollar value of stocks listed. The exchange depends on a computerized transaction system that handles a very high volume of activity throughout its operating day. Like all exchanges, the TSE is constantly working on developing new and increased capacity for trading activity. Glitches in the system can cause delayed processing of transactions and even shutdowns of the market itself for a number of hours.

For example, the TSE was able to operate for only 90 minutes on November 1, 2005, due to bugs with a newly installed transaction system, which was supposed to help deal with higher trading volumes. Trading was suspended for over four hours.

THINK CRITICALLY

What would happen if a stock exchange were to be hacked so that transactions were not secure? What is the global effect when stock exchanges close down on normal operating days? Who gets hurt?

©Redshinestudio/Shutterstock.com

---

out and given to the floor broker to carry out. When the transaction is completed, the brokers who bought and sold the stock report back to their respective brokerage firms. Then the buyer and seller are advised that the transaction has been concluded.

The NYSE is a form of **auction market** where buyers enter competitive bids and sellers enter competitive offers at the same time. Stock is sold to the highest bidder (buyer) and bought from the lowest offeror (seller).

NASDAQ is another popular U.S. securities exchange. It is a *dealer market*, not an auction market, because dealers (or stock traders) work directly with other dealers to buy and sell NASDAQ securities without the use of brokers. NASDAQ is a completely computerized network and does not have a physical location (trading floor).

Over-the-Counter Market

When securities are bought and sold through brokers but not through a stock exchange, the transaction is *over the counter* (OTC). The OTC market is a network of brokers who buy and sell securities of corporations that are not listed on a securities exchange. A stock might be traded in the OTC market because the company is small and unable to meet exchange listing requirements. However, some large, well-known companies are also traded over the counter. Brokers in the OTC market do not deal face to face with other brokers. Instead, trades with other brokers are completed by telephone or computer networks. Brokers operating in the OTC market use either the OTC Bulletin Board (OTCBB) or the OTC Link LLC. Both are electronic quotation systems that display quotes, last-sale prices, and volume information for stock that is not listed on a securities exchange. The difference between the two is that companies listed on the OTCBB are regulated by the Securities and Exchange Commission, whereas companies listed on the OTC Link are not.

✔ CHECKPOINT

How can you buy stocks that are listed on a stock exchange?

- -

You can approach investing with either a short- or long-term strategy. Generally, if you buy and sell stock within a short period of time, you are a *speculator* or *day trader*. If you hold your investment for a long period of time (a year or more), you are an *investor*.

Short-Term Techniques

When you buy and sell stocks for quick profits, you are "playing the stock market." The goal is to buy a stock that will soon increase in value. Then, when the price rises, you sell the stock. Many investors make short-term gains through processes called buying on margin and selling short.

Buy on Margin

Buying on margin involves borrowing money from your broker to buy stock. You must open a margin account and sign a contract with a broker called a *margin agreement*. To establish a margin account, you must deposit a minimum of $2,000 in cash or eligible securities (securities your broker considers valuable collateral) with a broker. Once the account is open, you can borrow up to 50 percent of the purchase price of a stock. This strategy is called leverage—the use of borrowed money to buy securities. You use less of your own money and, therefore, can buy more stocks with less cash. With a margin purchase, you are betting that the stock will increase in value. If it does, you sell the stock, repay the loan with interest and commission, and take your short-term profit. Figure 17.2 shows how buying on margin works.

Unfortunately, if the value of the stock does not increase, you will have to make up the difference. When the market value of a margined stock decreases to 25 percent of the original purchase price, you will receive a *margin call* from the broker. This means you must pledge additional cash or securities as

FIGURE 17.2 Buying on Margin

Buying on Margin

Example: You buy $2,000 worth of stock with $1,000 of your own money and $1,000 borrowed from your broker at 6% annual interest. The stock increases in value, and you sell it after 60 days for $2,800. Your broker's commission to buy and sell is $200.

Computing Profit:

Interest cost: $1,000 borrowed $\times$ .06 annual interest $\times \left(\dfrac{60 \text{ days}}{360 \text{ days in a year}} \right)$
= $10 interest on the 60-day loan

Costs: $1,000 from margin account + $1,000 borrowed + $10 interest + $200 commission = $2,210 total cost

Profit: $2,800 selling price − $2,210 cost = $590 total profit

Computing Return on Investment:

$\dfrac{\$590 \text{ profit}}{\$2,210 \text{ cost}}$ = 26.7% ROI

collateral for the loan. Buying on margin is used by experienced investors and those with a high-risk tolerance. A great deal of money can be made using leverage. At the same time, large sums of money can be "lost" in short periods of time, creating the need for immediate cash.

Sell Short

Short selling involves selling stock borrowed from a broker that must be replaced at a later time. To sell short, you borrow a certain number of shares from the broker. You then sell the borrowed stock, knowing that you must buy it back later and return it to the broker. You are betting that the price will drop, so that you can buy it back at a lower price than you sold it for, thus making a profit. However, if the stock price increases, you will lose money because you must replace the borrowed stock with stock purchased at a higher price. Figure 17.3 shows how selling short works. There is usually no broker fee for selling short. However, the broker receives a commission when the stock is bought or sold.

Long-Term Techniques

Investing in the stock market for short-term gains can be extremely risky. Most financial consultants advise you to invest for the long term. Records have shown that, over a long time, stock investments have consistently beaten rates for savings accounts, CDs, and other conservative options.

Buy and Hold

Most investors consider stock purchases as long-term investments. All stocks go up and down, but the overall trend of *nonspeculative stocks* (stocks with a low degree of risk) is moderately up. Remember, a profit or loss occurs only when you sell the stock. If you "buy and hold" stocks for many years, you can ride out the down times. When you are ready to sell years later, most likely your stock will have gained value. In addition, many stocks pay dividends, so you are earning income while you hold the stock.

FIGURE 17.3	Selling Short

Selling Short

Example: You borrow 100 shares of stock of XYZ Corporation from your broker. You then sell 100 shares of XYZ at $28 per share and pay a $100 commission.

Income from sale: 100 shares × $28 per share − $100 commission
= $2,700 initial income

Two weeks later, the stock price drops to $22 per share. You buy 100 shares to return to the stockbroker and pay a $100 commission.

Cost of buying back the shares: 100 shares × $22 per share + $100 commission = $2,300 cost

Profit from selling short: $2,700 income − $2,300 cost = $400 profit

Return on Investment: $\dfrac{\$400}{\$2,300} = 17.4\%$ ROI

A stock split can also add to the value of the stock over time. A **stock split** is an increase in the number of outstanding shares of a company's stock. When a company increases its number of outstanding shares, it lowers the selling price in direct proportion. For example, if there were 1,000 shares outstanding with a market value of $60, then a 2:1 (two-for-one) stock split would result in 2,000 shares outstanding selling for $30. Notice that the stock is still worth a total of $60,000. Because a stock split lowers the selling price of the stock, this makes the shares more affordable and encourages investors to buy more. As investors buy more stock at the lower price, the share price often rises. If you held the stock before the split, then this price increase makes your stock worth more.

Dollar-Cost Averaging

The **dollar-cost averaging** technique involves the systematic purchase of an equal dollar amount of the same stock at regular intervals, regardless of the share price. The result is usually a lower average cost per share. To calculate the average cost per share, divide the total amount invested by the total number of shares purchased. In the example shown in Figure 17.4, the investor purchased $100 worth of stock every quarter for one year. Over that time, the average price of the stock was $8. However, by investing at regular intervals over the time period, the investor's average cost per share was lower: $7.41.

Investors use this technique so they don't have to worry about timing their investment purchases. A regular purchase over a year's time will usually average out to a reasonable price per share. The investor profits when the selling price per share is higher than the average cost per share.

Direct Investment

You can save money using **direct investment**, or buying stock directly from a corporation. By buying directly, you avoid brokerage and other purchasing fees. You may also be able to obtain shares at prices lower than on open

---

FIGURE 17.4 **Dollar-Cost Averaging**

Dollar-Cost Averaging

Quarterly Investment Amount		Share Price ($)		Number of Shares
$100	÷	10	=	10
$100	÷	7	=	14 (rounded)
$100	÷	5	=	20
$100	÷	10	=	10
$400		$32		54
Total $ invested				Total number of shares

Average share price = $8
$32 ÷ 4

Your average cost per share = $7.41
Total $ invested ($400) ÷ Total number of shares (54)

Ending value = $540
Last share price ($10) × Number of shares (54)

exchanges. Direct investment is often available to existing stockholders who may have the privilege of buying additional shares at fixed prices at or below market value.

Reinvesting Dividends

You can also save money by reinvesting the dividends you earn. **Dividend reinvestment** is the use of dividends previously earned on the stock to buy more shares. Buying stock this way avoids a broker fee and other costs that apply, such as taxes, when you receive cash dividends on the stock.

✔ CHECKPOINT

What are four long-term investment techniques?

LO 2-3 Reading the Stock Listings

To make wise investments in the stock market, it is a good idea to track the progress of your investments to see how they are performing. You can track your stock through financial news publications, such as the *Wall Street Journal* or *Investor's Business Daily*, or online at various financial websites. Many sites allow you to sign up for daily portfolio e-mail updates, and some have smartphone apps that let you track your investments on the go. Whether you choose to follow your stock portfolio in the newspaper or online, you should see a listing similar to Figure 17.5. Follow along in the figure as you read the following explanations of each column.

- *Column 1.* This column lists stocks alphabetically by name. You will notice that stock names are abbreviated. This abbreviated name is called the stock's *ticker symbol*. If you are looking for stock quotes online, you can search for a company by its name or ticker symbol. You may see additional abbreviations, such as "pf" (which means "preferred stock"), beside the name of the stock. There will be a legend at the bottom of the listings that explains what these abbreviations mean.
- *Columns 2, 3, and 4.* These columns show the highest, lowest, and closing price for the stock on the previous day. The closing price is the final price at the end of the trading for the day.

FIGURE 17.5   Reading the Stock Listings

Excerpt from stock exchange listings:

Stock	High	Low	Close	Net Change	52 wks High	52 wks Low	Div	Yld%	P/E Ratio	Sales 100s
1	2	3	4	5	6	7	8	9	10	11
Eng pf	26.25	24.00	25.38	+.38	45.00	23.00	2.25	8.9	10	25
Enger	46.38	45.50	46.00	−.50	58.75	44.00	2.20	4.8	12	109
Entld	10.13	9.50	10.00	----	10.50	9.00	.10	1.0	3	8
Epsco	21.00	19.00	20.00	+.88	24.00	16.00	1.00	5.0	7	12
ExeB	46.00	43.00	44.00	+1.00	57.00	32.00	2.50	5.7	11	48
Exlab	5.75	5.12	5.50	----	6.38	4.00	----	----	15	300

- *Column 5.* This column, called net change, compares the closing price today with the closing price of the day before. A minus means the price has gone down. A plus means the price has risen.
- *Columns 6 and 7.* These columns show the highest and lowest price this stock sold for during the year. For the ExeB stock in Figure 17.5, the high for the last 52 weeks was 57.00 and the low was 32.00. This means the stock sold for $57 a share at one point (high) and $32 a share at another (low), though it may have sold for many prices in between these two amounts during the year.
- *Column 8.* This column shows the cash dividend per share for the year, listed in dollars and cents. For the ExeB stock, 2.50 means that if you owned 100 shares of this company, you would have received a dividend of $250 for the year. If this space is blank or has dashes, the company does not currently pay out dividends.
- *Column 9.* Yld% stands for percent yield, or the percentage of the current price the dividends represent. In other words, divide the amount of annual dividends (Column 8) by the closing price (Column 4).
- *Column 10.* The P/E ratio (price/earnings ratio) is the price of a share of stock divided by the corporation's earnings per share over the last 12 months. The P/E ratio is a key factor that serious investors use to evaluate stock investments. A low P/E ratio may indicate a solid investment, whereas a high P/E ratio may indicate higher risk.
- *Column 11.* This column shows sales in hundreds of shares (round lots) from the previous day. Multiply the number by 100 to get the number of shares.

Keeping track of your stock portfolio (or stock holdings) can be as simple as checking the closing prices periodically. The stocks shown in Figure 17.6 have been tracked for ten days straight. It does not take into account dividends received or the appreciation in value since the stock was purchased. The stock progress chart is merely a device for monitoring changes in the closing prices of stocks.

CHECKPOINT

What is meant by a "ticker symbol"?

FIGURE 17.6   Stock Progress Chart

Stock Progress Chart

| Stock Names | Closing Prices for 10 Days | | | | | | | | | | Total Change (+ or –) |
	1	2	3	4	5	6	7	8	9	10	
1. Eagle	28	28.12	29	28	27	28	28.50	29	29.50	30	+2
2. Glastn	38	40	41	41.50	--	40	39	38	38	38	0
3. Karbr pf	61	61.25	61.13	61	61.38	61	62	62.38	61	61.13	+.13
4. Maxln	50.13	49	50	50.25	51	51	51.13	52	52	53.50	+3.37
5. Totlmb	10	11	11.13	11.50	11	10.88	10	9	8	8.50	–1.50

Inflation: Who Gets Hurt?

Inflation is an increase in the general level of prices. It is measured yearly to see how much prices are rising. The *consumer price index* (*CPI*) is the instrument most often used as a measure of rising prices. The CPI measures price changes for a "market basket" of goods and services typically purchased by consumers. Inflation is also evident in rising interest rates. Interest rates reflect the cost of lending and borrowing money. As prices increase, interest rates go up as well.

Some people get hurt by rapidly rising prices and interest rates. People who are more likely to be affected by inflation include the following:

- *People on fixed incomes*. Many retired people live on a fixed monthly retirement benefit. When prices rise, their fixed income stays the same. Thus, they are unable to maintain the same standard of living in inflationary times.

- *People with a lot of debt*. During inflationary times, interest rates charged by credit card companies rise. As your interest rate goes up, so does your monthly payment. More of each month's payment goes toward interest rather than paying off the debt. This makes it difficult for people with a lot of debt to pay down their credit cards.

- *People who have to borrow*. If you need to borrow money, you will pay higher interest rates in times of inflation. As a result, your monthly payments will be higher or you will have to make payments for a longer time to pay off the loan.

- *People working as employees*. As an employee, you work for a salary or wage. Although you may get a yearly raise, it may not be enough to keep up with price increases. When inflation hits, you must adapt by making changes in your lifestyle. This lowers your standard of living because rapidly rising prices erode your purchasing power.

- *People who have fixed-rate investments*. Many investors buy fixed-income securities because they want a stable return on their investment, which comes in the form of interest payments. However, because the interest rate on fixed-income securities remains the same over time, the purchasing power of the interest payments declines as inflation rises.

To prepare for periods of inflation, you should save so that you will have resources during hard times. You should also look for investments that consistently (over time) bring you a rate of return that is higher than the rate of inflation so that your wealth is growing rather than falling behind as price levels continue to rise.

THINK CRITICALLY

1. Using the keyword "inflation," conduct online research and compare interest rates and rising prices in the United States to those in other countries, such as Brazil, Mexico, or France. Look at the rates over a three-year or five-year period of time. Report your findings.

2. Have you noticed goods or services you buy frequently increasing in price? How have prices of those goods or services affected your lifestyle?

KEY TERMS REVIEW

Match the terms with the definitions. Some terms may not be used.

___ 1. An increase in the number of outstanding shares of a company's stock

___ 2. The use of dividends previously earned on stock to buy more shares

___ 3. Selling borrowed stock that must be replaced at a later time

___ 4. Buying stock directly from a corporation

___ 5. An exchange where stock is sold to the highest bidder and bought from the lowest offeror

___ 6. The use of borrowed money to buy securities

___ 7. A marketplace where brokers who are representing investors meet to buy and sell securities

a. auction market
b. direct investment
c. dividend reinvestment
d. dollar-cost averaging
e. leverage
f. securities exchange
g. short selling
h. stock split

CHECK YOUR UNDERSTANDING

LO2-1 8. What kinds of stocks are traded over the counter?

LO2-2 9. Why is buying on margin risky?

LO2-2 10. How do you save money by reinvesting dividends?

APPLY YOUR KNOWLEDGE

LO2-2 11. Search online for investment advice. In no more than one page, summarize what experts are saying about which stocks are "hot" right now and which are not. Do the experts seem to agree or disagree with each other? (*Hint*: Some sites you might try include Forbes, CNN Money, MSN Money, Fortune, Kiplinger, and Barron's.)

THINK CRITICALLY

LO2-2 12. How can you save money by direct investment? Is this a good idea for long-term investing? Why or why not?

LO2-3 13. Look up the ticker symbol for two stocks you might like to buy. Using the table format presented in Figure 17.5, list the information for each stock. Based on the data given, do you think these are good stocks to purchase? Why or why not?

The Essential Question *Refer to The Essential Question on p. 410. Stocks are bought and sold through securities exchanges or in over-the-counter markets. When to buy or sell depends on your interpretation of how the stock is doing compared to other investment choices you have.*

SUMMARY

17.1

- *Stockholders profit through dividends and capital gains.*

- *Because preferred stock pays a fixed dividend, it is less risky than common stock, but generally earns a lower return when the company does well.*

- *Corporations that issue income stocks pay profits to stockholders in the form of dividends, whereas corporations that issue growth stocks reinvest profits in the business so that it can grow.*

- *Blue chip stocks provide a relatively safe but moderate return.*

- *Emerging stocks are issued by young, often small, companies and have a higher overall risk.*

- *Cyclical stocks are affected by ups and downs in the economy. They do well when the economy is growing but do poorly during recessions.*

- *Defensive (noncyclical) stocks are not affected by the ups and downs of business cycles. They remain relatively stable during both good and bad economic times.*

- *The par value printed on the stock certificate has nothing to do with the market value that investors actually pay for the stock.*

- *Stock price depends on the company's financial situation, current interest rates, the market for the company's products or services, the company's earnings per share, and the current conditions of the stock market.*

- *Dividends and capital gains are used to determine a stock's ROI.*

- *Investors use stock indexes to judge the performance of their investments.*

17.2

- *You can buy and sell securities through a securities exchange (physical place) or over the counter (by phone or computer).*

- *A securities exchange is a form of auction market where stock is sold to the highest bidder (buyer) and bought from the lowest offeror (seller).*

- *Short-term investors are speculators who try to make a quick profit by buying on margin or selling short.*

- *Long-term investment strategies are buy and hold, dollar-cost averaging, direct investment, and reinvestment of dividends.*

- *You can track your stock's progress by reading the stock listings in print publications and online.*

APPLY WHAT YOU KNOW

LO1-1 1. If you own 100 shares of common stock, which you purchased for $28 a share, and the company declares a cash dividend of $.88 (per share) for the quarter, how much will you receive in dividends?

LO1-2 2. Suppose you purchased 100 shares of stock in January for $48 a share. You received dividends of $1.25 a share on April 1 and July 1 and $.95 a share on September 1. You sold the stock in December for $50 a share. What would be the stock's return on investment for the year? Assume a broker commission of 3 percent on the purchase and 3 percent on the sale of the stock. (*Hint*: Use the formula in Figure 17.1.)

LO2-2 3. You decide to buy stock on margin. You have $2,500 in cash in a margin account and borrow $2,500 from your broker. You buy 50 shares of stock selling at $100 a share. Assume that the stock rises in value, and 30 days later you sell the stock for $110 a share. Interest on the amount borrowed is 7 percent. The total commission charged is $150. What is the total return on investment? Explain why buying on margin is a risky practice. (*Hint*: Use the formula in Figure 17.2.)

LO2-3 4. Select a stock listing on the NYSE and follow that stock for a week. Is it increasing or decreasing in value? (Is the price going up or down?) Conduct online research on the company to see if you can find information that would lead you to believe it will increase (or decrease) in the future. Prepare a short summary on the stock's performance and on your findings.

MAKE ACADEMIC CONNECTIONS

LO1-1 5. **History** The Securities and Exchange Commission (SEC) was formed in 1933 to protect investors from corporations that would deceive them into buying stock. Visit the SEC's website (www.sec.gov) and write a one-page report describing the role of the SEC in the past and today. What does it do to protect investors? What kinds of reports do corporations file with the SEC that are made available to the public on the SEC's website?

LO1-2 6. **Economics** Explain the relationship of the economy as a whole to the stock market. For example, stock prices are rising (bull market) when the economy is growing. Why is this true? Write a one-page report explaining how business cycles affect stock prices and what it means to you as an investor.

LO2-2 7. **Math** You wish to sell short. You arrange to borrow from your broker 100 shares of stock in XYZ Corporation on January 2. You immediately sell 100 shares of XYZ at $60 a share and pay a $100 commission. On April 1, you purchase 100 shares of XYZ at $53 a share to return to your broker. You pay a commission of $100. What is your return on investment for this transaction? (*Hint*: Use the formula in Figure 17.3.)

LO2-2 8. **Communication** You and your friend are thinking about investing in some stock together. You are trying to convince your friend that dollar-cost averaging will be your best choice as a long-term investment strategy. Write a paragraph that provides support for your position.

Solve Problems and Explore Issues

LO1-1 9. Your friend Janice has inherited $5,000 and is considering investing it in stocks. She won't need the money for five years, when she hopes to start medical school. Would you recommend common or preferred stock? Explain why.

LO1-1 10. Lucia and Carlos are married and are considering buying some stock to have a "nest egg" for their future children. Carlos wants to invest in a small local company that is just getting started. Lucia prefers to buy the stock of a well-known company that is listed on a major stock exchange. Discuss with them the pros and cons of each course of action.

LO1-1 11. Your neighbors Mr. and Mrs. Nelson are in their late fifties and plan to retire within the next five years. They want to take some of the money they have saved through the years and invest in the stock market. Which of these options would you recommend to them: Income or growth? Blue chip or emerging? Cyclical or defensive? Give a brief reason for each choice.

LO2-2 12. Suppose you decided to use dollar-cost averaging and purchased $200 worth of stock every quarter for one year. You paid the following share prices: Quarter 1, $5; Quarter 2, $10; Quarter 3, $8; Quarter 4, $4. Using Figure 17.4 as a guide, calculate these values: (a) average share price, (b) your average cost per share, and (c) ending value. Did you benefit from dollar-cost advertising? Explain.

EXTEND YOUR LEARNING

LO2-1 13. **Ethics and Legal Issues** In 2001 Enron Corporation and Arthur Andersen (accounting firm) were involved in a massive stock fraud scheme. Enron's stock plummeted, and it filed bankruptcy. Stockholders lost their entire investment. Prepare a history of the Enron scandal. What ethics issues were involved? Discuss reforms that were put in place as a result of the Enron stock scandal, such as the Sarbanes-Oxley (SOX) Act of 2002. How does SOX enhance corporate responsibility and protect you as an investor?

CHAPTER PROJECT

The Dow Jones Industrial Average lists the stocks for 30 of the largest and most influential companies in the United States. Over time, companies are added to and dropped from the list. Research the history of the Dow. What stocks were included 50 years ago? 25 years ago? What stocks are listed currently? What are the current criteria for being listed on the Dow? What kinds of corporations are being added? Prepare a report summarizing your findings. Use tables and other visual aids to support your findings.

> Complete the Guided Decision Making activity for Chapter 17 at **ngl.cengage.com/mypf**.

Overview

This simulation is designed to help you picture the stock selection process. In Part 1, you will seek appropriate advice; make stock selections; and determine the outcome, based on predetermined stock changes. In Part 2, you will consult financial pages and use real stock listing values to compute real outcomes.

PART 1 Getting Started

As a young person, you should begin investing with more conservative and less risky choices. For the purposes of this simulation, we are presuming that you have accomplished that, and you are now at the point where you are ready to do some direct, systematic investing in individual stocks that involve taking some risks.

You will be given a hypothetical listing of stocks on a typical day of trading on the New York Stock Exchange (NYSE). From the stock listings, you will choose the stocks in which you would like to invest. After one week, you will compute your gains or losses on your initial investments based on a data sheet that contains updated stock information provided by your instructor. After computing your first-week gains and losses, you will then have the opportunity to "move some shares of stock." For example, if some of your choices aren't doing as good as you had hoped, you may decide to sell them and purchase new stock instead. At the end of Week 2, you will once again compute your ending gains or losses based on a data sheet containing updated stock information provided by your instructor.

Before making your choices of stock, however, you should first seek advice from experts who will help you decide what kind of stock is right for you. You should also do some research on the corporation in which you are thinking of investing.

Investing Advice

This section contains advice that you received when you consulted the following sources: your full-service broker, a financial news magazine, an economist, a financial adviser, and a friend who is a successful investor.

Full-Service Broker:

"We are now in a bull market. Bull markets last longer than bear markets; however, we've been in this bull market for almost six months. I'm concerned that it won't last much longer. If I were you, I would consider investing in a stock of a well-known, large corporation. You might even consider buying one that is in the Dow itself. This will give you assurance that your stock will perform well, even if the bull market ends. And don't forget about risk.

© rosedesigns/Shutterstock.com

How much risk do you want to take? One way to measure risk is the price/earnings (P/E) ratio. It tells you how much the stock costs relative to its current performance. For example, a stock with a P/E ratio of 5 means that the stock is selling for five times its current performance. A P/E ratio of 20 means it is selling for 20 times that amount. The higher the P/E ratio, the more risk. However, the more risk involved, the greater the potential for a higher return!"

Financial Magazine Article:

"Many experts are now saying that the stock market could hit a bubble, just like the housing market did in 2007–2009. How high can it go? It just doesn't seem possible for it to continue rising at this level. There has to be a correction at some point, and it could be severe. We are projecting a 10–20 percent reduction in the value of stocks in the next year."

Economist:

"The Federal Reserve has had its stimulus package in place for a long time now. As it eases off, the economy will be on its own to hold the momentum. I think the momentum is there. We may see a brief downturn, but the economy will operate just fine when left alone. Market forces will bring prices up that are needed for economic growth, and vice versa. Interest rates need to rise to reward savers and investors. It's a normal economic recovery and growth stage. Thus, stocks likely will react in a similar manner. I'm betting on economic growth this year and next."

Financial Adviser:

"We are currently telling our clients who are in your age group and financial position to buy less risky investments—perhaps investments that will offset losses that might occur if we move into a bear market. At the same time, I'd like you to consider relying on dollar-cost averaging. The market may take a downturn, but in the long run, your returns will be there for you. After all, you don't need the money for many years to come."

Adviser Friend:

"I've been through these ups and downs in the market many times. Some people I know start buying and selling, hoping to make the right decisions. But they don't have a crystal ball, and neither do I. I check my investments twice a year and then consult with my broker. I'm content to leave things as they are and continue investing as usual. I don't see any need to panic."

Investing Research

Wise investors will also do research on the corporations in which they are considering investing. You can get information at the company's website, by looking at the company's annual report (which is available at the Securities and Exchange Commission's website and often at the corporate website), by reading newspaper and online articles about the company and its industry, and by reading expert opinions about the company and its stock. Like the advice you get from friends and others, the findings from your research may not always be consistent. Sometimes it may even be wrong. Therefore, you must base your decision on your own judgment and the sources of information that you trust.

Investment Choices

Figure 1 lists the stocks from which you will choose. These are real stocks on a hypothetical day of trading on the NYSE. Before making your choices, research the companies and the products/services they offer. Your total investment amount is $10,000, which you can invest in one of three ways:

1. You can purchase *round lots* (any group of shares that can be evenly divided by 100) of different stock. For example, you may decide to purchase 100 shares of AT&T stock and 200 shares of Coca-Cola stock.
2. You can purchase *odd lots* (a lot consisting of fewer than 100 shares or a lot that cannot be evenly divided by 100) of different stock. For example, you may decide to purchase 46 shares of Chevron stock and 208 shares of Xerox stock.
3. You can invest the $10,000 by putting lump sums into one or more stocks. For example, you can invest $5,000 into one stock and $5,000 into another stock, or you can invest the entire $10,000 in one stock.

The amount you invest cannot exceed $10,000. You must buy at the closing price (highlighted in Figure 1). That's the current market price that you would have paid at the end of that day of trading. You must also pay a brokerage fee of $10 per transaction. Therefore, if you buy one stock, the cost is $10; if you buy two stocks, it's $20 (2 × $10 each). Any amount left over (short of your $10,000) will be put into a savings account.

Complete Worksheet 1 (Week 1: Investment Choices) provided for you in the *Student Activity Guide* and presented for reference on the next page. Record the name and symbol of the stock(s) you will purchase, the closing price (what you will pay per share), the number of shares purchased, and the total investment in each stock (including broker fees).

FIGURE 1 Stock Listings

Stock	Symbol	Open	High	Low	Close	52-Week High	52-Week Low	Div.	P/E	YTD % Chg.
AT&T	T	33.74	33.81	33.51	33.62	39.00	32.76	1.84	23.68	−4.38
Bank of America	BAC	16.75	16.79	16.61	16.77	16.93	10.98	0.04	25.03	+7.71
Boeing	BA	142.79	142.80	140.90	141.90	142.80	72.68	2.92	24.92	+3.96
Chevron	CVX	122.50	122.84	120.37	121.01	127.83	110.80	4.00	9.83	−3.12
Coca-Cola	KO	39.96	40.29	39.90	40.13	43.43	36.52	2.79	20.47	−2.86
Delta Airlines	DAL	31.19	31.48	30.66	31.47	31.58	13.09	0.24	12.90	+14.56
Eli Lily	LLY	51.49	52.11	51.25	51.93	58.41	47.53	1.56	11.80	+1.82
FedEx	FDX	141.20	142.74	140.41	142.63	144.39	90.61	0.60	27.32	−0.79
Ford Motor	F	16.01	16.11	15.94	16.07	18.02	12.10	0.50	11.68	+4.15
General Electric	GE	27.19	27.23	26.86	26.96	28.09	21.01	0.88	19.29	−3.82
Johnson & Johnson	JNJ	94.64	94.97	94.14	94.74	95.99	72.00	2.64	20.60	+3.44
Macy's	M	55.98	56.09	55.26	55.84	56.25	36.75	1.00	15.43	+4.57
Oracle	ORCL	37.75	38.14	37.59	38.11	38.34	29.86	0.48	16.01	−0.39
Public Storage	PSA	153.04	154.60	153.04	154.26	176.68	145.04	5.60	32.64	+2.48
Target	TGT	62.89	63.63	62.16	62.62	73.50	59.72	1.72	16.65	−1.03
Xerox	XRX	12.06	12.07	11.94	11.99	12.28	7.17	1.92	12.62	−1.48

WORKSHEET 1
Week 1: Investment Choices

Directions: Using the stock listings in Figure 1 on p. 424, record the name and symbol of the stock(s) you want to purchase, the closing price, the number of shares you would like to purchase, and your total investment in each stock. (*Note:* Remember that each investment must include a $10 broker fee and that your total investment amount cannot exceed $10,000.)

Stock	Symbol	Close	# of Shares	Investment Amount
_____	_____	_____	_____	_____
_____	_____	_____	_____	_____
_____	_____	_____	_____	_____
_____	_____	_____	_____	_____
_____	_____	_____	_____	_____
_____	_____	_____	_____	_____
_____	_____	_____	_____	_____
_____	_____	_____	_____	_____
_____	_____	_____	_____	_____
_____	_____	_____	_____	_____

Total Investment $ _____

Week 1: Gains and Losses

At the end of the first week, your instructor will provide you with an updated sheet of the new closing prices for the stocks listed in Figure 1. You will use the updated closing prices to compute any gains or losses for each stock you own and your total investment balance. For example, assume you bought 100 shares of a stock at $30, which cost you $3,010 (100 shares × $30/share = $3,000 + $10 broker fee). At the end of Week 1, assume that the closing price of that same stock is $32. You now have $3,200 in that investment (100 × $32). You have effectively made $190 on your investment for the week ($3,200 − $3,010).

Do not assume any interest on your savings account (if you have one) at this point. The interest would be insignificant. If you had put your entire $10,000 into savings, you still would have $10,000 in savings. No gain, no loss.

Complete Worksheet 2 (Week 1: Gains or Losses) provided for you in the *Student Activity Guide* and also presented for reference on the next page. Use it to record the name and symbol of the stock(s) you purchased, the closing price at purchase, the new closing price at the end of Week 1 (provided by your instructor), the difference between the initial closing price and new closing price, your gain or loss on the investment (Difference in closing prices × Number of shares), and your new total investment in each stock (Original investment amount +/− Gain or loss).

WORKSHEET 2
Week 1: Gains or Losses

Directions: Record the name and symbol of the stock(s) you listed in Worksheet 1 on p. 425, the closing price at purchase and the closing price at the end of week 1, the difference between the closing price you paid at purchase and the closing price at the end of week 1, your gain or loss on the investment, and your new investment amount in each stock.

Stock	Symbol	Close at Purchase	Close at End of Week 1	Difference	Gain or Loss	New Investment Amount
_____	_____	_____	_____	_____	_____	_____
_____	_____	_____	_____	_____	_____	_____
_____	_____	_____	_____	_____	_____	_____
_____	_____	_____	_____	_____	_____	_____
_____	_____	_____	_____	_____	_____	_____
_____	_____	_____	_____	_____	_____	_____
_____	_____	_____	_____	_____	_____	_____
_____	_____	_____	_____	_____	_____	_____
_____	_____	_____	_____	_____	_____	_____
_____	_____	_____	_____	_____	_____	_____

Total Investment $_____

Decisions, Decisions

Refer to Worksheet 2 and look at the gain or loss for each of your investments. Perhaps one of your stocks took a significant loss. Also, refer to the data sheet that lists the new closing prices. Perhaps you see that the closing price for a stock you didn't purchase is much higher than the closing price in Figure 1. Based on this information, decide whether you want to sell some of your stock and buy others, or hold on to the current stock you own. When making buy/sell transactions, use the same closing prices as given at the end of Week 1. Also, assume that you will pay a $10 broker fee for each buy/sell transaction. If you have any money left over after completing your transactions, add it to your savings account.

Complete Worksheet 3 (Week 2: Investment Choices) provided for you in the *Student Activity Guide* and also presented for reference on the next page. List the stock(s) that you will continue to hold and any new stock(s) you want to purchase, the closing price at the end of Week 1 [for stock(s) you decide to hold on to and for any new stock(s) you decide to purchase], the number of shares purchased, and the total investment in each stock (including the broker fees). (Keep in mind that your new total investment amount may be greater or less than your initial $10,000 investment amount due to any gains or losses made.)

WORKSHEET 3
Week 2: Investment Choices

Directions: Record the name and symbol of the stock(s) you want to keep and any new stock(s) you want to purchase, the closing price at the end of week 1 [for the stock(s) you decide to hold on to and for any new stock(s) you decide to purchase], the number of shares you purchased/would like to purchase, and your total investment in each stock, including broker fees for new transactions. (*Note*: Remember that the total amount you have to invest may be greater or less than the initial $10,000 amount due to any gains or losses made.)

Stock	Symbol	Close at End of Week 1	# of Shares	Investment Amount
_____	____	_____	___	_____
_____	____	_____	___	_____
_____	____	_____	___	_____
_____	____	_____	___	_____
_____	____	_____	___	_____
_____	____	_____	___	_____
_____	____	_____	___	_____
_____	____	_____	___	_____
_____	____	_____	___	_____

Total Investment $ _____

Week 2: Gains and Losses

At the end of the second week, your instructor will once again provide you with an updated sheet containing new closing prices for the stocks listed in Figure 1. You will use the new closing prices to compute any gains or losses for each of your stock investments and your total investment balance.

Complete Worksheet 4 (Week 2: Gains or Losses) provided for you in the *Student Activity Guide* and also presented for reference on the next page. Use it to record the name and symbol of the stock(s) that you have listed in Worksheet 3, the closing price for that stock at the end of Week 1, the new closing price at the end of Week 2 (provided by your instructor), the difference between the closing price of Week 1 and the closing price of Week 2, your gain or loss on the investment (Difference in closing prices × Number of shares), and your new total investment in each stock (Week 2 investment amount +/− Gain or loss).

WORKSHEET 4
Week 2: Gains or Losses

Directions: Record the name and symbol of the stock(s) you listed in Worksheet 3 on p. 427, the closing price at the end of week 1 and the closing price at the end of week 2, the difference between the closing price at the end of week 1 and the closing price at the end of the week 2, your gain or loss on the investment, and your new investment amount in each stock.

Stock	Symbol	Close at End of Week 1	Close at End of Week 2	Difference	Gain or Loss	New Investment Amount
_____	____	____	____	____	____	____
_____	____	____	____	____	____	____
_____	____	____	____	____	____	____
_____	____	____	____	____	____	____
_____	____	____	____	____	____	____
_____	____	____	____	____	____	____
_____	____	____	____	____	____	____
_____	____	____	____	____	____	____
_____	____	____	____	____	____	____

Total Investment $ _____

PART 2 Your Stock Picks

In Part 2, you have the opportunity to select your own stocks from one of the major securities exchanges and follow them for two weeks.

Investment Choices

You can choose stocks listed on the Dow, NYSE, NASDAQ, or S&P 500. Stock listings can be found in daily financial news publications, such as The *Wall Street Journal*, or online at various financial and investor websites, such as Yahoo! Finance (finance.yahoo.com/stock-center).

As in Part 1, assume your total investment amount is $10,000. You can invest this by purchasing round lots of stock, by purchasing odd lots of stock, or by investing lump sums. Your investment(s) cannot exceed $10,000, you must purchase the stock at the closing price, and you must pay a broker fee of $10 per transaction.

Complete Worksheet 5 (Week 1: Investment Choices) provided for you in the *Student Activity Guide* and also presented for reference on the next page. Record the name and symbol of the stock(s) you want to purchase, the closing price, the number of shares purchased, and the total investment in each stock (including broker fees).

Week 1: Gains and Losses

At the end of one week, compute your gains/losses for your stock(s). To do this, refer to one of the financial newspapers or websites listed in the "Investment Choices" section on the previous page and look up the real-time data for your stock(s). Then complete Worksheet 6 (Week 1: Gains or Losses) provided for you in the *Student Activity Guide* and also presented for reference on the next page. Use it to record the name and symbol of the stock(s) you purchased, the closing price at purchase and the new closing price at the end of Week 1, the difference between the closing price you paid at purchase and new closing price, your gain or loss on the investment (Difference in closing prices × Number of shares), and your new total investment in each stock (Original investment amount +/− Gain or loss).

WORKSHEET 6
Week 1: Gains or Losses

Directions: Record the name and symbol of the stock(s) you listed in Worksheet 5 on p. 429, the closing price at purchase and the closing price at the end of week 1, the difference between the closing price you paid at purchase and the closing price at the end of week 1, your gain or loss on the investment, and your new investment amount in each stock.

Stock	Symbol	Close at Purchase	Close at End of Week 1	Difference	Gain or Loss	New Investment Amount
_____	____	_____	_____	_____	_____	_____
_____	____	_____	_____	_____	_____	_____
_____	____	_____	_____	_____	_____	_____
_____	____	_____	_____	_____	_____	_____
_____	____	_____	_____	_____	_____	_____
_____	____	_____	_____	_____	_____	_____
_____	____	_____	_____	_____	_____	_____
_____	____	_____	_____	_____	_____	_____
_____	____	_____	_____	_____	_____	_____
_____	____	_____	_____	_____	_____	_____

Total Investment $ _____

Buy, Sell, or Hold?

Based on the information you computed in Worksheet 6, you now have to decide whether you want to sell some of your stock and buy others, or hold on to the current stock you own. Complete Worksheet 7 (Week 2: Investment Choices) provided for you in the *Student Activity Guide* and also presented for reference on the next page. List the stock(s) that you will continue to hold and any new stock(s) you want to purchase, the closing price at the end of Week 1 for the stocks you will hold on to and for any new stock(s) you want to purchase, the number of shares purchased, and the total investment in each stock (including broker fees). (Keep in mind that your new total investment amount may be greater or less than your initial $10,000 investment amount due to any gains or losses made.)

WORKSHEET 7
Week 2: Investment Choices

Directions: Record the name and symbol of the stock(s) you want to keep and any new stock(s) you want to purchase, the current closing price [for the stock(s) you decide to hold on to and for any new stock(s) you decide to purchase], the number of shares you purchased/would like to purchase, and your total investment in each stock, including broker fees for new transactions. (*Note*: Remember that your total investment amount may be greater or less than the initial $10,000 amount due to any gains or losses made.)

Stock	Symbol	Close	# of Shares	Investment Amount
_____	_____	_____	_____	_____
_____	_____	_____	_____	_____
_____	_____	_____	_____	_____
_____	_____	_____	_____	_____
_____	_____	_____	_____	_____
_____	_____	_____	_____	_____
_____	_____	_____	_____	_____
_____	_____	_____	_____	_____
_____	_____	_____	_____	_____
_____	_____	_____	_____	_____

Total Investment $ _____

Week 2: Gains and Losses

You will now compute your gains and losses and total investment balance after two weeks of making your own stock choices. Once again, refer to one of the financial news publications or websites listed in the "Investment Choices" section on p. 428 and look up the real-time data for your stock(s). Then complete Worksheet 8 (Week 2: Gains or Losses) provided for you in the *Student Activity Guide* and also presented for reference on the next page. Use it to record the name and symbol of the stock(s) that you have listed in Worksheet 7, the closing price for that stock at the end of Week 1 and the new closing price at the end of Week 2, the difference between the closing price at the end of Week 1 and the closing price at the end of Week 2, your gain or loss on the investment (Difference in closing prices × Number of shares), and your new total investment in each stock (Week 2 investment amount +/− Gain or loss).

WORKSHEET 8
Week 2: Gains or Losses

Directions: Record the name and symbol of the stock(s) you listed in Worksheet 7 on p. 431, the closing price at the end of week 1 and the closing price at the end of week 2, the difference between the closing price at the end of week 1 and the closing price at the end of the week 2, your gain or loss on the investment, and your new investment amount in each stock.

Stock	Symbol	Close at End of Week 1	Close at End of Week 2	Difference	Gain or Loss	New Investment Amount
_____	___	_____	_____	_____	____	_____
_____	___	_____	_____	_____	____	_____
_____	___	_____	_____	_____	____	_____
_____	___	_____	_____	_____	____	_____
_____	___	_____	_____	_____	____	_____
_____	___	_____	_____	_____	____	_____
_____	___	_____	_____	_____	____	_____
_____	___	_____	_____	_____	____	_____
_____	___	_____	_____	_____	____	_____
_____	___	_____	_____	_____	____	_____

Total Investment $ _____

Follow-Up Assignment

As you assess your choices for Part 1 and/or Part 2 of the simulation, answer the questions below. (These questions are also provided for you in the *Student Activity Guide*.)

1. How did the stocks that you chose perform? Did you make good choices? Explain why you would (or would not) make the same choices again.
2. How did the stocks that you didn't choose perform? Which stock do you wish you had chosen? Why?
3. What information did you rely on to make your choices? What nonfinancial reasons might affect your choices?
4. Do you believe that making investments in stocks is a good idea for you as an individual, considering your risk aptitude? What are the pros and cons of investing in stocks?
5. How has this simulation changed your thoughts about the stock market?

CHAPTER 18

Investing in Bonds

18.1 Evaluating Bonds

18.2 Buying and Selling Bonds

Consider This...

Brenda is a conservative investor. She wants to be certain her money is safe and that it will be available to her in two years when she needs it to start her business.

"I want to get a better return than I can get for a certificate of deposit," she told her investment adviser. "I'm thinking about investing my money in bonds. I read in the financial section of today's paper that there are some tax-free municipal bonds that are paying 3.5 percent. I'm also considering a high-grade corporate bond that pays 6 percent. While the rate is higher on the corporate bond, interest earnings are taxable. There is also more risk involved investing in a corporate bond than in a municipal bond. I'm not sure which one to choose. What would you advise?"

The Essential Question *Why do investors include corporate and government bonds in their investment portfolios?*

LEARNING OBJECTIVES

> LO 1-1 Describe the characteristics and different types of corporate bonds.
> LO 1-2 Describe different types of government bonds.

KEY TERMS

- bond redemption, *434*
- face value, *434*
- debenture, *435*
- secured bond, *436*
- convertible bond, *436*
- callable bond, *436*
- zero-coupon bond, *436*
- municipal bond, *437*
- revenue bond, *437*
- general obligation (GO) bond, *438*
- agency bond, *439*

LO 1-1 Corporate Bonds

Companies need funds for new technology, long-term operating expenses, and expansion into new markets. While a corporation may use both bonds and stocks to finance business activities, there are important distinctions between the two. First, bonds are loans (debt) that must be repaid at maturity. Stocks are shares of ownership (equity) in the corporation, not loans. Second, corporations must make the semiannual interest payments on their bonds. Corporations are not required to pay dividends on stocks. The board of directors decides whether or not to pay stock dividends.

Characteristics of Corporate Bonds

Bonds are known as *fixed-rate investments* because they pay a specified amount of interest on a regular schedule. In other words, a bond's interest does not go up and down, unlike stock dividends. Usually, interest on bonds is paid to *bondholders* (those who invest in bonds) twice a year.

All bonds have a maturity date. Bond maturities typically range from 1 to 30 years. **Bond redemption** occurs when the bond is paid off at maturity. **Face value** is the amount the bondholder will be repaid at maturity. Face value is also referred to as par value because the face value is the dollar amount printed on the certificate. All corporate bonds are issued

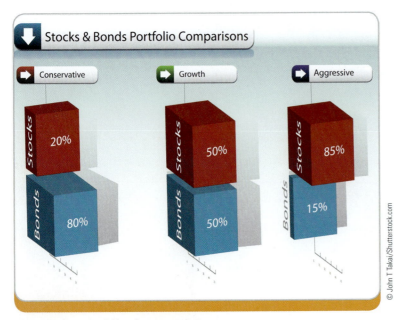

Stocks & Bonds Portfolio Comparisons

Conservative — Stocks 20% / Bonds 80%

Growth — Stocks 50% / Bonds 50%

Aggressive — Stocks 85% / Bonds 15%

© John T Takai/Shutterstock.com

How do bonds differ from stocks?

with a stated face value and fixed contract rate. A bond's *contract rate* (also called its interest rate) is the percentage of face value that the bondholder will receive as interest each year. Interest received on corporate bonds is taxable, and it must be reported as ordinary income on your tax return.

Figure 18.1 shows interest payments on a ten-year, 6 percent corporate bond with a face value of $10,000. Let's assume that the bond was issued on January 1, 2008, and interest payments are due on June 30 and December 31 of each year. The bondholder would receive semiannual payments of $300 for ten years. There is no compounding of interest. The bond has a maturity date of January 1, 2018, or ten years from the date of issue. On this date, the principal of $10,000 is repaid to the bondholder by the issuer.

The process for collecting the interest on a bond depends on whether it is a registered bond or a coupon bond. A *registered bond* is recorded in the owner's name by the issuing company. Interest checks for registered bonds are mailed semiannually, directly to the bondholder. A *coupon bond* (also called a *bearer bond*) is not registered by the issuing company. To collect interest on a coupon bond, bondholders must clip a coupon and then cash it in at a bank, following the procedures outlined by the issuer. Today, most bonds are registered.

A major disadvantage for individual investors is the cost of corporate bonds. Very few corporate bonds are sold in units of less than $1,000. Bonds are commonly sold in $5,000 units.

Types of Corporate Bonds

There are many types of corporate bonds. Some of the more common types include debentures, secured (mortgage) bonds, convertible bonds, callable bonds, and zero-coupon bonds.

Debentures

A **debenture** is a corporate bond that is based on the general creditworthiness and reputation of the company. The issuer does not pledge any specific assets to assure repayment of the loan. Because of this, debentures are considered

FIGURE 18.1 Earnings on a Ten-Year, 6% Corporate Bond

Year	June 30 Interest	December 31 Interest
1	$300.00	$300.00
2	300.00	300.00
3	300.00	300.00
4	300.00	300.00
5	300.00	300.00
6	300.00	300.00
7	300.00	300.00
8	300.00	300.00
9	300.00	300.00
10	300.00	300.00

January 1, 2018: $10,000 principal is repaid

unsecured bonds. An investor relies on the full faith and credit of the issuer of the bond for repayment of the interest and principal. When issued by reliable companies, debentures are relatively safe investments.

Secured Bonds

A **secured bond**, also called a *mortgage bond*, is backed by specific assets that serve as security to assure repayment of the debt. If the corporation fails to repay the loan as agreed, the bondholder may claim the property used as security for the debt. The asset most often used for security is real estate, a building, or some other type of property.

Convertible Bonds

A **convertible bond** is a corporate bond that can be converted to shares of common stock. The bondholder has the option of switching to a stock investment. If the bondholder converts to common stock, the bond is no longer due and payable at maturity. Convertible bonds can be exchanged for a certain number of common shares at a specific price per share. For example, say you purchase a $1,000 corporate bond which is convertible to 50 shares of the company's common stock. You should convert the bond to stock whenever the price of the company's common stock is $20 ($1,000 ÷ 50 shares) or higher. Assume the company's stock is selling for $22. In this situation, you would have an investment worth $1,100 ($22 × 50 shares) on conversion.

Callable Bonds

A bond may be issued with a call provision. A **callable bond** is a bond that the issuer has the right to pay off (call back) before its maturity date. The date when a bond can be called is identified at the time it is offered for sale. For example, a ten-year bond issued in 2015 with a maturity date of 2025 may be callable in the year 2020. If interest rates fall, corporations may choose to call the bonds because they can reissue them at a lower interest rate. Generally, it is cost-effective for corporations to pay the costs of calling and reissuing when interest rates drop by 2 percent or more. Corporations usually agree not to call bonds for the first five years after issuance. When the corporation does exercise its right to call the bond, it generally pays the bondholders a small *premium*— an amount above the face value of the bond. For example, a $1,000 bond may be called for $1,020.

Zero-Coupon Bonds

Another type of corporate bond is a zero-coupon bond. A **zero-coupon bond** is sold at a deep discount, makes no interest payments, and is redeemable for its face value at maturity. These bonds may also be issued by the U.S. government or municipalities. They are sold at as much as 50–75 percent below the face value of the bond. As the bond progresses toward maturity, it may increase in value. The bondholders make money by selling the bonds before maturity at a higher price than they paid for them. Or, they can hold the bonds to maturity and receive the face value and interest.

With a zero-coupon corporate bond, you must pay taxes on any "interest" you gain each year, even though you don't actually receive it until the bond is paid at maturity. Interest on zero-coupon municipal bonds, however, is not subject to taxation. Prices on zero-coupon bonds tend to fluctuate widely. Should you need to sell the bond before maturity, you may face a loss.

 **CHECKPOINT**

What are the different types of corporate bonds?

LO 1-2 Government Bonds

In addition to loaning money to corporations, you can also loan money to the government. Bonds are issued by the federal government as well as by state and local governments. There are four major types of government bonds: municipal bonds, savings bonds, Treasury securities, and agency bonds.

Municipal Bonds

A bond issued by state and local governments is called a **municipal bond**. The minimum investment in a municipal bond is usually $5,000, although brokers often ask for a multiple of this amount as a minimum investment. Municipal bonds generally pay a lower interest rate than corporate bonds. However, the interest is exempt from federal taxes (and often state and local taxes as well), so the effective rate is higher than the stated rate. As Figure 18.2 shows, the tax advantage of municipal bonds sometimes makes them a better deal than a corporate bond that pays a higher interest rate. Figure 18.2 calculates net interest on both kinds of bonds for an investor in the 28 percent tax bracket. Municipal bonds (also known as "munis") come in two varieties: revenue bonds and general obligation bonds.

Revenue Bonds

A **revenue bond** is a municipal bond issued to raise money for a public-works project. The revenues (income) generated by the project are used to pay the interest and repay the bonds at maturity. For example, if a revenue bond is issued to build a new toll road, the tolls that are collected from motorists who drive on the road are used to pay off the bond. In addition to toll roads, other major projects financed by revenue bonds include airports, hospitals, and public housing facilities.

FIGURE 18.2 — Comparing Taxable and Tax-Exempt Bonds

	Corporate Bond	Municipal Bond
Face value (Principal)	$10,000	$10,000
Rate of interest	× 6%	× 5%
Amount of annual interest	$ 600	$ 500
Tax on interest earned (28%)	−168	− 0
Net interest	$ 432	$ 500

The national debt consists of borrowing by the federal government. Each year, the national deficit (excess of spending over revenue collected) is added to that debt. In 2014 the national debt was over $17 trillion. In historical times, the national debt was used to finance wars. Currently, it is still used to fund the military, but it is also applied to funding recommendations outlined in the annual federal budgets. The national debt is represented by Treasury notes, bills, and bonds.

Many people feel the debt is overwhelming and represents obligations that must be paid by future generations. Others feel the national debt is needed to fund spending requirements, such as tax rebates to stimulate the economy, tax cuts, government programs to aid disaster relief, and so on.

THINK CRITICALLY

Which side do you agree with? Enter the keywords "national debt" in an online search engine and find out the current amount of the debt. What do you think the country should do about the national debt?

General Obligation Bonds

A **general obligation (GO) bond** is a municipal bond backed by the power of the issuing state or local government to levy taxes to pay back the debt. For example, school districts may issue bonds to finance construction of new buildings. A city may issue bonds to pay for a new police or administrative center. States may issue bonds to pay for a new college campus or a new road system.

A GO bond is repaid with the government's general revenue and borrowings. In contrast, a revenue bond is repaid from the revenue generated by the facility built with the borrowed funds. Cities pay off GO bonds by using funds collected from city income and sales taxes, fees, fines, and other sources. Schools and colleges pay off the bonds with property taxes, tuition, fees, state funding, and other sources.

Savings Bonds

U.S. savings bonds are available as Series EE and Series I bonds. Both types of savings bonds are sold at face value. The bonds are available in any amount from $25 to $10,000, and you can buy up to $10,000 worth of bonds in a year. The interest that both Series EE and Series I savings bonds earn is taxable at the federal level, but exempt from state and local income taxes.

You can no longer purchase Series EE or Series I savings bonds at a local bank, financial institution, or credit union. These savings bonds are sold online only at the U.S. Department of Treasury's TreasuryDirect website (www.treasurydirect.gov). Paper certificates are also no longer issued. The only exceptions are for those who (1) are replacing lost bonds or changing a beneficiary or co-owner name and (2) wish to exchange their tax refund for a Series I bond.

Treasury Securities

Treasury securities (Treasury bills, notes, and bonds) can be purchased at the TreasuryDirect website or through a bank or broker. They are no longer issued as engraved certificates, as are many stocks and corporate bonds. Instead, they are kept "electronically," and the investor receives a statement of account. Thus, these investments exist as bookkeeping entries in the records of the U.S. Department of Treasury itself or in the records of commercial banks. Like savings bonds, U.S. Treasury securities are taxed by the federal government but are exempt from state and local income taxes. They are virtually risk-free because they have the backing of the U.S. government.

Agency Bonds

A bond issued by government agencies and by *government-sponsored enterprises (GSEs)* is called an **agency bond**. GSEs are federally chartered corporations that are publicly owned by stockholders. They help investors create a more diversified portfolio without creating more credit or inflation risk. Examples of GSEs include the Federal Home Loan Mortgage Corporation (Freddie Mac), the Federal National Mortgage Association (Fannie Mae), and the Federal Farm Credit Banks. Because GSEs are owned by stockholders and are not part of the federal government, bonds issued by these corporations are not backed by the full faith and credit of the federal government and, thus, have a certain amount of default risk.

In contrast, bonds issued by government agencies, such as the Small Business Administration (SBA), the Federal Housing Administration (FHA), and the Government National Mortgage Association (Ginnie Mae), are backed by the full faith and credit of the U.S. federal government. These agencies may not issue bonds directly. Instead they may insure or guarantee securities issued by other companies.

When you purchase an agency bond, you are loaning money to one of these agencies. The agencies use this funding to finance activities related to specific purposes, such as increasing home ownership or providing agricultural assistance. There is usually a minimum investment required to buy an agency bond. For example, investing in a Ginnie Mae bond requires a $25,000 minimum investment.

Agency bonds help investors create a more diversified portfolio. They are basically risk-free and offer a slightly higher yield than Treasury securities. They are usually taxable at the federal level, but exempt from state and local income taxes. Agency bonds can be purchased through a bank or broker.

What is the purpose of an agency bond?

CHECKPOINT

What are the four major types of government bonds?

Hospitality

Those who work the front desk at a hotel, motel, or other lodging facility are in the hospitality industry. Most hospitality workers talk to and interact directly with customers. They have a variety of job tasks that include greeting customers; making, confirming, and canceling room reservations; making recommendations to guests regarding shopping, dining, or entertainment in the surrounding area; providing information on the facility's policies and services; processing payments; and presenting statements to and checking out departing guests. Front desk clerks must also coordinate regularly with other hotel staff, such as housekeeping or maintenance, to meet requests made by guests.

Most hotel clerks are employed full time. Because hotels are open 24 hours a day, 7 days a week, working evenings, weekends, and holidays is common.

Employment Outlook

- A slower-than-average rate of employment growth is expected.

Job Titles

- Front desk clerk
- Reservations specialist
- Hotel clerk
- Front desk associate

Needed Skills

- A high school diploma or equivalent is usually required.
- On-the-job training is needed as most hotel clerks learn their skills on the job.
- Strong customer service, interpersonal, and communication skills are needed.
- A professional, well-groomed appearance is desired.

What's it like to work in . . . *Hospitality*

Jamala works the 7 A.M. to 3 P.M. shift as a front desk clerk at a local hotel where she makes an annual salary of $24,500. She usually begins each day by reviewing any notes left by the front desk clerk who worked the previous shift. She then reviews charges for guests who are scheduled to depart that day and manages checkouts throughout the morning. After a guest has checked out, she notifies the housekeeping staff so that the room can be prepared for check-in, which begins at 3 P.M.

During her shift, she also answers phone calls, makes and cancels reservations, and assists guests who have any questions or requests. In addition to these routine tasks, today Jamala is helping with preparations for a technology conference that is being held in the hotel's banquet room tomorrow.

What About You?

Do you have good people skills and like interacting with others? Do you like serving others' needs? If so, the hospitality industry might be right for you.

The Career Clusters icons are being used with permission of the: States' Career Clusters Initiative, 2007, www.careerclusters.org

KEY TERMS REVIEW

Match the terms with the definitions. Some terms may not be used.

____ 1. A bond that is backed by specific assets as collateral

____ 2. The amount the bondholder will be repaid at maturity

____ 3. A bond issued by a state or local government

____ 4. A corporate bond that is based on the general creditworthiness and reputation of the company

____ 5. A bond issued to raise money for a public-works project

____ 6. A bond that the issuer has the right to pay off before its maturity date

____ 7. A bond backed by the power of the issuing state or local government to levy taxes to pay back the debt

____ 8. A bond that can be exchanged for shares of common stock

a. agency bond
b. bond redemption
c. callable bond
d. convertible bond
e. debenture
f. face value
g. general obligation (GO) bond
h. municipal bond
i. revenue bond
j. secured bond
k. zero-coupon bond

CHECK YOUR UNDERSTANDING

LO1-1 9. Why do corporations issue bonds?

LO1-1 10. What is a callable bond? Why does this feature make the bond more attractive to the investor?

LO1-2 11. What is a government-sponsored enterprise? Provide an example.

APPLY YOUR KNOWLEDGE

LO1-1 12. Why might an investor choose to buy bonds rather than stocks? As a bondholder, would your investment in a corporate bond be more secure than a stockholder's investment? Why or why not?

THINK CRITICALLY

LO1-1 13. Why might an investor choose to buy a secured bond rather than an unsecured bond? Why would an investor prefer a convertible bond?

LO1-2 14. Explain why you might choose to buy a municipal bond paying 5 percent over a corporate bond paying 7 percent.

The Essential Question *Refer to The Essential Question on p. 434. Corporate bonds pay a fixed rate of return and are relatively safe. Government bonds are usually tax-free for federal and/or state and local income tax purposes and also offer low-risk or risk-free investing.*

The Essential Question *How can investors buy bonds, earn a return, and lower their risk?*

LEARNING OBJECTIVES

> LO 2-1 Explain how to buy and sell bonds, considering both risk and return.
> LO 2-2 Explain how to read the bond listings.

KEY TERMS

- hedge, *442*
- primary market, *443*
- secondary market, *443*
- bond rating, *444*
- investment-grade bond, *444*
- junk bond, *444*
- bond default, *445*
- bond fund, *445*
- bond listings, *445*

LO 2-1 Owning Bonds

In addition to buying stock, many investors also choose to invest in bonds. Bonds are generally a safe investment because they have a fixed interest rate and represent a loan that the issuer must repay. Bonds play an important role in a diversified portfolio. Bond prices tend to remain steadier than do stock prices. Also, bond prices tend to react in the opposite direction of stock prices. When stock prices are falling, bond prices tend to rise, and vice versa. As a result, bond investments serve as a hedge to help offset the risk of the stocks in your portfolio. A **hedge** is any investment or action that helps offset against loss from another investment or action.

Full-service and discount brokers can assist you in buying and selling bonds. If you decide to use a broker, you will be charged a commission or flat fee for this service. Some bonds can also be purchased through banks.

Buying Bonds

You cannot purchase U.S. savings bonds at financial institutions. Instead, you can buy them at the TreasuryDirect website (www.treasurydirect.gov). To purchase a savings bond, you must have a TreasuryDirect account and a checking or savings account. When you buy a bond at TreasuryDirect, the purchase price is withdrawn from your designated bank account. When the bond matures, TreasuryDirect deposits the payment into your bank account.

TreasuryDirect also offers a payroll savings plan to buy savings bonds. Participating employers automatically withhold money from paychecks and directly deposit it into a TreasuryDirect account. The employee decides what type and dollar value of savings bond he or she wants to buy and TreasuryDirect automatically purchases it once there are enough funds in the employee's account.

You can also buy Treasury securities at the TreasuryDirect website. Interest earned is deposited directly into the bank account you designate when you set up your TreasuryDirect account. When the security matures, you can redeem it by having the principal deposited into your bank account, or you can reinvest it by using the proceeds from the matured security to buy another one. Treasury securities can also be bought through a bank or broker.

You can buy corporate bonds, municipal bonds, and agency bonds through banks or brokers. In most states, you can set up a bank account to buy municipal bonds. Often, you are purchasing a bond from the inventory your bank has on hand. Banks buy large blocks of municipal bonds and make them available to their customers. There is a fee for this service.

Primary and Secondary Markets

Corporate, municipal, and agency bonds can be purchased on the **primary market**, also known as the *new issue market* because investors can buy stocks and bonds when they are first issued by a company or group. However, most of these bonds are purchased on the **secondary market**, which is created when investors buy and sell previously issued stocks and bonds from one another with the help of brokers. One of the biggest differences between buying bonds on the primary market versus the secondary market is the price. In the primary market, investors pay only the face value of the bond. The issuing corporation—not the investor—pays the broker commission for the sale. In the secondary market, the price of the bond is affected by interest rates in the market and supply and demand.

Return on Bonds

Investors earn a return on bonds through interest that accumulates each day they own the bond and through the principal they receive when they redeem the bond for its face value at maturity. Investors can also earn a return if they sell the bond before maturity. While the interest rate on a bond is fixed, the *market price* (what the bond could sell for) can change. Bonds often appreciate in value, especially when interest rates are dropping, and bondholders may be able to sell the bond before maturity for a price higher than they paid for it. When bonds sell for more than their face value, they are selling at a *premium*. For example, Figure 18.3 shows that the *yield* (the return you get on a bond) is 6 percent on a $10,000, 6 percent bond selling for face value, or "100." But if the bond is sold for "104," it would have a premium of 4 percent. At 104, the market price would be $10,400.

$$\$10,000 \times .04 = \$400 \text{ premium}$$
$$\$10,000 + \$400 = \$10,400 \text{ market price}$$

FIGURE 18.3   Yield on a $10,000, 6% Bond

$$\frac{\text{Annual interest dollar amount}}{\text{Market price}} = \text{Yield}$$

	Annual Interest/Market Price	= Yield
If you buy the $10,000 bond at face value	$600/$10,000 =	6%
If you buy the bond at 104	$600/$10,400 =	5.8%
If you buy the bond at 96	$600/$9,600 =	6.3%

In this case (buying at a premium), the buyer's yield would be lower than 6 percent because the buyer had to pay more than face value to buy the bond.

Bonds can also sell below face value. Investors are not willing to pay face value for a bond yielding 6 percent when current interest rates are higher than 6 percent and rising. Therefore, the bond may have to be sold at a *discount*, or for an amount lower than face value, to attract buyers. If a bond sold for 96, it was sold at a 4 percent discount. The purchaser of the bond would pay only $9,600 for a $10,000 bond.

$$\$10,000 \times .04 = \$400 \text{ discount}$$
$$\$10,000 - \$400 = \$9,600 \text{ market price}$$

In this case (buying at a discount), the buyer's yield would be higher than 6 percent because the buyer paid less than face value for the bond. As these examples show, yield is not the same thing as the contract rate of interest.

Risk on Bonds

Like all investments, bonds have risk. However, the risk is not the same for all bonds. To help investors evaluate the risk level of different bonds, independent rating services rate bonds according to their safety. A **bond rating** tells the investor the risk category that has been assigned to a bond. Bond rating services, such as Moody's and Standard & Poor's, base their ratings on the creditworthiness of the issuing corporation or municipality. Figure 18.4 shows the bond rating scales for both Moody's and Standard & Poor's.

An **investment-grade bond** is considered a high-quality, low-risk bond. It has a rating of Baa or higher by Moody's or BBB or higher by Standard & Poor's. These bonds are considered safe because the issuers are stable and dependable. For example, U.S. Treasury bonds provide maximum safety because they are backed by the federal government itself. Unfortunately, the higher the bond's rating, the lower the interest rate you will earn.

If a company falls below a certain credit rating, its grade changes from investment quality to junk status. A **junk bond** has a low rating, or no rating at all. Any bond with a rating of Ba/BB or lower is called a junk bond and is categorized as *speculative*. Junk bonds have higher yields and, at times, appear to have reasonable levels of risk. However, in most cases, interest rates on junk bonds are high because they are at high risk, since the companies issuing them are not financially sound.

FIGURE 18.4	Bond Rating Scales		
Moody's	**Standard & Poor's**	**Grade**	**Risk**
Aaa	AAA	Investment	Highest quality
Aa	AA	Investment	High quality
A	A	Investment	Strong
Baa	BBB	Investment	Medium
Ba, B	BB, B	Junk	Speculative
Caa, Ca	CCC, CC, C	Junk	Highly speculative
C	D	Junk	In default

The European debt crisis is an ongoing economic crisis that has been affecting various countries of the Eurozone since 2008. Many Eurozone countries—Greece, Portugal, Ireland, Italy, and Spain, in particular—have, to varying degrees, failed to generate enough economic growth to pay back bondholders. As a result, ratings services downgraded the debt (bonds) of several of these countries. At one point, Greek bonds were moved to junk status. The effects of the crisis have been widespread. Government services have been reduced, many businesses have imposed massive layoffs, and cutbacks have been experienced at schools. The European Union and International Monetary Fund have taken action by implementing a series of bailouts for the troubled economies of these countries. One of the bailouts included a debt restructuring agreement with bondholders of Greek government bonds. As part of the debt restructuring, bondholders swapped their old Greek government bonds for new securities with a lower interest rate and longer maturity periods. This, in turn, reduced the country's debt level by over $100 billion. With debt relief, countries can once again begin to provide services and help to create jobs.

THINK CRITICALLY

How can government debt lead to loss of jobs for workers and cutback of government services? How can restructuring debt lead to economic recovery?

A bond with a rating of C by Moody's or D by Standard & Poor's indicates that the bond is in default. **Bond default** occurs when the bond issuer cannot meet the interest and/or principal payments. Because bonds are not insured, investors can lose their money if the corporation or municipality defaults.

Lowering Risk

To lower risk in owning bonds, many investors choose to buy into investment pools of various types of bonds rather than buying individual bonds. A **bond fund** is a group of bonds that have been bundled together and sold in shares (like stock) to investors. Typically, a bond fund will contain some investment-grade bonds along with bonds of some newer companies, foreign bonds, and a few junk bonds as well. Mutual funds, brokers, and investment services at financial institutions offer bond funds to their customers as a method of hedging against the risk of loss from other investments.

CHECKPOINT

How do bonds act as a hedge?

LO 2-2   Reading the Bond Listings

Bond listings are extensive tables that contain information about recent trades of bonds. You can find them in financial news publications such as the *Wall Street Journal*, *Investor's Business Daily*, and *Barron's* and at many financial and investor websites. Bond listings contain *bond quotes*, or the prices at which bonds are trading expressed as a percentage of face value. Interest rates effect bond prices. When interest rates rise, the value of bonds decreases. The bonds are paying less in comparison to other fixed-rate investments. Conversely,

©Redshinestudio/Shutterstock.com

when interest rates drop, fixed-rate bonds will become attractive because they are "locked in" at higher rates.

The bond listings you will find in newspapers or online will look similar to the one shown in Figure 18.5. To track bond prices, you need to understand the various columns in the bond listings.

- *Column 1.* This column lists the abbreviated name of the bond issuer.
- *Column 2.* This column indicates the type of bond and its rating. An "a" stands for senior bond, a "b" stands for split coupon, a "c" is a zero-coupon bond, a "d" is an unsecured bond, and an "e" is a secured bond.
- *Column 3.* This column shows the coupon rate of the bond (the guaranteed, fixed interest rate that will be paid annually on the bond).
- *Column 4.* This column shows the maturity date. Typically, the month and year are listed. For example, "12/20" means December 2020.
- *Column 5.* This column tells you what the final closing bid for the day was for the bond. It is similar to the closing price for stocks. Prices (bond quotes) are given as a percentage of face value, which is usually $1,000. For example, the last sale price for AK Steel was 98½, which translates into $985 on a $1,000 bond, or 98.5 percent of the face value.
- *Column 6.* This column compares the last price paid for the bond today with that paid on the previous day. A minus means the price has gone down; a plus means the price has risen. "Unch" means "unchanged"—the price has not changed from the previous day.
- *Column 7.* This column states the current yield for the bond. The current yield is computed by dividing the bond's coupon rate by its average market value (not its closing price). This yield figure varies as market interest conditions change; therefore, the current yield may be above or below the actual coupon rate. The current yield is an important indicator because it tells you what your bond is worth relative to other bonds you may have in your portfolio and other bond choices in the marketplace.

✔ CHECKPOINT

What is the significance of the current yield of a bond?

- -

| FIGURE 18.5 | Reading Corporate Bond Listings |

Excerpt from stock exchange (bond) listings:

Name	Type/ Rating	Coup.	Mat.	Last Sale	Net Chg.	Yld
1	2	3	4	5	6	7
AK Steel	a/BB	9.125	12/16	98½	+.38	9.46
Allied Waste	b/B	10.000	8/19	102	unch	9.57
Am Std	a/BB	7.375	2/18	98½	−1.25	7.56
Chanclr	b/BB	8.125	12/20	103	unch	7.36
Echostar	a/B	9.375	2/19	101¼	unch	9.52

What Are Some Investment Tax Strategies?

When choosing investment options, investors must keep one important consideration in mind—taxability. Some investments are fully taxable, while others are tax-free. There are numerous options in between. The choice of an investment might hinge on its tax status.

An investment is *tax-exempt* when there is no tax due on the interest income earned, either now or in the future. Tax-exempt investments include municipal bonds sold by state and local governments. However, to be free from both federal and state taxes, you must live in the state where the bond is issued. For example, if you live in California and own a municipal bond issued in the state of Oregon, the bond will be tax-free in Oregon but will be subject to state income taxes in California.

An investment is *tax-deferred* when income will be taxed at a later time. Tax-deferred investments include annuities, which will be discussed in Chapter 20. While earnings are credited to your account now, you do not pay taxes on the earnings until you withdraw them, often during retirement when you are in a lower tax bracket because your income is lower.

Taxes also are deferred on assets that appreciate in value. *Capital gains*, the profits from the sale of assets such as stocks, bonds, or real estate, are not taxed until the asset is sold. For example, if shares of stock you own are currently worth more than you paid for them, you will owe no taxes on the gain until you sell the stock.

Income and tax deductions can be *shifted* by postponing them to the following tax year, or by accelerating them forward into a current year, when they will be more beneficial. If your income is higher this year than usual, you can shift some deductions to help offset this increased income.

Taxes can be *avoided* by selling securities on which you lost money to offset gains on the sale of other securities. You can deduct losses to reduce capital gains on securities you sold at a profit. For example, you may sell shares of stock that are worth more than you paid for them and make a profit. However, you may own a bond that has dropped in value. If you sell the bond before maturity, you can use the losses from the sale of the bond to reduce the gains from the sale of stock. This strategy is called *tax avoidance*, and it is not the same as tax evasion, which is the use of illegal actions to reduce your taxes.

THINK CRITICALLY

1. Why is it important to consider tax consequences when choosing investment alternatives?

2. What type of investor would likely choose a tax-exempt investment? What type of investor would choose a tax-deferred investment?

3. Why should you seek professional advice when shifting income and avoiding taxes?

KEY TERMS REVIEW

Match the terms with the definitions. Some terms may not be used.

____ 1. *When a bond issuer cannot meet the interest and/or principal payments on a bond*

____ 2. *A bond with a low rating or no rating at all*

____ 3. *Any investment or action that helps offset against loss from another investment or action*

____ 4. *A high-quality, low-risk bond*

____ 5. *A group of bonds that have been bundled together and sold in shares to investors*

____ 6. *The risk category that has been assigned to a bond*

a. bond default
b. bond fund
c. bond listings
d. bond rating
e. hedge
f. investment-grade bond
g. junk bond
h. primary market
i. secondary market

CHECK YOUR UNDERSTANDING

L02-1 7. Under what conditions would bonds sell at a premium?

L02-1 8. What do bond ratings tell investors? How are they determined?

L02-2 9. What is a bond quote?

APPLY YOUR KNOWLEDGE

L02-2 10. Explain how bond prices are linked to interest rates. What causes the price of an existing bond to increase or decrease?

THINK CRITICALLY

L02-1 11. Would you choose to buy a Treasury security through a full-service broker, discount broker, bank, or TreasuryDirect? Why?

L02-1 12. You have the choice of buying a municipal bond with a rating of Aaa paying 4 percent interest or a corporate bond with a rating of Ba paying 8 percent interest. Which bond would be your choice? Explain why.

L02-2 13. Explain how a bond fund lowers the risk of owning bonds, which is already considered safer than owning stock.

The Essential Question *Refer to The Essential Question on p. 442. Investors can buy U.S. savings bonds and Treasury securities at the TreasuryDirect website. Other bonds can be purchased at banks or through brokers. A return on bonds is earned in one of three ways: (1) by collecting interest, (2) by redeeming the bond at maturity, and (3) by selling the bond for a premium before its maturity. The risk of owning bonds can be reduced by checking their ratings, buying a bond fund, and reading and understanding bond listings.*

SUMMARY

18.1

- *Bonds are loans that a corporation or government body must repay at face value, with interest. They are a fixed-rate investment because they pay a specified amount of interest at regular intervals.*

- *Debentures are unsecured bonds. Secured bonds (such as mortgage bonds) are secured by a specific asset.*

- *Owners of convertible bonds can exchange their bonds for common stock if they want to take advantage of higher stock prices.*

- *A callable bond may be "called" (paid off) by the issuer before maturity.*

- *Zero-coupon bonds sell at a deep discount and make no interest payments until maturity. Holders make money by selling them at a profit before maturity or redeeming them at face value at maturity.*

- *Municipal bonds generally are tax-free. Revenue bonds are issued to raise money for public projects. General obligation bonds are backed by the power of the issuing government unit to levy taxes to pay back the debt.*

- *U.S. savings bonds and Treasury securities are considered one of the safest investments because they are backed by the full faith and credit of the U.S. government.*

- *Agency bonds are issued by government agencies and by government-sponsored enterprises.*

18.2

- *You can buy corporate, municipal, and agency bonds through a bank or broker. U.S. savings bonds can only be purchased at the TreasuryDirect website, while Treasury securities can be purchased at the TreasuryDirect website or through a bank or broker.*

- *Investors can earn a return on bonds from interest, by redeeming the bonds for their face value at maturity, or by selling them before maturity for a price higher than they paid for them.*

- *Bonds whose interest rates are higher than the current market rate will sell at a premium. Bonds whose interest rates are lower than the current market rate will sell at a discount.*

- *Rating services rate bonds based on the financial condition of the issuing corporation or municipality. Investment-grade bonds are the highest-quality, lowest-risk bonds. Junk bonds have a low rating.*

- *Bond listings are extensive tables that contain information about bonds in recent trades.*

APPLY WHAT YOU KNOW

LO1-1 1. You bought a $10,000, 6 percent corporate bond at face value that matures in five years. What would be your total earnings during that five-year period?

LO1-2 2. Visit the TreasuryDirect website (www.treasurydirect.gov) and find the answers to these questions:

a. What are STRIPS?

b. How can you buy treasuries from this site?

c. How can you replace a lost, stolen, or destroyed savings bond?

LO2-1 3. Look up bonds in the financial section of your newspaper or online, including both corporate and government-issued bonds. Select two of each type and compare bond ratings. Keep track of the "net change" for each of these bonds for a week. What differences, if any, do you see?

LO2-1 4. A new bond you are considering buying has a face value of $1,000, an interest rate of 5 percent, and a maturity date eight years away. The average market price of the bond is 104. What is the yield? What amount of interest would you earn in that time period?

LO2-2 5. Three $1,000 bonds have the following closing bids: 95⅜, 103¼, and 99. What are the prices of the bonds in dollar amounts?

MAKE ACADEMIC CONNECTIONS

LO1-1 6. **Math** Marsha Clarke has just purchased a $10,000, 7.5 percent corporate bond that will pay interest semiannually for the next eight years. Prepare a chart showing how much interest she will receive for the next eight years (total interest payments are 16).

LO1-1 7. **Research** Choose a corporate bond listed on the New York Stock Exchange. Visit Moody's website (www.moodys.com) to answer the following questions about this bond. (*Note:* You will have to create a free account on Moody's website to view ratings.)

a. What is Moody's rating for the bond?

b. What is the purpose of the bond?

c. Does the bond have a call provision?

d. What collateral, if any, has been pledged as security for the bond?

Based on the information studied, would the bond be a good investment for you? Why or why not?

LO1-2 8. **Economics** The Federal Reserve System, known as the Fed, engages in monetary policy to help the economy grow without high inflation. One form of monetary policy is called "open market operations," where the Fed buys and sells U.S. securities (Treasury notes, bills, and bonds). Go to the Federal Reserve System's website (www.federalreserve.gov) to learn more about open market operations. Explain how this type of monetary policy helps the economy expand or contract (grow or shrink).

Solve Problems and Explore Issues

LO1-1 9. Your friend Jason has just inherited $10,000. He tells you that he is considering investing in the stock market. He also tells you that he wants to preserve the safety of the principal he invests. Explain to him why buying a bond would be a safer investment than buying a stock.

LO1-1 10. After your discussion with Jason, he asks you whether he should consider buying a corporate bond. Explain to him how bond investing works and the difference between the types of corporate bonds. What type of corporate bond would you recommend? Why?

LO1-2 11. Tatiana is considering purchasing a $10,000, 9 percent corporate bond. She also found that she can buy a $10,000, 7 percent municipal bond. Her federal income tax rate is 28 percent. Determine her net interest. Show your computations.

LO2-1 12. Les has chosen to buy a 5.5 percent, $1,000 corporate bond. The bond has an average selling price of 106. Compute his yield on the bond, and explain to him why yield is not the same as the stated interest rate.

LO2-1 13. In June 2009, corporate bonds of General Motors (GM) were at a default value of 12.5 cents on the dollar. The price fell because of the poor credit position of GM and the impending bailout needed from taxpayers. What happens when a bond defaults? What did GM do? What is the current rating for GM bonds?

EXTEND YOUR LEARNING

LO2-1 14. **Legal Issues** It is illegal for firms selling bonds to mislead or defraud investors. Investment firms have an obligation to inform their clients about the risks associated with the bonds. The Financial Industry Regulatory Authority (FINRA) is the largest nongovernmental agency that regulates bonds (and stocks). Use the Internet to learn more about FINRA. How does it help enforce federal securities laws and protect investors?

CHAPTER PROJECT

The bond market in the United States is a steady, but sometimes unpredictable, financial investment. People tend to buy bonds when certain conditions exist and reject them at other times. Conduct online research to see what experts are currently saying about the bond market. Write a one-page summary of your findings. Use and cite at least three different sources of information. Then assume that you have decided to invest in a corporate bond. Select a bond and create a bond listing for it following the format presented in Figure 18.5.

Complete the Guided Decision Making activity for Chapter 18 at ngl.cengage.com/mypf.

CHAPTER 19

Investing in Mutual Funds, Real Estate, and Other Choices

Consider This...

Patrick works 20 hours a week, lives at home with his parents, and can save $100 a month. He doesn't have a large lump sum to invest, but he's sure that he can set aside this amount regularly.

Patrick told his financial adviser, "I've thought about several kinds of investments. I researched several mutual funds online, and I think I'm ready to buy shares in a fund that specializes in growth stocks. The one I'm most interested in has averaged an 8 percent annual return over the last 15 years. That's good, considering the ups and downs of the stock market. An important benefit I'll have is the ability to check my account daily, if I want, by logging onto the fund's website. I can transfer my money from one fund to another electronically if I see that this would be a smart thing to do. And, once I buy in, I'm guaranteed to be able to keep buying shares of the fund, even if the fund is closed to new investors later."

The Essential Question *Why are mutual funds a good investment for beginning and less experienced investors?*

LEARNING OBJECTIVES

› **LO 1-1** Discuss mutual funds as an investment strategy.
› **LO 1-2** Explain how to buy and sell mutual funds.

KEY TERMS

- growth fund, *454*
- income fund, *454*
- growth and income fund, *455*
- balanced fund, *455*
- money market fund, *455*
- global fund, *456*
- index fund, *456*
- prospectus, *457*
- load, *458*
- net asset value (NAV), *458*

LO 1-1 Evaluating Mutual Funds

A *mutual fund* is a professionally managed group of investments bought using a pool of money from many investors. Individuals buy shares in the mutual fund. Mutual funds are operated by professional fund managers who use the pooled money to buy stocks, bonds, and other securities based on market research they have conducted. The kinds of securities they buy depend on the fund's stated investment objectives. For example, some mutual funds specialize in aggressive growth stocks. Others specialize in more conservative investments, such as bonds or money market securities.

Most mutual fund companies offer a *family of funds*, which is a variety of funds covering a whole range of investment objectives. You can choose the family member(s) that best match your own goals. You are allowed to move back and forth among the company's funds. For example, you can buy one type of fund (such as a stock fund) and later switch to another (such as a bond fund), all within the same family of funds.

Fund investors share in any profits made by the mutual fund. They receive profits as dividends and as capital gains, both of which may be reinvested in the fund or distributed to investors as cash payments. *Capital gains* come from the profits made when the managers sell some of the fund's securities for more than they paid for them.

Why do most mutual funds companies offer a family of funds?

© Pan Xunbin/Shutterstock.com

© JohnKwan/Shutterstock.com

Advantages of Mutual Funds

Investors often choose mutual funds for several good reasons:

- *Professional Management.* The primary advantage of investing in mutual funds is the professional management of your money. A mutual fund is a relatively inexpensive way for investors who do not have the time or expertise to manage their own portfolio to get a full-time manager to do so.
- *Diversification.* When you invest in mutual funds, you are diversifying because mutual funds purchase a variety of stocks and bonds. When you have enough money to invest in more than one fund, you can further diversify by buying shares in funds with different investment objectives. For example, you can buy some shares in riskier, aggressive mutual funds and limit the risk by also purchasing shares in more conservative funds.
- *Liquidity.* Mutual funds allow you to convert your shares into cash at any time. However, there is some risk of loss if the fund's price is low when you choose to sell.
- *Small Initial and Ongoing Purchases.* Many funds require only a small minimum investment. Once you buy into a fund, you can make additional purchases as often as you like. Also, by pooling your money with other investors in the fund, you can own, for example, part of a $10,000 government bond without having to pay $10,000 to buy the whole bond yourself.

Mutual Fund Risk

Individual funds within a family have different investment goals and risk levels. In their publications and on their websites, investment companies describe the investment goals and level of risk for each fund. You can choose funds that match your goals and risk tolerance. As with any investment, the greater the potential return, the higher the risk. Figure 19.1 shows the general risk/return profiles for general categories of mutual funds.

Growth Fund

A growth fund is a mutual fund whose investment goal is to buy stocks that will increase in value over time. To do this, the fund's managers select stocks in companies that reinvest their profit in the company rather than distribute it to investors as dividends. Investors in growth funds earn their return through capital gains rather than through dividends.

There are different levels of growth funds. An *aggressive growth fund* invests in stock of new or out-of-favor companies and industries that the fund managers think will achieve above-average increases in value. The philosophy behind aggressive growth funds is to accept high risk of loss in exchange for a chance to earn high returns. Other growth funds follow a less risky philosophy. They invest in more stable companies that the fund managers expect to increase in value but at a slower, steadier rate than the stocks of aggressive growth funds.

Income Funds

An income fund is a mutual fund whose investment goal is to produce current income on a steady basis in the form of interest or dividends. Investors in income funds are looking for income from their investments now rather than

FIGURE 19.1   Risk and Return Pyramid

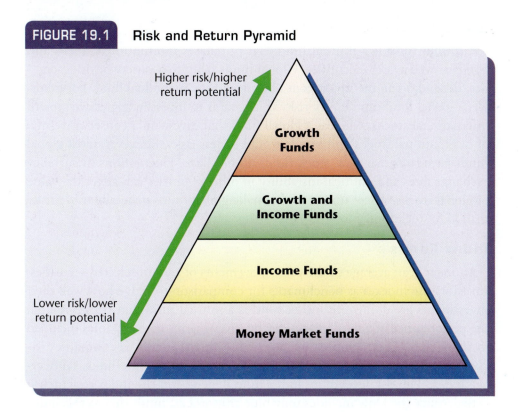

Higher risk/higher
return potential

Growth
Funds

Growth and
Income Funds

Income Funds

Lower risk/lower
return potential

Money Market Funds

capital gains later. Income funds are considered to be of low-to-moderate risk and less risky than growth funds.

Some income funds specialize in tax-exempt bonds. Their goal is to provide tax-free income for investors. Tax-exempt bond funds appeal to investors in high-income tax brackets.

Growth and Income Funds

A **growth and income fund** is a mutual fund whose investment goal is to earn returns from both dividends and capital gains. Managers of these funds try to select stocks that pay dividends as well as stocks that increase in market value over time. The risk level of this type of fund is moderate—between the riskier growth funds and less risky income funds.

A **balanced fund** is a mutual fund that seeks both growth and income but attempts to minimize risk by investing in a mixture of stocks and bonds rather than stocks alone. Like growth and income funds, the goal of a balanced fund is to earn returns from current income and capital gains. Balanced funds have moderate risk. They are a little less risky than growth and income funds that invest only in stocks.

Money Market Funds

A **money market fund** is a mutual fund that invests in safe, liquid securities, such as Treasury bills and bonds that mature in less than a year. These short-term maturities provide modest current income with little risk. The goals of a money market fund are the preservation of principal and high liquidity.

Many investors choose to put their money into money market funds while they are "waiting out" unfavorable market conditions. For example, if returns from income funds are dropping, an investor might transfer his or her balance to a money market fund until the income funds are rising once again.

Global Funds

A **global fund** is a mutual fund that purchases international stocks and bonds as well as U.S. securities. Global funds fall into a variety of risk categories, depending on the investment objective of the individual fund. For example, a global fund can be very risky if its goal is to invest in aggressive growth international stocks, whereas a global fund that invests in a conservative mix of international stocks and bonds would be less risky. However, most global funds have risks that U.S. stock funds do not have. Fluctuations in currency exchange rates and political instability in other countries can affect the value of global stocks. These uncertainties make global funds generally more risky than U.S. stock funds.

Index Funds

An *index* is an average of the price movements of certain selected securities. Investors use indexes as benchmarks for comparison to judge how well their investments are doing. An **index fund** is a mutual fund that tries to match the performance of a particular index by investing in the companies included in that index. For example, an index fund might invest in companies included in the Standard & Poor's 500 index or the Dow Jones Industrial Average index. The risk level of an index fund depends on the index to which it is tied. Since the Dow includes only blue chip stocks, funds tied to this index would be relatively low risk. The NASDAQ Composite index, on the other hand, includes stocks of some volatile high-tech companies. Funds tied to this index could be risky.

CHECKPOINT

What is the difference between a growth fund and an income fund?

LO 1-2 Buying and Selling Mutual Funds

There are thousands of mutual funds covering the whole range of investment objectives and risk levels. To choose the mutual fund that is right for you, you must know your own investment goals and risk tolerance. Do you want income from your investments now, or can you wait for capital gains in the future? Do you need a tax-free or tax-deferred investment to reduce your current income taxes? Are you comfortable with risking your investment for a chance at big returns, or do you prefer a safe, but lower, return? Once you know your own requirements, you can read about the objectives and risk profiles of different funds and find one that matches your requirements.

The Mutual Fund Company

The most important decision you will make with mutual fund investing is selecting the right mutual fund company or companies. Because mutual fund investments are not insured, the investor is taking a risk when placing money with these companies; therefore, it's a good idea to do extensive research on potential mutual fund companies.

To reduce your risk, you should choose a mutual fund company with the following characteristics:

- It has been in business for 20 or more years.
- It has a good track record of providing solid returns to its investors.
- It is a large company that manages investments for millions of investors.
- It is a well-known company that is highly respected among investment advisers and experts.
- It exists both in brick-and-mortar and in cyberspace.
- It is customer-friendly and responsive to customer questions and needs.
- It provides customers with easy-to-read statements and reports and offers daily online access.

Sources of Mutual Fund Information

Financial publications, such as *Forbes*, *Fortune*, and *Money*, regularly review and rank mutual funds. They compare one-year, five-year, and ten-year performances of various funds with similar objectives.

A great deal of information about mutual funds is available online. The Morningstar website issues reports that compare mutual funds. At the Yahoo! Finance website, you can get up-to-date news and market data on mutual funds. Another good website is the Mutual Fund Investor's Center. In addition to educational information and news articles, the site features daily pricing and performance information on more than 9,000 mutual funds. You can also search for the sites of fund families by name, such as Dreyfus and Vanguard. At these sites, you can find detailed descriptions, including risk/return profiles for all funds in their fund families.

The Prospectus

To find information on the mutual funds a company offers, you can refer to its prospectus. A **prospectus** is a legal document issued by an investment company that provides details about the securities it offers for sale. A fund prospectus contains a summary of the fund's portfolio of investments, its objectives and investment strategies, and financial statements showing past performance. In the United States, companies are required by law to provide potential buyers with a prospectus. They are also required to file their prospectus with the Securities and Exchange Commission (SEC). You can find company prospectuses at EDGAR, a database maintained by the SEC. You may also find a company's prospectus at its corporate website.

View Points

Some investors believe that once you have selected a mutual fund, you should check on it only periodically—maybe once every year or two—and resist making changes. Others believe that it is important to check your account balances almost daily. These investors frequently move their balances from one fund to another as they constantly look for choices that pay higher returns.

THINK CRITICALLY

Which view do you agree with? How often do you think you should check your mutual fund account balances and make changes?

© Vectomart/Shutterstock.com

Costs and Fees

You can buy and sell mutual funds through a broker or through the fund company directly. If you buy a mutual fund through a broker, you will likely have to pay a sales fee, called a **load**. The broker's commission comes from this fee. A *front-end load* is a sales charge paid when you buy an investment. Sometimes you pay this fee on reinvested dividends as well. A *back-end load* is a sales charge paid when you sell an investment. Either way, loads can range from 2 to 8 percent of the value of the shares purchased.

In some cases, you can buy mutual funds directly from the investment companies, often by phone or on their websites. This kind of fund, called a *no-load fund*, does not charge a sales fee when you buy or sell because no salespeople are involved.

Mutual fund companies make money by charging fees to their customers for the professional services provided. Funds often charge an annual management fee, which averages about 1 to 1½ percent of a fund's total assets. This charge is for the services of professional fund managers and for maintaining your account. The fund may also charge a "12b-1 fee" to cover the costs of marketing and distributing a mutual fund. These fees are part of the fund's *expense ratio*, which is expressed as a percentage of assets deducted each year for fund expenses. Mutual funds publish their expense ratios with their fund descriptions. When you consider investing in mutual funds, compare expense ratios as part of your evaluation.

Mutual Fund Prices

Unlike stocks, mutual fund prices are not determined by what people are willing to pay for them. They are determined by the net asset value. The **net asset value (NAV)** tells you the market price for a share of a mutual fund. The NAV is the total value of a fund's investment portfolio minus its liabilities, divided by the number of outstanding shares of the fund.

$$\text{NAV} = \frac{\text{Value of Portfolio} - \text{Liabilities}}{\text{Number of Shares}}$$

For example, suppose the value of all stocks in a fund's portfolio is currently $100,000. The fund has $90,000 in liabilities and has sold 500 shares of its fund to investors. The price for one of its shares, or its NAV, would be $20.

$$\frac{\$100,000 - \$90,000}{500} = \$20$$

Because the value of the portfolio changes as stocks and other securities are traded throughout the day, the NAV is calculated at the end of each business day. Thus, the value of your investment depends on that fund's performance in the securities market.

 **CHECKPOINT**

What are some features to look for in a mutual fund company?

Issues IN YOUR WORLD

How Do You Read the Mutual Funds Listings?

Mutual Fund Quotations

1	2	3	4	5	6	7	8
	Inv. Obj.	NAV	Offer Price	NAV Chg.	Return		
					YTD	26 Wks.	4 Yrs.
Ables Fund:							
AciBt1A	GRO	9.63	10.11	…	0.0	−0.1	NA
BiClo	BND	1.51	NL	−.01	−2.9	−1.6	+8.9
CoxDli	SML	8.61	NL	+.01	+1.6	+1.5	+18.6
DrixLt	G&I	26.54	NL	−.07	+6.1	+4.0	+18.0
BB&B Fund:							
Globl B	WOR	6.25	6.25	−.03	−4.3	−4.3	+2.7
MtgLtd	MTG	2.80	2.80	+.02	−2.3	−1.4	−1.0

- *Column 1*. This column lists the name of the mutual fund and its managing company. The name of the company that manages the funds is listed first. Its funds appear below in alphabetical order.

- *Column 2*. This column identifies the investment objective of the fund family. These companies offer investors a choice of growth (GRO), bond (BND), small company growth (SML), growth and income (G&I), global (WOR, for "world"), and mortgage (MTG) funds.

- *Column 3*. "NAV" stands for net asset value. It is the dollar value of one share of the fund, based on closing quotes.

- *Column 4*. The offer price reflects the NAV plus the broker's commission, if any. "NL" indicates a no-load fund.

- *Column 5*. This column indicates the gain or loss in the price for a share of the fund, based on the previous NAV quotation.

- *Column 6*. The "YTD" (year-to-date) column tells you how much the fund has gone up or down since January 1 of the current year.

- *Column 7*. This column shows the average earnings the fund has returned to investors in the last 26 weeks (six months), stated as a percentage return on investment.

- *Column 8*. This column shows the average earnings the fund has returned to investors for the last four years, stated as a percentage return on investment.

THINK CRITICALLY

1. Which of the mutual funds in the listing seems to be the best investment? Why?

2. Why is it important to know the investment objective?

KEY TERMS REVIEW

Match the terms with the definitions. Some terms may not be used.

____ 1. The sales fee charged for buying mutual funds

____ 2. A mutual fund that invests in safe, liquid securities

____ 3. A mutual fund that tries to match the performance of a particular index

____ 4. A mutual fund that purchases international stocks and bonds as well as U.S. securities

____ 5. A mutual fund that minimizes risk by investing in a mixture of stocks and bonds

____ 6. A mutual fund whose goal is to buy stocks that will increase in value over time

____ 7. A legal document issued by an investment company that provides details about the securities that the company offers for sale

a. balanced fund
b. global fund
c. growth and income fund
d. growth fund
e. income fund
f. index fund
g. load
h. money market fund
i. net asset value (NAV)
j. prospectus

CHECK YOUR UNDERSTANDING

LO1-1 8. Which type of mutual fund has the highest risk/return potential? Which type of mutual fund has the lowest?

LO1-2 9. What is NAV, and how is it computed?

APPLY YOUR KNOWLEDGE

LO1-1 10. Describe the type of investor (in terms of goals and risk tolerance) who would be interested in each of the following types of mutual funds: (a) growth funds, (b) income funds, (c) growth and income funds, and (d) money market funds.

THINK CRITICALLY

LO1-1 11. How can you lower risk when choosing mutual funds?

LO1-2 12. Why is it important to choose a mutual fund company that has been in business for a long time?

LO1-2 13. Why would you choose a no-load fund rather than a front-load fund for an investment?

The Essential Question *Refer to The Essential Question on p. 453. Mutual funds are good investments for beginning and less experienced investors because they are operated by professional fund managers, are comprised of a diversified group of investments, are highly liquid, require only a small minimum investment, and are focused on particular investment goals.*

The Essential Question *How is investing in real estate and investing in collectibles and commodities similar and different in terms of risk and reward?*

LEARNING OBJECTIVES

> LO 2-1 Explain real estate investing, both direct and indirect.
> LO 2-2 Describe other investments, including metals, gems, collectibles, and financial instruments.

KEY TERMS

- commercial property, *461*
- real estate investment trust (REIT), *464*
- real estate syndicate, *464*
- certificate of participation, *465*
- precious metals, *466*
- gems, *466*
- commodities, *467*

LO 2-1 Real Estate Investing

When you invest in real estate, you are buying land and any buildings on it. **Commercial property** is land and buildings that produce income through leasing or renting. Such property includes office buildings, stores, hotels, duplexes, and multi-unit apartments. Investing in real estate is considered a good way to combat inflation, because it usually increases in value over the years at rates equal to or higher than inflation. However, real estate is one of the least liquid investments you can make because a property can take months or even years to sell. Also, some real estate investments are speculative and can result in a substantial loss. You can invest in real estate directly or indirectly.

Direct Investing

With *direct investing*, the investor holds legal title to the property and has control over management decisions. There are numerous types of real estate properties that you can buy directly. These include vacant land; single-family houses; rental properties, such as apartments, condominiums, and duplexes; and vacation homes.

Vacant Land

Vacant land, or unimproved property, usually is considered a speculative investment. Investors hold the property expecting it to increase substantially in value over time. Other people purchase a vacant lot with plans for building a house or a small business on it. In either case, you may have to pay cash for vacant land. Because it is considered speculative, some banks are unwilling to make loans. When purchasing vacant land, it's important to check zoning laws that regulate what type of structure can be built on the property.

© Pan Xunbin/Shutterstock.com

Single-Family Houses

In addition to owning your own home, you might wish to purchase a single-family house and rent it to others. Because the property is not owner-occupied, you may find that banks are reluctant to grant you a mortgage loan to buy a house as rental property. As a condition for a loan, you may have to make a larger down payment or pay a higher interest rate.

When a renter takes possession of your house, you still have responsibilities as the owner. For example, you must maintain the premises in a livable condition. This involves providing running water, electricity, sewer or septic hookups, and normal repairs and maintenance.

Rental Properties

There are several types of *rental properties*, or real estate designed for owners to rent to tenants on an ongoing basis.

- An *apartment complex* is a large building or group of buildings that contain many housing units and have common facilities such as a recreation area, clubhouse, laundry room, and parking lots.
- A *condominium* (or *condo*) is an individually owned unit in an apartment-style complex with shared ownership of common areas. The owner of a condo owns the individual apartment as well as a proportional share of common areas, such as the lobby, yard, and hallways. Condo owners usually pay a monthly fee for the upkeep of the common areas.
- A *duplex* is a building with two separate living units that share a common wall. A *triplex* is a building with three individual housing units, while a *quad* has four individual housing units. Usually, the living areas are the same with separate entrances.

By pooling your cash with that of other investors, you can afford to buy larger and more expensive pieces of property. For example, if you and three others formed a partnership to buy an eight-unit apartment building, each of you would have to pay only one-fourth of the total costs of buying and maintaining the property.

Vacation Homes

Many people buy second homes for vacations, which may become their primary residence after they retire. Often, the owners rent these properties out to others to generate income during the times when they are not using them.

Vacation property includes beach and mountain cabins and even vacant land near recreational sites such as rivers, lakes, or an ocean. The owner can use and enjoy the property on weekends and during vacations and at other times rent out the property.

© Anastasija Popova/Shutterstock.com

Do you think vacation homes are good investments? Why or why not?

However, absent owners may need to arrange for someone else to take care of the property and manage the rental process. Real estate companies in popular vacation areas can provide these services for a fee.

Buying and Owning Rental Property

When buying real estate directly, most people make a down payment and get a mortgage (or trust deed) to pay the balance. A mortgage is a loan to purchase real estate. Borrowing money to buy an investment is called *leverage*, which means only a small amount of the purchase price is your own money. For example, if you buy a duplex for $300,000 and make a down payment of $60,000 (a 20 percent down payment is usually required for rental property), you are borrowing $240,000 from the bank. As the property gains in value, the mortgage payments remain fixed. When you eventually sell the property, you keep the difference between the sales price and the balance of the mortgage. This difference is the *equity*, or ownership interest.

Monthly Payments

As your tenant makes rent payments, you make the mortgage payments to the bank. You would use the difference between the amount of rent collected and the mortgage payment to pay property taxes and the cost of upkeep on the property. If you have money left over after paying these expenses, you have a *positive cash flow*. If, however, you cannot collect enough rent to pay the mortgage, property taxes, repairs, and maintenance, then you have a *negative cash flow* and must make up the shortfall from your own pocket.

Managing Rental Property

To manage a multi-unit rental property, you can be a resident landlord or hire a resident landlord or property manager. A *resident landlord* lives at the rental site, takes care of all repairs and maintenance, collects the rent, and assures suitable living conditions. A *property manager* collects rent, hires and pays people to make repairs and maintain the property, charges a fee for his or her services, and remits the difference to the property owner. Property managers do not live on site and usually manage several rental properties at the same time.

Tax Advantages

Depreciation is the decline in the value of property due to normal wear and tear. Even though your property may be increasing in overall market value, you can deduct depreciation expense on your rental property when filing your tax return. In addition, property taxes and other expenses of maintaining rental property can be deducted to help reduce the taxes you have to pay on your rental income. However, when you sell your rental property, you will have to pay taxes on the capital gain.

Risks of Owning Rentals

You should consider the risks of owning and renting property. Renters can damage or destroy your property to a degree far exceeding what a security deposit will cover. When your units have vacancies, your rental income will decline, yet you still have to pay the mortgage and other expenses, thus cutting into your profits.

Real estate is also subject to zoning laws and other local use restrictions. Cities have laws that regulate what type of structure (for example, single-family residence, apartment complex, office building) can be built in each area of the city. Before buying property, you should check the zoning laws to make sure you will be allowed to use the property as you intend.

Indirect Investing

With *indirect investing*, investors have a third person do the actual buying and selling of property. A *trustee* is an individual or institution that manages assets for someone else. The trustee holds the title to the property. Real estate investment trusts, real estate syndicates, and mortgage pools (in the form of certificates of participation) are examples of indirect investments using a third-party trustee.

Real Estate Investment Trusts

A **real estate investment trust (REIT)** is a corporation that pools the money of many individuals to invest in a diversified class of properties. Properties may include warehouses, shopping malls, apartment buildings, and hotels. A REIT is similar to a mutual fund in that it makes all buy-and-sell decisions for properties. REITs may invest in the properties themselves, generating income through the collection of rent, or they may invest in mortgages tied to the properties, generating income through the interest they earn on the mortgage loans.

REITs allow you to invest in the portfolios of large-scale properties through the purchase of shares of stock. You can buy and sell REIT shares at will, making them highly liquid. REITs are traded on stock exchanges or over the counter. Like stocks, REIT shares fluctuate with market conditions, and dividends are paid when the real estate investments do well. REIT listings can be found online at various financial websites and also in the financial section of newspapers along with stock, bond, and mutual fund price quotations.

Real Estate Syndicates

A **real estate syndicate** (often called a *limited partnership*) is a group of investors who pool their money to purchase high-priced real estate as a short-term investment. This is a temporary association of individuals organized for the purpose of raising a large amount of capital. A real estate syndicate often owns several properties for diversification, which are managed professionally. Unlike a REIT that pays dividends periodically, a real estate syndicate does not distribute cash until the end of the investment.

The organizer of the syndicate is called the *general partner* or syndicator. The people who contribute the capital are called *limited partners*. In a real estate syndicate, the general partner forms a partnership and assumes unlimited liability for all of the obligations (debts) of the partnership. By assuming unlimited liability, the general partner's responsibility extends beyond the initial investment to his or her personal assets if the investment incurs debt. The general partner then sells participation units to limited partners whose liability is limited to the amount of their investment. This means that the limited partners can lose no more than they invested if the investment fails. *Limited liability* is especially important in real estate partnerships because the mortgage acquired to purchase real estate often exceeds the net worth of the individual partners.

Certificates of Participation

A **certificate of participation** (COP) is an investment in a pool of mortgages that have been purchased by a government agency or government-sponsored enterprise. COPs (also known as *pass-through securities*) are issued by the Government National Mortgage Association (Ginnie Mae), the Federal Home Loan Mortgage Corporation (Freddie Mac), and the Federal National Mortgage Association (Fannie Mae). As the name suggests, the cash flow from the mortgage payments is "passed through" to the investor in the form of monthly payments of principal and interest.

COPs are also issued when individuals buy shares of lease revenues associated with government projects. Payments are made to the investor for the duration of the project, based on the percentage of shares the investor has in the lease agreement.

✔ CHECKPOINT

What are some types of direct and indirect real estate investments?

LO 2-2 Other Investing Choices

You may be willing to invest your money in just about anything you think will bring you a return in value over time or provide some other form of income. Often these choices depend on personal values and tastes.

Metals, Gems, and Collectibles

Investments in this category are often speculative. They can return large profits or losses when sold. In some cases, the enjoyment of having the investment will far exceed any resale value. Although not inexpensive, precious metals, gems, and collectibles are easy to purchase. However, they can be very difficult to sell in a hurry and do not provide any current income in the form of interest or dividends. Therefore, be cautious when making this type of investment.

Global View

©Redshinestudio/Shutterstock.com

A *bitcoin* is a new digital "currency" created in 2009 as open source software by an unknown person using the alias of Satoshi Nakamoto. Bitcoins allow transactions without middlemen—no banks or credit card companies. Without transaction fees, people can do business anonymously. More online merchants are beginning to accept bitcoins as a form of payment. In addition, international payments are easy and cheap because bitcoins are not tied to any country and are not being regulated. Because they are mostly unregulated, governments are concerned about their lack of control over the currency.

THINK CRITICALLY

Some people buy bitcoins as an investment, expecting them to increase in value. Would you consider investing in bitcoins? Why or why not? Do you think bitcoins will become an integral part of the global financial system in the future? Do you see them as a possible competitor to paper currency?

Precious Metals

Precious metals are tangible metals that have known and universal value around the world. Examples include gold, silver, and platinum. They are usually rare, natural substances that have high economic value. However, prices of precious metals can swing widely over time. These swings are what make investments in precious metals very risky.

You can buy gold, silver, and platinum as coins, medallions, jewelry, and bullion. Storing precious metals safely may be a problem because of bulk and weight. Instead of storing your investment yourself, you can buy gold and silver in the form of a certificate stating how much you own of the metal being stored for you. You also can own gold indirectly by investing in gold-mining stocks or in mutual funds specializing in these stocks. Other metals in which you can invest include aluminum, tin, copper, lead, nickel, and zinc. Prices for precious metals can be found in the financial pages of newspapers and online at various financial sites.

Gems and Jewelry

Gems are natural, precious stones, such as diamonds, rubies, sapphires, and emeralds. Their prices are high and subject to drastic change. Gems have their greatest value as jewelry. However, when you purchase jewelry at retail prices, you are paying markups of 50 to 500 percent or more. Prices must increase substantially in the world market before you can recover the cost and make a profit from reselling your jewelry.

The biggest disadvantage of investing in gems is the risk that you won't be able to resell them. The gems market can be very small and unpredictable, and no ready market may exist when you decide to sell. The process of buying and selling can also be hazardous, as most such transactions require the use of cash. Fraud is also a common risk that investors will face when purchasing gems. Unless you are working with a professional appraiser, judging whether a stone is real can be very difficult. However, despite these drawbacks, the returns from investing in gems can be high.

Collectibles

Collectibles are physical assets that appreciate in value over time because they are rare or desired by many. Collectibles can be things such as antiques, art, baseball cards, stamps, and comic books. Collectibles are valuable because they are old, no longer produced, unusual, irreplaceable, or of historic importance. Coins are the most commonly collected items. Silver coins (rather than today's alloy coins) often are worth more than 20 times their face value.

People collect items in hopes that someday their collection will be valuable. If you collect an item that goes up in value rapidly, you can reap large rewards.

Photodisc/Getty Images

Why might you want to avoid investing in gems?

Collectibles attract a certain type of "investor." They can be found about anywhere—swap meets, flea markets, antique stores, auctions, and garage sales. They also can be found online at websites such as eBay and Craigslist. You will find all types of things offered to buy, sell, and exchange.

Review the "Collectibles" section(s) in your local newspaper's classified ads or on a website. What types of items are offered for sale? In contrast, what items are people looking to buy? Prepare a summary of your findings to share in a class discussion.

Unfortunately, collectibles can take a very long time to increase in value, and may not increase in value at all, making them a risky investment. If you want to be a collector, buy what you can personally appreciate and enjoy through the years, knowing that your collection may or may not result in a profit when you decide to sell it.

Financial Instruments

A *futures* contract obligates the buyer to purchase (or the seller to sell) stock or a commodity for a specified price on a specified date in the future. **Commodities** are products that are mined or grown. These include farm products (such as wheat, corn, and cattle) and metals (such as gold and silver). Commodity prices are volatile because supply and demand for commodities are disrupted by all kinds of mostly unpredictable situations, from political upheaval to the weather.

Commodities may be sold for cash or traded in the futures market. People enter the futures market for protection against volatile prices. For example, a farmer could sell a futures contract to deliver 5,000 bushels of wheat one year from today. In this case, the farmer knows in advance what he will be paid for the wheat. If prices of wheat fall during the year, the farmer can make money because he or she is being paid a set price; if prices rise, however, the farmer will lose money. Thus, trading in futures can be very risky.

An *option* is the right, but not the obligation, to buy (or sell) stock or a commodity for a specified price within a specified time period. A *call option* is the right to buy shares of stock at a set price by a certain expiration date. You can exercise the right at any time before the option expires. A *put option* is the right to sell stock at a fixed price until the expiration date. An investor who thinks a stock's price will increase during a short period of time may decide to purchase a call option. On the other hand, an investor who feels a stock's price will decrease during a short period of time may purchase a put option to safeguard the investment. Options are risky business and not for the inexperienced investor.

✔ CHECKPOINT

Why are collectibles risky investments?

Manufacturing

People who work in manufacturing plants are involved in creating new products for the marketplace. In many cases, they work on an assembly line, where their role in the entire process is small. In other cases, they may install a part or complete the assembly of a product to be shipped to a wholesaler, retailer, or the general public.

Most work done in manufacturing is very precise. Robotics and computerized production lines create consistently high-quality products. Workers who run and maintain these machines and tools are highly skilled technicians who can detect even small differences in performance and output.

Those who work in manufacturing are members of a team. They must all work together to use a wide range of skills and knowledge to perform multiple tasks. Many times, team members rotate through different tasks, rather than specializing in a single task.

Employment Outlook

- A slower-than-average rate of employment growth is expected.

Job Titles

- Machine technician
- Machinist
- Assembly line worker

Needed Skills

- A high school diploma or equivalent is typically required.
- On-the-job or specialized training may be required.
- Good math and technical skills, dexterity, and physical strength are desirable.

What's it like to work in . . . *Manufacturing*

Amelia has worked as a team assembler for a local electronics manufacturer for the past five years. She makes an hourly wage of just over $15. She works full time and often has the opportunity for overtime.

Amelia begins her day at the factory at 8 A.M. She uses mechanically controlled tools and instruments to install precision metal parts, which are then passed to the next stage of production. She has rotated among the various assembly line jobs, helping her learn most of the steps in the production and assembly of the parts. This makes it possible for her to work on other parts of the assembly line if needed.

Today, Amelia is attending a training session to learn about a new computerized manufacturing system that is being installed to increase workers' output. She will learn how to operate the system and how it will change her job duties.

What About You?

Are you interested in working with computer-controlled or mechanically controlled machines? Do you work well as a team member? If so, a job in manufacturing might be right for you.

The Career Clusters icons are being used with permission of the: States' Career Clusters Initiative, 2007, www.careerclusters.org

KEY TERMS REVIEW

Match the terms with the definitions. Some terms may not be used.

____ 1. Tangible metals that have known and universal value worldwide

____ 2. Products that are mined or grown

____ 3. Natural, precious stones, such as diamonds, rubies, sapphires, and emeralds

____ 4. Land and buildings that produce income through leasing, renting, or price appreciation

____ 5. A group of investors in the form of a limited partnership who pool their money to buy high-priced real estate as a short-term investment

____ 6. An investment in a pool of mortgages that have been purchased by a government agency or government-sponsored enterprise

a. certificate of participation
b. commercial property
c. commodities
d. gems
e. precious metals
f. real estate investment trust (REIT)
g. real estate syndicate

CHECK YOUR UNDERSTANDING

LO2-1 7. What are some advantages of owning real estate as an investment?

LO2-1 8. How is direct investing in real estate different from indirect investing?

LO2-2 9. Explain how futures contracts work.

APPLY YOUR KNOWLEDGE

LO2-1 10. Describe what it would be like to be a landlord (your responsibilities and duties) if you owned: (a) a single-family house rented to a family, (b) an eight-unit apartment building where you were the resident landlord, and (c) a second home on the beach that you rented to vacationers.

THINK CRITICALLY

LO2-1 11. When it comes to buying and owning rental property, explain the concept of leverage and the need for a positive cash flow.

LO2-2 12. Price changes for precious metals can be very unpredictable. Why would anyone want to invest in these items?

LO2-2 13. Name some collectible items that have increased in value over the years. What do/would you like to collect and why?

The Essential Question *Refer to The Essential Question on p. 461. Real estate, collectibles, and commodities are similar in that they can be difficult to sell and can sometimes result in large losses when sold. However, real estate investments have ongoing value, whereas collectibles and commodities do not provide any current income until sold.*

SUMMARY

19.1

- *Mutual funds use money pooled from many investors to buy securities that fit the fund's stated objectives.*

- *Investors choose mutual funds for the professional management, diversification, liquidity, and relatively small minimum investment required.*

- *Growth funds invest in stocks that are expected to earn future capital gains, whereas income funds invest to provide current income on a steady basis in the form of interest and dividends.*

- *Growth and income funds and balanced funds seek returns from both dividends and capital gains.*

- *Money market funds invest in safe, liquid securities.*

- *Global funds invest in international stocks and bonds as well as U.S. securities.*

- *Index funds try to match the performance of a particular index.*

- *To evaluate a mutual fund, examine its prospectus and other published information on the fund and learn about the fees involved.*

- *Net asset value (NAV) is calculated as the total value of the fund's investments minus its liabilities, divided by the number of outstanding shares.*

19.2

- *If you invest in real estate directly, you own legal title to it. If you invest indirectly, a trustee holds legal title on behalf of the investor group.*

- *Types of real estate properties you can invest in directly include vacant land; single-family houses; rental properties, such as apartment units, condominiums, and duplexes; and vacation homes.*

- *As the owner of rental property, you benefit from tax advantages for depreciation and other expenses. However, there is a risk of having bad tenants or prolonged vacancies, and it may be difficult to resell.*

- *If your rental income from rental property exceeds your mortgage payment, property taxes, and upkeep expenses, then you have a positive cash flow.*

- *You can invest in real estate indirectly through real estate investment trusts (REITs), real estate syndicates, or mortgage pools (in the form of certificates of participation).*

- *Investments in precious metals, gems, collectibles, futures contracts, and options are risky and not for the novice investor.*

APPLY WHAT YOU KNOW

L01-1 1. What makes mutual funds an attractive investment?

L01-1 2. To what type of investor would a money market fund appeal?

L01-2 3. Why should a new investor read the prospectus of a mutual fund carefully before investing in the fund?

L02-1 4. Why might an investor want to buy a piece of vacant land? Why is it important to check a city's zoning laws before purchasing vacant land?

L02-1 5. What benefits does a vacation home offer to an investor? If you don't plan on living in the home full time until you retire, why might you buy it now?

L02-1 6. Why would a bank charge you a higher interest rate on a mortgage for a single-family house that you plan to rent out?

L02-1 7. What is the meaning of the following statement: "Real estate is an illiquid investment"?

L02-2 8. The Internet has provided a new way for buyers and sellers of collectibles to find each other. Search the Internet for websites dealing with a collectible that interests you. How is this item bought and sold online? Is there an association or club for your collectible? If so, how does the site help collectors?

MAKE ACADEMIC CONNECTIONS

L01-1 9. **Communication** Mutual funds are often the best choice for young investors and those wishing to get started investing for the first time. Suppose a person had $500 to invest initially and planned to invest $50 a month thereafter. Write a one-page paper explaining why mutual funds might be a better way to invest this money than collectibles (such as buying Barbie dolls or baseball cards).

L01-1 10. **Research** Visit the website of an investment company that offers a family of mutual funds, such as Vanguard, Fidelity, or Goldman Sachs. Select five of the company's funds that are very different from each other. Describe the investment objective(s) and risk level for each of the five funds. Prepare a graphic that visually displays risk level, going from least risky to most risky. On the graph, identify the most risky fund and the least risky fund that you selected. Then place the three other funds at their appropriate risk levels in between the two extremes. In a paragraph, summarize what you learned about mutual funds and risk.

L02-2 11. **Economics** Gold is a commodity. Most of the U.S. gold supply is stored at Fort Knox. Also stored at Fort Knox is the gold supply of many foreign countries. What is meant by "the gold standard"? Does the United States have a gold standard today? How much gold does the United States have? Conduct online research and prepare a brief history of the importance of gold to the U.S. economy.

L01-1 12. Antonio and Barbara have been married for three years and have managed to save some money to invest. They have decided on mutual funds but don't want to take too much risk. Still, they would like to have some additional income now and also be able to sell the shares for a good profit in five to ten years. Suggest to them some types of mutual funds that might fit their investment goals and risk tolerance levels.

L01-2 13. Compute the NAV for the following three mutual funds:

    a. Fund A is a portfolio worth $12 million that has liabilities of $2 million and 500,000 shares outstanding.

    b. Fund B is a portfolio worth $33 million with liabilities of $6 million and outstanding shares of 850,000.

    c. Fund C is a portfolio worth $1.6 billion that has liabilities of $22 million and outstanding shares of 12.8 million.

L02-1 14. Alena has decided to invest in real estate. She can't decide whether to buy a vacant lot for $25,000 or a one-fourth interest in a four-unit apartment building selling for $400,000. Explain to her the pros and cons of both of these alternatives.

L02-2 15. Your friend George wants to buy a ruby ring at a local jewelry store. He believes that it will be an excellent investment for the future because he intends to sell the ring and make a profit. Explain to him the pros and cons of this type of investment.

EXTEND YOUR LEARNING

L02-1 16. **Legal Issues** Every state has requirements for becoming a licensed real estate broker. What are the requirements in your state? Why do you think those requirements are necessary? What other laws or regulations exist that aim to protect consumers in real estate transactions? If these laws didn't exist, what legal issues might arise?

CHAPTER PROJECT

Obtain a prospectus for a specific mutual fund from a brokerage firm or financial adviser or at an investment company's website. You can also find a prospectus at the SEC's website using its EDGAR search tools. Read the prospectus and report on your findings regarding the objectives (goals) of the fund, risk profile, tax or tax-exempt status, and performance of the fund over the last year and the last five years. Based on your research, would you choose the mutual fund as an investment? Why or why not?

Complete the Guided Decision Making activity for Chapter 19 at ngl.cengage.com/mypf.

Retirement and Estate Planning

20.1 **Planning for Retirement**

20.2 **Saving for Retirement**

Consider This...

"My grandparents said the time to think about retirement is when I get my first job," Susan told her coworkers. "But this isn't really my first job; it's just a part-time job while I go to school. When I get my first career-type job, then I'll start thinking about saving for retirement."

"Your grandparents are right," replied Andrew. "I have a great-uncle who is getting Social Security benefits. He barely has enough money to buy his groceries, pay the rent, and pay for his monthly medication. One of his prescriptions costs over $400 a month. Every time prices go up, he gets stressed out because, in his words, he 'won't get a pay increase to make up for it.' I'm already thinking about the time when I won't be able to work. I think it's important to have enough money to live comfortably. I don't want to have to worry about not having enough money to pay my bills when I retire. I wonder what I need to do to start saving for retirement?"

© Pan Xunbin/Shutterstock.com

Planning for Retirement

LEARNING OBJECTIVES

> LO 1-1 Describe retirement needs for most individuals and families.
> LO 1-2 Discuss estate planning documents and methods to minimize taxes on estates.

KEY TERMS

- reverse mortgage, *475*
- estate, *477*
- will, *477*
- codicil, *478*
- trust, *479*
- probate, *479*
- power of attorney, *480*
- estate tax, *480*
- inheritance tax, *482*
- gift tax, *482*

LO 1-1 Retirement Needs

When you get ready to retire, you will want to have enough financial resources to live comfortably. At that point, many people also want to be able to afford to do the things they didn't have time for while they were working. Social Security and a company-sponsored retirement plan may not be enough to cover the costs of living because inflation will decrease the purchasing power of your retirement savings.

Why is it important to save for retirement during your work life?

How Much Income Will You Need?

Many financial advisers suggest that you will need between 75 and 85 percent of your preretirement income to live comfortably. This percentage may seem high. You may wonder how you can have that kind of income when you are no longer working. In order to have a comfortable retirement, most people need to limit current spending and start saving at the beginning of their work life.

There will be times when you won't have much cash to set aside. You may be paying for a college education, cars, houses, furniture, and so on. However, it is important to save when you can. As your expenses go down, you can save more. With regular saving and investing, your nest egg will grow.

Keep the House or Move?

Once their children are adults, and after retiring, couples are faced with the decision of whether to keep their family home or move. Many couples choose to keep their house because it is paid off and moving can be very expensive. Other couples choose to sell their family home and find something smaller and easier to maintain. Current tax law allows married couples to sell the house they have lived in at least two years without paying taxes on the profits of up to $500,000. (For single people, the tax-free profit limit is $250,000.) Thus, if you choose to sell the family home, you will have the opportunity to keep the proceeds.

The value of most homes appreciates, or increases in value, over time. *Appreciation* is one way that the equity in your home increases. *Equity* in a house is the difference between the property's market value (the amount for which you could sell your home now) and the mortgage balance (the amount you owe on it). As you make mortgage payments over the years, the equity in your home increases while the mortgage decreases. However, equity is not income. It is money "tied up" in property. You can turn equity into income without selling your house by getting a reverse mortgage.

A **reverse mortgage** is a loan available to homeowners age 62 or older that allows them to convert part of their home equity into income. It works the opposite of a mortgage, hence the name "reverse mortgage." Instead of making payments to the lender, the lender makes tax-free monthly payments to the homeowner. This is a loan, however, and it must be repaid in the future. Also, there is a limit on the loan amount. Most reverse mortgages are a percentage of equity. The monthly payments to you will continue until they add up, together with interest, to the amount of equity (loan amount). (See how a reverse mortgage is calculated in the Math Minute on the next page.) Once the full loan amount has been reached, you may have to sell the home or get a regular mortgage to pay off the loan. If you die during the term of the loan, your heirs will have to pay it off. An *heir* is a person who will inherit property from someone who dies. Typically, heirs are the deceased's spouse and/or children. If the property has to be sold in order to pay off the mortgage, the property will not pass to heirs.

What Type of Investment Strategy?

Retired people view investments from a different perspective than when they were younger. Rather than saving for the future, investors at this stage are trying to preserve their financial position—that is, safeguard principal while earning a reasonable return. Thus, fixed-income (low-risk) investments become a more practical choice. Many retirees and people approaching retirement move more of their investments into low-risk options, trading high-potential earnings for lower, but more certain, returns. Also, because monthly income is often their main need, retirees may want to take dividends rather than reinvest them. They often move some of their money out of growth stocks, which earn capital gains in the future, and into income stocks and bonds that produce interest and dividends now.

How Much Insurance?

When you retire, your insurance needs also change. While your need for life insurance decreases, your need for other types of insurance increases.

For retired people, the crucial need for insurance falls in the area of health—being sure that an illness or injury will not wipe out a lifetime of saving and investing. The rapidly rising cost of prescription medications may be a major obstacle, along with high payments for health insurance coverage.

Reverse Mortgage Amount and Payments

A couple owns a home with a market value of $200,000. The unpaid mortgage balance is $40,000. With a reverse mortgage that allows them to borrow up to 80 percent of their equity, they could borrow $128,000 ($160,000 ✕ .80). Amortized over their remaining life expectancy of 20 years and at 7 percent interest, how much could they receive in monthly payments? (*Hint*: Find a mortgage payment calculator online and plug in the years and the interest rate to determine payment.)

Solution:

As determined using a mortgage payment calculator and inserting inputs given, they would receive monthly payments of $992.38.

Mortgage Payment Calculator

Principal	128,000
Interest	7
Number of Years:	20

Calculate

In the United States, *Medicare* is a national social insurance program administered by the U.S. government that guarantees access to health insurance for Americans age 65 and older who have worked and paid into the system. However, since you must be age 65 to be eligible for Medicare, there may be an interim period between your retirement and the start of your Medicare coverage. In this case, you will have to pay for your own health insurance. Also, Medicare may not cover all health care costs. So you will likely need supplemental insurance to cover out-of-pocket expenses. In addition, retired people may need coverage for long-term care in a nursing facility.

How Do You Beat Inflation?

The probable loss of buying power due to inflation is one reason that planning for retirement is so important. As you will recall, *inflation* is a general increase in prices. Because of inflation, the cost of living goes up over time. Price increases reduce buying power. For instance, if prices are increasing at a faster rate than your retirement income, you'll have to cut out something from your budget or dip into your principal to maintain your living standard. Therefore, budgeting must continue throughout retirement. Many seniors choose to work part time to earn more income to offset inflation.

✔ CHECKPOINT

What types of investments should retirees choose?

© simo988/Shutterstock.com

An **estate** is all that a person owns, less debts owed, at the time of the person's death. When people die, their possessions pass to other people, either as directed by the person who died (called the *decedent*) or by the laws of the state in which the person died. The estate may be taxed by the federal and/or state governments. *Estate planning* involves preparing a plan for transferring property during one's lifetime and at one's death. Your goals in estate planning should be to minimize taxes on the estate, to make known how you want your possessions distributed, and to provide for a smooth transfer of your possessions to your loved ones upon your death.

What are the various goals of estate planning?

Estate Planning Tools

To provide for proper disposal of assets and to avoid taxes whenever possible, there are a number of good estate planning tools. These include wills, trusts, joint ownership of assets, and powers of attorney.

Wills

A **will**, or *testament*, is a legal document that tells how an estate is to be distributed when a person dies. The person who makes the will is called the *testator*. In your will, you name an *executor* (also called a personal representative) to carry out your wishes when you die.

Any person who is age 18 or older and of sound mind can make a legally valid will. If your estate is relatively uncomplicated, you can prepare a simple will yourself. A *simple will* is a short document that lists the people whom you want to be your heirs and what you want each to receive. Simple wills take a short time to prepare, and they are fairly standard documents. They can be prepared using an inexpensive kit or software, such as Quicken® WillMaker Plus, that can be purchased online or at an office supplies store. Regardless of whether you draft your will yourself or use a lawyer, you will need two witnesses to your signature. Usually, the witnesses must be people not mentioned in the will who are age 18 or older, unrelated to you, and able to attest to your mental competency at the time you signed the will. An example of a simple will is shown in Figure 20.1.

A *holographic will* is written in a person's own handwriting. It does not require witnesses. In some states, a handwritten will is legally valid if it is entirely written in your own handwriting, is dated and signed, and clearly expresses your intent to make it your will. When handwritten, people may be more likely to *contest the will*, which means that a lawsuit is filed challenging the validity of the will.

FIGURE 20.1 Simple Will

LAST WILL AND TESTAMENT OF ANTHONY JOHN HINTON

I, Anthony John Hinton, of the city of Dayton and state of Ohio, do make, publish, and declare this to be my Last Will and Testament in manner following:

FIRST: I direct that all of my just debts, funeral expenses, and the cost of administering my estate be paid by my personal representative hereinafter named.

SECOND: I give, devise, and bequeath to my beloved daughter, Carol Hinton Campbell, now residing in Englewood, New Jersey, that certain piece of real estate, with all improvements thereon, situated in the same city and at the corner of Hudson Avenue and Tenafly Road.

THIRD: All the remainder and residue of my property, real, personal, and mixed, I give to my beloved wife, Kimberly Sue Hinton, personal representative of this, my Last Will and Testament, and I direct that she not be required to give bond or security for the performance of her duties as such.

LASTLY: I hereby revoke any and all former wills by me made.

IN WITNESS WHEREOF, I have hereunto set my hand this tenth day of October, in the year two thousand --.

Anthony John Hinton
————————————————————
Anthony John Hinton

We, the undersigned, certify that the foregoing instrument was, on the date thereof, signed and declared by Anthony John Hinton as his Last Will and Testament, in the presence of us who, in his presence and in the presence of each other, have, at his request, hereunto signed our names as witnesses of the execution thereof, this tenth day of October 20--; and we hereby certify that we believe the said Anthony John Hinton to be of sound mind and memory.

Vilbin Schaenbar	residing at	251 Wonderly Avenue Dayton, Ohio 45419-2521
Samuel Vance	residing at	3024 James Hill Road Kettering, Ohio 45429-2454
Irene Vasilhous	residing at	423 Goldengate Drive Centerville, Ohio 45459-2459

A person can make a will and make small changes at a later time. A **codicil** is a legal document that modifies parts of a will and reaffirms the rest. A will cannot be legally amended by crossing out or adding words, by removing or adding pages, or by making erasures. A codicil is drawn by an attorney and is executed and witnessed the same as a will.

When people die without a will, they are said to be *intestate*. In that event, the person's property is distributed according to the laws of the state where the decedent died. By having a valid will, you can control what your heirs get, rather than allowing the state to make those decisions. Property reverts to the state when a person dies without heirs.

Trusts

A **trust** is a legal document in which an individual (the *trustor*) gives someone else (the *trustee*) control of property, for ultimate distribution to another person (the *beneficiary*). The trustee may be a financial institution or a person, while the beneficiary can be one or multiple parties.

There are two types of trusts. A trust that exists during the lifetime of the trustor is called *inter vivos*, or a living trust. With a living trust, you simply transfer some property to a trustee, giving him or her instructions regarding its management and disposition while you are alive and after your death.

The other type of trust is called a *testamentary trust* or *trust will*. It takes effect upon the death of a trustor. This type of trust is often used when a trustor wants to leave assets to a beneficiary but doesn't want the beneficiary to receive the assets until a specified time. Such a trust can be valuable if your beneficiaries are minor children. In order for money and property to be left to a minor child, the child must have a *legal guardian* who makes accountings of the child's property and money. Parents of small children typically create trust wills to provide for their children's education and living expenses. Then the balance of the estate is given to the children at some later age when they have reached adulthood.

The purpose of a trust is twofold. First, trusts provide for beneficiaries who might not be able to effectively manage assets for themselves. The trustee is held accountable for how money is spent and how the trust is administered. The trustee must file papers yearly with the court, reporting on how the trust is progressing. Also, the trustee typically receives a fee for these services. Second, a trust can minimize inheritance or estate taxes and avoid probate. **Probate** is the legal process of proving that a deceased person's will is valid and then administering and distributing that person's estate upon death. Probate can be a lengthy process because the estate pays all creditors and probate fees before the balance of the estate is distributed to heirs. Property held in a trust is not subject to probate. Therefore, the property can pass to beneficiaries quickly without a prolonged court proceeding and without the costs of probate.

Joint Ownership

Many people opt to hold title to property through joint ownership. By putting property in joint ownership, two or more people own an undivided interest in the property. Joint ownership of property can exist between spouses, parents and children, other relatives, or any two or more people.

Joint tenancy between spouses is perhaps the most widely used property ownership arrangement. If you and your spouse own property as *joint tenants with right of*

How does joint ownership between spouses affect an estate?

survivorship (JTWROS), the ownership is split 50/50 for the purpose of the estate. If one spouse dies, the surviving spouse automatically becomes the sole owner of the property. No legal action is necessary to transfer title. This form of ownership is commonly used for land, automobiles, residences, bank accounts, and securities.

Two or more people can own property without survivorship. This form of property ownership is known as *tenancy in common*. With tenancy in common, the interest in the property does not automatically pass to the remaining owners as in JTWROS. Instead, each owner leaves his or her share of the property to a beneficiary of his or her choosing.

Joint ownership offers many advantages over holding ownership of property singly. Upon death, title to the property automatically passes to the joint owner or named beneficiary, making probate unnecessary. Joint ownership is also an effective way to avoid inheritance taxes in some states.

Power of Attorney

At some time in your life, you may become incapacitated and unable to make your own decisions. A **power of attorney** is a legal document authorizing someone to act on your behalf. For example, if you become incapable of caring for yourself, the power of attorney gives your appointed person the power to use money from your savings and other accounts or assets to pay your bills and hire people to care for you.

The power of attorney may be limited or general in time or in scope. A *limited power of attorney* may be good for a specified amount of time, such as 30 days or a year, or it may pertain to a particular transaction. A *general power of attorney* gives another person the right to act for you completely.

When you give a power of attorney to another person, you give that person the power to do anything you could have done. Therefore, you should choose a trusted family member, a proven friend, or a reputable and honest professional.

Figure 20.2 shows a power of attorney form. You can hire a lawyer to write your power of attorney, or you can do your own using a kit or software designed for creating legal documents. Often software packages for writing wills contain templates for creating powers of attorney. Websites such as Legal-Zoom also provide power of attorney forms.

Taxation of Estates

Federal and state governments levy various types of taxes that must be taken into consideration when planning your estate, including estate, inheritance, and gift taxes.

Federal Estate Tax

The federal government levies an **estate tax**, which is a tax on property transferred from an estate to its heirs. An estate must be worth more than a certain amount ($5.34 million in 2014) to be subject to this tax. The estate tax is paid from the assets of the estate before anything can be distributed to heirs. An estate may have to sell property or investments in order to pay this tax.

FIGURE 20.2 Power of Attorney

GENERAL POWER OF ATTORNEY

I, [YOUR FULL LEGAL NAME], residing at [YOUR FULL ADDRESS], hereby appoint
_____ of _____, as my Attorney-in-Fact ("Agent").

I hereby revoke any and all general powers of attorney that previously have been signed by me. However, the preceding sentence shall not have the effect of revoking any powers of attorney that are directly related to my health care that previously have been signed by me.

My Agent shall have full power and authority to act on my behalf. This power and authority shall authorize my Agent to manage and conduct all of my affairs and to exercise all of my legal rights and powers, including all rights and powers that I may acquire in the future. My Agent's powers shall include, but not be limited to, the power to:

1. Open, maintain, or close bank accounts (including, but not limited to, checking accounts, savings accounts, and certificates of deposit), brokerage accounts, and other similar accounts with financial institutions.

2. Sell, exchange, buy, invest, or reinvest any assets or property owned by me. Such assets or property may include income-producing or non-income-producing assets and property.

3. Purchase and/or maintain insurance, including life insurance upon my life or the life of any other appropriate person.

4. Take any and all legal steps necessary to collect any amount or debt owed to me, or to settle any claim, whether made against me or asserted on my behalf against any other person or entity.

5. Enter into binding contracts on my behalf.

6. Exercise all stock rights on my behalf as my proxy, including all rights with respect to stocks, bonds, debentures, or other investments.

7. Maintain and/or operate any business that I may own.

My Agent shall be entitled to reasonable compensation for any services provided as my Agent. My Agent shall be entitled to reimbursement of all reasonable expenses incurred in connection with this Power of Attorney.

My Agent shall provide an accounting for all funds handled and all acts performed as my Agent, if I so request or if such a request is made by any authorized personal representative or fiduciary acting on my behalf.

This Power of Attorney shall become effective immediately, and shall not be affected by my disability or lack of mental competence, except as may be provided otherwise by an applicable state statute. This is a Durable Power of Attorney. This Power of Attorney shall continue effective until my death. This Power of Attorney may be revoked by me at any time by providing written notice to my Agent.

Dated _____, 20-- at _____, _____.

[YOUR SIGNATURE]

_____
[YOUR FULL LEGAL NAME]

[WITNESS' SIGNATURE]   [WITNESS' SIGNATURE]

_____   _____
[WITNESS' FULL LEGAL NAME]   [WITNESS' FULL LEGAL NAME]

STATE OF _____, COUNTY OF _____, ss:

The foregoing instrument was acknowledged before me this _____ day of _____, 20-- by [YOUR FULL LEGAL NAME], who is personally known to me or who has produced _____ as identification.

_____
Signature of person taking acknowledgment

_____
Name typed, printed, or stamped

_____
Title or rank

_____
Serial number (if applicable)

State Inheritance Tax

People who inherit property may also have to pay a separate state inheritance tax. The state **inheritance tax** is imposed on an heir who inherits property from an estate. The difference between the federal estate tax and a state inheritance tax lies in who pays the tax. The estate tax is deducted from the value of the estate before distribution to heirs, but the heir pays inheritance taxes on property received. The amount of tax is based on the value of the property in the estate. In states where inheritance taxes are imposed, laws vary widely as to the rate of taxation and the treatment of property to be taxed.

Federal Gift Tax

Gifts are a popular way of distributing some property to loved ones before death to avoid estate and inheritance taxes. However, if you give someone money or property during your life, you may be subject to federal gift tax. A **gift tax** is a tax applied to a gift of money or property. The gift tax is paid by the giver, not the receiver, of the gift.

In 2014 you could have given up to $14,000 per person per year without having to pay a gift tax. A husband and wife may use a technique called *gift splitting*, which allows a married couple to combine their annual exclusion amounts. Therefore, in 2014 a husband and wife together could have given as much as $28,000 to any one person, tax-free. For gifts that exceed the limit, you can either pay the tax on the excess or take advantage of the *unified gift tax credit*, which allows a person to give away up to a specific amount ($5.34 million in 2014) during his or her lifetime. Gifts to your spouse or to a charity are exempt from the gift tax.

The timing of the gift also matters. A gift of personal property (not real estate) given within three years of a person's death may be considered a "gift in contemplation of death." In this event, the gift is included in the value of the estate, rather than making the gift subject to a separate federal gift tax that would be charged to the gift giver. The gift receiver would have to pay the appropriate inheritance taxes on the value of the gift.

It's important not to distribute property that you need in order to live comfortably prior to your death. One way to retain possession is to create a life estate. A *life estate* allows you to pass title to real property to a loved one but retain your right to live on the premises for as long as you live. This means that you cannot be evicted even after the property is in another person's name.

Federal/State Income Taxes

When someone dies, income taxes must be paid on the income that the decedent earned that year and on any income earned by the estate while its assets remain undistributed (such as interest or dividends). The executor or attorney representing the estate must file this tax return and pay the taxes from the estate before the estate can be distributed to heirs.

✔ **CHECKPOINT**

What purposes does a trust serve?

Estate Planning

Estate planners and financial advisers help people prepare for retirement. Their advice includes both analysis and guidance in making investment choices to meet their clients' long-term objectives.

Estate planners use their knowledge of investments, tax laws, and insurance to recommend options for individuals. They develop a comprehensive plan that identifies problem areas, makes recommendations for improvement, and selects investments compatible with the client's goals. They monitor the client's investments and usually meet with each client on a yearly basis to update the client on potential investments and to adjust the client's financial plan if needed.

Planners typically earn their income from commissions on financial products that they sell. In addition, they may also earn a salary or charge an hourly fee.

Employment Outlook

- A much faster-than-average rate of employment growth is expected.

Job Titles

- Estate planner
- Financial adviser
- Personal finance analyst
- Wealth manager

Needed Skills

- A bachelor's or master's degree is required, with emphasis in finance, business, or accounting.
- Financial advisers who buy or sell securities and insurance policies need licenses based on the products they sell.
- A CEP (certified estate planner) certification is recommended for estate planners.
- Excellent math, analytical, and interpersonal skills are needed.

What's it like to work in . . . *Estate Planning*

Ruth is a self-employed estate planner. She has a CEP certification and also has a stockbroker's license, enabling her to sell securities to investors. Her average annual income is $71,000, which she earns by charging a percentage of the clients' assets that she manages.

Ruth currently maintains retirement portfolios for a group of 15 clients. They are a variety of ages, but many are already retired. She provides financial planning advice for her clients, based on their age, life stage, and financial goals.

Ruth's days consist of reviewing her clients' accounts, watching financial and market conditions, and making recommendations for changes. Today she is meeting with one of her clients to review his financial plan and answer questions he may have about current and projected market conditions.

What About You?

Would you like working with people to help them achieve their lifelong goals? Do you enjoy working with financial analysis and numbers? Would you like to be a financial adviser or an estate planner?

KEY TERMS REVIEW

Match the terms with the definitions. Some terms may not be used.

a. codicil
b. estate
c. estate tax
d. gift tax
e. inheritance tax
f. power of attorney
g. probate
h. reverse mortgage
i. trust
j. will

____ 1. A legal document that modifies parts of a will and reaffirms the rest

____ 2. A legal document authorizing someone to act on your behalf

____ 3. A federal tax on property transferred from an estate to its heirs

____ 4. All that a person owns, less debts owed, at the time of the person's death

____ 5. A state tax imposed on an heir who inherits property from an estate

____ 6. The legal process of proving the validity of a deceased person's will and then administrating and distributing the estate upon death

____ 7. A legal document in which an individual gives someone else control of property, for ultimate distribution to another person

CHECK YOUR UNDERSTANDING

LO1-1 8. What is a reverse mortgage? How does a reverse mortgage work?

LO1-2 9. Why is it important to have a will?

APPLY YOUR KNOWLEDGE

LO1-1 10. At what age would you like to retire? Briefly describe your plans for retirement, such as travel and recreation. What things should you consider in the near future in order to meet your retirement goals?

THINK CRITICALLY

LO1-1 11. Why are many young people often reluctant to plan for retirement?

LO1-1 12. Explain how you might invest your money to be sure your income keeps up with inflation.

LO1-2 13. What is a testamentary trust (trust will)? Why is it important? Explain how it is used in estate planning.

The Essential Question *Refer to The Essential Question on p. 474. Planning for retirement involves such things as determining how much income you will need to live comfortably, deciding whether to keep the family home or move, determining an investment strategy, determining your insurance needs, and preparing a plan for transferring property.*

20.2 Saving for Retirement

The Essential Question *What are personal, employer-sponsored, and government sources of retirement income?*

LEARNING OBJECTIVES

> LO 2-1 Discuss features and types of personal retirement plans.
> LO 2-2 Discuss features and types of employer-sponsored retirement plans.
> LO 2-3 Explain benefits available through government-sponsored plans.

KEY TERMS

- individual retirement account (IRA), *485*
- traditional IRA, *485*
- Roth IRA, *486*
- Keogh plan, *486*
- Simplified Employee Pension (SEP) plan, *486*
- defined-benefit plan, *488*
- defined-contribution plan, *488*
- 401(k) plan, *488*
- 403(b) plan, *489*

LO 2-1 Personal Retirement Plans

Personal or individual retirement accounts are a good way to set aside money for the future. For those who are self-employed or who are not covered by employer-sponsored plans, personal retirement plans are very important. You can select from tax-sheltered plans, such as individual retirement accounts, Keoghs, and simplified employee pensions if you qualify, as well as annuities. You should also include some savings and investments on which you have paid taxes along the way.

Individual Retirement Accounts

An **individual retirement account (IRA)** is a retirement savings plan that offers tax advantages and allows individuals to set aside a specified amount each year. The total amount that can be contributed to an IRA is limited. In 2014 the contribution limit was $5,500 per year (or $6,500 if you are age 50 or older). People not covered by a retirement plan at work may contribute the full amount per year, if they wish. Those who do participate in a retirement plan at work can also contribute to an IRA, but they may not be able to contribute the maximum, depending on their income.

There are different types of IRAs, each with their own tax implications. With a **traditional IRA**, you can deduct your contribution each year from your taxable income. This allows you to delay paying tax on that income and the earnings it accumulates until you begin withdrawing the money after age 59½. At that time, your income will likely be lower than it was while you were working. As a result, you would be in a lower tax bracket and would pay less tax. Although you don't have to start making withdrawals when you turn 59½, you must begin making withdrawals, or *required minimum distributions (RMDs)*, from your traditional IRA by age 70½; otherwise, a penalty will be assessed.

© Pan Xunbin/Shutterstock.com

What are the benefits of contributing to a traditional IRA?

A **Roth IRA** is a type of IRA where contributions are taxed, but earnings are not. With a Roth IRA, you pay tax on your income before you put it into the account. After a five-year holding period, and at age 59½, you can begin making tax-free withdrawals. This is the opposite of a traditional IRA, for which you pay tax on the earnings as well as the contributions when you withdraw the money at retirement. RMDs do not apply to Roth IRAs.

For early withdrawals from a traditional or Roth IRA (prior to age 59½ or prior to having the account for 5 years), a 10 percent tax penalty will be applied. In addition, the money withdrawn is subject to federal and state income taxes in the year of withdrawal.

To help lessen your expenses during your retirement, you may want to set up a *Coverdell Education Savings Account (CESA)*, formerly called an educational IRA, if you have children under age 18. Contributions to a CESA are not tax-deductible. It is a trust created for the purpose of paying higher education expenses. Withdrawals for qualified expenses, such as tuition, books, fees, and supplies, are not taxable when withdrawn. This is similar to how a Roth IRA works.

Keogh Plans

A **Keogh plan** is a tax-deferred retirement savings plan available to self-employed individuals. In addition, if you own a small business and have employees, they are eligible to participate in your Keogh plan. However, employees do not contribute to the plan. All contributions come from the business owner, and the contribution rate set by the business owner must be applied uniformly to all employees.

Keogh plans can be structured in various ways. A self-employed person may set an annual goal for funding the plan. In 2014 Keogh contributions were limited to $210,000 or 100 percent of self-employment income (whichever is less). This type of plan may allow high-earning self-employed individuals to save more for retirement than many other plans. Contributions to Keogh plans that are based on profit-sharing were restricted to $52,000 or 25 percent of earned income (whichever is less) in 2014. *Earned income* is your net income after subtracting business expenses, including any contributions to the plan for employees.

The amounts that a self-employed individual contributes are fully tax-deductible. Earnings on Keogh plans are also tax-deferred. Withdrawals cannot be made before age 59½ without penalty, and withdrawals must begin by age 70½.

Simplified Employee Pension Plans

A **Simplified Employee Pension (SEP) plan**, also known as a SEP-IRA, is a tax-deferred retirement plan available to small businesses. SEPs were authorized by Congress to encourage smaller employers to establish employee pension plans with IRAs as a funding method. Many self-employed individuals also use SEPs because they are easier to set up than Keogh plans.

With a SEP plan, all contributions come from the employer; employees cannot contribute. Employers can make an annual tax-deductible contribution of up to 25 percent of the employee's salary or $52,000 (in 2014), whichever is less. These contributions go into a traditional IRA that each employee sets up at a financial institution. Withdrawals cannot be made before age 59½ without penalty and must begin by age 70½. The SEP-IRA works much the same way for self-employed individuals.

Annuities

An *annuity* is a contract between you and an insurance company in which you make a lump-sum payment or series of payments that earn interest in return for regular disbursements, often at retirement. You have the option of receiving your payments for a specific period of time, such as 20 years, or receiving them until your death. In recent years, *tax-sheltered annuities (TSAs)* have become popular because of the tax-free buildup of interest or dividends during the time the annuity contract remains in effect. Such annuities are often used by younger people to save money toward retirement. Before purchasing an annuity, be sure to check the financial standing of the insurance company offering it. Ask about charges, fees, and the expected rate of return.

Pretaxed Savings

Not all of your retirement savings should be tax-deferred. Some should be savings and investments made with *pretaxed income* (income on which you have already paid tax). In fact, many financial advisers recommend that at least half of your retirement savings be pretaxed. By having pretaxed savings and investments as part of your personal retirement plan, you will be able to withdraw these funds at any time, without tax consequences. However, because there is no early withdrawal penalty for these funds, you will have to restrain yourself from spending this part of your nest egg, so that it will be there when you retire.

✔ CHECKPOINT

What is the difference between a traditional IRA and a Roth IRA?

LO 2-2 Employer-Sponsored Retirement Plans

Another source of retirement income may be the retirement plan offered by your company. With *employer-sponsored retirement plans*, you and often your employer contribute to your retirement savings. Contributions and earnings on employer-sponsored plans accumulate tax-free until you receive them.

When participating in employer-sponsored retirement plans, employees are protected under the Employee Retirement Income Security Act (ERISA), enacted in 1974. In addition to safeguarding retirement funds from employer mismanagement, ERISA does the following:

- Requires employers to provide participants with information about the plan's features and funding
- Requires that all participants be treated equally under the plan
- Defines how long a person may be required to work before becoming eligible to participate in a plan, to accumulate benefits, and to have a nonforfeitable right to those benefits (vesting)
- Guarantees payment of certain benefits if a defined plan is terminated

Defined-Benefit Plans

Many larger employers provide defined-benefit plans or pensions for their employees. A **defined-benefit plan** is a company-sponsored retirement plan in which employees receive a set monthly amount for life beginning at retirement based on wages earned and number of years of service. Employees typically do not contribute to the plan; instead, the employer makes the entire contribution to the plan. To become *vested*, or entitled to the full amount in the plan, you may have to work for the company for a specified number of years.

Employees who are vested but leave the company before retirement may withdraw the account balance in cash or "roll it over" (transfer it) to an IRA. In this situation, most people choose to roll the money into an IRA to delay paying taxes on it until retirement. If they take it as cash when they leave the company, they will have to pay tax on the full amount that year plus a 10 percent penalty if they are under age 59½.

Defined-Contribution Plans

A **defined-contribution plan** is a company-sponsored retirement plan in which employees receive a periodic or lump-sum payment based on their account balance and the performance of the investments in their account. Defined-contribution plans are more common than defined-benefit plans at most companies today.

Each company's plan specifies the percentage of salary that an employee may contribute to his or her own account each year. These contributions are often tax-deferred until withdrawn at retirement. The employer may or may not make contributions to the plan. The plan specifies the amount the employer will contribute, if anything. When a plan participant retires or otherwise becomes eligible, his or her benefit is the total amount of money accumulated in the account, including investment earnings on contributions to the account. Two types of defined-contribution plans are 401(k) and 403(b) plans.

401(k) Plans

A **401(k) plan** is a defined-contribution plan for employees of companies that operate for a profit. Under a 401(k) plan, employees choose the percentage of salary they want to contribute to their account. The employer deducts this amount from their paychecks and puts it into the employees' individual accounts. This amount is not part of the employees' taxable income for the year, so they do not have to pay taxes on it until they withdraw the money at retirement. An investment company manages the accounts and invests the money. Usually, employees may select the types of investments they want from among several options offered by the plan.

Frequently, employers match employee contributions by some percentage. For example, for every $1 of salary that employees contribute to their account, the employer may add 50 cents (a 50 percent match). This contribution is pure profit to the employee. In the preceding example, the 50 percent match is the same as making an immediate 50 percent return on your investment!

Employees cannot withdraw funds from their 401(k) without penalty before age 59½, except in the event of death, disability, or financial hardship. They must also begin making withdrawals by age 70½ or otherwise pay a penalty.

Why are 401(k) plans a wise investment choice?

403(b) Plans

A **403(b) plan** is a defined-contribution plan for employees of schools, nonprofit organizations, and government units. Under a 403(b) plan, employees contribute a percentage of their salary toward this tax-deferred account. While the rules may vary slightly, the 403(b) plan operates like a 401(k).

These plans are also known as tax-sheltered annuities because originally annuities were the only type of investments in these plans as permitted by law. Today, 403(b) plans are no longer restricted to annuities and can choose other investments, such as mutual funds. Investment options are still fewer than under a 401(k) plan, however. Earnings are tax-deferred, and early withdrawal penalties apply. Should an employee leave his or her employer, the 403(b) funds can be rolled into an IRA (within a certain time period).

✔ **CHECKPOINT**

What is the main difference between a 401(k) plan and a 403(b) plan?

LO 2-3   **Government-Sponsored Plans**

You may be entitled to benefits from the federal government—in the form of Social Security, military retirement, or veterans' benefits. Many state, county, and city governments also have retirement plans for their employees.

Social Security Benefits

When you retire, you will be eligible for Social Security benefits if you worked for the required number of years (generally, ten years) and paid Social Security taxes during this time. The amount of your benefit is based on your earnings and contributions to Social Security over your lifetime.

Benefits are funded by taxes imposed on wages of employees and self-employed individuals. The employer and employee are each responsible for one-half of the Social Security tax, with the employee's half withheld from his or her paycheck. Self-employed workers are responsible for the entire amount of Social Security tax.

Social Security replaces only about 40 percent of an average wage earner's income after retiring; therefore, it was never intended to fully support people in retirement. Instead, Social Security is designed as a safety net, or supplement to an individual's own retirement savings. To retire comfortably, you must have accumulated your own nest egg apart from Social Security. Social Security laws allow seniors at retirement age to continue working without losing Social Security benefits, which many seniors choose to do to supplement their Social Security income.

Once you have started paying into the system, you can view and print a Social Security benefits statement online by signing up for an account at the Social Security Administration's website (www.ssa.gov). This statement shows a record of the income on which you paid Social Security taxes, how much you can expect to earn in monthly Social Security benefits when you hit retirement age, plus your estimated disability and Medicare benefits. Medicare premiums are deducted from your monthly Social Security payments.

Full Social Security retirement benefits (100 percent) are available at full retirement age (age 67 for people born after 1960). If you delay collecting your Social Security benefits beyond your full retirement age, benefits are increased by a certain percentage up to age 70. The earliest age at which reduced benefits are payable is 62. In addition, if you were married for ten years or more, you may be entitled to receive Social Security benefits based on your spouse's income, even if you are divorced.

Most or all of Social Security retirement benefits are taxable if your total income from all sources exceeds maximum limits that are adjusted from time to time. Cost-of-living adjustments to Social Security benefits are made periodically, subject to the approval of Congress.

Military Benefits

Retired military personnel receive pensions after 20 years of active duty in the U.S. armed forces. Pensions are payable in full regardless of other sources of income and are subject to income taxes. In addition, military retirees may have special privileges, such as the ability to purchase goods through military posts. These benefits can be very attractive, especially for people who retire from the military in their early forties and continue working in different jobs until they reach retirement age.

The Veterans Administration provides regular pensions for survivors of men and women who died while in the armed forces and disability pensions for veterans who were permanently injured while in the armed forces. Veterans may also be entitled to additional benefits, such as low-interest mortgage loans; educational assistance; burial and memorial services; and low-rate car, home, and life insurance.

CHECKPOINT

Why should you not rely solely on Social Security benefits for retirement?

What Is a "myRA"?

In his State of the Union address on January 28, 2014, President Obama announced the creation a new myRA (My Retirement Account) program aimed at helping millions of Americans to start building a nest egg. The myRA program targets low- and middle-income Americans who are not covered by employer-sponsored retirement plans. Anyone with individual income under $129,000 a year, or household income under $191,000 a year, is eligible to invest in these accounts.

Employers who offer the myRA program will not have to administer the plan nor will they be required to contribute to it. Instead, employees who sign up will automatically have a portion of their paycheck directly deposited into their myRA every payday. A minimum contribution of $25 is required to set up a myRA. Workers can contribute as little as $5 per paycheck, and up to $5,500 in contributions can be made in a year.

The account will function like a Roth IRA in that it will allow individuals to invest after-tax dollars and withdraw the money tax-free when they retire. Also, similar to a Roth IRA, the principal can be withdrawn at any time tax-free. However, anyone who withdraws the interest earned on the account before age 59½ will get hit with taxes and has to pay an early withdrawal penalty. The myRA differs from a Roth IRA opened through a bank, brokerage firm, or other financial institution in that it will have no administrative fees. The account will also be invested solely in U.S. government savings bonds, which are backed by the full faith and credit of the U.S. government. This guarantees that employees cannot lose their principal investment.

Employees may keep their myRA if they change jobs. They can also contribute to the account from multiple part-time jobs. Individuals can save up to $15,000, or for a maximum of 30 years (whichever occurs first), and then roll over their myRA to a Roth IRA, which invests in stocks and other securities that provide higher earnings.

It is estimated that half of all full-time workers and 75 percent of all part-time workers are not covered by employer-sponsored retirement plans. Many retirement advocates think the myRA program is an important step toward encouraging millions of Americans with little or no retirement savings to get started.

THINK CRITICALLY

1. Assume that you work for an employer that does not offer an employer-sponsored retirement plan. Would you consider investing in a myRA? Why or why not?

2. What do you see as some of the advantages of the myRA plan?

KEY TERMS REVIEW

Match the terms with the definitions. Some terms may not be used.

____ 1. *A type of IRA where contributions are taxed, but earnings are not*

____ 2. *A tax-deferred retirement plan available to small businesses*

____ 3. *A type of IRA for which you can deduct your contribution each year from your taxable income*

____ 4. *A defined-contribution plan for employees of companies that operate for a profit*

____ 5. *A defined-contribution plan for employees of schools, nonprofit organizations, and government units*

____ 6. *A company-sponsored retirement plan in which employees receive a periodic or lump-sum payment based on their account balance and the performance of investments in their account*

a. 401(k) plan
b. 403(b) plan
c. defined-benefit plan
d. defined-contribution plan
e. individual retirement account (IRA)
f. Keogh plan
g. Roth IRA
h. Simplified Employee Pension (SEP) plan
i. traditional IRA

CHECK YOUR UNDERSTANDING

LO2-1 7. What are required minimum distributions (RMDs)?

LO2-1 8. What is a defined-benefit plan?

LO2-3 9. Who is eligible to collect Social Security retirement benefits?

APPLY YOUR KNOWLEDGE

LO2-2 10. Find an online retirement calculator and input reasonable numbers into the required fields. How can this tool help with retirement planning?

THINK CRITICALLY

LO2-1 11. Explain why your personal retirement plan should contain both tax-deferred options and some pretaxed savings.

LO2-2 12. Suppose your employer offers a 401(k) plan with 50 percent matching. How would contributing to this plan affect your current income? Future income? Do you think participating in this plan is a good idea? Explain.

The Essential Question *Refer to The Essential Question on p. 485. Personal retirement plans include IRAs, Keogh plans, SEP-IRAs, and annuities. Employer-sponsored retirement plans include 401(k) plans and 403(b) plans. Government sources include Social Security and military benefits.*

Assessment

SUMMARY

20.1

- *To have a comfortable retirement, you need to start saving at the beginning of your work life.*

- *The equity you build in your home can be a source of retirement income with a reverse mortgage.*

- *As you near retirement, you may want to switch to less risky investments that emphasize current income over future capital gains.*

- *Estate planning involves preparing a plan for transferring property during one's lifetime and at one's death.*

- *A will specifies how to distribute your assets. A trust is a legal document in which an individual gives someone else control of property, for ultimate distribution to another person.*

- *Joint tenants with right of survivorship (JTWROS) transfers property at death without the costs and time involved in probate.*

- *A power of attorney empowers someone else to act on your behalf.*

- *Various federal and state taxes, such as estate taxes, inheritance taxes, and gift taxes, may be applied to an estate.*

20.2

- *A traditional IRA allows you to delay paying income tax on the contributions until you withdraw the money at retirement age.*

- *With a Roth IRA, you pay taxes on the contributions but pay no taxes on the earnings when withdrawals are made at retirement.*

- *A Keogh plan is a tax-deferred plan for self-employed people. SEP plans are tax-deferred plans for employees of small businesses.*

- *An annuity is a contract between you and an insurance company in which you make a lump-sum payment or series of payments that earn interest in return for regular disbursements, often at retirement.*

- *Under a defined-benefit plan, retired employees receive a set monthly amount for life based on wages earned and number of years of service.*

- *Defined-contribution plans, such as 401(k) and 403(b) plans, allow employees to contribute part of their salary to tax-deferred investments. Employers may or may not contribute matching funds.*

- *You will be eligible for Social Security benefits at retirement if you worked and paid Social Security taxes for the required number of years (generally, ten years).*

APPLY WHAT YOU KNOW

L01-2   1. Visit the Nolo website, which offers legal information for individuals and small businesses. Follow the links to wills, trusts, and probate. Select an article that interests you. Write a paragraph summarizing the key points of the article.

L01-2   2. Prepare a simple will for yourself, using Figure 20.1 as a guide. What would happen to your property if you did not have a will?

L01-2   3. If you had minor children, you might create a trust to provide for them if you were to die while they were still young. Explain why a trust fund is important for managing the financial needs of minors.

L01-2   4. What are some advantages of owning property jointly with another person? Why would people own property as joint tenants with right of survivorship?

L01-2   5. Suppose you gave a $20,000 gift to a friend. Would you pay a gift tax on $20,000 if you were single? If so, how much of the gift amount would be taxed?

L02-1   6. Use the Internet to learn more about Roth IRAs. From the information you find, write a paragraph about Roth IRAs. Who would choose them and why?

L02-1   7. Explain the difference between a traditional IRA and a SEP-IRA. Explain who can have these types of accounts.

MAKE ACADEMIC CONNECTIONS

L01-1   8. **Math** The Andersons, a retired couple, own their house free and clear. It has a current market value of $280,000. They are considering a reverse mortgage with a loan of 80 percent of market value. How much could they borrow? What would they receive in monthly income, for a period of 20 years (12 payments per year) at an assumed interest rate of 5 percent? 6 percent? 7 percent? (*Hint*: Use an online mortgage calculator.)

L01-1   9. **Economics** Inflation is a major consideration for those on fixed incomes, such as retirees. As prices rise, their incomes remain flat. What can retired people do to preserve their purchasing power? Conduct online research on the history of inflation in the United States. Prepare a multimedia presentation that summarizes your findings and explains the best ways to protect your retirement income from the effects of inflation.

L01-2   10. **Communication** Retirement and estate planning is a field of study, with many professionals making a career of providing advice in this area. Some advisers charge fees for their services; others make money based on the retirement tools they sell to customers. Research the types of retirement and estate planning experts who are available to consumers. Report your findings in a two-page paper, citing your sources of information and briefly evaluating each source. Include private-sector as well as government resources.

Solve Problems and Explore Issues

LO1-1 11. Violeta Ramirez has an employer-paid pension of $300 a month and Social Security benefits of $1,100 a month. She owns her home free and clear but has high medical bills. Explain to her how she can use her house equity to generate monthly income for her retirement years.

LO1-2 12. Renee and Ryan own a new car jointly with right of survivorship. Can Renee leave her share of the car to another person when she creates her will? Why or why not?

LO2-1 13. Bob works and earns under $25,000 a year. He has never had an IRA because he thinks that Social Security will be enough for retirement income. Explain how an IRA works and why he needs one.

LO2-1 14. Tanya is self-employed. Every year, she has extra money she could save, but spends it on trips and jewelry instead. She earns above-average income from her business, putting her in a high tax bracket. Explain to her why she should consider a Keogh plan or SEP-IRA.

LO2-3 15. Jackson has worked for over 45 years. He served in the military for 20 of those years. He reaches full retirement age next year. Explain to him the benefits that he might expect to receive.

EXTEND YOUR LEARNING

LO1-2 16. **Legal Issues** Senior citizens often fall victim to scams. One such scam was reported in California. A real estate broker searched for unoccupied homes with delinquent taxes, many of which were owned by senior citizens staying in nursing homes. The broker paid the delinquent taxes and fraudulently transferred the property to his name without the owners' consent. He then rented the homes and kept the money. This crook defrauded homeowners of more than $5 million. How can elderly people protect themselves and their property from scams like this?

CHAPTER PROJECT

When people die, they often leave their estates (assets) to beneficiaries. What is the difference between estate taxes and inheritance taxes? If you inherited $25,000, what federal, state, or other taxes would you have to pay? Could these taxes have been avoided? Explain why or why not. How might you invest your large inheritance for retirement? Find a retirement calculator to estimate how much you can save by the age of 65 if you deposit the full $25,000 into an investment with an expected rate of return of 7 percent. Prepare a report explaining your findings on taxes and your investment choices. Include tables and graphs as visual aids.

Complete the Guided Decision Making activity for Chapter 20 at ngl.cengage.com/mypf.

Warren Buffett

Warren Edward Buffett was born in Omaha, Nebraska, on August 30, 1930. As a child, Buffett displayed an interest in making and saving money. He went door to door selling gum, Coca-Cola, and magazines. For a while, he worked in his grandfather's grocery store. In high school, he also delivered newspapers, sold golf balls and stamps, and detailed cars to earn money he could set aside.

Buffett also developed an interest in the stock market and investing during his childhood. He visited the New York Stock Exchange (NYSE) when he was 10. At age 11, he bought his first shares of stock (three shares of Cities Service Preferred).

LUCAS JACKSON/Reuters /Landov

Buffett enrolled at the Wharton School of Business at the University of Pennsylvania at age 16. He then transferred to the University of Nebraska in 1950, earning his bachelor's degree in business administration. Buffett earned his master's degree in economics from Columbia University in 1951.

In 1956 he formed Buffett Partnership, an investment firm, in his hometown of Omaha. By 1960 Buffett had seven partnerships operating. Because of his partnerships, Buffett became a millionaire by 1962. In that same year, Buffett began buying stock in Berkshire Hathaway, a textile manufacturing firm. He eventually took control of the company in 1966 and is currently the firm's chairman, CEO, and largest shareholder.

Throughout the years, Buffett's practice of "value investing," or investing in stocks of well-known, undervalued companies, made him extremely rich. By 1990 Buffett was a billionaire and was ranked as the world's wealthiest person in 2008 by *Forbes*. Buffett is also one of the world's greatest philanthropists. In June 2006 he announced that he would be giving 99 percent of his fortune away to charity, committing 85 percent of it to the Bill and Melinda Gates Foundation. This donation became the largest act of charitable giving in U.S. history.

THINK CRITICALLY

1. How did Mr. Buffett's childhood experiences and his education help him to succeed as an investor and as a business executive?

2. As a billionaire, Mr. Buffett is an influential man, both nationally and internationally. He is very vocal about financial practices. What does he do with his knowledge and wealth to help others?

Assessing Your Financial Security

Overview

At the end of Unit 3, you explored how to manage your resources. Now you will continue to improve your financial planning. You can protect your financial security through savings, investments, and retirement and estate planning.

Savings

Although saving money takes self-discipline and motivation, it is a key principle of life. People who make a habit of saving regularly, even small amounts, are well on their way to success. Money you set aside today will allow you to make purchases later. It also helps you to plan for life events and be ready for unplanned or emergency needs.

Future Value

When money is deposited in savings, it gains interest until some point in the future when it is withdrawn and spent. *Future value* is the final compounded value of a deposit or series of deposits. By using future value tables (which are built into financial calculators), you can determine how much money you need to set aside today in order to reach a future goal.

Figure U4.1 shows the future value (compound sum) factors to use when computing interest earned at numerous interest rates and allowed to compound for a number of compounding periods. Rather than compute interest

© STILLFX/Shutterstock.com

| FIGURE U4.1 | | Future Value (Compound Sum) of $1 | | | | | | | |

Period					Percent				
	3%	4%	5%	6%	7%	8%	9%	10%	11%
1	1.03000	1.04000	1.05000	1.06000	1.07000	1.08000	1.09000	1.10000	1.11000
2	1.06090	1.08160	1.10250	1.12360	1.14990	1.16640	1.11810	1.21000	1.23210
3	1.09273	1.12486	1.15723	1.19102	1.22504	1.25971	1.29503	1.33100	1.36763
4	1.12551	1.16986	1.21551	1.26248	1.31080	1.36049	1.41158	1.46410	1.51807
5	1.15927	1.21665	1.27628	1.33823	1.40255	1.46933	1.53862	1.61051	1.68506
6	1.19405	1.26532	1.34010	1.41852	1.50073	1.58687	1.66710	1.77156	1.87042
7	1.22987	1.31593	1.40710	1.50363	1.60578	1.71382	1.82804	1.94872	2.07616
8	1.26677	1.36857	1.47746	1.59385	1.71819	1.85093	1.99256	2.14359	2.30454
9	1.30477	1.42331	1.55133	1.68948	1.83846	1.99901	2.17189	2.35795	2.55804
10	1.34392	1.48024	1.62890	1.79085	1.96715	2.15893	2.36736	2.59374	2.83942
11	1.38423	1.53945	1.71034	1.89830	2.10485	2.33164	2.58043	2.85312	3.15176
12	1.42576	1.60103	1.79586	2.01220	2.25219	2.51817	2.81266	3.13843	3.49845
13	1.46853	1.66507	1.88565	2.13203	2.40985	2.71962	3.06581	3.45227	3.88328
14	1.51259	1.73168	1.97993	2.26090	2.57853	2.93719	3.34173	3.79750	4.31044
15	1.55797	1.80094	2.07893	2.39656	2.75903	3.17217	3.64248	4.17725	4.78459
16	1.60471	1.87298	2.18288	2.54035	2.95216	3.42594	3.97031	4.59497	5.31089
17	1.65285	1.94790	2.29202	2.69377	3.15882	3.70002	4.32763	5.05447	5.89509
18	1.70243	2.02582	2.40662	2.54035	3.37993	3.99602	4.71712	5.55992	6.54355
19	1.75351	2.10685	2.52695	3.02560	3.61653	4.31570	5.14166	6.11591	7.26334
20	1.80611	2.19112	2.65330	3.20714	3.86968	4.66096	5.60441	6.72750	8.06231

for each period and add it to the previous balance, you can use this table. For example, if you deposit $5,000 at 8 percent and leave it for five years, compounded semiannually, you would use the table as follows: 8 percent a year is 4 percent per compounding period (8 ÷ 2). Five years, compounded semiannually, is 10 compounding periods (5 × 2). In the table, the factor for 4 percent and 10 periods is 1.48024. Multiply $5,000 by 1.48024, and the account total will be $7,401.20 after 5 years, at 8 percent interest, compounded semiannually.

When you make regular payments (rather than deposit a lump sum at irregular intervals) to your account, you can use another table to shortcut the calculations. Figure U4.2 shows the future value (compound sum) factors used to compute future value of an annuity. (You will recall that an annuity is a sum of money set aside regularly, such as monthly, for the future.) Instead of calculating interest, adding a deposit, calculating interest, and so on, the table shown in Figure U4.2 simplifies the procedure. For example, assume you deposit $1,000 per year for 12 years, earning 6 percent interest a year. In the table, the factor for 6 percent and 12 periods is 16.86994. Multiplying $1,000 by 16.86994, you get $16,869.94, which is the value of the deposits at the end of 12 years.

Using the two tables shown in Figures U4.1 and U4.2, complete Worksheet 1 (Future Values) provided for you in the *Student Activity Guide* and also presented for reference on the next page.

Future Value (Compound Sum) of an Annuity of $1

Period					Percent				
	3%	4%	5%	6%	7%	8%	9%	10%	11%
1	1.00000	1.00000	1.00000	1.00000	1.00000	1.00000	1.00000	1.00000	1.00000
2	2.03000	2.04000	2.05000	2.06000	2.07000	2.08000	2.09000	2.10000	2.11000
3	3.09090	3.12160	3.15250	3.18360	3.21490	3.24640	3.27810	3.31000	3.34210
4	4.18363	4.24646	4.31013	4.37462	4.43994	4.50611	4.57313	4.64100	4.70973
5	5.30914	5.41632	5.52563	5.63709	5.75074	5.86660	5.98471	6.10510	6.22780
6	6.46841	6.63298	6.80191	6.97532	7.15329	7.33593	7.52334	7.71561	7.91286
7	7.66246	7.89829	8.14201	8.39384	8.65402	8.92280	9.20044	9.48717	9.78327
8	8.89234	9.21427	9.54911	9.89747	10.25980	10.63663	11.02847	11.43589	11.85943
9	10.15911	10.58280	11.02656	11.49132	11.97799	12.48756	13.02104	13.57948	14.16397
10	11.46388	12.00611	12.57789	13.18080	13.81645	14.48656	15.19293	15.93743	16.72201
11	12.80780	13.48635	14.20679	14.97164	15.79360	16.64549	17.56029	18.53117	19.56143
12	14.19203	15.02581	15.91713	16.86994	17.88845	18.97713	20.14072	21.38428	22.71319
13	15.61779	16.62684	17.71298	18.88214	20.14064	21.49530	22.95339	24.52271	26.21164
14	17.08632	18.29191	19.59863	21.10507	22.55049	24.21492	26.01919	27.97498	30.09492
15	18.59891	20.02359	21.57856	23.27597	25.12902	27.15211	29.36092	31.77248	34.40536
16	20.15688	21.82453	23.65749	25.67253	27.88805	30.32428	33.00340	35.94973	39.18995
17	21.76159	23.69751	25.84037	28.21288	30.84022	33.75023	36.97371	40.54470	44.50084
18	23.41444	25.64541	28.13239	30.90565	33.99903	37.45024	41.30134	45.59917	50.39594
19	25.11687	27.67123	30.53900	33.75999	37.37897	41.44626	46.01846	51.15909	56.93949
20	26.87037	29.77808	33.06595	36.78559	40.99549	45.76196	51.16012	57.27500	64.20283

WORKSHEET 1
Future Values

Directions: For numbers 1–4, use Figure U4.1 to compute the value of each deposit at the rate given. For numbers 5–8, use Figure U4.2 to compute the value of each annuity at the given rate.

Future Value (Compound Sum) of $1

Deposit	Time	Annual Rate	Value
1. $5,000 Compounded quarterly	4 years	12%	$_____
2. $1,000 Compounded semiannually	10 years	6%	$_____
3. $7,500 Compounded annually	8 years	8%	$_____
4. $3,850 Compounded semiannually	2 years	8%	$_____

Future Value (Compound Sum) of an Annuity

Deposit	Time	Annual Rate	Value
5. $500/year	5 years	6%	$_____
6. $100/year	10 years	9%	$_____
7. $900/year	2 years	8%	$_____
8. $250/year	10 years	5%	$_____

Your Savings Plan

For your own personal savings plan, you should set aside a predetermined amount each month. It is often more difficult to set aside lump sums. However, should you inherit money or earn a large bonus, you can always make lump-sum deposits. Complete Worksheet 2 (Your Savings Plan) provided for you in the *Student Activity Guide*, and also presented for reference below, to see how funds set aside now can grow larger in the future.

Investments

After you have provided for savings, you can then begin investing. Investments can bring higher returns than savings, but they also carry higher risk.

WORKSHEET 2
Your Savings Plan

Directions: In the spaces, project what you could save presently (either lump sum or monthly payment), and calculate the future value in 5, 10, and 20 years at the interest rate shown. Then project what you would like to be able to save (lump sum or monthly payment) in 5, 10, and 20 years.

Savings Amount	Interest Rates	Future Value
$_____ What you could set aside today	6% per year, compounded annually, in 5 years	$_____
	6% per year, compounded annually, in 10 years	$_____
	6% per year, compounded annually, in 20 years	$_____
$_____ What you want to be able to save 5 years from now	8% per year, compounded semi-annually, in 10 years	$_____
	6% per year, compounded annually, in 20 years	$_____
$_____ What you want to be able to save 10 years from now	5% per year, compounded annually, in 20 years	$_____
	6% per year, compounded semi-annually, in 5 years	$_____

Make a plan for the amount of money you will set aside now and in the future.

Directions: In the spaces below, write when you will set aside money, how much you will set aside and how often, your goal amount, and the future purpose of the amount saved.

Date	Amount Set Aside/How Often/Goal	Future Purpose of Saved Amount
_____	$_____ / _____ / _____	_____
_____	_____ / _____ / _____	_____
_____	_____ / _____ / _____	_____

Investments and Risk

When choosing investments, you should first determine your risk comfort level. Complete Worksheet 3 (Risk Aptitude Test) provided for you in the *Student Activity Guide* and also presented for reference below.

WORKSHEET 3
Risk Aptitude Test

Directions: Answer the following questions, recording your answers in the spaces provided. Then compute your risk aptitude score as shown.

_____ 1. You have an extra $100 left over from your year-end bonus. Would you rather (a) put it all in savings, (b) spend some and save a little, (c) bet it on a lottery.

_____ 2. You are ready to buy a new car. Will it be a (a) small economy car, (b) conventional, standard car with a variety of options, (c) sports car emphasizing speed, style, or performance.

_____ 3. You have won a weekend trip of your choice. Will you (a) take the cash value of the prize instead, (b) go on a cruise or sightseeing trip, (c) fly to a mountain lodge for skiing.

_____ 4. You are looking for a job. Which of these is most important to you? (a) job security (permanent employment), (b) higher salary with moderate security, (c) higher pay and less job security.

_____ 5. You are betting on a horse race. Which wager will you make? (a) bet on the favorite, even though winnings will be small, (b) select a horse with a good chance of winning and moderate payback if it does, (c) pick a long shot with high payback.

_____ 6. You have a mortgage on your home. Will you (a) make regular payments, paying off the loan on schedule, (b) repay the loan quicker than required so you can save interest, (c) refinance the loan and use the extra cash for other investments.

_____ 7. You are considering changing jobs. Which sounds best? (a) joining a well-established firm and doing similar work, (b) associating with a new company in a newly created position, (c) going into business for yourself.

_____ 8. You have a schedule conflict. The following three events are all scheduled for the same day and time. Which will you choose? (a) attending a seminar, (b) working on a committee, (c) giving a speech to a group of students.

_____ 9. Your dinner is "on the house." Which will you choose? (a) cold turkey sandwich and salad, (b) enchilada with hot peppers, (c) rare sirloin with fries.

_____ 10. You have a delayed flight, and your plane will be four hours late. Will you (a) read a book and wait, (b) take in a short sightseeing trip, (c) book another flight.

Scoring: Give yourself 1 point for each question you marked (a); 3 points for each (b); and 5 points for each (c). Scores 40 and above indicate willingness to take risk (you are a risk taker); scores between 25 and 40 indicate a willingness to take moderate risk; and scores below 25 show high risk aversion. A score of 30 is average.

Analyzing Your Score:

Based on your score, what are some investments that have the amount of risk you are willing to take? (See Chapter 16.)

Worksheet 3 will help you assess your tolerance for risk. If you find that you are risk averse, you should choose low-risk investments to avoid stress. If you determine that you are a risk-taker, you can take maximum risks and enjoy the excitement of uncertainty. Most people fall somewhere in the middle and should try to balance their investments.

Investment Strategy

An *investment strategy* is a plan that examines potential returns and rates investments according to desirability. To measure investment potential, two standards apply: the rate of inflation and the overall performance of the stock market. Inflation may be averaging 3 to 6 percent, and if your investment matches or exceeds that rate, you've done well. To estimate the return you're getting, follow the formula in Figure U4.3.

Suppose that four years ago you purchased ten shares of stock at $35 each. The stock is now trading at $38.50 per share. You have received dividends of $.50 per share for four years. Computation of the average rate of return is shown in Figure U4.4.

If inflation averaged less than 3.9 percent during those four years, your investment was worthwhile. However, if the inflation rate was higher than your average return of 3.9 percent, you should sell that investment.

FIGURE U4.3	Average Rate of Return Formula

Current market value of investment	$ _____	A
Less: Original price paid for investment	_____	B
Gain (loss) (A − B)	$ _____	C
Plus: Dividends, interest, and other revenue you've received from the investment	_____	D
Total gain (loss) (C + D)	$ _____	E
Average yearly gain (loss) (E ÷ years owned)	$ _____	F
Average rate of return (F ÷ B)	$ _____%	G

FIGURE U4.4	Example Calculation of Average Rate of Return

Current market value ($38.50 × 10 shares)..................	$ 385.00	A
Less: Original price ($35.00 × 10 shares)......................	−350.00	B
Gain..	$ 35.00	C
Plus: Dividends ($0.50 × 10 shares × 4 years)..............	20.00	D
Total gain..	$ 55.00	E
Average yearly gain ($55.00 ÷ 4 years)........................	$ 13.75	F
Average rate of return ($13.75 ÷ $350.00)....................	3.9%	G

Now you can use this same formula to evaluate and rank a group of investments. Complete Worksheet 4 (Investment Analysis) provided for you in the *Student Activity Guide* and also presented for reference below.

WORKSHEET 4
Investment Analysis

Directions: Calculate the average gain per year and average rate of return on investments shown, and rank the investments in order of desirability.

Asset Purchased	Original Price	Years Held	Current Value	Dividends or Interest Received	Avg. Yearly Gain	Avg. Rate of Return	Rank
H&H Stock 25 shares	$14.00/sh	10	$16.00	$.30/share/ year	_____	_____	_____
Time CD	$5,000	5	$5,000	$1,055	_____	_____	_____
Mutual Funds 33 shares	$18.50/sh	7	$17.50	$.35/share/ year	_____	_____	_____
Gold 50 troy oz.	$1,325/oz.	3	$1,262/oz.	0	_____	_____	_____
ATZ Stock 50 shares	$29.50/sh	5	$35.50	$.50/share/ year	_____	_____	_____

Your Investment Plan

A good investment plan should start with low-risk, predictable, and stable options. Then as your comfort level increases and you have more money to risk, expand into moderate and high-risk ventures with greater potential profits. Complete Worksheet 5 (Investment Plan) provided for you in the *Student Activity Guide* and also presented for reference on the next page. You may wish to refer to Chapters 17–19 to examine your options as you plan for future investments.

Retirement

The time to begin planning for retirement is now—at the beginning of your work career. Because people are living longer and enjoying healthier lives, it is important to consider those post-working years. With adequate financial resources, retirement can be fun, satisfying, and enjoyable.

The most difficult part of retirement planning is estimating your postretirement income and needs. Although living expenses generally decrease following retirement, many financial advisers suggest that you will still need between 75 and 85 percent of your preretirement income to live comfortably. The types of expenses also change. Health care will become a major budget item, while house payments disappear as mortgages are paid off.

Between today and the day you retire, inflation will likely continue to be an issue. However, your investments and savings should grow at a slightly faster pace. Therefore, when planning for retirement needs, prepare a budget based on today's dollars. Complete Worksheet 6 (Retirement Plan) provided for you in the *Student Activity Guide* and also presented for reference on the next page.

Completing the retirement plan in Worksheet 6 should convince most people of the need for multiple sources of income. You cannot rely on Social Security benefits alone. Keep in mind that some income sources will have a tax advantage and others will not. For example, when you make withdrawals from a traditional IRA or other tax-deferred account, such as a 401(k) or 403(b), you will pay income taxes on the withdrawn amounts as current income. When computing the future monthly income to be derived from such sources, be sure to subtract the taxes. (A good rule of thumb is to subtract 25 percent for taxes.)

Estate Planning

You learned about many aspects of estate planning in Chapter 20, but there are additional matters to consider. If you become ill and incapacitated, you should devise an advance directive in the event that you are unable to make medical care decisions on your own behalf. An *advance directive* is a written statement of a person's wishes regarding medical treatment. The two most common types of advance directives are the physician's directive and the health care power of attorney.

A *physician's directive*, also known as a *health care directive* or *living will*, states the kind of medical or life-sustaining treatments a person would want if he or she becomes seriously or terminally ill. It is used only if the individual has become unable to give informed consent or refusal due to incapacity. Figure U4.5 is a sample physician's directive.

A *health care power of attorney* is a written authorization that names another person (typically a loved one or family member) as a representative and allows that person to make medical decisions on one's behalf should one become incapacitated and unable to make their own decisions. Unlike the physician's directive, the health care power of attorney is nonspecific in the decisions that a representative will make; it leaves some discretion to the representative.

You should make copies of your advance directives and give them to loved ones and/or family members who might have input in decisions on your behalf. You should also give copies of your advance directives to your physicians and ask that they be made part of your medical record.

FIGURE U4.5 Physician's Directive

PHYSICIAN'S DIRECTIVE

To My Physicians and Health Care Providers:

In the event that I become incapacitated and unable to make my own choices, I specifically make the following directive(s) regarding my health care (I have checked all that apply):

_____ If I am in a continuous state of nonresponsiveness for a period of a week or longer and two or more doctors have determined that I will not recover, then I wish to have all life support removed within 24 hours of such determination.

_____ If I am in a continuous state of nonresponsiveness for a period of a week or longer and two or more doctors have determined that I will not recover, then I wish to have nutrition and comfort services only.

_____ If I am in a continuous state of nonresponsiveness for a period of a week or longer and two or more doctors have determined that I will not recover, then I wish to have all efforts continue to be made until one month or 30 days have passed. If I continue to show no signs of responsiveness, then I request that all life support be removed within 24 hours of such determination.

_____ I specifically request a do-not-resuscitate (DNR) order. Take no extraordinary measures to revive me through CPR should I suffer a condition that causes my heart and breathing to stop.

Date: _____ Signature: _____

Risk Management

© Monkey Business Images/Shutterstock.com

Unit 5 introduces you to risk. In Chapter 21, you will find out what it is and how it will affect you. Insurance is the concept of sharing risk based on the laws of probability. You will learn about insurance and how to manage your risks by devising a risk management plan.

In Chapter 22, you will learn about property and liability insurance. Although you may not own real property now, you most likely own personal property, from technological devices to collections of popular items of culture. Currently, your property is covered by your parents' homeowners insurance. However, when you establish your own household, you need to consider purchasing your own insurance.

The unit concludes with a discussion on health insurance. In Chapter 23, you will learn about the various group and individual health care plans offered. This chapter also explores the importance of having life insurance.

© Pan Xunbin/Shutterstock.com

CHAPTER 21

Introduction to Risk Management

21.1 Understanding Risk

21.2 Managing Risk

Consider This...

Giang was visiting with her financial planner and discussing plans for purchases and investments in the future. Her planner asked about her risk management plan.

"I have basic insurance on my car," she answered, "but I don't really know whether it's adequate. I hear a lot about life insurance, but I haven't bought a policy. I'm renting an apartment, so I have considered getting renters insurance. However, I don't have much room in my budget, and I can't afford to make big insurance payments. Still, I don't want to take chances that could drain my savings if I'm not properly insured. You've mentioned having a risk management plan. What is that? Is that the same thing as buying insurance?"

© Pan Xunbin/Shutterstock.com

The Essential Question *What are types of risk, and how can you spread that risk to lower your financial burden?*

LO 1-1 Types of Risk

Risk is a state of uncertainty where certain situations may result in loss or another undesirable outcome. *Uncertainty* is the likelihood that something will or will not happen. In other words, there is more than one possibility. For example, the weather forecast may call for a 50 percent chance of rain.

Chapter 16 described one type of risk (investing risk) as the chance of financial loss from a decline in an investment's value. There are many other types of risk you will face in your lifetime.

Pure Risk

Pure risk is a chance of loss with no chance for gain. Pure risks are random, meaning they can happen to anyone. Examples of pure risk include:

- Accidents resulting in physical injury and damage to property
- Illnesses that people get throughout life, as a part of aging
- Acts of nature, resulting in damage to persons and property

However, it is possible to do things to help protect yourself from the consequences of these types of risk. Everyone should have a plan in place in the event of a pure risk because the consequences are often serious and can even be catastrophic, affecting both your life and your lifestyle.

Insurable Risk

You can reduce negative consequences of pure risk by purchasing insurance. **Insurance** is a

What are some types of risk that we experience during our lives?

method for spreading individual risk among a large group of people to make losses more affordable for all. An **insurable risk** is a pure risk that is faced by a large number of people and for which the amount of the loss can be predicted. Insurance companies can make these predictions by examining the amount of loss incurred from past events, such as flooding.

To purchase insurance, you must have an insurable interest to protect. An **insurable interest** is any financial interest in life or property such that, if the life or property were lost or harmed, the insured would suffer financially. For example, you cannot buy insurance on someone else's house. Unless you own the house, you would not suffer a financial loss if it burned down. However, if you depend on your spouse's income to live, then you have an insurable interest in your spouse and can buy insurance on his or her life.

There are three major insurable risks: personal, property, and liability. You should consider each of these risks as you make plans to protect your financial interests. Figure 21.1 gives examples of common insurable risks and ways to protect yourself or to reduce their impact on you financially.

Personal Risk

A **personal risk** is the chance of loss involving your income and standard of living. You can protect yourself and others who depend on your income from personal risks by buying life, health, and disability insurance.

Property Risk

The chance of loss or harm to personal or real property is called **property risk**. For example, your home, car, or other possessions could be damaged or destroyed by fire, theft, wind, rain, accident, and other hazards. To protect against such risks, you can buy property insurance.

FIGURE 21.1   Common Risks

Risks	Causes (Perils)	Ways to Protect Yourself
1. Losing job (income)	Poor economy Company's financial condition Job-skills obsolescence	Unemployment insurance Learn new skills; make 　yourself more valuable
2. Illness or injury	On-the-job accident Chronic health condition or handicap	Health insurance Disability insurance Retraining programs
3. Death of wage earner	Dangerous activities including 　sports or job Illness	Life insurance Get training/lessons Take safety precautions
4. Liability for others' injuries	Careless driving Hazard at home/place of work	Liability insurance Signs, warnings, 　supervised uses
5. Loss of property to theft	Vehicle stolen Robbery	Property insurance Park in well-lit and 　secure places Locks/security devices

Liability Risk

A **liability risk** is the chance of loss that may occur when your errors or actions result in injuries to others or damages to their property. For example, you could accidentally cause injury or damage to others or their property while driving a car. Or a person could fall and break an arm because of your home's crumbling front steps. Liability insurance will protect you if others sue you for injuring them or damaging their property.

Economic Risk

Everyone faces risks due to the current state of the economy. **Economic risk** may result in gain or loss because of changing economic conditions. For example, when the business cycle is in a period of recovery or growth, most people and businesses are realizing gains in their financial position. However, the economy can slow down (and go into a recession if the slowdown lasts for very long). During this time, many people lose their jobs and are unable to buy goods and services. As a result, many businesses find themselves unable to meet their debts. Figure 21.2 is an illustration of the business cycle.

FIGURE 21.2 The Business Cycle

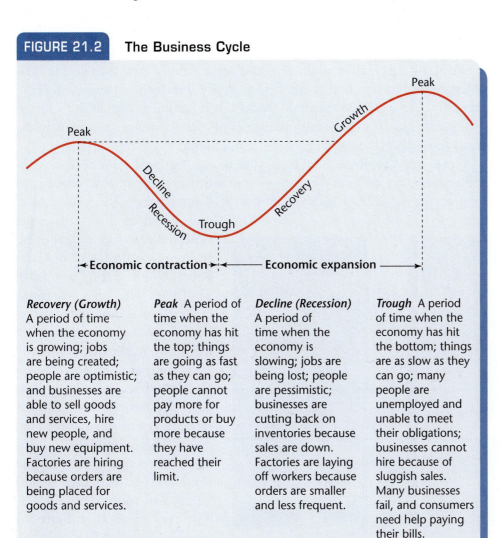

Recovery (Growth) A period of time when the economy is growing; jobs are being created; people are optimistic; and businesses are able to sell goods and services, hire new people, and buy new equipment. Factories are hiring because orders are being placed for goods and services.

Peak A period of time when the economy has hit the top; things are going as fast as they can go; people cannot pay more for products or buy more because they have reached their limit.

Decline (Recession) A period of time when the economy is slowing; jobs are being lost; people are pessimistic; businesses are cutting back on inventories because sales are down. Factories are laying off workers because orders are smaller and less frequent.

Trough A period of time when the economy has hit the bottom; things are as slow as they can go; many people are unemployed and unable to meet their obligations; businesses cannot hire because of sluggish sales. Many businesses fail, and consumers need help paying their bills.

Speculative Risk

A **speculative risk** may result in either gain or loss. For example, if you buy gold, futures, options, or commodities as investments, you could either make a lot of money or lose a lot of money. Because speculative risks are not "accidental" or random and may result in either gain or loss, you cannot protect yourself from losses in a traditional manner. While *hedging* (making an investment to help offset against loss) is a technique used to help reduce losses from such risky acts, it does not reduce the risk itself.

✔ CHECKPOINT

What are the three types of insurable risk?

LO 1-2   Spreading the Risk

You face risks every day. From the moment you get out of bed, you take chances. You could slip and fall. You could have an accident in the kitchen. You could have your stereo stolen or injure another person or property while driving your car. Insurance serves as an excellent risk management tool. It provides relief from fear of severe financial loss due to events beyond your control. Although most adults purchase some form of insurance during their lifetime, such as life, health, liability, disability, homeowners, and auto, many do not understand how insurance works. It is helpful to familiarize yourself with some basic insurance terminology. Figure 21.3 illustrates the many insurance terms that all consumers need to understand.

Here's an example of how insurance works. Suppose your textbook for this class costs $60. If you lose it, you will have to pay that amount to replace it. An average of 1 out of every 10 textbooks is lost each school year. Based on this statistic, the expected losses in a class of 30 students would be 3 books, at a total cost of $180 (3 × $60). To lower the cost of these expected losses to each student, the class could establish an insurance company. An insurance company, or *insurer*, is a business that agrees to pay the cost of potential future losses in exchange for regular fee payments. If every student contributed $6 to the company, the total of $180 collected would be used to replace lost books. The cost to each student for a lost book would be only $6, rather than the full $60.

How does insurance help protect you from financial loss?

© iStock.com/BrianAJackson

FIGURE 21.3 **Insurance Terminology** 513

Actuarial table A table of premium rates based on ages and life expectancies

Actuary A specialist in insurance calculations and statistics

Beneficiary A person named on an insurance policy to receive the benefits from the policy

Benefits Sums of money to be paid for specific types of losses under the terms of an insurance policy

Cash value The amount of money payable to a policyholder upon discontinuation of a life insurance policy

Claim A policyholder's request for reimbursement for a loss under the terms of an insurance policy

Coverage Protection provided by the terms of an insurance policy

Deductible The specified amount of a loss that the policyholder pays before the insurer is obligated to pay anything; the insurance company pays only the amount in excess of the deductible

Exclusions Specified losses that the insurance policy does not cover

Face amount The amount stated in a life insurance policy to be paid upon death

Grace period The additional time after the premium due date that the insurer allows the policyholder to make the payment without penalty (usually 30 days)

Hazard A condition that creates or increases the likelihood of some loss; for example, defective house wiring can increase the likelihood of a fire

Insurance agent A professional insurance salesperson who acts for the insurer in negotiating, servicing, or writing an insurance policy

Insured The person or company protected against loss (not always the owner of the policy)

Insurer The insurance company who provides insurance coverage for a policyholder

Loss An unexpected reduction in value of the insured's property caused by a covered peril; the basis of a valid claim for reimbursement under the terms of an insurance policy

Peril An event whose occurrence can cause a loss; people buy policies for protection against such perils as a fire, storm, explosion, accident, or robbery

Probability The mathematics of chance, or statistical likelihood that something will happen

Proof of loss The written verification of the amount of a loss that must be provided by the insured to the insurer before a claim can be settled

Standard policy The contract form that has been adopted by many insurers, approved by state insurance departments, or prescribed by law (modifications are made to suit the needs of the individual)

Unearned premium The portion of a paid premium that the insurer has not yet earned because the policy term has not ended; the unearned premium is returned to the policyholder when a policy is canceled

Experts believe that in order to reduce teen driving accidents, the most effective tactic is to limit teens' driving risk exposure. For example, some states impose night driving and passenger restrictions for beginning drivers and require higher ages for initial licensure. At the same time, very few states have laws that regulate elderly drivers. This group often continues to drive after their vision, reflexes, hearing, and other skills necessary for safe driving have diminished.

THINK CRITICALLY

Do you think that stricter teen driving rules are effective? Do they infringe on teens' rights? Do you think that restrictions should be placed on older drivers? What would you recommend? Explain your answer.

When people buy insurance, they join a risk-sharing group by purchasing a written insurance contract (a policy). Under the policy, the insurer agrees to assume an identified risk for a fee, called the **premium**, usually paid at regular intervals by the owner of the policy (the policyholder). The insurer collects insurance premiums from policyholders under the assumption that only a few policyholders will have financial losses at any given time.

Insurers set premiums based on *statistical probability*. In other words, they estimate the likelihood of potential losses. They gather and analyze historical data to determine how many of a particular type of loss occurred, on average, in a population over a given time period. From this analysis, they can predict approximately how many such losses to expect among their policyholders over a similar future time period, such as a year. For example, in a sample of 100,000 drivers under the age of 18, an insurer can predict approximately how many will have accidents in a given year.

The higher the probability of a loss occurring, the higher the premium for insuring against it. Remember that insurers deal in averages. They cannot predict which specific individuals will suffer losses. To make a profit, the insurer must collect more in premiums than it pays out for losses and operating expenses. In years when a catastrophic disaster or multiple major disasters occur, such as hurricanes, floods, and earthquakes, an insurer may pay out more in benefits than it receives in premiums. This is why in some states, such as Florida, the cost of homeowners insurance is so high. The probability of a hurricane or other large storm is very likely to happen, so the insurance companies are taking considerable risk with these policies.

Insurance is not meant to enrich—only to compensate for actual losses incurred. This principle is called indemnification. **Indemnification** is the process of putting the policyholder back in the same financial condition he or she was in before the loss occurred. If the insured tries to make money by filing false insurance claims, he or she is committing *insurance fraud*, which is deception for the purpose of unlawful gain. Insurance fraud is a crime punishable by law, and it results in higher insurance rates for everyone.

✔ CHECKPOINT

How do insurance companies determine the cost of premiums?

Insurance

Insurance agents help people select insurance policies that provide the best protection for their lives, health, and property. Many insurance agents also offer financial planning services, such as retirement planning and estate planning.

Insurance sales agents spend much of their time contacting potential customers. They also maintain records, handle policy renewals, and help policyholders settle claims.

Insurance agents may work exclusively for one insurance company (captive agents), or they may work for an insurance brokerage (independent insurance agents). Captive agents sell only policies provided by the company that employs them, whereas independent insurance agents sell the policies of several companies. They match clients' needs with the companies that offer the best rates and coverage.

Employment Outlook

- An average rate of employment growth is expected.

Job Titles

- Insurance agent
- Insurance broker
- Claims adjuster

Needed Skills

- A high school diploma is typically required, although a bachelor's degree in business, finance, or economics can improve job prospects.
- Agents must obtain a license in the states where they work. In most states, licenses are issued only to those who pass state exams. Continuing education courses are also often required.
- Analytical and communication skills are important.

What's it like to work in . . . *Insurance*

Mylee works as an independent insurance agent. She received her license shortly after graduating from college, where she earned a bachelor's degree in finance. On average, she earns $51,500 yearly through commissions based on the type and amount of insurance she sells.

This morning, Mylee is meeting with new clients—a young married couple who have just purchased their first home. She will describe the kinds of risks the couple may face at this stage of their lives, including personal, property, and liability risks, and explain the types of coverage available that will help minimize their financial risk. She will use the information gathered to put together an insurance policy that will meet their needs.

Mylee will check coverage and rates with several insurance companies to see which one offers the best policy for her new clients. After selling the policy, she will meet with the couple to ensure that they understand the deductibles, exclusions, and claim procedures outlined in the policy.

What About You?

Would you like to help people assess and plan for risks? Would a career in insurance be right for you?

The Career Clusters icons are being used with permission of the: States' Career Clusters Initiative, 2007, www.careerclusters.org

KEY TERMS REVIEW

Match the terms with the definitions. Some terms may not be used.

____ 1. A fee paid by the policyholder at regular intervals to the insurer for insurance

____ 2. A risk that may result in either gain or loss

____ 3. The process of putting the policyholder back in the same financial condition he or she was in before a loss occurred

____ 4. A financial interest in life or property

____ 5. A chance of loss with no chance for gain

____ 6. A risk that may result in gain or loss because of changing economic conditions

____ 7. A pure risk that is faced by a large number of people and for which the amount of the loss can be predicted

____ 8. The chance of loss or harm to personal or real property

a. economic risk
b. indemnification
c. insurable interest
d. insurable risk
e. insurance
f. liability risk
g. personal risk
h. premium
i. property risk
j. pure risk
k. speculative risk

CHECK YOUR UNDERSTANDING

LO1-1 9. Explain the concept of an insurable risk.

LO1-2 10. What is the purpose of insurance?

APPLY YOUR KNOWLEDGE

LO1-2 11. What is the difference between pure risk and speculative risk? Provide an example of each type of risk.

THINK CRITICALLY

LO1-1 12. The economy is not under your control, but there are things you can do to prepare for changing economic conditions. What can an individual consumer do to be better prepared for times of recession?

LO1-2 13. Explain how a peril is different from a hazard. Explain why insurance companies charge higher premiums if property does not meet minimum standards of safety or quality, or is hazardous.

LO1-2 14. Insurance policies are based on statistical averages. Based on this statement, what groups of drivers do you think pay the highest premiums for automobile insurance? Explain.

The Essential Question *Refer to The Essential Question on p. 509. Types of risk include pure risk; insurable risks (personal, property, and liability risks); economic risk; and speculative risk. You can purchase insurance to spread the costs of insurable risk and lower your financial exposure.*

The Essential Question *What is risk management, and how can you use it to reduce your costs of insurance?*

LEARNING OBJECTIVES

> LO 2-1 Explain the risk management process.
> LO 2-2 Create a risk management plan.
> LO 2-3 Identify ways to reduce the costs of insurance.

KEY TERMS

- risk management, *517*
- risk assessment, *517*
- risk shifting, *518*
- risk avoidance, *518*
- risk reduction, *519*
- risk assumption, *519*
- deductible, *521*
- multi-policy discount, *521*
- multi-line discount, *521*

LO 2-1 The Risk Management Process

While you cannot eliminate risk, you can manage it so that a loss does not become financially devastating. **Risk management** is an organized strategy for controlling financial loss from pure risks. It begins as soon as you have something to lose. In other words, as soon as you have assets, wealth, income, and anything that others could take from you, you must begin to think about how you can protect yourself from loss. Risk management should remain in effect throughout your life. Even after death your estate can be vulnerable, so steps should be taken to protect it.

Risk management involves more than buying insurance for every possible hazard that could occur. Some risks are not serious enough to insure. Others are better handled by taking steps to avoid the risk or reduce the chances that the risk will occur. Risk management is a three-step process, as illustrated in Figure 21.4.

Step 1: Identify Risks of Loss

The first step in risk management is to identify potential risks. Begin by asking yourself what financial risks you take on a regular basis, such as the risks you incur by driving a car or renting an apartment. As you will see in later chapters, many potential losses could occur. Even though they may not happen as a result of your error or fault, you still can be held responsible for damages to others and to property.

Step 2: Assess Seriousness of Risks

Once risks have been identified, they should be assessed to determine the probability of occurrence and the potential severity and impact on you if they do occur. **Risk assessment** is a systematic study of the risks that you face. It involves understanding the types of risk you will face and their potential consequences.

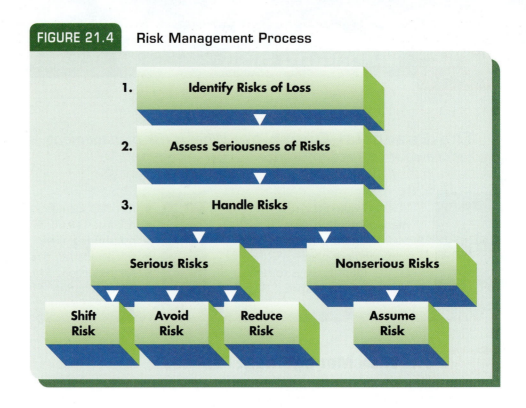

FIGURE 21.4 Risk Management Process

1. Identify Risks of Loss
2. Assess Seriousness of Risks
3. Handle Risks

Serious Risks
- Shift Risk
- Avoid Risk
- Reduce Risk

Nonserious Risks
- Assume Risk

Human activities and the ownership of property reflect a certain amount of risk. Some risks are high priority because they could have serious financial consequences. For example, when driving your car, you could destroy the property of others, injure others, or even kill someone. Because potential losses are very great, driving is a high-priority risk. Other types of risk may have a relatively low financial consequence or may have a very small chance of occurring. Therefore, these types of risk are a lower priority. By understanding the risks you face and their consequences, you can better plan to protect yourself and others.

Step 3: Handle Risks

Based on the nature and seriousness of the risks you identify, you should select a risk management technique that best addresses each risk. There are four techniques you can consider to handle risk: shifting, avoiding, reducing, or assuming risk. A good risk management plan uses a combination of these strategies to balance risk, the cost of insurance, and your potential losses.

1. **Risk shifting**, also called *risk transfer*, passes risk to another party. An example is when you buy insurance to cover financial losses caused by damaging events, such as auto accidents, fire, theft, injury, or death. By making insurance premium payments, you shift the risk of major financial loss to the insurance company. This is the most common method of dealing with pure risks that can carry high costs.

2. **Risk avoidance** lowers the chance for loss by not engaging in the activity that could result in the loss. For example, instead of having a party at your house and risking damage, you could reserve a section of a restaurant. Instead of participating in a dangerous sport, such as bungee jumping, you could go camping. You can avoid certain health issues by not smoking.

On December 26, 2004, an earthquake with a magnitude of 9.1 (the third largest ever recorded) had its epicenter off the west coast of Indonesia. The earthquake triggered a series of devastating tsunamis along the Indian Ocean, killing more than 225,000 people in 14 countries. Coastal communities were hit with waves more than 30 meters (100 feet) tall. Hardest hit were Indonesia, Sri Lanka, India, and Thailand. Many villages and towns along coastlines were completely destroyed. Local residents and tourists alike were killed as the waves hit the beaches. Despite a lag of several hours between the earthquake and the impact of the tsunami, nearly all of the victims were taken by surprise. There were no warning systems in the Indian Ocean to detect tsunamis or to warn coastal communities.

THINK CRITICALLY

Is it possible to protect yourself against all types of risks? If you choose to do nothing to lower your risks, what costs can result? How do those costs compare with the cost of risk management?

3. **Risk reduction** lowers the chance of loss by taking measures to lessen the frequency or severity of losses that may occur. For example, you may put studded snow tires on your car, install fire alarms or sprinklers in your home, or use seat belts. All of these steps would lessen the financial risk of potential losses as well as the severity of damages.

4. **Risk assumption** is the process of accepting the consequences of risk. To help cushion your financial burden, you could establish a monetary fund to help cover the cost of a loss. People who *self-insure* plan to absorb the costs of some risks themselves. This strategy can reduce the cost of insurance. In some cases, the cost of insuring against a particular risk may be too great, or the probability that the risk will occur may be too low, to justify paying an insurance premium. For example, an older car may not be worth much money. So instead of fully insuring it, you may assume the risk of paying for repairs yourself if it is damaged.

CHECKPOINT

What are the four techniques used to handle risk?

LO 2-2   The Risk Management Plan

Everyone faces risks and the potential losses they bring. Some people choose to do nothing—but this is, in fact, a choice. When you allow events to control your life, they can drain your finances unpredictably. To avoid possible financial disaster, you should create a *risk management plan*, which lists the risks you have identified, your assessment of their financial impacts, and the techniques that you plan to use to manage each risk.

Figure 21.5 outlines a risk management plan that a young person might develop. A good risk management plan uses various techniques to lower overall risk. As you progress through life, your priorities will change, and you will need to adjust your plan. For example, life insurance may become a higher priority when you have children who depend on your income.

Insurance is an important part of any risk management plan. In general, financial advisers say that a basic insurance plan should help reduce risk and protect against the following:

- Potential loss of income due to the premature death, illness, accident, or unemployment of a wage earner.
- Potential loss of income and extra expense resulting from the illness, disability, or death of a spouse or other family member.
- Potential loss of real or personal property due to fire, theft, or other hazards.
- Potential loss of income, savings, and property resulting from personal liability (injuring a person or damaging the property of others).

When a risk is significant and can have drastic consequences, shifting the risk by purchasing insurance is a good idea. In Chapters 22 and 23, you will learn more about types of insurance.

✔ CHECKPOINT

What is a risk management plan?

FIGURE 21.5   Risk Management Plan

Risk	Seriousness of Financial Impact	Method for Handling
1. Auto accidents	High	Collision and liability insurance Reduce risk—driver's education class
2. Theft or damage to personal property in my apartment	Medium	Renters insurance Reduce risk—add deadbolt lock to door
3. Theft or damage to personal property at work or in my car	Medium	Renters/homeowners standard policy Floater policy (for higher-priced items) Reduce risk—install an alarm in my car; keep items locked and out of sight
4. Injury to my apartment visitors	Medium	Renters insurance Low probability of occurring—assume risk above renters insurance coverage
5. Personal illness and sports injuries	High	Health insurance Avoid some risk—stop bungee jumping Reduce some risk—wear a helmet for mountain biking Reduce risk—get special training
6. Vision and dental needs	Low	Assume risk—contribute $10 a month to a fund to pay for new glasses and dental work when needed (self-insure)
7. Income protection	Medium/low (depending on life situation)	Life insurance (to protect dependents) Disability insurance (to provide income if I can't work) Insurance to make minimum payments when I am unemployed

Insurance can be expensive. As you consider an insurance plan, think about the following ways to save on insurance costs.

- *Increase deductibles.* A **deductible** is the specified amount of a loss that the insured must pay. The insurer's obligation to pay begins only after you have paid your full deductible. Generally, the higher the deductible, the lower the insurance premium. For example, premiums for a policy with a $100 deductible will be higher than for a policy with a $500 deductible. To reduce your premiums, accept a higher deductible.

- *Purchase group insurance.* Premiums for group plans are usually much lower than for individual plans, especially for health insurance. If group plans are available through your job, credit union, a social or professional organization, or other similar group, you will likely save money by enrolling in them.

- *Consider payment options.* How you pay premiums can save you considerable money over a short period of time. Monthly payments usually contain an extra charge, whereas annual or semiannual payments do not. Agreeing to have your premiums automatically deducted from your checking account or paying electronically may also reduce your costs.

- *Look for discount opportunities.* Many insurance companies offer discounts for special conditions. For example, nonsmokers can get lower premiums on health insurance. Taking driver's education courses and getting good grades can reduce auto insurance costs for teenagers. Good driving records can lower costs. Insuring more than one vehicle with the same company can result in a **multi-policy discount**. Having more than one type of policy (such as auto insurance and homeowners insurance) with a company can result in a **multi-line discount**.

- *Comparison shop.* Like many other things you buy, it pays to shop around for insurance. Get quotes from several insurers. Be sure to give each insurer the same information so that you can compare exact coverage and costs. It's also important to know exactly what coverage you need—and don't need—before talking to insurers.

There are many sources that can help you when shopping for insurance. For example, ask people you know for recommendations about insurers they have used. Also, check with your state insurance commissioner to see which companies are legally doing business in the state and whether any complaints have been filed against them. The financial strength of the insurer may be a major factor in keeping down insurance costs. You can find ratings for different insurers in print and online publications of A.M. Best Company and Standard & Poor's.

You should consider looking for a new insurance company when premiums rise. Many companies offer low rates to new customers, but then steadily raise them after a few years. It pays to shop around periodically.

 CHECKPOINT

What can you do to save money on insurance premiums?

What Are Government Transfer Payment Programs?

Since the Great Depression, the United States has had many programs designed to protect people from the harsh realities of risk in their lives. *Transfer payments* are government grants to some citizens that are paid with taxes collected from other citizens. Essentially, the government uses taxes to transfer some wealth from those who have it to those who do not. Some transfer payments are made in cash; others are made "in kind." That is, the government provides the needed item rather than cash. The following programs are available to U.S. citizens:

In-Cash Payments

- *Unemployment Compensation.* When workers are laid off, they are eligible to receive a percentage of their pay for a specified number of weeks, or until they get a new job (whichever comes first).

- *Disability Payments.* For injured workers, the disability portion of Social Security pays a monthly benefit until the workers recover, or for the rest of their lives if they remain disabled.

- *Temporary Assistance for Needy Families (TANF).* Low-income families with children can receive a monthly payment for a maximum of five years. To receive the benefit, adults in the family must work a minimum of 30 hours per week (20 hours for parents with children under 6 years old) to gain the experience needed to become economically self-sufficient.

In-Kind Payments

- *Supplemental Nutritional Assistance Program (SNAP).* People with insufficient income or resources to buy food may qualify to receive food stamps, which are government vouchers or debit cards that can be exchanged for food items.

- *Housing Subsidies.* Special housing programs allow low-income individuals and families to rent apartments and other residences at a lower rate than the market rate. The difference is "subsidized," or paid by the government.

- *National School Lunch Program.* Children from low-income families may receive free or low-cost lunches at school. The schools receive cash subsidies and donated food from the government for each meal they serve.

- *Medicaid.* Medicaid is government-sponsored health insurance for people living in poverty who cannot afford private health insurance.

These programs are temporary, rather than permanent, solutions. They are designed to help sustain people while they are retraining, recovering, or working to get back on their feet financially.

THINK CRITICALLY

1. What would you do if you lost your job and had no immediate source of cash for food and other necessities? How would you cope?

2. Visit your state government website and list resources that are available to people in need.

KEY TERMS REVIEW

Match the terms with the definitions. Some terms may not be used.

a. deductible
b. multi-line discount
c. multi-policy discount
d. risk assessment
e. risk assumption
f. risk avoidance
g. risk management
h. risk reduction
i. risk shifting

____ 1. An organized strategy for controlling financial loss from pure risks

____ 2. Lowering the chance of loss by taking measures to lessen the frequency or severity of losses that might occur

____ 3. Lowering the chance of loss by not engaging in an activity that could result in a loss

____ 4. A systematic study of the risks that you face

____ 5. Accepting the consequences of risk by self-insuring to absorb the loss

____ 6. A discount from insuring more than one vehicle with the same company

____ 7. The specified amount of a loss that the insured must pay

CHECK YOUR UNDERSTANDING

L02-1 8. Provide an example of risk shifting, risk avoidance, risk reduction, and risk assumption.

L02-2 9. What role does insurance play in a risk management plan?

L02-3 10. How can changing the deductible reduce an insurance premium?

APPLY YOUR KNOWLEDGE

L02-1 11. Why is it important to perform a risk assessment before developing a plan to manage risk?

THINK CRITICALLY

L02-1 12. Why is it important to handle risks in ways other than buying insurance to protect you from every financial loss? As a responsible adult, how will you handle the risks in your life?

L02-2 13. How might a risk management plan be different for a person with a spouse and children than for a person nearing retirement?

L02-3 14. What are some things you and your family can do now to reduce your overall automobile insurance premium costs?

The Essential Question *Refer to The Essential Question on p. 517. Risk management is an organized strategy for controlling financial loss from pure risks. The purpose of a risk management plan is to lower overall financial risk and protect from loss of income, property, and other forms of wealth.*

SUMMARY

21.1

- *Pure risk is a chance of loss with no chance for gain. Pure risks are random and related to events that are beyond the risk-taker's control.*

- *Insurance is a method of spreading risk across a large group, so that no one member must endure the full cost of a devastating loss.*

- *To be insurable, a risk must be a pure risk faced by a large number of people and for which the amount of the loss can be predicted. Insurable risks include personal risks, property risks, and liability risks.*

- *Everyone is affected by what happens in the economy; economic risk is not avoidable, but there are ways to lessen its impact (such as to save during good economic times to help prepare for slow economic times).*

- *Speculative risk may result in either loss or gain.*

- *Insurers analyze historical data to help predict how many losses to expect among their policyholders over a given time period. They base premiums on these statistical averages.*

- *Insurers make a profit by collecting more in premiums than they pay out in losses and operating expenses.*

- *Insurance is not meant to enrich, but to provide indemnification, or return the policyholder to the same financial condition as before the loss occurred.*

21.2

- *Risk management is an organized strategy for controlling financial loss from pure risks.*

- *The risk management process is a three-step process that involves identifying risks, assessing the seriousness of the risks, and considering the techniques for handling the risks.*

- *You can choose to handle risks through risk shifting (transfer), risk avoidance, risk reduction, or risk assumption.*

- *A good risk management plan uses a combination of techniques to lower overall risk.*

- *To reduce insurance costs, increase your deductibles, buy group plans, choose cost-effective payment options, take advantage of discounts, and comparison shop.*

© Pan Xunbin/Shutterstock.com

APPLY WHAT YOU KNOW

LO1-1   1. Based on Figure 21.1, list any current or anticipated risks that you and your family face or will face in the near future. Analyze your current personal, property, and liability risks. Then assume that you are now ten years older. Based on being where you would like to be and doing what your current goals dictate, analyze your personal, property, and liability risks for this stage in your life.

LO1-2   2. Insurance premiums are based on statistical probability. Explain what this means and what you can do to improve your position.

LO2-1   3. Using the three-step risk management process (see Figure 21.4), interview a family member or another person at a later life stage than your own to help identify, assess, and handle their risks. Then using Figure 21.5 as a guide, prepare a risk management plan for them.

LO2-3   4. Visit the website of your state insurance commissioner. Print out the complaint form, if one is available, and write a paragraph about what recourse you have when you feel that an insurer is treating you unfairly.

LO2-3   5. Visit Standard & Poor's website and look up the financial strength ratings for insurance companies until you find two with different ratings. Then look up the meaning of these ratings. Which company did Standard & Poor's judge to be financially stronger? Why?

MAKE ACADEMIC CONNECTIONS

LO1-1   6. **Economics** Write a report about the business cycle (see Figure 21.2). Compare business cycles over time. How long do slowdowns usually last? When was our last trough? How long did it last? Explain how to survive financially during the different stages of the business cycle.

LO1-1   7. **History** Using the Internet, search for the "Great Depression" and locate several sources of information. Write a paper presenting a narrative of what it was, how long it lasted, how people were affected, and what President Franklin D. Roosevelt did to help end the Depression and get people working again.

LO2-1   8. **Research** The design of the automobile has changed significantly throughout the years, with safety becoming a bigger factor. Conduct research to learn about safety features that have been incorporated in the design of automobiles over the years. Present your findings to the class. Use visual aids to showcase the safety features. Explain how these safety features have reduced risks faced by consumers.

LO2-3   9. **Technology** Describe how technology has affected the insurance industry. Discuss how consumers apply for insurance coverage, how insurance agents use the Internet, and how costs for premiums are affected because information is readily available online. Interview an insurance agent to discuss how his or her life has changed because of technology.

Solve Problems and Explore Issues

L02-1 10. Your cousin Jerry has decided to take up snow skiing. How can he minimize the risks and costs that could occur as a result of skiing?

L02-2 11. Lydia is single and age 24. She has a full-time job, and group health insurance is available through her employer. She has a car and has had no accidents or traffic tickets. She has an apartment that contains furnishings and personal belongings. Prepare a list of the risks that she may face. What types of insurance coverage may she need?

L02-2 12. Zoe and Richard are planning to get married next summer. They don't own a car and plan to rent an apartment. They intend to have children in the next few years. What advice can you give them about risk and risk management? When should they consider buying insurance?

L02-3 13. Jeremy made the following statement: "I don't take any chances. Everything I own is insured, including my life and ability to provide money for my family. In fact, I pay so much in insurance premiums that there is little money left for entertainment. Am I doing something wrong?" What advice would you give to Jeremy?

EXTEND YOUR LEARNING

L01-1 14. **Ethics** Government programs to help people through difficult times have existed since the 1930s. When the Great Depression began (1929) there was no Social Security, welfare, unemployment, or other safety nets to help people. Today, these programs continue to exist. Although they were not designed to be a person's sole or permanent refuge, many people—possibly millions—abuse the system to avoid working and providing for their own needs. As a result, the system is strained, leading to tax increases for employers and employees to fund these programs. Is it ethical to use the system long after you are able to support yourself? Do you think it's the government's responsibility to provide services to those in need? How does the government promote self-sufficiency?

CHAPTER PROJECT

Assume you will be attending college next year. Using Figure 21.4 as a guide, identify your most significant risks as a college student and the perils that cause them. Then list ways that you can protect yourself by shifting, avoiding, or reducing the risks and financial impact. Then based on the risks you identified, use Figure 21.5 as a guide to prepare a risk management plan for yourself. Present your plan to the class.

Complete the Guided Decision Making activity for Chapter 21 at **ngl.cengage.com/mypf.**

CHAPTER 22

Property and Liability Insurance

22.1 **Property Insurance**

22.2 **Auto and Umbrella Insurance**

Consider This...

Andy attends college full time and shares an apartment with two housemates. "As renters, we need to insure our personal possessions, and we're responsible for what happens on the property, even though we're only renting," he tells his housemates. "I've talked to my insurance agent about renters insurance. It would protect us in case of theft, fire, or freezing pipes. It would even cover people's injuries if they were visiting us and had some kind of accident at our apartment. The good news is that we won't have to pay very much—probably between $150 and $300 a year. That's about $50 to $100 per person for the year. It's good coverage for the price, and it takes care of risks that we face as renters. I think we should include it in our monthly budget. What do you think?"

The Essential Question *Why do renters and homeowners need liability insurance as well as coverage for their personal property?*

LEARNING OBJECTIVES

> LO 1-1 Explain the purpose and provisions of renters insurance.
> LO 1-2 Describe the need for and coverage provided by homeowners insurance.

KEY TERMS

- renters insurance, *528*
- homeowners insurance, *529*
- personal property floater, *531*
- liability coverage, *531*
- guest, *531*
- uninvited guest, *531*
- trespasser, *531*
- attractive nuisance, *531*
- endorsement, *531*
- overinsuring, *532*
- replacement value, *532*
- coinsurance clause, *532*

LO 1-1 Renters Insurance

If you rent your residence, you don't have to worry about insuring the building; that is the landlord's responsibility. However, your personal belongings are your responsibility to protect—not the landlord's (the landlord has no "insurable interest" in your assets). You are also responsible for personal injuries that occur inside your home. **Renters insurance** protects renters from property and liability risks. For example, it protects you from damage to personal property, loss of personal possessions you carry with you outside the home, and liability for injuries to your guests. Increasingly, renters insurance is being required by many landlords.

Personal Property

Personal possessions inside the rental property can be damaged or destroyed by fire, smoke, water, moisture, freezing temperatures, or heat. For example, if you rent an apartment and there is a fire in the building, your personal property (couch, chairs, bed, clothing, and so on) may suffer damage. Your rental insurance policy will cover the costs of repairing or replacing damaged or destroyed property.

Personal Liability

The landlord is not responsible for what happens inside your residence; that is your responsibility because you have control over those events.

What protection is available with renters insurance?

Renters insurance can help protect you if someone is injured while in your rented home. For example, if someone trips and falls at your home, injuring themselves seriously enough to warrant medical attention, your renters insurance policy will pay for his or her medical costs. It is important to note that you can be held legally liable whether or not the injury was your fault.

Extended Coverage

A renters insurance policy may also cover the contents of your vehicle and luggage while traveling. For example, if an item is stolen from your vehicle, it likely will be covered by renters insurance. Also, if your suitcase is lost, most airlines will reimburse customers only up to a certain amount. Renters insurance may cover the remaining cost of the lost items.

If you have particularly valuable possessions at your home, in storage, or with you as you travel, you might need to buy special coverage for the items. For example, expensive jewelry, computers or other technology, or valuable antiques beyond the basic policy's limits may need *extended coverage*. To insure such items, you likely will need to get an *appraisal*, or an expert's opinion on the market value of the asset. An appraisal will give you proof of value in the event the item is damaged, stolen, or destroyed. Appraisals cost anywhere from $50 to $300 or more, depending on the value of the property.

Cost of Renters Insurance

Renters insurance rates vary from state to state. Further, the cost of renters insurance depends on the insurance company, the amount of coverage, and the deductible you select. However, renters insurance is relatively inexpensive. The average policy costs between $15 and $30 a month. Most people's personal property (furniture, clothing, television, computer, and other such items) would cost $25,000 or more out of pocket to replace. To make sure that your personal property is protected from loss, purchasing renters insurance is a very good idea.

 CHECKPOINT

Why do you need insurance as a renter?

LO 1-2 Homeowners Insurance

When you buy a home, you will spend a large amount of money on the house and its contents. You need to protect your investment by limiting your risks. **Homeowners insurance** protects property owners from property and liability risks. It is similar to renters insurance, except that it includes coverage for the building in addition to the owner's personal possessions inside the building. Homeowners insurance policies offer various levels of protection depending on the needs of the homeowner. Figure 22.1 lists common types of homeowners insurance policies. *Package policies* that include several types of coverage in a single contract usually carry a lower premium than you would pay for each type of coverage purchased separately.

FIGURE 22.1 Homeowners Insurance Policy Coverage

HO-1	Basic Coverage	Fire, lightning, windstorm, hail, explosion, riot, civil commotion, aircraft, nonowned vehicles, smoke, vandalism, malicious mischief, theft, and glass breakage. Limits apply, such as $500 or 5 percent of policy value.
HO-2	Broad Form	Broader list of perils; broader definition; still has restrictions and limits, such as fire from fireplaces being excluded; limit of $1,000 or 10 percent of policy value.
HO-3	Special Form	All-risk coverage on dwelling itself; a loss not specifically excluded (such as flood) is covered.
HO-4	Renters	Insuring personal property on a broad-form basis with advantages of homeowners policy (such as special coverage in event of flood or water damage).
HO-5	Comprehensive	Most complete coverage available; dwelling and contents are covered on an all-risk basis.
HO-6	Condominium Owner's	HO-4 coverage for condominium owners (wording is adjusted to fit legal status of condominium owner).
HO-7	Mobile Homes	Protects owners of manufactured homes.
HO-8	Older Homes	Meets special needs of owners of older buildings with high replacement costs (actual cash value basis rather than replacement cost basis).

Homeowners insurance typically covers property owners' losses from these three types of risks:

1. *Hazards*—fire, water, wind, and smoke that may cause physical damages
2. *Crimes*—criminal activity, such as robbery, burglary, arson, and vandalism
3. *Liability*—the cost of another person's losses for injuries at your property

Physical Damage Coverage

The main component of homeowners insurance is protection against financial loss due to damage or destruction. Hazards such as fire, water, wind, and smoke may damage or destroy your home or cause you to lose use of it temporarily. Coverage extends to household belongings, including appliances, clothing, and furniture. Some policies will even provide limited coverage for refrigerated items that spoil due to a power outage. Detached structures on your property, such as a garage or shed as well as trees, plants, and fences, are also covered by homeowners insurance. If damage from a covered hazard prevents you from using your property while it is being repaired or replaced, your homeowners insurance policy will pay for temporary housing for a limited time.

Theft and Vandalism Coverage

Theft and vandalism coverage protects your personal belongings against loss from criminal activity, such as robbery and physical damage from vandals. Not only does homeowners insurance cover your possessions when they are in your home, but most policies contain off-premises coverage to protect your possessions if they are with you when you are away.

A **personal property floater** is additional insurance coverage for valuable items not covered by the basic policy. People often buy floaters to protect items of high value, such as jewelry, coin and stamp collections, fine art, musical instruments, and the like. A standard homeowners insurance policy has limits on coverage of personal property. For example, your policy may pay up to only $2,000 for jewelry and $1,000 for collections and collectibles. If, in fact, you have personal property worth more than these minimum amounts, you can protect it with a floater. You may need to get an appraisal to insure these items.

Liability Coverage

Liability coverage is insurance to protect against claims for bodily injury to another person or damage to another person's property. For instance, if a guest in your home falls and breaks a leg, you may be held liable for medical expenses. If you own a dog, you are responsible if the dog bites someone or another dog. If your child hits a baseball through your neighbor's window, you are responsible for the damage.

Homeowners are responsible for acts occurring on their property, both for guests and for uninvited guests. A **guest** is someone you specifically ask to come to your house. An **uninvited guest** is presumed to have permission to be on your property, such as door-to-door solicitors or delivery people. In most cases, homeowners will not be held liable for damages caused by or injuries to a **trespasser**, or an unlawful intruder.

An **attractive nuisance** is a dangerous place, condition, or object that is particularly attractive to children, such as a swimming pool. For example, if a child sneaks into a private pool without permission and is hurt, the homeowner will be held liable for the child's injuries, even if the homeowner has taken steps to prevent entry into the pool.

What's Not Covered

While homeowners insurance covers most losses, not every loss will be covered. *Exclusions* are items that homeowners insurance policies specifically will not cover, as shown in Figure 22.2.

Damage that is the result of floods and earthquakes is generally not covered in a basic policy. For these types of perils, policyholders often use endorsements to add coverage to their policy for an additional premium. An **endorsement** is a written amendment to an insurance policy that reflects changes to it. For example, you can add flood or earthquake insurance as an endorsement to your homeowners insurance policy.

How Much Coverage Is Needed?

Generally, people insure the contents of their home for at least half the value of the building. For example, a building insured for $200,000 is likely to have contents covered for at least $100,000. This includes all types of personal possessions, from furniture and appliances to clothing and other personal property and assets kept at the property.

FIGURE 22.2   Exclusions from Homeowners Insurance

Items Not Covered by Most Homeowners Insurance Policies:

- Articles insured separately (floater) such as jewelry, collections, and fine art

- Animals, birds, fish, and other pets

- Motorized land vehicles (licensed for use), except for lawn mowers and things used on the property exclusively

- Stereos, radios, CBs, cell phones, or CD or DVD players in vehicles

- Aircraft and parts of aircraft

- Property of renters, boarders, and other tenants (unless they are related to the owner and not paying rent)

- Business property in storage, such as samples

- Business property pertaining to a business that is conducted at the residence (separate insurance is required)

- Business property away from the residence

To be sure that you are reimbursed for all damaged or destroyed property, you should complete a household inventory, as shown in Figure 22.3. This inventory is similar to the personal property inventory you prepared in Chapter 4, except that a homeowner's inventory usually needs to be more detailed. Your inventory should include documentation that shows proof of ownership and value. Some people keep receipts and take pictures or record a video. Keep this documentation in a safe place, such as a safe deposit box or a fireproof vault. If you have an appraisal that was prepared, that document should be stored with the inventory as well.

Avoid **overinsuring**—that is, buying more insurance than is necessary. An insurer will pay no more than the actual replacement value of the house. The **replacement value** is the cost of replacing an item regardless of its actual cash (market) value. For example, if your house has a market value of $150,000, due to rising costs, it may cost $200,000 to rebuild it using material of similar quality if lost in a fire. If a house with a replacement value of $200,000 and contents worth $100,000 were totally destroyed, the insurer would pay no more than $300,000 ($200,000 + $100,000). If you owned a $400,000 homeowners insurance policy, you would still receive reimbursement of no more than $300,000. As you learned in Chapter 21, insurance follows the legal principle of *indemnification*. It will reimburse the actual cash value of a loss (which includes depreciation), unless your policy includes a replacement value clause, in which case it will reimburse the amount needed to restore you to your pre-loss financial position (up to the amount of insurance you purchased).

Claims adjusters, also known as *insurance adjusters*, determine the value of the property destroyed or damaged by a covered hazard. Also, insurers employ *insurance investigators* who look for evidence of destroyed or damaged property. They also look into cases where people fraudulently claim damages that did not occur.

Most property insurance policies contain a **coinsurance clause**, which is a provision requiring policyholders to insure their building for a stated percentage of its replacement value in order to receive full reimbursement for a loss.

FIGURE 22.3 **Household Inventory for Insurance**

HOUSEHOLD INVENTORY

Room	Type of Property	Replacement Cost	Receipt/Proof
Kitchen	Appliances:		
	Stove/oven	$ 600	Sears, 7/12
	Microwave	400	JCPenney, 9/11
	Toaster	25	Gift
	Mixer/blender	125	Shaleys, 1/13
	Bread maker	150	Kmart, 6/13
	Cabinets and contents:		
	Dishes	500	
	Pots and pans	500	
	Silverware	800	Oneida, 2/10
	Clock on wall	100	Gift
	Table and chairs	1,200	Dixons, 5/13
	Curtains	500	Wards, 8/12
Family Room	Bookcase, books	2,000	
	Couch and chair	1,000	Dixons, 2/13
	End tables/lamps	800	Dixons, 2/13
	Television	1,000	Mel's, 3/14
	Stereo	1,200	Mel's, 3/14
	Paintings	700	Dixons, 2/13
Bedroom	Antique bedroom set	5,000	Appraisal
	Clothing	2,000	
	Jewelry	500	
	Picture/mirrors	800	Dixons, 2/13
Garage	Lawn mower	900	Swath's, 3/12
	Garden tools	300	
	Camping equipment	800	Mel's, 3/14
	Bicycles	1,800	Jon's, 3/14
Utility Room	Washer/dryer	1,200	Sears, 3/12
	Cleaning supplies	100	

The percentage is usually at least 80 percent. Insurers do not require 100 percent coverage because even if your property is completely destroyed, the land and the building foundation will probably still be usable. If you do not meet the coinsurance minimum coverage, you will receive less than the full amount of the damages.

Cost of Homeowners Insurance

As with renters insurance, rates for homeowners insurance vary from state to state. The priciest states to insure your home are the states most susceptible to large-scale natural disasters, such as tornadoes and hurricanes. The cost of homeowners insurance also depends on the insurance company that you select, how much coverage you opt to have, and the amount of your deductible. Other variables that can affect the cost of homeowners insurance include your zip code (whether the house you are insuring is in a high-crime area), the size of the house, and its condition.

Calculating Insurance Reimbursements (Coinsurance)

The coinsurance clause in a homeowners policy requires that you buy coverage equal to a stated percentage of the property's replacement value in order to receive full reimbursement for a loss. For example, an 80 percent coinsurance clause would require the following coverage on a $150,000 house:

$$\$150,000 \times .80 = \$120,000 \text{ coverage required}$$

Many homeowners believe they can save money by underinsuring. Say the owners of the home in our example decide to buy only $100,000 of insurance instead of the required $120,000, thinking that $100,000 will cover most losses. Then they have a fire that results in a loss valued at $50,000. They think their $100,000 policy will cover the loss, but that isn't the case. Because they did not meet the $120,000 requirement, the insurer will reimburse based on the percentage of coverage they do have:

$$\$100,000 \div \$120,000 = .833 \text{ or } 83.3\%$$

To determine the amount of reimbursement, the insurer will multiply the value of the loss by this percentage:

$$\$50,000 \times .833 = \$41,650$$

Thus, for a $50,000 loss, the homeowners will receive only $41,650, or 83.3 percent of the loss.

Based on the preceding example, compute the insurance reimbursement in the following situation:

Daniel bought a house for $200,000. His coinsurance requirement is 85 percent. Daniel bought insurance for $120,000 to save money on insurance premiums. Last month, a storm caused $60,000 damage to his house. How much will the insurer reimburse?

Solution: $200,000 × .85 = $170,000 required coverage

$120,000 ÷ $170,000 = .706 or 70.6%

$60,000 × .706 = $42,360 reimbursement

When shopping for homeowners insurance, the Internet is a valuable resource. Many insurers have websites where you can get information about the policies and premiums they offer. There are also websites, such as Insure.com and NetQuote, that allow you to comparison shop for quotes.

✔ CHECKPOINT

What are the three types of risks that homeowners insurance covers?

Emergency Services

Emergency medical technicians (EMTs) and paramedics respond to 911 calls for emergency medical assistance. They provide medical services on site and then transport patients to medical facilities.

EMTs and paramedics work in teams to assure that the needs of the patient can be met. They care for the patient in route, using equipment and in some cases communicating with doctors to be sure they are keeping the patient stable.

The specific duties of EMTs and paramedics vary. EMTs have the skills to assess a patient's condition and to manage respiratory, cardiac, and trauma emergencies. Many also have instruction in administering intravenous fluids and other medications. Paramedics provide more extensive pre-hospital care than do EMTs. In addition to being able to carry out the tasks of EMTs, paramedics can administer medications, interpret EKGs, and operate complex equipment.

Employment Outlook

- A much faster-than-average rate of employment growth is expected.

Job Titles

- Emergency medical technician
- Paramedic

Needed Skills

- Completion of a post-secondary education program is required.
- All states require EMTs and paramedics to be licensed.
- Compassion, interpersonal skills, and physical strength are needed.

What's it like to work in . . . *Emergency Services*

Khim works full time as an EMT. He received his license two years ago and works for an emergency services company in his town. His annual salary is $34,000.

Khim's workday may start at any time of the day or night and often goes for a full 24 hours before the shift is over. He must always be ready to answer a call from emergency services dispatchers.

Once at the scene, Khim notes the symptoms of the person in need of aid. If treatment is needed beyond what Khim can give, he will attempt to stabilize the person's condition by using intravenous fluids, drugs, and/or bandages. Khim helps load the patient into the back of the ambulance and stays with the patient to monitor his or her vital signs on the way to the hospital. At the hospital, Khim takes the patient to the emergency room and informs the doctors and nurses on staff about the patient's condition and any treatments administered.

What About You?

Would you like to work in a field where you are called to emergencies and render life-saving services? Would you like to be an EMT or paramedic?

KEY TERMS REVIEW

Match the terms with the definitions. Some terms may not be used.

____ 1. *A written amendment to an insurance policy that reflects changes to it*

____ 2. *A person presumed to have permission to be on your property*

____ 3. *Insurance that protects renters from property and liability risks*

____ 4. *A dangerous place, condition, or object that is particularly attractive to children*

____ 5. *Insurance that protects property owners from property and liability risks*

____ 6. *Additional insurance coverage for valuable items not covered by the basic policy*

____ 7. *Provision requiring policyholders to insure their building for a stated percentage of its replacement value*

____ 8. *Insurance to protect against claims for bodily injury to another person or damage to another person's property*

a. attractive nuisance
b. coinsurance clause
c. endorsement
d. guest
e. homeowners insurance
f. liability coverage
g. overinsuring
h. personal property floater
i. renters insurance
j. replacement value
k. trespasser
l. uninvited guest

CHECK YOUR UNDERSTANDING

LO1-1 9. What is the purpose of a personal property floater?

LO1-2 10. Why is it important to avoid overinsuring your property?

APPLY YOUR KNOWLEDGE

LO1-2 11. Explain the concept of a coinsurance clause. Why do most homeowners insurance policies contain this clause?

THINK CRITICALLY

LO1-1 12. Explain why renters and homeowners have liability for injuries to invited and uninvited guests. What can they do to lower the risks?

LO1-2 13. Why are homeowners insurance premiums significantly higher than renters insurance premiums?

LO1-2 14. Explain why homeowners with an attractive nuisance should take extra precautions in addition to increasing their liability insurance coverage. Why do homeowners have such a responsibility?

The Essential Question *Refer to The Essential Question on p. 528. Renters and homeowners need liability coverage in case another person is injured on their property. They also need to cover personal property from damage or loss.*

22.2 Auto and Umbrella Insurance

The Essential Question *Why is it a good idea to have full-coverage auto insurance together with an umbrella liability policy?*

LEARNING OBJECTIVES

> LO 2-1 Identify common types of auto insurance coverage.
> LO 2-2 Explain the concept of umbrella liability insurance.

KEY TERMS

- driving record, *538*
- full coverage, *539*
- collision coverage, *540*
- comprehensive coverage, *540*
- personal injury protection (PIP), *541*
- uninsured/underinsured motorist coverage, *541*
- no-fault insurance, *541*
- assigned risk pool, *541*
- umbrella liability insurance, *542*

LO 2-1 Auto Insurance

Auto insurance covers costs of damage to the vehicle, its owner, and any passengers. It also covers costs of repairs to other vehicles, medical expenses of occupants in other vehicles, and property damage (shrubs, trees, and fences) caused by an accident. Standard policies also cover theft of the vehicle and/or its contents.

Cost of Auto Insurance

People pay *premiums* to an insurance company to insure their vehicles. In return, the company pays all or most of the costs associated with an accident or other vehicle damage. Premiums are based on a number of factors, such as:

- Type of car (model, style, age)
- Driver classification (age, sex, marital status)
- Driving record
- Location (city, county) of the driver and car
- Distances driven
- Purpose of driving (such as work)
- Age, sex, and marital status of other regular drivers of the car

Premium discounts are available for certain conditions, such as insuring more than one vehicle with the same company, taking driver's education

How are premiums set for car insurance?

courses, having safety features (such as airbags and rear view cameras) in your car, and getting good grades in high school and college (usually a "B" average or better).

Type of Car

Except for vintage (antique) cars, older cars should require less insurance than newer cars because older cars are worth less. New and expensive cars cost more to insure because they are worth more and would therefore be more expensive to repair or replace. Statistics show that sports cars have an increased risk of being in an accident and that the accident will be more serious. Thus, sports cars often have higher premiums.

Different makes and models of cars are rated by insurance companies as to risk of damage, both to the vehicle and its occupants, and to other cars and their occupants. These ratings can cause premium increases. The results of *crash tests,* where cars are intentionally wrecked to see how they will perform, can also affect premiums. In addition, vehicles that are common targets among thieves usually carry higher auto insurance premiums.

Driver Classification

As you learned in Chapter 21, insurers base their premiums on statistical probabilities. From their analysis, insurers determine that some drivers have a higher probability of getting into accidents than others. For example, young, single drivers are statistically more likely to be involved in an accident than married drivers over age 25. Thus, young drivers pay higher premiums. Also, women are generally better risks on the road than men and pay less for auto insurance.

Driving Record

Your **driving record** includes the number and type of traffic tickets you've received for driving infractions and misdemeanors along with the number of accidents in which you've been involved. An *infraction* is a minor violation and is punishable only by a fine. Infractions can be moving violations or non-moving violations.

A *moving violation* is any violation of the law committed by the driver of a vehicle while it is in motion. Moving violations include things such as failing to come to a complete stop at a stop sign, making an improper left-hand turn, or following too close to the vehicle in front of you. A *nonmoving violation* is any violation of the law involving a vehicle that is not in motion. Nonmoving violations may include expired license tags, malfunctioning equipment (such as a headlight or turn signal light that is out), excessive noise, and parking tickets.

More serious offenses, called *misdemeanors,* may incur fines as well as jail time. Examples include speeding, driving without a license, and reckless driving. Very serious traffic violations, such as driving under the influence of alcohol or drugs, hit and run, or leaving the scene of an accident, can cause insurance premiums to rise dramatically.

Many insurance companies use *point systems* to calculate premiums. For example, an infraction might count as 1 point and a misdemeanor might count as 5 points. When you reach 3 points, your premiums rise. If you reach 10 points, your policy could be canceled.

Other Factors

There are other factors that determine auto insurance premiums. For example, certain geographic locations (such as large cities) have higher accident rates. As a result, insurers charge higher premiums to drivers in these areas. In addition, how much you drive influences how much your auto insurance is. For example, someone commuting 50 miles a day may pay a higher premium than someone whose commute is only 10 miles, because more miles behind the wheel means more exposure to risk. Who will be driving the car is also a factor in setting premiums. Adding a teenage driver to an existing policy will increase premiums.

Another important consideration is the number of claims filed. When you file too many claims, your premiums rise. Also, when you are in an accident that is your fault and your insurance company has to pay claims, you are likely to see a *surcharge*, which effectively increases your premium for three years or longer.

Types of Auto Insurance Coverage

There are five basic types of auto insurance:

- Liability
- Collision
- Comprehensive
- Personal injury protection (PIP)
- Uninsured/underinsured motorist

When all of these types are purchased together in a single policy, it is known as **full coverage**. When you get a loan for a new car, the lender will require full coverage to protect its interests. Figure 22.4 shows a comparison of coverage for auto insurance.

FIGURE 22.4 Auto Insurance

	Who Is Protected	
	Policyholder	**Other Persons**
Liability coverage:		
Personal injuries	No	Yes
Property damage	No	Yes
Collision coverage:		
Damage to insured vehicle	Yes	No
No-fault provision	Yes	No
Comprehensive coverage:		
Damage to insured vehicle	Yes	No
Personal injury protection:		
Medical payments	Yes	Yes
Pedestrian coverage	Yes	No
Uninsured/underinsured motorist coverage:		
Bodily injury	Yes	Yes

Liability Coverage

Most states require all drivers to at least carry liability coverage. Each state sets its own minimum limits for liability coverage that drivers must carry on their car insurance policies. The purpose of liability coverage is to protect the insured against claims for bodily injury to another person or damage to another person's property. It pays nothing toward the insured's own losses, either personal injury or damage to the vehicle. However, if an accident is legally not your fault, the other driver's liability coverage will pay for damages to your car. If the accident is your fault and all you have is liability coverage, your insurance will not pay for the damages to your car.

Liability insurance coverage usually is described using a series of numbers, such as 100/300/50. These numbers mean that the insurer will pay up to $100,000 for injury to one person, $300,000 total for all people, and $50,000 for property damage per accident. Premiums charged for liability insurance vary according to the amount of coverage.

Collision Coverage

Collision coverage is auto insurance that protects your own car against damage from accidents or vehicle overturning. This coverage will pay for the damage to your car in the event you are at fault and the other driver's liability insurance does not have to pay.

Most collision coverage has a deductible. For example, you may have to pay the first $500 (or whatever deductible is specified by your policy) for repairs, and the insurer will pay the rest. Many minor traffic accidents involve damage that costs less than the deductible. However, it may be wise to have a higher deductible and pay lower premiums to save money. In other words, paying the first $1,000 for each accident would be less expensive in the long run than having a $500 deductible and paying higher premiums.

Comprehensive Coverage

Comprehensive coverage is auto insurance that protects you from damage to your car from causes other than collision or vehicle overturning. The causes might be fire, theft, severe weather, natural disasters, falling objects, acts of vandalism, and impacts from hitting an animal, such as a deer. For example, if your car gets hail damage from a storm, your comprehensive insurance pays for the repair.

As with collision coverage, comprehensive coverage has a deductible. The higher you set your deductible, the lower your premium.

What is the difference between collision coverage and comprehensive coverage?

Personal Injury Protection

Also known as medical coverage insurance, **personal injury protection (PIP)** is auto insurance that pays for medical, hospital, and funeral costs of the insured and his or her family and passengers, regardless of fault. If the insured is injured as a pedestrian or bicyclist, this insurance will pay the medical costs. In some cases, PIP will also cover lost wages if the insured is unable to work due to accident-related injuries.

PIP coverage is mandatory in some states. If you have health insurance with excellent post-accident benefits, the lowest legally required PIP limits may be sufficient. On the other hand, if you don't have good health insurance or have a plan that doesn't offer all of the benefits of PIP, it might be in your best interest to get as much PIP coverage as you can comfortably afford. To reduce costs for this kind of insurance, consider buying a car with extra airbags, antilock brakes, and other safety devices that lower the risk of injury.

Uninsured/Underinsured Motorist Coverage

Uninsured/underinsured motorist coverage is auto insurance that pays for injuries to you and your passengers when the other driver is legally liable but unable to pay. In other words, if the other driver is legally at fault for the accident but has no insurance or insurance that is insufficient to cover the costs, your insurer will pay your medical costs. This coverage also protects you as a pedestrian or a bicyclist if you are hit by an uninsured vehicle. Because of the high number of uninsured drivers on the road, many states require drivers to carry at least uninsured motorist coverage.

No-Fault Insurance

Many states have passed no-fault insurance laws. These laws set up a system of compensation for auto accidents that does not require a legal determination of who was at fault before claims are paid. **No-fault insurance** is auto insurance in which drivers receive reimbursement for their expenses from their own insurer, no matter who caused the accident.

The basic idea behind no-fault insurance is to avoid the years of legal battling required to settle a case and determine fault. Even then, drivers with no assets and no insurance would not be able to fix the other driver's car or pay for damages resulting from their negligence. Also, by reducing the number of lawsuits, more money can go to injured people in a shorter timeframe and lower the costs of insurance.

Assigned Risk Policies

If you have an accident that costs your insurer large sums of money, the insurer may cancel your policy. The number of traffic citations and fines on your driving record may also cause your insurer to drop you. If so, you may be deemed a "high-risk driver" by the state and may not be able to find another insurer willing to insure you.

Every state has an **assigned risk pool** that consists of people who are unable to obtain auto insurance due to the high risk they present. The state assigns these people to different insurers in the state. The insurers must then provide coverage. However, the insurance premiums may cost the insured considerably

Communication Connection

Assume you work for an insurance agency and have been asked to create a sales pamphlet of one or two pages that explains the need for auto insurance and describes the different types of coverage available from your company, including a high-risk pool plan for drivers with less-than-perfect driving records. Put together an attractive brochure, including a company logo. Add photos or other types of images if possible.

more than the normal rate until the risky driver is able to reestablish a good driving record. In addition, basic liability coverage may be all that is available for the high-risk pool.

✔ CHECKPOINT

What are the five basic types of auto insurance?

LO 2-2 Umbrella Liability Insurance

People who maintain required liability coverage on their vehicle and residence can also purchase an umbrella policy that picks up where the other coverage leaves off. **Umbrella liability insurance** supplements your basic auto and property liability coverage by expanding limits and including additional risks. It provides an additional layer of security to those who are at risk for being sued for injuries caused to others in an accident or damages to their property. It also provides protection against libel, vandalism, slander, and invasion of privacy. With personal injury lawsuits yielding verdicts in the millions of dollars, it is a good idea when you have built up your assets and your income to protect yourself from this type of catastrophic loss.

Umbrella liability insurance protects you from *extraordinary losses*, which are extremely high claims because of unusual circumstances. It can be very beneficial if you are sued and the dollar limit of your original policy has been exhausted. For example, you may be involved in a car accident in which a person receives a permanent injury. If you are sued and found liable for $1 million but your auto liability policy covers only $250,000, you'd be responsible for the remaining $750,000. However, if you have $1 million in umbrella liability insurance coverage, your umbrella policy will cover it.

Insurance companies that offer auto and property (renters and homeowners) insurance policies also offer umbrella policies. Premiums for umbrella insurance are reasonable. For example, a policy for $1 million would typically cost between $150 and $300 a year, depending on where you live and the probabilities calculated by the insurance company for your particular geographic area. This premium is in addition to the premiums for your auto insurance and your renters or homeowners insurance.

✔ CHECKPOINT

Why does a person or family need umbrella liability insurance?

Why Is It a Bad Idea to Drive Uninsured?

In most states, drivers are legally required to have liability insurance. This insurance protects others from loss when the accident is not their fault. Still, many people drive uninsured, even though it is against the law. In fact, it is estimated that one in seven drivers go uninsured. Some likely consequences for uninsured drivers include the following:

- They may be cited for failure to have insurance. The fine for this offense can be severe. Continued lack of insurance, following a citation, can result in jail time, loss of driving privileges, and large fines.

- Their citation may subject them to state financial responsibility laws. These laws would require them to file a special form (an SR-22) with the state for a period of one to three years, proving they have insurance or the ability to pay for damages they may cause. Filing these forms will result in even higher insurance rates.

- Because they do not have insurance, an accident may be deemed their fault automatically, requiring them to pay for damages.

Uninsured motorists also cause consequences to others on the road.

- Because people drive without insurance, or without enough insurance, other drivers must carry uninsured/underinsured motorist coverage. This raises the cost of insurance for everyone.

- When insured drivers file claims that their insurance company must pay because the other driver is uninsured, this loss may be counted against the policyholders. Thus, another person's failure to have insurance can result in your premiums being increased.

- It may take longer to process claims and get your car repaired when an uninsured driver is at fault.

As you can see, it's a bad idea to drive uninsured. You should obey the law and carry the required insurance. You as well as everyone else will benefit.

THINK CRITICALLY

1. Do you know of someone or have you read about a person who had an accident in which the party at fault had no insurance? What were the consequences?

2. What are the requirements for car insurance in your state? Does your state have a no-fault law? What is the penalty for those who disobey your state law?

KEY TERMS REVIEW

Match the terms with the definitions. Some terms may not be used.

____ 1. People who are unable to obtain auto insurance due to the high risk they present

____ 2. Auto insurance that protects you from damage to your car from causes other than collision or vehicle overturning

____ 3. Auto insurance that protects your own car against damage from accidents or vehicle overturning

____ 4. Auto insurance in which drivers receive reimbursement for their expenses from their own insurer, no matter who caused the accident

____ 5. Insurance that supplements your basic auto and property liability coverage by expanding limits and including additional risks

____ 6. The number and type of traffic tickets you've received along with the number of accidents in which you've been involved

____ 7. All five basic types of auto insurance purchased together in a single policy

a. assigned risk pool
b. collision coverage
c. comprehensive coverage
d. driving record
e. full coverage
f. no-fault insurance
g. personal injury protection (PIP)
h. umbrella liability insurance
i. uninsured/ underinsured motorist coverage

CHECK YOUR UNDERSTANDING

L02-1 8. What is the purpose of no-fault insurance laws?

L02-2 9. What types of protection does umbrella liability insurance provide?

APPLY YOUR KNOWLEDGE

L02-1 10. Liability coverage is required in most states. What is the reasoning behind this requirement?

THINK CRITICALLY

L02-1 11. Explain why comprehensive coverage is of lesser value to drivers of older (but not classic) cars.

L02-1 12. What are some things you and your family can do now to reduce overall auto insurance premium costs?

L02-2 13. Explain why a person who has substantial assets and income should consider adding an umbrella policy to his or her insurance coverage.

The Essential Question *Refer to The Essential Question on p. 537. Full-coverage auto insurance with an umbrella policy will protect you from exposure to risk and lawsuits resulting in personal liability.*

SUMMARY

22.1

- *Renters insurance protects you from damage to personal property, loss of personal possessions you carry with you outside the home, and liability for injuries to guests in your rented home.*

- *Homeowners insurance includes personal property and liability protections plus coverage for the building itself. It protects against three types of risks: hazards, crimes, and liability.*

- *A personal property floater is additional insurance coverage for specific items generally not covered by basic policies.*

- *Liability coverage protects you if a guest, invited or uninvited, is injured on your property and for damage caused to others' property.*

- *An endorsement is a written amendment to an insurance policy often used to add coverage, such as for damage caused by a flood or earthquake.*

- *Insurers will reimburse no more than the replacement value; therefore, overinsuring will result in higher premiums with no additional benefits.*

- *The coinsurance clause requires you to insure your building for a stated percentage of its replacement value to receive full reimbursement for a loss.*

22.2

- *Factors such as type of car, driver classification, driving record, coverage desired, distances driven, purpose of driving, and deductibles affect auto insurance premiums.*

- *Liability coverage protects others who may be injured or have property damage as a result of your actions or negligence.*

- *Collision coverage pays for damage to your vehicle when you are at fault in an accident.*

- *Comprehensive coverage protects your vehicle from non-collision losses, such as from theft, storms, and falling objects.*

- *Uninsured/underinsured motorist coverage protects you in the event the other driver is uninsured or does not have enough insurance.*

- *No-fault insurance laws require insurers to pay the losses of their own policyholders rather than require the at-fault driver's insurer to pay.*

- *Umbrella liability insurance may be purchased to expand coverage and reimbursement limits.*

APPLY WHAT YOU KNOW

LO1-1   1. Explain what types of coverage are included in a renters insurance policy. Why is purchasing renters insurance a good idea, even for someone on a limited budget?

LO1-2   2. Outline ways that you can protect valuables from being stolen from your home or vehicle. Research the cost of protection devices or services.

LO1-2   3. Explain the difference between a guest, an uninvited guest, and a trespasser. Who is responsible for damages to the property of the insured with regards to each of these individuals?

LO1-2   4. Write a paper discussing the perils of overinsuring or underinsuring property. Be specific in the consequences that may result in either case. How can you be sure that you are insuring property for its appropriate replacement value?

LO2-1   5. The Internet makes it easy to get auto insurance quotes. Locate an auto insurance website. Compile a list of questions that you must answer at the website in order to get a quote.

LO2-2   6. Interview an insurance agent about the need for umbrella liability insurance in your state. Ask questions about coverage availability, maximum policy limits, and premium costs. Also ask about exclusions. What situations would not be covered by the umbrella policy?

MAKE ACADEMIC CONNECTIONS

LO1-2   7. **Math** Your friend owns a home that has a value of $180,000. Her insurance policy has an 80 percent coinsurance clause. She has the property insured for $140,000. Later that year, a tree falls on her house during a storm, causing damages of $25,000. Compute the reimbursement that she will be able to collect.

LO1-2, LO2-1   8. **Communication** Write a paper about the type of insurance (property and vehicle) that you and your family need to have at this point. Explain how that will change over time, both for you and for your family. Include the reason why you have chosen insurance over some other form of risk management.

LO2-1   9. **Research** Your driving record can greatly impact auto insurance premiums. A safe-driving agreement contains rules that teens should follow to help keep everyone safe on the roads. Search for sample agreements online and use them to create your own agreement. Include rules regarding risky behaviors that you have witnessed.

LO2-1   10. **Geography** Do a comparative study of auto insurance laws in two states, or between two countries. Create a table that outlines how they are similar and how they are different. Cite your sources of information.

LO2-1   11. **Technology** Conduct online research about the impact of the digital age on the field of insurance. How have insurance companies changed? How has it affected consumers? Write a paper explaining the positive and negative consequences.

Solve Problems and Explore Issues

LO1-1 12. Megan is renting an apartment. She has some antique furniture. Last year, the pipes burst in her apartment building but her furnishings were not damaged. She does not have renters insurance, but the landlord has property insurance. How would you advise her?

LO1-2 13. As a first-time homebuyer, Curtis is considering what type of insurance to buy. Describe the types of insurance that he might consider. (Refer to Figure 22.1.)

LO2-1 14. Luis would like to own his own car; however, at age 19, he feels he can't afford the auto insurance premiums. How can he reduce them?

LO2-1 15. Tia has the following auto insurance coverage: comprehensive ($250 deductible); bodily injury and property liability (100/200/25); collision ($250 deductible). As a result of an accident that was her fault, the other driver was awarded $9,800 for injuries and $2,100 in damages to his car. Tia's car was damaged at a cost of $820. Her medical bills were $135. How much did the insurer have to pay in accident claims? What is the most that Tia's policy would pay for injuries to the other driver?

EXTEND YOUR LEARNING

LO1-2, LO2-1 16. **Legal Issues** Tort lawsuits (person vs. person) are civil (as opposed to criminal) actions that involve injuries caused to other persons. Negligence is a tort, and it is based on foreseeable risk. You have a duty of care to others when there is a foreseeable risk that your actions could cause injuries. Thus, even though you do not have intent to injure another, the fact that you have a duty of care that was breached and led to another's injury will make you responsible for his or her injuries. You can also be held liable for criminal acts when your behavior causes injuries to others. How can you reduce your civil and criminal liability?

CHAPTER PROJECT

Assume you are helping your family with its insurance needs. For insurance claim purposes, prepare a household inventory, listing the contents of each room in your home. Use Figure 22.3 as an example. Next to each item, record its approximate value and indicate whether you have a receipt to prove its cost. Take a photo of particularly valuable or collectible items to include with the inventory. Then help your family find insurance for a new car of your choice that you will be permitted to drive. Get a price quote for full-coverage auto insurance. Determine ways to reduce premium costs through discounts or other methods. Organize all of the information you have collected in a folder.

Complete the Guided Decision Making activity for Chapter 22 at ngl.cengage.com/mypf.

CHAPTER 23

Health and Life Insurance

23.1 Health Insurance

23.2 Disability and Life Insurance

Consider This...

Corrie wasn't feeling well and was sure it was strep throat. Because she'd had it before, she knew the symptoms.

"I need a doctor's appointment," she told her friend. "I'm insured under my mother's policy at work. I have an insurance card that allows me to see the doctor, but I have to pay a $30 co-payment at the time I go to the clinic. The doctor will give me a test called a 'lab culture' to be sure that I have strep. I'll have to pay 20 percent of the cost of that test. Then I'll get a prescription, and I have a $20 co-payment for that. Even with insurance, this illness will cost me $75 plus another $80 for time lost from work. Health care is expensive! Soon I won't be able to stay on my mom's policy any longer and will need to get my own insurance if I'm not employed. This really worries me."

The Essential Question *What is the difference between group and individual health insurance, and what types of coverage and plans are available?*

LEARNING OBJECTIVES

> LO 1-1 Describe group and individual health insurance choices.
> LO 1-2 List and explain common types of health insurance coverage and plans.

KEY TERMS

- health insurance, *549*
- group insurance, *549*
- COBRA, *550*
- preexisting condition, *550*
- coordination of benefits, *550*
- Flex 125 Plan, *550*
- health insurance exchange, *551*
- basic health coverage, *552*
- major medical coverage, *552*
- stop-loss provision, *553*
- health savings account (HSA), *553*

LO 1-1 Group and Individual Health Insurance

Health insurance is a plan for sharing the risk of high medical costs resulting from injury or illness. Like other forms of insurance, health insurance reduces individual risk by spreading it among many people. In exchange for regular premiums, the insurer promises to pay medical expenses for the treatments covered by the policy.

If you are employed, health insurance may be provided through your employer. On the other hand, if you are self-employed, unemployed, or work for an employer that does not provide health insurance, you may find that purchasing an individual health insurance policy is your only option. Monthly premiums for individual plans are often high, and many people cannot afford coverage. Many of the reforms instituted by the Affordable Care Act of 2010 were designed to extend health care coverage to those without it.

Group Policies

The most common type of health insurance is **group insurance**, in which all those insured have the same coverage and pay a set premium. It is most often obtained through employers. Because a group represents a large portion of potential business for an insurer, a group can usually negotiate better coverage and lower premiums than individuals can get on their own.

Some employers pay the premiums as a benefit to their employees. More commonly, however, both share the premium costs. Due to rising insurance costs, many employers are requiring employees to pay a higher portion of health care costs and insurance. The rationale is that if employees share more of the costs, they will better manage their use of health care services.

© Pan Xunbin/Shutterstock.com

COBRA

The *Consolidated Omnibus Budget Reconciliation Act*, or **COBRA**, is a federal law enacted in 1986 that allows people who leave their job to continue their health insurance under the company plan for a limited period of time (usually 18 months). During this period, former employees pay premiums individually for the same group coverage they had while employed. The purpose of this law is to give former employees an element of financial security while trying to obtain other insurance, either on their own or through a new employer.

HIPAA

The *Health Insurance Portability and Accountability Act (HIPAA)* is a federal law enacted in 1996 to provide protections for people seeking group health care. HIPAA limits the preexisting conditions that group plans may exclude. A **preexisting condition** is any medical condition that a person has before being enrolled in an insurance plan. HIPAA also makes it illegal for an insurer to deny coverage based on health status (though it does not limit the amount the insurer may charge for coverage). The purpose of the law is to increase your ability to obtain insurance when you start a new job and lower your chances of losing your current health insurance.

Double Coverage

If a family has more than one group insurance plan, the insurers will share the costs of a claim. **Coordination of benefits** is a group health insurance provision that specifies how the insurers will share the cost when more than one policy covers a claim. This provision assures that reimbursement will not exceed 100 percent of allowable expenses. For example, if a couple has two policies—one through the husband's employer and one through the wife's employer—then one policy may pay 80 percent of the medical expenses and the other the remaining 20 percent.

Flex Plans

Many employers provide flexible benefit plans. A Section 125 Flex Plan, or **Flex 125 Plan**, is an employee benefit program that allows employees to set aside money, pretax, to help pay deductibles, co-payments, and other health expenses during the year that are not covered by insurance. A Flex 125 Plan is often offered as part of a *cafeteria-style plan*, which is an employee benefits program that allows employees to choose the types of benefits that best meet their needs. However, the Flex 125 Plan has one big disadvantage: the money that the employee sets aside is forfeited at the end of the year if not used (the employer keeps it).

Individual Policies

People can also buy individual health insurance policies. The premiums are often high, depending on the type of coverage. Unlike group plans, some individual policies require a physical exam, and insurers may refuse to cover individuals with health problems (unless there are state laws prohibiting this practice). Also, individuals may have a waiting period of 30 to 90 days before coverage begins. (Members of group plans usually receive immediate coverage.)

Many states require insurers to make some type of individual policy available for purchase by individuals who do not have group policies. States may also have high-risk health insurance pools, whereby people with preexisting conditions (such as diabetes) can buy insurance. Unfortunately, the premiums can be very high, and placement on a waiting list can exclude people from coverage when they need it.

Sometimes medical costs can exceed the limits of a standard health policy. To protect against this risk, people can buy *supplemental health insurance*. This secondary policy is designed to pay high deductibles and co-payments as well as medical fees that are higher than the insured's standard policy allows. For example, a standard plan may pay up to $450 a day for a hospital room, but the actual charges may come to $500 a day. A supplemental policy would pay the difference of $50 a day.

Health Insurance Exchanges

The *Affordable Care Act*, also known as *Obamacare*, was signed into law on March 23, 2010. This sweeping law was advocated by President Barack Obama in the largest health reform in the nation's history. The purpose of this law was to increase the availability and affordability of health insurance while controlling rising medical costs for individuals and the government.

The law mandates that everyone have health insurance or face a penalty for failing to do so. The rationale is that if everyone is insured, the overall cost of insurance should drop because younger people (with lower health risks), who were choosing to be uninsured previously, would now be added to the pool. Thus, the risk is spread, and everyone pays a minimum insurance rate based on age rather than physical condition or other arbitrary factors.

The law set up health insurance exchanges to facilitate the purchase of health insurance in each state. A **health insurance exchange** provides a set of government-regulated and standardized health care plans from which uninsured and underinsured individuals may purchase health insurance policies. The cost of coverage is controlled by the states to help ensure premium rates are reasonable. Individuals who meet low-income requirements are eligible to receive federal subsidies to help pay premium costs of insurance purchased through a health insurance exchange.

What is the purpose of the Affordable Care Act?

The Affordable Care Act mandates that the exchanges meet certain minimum requirements.

- Health plans cannot limit or deny benefits due to preexisting conditions.
- Insurers cannot cancel coverage because of the number of claims made.
- Health insurance plans cannot place a limit on lifetime benefits.
- Preventive medical care must be provided without co-pays.
- Patients can choose their own primary care doctors.
- Mental health coverage is mandated, including both inpatient and outpatient services.

Health insurance exchanges began operating in every state on October 1, 2013. By April 2014, President Obama announced that more than 8 million Americans had selected an exchange plan, with 28 percent being young individuals. Those numbers are expected to grow.

CHECKPOINT

Name three ways that you can obtain health insurance.

LO 1-2 Types of Coverage and Plans

Both group and individual health insurance have very similar types of coverage and plans available. In most cases, there is an *annual enrollment period* where the insured can make changes to their plans, adding or deleting certain types of coverage and/or changing health plans.

Types of Coverage

Health insurance policies typically cover basic health expenses (medical, hospital, and surgical) and major medical costs. These kinds of coverage help protect consumers from doctor and hospital bills that could ruin them financially. Some policies cover dental and vision needs for a higher premium.

Basic Health Insurance

Basic health coverage includes medical, hospital, and surgical costs. Medical coverage helps pay for routine physician services, including doctor office visits, annual physical exams, recommended immunizations, screenings, X-rays, and laboratory tests. When the policy covers prescriptions, it often requires the use of generic rather than name-brand drugs. Hospital coverage pays hospital bills for room, board, and medication. Surgical coverage pays for part or all of a surgeon's fees for an operation. Usually, basic health insurance covers only necessary (not cosmetic or elective) surgery and excludes certain types of procedures.

Major Medical Insurance

Major medical coverage provides protection against the catastrophic expenses of a serious injury or illness. For example, when a patient is admitted to the hospital for an organ transplant or some other major surgery, the cost can easily be $500,000 or more. Major medical coverage is beyond basic health insurance, and by law, there can no longer be a limit on the amount of lifetime benefits paid.

Major medical coverage often has a coinsurance provision requiring the insured to pay some portion (such as 20 percent) of all bills. For a higher premium, a stop-loss provision is often included. A **stop-loss provision** is an insurance clause that caps or sets a maximum that the insured has to pay out of pocket during any calendar year. For example, a $5,000 stop-loss means the insured would have to pay no more than $5,000 for co-payments and deductibles in a year.

Dental and Vision Insurance

Dental insurance covers basic dental services, such as exams, cleanings, X-rays, and fillings. Dental plans usually have low deductibles and coinsurance requirements of 20 percent or more. They often state upper limits, such as $1,500 per year per person. Insurers typically pay less (such as 50 percent) for some services, such as crowns or bridges.

Why is major medical coverage so important?

In some cases, insurers cover only certain types of services. For example, the cost of an amalgam filling (metal) is far less than a porcelain filling. Most dental policies will pay only for amalgams except when the filling is in the front teeth. If you want a porcelain filling for a back tooth, you would have to pay the difference in cost. For instance, if your dentist charges $180 for a porcelain filling and your insurance allows only $90 and will pay 80 percent of the cost, you must pay $18 ($90 × .20). In addition, you must pay the $90 difference between the dentist's fee ($180) and the allowable amount ($90).

Vision insurance often pays for exams for eye disease as well as for prescription adjustments and lenses. Policies usually cover an eye examination on a regular basis—once every year or two—and the purchase of single-vision corrective lenses and frames. Some policies offer limited coverage for prescription sunglasses and contact lenses.

Types of Private Health Care Plans

Employee or private health care plans are grouped into two categories: unmanaged and managed.

Unmanaged Care

Unmanaged care (traditional fee-for-service) plans allow participants to choose any doctor and be reimbursed for a portion of the expenses (usually 80 percent) incurred after a deductible is met. Deductibles often range from $100 to $1,000 per patient, or $500 or more per family. This plan is often the most expensive because control over costs and services is less strict.

A **health savings account (HSA)** is used in association with a medical plan that carries a higher annual deductible than typical health plans. The insured basically takes the money that would have gone toward the premiums for basic health coverage and has it deposited into an HSA.

Math Minute

Calculating Costs of Services Not Fully Paid by Insurance

John needs to have a root canal. His dental insurance will pay 80 percent of the cost. The policy sets an allowable limit for a root canal at $600. The dentist bills John's insurer for $800. How much will insurance pay? How much will John have to pay?

First, compute how much insurance will pay on the root canal:

$600 × .80 = $480 will be paid by insurance

Then subtract the amount paid by insurance from the total for the root canal:

$800 − $480 = $320 due from John

Based on the preceding example, compute the out-of-pocket expenses in the following situation:

Fran's dental insurance will pay 70 percent of the cost of a porcelain crown. The policy sets an allowable limit for a crown at $800. The dentist bills Fran's insurer for $1,000. How much will Fran have to pay?

Solution: $800 × .70 = $560 will be paid by insurance

$1,000 − $560 = $440 due from Fran

The account is then used to pay qualified medical expenses not covered by insurance, including deductibles and co-payments. Contributions to the account are made pretax and are tax-deductible. If the HSA is sponsored through the employer, it may contribute to the account as well. Money withdrawn from an HSA to pay qualified medical expenses is tax-free. Unlike the Flex 125 Plan, unused money in an HSA isn't forfeited at the end of the year; it continues to grow on a tax-deferred basis, like an IRA.

Managed Care

Managed care plans rely on a network of health care providers. To receive maximum reimbursement, participants in a managed care plan must select doctors who belong to the network. The policy requires participants to obtain preapproval for any surgery or hospital admission and two or three doctors' opinions before a major procedure can be performed. The insurer exercises significant control over the types of services provided and the maximum benefits allowed for those services. Health maintenance organizations (HMOs), preferred provider organizations (PPOs), and point of service (POS) plans are the most common types of managed care plans.

Health Maintenance Organization (HMO) A *health maintenance organization (HMO)* is a group plan offering prepaid medical care to its members. An HMO often has its own facilities and provides a full range of medical services. Patients must choose doctors on the HMO staff, including one doctor to be their *primary care physician (PCP)*, or main provider. To see a specialist, patients must get a referral from their PCP first. Otherwise, the insurance will not cover the visit to the specialist. In this way, the PCP acts as a "gatekeeper." HMO patients usually make a co-payment of $25 to $50 for an office visit. HMOs that are *capitated* (meaning "per person") receive a fixed monthly premium for each patient, regardless of whether the patient seeks medical care.

An advantage of belonging to an HMO is that *preventive care*, such as routine physical exams and vaccinations, are generally covered at 100 percent. The idea is to encourage people to come in for treatment before a minor ailment becomes a major (and expensive) problem.

Preferred Provider Organization (PPO) A *preferred provider organization (PPO)* is a group of health care providers (doctors and hospitals, for example) who band together to provide health services for set fees. Patients can choose doctors from an approved provider list, but they can also go outside of the plan for care. However, if they choose to do so, they will have to pay a larger percentage of the fee. Patients are not required to choose a primary care physician and do not need a referral to see a specialist, but the cost will be higher. There are limits on types of services that can be provided and fees that can be charged. Patients who stay within the network of providers usually must make a small co-payment, such as $25 per office visit or per prescription. Because this type of plan is more flexible than an HMO, it is more expensive.

Point of Service (POS) Hybrid medical insurance plans are rare but are available in some locations. *Point of service (POS)* plans give people more choice and control over medical services. These plans combine the features of HMOs and PPOs. Like an HMO, patients must choose a primary care physician, but like a PPO, patients can choose to go outside of the plan for health care. However, unless referred by the primary care physician, patients will pay more for going outside the plan than they would with a PPO. Although a POS gives you more flexibility than an HMO, its cost structure is designed to encourage participants to stay within the plan. (HSA plans may offer this type of option for maximum flexibility.)

Types of Government Health Care Plans

Medicare and Medicaid are both government-sponsored programs designed to help cover health care costs. While both programs were established by the federal government in 1965 and are taxpayer funded, they are actually very different programs with differing eligibility requirements and coverage. People who have Medicare and Medicaid do not qualify for the health insurance exchanges set up by the Affordable Care Act.

Medicare

Medicare is government-sponsored health insurance for people age 65 or older. Medicare is run by the Social Security Administration (SSA) and funded by employee payroll deductions and matching employer contributions. Like other plans, there are maximum benefits, exclusions, and other requirements. Retired people pay a monthly premium for Medicare insurance, which is deducted from their Social Security payments.

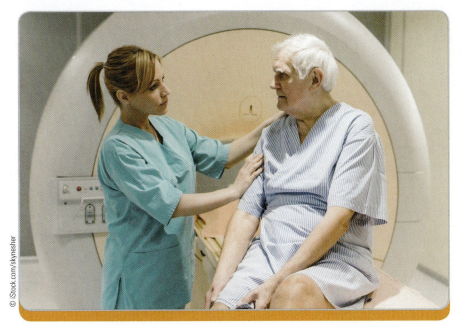

Why do many Medicare enrollees purchase Medigap insurance?

Medicare has four parts: Part A (hospital insurance), Part B (medical insurance), Part C (Medicare Advantage health plans), and Part D (prescription drug costs). Part A provides payments for inpatient hospital or nursing care facility services, home health care services, and hospice care. Part B provides payments to physicians and surgeons as well as for medically necessary outpatient hospital services, such as ER, laboratory tests, and X-rays. Part C is not actually a benefit but rather an option. It allows private health insurance companies to provide Medicare benefits. *Medicare Advantage plans* must offer at least the same benefits as Parts A and B but can do so with different costs and coverage restrictions. Part D of Medicare covers prescription drugs. It is provided only through private insurance companies that have contracts with the government. Anyone with Part A or B is eligible for Part D. Medicare Advantage plans may also provide prescription drug coverage.

Medicare will not cover all health care costs for Medicare enrollees (called "beneficiaries"). Many beneficiaries purchase supplemental (or *Medigap*) insurance to help pay the co-payments and deductibles not covered by Medicare. Medigap insurance is sold by private insurance companies.

Medicaid

Medicaid is government-sponsored health insurance for people with low incomes and limited resources. This program helps families who live in poverty and cannot afford private health insurance to pay the costs associated with long-term medical and custodial care.

Unlike Medicare, which is solely a federal program, Medicaid is a joint federal and state program. Each state operates its own Medicaid system. The federal government funds up to 50 percent of the cost of each state's Medicaid program. All states are required to cover certain mandatory benefits, such as comprehensive inpatient and outpatient health care coverage.

Not everyone is eligible for Medicaid. There are income, age, disability, and citizenship requirements that must be met. The Affordable Care Act expanded Medicaid eligibility starting in 2014. Under the law, states that choose to participate in the Expanded Medicaid program are required to allow people with income up to 133 percent of the poverty line to qualify for coverage. Those enrolled in Medicaid receive coverage that is similar to that provided by the Affordable Care Act, but at little or no cost to them.

✔ **CHECKPOINT**

How does basic health coverage differ from major medical coverage?

What Is Obamacare, and Why Do We Need It?

The Patient Protection and Affordable Care Act, commonly called the Affordable Care Act or Obamacare, is a federal statute signed into law by President Barack Obama on March 23, 2010. Together with the Health Care and Education Reconciliation Act, it became the most significant overhaul of the health care system since the passage of Medicare and Medicaid in 1965. The goals of the new law are to decrease the number of uninsured, to expand public and private health insurance coverage, and to reduce overall costs of health care.

There are many critics of the new law. Opponents are against mandatory coverage that requires all citizens to buy insurance or face penalties. On June 28, 2012, the U.S. Supreme Court upheld the constitutionality of the law's mandate to obtain insurance. However, many conservative political advocacy groups, small business organizations, and some state governments continue to challenge the law, and many individuals refuse to enroll in Obamacare.

On the other hand, proponents say that the Affordable Care Act puts consumers back in charge of their health care. Under this law, a new "Patient's Bill of Rights" gives the American people the stability and flexibility they need to make informed choices about their health. Supporters argue that lack of health insurance results in poor health and shorter lives for many Americans. They also argue that there are costs to society as well, such as the following:

- Developmental deficiencies from insufficient health care during infancy
- Expenses for chronic health conditions not treated until they become emergencies
- Lost income due to reduced job productivity and employment
- Health care expenses paid by taxpayers for uninsured patients
- Social inequality (with lower-income Americans being at a definite health disadvantage)

Many people propose other ways to provide access to affordable health care. Some say a single-payer, government-sponsored health plan is the answer. In a single-payer system, individuals and businesses pay taxes to raise revenue that covers insurance expenses for the entire population. This type of system exists in many other nations, such as Canada and most western European countries. Others say we can reform the system we have so that health insurance becomes portable—meaning you can take it with you from job to job. Whatever the answer, we as a country must find a way to reduce the costs of health care and provide access to affordable health insurance for all Americans.

THINK CRITICALLY

1. Suppose you have no health insurance. How would this fact affect the decisions you make about your health care?

2. Do you believe it is a violation of your freedom of choice (life, liberty, and pursuit of happiness) to be required to buy health insurance?

KEY TERMS REVIEW

Match the terms with the definitions. Some terms may not be used.

____ 1. Health insurance obtained through employers in which all those insured have the same coverage and pay a set premium

____ 2. An insurance clause that caps or sets a maximum that the insured has to pay out of pocket during any calendar year

____ 3. Insurance coverage for medical, hospital, and surgical costs

____ 4. Any medical condition that a person has before being enrolled in an insurance plan

____ 5. A plan for sharing the risk of high medical costs resulting from injury or illness

____ 6. Coverage against catastrophic medical expenses of a serious injury or illness

____ 7. Law that allows insurance to continue after an employee leaves his or her job

a. basic health coverage
b. COBRA
c. coordination of benefits
d. Flex 125 Plan
e. group insurance
f. health insurance
g. health insurance exchange
h. health savings account (HSA)
i. major medical coverage
j. preexisting condition
k. stop-loss provision

CHECK YOUR UNDERSTANDING

L01-1 8. Why is group insurance generally less expensive than individual policies?

L01-2 9. How is Medicaid different from Medicare?

APPLY YOUR KNOWLEDGE

L01-2 10. Explain the advantages and disadvantages of choosing a managed care plan over an unmanaged care plan.

THINK CRITICALLY

L01-1 11. Why are an increasing number of employers expecting employees to pay a larger portion of their health care costs?

L01-1 12. What is the purpose of health insurance exchanges?

L01-2 13. Explain why people who are in good health might prefer to have high-deductible medical insurance with a health savings account (HSA).

The Essential Question *Refer to The Essential Question on p. 549. With group insurance, all those insured have the same coverage and pay a set premium, which is usually lower than individuals can get on their own. Basic health coverage, major medical coverage, and dental and vision insurance are available through unmanaged and managed care plans, such as HMOs and PPOs. Medicare and Medicaid are government-sponsored health insurance plans.*

The Essential Question *Why do individuals need disability insurance and life insurance?*

LEARNING OBJECTIVES

> LO 2-1 Discuss different types of disability insurance.
> LO 2-2 Describe the characteristics of different life insurance plans.

KEY TERMS

- disability insurance, *559*
- life insurance, *561*
- portability, *562*
- incontestable clause, *562*
- double indemnity, *563*
- acceleration of benefits, *563*
- temporary life insurance, *563*
- permanent life insurance, *564*
- cash value, *564*

LO 2-1 | Disability Insurance

Of all the types of insurance, disability insurance is the most overlooked. **Disability insurance** is an insurance plan that makes regular payments (usually monthly) to replace income lost when illness or injury prevents the insured from working. This type of insurance is often referred to as *income protection*, because coverage compensates workers for loss of income resulting from serious illness or injury. People think nothing can happen to them that will interrupt their earning power. Unfortunately, recovery from an accident or an illness can go on for weeks or even months. Yet while you are disabled (unable to perform your job), your regular living expenses go on.

Generally, there are two types of disability insurance: short term and long term. *Short-term disability* insurance usually lasts between three and six months. *Long-term disability* insurance usually picks up where short-term disability leaves off and can provide coverage up to retirement. Short-term and long-term disability plans typically cover 50 to 70 percent of monthly salary.

Most employers offer both short-term and long-term disability group plans. In many cases, the employer pays for part or all of the plan. However, the insurance is good only as long as you

What is the main purpose of disability insurance?

© Chris Singshinsuk/Shutterstock.com

© Pan Xunbin/Shutterstock.com

work for the employer. If you leave the company, you lose all policy rights. If your employer does not have a group plan, individual coverage can be provided through private insurance at a higher premium.

Disability benefits don't begin the day you become disabled. Instead, coverage requires a *waiting period* (or *elimination period*). The waiting period can range from 30 days to 90 days or longer. During this time, you may be on sick leave from work collecting regular pay. Private disability insurance policies that require longer waiting periods have lower premiums.

The maximum *duration of benefits* under most disability policies is until age 65 or early retirement if you qualify. A few policies pay benefits for life if you become permanently disabled.

Guaranteed renewability of coverage will protect you against cancellation if your health declines. Without this provision, an insurer could refuse to renew your insurance. The premium for a policy with guaranteed renewability is higher, but the coverage may be worth the extra cost.

Social Security Disability Insurance

Most workers in the United States participate in the Social Security program. Social Security is more than retirement income. It is OASD (old age, survivors, and disability insurance) as well as HI (health insurance—Medicare). If you have Social Security taxes deducted from your paycheck, you are entitled to disability payments from Social Security in the event you become disabled and cannot work.

To qualify, you will have to prove the extent of your disability, fill out forms, and have medical exams as required by the Social Security Administration. Workers are considered disabled if they have a physical or mental condition that prevents them from doing any gainful work and the condition is expected to last for at least 12 months or result in death. Benefits are determined in part by your pay and in part by the number of years you have been covered under Social Security. The work requirement may be waived for certain individuals, including the blind, widows or widowers with disabilities, children with disabilities, and wounded military service members.

Workers' Compensation Insurance

Workers' compensation is a form of insurance that provides coverage for an employee who has suffered an injury or illness resulting from job-related duties. Coverage includes payment of medical bills and compensation for lost wages. This insurance also carries a death benefit. It provides a burial payment and an allowance for living expenses for survivors of people killed on the job. Like Social Security benefits, these benefits are determined by your earnings and your work history.

Workers' compensation insurance is administered at the state level. Each state has its own laws and programs for workers' compensation. In most states, workers' compensation coverage is not optional; almost all employers must carry this insurance.

Workers' compensation should not be confused with short-term and long-term disability; it pays workers only when they are injured on the job, whereas disability insurance pays regardless of when or where the insured is injured or disabled.

LO 2-2 Life Insurance

Life insurance provides funds to the beneficiaries when the insured dies. Consider the financial needs that a family will face after the death of a wage earner—and how much income will be needed to pay the ongoing expenses of daily living. The main purpose of life insurance, then, is to provide for those who depend on you as a source of income. There are also other purposes that life insurance can fulfill, as shown in Figure 23.1. As you can see, in addition to death benefits, life insurance can also provide savings benefits.

Like all types of insurance, life insurance is based on risk sharing and probability. To predict the probability of death at different ages, insurers use *mortality tables*. These tables are based on statistics gathered about life expectancy and death rates among various groups of people. Insurers set premiums based on these tables. For example, older people have a higher probability of dying while the policy is in effect than do younger people. As a result, insurers generally charge older adults higher premiums. Other factors enter the calculation as well. For example, smokers tend to die sooner than nonsmokers, and premiums reflect this.

To buy an individual life insurance policy, you will have to supply a detailed medical history. You also may be required to have a medical exam, especially for large policies. Someone with a serious health problem, such as heart disease, may not be able to buy an individual life insurance policy at all.

You may be able to buy group life insurance through your employer. A *group life insurance plan* insures a large number of people under the terms of a single policy without requiring a medical exam. Employers often provide

---

FIGURE 23.1   Purposes of Life Insurance

Why You Should Purchase Life Insurance

- to provide cash to pay for a funeral
- to pay off a home mortgage and other debts at the time of death
- to provide a lump-sum payment to children when they reach a specified age
- to provide an education or income for children
- to make charitable bequests after death
- to provide for retirement income
- to accumulate savings
- to make estate and inheritance tax payments
- to take care of children's needs as they are growing up (including child care services in the event of the death of a parent)
- to provide cash value that can be borrowed

group life insurance as an employee benefit. Group coverage costs much less than an individual policy. Today, recent laws require that group policies be portable. **Portability** means that when you leave your employer, you are able to continue paying the premiums and convert your group policy into an individual policy.

Provisions of Life Insurance Policies

Although life insurance policies differ from company to company, there are a number of standard provisions that are usually found in all policies. It is important to understand these provisions before purchasing a life insurance policy so that you know what is expected of you and the insurer.

Beneficiary Clause

An important provision in a life insurance policy is the right to name your beneficiaries. As you previously learned, *beneficiaries* are the people named in an insurance policy who will receive the benefits of the policy. The beneficiaries of a life insurance policy will receive the amount specified in the policy upon the death of the insured. Beneficiaries can be anyone; if children are minors, parents may name a trustee or guardian to handle the money on behalf of the children. Both primary and secondary beneficiaries can be designated. If the primary beneficiary is deceased, the benefits will go to the secondary beneficiary. You also can change the beneficiaries anytime during the term of the policy.

Incontestable Clause

An **incontestable clause** is a provision of a life insurance policy stating that once the policy has been in effect for a stated period of time (usually two years), the insurer may no longer question items on the application in order to deny coverage. For example, an applicant may lie about his or her age or conceal a serious medical condition in order to get a lower premium. If the insurer discovers this, it will not pay the claim on the death of the insured if it occurs during the first two years (or other specified time period) of the policy. After the specified period, the insurer cannot dispute the policy's validity during the lifetime and after the death of the insured for any reason. One reason for this provision is to protect the beneficiaries from financial loss. They should not be made to suffer because of acts of the insured.

Suicide Clause

A *suicide clause* is a provision of a life insurance policy that specifies that the insurance company will not pay the claim if the insured commits suicide within the first two years (or other specified time period)

What are the various provisions commonly found in life insurance policies?

of the policy. If the insured's death is a result of suicide, the insurer will likely only return previously paid premiums to the family. Some policies will pay death benefits after a waiting period (such as two years) from the date of death.

Riders

Insurers offer a variety of riders to life insurance policies. A life insurance *rider* is a small insurance addendum that modifies the coverage of the main policy. A rider usually adds or excludes some types of coverage or alters policy benefits. Riders result in higher premiums.

A *waiver of premium* rider allows you to stop paying premiums and keep your coverage in force if you become disabled and cannot work. This rider usually does not kick in until you've been disabled at least six months.

Guaranteed insurability riders give you the right to renew a policy or buy additional coverage regardless of changes in health. If your health starts to decline with age, you can apply for extra coverage without undergoing a medical exam.

Many insurers also offer *accidental death* riders. In the case of accidental death, some riders provide for double indemnity. **Double indemnity** means that the beneficiary is paid double the face amount of the insurance policy.

The acceleration of benefits rider is also offered by many insurers. **Acceleration of benefits** allows people who have been diagnosed with a serious medical condition that will likely lead to their death in 12 or 24 months (or other specified time period) to collect a portion of their life insurance benefits before death. Typical benefits are anywhere between 50 to 90 percent of the face value of the policy, depending on the insurer. The purpose of this provision is to allow the person to pay off debts and prepare for expenses that will occur. If the person does not die within the specified time period, he or she does not have to repay the accelerated benefits received.

Types of Life Insurance

There are two main types of life insurance: temporary and permanent. Both types come in different forms and have advantages and disadvantages.

Temporary Life Insurance

Temporary life insurance remains in effect for a specified period of time, such as 20 years. If the insured survives beyond that time, coverage ceases with no remaining value. Temporary life insurance is often referred to as *term life insurance*. Term policies are sometimes called "pure" life insurance, because they have value only if the covered risk (death) occurs while the policy is in effect. They have no savings component, as permanent life policies do. However, the premiums for these types of policies are significantly lower than the costs for permanent life insurance. Parents often buy term policies to cover the financial needs of their children in case they should die while the children are still young. By the time the term policy ends, the children will be grown and out on their own, so the parents no longer feel a need to provide for their children.

An insurance agent's income is usually based on commissions. Some people believe that insurance agents will sell as much insurance as possible, with little regard to the actual needs of their customers. They may encourage people to buy permanent life insurance with a high face value as an investment when, in reality, only term life insurance is needed to meet temporary needs. These people believe that permanent life insurance is a poor savings and investing plan. Others believe that people should carry large amounts of life insurance as a way to leave an estate for their heirs. They also feel that permanent life insurance is a good investment because it forces you to save money.

THINK CRITICALLY

With which side do you agree? Why? How much insurance do you think is needed by the average person of your age? What factors should you consider when deciding whether to buy insurance?

There are several variations of term life insurance. With *decreasing term insurance*, the amount of coverage decreases each year while the premium remains the same. For example, assume a person buys a 20-year decreasing term policy worth $100,000. The policy decreases in coverage each year until the value reaches zero at the end of 20 years. If the insured dies during the first year of the policy, it pays the full benefit ($100,000). If the insured dies during the second year, death benefits decrease to $95,000. If the insured dies during the third year, benefits decrease to $90,000, and so on. Therefore, the coverage of the policy decreases by a specified amount each year. In contrast, the death benefit on *level term insurance* remains constant from beginning to end, while the premium increases at designated intervals (such as five years). Although it can be used for any purpose, decreasing term insurance is often sold for the purpose of paying off a mortgage in the event of death. The value of decreasing term insurance decreases over time as does the principal in a mortgage.

Renewable term insurance gives the insured the right to renew the policy each year, without having to pass a physical exam. Premiums increase with each renewal because the policyholder is older (and the risk of death greater), but the death benefits remain the same.

Convertible term insurance permits the insured to convert the policy to permanent coverage within a specific time period without providing additional evidence of insurability, such as a medical exam. This type of policy provides the benefit of purchasing less expensive term life insurance now with the option to convert to a permanent policy at a later date, as insurance needs and financial resources change. Converting the policy to permanent insurance will raise the premium.

Permanent Life Insurance

Permanent life insurance remains in effect for the insured's lifetime and builds a cash value. **Cash value** is the savings accumulated in a permanent life insurance policy that you would receive if you canceled your policy. To build cash value, a portion of your premiums is deposited into an investment account where it earns interest. The interest rate varies with short-term rates in the economy. You can borrow money using your policy's cash value as collateral. If you do not repay the loan, the policy will repay it out of the death benefit when you die. For example, if you have a $100,000 policy and you borrow $20,000 but do not repay it, your beneficiaries will receive only $80,000 upon your death.

Permanent life insurance comes in many forms. Four common types of permanent life policies are whole life, limited-pay life, universal life, and variable life.

Is it wise to borrow against the cash value of your life insurance policy? Why or why not?

Whole Life

A *whole life* policy (also known as straight or ordinary life) is insurance for which you pay fixed premiums throughout your life, and upon your death, a stated sum is paid to your beneficiary. The amount of your premium depends primarily on the age at which you purchase the policy. The premiums are high enough to pay for the death benefit plus contribute to the policy's cash value.

Limited-Pay Life

With a *limited-pay life* policy, premiums are limited to a specific number of years or until age 65. At the end of the payment period, the policy is considered "paid up." However, you remain insured for life, and the company will pay the face value of the policy at your death.

Universal Life

Unlike the other types of permanent life policies, the premiums and death benefit on a *universal life* policy are not fixed. The policyholder can choose to change the death benefit and the amount or timing of premiums during the life of the policy. Thus, the face value of the policy can be lowered or raised without rewriting the policy. When interest rates are high, you can move large sums of money into your policy (by paying higher premiums) and let the earnings grow tax-deferred.

Variable Life

Variable life combines a death benefit with investment options. At the designation of the policyholder, the insurer invests part of the premium in securities (such as stocks, bonds, and money market funds) within the insurance company's portfolio. Both the death benefit and cash value rise (or fall) with the investment results. While a minimum death benefit is guaranteed, there is no guaranteed cash value. With some variable life policies, policyholders pay fixed premiums. With others, the premiums can fluctuate because the interest earned on investments may be applied to the premiums, thus reducing the amount the policyholder pays.

CHECKPOINT

How do temporary life insurance and permanent life insurance differ?

Insurance Underwriting

Insurance companies write policies to protect consumers from financial loss. Underwriters decide if insurance will be provided to applicants and under what terms. They use computer software programs to help them do a careful analysis of risk factors in order to make recommendations on coverage and premiums.

Insurance underwriters must achieve a balance between risky and cautious decisions. When they underestimate the risk, the insurance company pays out excessive claims. When they overestimate risk, the insurance company loses customers.

Underwriters typically work in four main types of insurance: life, health, mortgage, or property. Life and health insurance underwriters specialize in group or individual policies.

Employment Outlook

- A slower-than-average employment growth is expected.

Job Titles

- Insurance underwriter
- Property value analyst
- Group risk analyst

Needed Skills

- A bachelor's degree is preferred, especially in business, accounting, or finance.
- Certification is often necessary for advancement.
- Good judgment, excellent analytical skills, and strong computer skills are essential.

What's it like to work in . . . *Insurance Underwriting*

Stefanie has worked as a group health insurance underwriter for a local insurance firm for the past five years. Her annual salary is $65,000. She is also currently working on her RHU (Registered Health Underwriter) certification.

Stefanie analyzes data for a group of similarly sized employers and develops a risk assessment that will be used to set their annual premiums. She works mostly in her office at the computer and uses the Internet to connect to databases that help her analyze information on applications. She also spends time contacting field representatives, medical personnel, and others to obtain additional information on applicants. To stay current, she meets with other underwriters to share and compare underwriting trends and techniques.

Stefanie is detail oriented and takes the time to do a thorough and accurate job. She realizes the importance of assessing risk accurately so that premiums reflect a positive profitability ratio for her company.

What About You?

Would you like to work with numbers and large amounts of data? Are you analytical, accurate, and detail oriented? Would you enjoy working as an insurance underwriter where you can assess and predict risk?

The Career Clusters icons are being used with permission of the: States' Career Clusters Initiative, 2007, www.careerclusters.org

KEY TERMS REVIEW

Match the terms with the definitions. Some terms may not be used.

a. acceleration of benefits
b. cash value
c. disability insurance
d. double indemnity
e. incontestable clause
f. life insurance
g. permanent life insurance
h. portability
i. temporary life insurance

____ 1. The feature that allows a group policy to be converted into an individual policy

____ 2. Savings accumulated in a permanent life insurance policy that you would receive if you canceled your policy

____ 3. Insurance that provides funds to the beneficiaries when the insured dies

____ 4. A rider that allows the beneficiary to be paid double the face amount of the insurance policy

____ 5. Insurance that remains in effect for the insured's lifetime and builds a cash value

____ 6. An insurance plan that makes regular payments to replace income lost when illness or injury prevents the insured from working

____ 7. A rider that allows people who have been diagnosed with a serious medical condition to collect a portion of their life insurance benefits before death

CHECK YOUR UNDERSTANDING

LO2-1 8. What is the difference between short-term disability insurance and long-term disability insurance?

LO2-2 9. Why do insurers use mortality tables?

APPLY YOUR KNOWLEDGE

LO2-2 10. How will your life insurance needs change over your lifetime?

THINK CRITICALLY

LO2-1 11. If you have workers' compensation insurance, why would you need disability insurance?

LO2-2 12. Explain why portable group life insurance policies are a good idea for many workers.

LO2-2 13. Why might a financial adviser recommend term insurance instead of permanent insurance?

The Essential Question *Refer to The Essential Question on p. 559. Disability insurance protects the family from loss of income when the wage earner cannot work. Life insurance protects those left behind when a wage earner dies.*

SUMMARY

23.1

- *Group health insurance policies provide broad coverage at lower premiums than do individual policies.*

- *COBRA allows people who leave their jobs to keep their employer-provided health insurance for a limited time.*

- *HIPAA limits exclusions for preexisting conditions and makes it illegal to deny coverage based on health status.*

- *A Flex 125 Plan allows employees to set aside money, pretax, to help pay deductibles, co-payments, and other health expenses that are not covered by insurance.*

- *People without a group plan can buy individual health insurance, but they may have to meet certain requirements.*

- *Health insurance exchanges provide a set of government-regulated and standardized health care plans from which uninsured and underinsured individuals may purchase health insurance policies.*

- *Typical health insurance includes basic medical and major medical coverage. Some cover dental and vision needs for a higher premium.*

- *Unmanaged care plans allow employees to select their own providers and be reimbursed a percentage of expenses after a deductible is met. Managed care plans contract with a network of health care providers.*

- *Medicare is government-sponsored health insurance for people age 65 or older. Medicaid is government-sponsored health insurance for people with low incomes and limited resources.*

23.2

- *Disability insurance replaces income if you are injured or ill and cannot work. Social Security and workers' compensation insurance also provide disability coverage.*

- *Life insurance provides funds to beneficiaries when the insured dies.*

- *Insurers set life insurance premiums based on life expectancy and death rates compiled in mortality tables.*

- *Temporary life insurance, commonly known as term life insurance, remains in effect for a specified time. If the insured survives beyond that time, coverage ceases with no remaining value.*

- *Permanent life insurance remains in effect for the insured's lifetime and has a savings component (cash value) as well as a death benefit. Common types of permanent life policies are whole life, limited-pay life, universal life, and variable life.*

APPLY WHAT YOU KNOW

L01-1 1. Obtain a brochure describing the benefits of a group health insurance plan. If you don't know someone who belongs to a group plan, the Internet will have information about these plans. Write a paper summarizing your findings regarding the types of coverage available and the plan's provisions for deductibles, co-payments, exclusions, and so on.

L01-2 2. Interview a person who has recently had surgery or been in the hospital for several days or longer. Ask this person about the type of services provided and the approximate cost per day of those services. Ask him or her how much of the cost was paid by insurance and how much (percentage or dollar amount) he or she will have to pay out of pocket. Write a report on your findings.

L02-1 3. Assuming that you are working full time, are married, and have one child, prepare an analysis of your disability insurance needs. Select a career that you would like to have and use a realistic income figure for someone with one to three years of experience.

L02-2 4. Examine the various purposes of life insurance in Figure 23.1. Can you add anything to this list? Would you delete anything? Prepare a list of reasons for purchasing life insurance based on your personal situation as you imagine it will be in ten years.

MAKE ACADEMIC CONNECTIONS

L01-1 5. **Communication** Write a paper about the Affordable Care Act (Obamacare) and how it is perceived in terms of reducing costs and providing coverage for the uninsured and underinsured in this country. Conduct online research to get current statistics on how many Americans are still uninsured. What can be done to resolve the problem? How can we control medical costs and make medical care affordable to all citizens?

L01-2 6. **Math** Compute the out-of-pocket expenses in the following situation: Tom's medical insurance will pay 80 percent of the cost of a procedure. The policy sets an allowable limit for the procedure at $1,000. Tom's doctor bills the insurer for $1,300. How much will Tom have to pay?

L02-1 7. **Economics** Explain the effect on the economy when people receive Social Security Disability Insurance (SSDI). Conduct online research to find out how much money is paid each year to people receiving SSDI versus how much money is collected through Social Security taxes. What effect would insolvency (financial collapse) of SSDI or Social Security have on future generations? What ideas are being suggested to save the program from insolvency? Write a two-page paper on your findings. Include charts, tables, or graphs to enhance your report.

L02-2 8. **Research** Choose a permanent life insurance policy and decide on the amount of coverage you want. Visit an insurer in person or online to find out more about the policy and its premiums. Write a report summarizing why you selected the policy and what you learned about it from the insurer.

Solve Problems and Explore Issues

LO1-1 9. Your friend is considering two career opportunities—one in which she would be self-employed and have no benefits, and one in which she would work as an employee of a company and have full health insurance. Explain to her the importance of having health insurance and how her options for insurance might differ, depending on her career choice.

LO1-2 10. A young married couple needs affordable health coverage. Neither employer provides spousal coverage without a very high premium. One spouse is considering an HSA, while the other is considering an HMO. What are the advantages and disadvantages of these plans?

LO2-1 11. Your friend Devon is working full time at two jobs in order to make house payments and buy a new car. His wife, Cara, is working nights so she can care for the children during the day. Devon can purchase both short-term and long-term disability insurance for a small premium ($10 a month) through his employer's group insurance plan. Explain to them the importance of having disability insurance.

LO2-2 12. As a young, unmarried person, you are contemplating college next year and the pursuit of a professional degree that will take six years or more to complete. A neighbor sells life insurance and wants you to buy a universal life policy with a $100,000 face value. Explain whether or not you would consider purchasing this policy. Would you consider purchasing a different type of life insurance policy? Explain your answer.

EXTEND YOUR LEARNING

LO1-1 13. **Ethics** It is becoming common practice today for employers to require employees to participate in wellness programs to manage their health. These programs include mandatory exercise and diet programs and weight management. If employees refuse to participate, they pay higher premiums for their health insurance. Do you feel this practice invades a person's rights? Or do you believe that forcing people to get well and stay well is a benefit worth having? Explain your answer.

CHAPTER PROJECT

Conduct research on Medicare by visiting the U.S. government's official site on Medicare (www.medicare.gov). What types of coverage are available, and how much do Medicare beneficiaries pay for this coverage? Explain how Medicare Advantage plans work, and provide information on Medigap insurance. What is the "donut hole" for prescription drug coverage? What is the total cost of Medicare to a retired person? Prepare a report on your findings using visual aids.

Complete the Guided Decision Making activity for Chapter 23 at ngl.cengage.com/mypf.

Janet Yellen

BAO DANDAN/Xinhua /Landov

Janet Louise Yellen was born in Brooklyn, New York, in 1946. She is the chair of the Board of Governors of the Federal Reserve System. Yellen graduated from Pembroke College (now Brown University) with a degree in economics in 1967. She earned her PhD in economics from Yale University in 1971. From 1971 to 1976, she was an assistant professor at Harvard University and was an economist with the Federal Reserve Board of Governors in 1977–1978. She taught at The London School of Economics and Political Science from 1978 to 1980. In 1980 she began teaching at the University of California, Berkeley's Haas School of Business, where twice she was awarded the Haas School's outstanding teaching award. Yellen was appointed as a member of the Federal Reserve System's Board of Governors from 1994 to 1997 and served as chair of President Clinton's Council of Economic Advisers from 1997 to 1999. From 2004 to 2010, she was the president and CEO of the Federal Reserve Bank of San Francisco and a voting member of the Federal Open Market Committee in 2009. In 2010 President Obama nominated Yellen as vice chair of the Federal Reserve System, and in October 2013, Yellen was officially nominated to replace Ben Bernanke as head of the Federal Reserve. Yellen was sworn in on February 3, 2014, making her the first woman to hold the position.

Actions of the Federal Reserve affect all Americans in the form of economic risk. As chair of the Federal Reserve, Yellen pledged to "meet the great responsibilities that Congress has entrusted to the Federal Reserve—to promote maximum employment, stable prices, and a strong and stable financial system." As a monetary "dove" (as opposed to a monetary "hawk"), she has been an outspoken advocate for using the powers of the Federal Reserve to reduce unemployment and has seemed more willing than other economists to risk slightly higher inflation to accomplish this goal.

THINK CRITICALLY

1. How did Janet Yellen's career moves lead to her new position as chair of the Federal Reserve? Do you think she's qualified for her job?

2. How might the actions of the Federal Reserve affect the economy in the United States as well as worldwide? What risks do Americans face as a result of these actions?

Managing Risk

Overview

In this project, you will apply risk and insurance concepts. You will also do some further exploring and assessing of your insurance needs. You'll learn how to compute the true cost of insurance, how to file an insurance claim, what to do if you have a car accident, how you can reduce health insurance costs, how to use mortality tables, and how to build a good lifetime risk management plan.

You will also learn about workplace safety and emergency planning. Knowing what to do ahead of time will prevent injuries and lower overall risk to yourself and others.

The True Cost of Insurance

People buy insurance for protection against the risks of financial uncertainty and unexpected losses. The alternative—being uninsured—may represent large and undefined risks that can leave you feeling uncomfortable. Since the alternative of not being insured is often unacceptable, most people are covered by some type of insurance most of their lives. Although insurance can be costly, there are ways in which you can save money when buying a policy.

Auto Insurance

Let's look at auto insurance first. Your full-coverage policy might offer the type of coverage and annual cost shown on the next page.

© Deymos Photo/Shutterstock.com

Liability coverage, 100/300/50	$560
Collision coverage, $50 deductible	180
Comprehensive coverage, $50 deductible	90
Personal injury protection	80
Uninsured/underinsured motorist	60
Towing	15
Total annual cost	$985

If you were willing to increase the deductibles, your savings could be considerable. Let's assume that a $500 collision deductible would reduce the cost of the coverage in our example by $100 a year. Over a five-year period, your total insurance costs would be:

Full coverage, $50 deductible: $985 × 5 = $4,925
Full coverage, $500 deductible: $885 × 5 =   4,425
Savings $ 500

In five years, you would have saved enough in premiums to pay a $500 loss, should it occur. Therefore, it is wise to check your options for saving on insurance premiums. Calculate the savings over time and decide whether you would likely save more in premium reductions than you would likely pay out in losses.

You can also lower your premiums by reducing the limits of liability coverage from 100/300/50 to your state's minimum. However, when using this method of lowering your premiums, you risk greater loss if you are at fault in an accident.

You may also be able to lower your premiums by choosing to reduce or drop collision coverage from your policy. Figure U5.1 illustrates when it would be wise to reduce or drop collision coverage on your car to save on premiums.

FIGURE U5.1   Reduce or Drop Coverage (Collision)

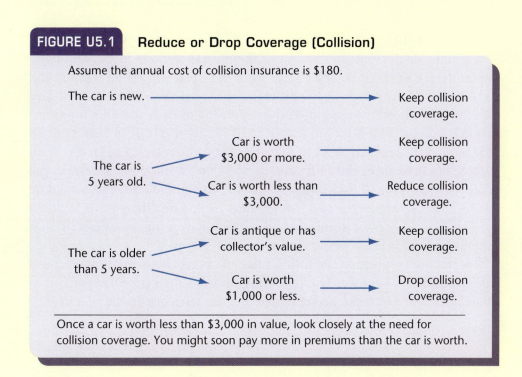

Assume the annual cost of collision insurance is $180.

The car is new. ──────────────────────→ Keep collision coverage.

The car is 5 years old.
→ Car is worth $3,000 or more. → Keep collision coverage.
→ Car is worth less than $3,000. → Reduce collision coverage.

The car is older than 5 years.
→ Car is antique or has collector's value. → Keep collision coverage.
→ Car is worth $1,000 or less. → Drop collision coverage.

Once a car is worth less than $3,000 in value, look closely at the need for collision coverage. You might soon pay more in premiums than the car is worth.

Life Insurance

Let's now compute the cost of a whole life insurance policy and compare the results to the purchase of term insurance. To do this, we must use the time value of money concept—the fact that money will grow over time because it is earning interest.

Suppose you are age 25 and purchased a $100,000 face value whole life policy. The annual premium for this policy is $250. The policy will pay a guaranteed rate of 6 percent (on the policy's cash value) after the first year. At the end of the first year, there is no cash value. The entire premium is used to cover commissions and policy costs. After the first year, a portion of the premium covers the cost of insurance, and the rest is deposited in a savings plan. The amount deposited accumulates as cash value. The death benefit remains at $100,000 over a five-year period. During this time, the cost of insurance rises slightly each year, leaving a smaller amount of the premium for savings. Assuming the 6 percent rate holds, the cash value of the policy after five years would be $634.95.

Whole Life Policy

			Savings Plan			
Year	Premium	Insurance Cost*	Deposit	+	Interest	Cash Value at Beg. Year
1	$ 250.00	$100.00	$ 0.00			$ 0.00
2	250.00	102.00	148.00	+	$ 0.00	148.00
3	250.00	104.00	146.00	+	8.88	302.88**
4	250.00	106.00	144.00	+	18.17	465.05
5	250.00	108.00	142.00	+	27.90	634.95
Totals	$1,250.00	$520.00	$580.00		$54.95	$634.95

*This amount represents only policy costs. Commissions are not included.

**Assume the full premium is paid at the beginning of each year. To compute the interest earned at the end of Year 2, multiply $148 by 6 percent. Then add the deposits of $148 and $146 to interest earned of $8.88 to derive the Year 3 cash balance of $302.88.

As an alternative, you could purchase term life insurance. Assume the term premiums are the same as the cost of the insurance alone in the whole life example: $100 (Year 1), $102 (Year 2), $104 (Year 3), $106 (Year 4), and $108 (Year 5). You deposit the difference between the whole life premium ($250) and the term premium at the beginning of each year in a 6 percent savings account. That is, you invest $150 ($250 − $100) in Year 1; $148 ($250 − $102) in Year 2; $146 ($250 − $104) in Year 3; and so on. With whole life insurance, the cash value is $634.95. With term insurance, the accumulated value of the savings account at the end of five years would be $873.79, as shown in the table on the next page. The difference is $238.84 ($873.79 − $634.95). In this case, you can achieve a higher savings balance through buying term insurance and saving on your own.

To practice computing the future value of savings between different policies, complete Worksheet 1 (Computing Future Value) provided for you in the *Student Activity Guide* and also presented for reference on the next page.

Invested Savings with Term Insurance Policy

Year	Beginning Balance	Deposit	Interest	Ending Balance
1	$ 0.00	$150.00	$ 9.00	$159.00
2	159.00	148.00	18.42	325.42
3	325.42	146.00	28.29	499.71
4	499.71	144.00	38.62	682.33
5	682.33	142.00	49.46	873.79*

*The total saved at the end of five years is $873.79.

How to File an Insurance Claim

When you have sustained a loss, such as fire damage to your home, you must file an insurance claim. Before filing a claim, you should know your policy and its coverages, limitations, and exclusions. To receive compensation, you must be organized before you file the claim.

Keep receipts and other documentation of value. If you own antiques, collectibles, or other items for which you have no receipt, have the items *appraised* so that you will have a certificate of authenticated value. Such an appraisal may cost $100 or more, but it will help you receive the full reimbursement due to you when you file a claim.

If property is stolen, call the police and fill out a report. Without evidence of a theft and a *police report* as documentation, the insurance company has no way to verify that the incident took place. You should have good notes about what was taken, witnesses, time of day, what you observed, and so on. This allows you to provide as much information as possible when filling out the police report. Also, you must take ordinary precautions against theft.

If, for example, you leave your car unlocked, the insurer may not pay benefits for stolen property.

If property is damaged, you will need to get repair estimates—usually more than one. Contact your insurer right away and have documentation and notes ready. The insurance adjuster will take your report and ask you questions. It's important to be clear and accurate when supplying information. You must also take reasonable precautions to avoid further damage. For example, if a storm creates a hole in your roof, you must cover the hole as soon as possible with some type of protective covering to avoid rain damage to your home's contents. If you fail to take this step, the insurer may not pay for the extra damage.

Complete Worksheet 2 (Insurance Claim Form) provided for you in the *Student Activity Guide* and also presented for reference on the next page. It provides hypothetical information and a sample claim form, similar to one that your insurer would require you to complete to report property damage.

What to Do If You Have a Car Accident

Sooner or later, either as a driver or as a passenger, you are likely to be involved in an automobile accident. Most car accidents are the result of human error. The higher the speed, the higher the likelihood of a serious injury and damage to property.

If you are involved in an automobile accident, there are several things you must do. Figure U5.2 lists standard procedures to follow. Your state may have additional things you should, or should not, do following an accident. Failure to comply with these laws can lead to suspension of your driving privileges, fines, and other types of punishment. You will find this information in your state's driver's manual or online at your state's Department of Motor Vehicles website. You should be familiar with this information before an accident occurs.

FIGURE U5.2   **What to Do If You're in a Car Accident**

If you are involved in a motor vehicle accident, standard requirements are as follows:

1. Stop your vehicle, turn off the ignition, and remain at the scene of the accident. If feasible, pull your car to the side of the road so you won't impede traffic.

2. Get the names and addresses of other drivers, passengers, and witnesses. Make notes of what happened, including time of day, weather conditions, roadway location, signal lights, and so on. Write down vehicle license numbers.

3. Fill out the necessary accident report forms within the time requirements in your state (usually three days). Give a copy of the report to your insurance company. Also obtain a copy of the police report, if any.

4. Provide assistance to persons who are injured; seek medical help if needed. Stay at the scene of the accident until all needed information is exchanged and all involved parties leave the scene.

5. Always have your insurance and vehicle registration information with you. Get insurance and vehicle registration information from the other driver; copy it from the documentation or enter it into electronic media so it can be stored.

6. Know the laws of your state. There may be additional requirements where you live.

Your state has accident reporting forms. Get one and fill it out for a fictional situation. In most cases, you may have only three days (72 hours) to fill out an accident report once you are in an accident.

WORKSHEET 2
Insurance Claim Form

Directions: Fill out the claim form below based on the following information. The insured is Mary B. Ownbey, who lives at 845 Oak Street, Wellington, Ohio 44090. Her phone number is (440) 555-0180. Her policy number is KN338-44-2281, and her agent is G. Smiley. Her home was broken into sometime between 8 p.m. and 2 a.m. (Friday evening) while she was away. The kitchen was vandalized (spray paint on the walls and eggs thrown on the floor); the carpeting in the dining room was stained as well. A police report was filed (Case 95-2288) by Officer K. Bridges. There were no witnesses. The walls in the kitchen must be scraped and painted; the carpeting must be cleaned or replaced if the stain cannot be removed. The value of the damage is estimated at $500. The house was painted last year ($100 for the kitchen walls); the carpet was new a year ago ($2,000 for the damaged carpeting). Both were purchased at Excel Interiors, and she has a receipt. The property is located in the home at the above address. Use today's date.

Claim No. _____

Name of Insured _____

Address _____

_____ Phone _____

Policy No. _____ Agent _____

Describe what happened: _____

_____

_____

_____

Was a police report filed? _____ Case No. _____
(Attach copy)

Police officer taking report _____

Were there any witnesses? _____ List their names and addresses:

_____

_____

Description of property damaged _____

Value of property _____

Date purchased _____ Purchase price _____

Where purchased _____ Receipt? _____

Where is property now located (for inspection)? _____

_____

_____   _____

Date   Signature of Insured

How to Reduce Health Care Costs

The best way to avoid high medical costs is to stay well. Corporations across America are realizing the importance of "wellness" programs in an attempt to keep their employees healthy. Here are some suggestions of how to avoid illness and injury:

- Eat a balanced diet and keep your weight within reasonable limits.
- Avoid smoking.
- Don't drink to excess.
- Get sufficient rest and relaxation.
- Know your body's limitations; don't overdo it.
- Never get in a vehicle where the driver's abilities are impaired by alcohol, anger, or any other condition.
- Don't drive if you have had anything that could impair your ability to drive, including over-the-counter and prescription drugs.
- Drive carefully; avoid and reduce risks where possible. For example, don't drive in freezing rain. If you must drive, use safety devices.

When you do use health care services, there are additional ways to minimize your costs and your insurer's costs. Figure U5.3 lists some methods of reducing health care costs and maximizing the benefit from services that you can use.

To assess how you personally reduce health care costs, complete Worksheet 3 (Reducing Health Care Costs) provided for you in the *Student Activity Guide* and also presented for reference on the next page.

FIGURE U5.3 **How to Cut Health Care Costs**

When you are the patient, whether or not insurance is involved, you can maximize your health care dollars with the following actions:

1. Know your insurance coverage, limitations, and exclusions.

2. Take insurance information with you when visiting a hospital or doctor's office and when picking up prescriptions.

3. Take a list of questions with you to the doctor. Take notes so you will remember specific answers.

4. Give your doctor information needed to make correct diagnoses. Write down symptoms, relevant past history, what you have done or taken so far, and related information.

5. Ask the doctor about short- and long-term side effects of prescriptions. Read prescription directions and information supplied by a pharmacist and manufacturer. Do online research at sites such as WebMD.

6. Get second (and third) opinions for any type of surgery or medication with serious risks or potential side effects.

7. Predetermine fees for routine tests and services and look for less expensive providers. For example, have your cholesterol tested at a local clinic rather than the doctor's office.

8. Use generic medicines when possible.

9. Be cautious and ask lots of questions. Remember: You are in charge of your health, and the doctor is there to assist you, not the other way around. Take charge of your own life, nutrition, and lifestyle and know what it takes to stay healthy and strong.

WORKSHEET 3
Reducing Health Care Costs

Directions: Answer the following questions about ways you can reduce health care costs.

1. Do you eat well-balanced meals and exercise regularly?

2. Do you get sufficient rest and relaxation?

3. Do you know your health insurance coverages, limitations, and exclusions?

4. Do you use generic prescriptions when possible? (Generic drugs are less expensive versions of brand-name drugs. Because there is no advertising or other expenses of mass marketing, the cost is lower.)

5. Do you shop around for the best prices for (a) dental work, (b) vision care and glasses, (c) prescriptions, (d) charges for office visits, and (e) supplies, vitamins, and other health care purchases?

6. List some things you and your family can do to reduce health care costs.

7. Explain why it is important to ask questions when you visit your doctor.

How to Use Mortality Tables

A *mortality table* lists the number of people per 1,000 living of a specific age who are expected to die in a given year. A mortality table also tells you the average number of years that a person of a specific age would be expected to live. These tables are typically constructed separately for men and women.

Mortality tables (or *life expectancy tables*) are used by insurance actuaries in setting life insurance premiums. A mortality table matches age with a mortality rate and sets a premium accordingly.

Figure U5.4 shows part of a mortality table that would be used by insurance actuaries in determining the premium for a life insurance policy. Use this table to complete Worksheet 4 (Using Mortality Tables) provided for you in the *Student Activity Guide* and also presented for reference on the next page.

FIGURE U5.4 Partial Mortality Table

Age	Male Deaths per 1,000	Male Life Expectancy (Years)	Female Deaths per 1,000	Female Life Expectancy (Years)
25	1.1	52.5	0.5	56.4
30	1.1	47.8	0.7	51.6
35	1.2	43.1	1.0	46.8
40	1.7	38.3	1.3	42.0
45	2.7	33.7	1.9	37.3
50	3.8	29.2	3.1	32.7
55	6.2	24.8	5.1	28.3
60	9.9	20.6	8.0	24.1
65	16.9	16.8	11.9	20.1
70	25.8	13.3	17.8	16.4
75	41.9	10.2	27.9	13.0

WORKSHEET 4
Using Mortality Tables

Directions: Based on the mortality table above, answer the following questions:

1. At the bottom of the Life Expectancy column, what does the number 13.0 mean?

2. On average, people who are 50 years old now could be expected to live to be what age?

3. In the Deaths per 1,000 column, what does the number 1.2 mean?

4. In a group of 10,000 males, all age 40, an average of how many could be expected to die in the next year?

A Personal Insurance Plan

As you make choices about the type and amount of insurance you will buy, keep the following guidelines in mind:

- *Reduce billing fees.* If your financial situation allows you to, pay your insurance policy either annually or semiannually. Many insurers offer discounts to customers who choose to make one or two payments each year instead of paying in monthly installments.
- *Read the policy carefully.* If you discover a clause that you do not understand, call your agent for clarification.
- *Review your policies regularly to see if the coverage meets your needs.* As your family situation changes, you might wish to modify your life insurance coverage. As your car gets older, you should consider dropping collision coverage.
- *Don't hold on to policies or stay with companies for sentimental reasons.* Be a wise comparison shopper. When you are certain you can do better with another company and have taken proper precautions, move forward to secure a new policy. For example, you may find better rates through a professional organization or other group, such as a credit union.
- *Consider carefully the outcome of switching insurers or changing policies.* If you do switch, be sure you are approved for the new insurance—and that it is correct as represented—before dropping your old insurance.
- *Get to know your insurance agent.* Use his or her expertise. Ask lots of questions and be sure you understand all your coverage options, limitations, and exclusions. Discuss your changing needs and get recommendations, but make your own decisions.
- *Don't keep overlapping policies with the hope of making a quick profit off insurance claims.* Group policies require coordination of benefits. Private policies that overlap coverage in a group policy can be very expensive.
- *Use deductibles wisely.* By paying the first part of an expense yourself, you can save a bundle on insurance rates.
- *Keep your insurance up to date.* Pay premiums promptly and take advantage of any discounts. Ask your insurance agent about discounts available to reduce premiums, such as discounts for nonsmokers.
- *Consider risk management strategies of risk avoidance, risk assumption, and risk reduction.* As you experience life changes, such as having a family, your risks—and, thus, your insurance needs—will change. For example, you might choose to save premium dollars by reducing your collision coverage on your car while increasing your coverage for term life insurance.

To review what you have learned about preparing a personal insurance plan, complete Worksheet 5 (Personal Insurance Plan) provided for you in the *Student Activity Guide* and also presented for reference on the next page.

WORKSHEET 5
Personal Insurance Plan

1. Explain the purpose of each of the following types of insurance.

   a. Homeowners insurance

   b. Automobile insurance

   c. Liability insurance

   d. Health insurance

   e. Disability insurance

   f. Life insurance

2. Based on your current situation, what types of insurance do you currently purchase?

   a. Homeowners insurance

   b. Automobile insurance

   c. Liability insurance

   d. Health insurance

   e. Disability insurance

   f. Life insurance

3. How do you anticipate that your need for each of these insurance coverages will change in the next five years?

   a. Homeowners insurance

   b. Automobile insurance

   c. Liability insurance

   d. Health insurance

   e. Disability insurance

   f. Life insurance

4. List several guidelines for building a plan for purchasing all types of insurance.

Workplace Safety

Americans spend a large percentage of their time at work, yet work can be one of the most dangerous places to be. All workers are entitled by law to a safe place to work. However, workplace injuries are common. Major work-related accidents and injuries are related to the following factors:

- Unsafe working conditions
- Hazards that can lead to injuries of some or all workers
- Tasks that require constant focus to prevent injuries
- Machinery, equipment, or other conditions that require well-developed skills and training
- Carelessness of workers
- Failure to use safety equipment
- Lack of awareness of dangers
- Not knowing how to avoid and reduce risks
- Lack of a practiced and workable emergency plan

Safety is part of everyone's job. Where potentially dangerous conditions exist, workers must know and appreciate the risks that are involved, understand safety needs, and make safety a priority. Therefore, safety training should be required for all employees, even though they may not be directly involved with dangerous work. Having a safe workplace and reducing the number of accidents or injuries will benefit not only the workers but the company as well. Workers' compensation costs are partially based on the safety record of the company.

Emergency Planning

An *emergency plan* is a vital part of workplace safety. An effective emergency plan provides for the safety of workers, employees, visitors, and others. A good emergency plan has the following components:

- Detailed steps to follow in an emergency
- A list of who is responsible for each activity
- A list of who has backup roles
- A secondary plan in case the first course of action fails
- A data backup system
- A process to communicate status inside and outside the company
- Practice drills so that everyone will know what to do in case of a real emergency

Emergency plans should be in writing and shared with everyone. If special training is required, it should be completed and practiced regularly.

Sometimes a safety committee draws up and tests the plan. A safety committee should have representatives for each part of the plan and from each part of the organization. For example, if the organization is a high school campus, every building, floor, or other subunit should have representation.

Emergency plans should include both "expected" events, such as windstorms, fire, and freezing conditions, and "unexpected" or nonroutine events, such as bomb threats, explosions, shootings, or terrorist acts. When companies focus on what could happen, they can identify weak points and take all possible precautions.

Having an emergency plan not only applies to workplaces but also to homes as well. It is important to make sure that the entire family is prepared and informed in the event of a disaster or emergency. Figure U5.5 is an emergency plan for a family in the event they lose power and are unable to go for help. It is suggested by the Federal Emergency Management Agency (FEMA) that all families have such a plan and be able to survive on their own for at least a week.

FIGURE U5.5	Emergency Plan (for Inclement Weather)
Event:	• Weather or other event that leaves us without power (electricity and/or gas) for a week and also prevents us from driving or walking to get food and water
What to do:	• Close up the house to preserve as much heat as possible • Use blankets and a wood-burning fireplace for heat • Move everyone into one room to share the warmth
What to have:	• Food for seven days, to include canned food (tuna, beans, and other items that are not perishable) • Dry pet food in sacks • Water for seven days • Firewood; Pres-to-Logs for fireplace fuel • Blankets • Flashlights, candles, and matches • Emergency supplies in case of injuries (bandages, antiseptic) • Battery-powered radio • Extra batteries
Notes:	• Food has to be rotated to make sure it is fresh and edible • Batteries have to be rotated to be sure they are good

Consumer Rights and Responsibilities

Unit 6 focuses on the role of consumers in a market economy. In Chapter 24, you will examine types of economic systems, how the market economy works, and the role of money. You'll also look at ways to detect and protect yourself from deceptive practices and fraud. Finally, you'll examine ways you can gain redress when you have a complaint.

In Chapter 25, you will take a look at federal laws and agencies that have been formed to help protect you as a consumer.

Chapter 26 examines the legal system of the United States. You'll learn about the trial process, including the people, the paperwork, and the legal remedies available to you. You will also discover other methods of reaching redress, from the informal steps of alternative dispute resolution to small claims court and forms of government assistance.

CHAPTER 24

Role of Consumers in a Market Economy

24.1   **Our Market Economy**

24.2   **Consumer Responsibilities**

Consider This...

Steven is a full-time student. He works part time at a gym to earn money during the school year. He wants many things, but he doesn't have enough money for all of them. He just heard about a new electronic device that uses the latest technology for downloading, storing, and playing music and videos, but the price is very high. He doesn't have enough money, but he could use credit to purchase it.

"If I wait to buy this device until I can save enough money for it, I won't be able to enjoy it now while it's on the cutting edge. On the other hand, if I wait, the price will come down, and then I can afford it. By then, similar alternatives may be on the market. I'm not sure how the law of supply and demand works, but I do know that my resources are limited and I want to get the most for each dollar spent. What would you do?" he asked his friend.

The Essential Question *What are the characteristics of the various types of economic systems, and what is the role of money?*

LEARNING OBJECTIVES

> LO 1-1 Compare and contrast economic systems.
> LO 1-2 Discuss the basic characteristics of a market economy.
> LO 1-3 Explain the role of money in a market economy.

KEY TERMS

- communist economic system, *587*
- socialist economic system, *588*
- traditional economic system, *588*
- capitalism, *588*
- market economy, *588*
- scarcity, *589*
- competition, *591*
- monopoly, *591*
- money, *592*
- fiat money, *593*

LO 1-1 Economic Systems

An *economic system* refers to the process used by a society to decide what to produce, how to produce it, and for whom (how to distribute it among the population). There are three major types of economic systems: hands-on, hands-off, and compromise.

Hands-On Systems

A *hands-on system* is one where the government or central authority controls most of the decisions involving what will be produced, how, and for whom. This type of system grew from the feudalism of the middle ages, where people lived together for safety and to provide for group needs. Today, there are two basic types of hands-on economic systems: communism and socialism.

- *Communism.* Within a **communist economic system** (also known as a *command system*), the government owns and controls most, if not all, of the productive resources of a nation. Parts of China and the former USSR are examples of the communist, classless system. Based on the Marxist theories of sharing resources for the greater benefit of all, this system excludes most private property and ownership of resources; it also limits individual choices.

How is a hands-on economic system different from a hands-off system?

© iStock.com/Kzenon

© Pan Xunbin/Shutterstock.com

- *Socialism.* A socialist economic system (also called a *planned system*) is characterized by a large degree of government control of many of the decisions within the nation. Examples include Sweden, Germany, and other nations that have high tax rates but provide universal access to services, such as education and health care, and guaranteed jobs for all citizens. While there is private ownership of resources and property, many of the nation's choices are predetermined.

Hands-Off Systems

A *hands-off system* is one where there is little or limited role for government or a central authority. Decisions about what will be produced, how, and for whom are made by the people, acting as a whole rather than individually.

- *Traditional.* Within a traditional economic system, the people decide what decisions will be made and how they will be made. Often these systems are based on long-established traditions, religion, or cultural values. Middle-Eastern countries and some small nations in Africa and Asia are organized as traditional economies.
- *Capitalism.* When our country first began, it started as a pure free-enterprise, or capitalist, system. Capitalism is an economic system in which producers and consumers are free to operate and compete in business transactions with minimal, if any, government interference or regulation. Within a "laissez-faire" (hands-off) economy, the power to make decisions regarding resources belongs to individuals and businesses rather than society as a whole, without much, if any, governmental interference.
- *Others.* There are other hands-off economic models, including anarchism, mutualism, and libertarianism. These models reject the role of government or other forms of "group-think," and instead embrace self-rule for all choices.

Compromise Systems

Most nations today have some form of *mixed economy*, which contains elements of more than one type of economic system. For example, over time a capitalist system can become a "survival of the fittest" society unless it accepts a growing need to protect those who would not otherwise survive. Our U.S. economy is considered a market economy, because both market forces (based on individual freedoms) and government decisions determine which goods and services are produced and how they are distributed. The government produces some goods and services, rather than leaving them to private enterprise.

In a market economy, the government also influences and controls some choices. For example, the government collects taxes and borrows money that it spends and redistributes according to its own priorities. Government is also able to impose price controls and other regulations. For example, a *price floor* is imposed on the market when government sets a minimum wage. Employers cannot pay less, or below the floor. When government sets a *price ceiling*, then sellers cannot charge more. The government does this to protect some buyers who may not be able to afford certain items. For example, the government

Many people in the United States believe that a market economy will work most efficiently if it is left alone; that is, without government intervention (fiscal policy) when the economy is faltering. When the government takes actions such as bailouts (government loans to privately held companies to save them from bankruptcy), as it did for General Motors and AIG at the beginning of the Great Recession, it saved many thousands of jobs. But taxpayers ultimately paid the bill. Some people feel that the bailouts did little for the economy, which would have recovered on its own, although at a slower pace, and that the money spent on bailouts could have been used to create new jobs or for some other better purpose. Others argue that bailouts are needed in order to save jobs, especially when tens of thousands of jobs are at stake, and that it is government's responsibility to save jobs whenever it can.

THINK CRITICALLY

Whose side do you agree with in this argument? Do you feel that government should step in to prevent large companies from failing because of the overall effect on the economy resulting from the loss of numerous jobs? Explain your answer.

might set a price ceiling on milk and insulin to protect young families and those with diabetes.

In our market economy, government influence also exists in the form of fiscal policy. *Fiscal policy* refers to actions of the government to stimulate or slow the economy, such as tax increases or decreases and tax rebates. A market economy recognizes the need for such actions in order to protect consumers from adverse economic conditions.

Today, there are few if any pure economic systems. For example, a country may be a command system mixed with individual choices and ownership of some resources. Or it may be a free-enterprise system mixed with some degree of governmental controls. The degree of those centralized or group decisions determines the classification for each country.

 CHECKPOINT

What is a market economy?

- -

LO 1-2 **Elements of a Market Economy**

In a market economy, both producers and consumers must play active roles. *Producers* are the manufacturers or makers of goods and services for sale. *Consumers* are the buyers and users of goods and services. Both producers and consumers engage in *self-interest behavior* that forces the wise use of scarce resources.

Scarcity

In any economy, consumers' wants are unlimited, while the resources for producing the products to satisfy these wants are limited. This basic economic problem is called scarcity. A country's economic system determines what products will be produced with its limited resources. In our market economy, consumers play a key role in determining what is produced.

As an individual consumer, you have limited resources. You must decide what to buy with your limited income to achieve the greatest satisfaction or *utility* (measurement of something's usefulness). Your spending decisions and those of other consumers determine which products will succeed and which will fail and leave the market. Producers take cues from the marketplace to know which products will be profitable.

Supply and Demand

Supply is the quantity of goods and services that producers are willing and able to provide at various prices. *Demand* is the willingness and ability of consumers to purchase goods and services at various prices. Generally, if enough consumers demand a product (are willing and able to buy it), producers are willing to produce and sell it. The system works like this:

1. Increased demand creates a situation in which the supply of the product is not sufficient to satisfy all consumers who want to buy it. As a result, producers can raise their prices.
2. The high prices bring large profits to the producers.
3. Large profits prompt current producers to make more of the product and attract other producers to start providing the product, thus increasing supply.
4. Supply then exceeds demand, and consumers have more of a selection. In order to entice consumers to buy their product instead of their competitors' products, producers must reduce their prices.
5. Reducing prices, in turn, lowers profits, and producers begin to produce less.
6. Eventually, the product reaches the *equilibrium price*. This is the price at which the quantity supplied equals the quantity demanded of the product. At this price, there is just enough of the product available for all consumers who want to buy it.

Consumer Power

Consumers have the ultimate power in a market economy; this is known as *consumer sovereignty*. Consumers determine what is produced and at what price. Collectively, consumer buying decisions direct the production of goods and services. When consumers purchase a good or service, they are casting dollar "votes" for its continued production.

If consumers refuse to buy a good or service, the price will drop. If the good or service still does not sell or sales do not generate a profit, producers will no longer provide it.

Producer Power

Producers also have power in a free-enterprise system because they can employ various techniques to influence consumer buying decisions. They use advertising and

What is meant by consumer sovereignty?

© iStock.com/Yongyuan

other marketing strategies to try to increase demand for their products. Advertising can be informative and provide important facts about the quality and features of products. Unfortunately, it can also be false and misleading—thus, the saying, "Let the buyer beware."

Parts of the Economic System

Three essential parts of a market economy are: (1) competition, (2) purchasing power, and (3) informed consumers. If one of these parts is missing or not functioning properly, the system begins to fail. The economy gains strength when each component functions properly.

Competition

In order for prices to rise and fall with changes in supply and demand, competition must exist. **Competition** is the rivalry among sellers in the same market to win customers. There are three forms of competition in a market economy:

1. *Pure Competition.* With *pure competition*, there are many sellers in the market producing nearly identical products, resulting in improved quality and lower prices. Because of the freedom of both producers and consumers to enter and leave the market, supply and demand are free to interact to set equilibrium prices.
2. *Oligopoly.* An *oligopoly* exists where there are only a few sellers producing a very similar product or service. Because of the dominance of a few businesses, it is difficult for competitors to enter the industry. For example, the automobile industry has only a few manufacturers. An oligopoly works properly when buyers shop carefully and negotiate prices effectively.
3. *Monopoly.* A **monopoly** is a market with many buyers but only one seller. Without competition, the one seller has no incentive to improve quality or lower prices. Sometimes a monopoly is necessary within a market economy. Examples of monopolies include power and utility companies. Because consumers cannot shop for the product or service elsewhere, monopolies must be controlled (by government) to ensure they provide fair prices to consumers.

Illegal business practices can reduce competition and result in higher prices. *Price fixing* is an illegal agreement among competitors to sell a good or service for a set price. There is no real competition because prices have been predetermined, or fixed. Because price fixing prevents the forces of supply and demand from determining prices freely in the marketplace, it impedes free enterprise. Therefore, laws were passed to make it illegal.

Purchasing Power

For a market economy to operate, citizens must have the ability to buy. In the United States, most adults have income from their jobs that they can spend on goods and services. However, the purchasing power of the dollar goes up or down with the economy. *Purchasing power* is the value of money, measured in the amount of goods and services that it can buy.

In a period of *inflation*, when prices are generally rising in the economy, purchasing power decreases. For example, if the price of a juice drink rises from

$1.50 to $2.00, then your income won't buy as many juice drinks. Purchasing power also declines during periods of *recession*, when production, employment, and income are declining. People who lose their jobs or have their wages reduced cannot buy as many goods. The result is an overall loss of purchasing power in the economy.

The government also shifts purchasing power among citizens by making *transfer payments*, which are government grants to some citizens paid with money collected from other citizens, generally through taxes. Transfer payments are unearned income for the recipients because they are not providing any services in exchange for the payments. However, transfer payments provide purchasing power for needy people. Welfare, Social Security, and veterans' benefits are all transfer payments. SNAP benefits (formerly known as food stamps), reduced-price school lunches, and housing assistance also fall into this category.

Informed Consumers

A market economy must have informed consumers who know their rights and responsibilities in the marketplace. Informed consumers compare products and prices. When consumers make wise decisions, the system works to weed out inferior products and keep prices at acceptable levels. When consumers do not act in a responsible manner, prices increase.

✔ CHECKPOINT

What role does scarcity play in a market economy?

LO 1-3 The Role of Money

All economic systems use some form of money or medium of exchange. **Money** is anything that can be used to settle debt. It should be easily exchangeable and readily accepted in the marketplace. To meet these requirements and be functional, money must be readily divisible, durable, and recognizable as a store of value.

- *Divisibility*. In the United States, money, or *currency*, is divided into denominations for ease in completing transactions. The dollar bill is easily recognizable, and for sums less than a dollar, coins are used. The largest denomination produced for circulation is the $100 bill. In recent years, the Bureau of Engraving and Printing has added color and new security features to help prevent counterfeiting. When money is counted, it is divided into units. For example, 50 cents is one-half of a dollar. Ten dollars is ten times one dollar. Because money is readily *divisible*, you can buy and sell goods and give and receive the exact "change" for your money.

- *Durability*. Money must be transferred from one person to another. Currency lasts a long time (durability) before it must be reissued. Coins are produced by the U.S. Mint; paper money is produced by the Bureau of Engraving and Printing. As money wears out, new coins and bills replace old ones, which are destroyed.

- *Store of Value.* To serve as a medium of exchange, money must have a store of value, or be recognized to represent that value. For example, a $5 bill is readily exchangeable for merchandise of that value. When you accept a $5 bill for something you have sold, you expect to be able to reuse that $5 bill when you wish to do so. Because you have confidence that the paper money can be used again, you will accept it in exchange for goods and services.

The Gold Standard

When our nation was young, our money was based on a gold standard. With a *gold standard*, each dollar bill was backed by that same amount of gold in storage at a safe place. Much of the U.S. gold supply is stored at Ft. Knox, Kentucky. In the early days of our country, a citizen could go into a bank and demand $20 of gold in exchange for a $20 bill. Banks issued their own money, called "gold certificates" or "silver certificates," because they were able to produce the gold or silver on demand.

Today our money is referred to as **fiat money**, which is not backed by gold, but by faith in the general economy and government of the country. You readily accept dollar bills and other currency because you are confident that you will be able to exchange them for other goods and services when you wish.

Supply and Demand of Money

Like most other commodities, money is also subject to the forces of supply and demand. The government's efforts to stabilize the economy by managing the money supply and setting interest rates are referred to as the *monetary policy*. The Federal Reserve System (the Fed) controls our *money supply*, or the total amount of money in circulation. Using the reserve requirement, the Fed can increase or decrease the money supply. The *reserve requirement* indicates how much money a bank can loan out from its transaction deposits (money on deposit from customers) and how much it must keep "on reserve." For example, with a 20 percent reserve requirement, 20 percent of all demand account deposits (such as checking accounts) must be retained by the bank in its vaults. Raising that percentage means the banks have less money they can lend. When they have less to lend, the price of borrowing (the interest rate) will rise.

The Fed also controls the discount rate and the federal funds rate. The *discount rate* is the interest rate charged to banks that borrow from the Fed. The *federal funds rate* is the interest rate at which banks are able to borrow from the excess reserves of other banks. As these rates increase, the money supply shrinks because it is more expensive to borrow money. As these rates drop, banks

© iStock.com/Kali9

What is the purpose of the reserve requirement?

The World Bank provides financial assistance to developing countries around the world. It is owned by over 180 member countries. One of its goals is to reduce poverty and improve living standards around the world. The World Bank does this through low-interest loans, interest-free credit, and grants to developing countries for education, health, infrastructure, communication, and other purposes. For example, it provided financial support to improve and expand the electricity supply to 25 million people in the rural areas of Bangladesh, where only 42 percent of the rural population has access to electricity. Access to electricity will have a positive impact on the economy by helping to reduce poverty.

THINK CRITICALLY

Visit the World Bank online at www.worldbank.org. What has been accomplished by this international organization? Do you think its mission is worthwhile? Why or why not?

are able to borrow and loan more money. When more money is available, its price (interest rate) will be lower.

The creation of money helps the economy to grow. A growing economy is able to provide more jobs for workers and more products for consumers to purchase. Thus, the supply and demand for money affects our lives in a very real and significant way.

The Money Multiplier

When banks are able to lend money that they have on deposit from customers (transaction deposits), they are able to "create" more money. The *money multiplier* indicates how much more money can be created when banks can lend out a portion of each customer's deposit. The formula is as follows:

$$\text{Money Multiplier (MM)} = \frac{1}{\text{RR}} \text{ (reserve requirement)}$$

With a reserve requirement of 20 percent, the formula would work like this:

$$\text{MM} = \frac{1}{.20} = 5$$

Thus, if one customer deposits $100 in his or her checking account, the bank must keep 20 percent on reserve, or $20, and can lend the rest of the deposit, $80, to another customer, which creates a new deposit in another account. Of that new $80, 80 percent, or $64, can also be loaned to others, and so on. This will result in a multiplier of 5, or a maximum of $500 ($100 × 5) in additional money that can be created from the initial deposit.

If the Fed lowers the reserve requirement, the money multiplier gets larger. If the Fed raises the reserve requirement, the money multiplier gets smaller.

 CHECKPOINT

Describe the three characteristics of money that make it functional.

Construction

Whenever anything is built, from a building to a highway to a factory, there are construction workers who make it happen. They work in the sun, rain, heat, and cold year round so that our lives can be made more comfortable. The construction industry is vitally important to the economy. It is often a predictor of economic growth.

Construction workers do physically demanding work. They lift and carry heavy objects; they stoop, kneel, and crawl in awkward positions. Some work at great heights or in extremely small and uncomfortable spaces.

When Hoover Dam was completed in 1935, it was the world's largest concrete structure. Located on the border between Arizona and Nevada, it impounds the Colorado River and creates Lake Mead. There were 7,000 construction workers, of which 112 died due to the hazards of their job. Today, Hoover Dam is a landmark, a recreation site, and a major power facility attracting more than 7 million visitors annually.

Employment Outlook

- A much faster than average employment growth is expected.

Job Titles

- Construction worker
- Carpenter
- Brickmason
- Painter
- Roofer

Needed Skills

- No specific degrees are required, but apprenticeship and specialized skills are desirable.
- Trade-related training is available through vocational schools and community colleges.

What's it like to work in . . . *Construction*

Jim started working in construction through an apprenticeship program five years ago. Today he is the leader of a crew and earns $33,000 a year. He starts his day at the work site by putting on his helmet, safety goggles, and protective gear. Then he begins unloading, identifying, and distributing building materials. He also checks the machines to be sure they are operational.

He talks to the roofer and his crew that will be working on the first house and instructs them on what needs to be completed that day. Then he greets the brickmason who is setting up to build the chimney and brick façade for a second house. Once all of the work is underway, Jim jumps in to help install the drywall in another house on the work site. Throughout the day, Jim reports to the construction foreman, who wants updates on progress at the site.

What About You?

Why is the construction industry important to our economy? What work characteristics of this career do you like and dislike?

The Career Clusters icons are being used with permission of the: States' Career Clusters Initiative, 2007, www.careerclusters.org

KEY TERMS REVIEW

Match the terms with the definitions. Some terms may not be used.

___ 1. Money backed by faith in the general economy and government of the country

___ 2. A system characterized by a large degree of government control of many of the decisions within the nation

___ 3. A situation in which consumers' wants are unlimited, while the resources for producing the products to satisfy those wants are limited

___ 4. A system in which the government owns and controls most of the productive resources of a nation

___ 5. Anything that can be used to settle debt

___ 6. The rivalry among sellers in the same market to win customers

___ 7. A market with many buyers but only one seller

a. capitalism
b. communist economic system
c. competition
d. fiat money
e. market economy
f. money
g. monopoly
h. scarcity
i. socialist economic system
j. traditional economic system

CHECK YOUR UNDERSTANDING

L01-1 8. What group, as a whole, has the ultimate power to determine what will be produced and at what prices in a market economy?

L01-2 9. Why is purchasing power important in a market economy?

APPLY YOUR KNOWLEDGE

L01-2 10. How is the market price of a good or service affected by (a) an increase in demand; (b) a decrease in demand; (c) an increase in supply; and (d) a decrease in supply?

THINK CRITICALLY

L01-1 11. Most economic systems today are compromise, or mixed, systems. Why is this the case?

L01-2 12. If you were given $100 to spend however you wanted, how would utility play a factor in what you would buy and how much you would spend?

L01-3 13. How does the money multiplier "create" new money?

The Essential Question *Refer to The Essential Question on p. 587. Hands-on and hands-off economic systems are characterized by the degree of government control. The United States has a market economy in which the concept of supply and demand, not government control, has a major impact. Money provides a medium of exchange that is divisible, durable, and a store of value.*

24.2 Consumer Responsibilities

The Essential Question *What are some major forms of deception in the marketplace, and how can consumers protect themselves?*

LEARNING OBJECTIVES

› LO 2-1 Recognize deceptive practices used to defraud consumers.
› LO 2-2 Discuss how to be a responsible consumer and protect yourself from fraudsters.

KEY TERMS

- deception, *597*
- bait and switch, *597*
- fake sale, *597*
- low-balling, *598*
- pyramid scheme, *598*
- pigeon drop, *599*
- Ponzi scheme, *599*
- infomercial, *601*
- clearance, *602*
- liquidation, *602*
- redress, *605*

LO 2-1 Recognizing Fraud and Deception

The marketplace is full of deceptive and misleading promotions that persuade consumers to buy goods and services that are of inferior quality or that they do not really need or want. **Deception** occurs when false or misleading claims are made about the quality, the price, or the purpose of a particular product. In many cases, little can be done once the consumer has been fooled into making a purchase. Dishonest sellers quickly disappear or deny wrongdoing. In a market economy, consumers must educate themselves to recognize a potential fraud before they become victims. Prevention is still the best safeguard against financial misfortune.

Bait and Switch

Bait and switch is an illegal sales technique in which a seller advertises a product with the intention of persuading consumers to buy a more expensive product. The "bait" is the bargain product that gets customers into the store. When they arrive to purchase the advertised product, however, the salesperson strongly urges them to purchase a higher-quality, more expensive product. In other cases, when customers ask for the bait merchandise, they are told that it is sold out (even if it isn't) and are shown comparable merchandise available for more money.

To avoid the bait-and-switch trap, educate yourself about products and prices. When a product is advertised at a special price, find out its regular price and do research to learn about its quality. Shop around before making major purchases.

Fake Sales

Probably the most common of all consumer frauds is the **fake sale**, which occurs when a merchant advertises a big sale but keeps the items at regular price or alters the price tags to make them look like there has been a price reduction

© Pan Xunbin/Shutterstock.com

How do repair shops use the low-balling strategy?

when there actually is none. Often the merchant increases the prices just prior to the sale and alters the price tags to show the so-called "markdowns."

The best way for consumers to protect themselves from fake sales is to compare products and prices offered at other stores. Just because a flashy sign shouts "SUPER SAVINGS" does not mean that prices have been reduced. Product and price knowledge can help you identify a real bargain.

Low-Balling

Repair shops sometimes use a deceptive practice called "low-balling." **Low-balling** is a technique whereby a company advertises a product or service at a low price to lure in customers and then attempts to persuade them that they need additional products or services. For example, an appliance repairperson quotes a price, but after dismantling the appliance, he or she discovers other "necessary" repairs that will cost extra. If the consumer refuses to make the additional repairs, the repairperson may charge extra fees for reassembly.

Another form of low-balling involves applying pressure to convince car owners that their cars need additional work for safe operation. For example, a repair shop may offer a special on brake replacements. But when the mechanics inspect the brakes, they find several other "necessary" repairs. Customers may wind up with a front-end alignment, wheel balancing, or other repairs that are not really as urgent as they are led to believe.

To protect yourself from this type of low-balling, state that you want no repairs other than those agreed upon unless the repair shop informs you of the additional cost ahead of time and you choose to authorize the extra repairs. You should not pay for unauthorized work. Before having major work done, get a second opinion. Discuss major car repairs with someone you trust who knows about the mechanical aspects of cars. Find a mechanic you know and can trust. Don't take your vehicle to repair shops you know nothing about.

Pyramid Schemes

A **pyramid scheme** is a multilevel marketing plan that promises members (distributors) commissions from their own sales and those of other members they recruit. A cash investment of some kind is usually required to become a distributor of the product being sold. The pyramid consists of managers at the top and many middle and lower distributors who arrange parties where they can sell products to friends and acquaintances and recruit new distributors. The managers at the top make big profits by selling the products to the distributors below them in the pyramid—not to the general public. However, most distributors lower in the pyramid never make a profit or recover their initial investment. Instead, they are left with a lot of low-quality products that no one wants to buy and are unable to find new members to recruit.

The best defense against pyramid sales schemes is to remember that you cannot expect to make big profits without hard work. Before committing to such a plan, investigate it. Talk to people who have purchased the products. Check with local consumer protection agencies. Think it through. What is the company's track record? Does the company have evidence to back up its claims? Who will buy this product? Will your commission depend on recruiting other distributors? Be skeptical if the company requires you to buy a "starter kit" of sales brochures and product inventory.

Pigeon Drop

A scam in which a con artist convinces people to give up their money (or personal information) in return for a share of a larger sum of money is called a **pigeon drop**. The "pigeon" is the unsuspecting consumer. Con artists often target trusting people who have a source of money, such as senior citizens. One of the most common pigeon drop scams occurs when a con artist approaches a victim by claiming to have found a large sum of money and offering to split it. The con artist sets up a meeting to discuss dividing up the money. In the meantime, the con artist asks the victim to put up some of his or her own money as collateral to prove that he or she is trustworthy. Later, when the victim arrives at the meeting spot, the con artist and the victim's money are nowhere to be found. In another pigeon drop scam, a con artist convinces victims to use their checking account to assist in the transfer of a large international deposit in return for a portion of the money. The victims hand out their checking account information, which is used by the con artist to clean out the account. If someone approaches you with a suspicious deal that sounds too good to be true, it probably is. Do not hand over your money or personal information to someone you don't know and trust.

Ponzi Schemes

A **Ponzi scheme** is a fraudulent investment operation in which money collected from new investors is used to pay off earlier investors. A person represents himself or herself as an expert financial adviser. The "expert" promises solid investment returns, usually much higher than the market in general. For a while, the fraudster maintains the appearance of a legitimate business and pays dividends to the victims. This helps lure in new investors, often through recommendations. But actually, the dividends are being paid with money from new investors, while the fraudster pockets the rest of the money to live a lavish lifestyle. Eventually, the investment accounts fail, and the investors lose their money. The fraudster is prosecuted, but the money is often never recovered.

The best protection against this type of swindle is the local Better Business Bureau. The Bureau is equipped to investigate unsound businesses. Insist upon seeing credentials, annual financial reports, and proof of past dealings. Invest only in established firms with a proven track record.

Fraudulent Representation

Consumers lose billions of dollars each year to *telemarketing fraud*. One warning sign is the offer of a "free" prize if you pay shipping and handling. A truly free prize never requires that you pay a fee. Foreign lotteries are illegal, and sweepstakes requiring you to pay any money are not legitimate.

How can you avoid telemarketing scams?

Fraudulent telemarketers will ask you to wire money to them or give a credit card number to claim your prize. Unsolicited calls from telemarketers who know a lot about you should sound an alarm. Promises of big prizes, wonderful vacations, and no-risk investments usually turn out to be fraudulent. The telemarketers collect the tax, fees, delivery charges, and other "costs" from you, and then you never receive your prize.

Many companies use telemarketing to sell customers products they do not need. You can protect yourself from these calls by saying "no, thank you" and hanging up. You can greatly reduce the number of unwanted telemarketing calls you receive by signing up with the government's National Do Not Call Registry. You can register for free online at www.donotcall.gov.

Around holidays and after disasters, fraudulent telemarketers and door-to-door solicitors may claim to represent charities and ask for donations. Door-to-door solicitors may also claim to represent well-known companies. Consumers buy their products and then learn that the products have been rebuilt, stolen, or made from inferior-quality parts. In some cases, the product is worthless or unusable. One such scam involves the sale of a book of discount coupons to be used at local restaurants and businesses. When the buyers try to use them, they discover that the merchants have not authorized the coupons.

Before giving money to someone claiming to represent a major company or charity, check with the organization to verify the person's claims. The local Better Business Bureau will have a record of solicitors who repeatedly engage in questionable practices.

Internet Fraud

When you are online, you will be bombarded by advertisements, from banners to e-mail. Some of these are legitimate; others are not. *Phishing* scams make fake websites and e-mails appear genuine by designing them to look just like their legitimate business counterparts. Don't assume that a professional-looking website means that the company is legitimate. You may order and pay for goods and never receive them. When you give credit card numbers and other personal information to these scam artists, you may become a victim of *identity theft*, whereby your personal information, such as credit card numbers and Social Security numbers, are stolen to gain access to your finances. Don't click on advertising links. Instead, look up the legitimate web addresses of companies with which you would like to do business. Report any look-alike websites and e-mails to the actual businesses.

Health and Medical Product Frauds

A common type of swindle involves deceptive advertising for expensive "miracle" pills, creams, and other products to enhance the consumer's health and beauty. The ads are designed to appeal to the consumer's desire to be healthy and attractive. Usually, deceptive health and medical advertisements carry endorsements and pictures of people who have had success using the product. Magazines, newspapers, websites, e-mails, and flashy tabloids often carry these advertisements. Sometimes you send money but never receive the product. If you do receive the product, it may be totally ineffective.

Infomercials

An **infomercial** is a lengthy paid TV advertisement that includes testimonials and product demonstrations. These advertisements generally last 15 to 30 minutes and target people with specific needs that are usually emotional—from weight loss to hair growth. While the product may be reputable, there is no guarantee, and claims about results may be greatly exaggerated. With infomercials, it is important to find out whether the business is reputable and the product works before you buy. Be cautious about giving credit card numbers over the telephone. Don't assume that because something "worked" for the paid actors describing the product on television that you will receive the same results. You must also beware of add-ons, such as high shipping and handling charges and club memberships. Although you may get your initial shipment at a reduced price, you unknowingly may be signing up for some other hidden commitment, such as regular monthly shipments.

 **CHECKPOINT**

Why do many people fall victim to Internet scams?

LO 2-2 Being a Responsible Consumer

Learning to identify various deceptive marketing tactics is the first step toward being a responsible consumer. Prevention is your best choice. After you have been swindled, it is difficult to undo the financial damage. To protect yourself, be alert for the warning signs of a scam. Educate yourself on products and prices, and seek redress when necessary.

Identify Deceptive Practices

When you hear unrealistic claims, be suspicious. Watch for warning signals in claims or offers made through advertising and by salespeople. Figure 24.1 lists common warning signals of possible deception that should catch your attention. Protect yourself by knowing these warning signs.

Shop Smart

Our economy produces a large assortment of products from which to choose. The methods used to sell them are sometimes misleading. Although the Internet provides helpful shopping tools, it also presents hidden dangers. There are many things you can do to help make wise buying decisions.

- *Shop at several stores. Comparison shopping* involves comparing the quality, price, and warranties for the same products at several different stores. Online price-comparison search tools are very useful for this.

FIGURE 24.1 Warning Signals

Watch Out When You Hear This:

- You can get something for nothing.
- You will receive a free gift if you reply now.
- You or your home has been specially selected.
- You can make high earnings with no experience or little effort.
- You have been selected to complete an advertising questionnaire.
- You may attend a demonstration with no obligation to buy.
- If you don't decide now, you will lose a golden opportunity.
- You can buy a high-quality product for an incredibly low price.
- To receive a product or service, you must first send money.
- To receive your prize, you must supply your credit card or checking account number.

■ *Be aware of prices.* Know regular or "list" prices of common items. Terms often used in advertising, such as "manufacturer's list price" and "suggested retail price" and phrases such as "$40 value for only $35," attract your attention. But the prices actually may not be reduced.

■ *Understand sale terminology. Sale* means that goods are being offered "for sale" but not necessarily at reduced prices. **Clearance** means that the merchant wants to clear out all of the advertised merchandise, but not necessarily at a reduced price. **Liquidation** means that the merchant wants to sell the inventory (merchandise) immediately to turn it into cash. Again, prices may not be reduced. These terms often are used interchangeably, and no reduction in price is given.

■ *Avoid impulse buying.* Take a list with you when you shop, and buy only what is on the list. Avoid displays of products that attract your attention but are unnecessary. Don't let the convenience of online shopping lure you into buying something you don't need.

■ *Plan your purchases.* Thoroughly research major purchases before making your choice. Read online and printed product information and comparative reviews. Do not make major purchases when you are emotionally stressed or your judgment is impaired. Ask questions so you are sure that you understand claims, features, prices, and terms. For example, the product may show the net price after a mail-in rebate. However, you may not qualify for the rebate, or it may have expired.

■ *Compute unit prices.* Unit pricing is the cost for one unit of an item sold in packages of more than one unit. For example, to compare the price of a 15-ounce box with the price of a 24-ounce box, divide the total price of each box by the number of ounces in it. The result is the price per ounce. The lowest unit price for products of comparable quality is the best buy.

■ *Read labels.* Know ingredients and materials and what they mean. For example, a shirt that is 100 percent cotton may shrink, or if it is a dress shirt, it will probably have to be pressed each time you wear it. A product that is labeled "Dry Clean Only" will be more expensive to maintain.

Computing Unit Prices

Which is better: 24 ounces for $2.59 or 15 ounces for $1.89? To determine which is better, you'll need to know the cost per unit. To compute cost per unit, divide the total cost by total units:

$$\$2.59 \div 24 \text{ ounces} = \$0.108 \text{ per ounce}$$

$$\$1.89 \div 15 \text{ ounces} = \$0.126 \text{ per ounce}$$

In this case, the 24-ounce container is the better buy.

Based on the previous example, determine which of the following is the better buy: 3 packages for $0.89 or 6 packages for $1.99?

Solution: $\$0.89 \div 3 = \$0.297 \text{ per package}$

$\$1.99 \div 6 = \$0.332 \text{ per package}$

Thus, 3 packages for $0.89 is the better buy.

- *Check containers carefully*. Be sure packages have not been opened or damaged. Report any suspicious openings in packages to the store manager.
- *Read contracts*. Read and understand contracts and agreements before signing them.
- *Keep receipts and warranties*. Print out warranty statements and sales receipts from online purchases. For all major purchases, keep receipts along with warranties, guarantees, or other written promises in case you need to make returns or get replacements later.
- *Compute total cost*. Check the total cost of an item, including supplementary items (such as batteries), delivery charges, finance charges, and other add-on costs. In some cases, the base price may be lower than for similar products, but once you add up all of the related charges, you will find that the total cost exceeds other choices.
- *Ask for references*. Ask company representatives for references to be sure they really do represent the company. Call the company to check.
- *Be loyal*. Patronize online and bricks-and-mortar businesses that have good reputations and have served you well in the past. Tell others when you have a good experience, and ask others for recommendations of doctors, accountants, repair shops, and other service businesses.
- *Check up on businesses*. Check for valid certifications, licenses, bonding, and endorsements. Use your local Better Business Bureau and your state's business records division to be sure you are getting service from qualified and reputable professionals.
- *Wait a day for major purchases*. Try waiting at least 24 hours before making a major purchase to be sure you are not making the purchase on impulse or being pressured into buying it. Many people change their minds after a "cooling-off" period. If you still want the product after further consideration, then you can be sure you are buying for the right reasons.

Online Shopping

You are responsible for protecting yourself if you shop online. Here are some tips to follow when shopping over the Internet:

- *Shop at secure websites.* Look for "https" in the web address. The "s" indicates "secure."
- *Check the website address, called the Uniform Resource Locator (URL).* A business address should be followed by .com; a government address should be followed by .gov; a nonprofit organization address often uses .org; a college or university address uses .edu; and so on. Be suspicious of URL addresses that are not in the approved domains.
- *Research the website before you order.* Look for the business address and the telephone number.
- *Read the website's privacy and security policies.* These policies are usually listed in a section entitled Privacy and Security. Determine if the site intends to share your information with a third party or another company. If the policies are not posted, do not trust the site.
- *Shop safely.* The safest way to shop on the Internet is with a credit card or a prepaid gift card (Visa) on a secure site. If something goes wrong, you can protest the charge through your credit card company. With a prepaid gift card, you do not have to supply personal information, thus preventing identity theft.
- *Share only the essentials when you order.* Never provide a Social Security number, date of birth, or other information not relevant to the purchase.
- *Print and keep the confirmation order.* Print at least one copy of what you have ordered as well as the page showing the company name, address, phone number, and legal terms.
- *Know shipping and return policies.* Check the website for cancellation and return policies.
- *Use common sense.* If it seems too good to be true, it probably is!

Stay Informed

You are responsible for educating yourself about products and services before you buy. To protect yourself, actively seek consumer information in the following ways:

- Become familiar with sources of information on goods and services, such as *Consumer Reports* and consumer-oriented websites.
- Read warranties and guarantees. Ask questions so that you can fully understand performance claims. Get written guarantees and warranties whenever possible.
- Read and understand care instructions before using a product.
- Analyze advertisements about products before buying. Know why you are interested in the product or service and decide what you want before you buy.
- Know the protections offered by consumer protection laws, and know how to seek a remedy to consumer problems. Inform consumer protection agencies of fraudulent or unsafe performance of products and services. Make your dissatisfaction known to help others avoid the same problem and to prompt producers to improve their product or service.

- Post comments (both positive and negative) about products at websites and blogs so that others can benefit from your experience. Read through similar postings before you buy or do business with a company.
- Report wants, likes, and dislikes, as well as suggested improvements and complaints, to retailers and manufacturers.
- Keep good records of complaints, product defects, actions taken to resolve problems, names of people you have talked to, and so on. You will need these forms of evidence to support your claims.

Seek Redress

When you have a complaint or need to solve a problem related to a product or service, you have the right to seek redress. **Redress** is a remedy to a problem. When you have a consumer problem, you have the right to expect the business to work with you to resolve the problem. The remedy might be your money back, a repair, or some other compensation. Here are some suggestions for filing a complaint and resolving problems:

1. Take the product back to the store where you bought it. Calmly explain the problem to a salesperson there. If necessary, talk to a manager. If you bought the item online, then talk to a customer service representative on the phone. Explain the specifics about the problem and provide evidence. Keep all warranties, sales receipts, and related materials. If needed, provide photocopies of information to explain and support your position.
2. Stay firm but not angry. State that you are dissatisfied and explain why. Be specific about the type of adjustment you want: refund, repair, replacement, or other action. Many consumer problems can be resolved by discussing them reasonably with the retailer.
3. If you are not satisfied with the manager's remedy, put your complaint in writing to the store's owner or headquarters. If you do not receive satisfaction, write to the manufacturer or distributor and state your complaint. In any written correspondence, describe your previous interactions with store personnel and explain why you are dissatisfied with the result. Be specific.
4. Keep good records. Be prepared to send photocopies of evidence, such as sales receipts, warranties, or anything else that will help you support your position. Be firm and once again state the type of adjustment you want. Specify a reasonable time limit in which to resolve the problem.
5. If you are still dissatisfied with the result, file a complaint with the appropriate government agency for consumer protection. There may be more than one private or public agency to assist you in solving the problem.
6. Finally, you may need to seek legal recourse to get the desired result. Attorneys' fees are expensive, so it is better to try to resolve the issue yourself, if possible. Small claims court and other legal remedies are discussed in Chapter 26.

✔ **CHECKPOINT**

Name and describe two ways to shop smarter.

What Are Mouse Tracks on the Web?

When you explore different websites, be aware that you are not always anonymous. Some sites can immediately determine certain information about you when you visit that site, such as the type of computer system you use, the company you use to access the Internet, and the last web page you visited.

At some websites you must log in, register, and/or give information about yourself. This information is saved and often shared with others. These "mouse tracks" enable companies to determine whether you are a potential customer and what types of interests you have.

Some businesses electronically record information about your visit to their site by depositing a piece of information called a *cookie* onto your computer. Once a cookie is saved on your computer, that website can keep track of information about your visit, such as which parts of the site you visit. This helps site operators determine the most popular areas of their site. It also helps them improve the site and its offerings. Cookies also allow for more efficiency when revisiting a site because:

- Your preferences for visiting certain areas of the site are stored in your cookie file. The next time you return, the section you like best may already be displayed for you.

- You may be alerted to new areas of interest based on web pages you have previously visited.

- Your past purchases may be recorded in the cookie file so that the site knows what you like; thus, you may be shown special offers on products and services tailored to your interests.

Some versions of browser software can be set to notify you before a website places a cookie on your computer. Then you can choose to accept or reject the cookie. Some browsers will allow you to deactivate a cookie. You can also delete cookie files, but you will lose the personal customization offered by the sites. Many computer users find it important to systematically remove cookies and other information linking their computer usage to specific sites. This helps protect your privacy.

THINK CRITICALLY

1. What websites do you visit regularly? What information have you given them about yourself?

2. What are the advantages and disadvantages of having cookies stored on your computer?

KEY TERMS REVIEW

Match the terms with the definitions. Some terms may not be used.

____ 1. A remedy to a problem

____ 2. Making false or misleading claims about quality, price, or purpose of a product

____ 3. An illegal sales technique in which a seller advertises a product with the intention of persuading consumers to buy a more expensive product

____ 4. The intent to sell inventory immediately to turn it into cash

____ 5. A lengthy paid TV advertisement that includes testimonials and product demonstrations

____ 6. A multilevel marketing plan that promises members commissions from their own sales and those of other members they recruit

____ 7. A fraudulent investment operation in which money collected from new investors is used to pay off earlier investors

a. bait and switch
b. clearance
c. deception
d. fake sale
e. infomercial
f. liquidation
g. low-balling
h. pigeon drop
i. Ponzi scheme
j. pyramid scheme
k. redress

CHECK YOUR UNDERSTANDING

LO2-1 8. What makes a sale a "fake sale"?

LO2-2 9. What is the first step toward being a responsible consumer?

APPLY YOUR KNOWLEDGE

LO2-1 10. Locate a product advertisement with an unusually low price or a claim to perform in extraordinary ways. Explain how such an advertisement can lead to consumer deception.

THINK CRITICALLY

LO2-1 11. Have you ever gone to a store to purchase an advertised product only to find that it was not available, but another, more expensive product was available? How did you react? Did you purchase the other product?

LO2-2 12. Under what circumstances would you consider seeking redress for a consumer problem? What procedures would you follow before seeking legal advice?

The Essential Question *Refer to The Essential Question on p. 597. Major forms of deception include bait and switch, fake sales, low-balling, pyramid schemes, pigeon drop, Ponzi schemes, fraudulent representation, Internet fraud, health product frauds, and infomercials. To protect themselves, consumers can shop smart, use precautions when online, stay informed, and seek redress.*

SUMMARY

24.1

- *Hands-on economic systems involve government controls over the way decisions are made. Examples are communism and socialism.*

- *Hands-off economic systems do not involve central authority; individuals make the choices. Traditional and pure capitalism are examples.*

- *Most economies today are mixed. A free-enterprise system with some governmental controls is today's market economy.*

- *All economies face the problem of scarcity because resources are limited but consumer wants and needs are increasing and unlimited.*

- *In a market economy, the interaction of supply and demand determines what will be produced, in what quantities, and at what prices.*

- *To function smoothly, a market economy needs competition, purchasing power, and informed consumers.*

- *All economic systems use some form of money or medium of exchange. Fiat money is backed by the faith in the general economy and government of the country.*

24.2

- *Bait-and-switch scams lure customers into the store with advertised bargains and then switch customers to a more expensive product.*

- *Fake sales make customers think prices are reduced when they really aren't.*

- *Repair shops use low-balling when they offer a repair at a low price but then suggest other "necessary" services to run up the price.*

- *Pyramid schemes depend on recruiting multiple levels of distributors.*

- *Pigeon drops are scams that convince people to give up their money (or personal information) in return for a share of a larger sum of money.*

- *Ponzi schemes lure in potential investors with promises of high returns, but in fact, dividends are paid from new investors' money.*

- *Internet fraud can lead to identity theft, which involves stealing personal information, such as credit card numbers and Social Security numbers, to gain access to a person's finances.*

- *Fraudulent representation can occur through telemarketing and door-to-door solicitations.*

- *To be a responsible consumer, learn to identify deceptive practices, follow wise buying habits, stay informed, and seek redress for consumer problems.*

APPLY WHAT YOU KNOW

L01-1   1. Compare and contrast the three major ways economies can be organized. What type of economy exists in the United States? Do you think another type of economy would be better? Explain your answer.

L01-2   2. Select a commonly used product, such as gasoline or milk, and track the prices of this product over a 20-year period by creating a line graph. Explain price increases and decreases based on supply and demand.

L01-3   3. Explain how the Federal Reserve Bank affects the money supply in the United States. How do the Fed's actions, including setting reserve requirements and controlling discount rates, speed up or slow down the economy?

L02-1   4. Visit the Federal Trade Commission's website to learn about the latest frauds and schemes being carried out against consumers. Write a one-page report on a new scheme that is not discussed in the textbook.

L02-1   5. Search magazines, newspapers, and the Internet for advertisements. Collect or print out ads that offer the following: (a) something for nothing, (b) bonus for early reply, (c) offers of gifts and prizes, and (d) very short time limit for response to get a special deal. Evaluate the authenticity of the ads.

L02-2   6. Choose five food, beauty, or household products you find in your home. Visit a local store and compare three different sizes of the product and compute unit prices. Compile the information gathered in a chart. For each product, indicate whether the larger size saves you money or costs more per unit.

MAKE ACADEMIC CONNECTIONS

L01-1   7. **Economics** Select a country with an economic system that is considered communist or socialist. Conduct online research about quality of life, life expectancy rates, tax rates, income and education levels, and other lifestyle data from this country. Locate the same data for the United States. Based on your findings, write a two-page report in which you compare and contrast consumers in both economies.

L01-2   8. **Social Studies** Conduct a survey of at least three people of varied ages based on the following question. "How is the U.S. economy impacting your life?" As a class, compare and discuss the results.

L01-3   9. **International Studies** Using the Internet, compare the value of the dollar to the value of worldwide currencies. Find the value of the Japanese yen, British pound, Chinese yuan, Euro, Canadian dollar, and Mexican peso. Make a chart that shows the value of each.

L02-1 10. **Research** Perform research to find a recent news story about a business that used deceptive marketing practices, such as price fixing, bait and switch, fake sales, low-balling, or another scam. Write a one-page report describing the deception and the final outcome.

Solve Problems and Explore Issues

LO2-2 11. Compute unit prices for the following pairs and determine which of the two is the better deal: (a) 3 for $0.98 or 8 for $2.99, (b) 4 for $1.00 or 12 for $3.39, (c) 24 oz. for $1.98 or 36 oz. for $2.49, and (d) 2 lbs. for $2.19 or 5 lbs. for $5.89?

LO2-2 12. Copy the ingredients from the labels of the following products: (a) deodorant, (b) liquid cleaning product, (c) bug spray, and (d) breakfast cereal. Do any of the labels carry warnings? What types of precautions are suggested? Why is it important that customers are informed of product ingredients?

LO2-2 13. Read the warranty or guarantee for a household product that your family has purchased (examples: coffee maker, blender, or electronic device). What does the manufacturer agree to do? What exceptions are stated? What actions does the manufacturer state it will not agree to do?

LO2-2 14. Visit *Consumer Reports* online or obtain an issue from your library and answer the following questions: (a) Who publishes the magazine? (b) Who advertises in the magazine? (c) How are products tested and compared for quality? Select a tested product and summarize three key findings that would influence your buying decision.

EXTEND YOUR LEARNING

LO2-1 15. **Ethics** Some celebrities lend their names to products that later turn out to be ineffective or harmful to consumers. The celebrities are paid to endorse the product by claiming they have used it. But in many cases, the celebrities know very little about it. Some celebrities have been held legally liable because people relied on their claims. When a celebrity—whether an entertainer or athlete—endorses a product or service, do you seek to buy it based on his or her opinion alone? Do you think this marketing tactic is effective? Is it ethical? Explain why or why not.

CHAPTER PROJECT

You bought a new smartphone. Two weeks later, it stopped working and you had to replace the battery. Now the phone won't hold a charge for long. At times, the phone shuts off randomly, and there is an audible hiss in the background during calls. Although the camera in the phone was promoted as the "best" on the market, it takes blurry photos. In addition, the display is too dark. You returned to the store for help, but the manager told you that you would have to contact the manufacturer directly. Write a complaint letter to the manufacturer. (For this activity, make up information about the manufacturer, receipt, and warranty.) Request a replacement or a refund. Also, prepare a "post" about the product for a consumer review website.

Complete the Guided Decision Making activity for Chapter 24 at ngl.cengage.com/mypf.

CHAPTER 25

Consumer Protection

25.1 **Consumer Rights and Laws**

25.2 **Consumer Agencies**

Consider This...

Diego bought a computer at an online auction website. He provided his credit card number and expiration date, along with his name and home address for shipping.

"I think you can get a pretty good deal when you buy online," he told his instructor. "But at the same time, I worry about giving personal information to a vendor that I don't know. Before I made the purchase, I checked the Better Business Bureau's website and learned that this company meets its criteria and that there are no complaints filed against it. I also checked some other consumer complaint websites and didn't find any complaints posted about the company. That makes me feel a little better, but I know I'm still taking a risk. Do you think there are any other ways I can protect myself when shopping online?"

The Essential Question *What rights do you have as a consumer, and what types of protection are provided by consumer laws?*

LO 1-1 Consumer Rights

For many years, the consumer's position in the marketplace was known as "buyer beware." Consumers had little protection against unfair business practices. Since 1960, however, things have changed. As abuses have become apparent, new rights for citizens and consumers have arisen.

Consumer Bill of Rights

One of the most important steps in the direction of consumer protection was the adoption of the *Consumer Bill of Rights*. This law was proposed by President Kennedy in 1962. It outlines the four basic rights of consumers:

What are the basic provisions of the Consumer Bill of Rights?

1. *The right to safety.* This right protects consumers against products that are hazardous to life or health. It implies that products should cause no harm to their users if used for their intended purpose.
2. *The right to be informed.* This right protects consumers from product information that is fraudulent, deceitful, or misleading and assures them that they will be given the facts needed to make intelligent and informed product choices.
3. *The right to choose.* This right ensures consumers that they will have access to a variety of quality products and services offered at competitive prices.
4. *The right to be heard.* This right gives consumers the ability to voice complaints and concerns about a product or service. It also gives consumers a voice in formulating government policies related to consumer interests.

In 1985 consumer rights were endorsed by the United Nations through the United Nations Guidelines for Consumer Protection, and they were expanded to include four more consumer rights, for a total of eight basic rights:

5. *The right to satisfaction of basic needs.* This right demands that people have access to basic, essential goods and services, including adequate food, clothing, shelter, health care, education, public utilities, water, and sanitation.

6. *The right to redress.* This right provides assurance that buyers can receive fair settlement (such as compensation) for valid claims involving misrepresentation, inferior products, or unsatisfactory services.

7. *The right to consumer education.* This right gives consumers access to information and programs that help them acquire the necessary knowledge and skills to make better marketplace decisions. When consumers are educated, they are aware of basic consumer rights and responsibilities and know how to act on them.

8. *The right to a healthy environment.* This right asserts that people should live and work in a clean, safe, healthy environment that is nonthreatening to the well-being of present and future generations.

Airline Passenger Rights

In 1999 it became apparent that airline passengers were being treated unfairly. Thus, many saw the need for a bill of rights for airline passengers. In 2009 and 2011, the U.S. Department of Transportation (DOT) expanded these rights by adding several more rules. Basic protections for airline passengers now include the following:

- *Reservations.* Once you have a confirmed reservation, you will be provided a seat on that flight even if there is no record of your reservation in the airline's computer system. If you have a ticket or printout, an agent cannot deny boarding because there's no reservation "in the computer." (However, if you don't show up for a flight and fail to cancel the reservation, you are considered a no-show and the airline can cancel any continuing or return reservations.)

- *Refunds.* If you cancel a ticket for a "nonrefundable fare," you may be able to apply the fare toward a future flight, minus any applicable charges or cancellation fees. If you cancel a refundable ticket, your refund will be issued in the same manner as your purchase (for example, if you used a credit card, the credit card will be credited).

- *Delays and cancellations.* Airlines are not required to compensate passengers for delayed or canceled flights, but they must promptly notify consumers of delays of over 30 minutes as well as cancellations and diversions.

- *Bumped flights.* Compensation is required if you are "bumped" from a flight that is oversold. The only exception to this requirement is if the airline can claim extraordinary circumstances, such as weather or security issues. If you are voluntarily bumped, you may receive a free ticket or voucher. If you are involuntarily bumped, you have the right to compensation, which can be as much as 200 to 400 percent of the cost of your one-way fare.

Do you think there is a need for an airline passengers' bill of rights? Why or why not?

- *Extended tarmac delays.* U.S. airlines operating domestic flights cannot permit an aircraft to remain on the tarmac for more than three hours, with exceptions for safety, security, and air traffic control-related reasons. The rule also requires U.S. airlines to provide basic services, such as access to working lavatories and food and water. In April 2010, this rule was expanded to include a four-hour limit on the tarmac for international flights experiencing delays.
- *Fee disclosures.* Airlines must disclose all potential fees on their websites, including but not limited to fees for baggage, meals, canceling or changing reservations, or advanced or upgraded seating.

Consumer Technology Bill of Rights

As a result of technology and its widespread use by consumers, a *Consumer Technology Bill of Rights* was introduced by Congress in 2002. It recognizes the reasonable, personal, and noncommercial rights of consumers related to technology. Provisions include the following:

- *Time-shifting.* Consumers have the right to time-shift content that they have legally acquired. Consumers are **time-shifting** when they record video or audio for later viewing or listening. For example, you can record a TV show and watch it later.
- *Space-shifting.* Consumers have the right to use content that they have legally acquired in different places, as long as the use is personal and non-commercial. **Space-shifting** allows media, such as music or films, stored on one device to be accessed from another place through another device. For example, you can copy the contents of a CD to a portable music player so that you can listen to it while jogging.
- *Backup copies.* Consumers have the right to make archival copies of purchased CDs and other electronic media to protect against the event that the original copy is destroyed.
- *Platform of choice.* Consumers have the right to use legally acquired content on whatever device they choose. For example, you can listen to music on your iPod, watch TV on your iMac, and view DVDs on your HP notebook.
- *Translation.* Consumers have the right to translate legally acquired content into a format that makes it more usable to them. For example, a visually challenged person can modify an electronic book so that it can be read out loud.

Patients' Bill of Rights

Abuses in managed care and other related institutions created the need for a patients' bill of rights. These policies were adopted by the President's Advisory Commission on Consumer Protection and Quality in the Health Care

Industry in 1998. Further rights were proposed in 2001. Broadly, patients have the following rights:

- *Information disclosure.* Patients have the right to receive accurate, easily understood information in order to make informed health care decisions.
- *Choice of providers and plans.* Patients have the right to choose their own doctors and other health care providers who can give them high-quality health care when they need it.
- *Access to emergency services.* Patients have the right to access health care services whenever and wherever the need arises. A health plan must pay for costs that a **prudent layperson** (a reasonable, untrained person in a similar position) would reasonably expect the plan to cover. For example, your health plan may say that you must use a particular hospital. But if a prudent layperson would go to the closest hospital to avoid death or serious consequences, then those costs must be covered.
- *Treatment decisions.* Patients have the right to fully participate in all decisions related to their health care. Patients who are unable to fully participate in treatment decisions have the right to be represented by parents, guardians, and family members.
- *Respect and nondiscrimination.* Patients have the right to considerate, respectful care from all members of the health care system at all times and under all circumstances.
- *Confidentiality.* Patients have the right to have the confidentiality of their individually identifiable health care information protected. Patients also have the right to review and copy their own medical record and have their record amended if it is incorrect or incomplete.
- *Complaints and appeals.* Patients have the right to a fair, fast, and objective review of any complaint they have against doctors, hospitals, or other health care personnel.

CHECKPOINT

What is the difference between time-shifting and space-shifting?

LO 1-2   Consumer Protection Laws

Over the years, Congress has passed many laws to protect consumers from unsafe products and unfair or deceptive business practices. These laws help ensure that consumers get quality goods and services for their hard-earned dollars.

Food, Drug, and Cosmetic Act

In 1937 a Tennessee drug company marketed a new wonder drug that would appeal to pediatric patients. However, the solvent in this untested product was a highly toxic chemical similar to antifreeze. Over 100 people died, many of whom were children. The public outcry reshaped the drug provisions of a new law proposed that year to prevent such an event from happening again. The *Food, Drug, and Cosmetic Act* of 1938 requires that foods be safe, pure, and wholesome; that drugs and medical devices be safe and effective; and that cosmetics be safe. The law also requires *truthful labeling* on these products, including the name and address of the manufacturer. In addition, the law mandates that the U.S. Food and Drug Administration (FDA) approve drugs before they can be sold.

Flammable Fabrics Act

The *Flammable Fabrics Act* of 1953 enabled the Consumer Product Safety Commission to set flammability standards for clothing, children's sleepwear, carpets, rugs, and mattresses. **Flammability** is the capacity for catching on fire. The law prohibits the selling of wearable apparel made of easily ignited material. The flammability standard for children's sleepwear requires that the garment will not catch fire when exposed to a match or small fire. The flame-retardant finish must last for 50 washings and dryings. In 1967 Congress amended the Flammable Fabrics Act to expand its coverage to include interior furnishings as well as paper, plastic, foam, and other materials used in consumer products.

Meat Inspection Laws

Numerous acts that standardize inspection procedures have been passed to protect consumers who purchase chicken and beef. The *Poultry Products Inspection Act* of 1957 requires poultry to be inspected for harmful contaminants. These requirements also apply to imported meat and poultry products, which must be inspected under equivalent foreign standards. In 1967 the *Wholesome Meat Act*, an update to the Meat Inspection Act of 1906, provided for stricter standards for processing facilities of meat products. States are required to have meat inspection programs equal to that of the federal government, which are administered by the United States Department of Agriculture (USDA).

Hazardous Substances Act

The *Hazardous Substances Act* of 1960 requires that warning labels appear on all household products that are potentially dangerous to the consumer. The purpose of the warning labels is to help consumers safely store and use these products and to provide information about first-aid steps to take if an accident happens. In most cases, products found to be unacceptably hazardous must be recalled. A **recall** is a request for consumers to return a defective product to the manufacturer for a refund or repair.

What purpose do warning labels serve?

Kefauver-Harris Drug Amendment

As a result of the *Kefauver-Harris Drug Amendment* of 1962, drug manufacturers must test drugs for safety and effectiveness before they are sold to consumers. This law was a reaction to the Thalidomide tragedy in which thousands of children were born with birth defects as a result of their mothers taking thalidomide for morning sickness during pregnancy. In addition, the amendment requires drug advertising to disclose accurate information about potential side effects of medications.

This amendment also provides for the manufacture and sale of generic drugs. **Generic drugs** are medications with the same composition as the equivalent brand-name drugs, but they are generally less expensive. National brand names are expensive because of the costs of development and marketing. To allow drug companies to recoup the costs of developing new drugs, the law offers patent protection, which gives companies the exclusive right to market the drug for a number of years before competitors can sell the generic equivalents.

Cigarette Labeling and Advertising Act

The *Cigarette Labeling and Advertising Act* of 1965 requires tobacco companies to place a warning label on cigarette packaging. The warning label advises consumers of health hazards from smoking. Original labels read: "Caution: Cigarette Smoking May Be Hazardous to Your Health." Today these warning labels are even more specific. Current labels read: "Surgeon General's Warning: Smoking Causes Lung Cancer, Heart Disease, Emphysema, and May Complicate Pregnancy."

National Traffic and Motor Vehicle Safety Act

The *National Traffic and Motor Vehicle Safety Act* of 1966 established national safety standards for automobiles. It was enacted to reduce traffic accidents as well as the number of deaths and injuries to people involved in traffic accidents. The National Highway Traffic Safety Administration enforces provisions of the act. Its responsibilities include increasing public awareness of the need for safety devices, testing for safety, and inspecting vehicles for proper safety equipment.

Fair Packaging and Labeling Act

The *Fair Packaging and Labeling Act* of 1967 requires product labels to contain accurate names, quantities, and weights. These rules apply to all types of products, such as groceries, cosmetics, cleaners, and chemicals.

Amendments to the Fair Packaging and Labeling Act were passed in 1992. These laws require labels to include conversion of quantities into a metric measurement in addition to the U.S. system of weights and measures.

Toy Safety Laws

The *Child Protection and Toy Safety Act* of 1969 bans the sale of toys and children's articles that contain hazardous substances or pose electrical, mechanical, or thermal dangers. Such products can be inspected and removed from the marketplace. The act requires special labeling for children's products, along with devices that make potentially dangerous products **childproof**, or resistant to tampering by young children.

Other toy safety laws have been enacted over the years. The *Toy Safety Act* of 1984 permits quick recall of toys and other articles intended for use by children that might present a substantial risk of injury.

In 1994 Congress passed the *Child Safety Protection Act*, which strengthened earlier standards and imposed strict labeling laws for manufacturers and retailers of children's toys that may present a danger to small children, such as small balls, marbles, and balloons. The *Consumer Product Safety Improvement Act* of 2008 requires that children's toys and infant products undergo testing before sale. The legislation further banned use of toxic chemicals, such as lead paint, from toys and other products.

Care Labeling Rule

The *Care Labeling Rule* of 1971 requires that clothing and fabrics be labeled permanently with laundering and care instructions. Care labels give instructions for cleaning, wash and dry temperatures, and other care needed to preserve the product. The labels must stay attached and be easy to read for the life of the garment. This law was amended in 1984 to allow for exceptions to the rule for fabrics that may be damaged as a result of having a permanent label. These fabrics include leather, gloves, hats, and reversible clothing. In 1997 the law was updated to allow for the use of symbols on labels instead of written instructions.

Family and Educational Rights and Privacy Act

The *Family and Educational Rights and Privacy Act (FERPA)* of 1974 is a federal law that protects the privacy of student education records. Parents and students 18 years of age or older have the right to inspect and review the students' education records maintained by the school. Errors or misleading information may be corrected. Schools must obtain written permission from the parent or student before releasing any information from a student's education record. Only directory-type information, such as name, address, phone number, and date of birth, may be disclosed without consent. Parents and students may request that even this information not be disclosed. One important requirement is that Social Security numbers cannot be used as student ID numbers.

Generic Drug Act

The *Drug Price Competition and Patent Term Restoration Act* of 1984 (also called the *Hatch-Waxman Act* or *Generic Drug Act*) established the modern system of generic drugs. It speeds up the FDA approval process of generic versions of drugs. It attempts to protect the consumer more quickly than in the past by reducing roadblocks that would keep drug prices high.

Nutrition Labeling and Education Act

The *Nutrition Labeling and Education Act* of 1990 requires that all packaged foods contain a uniform "Nutrition Facts" label that includes specific information about key vitamins and minerals as well as nutrients (fat, saturated fat, sodium, and cholesterol) that contribute to increased chronic disease. The act also developed guidelines regarding the use of nutritional claims. Terms such as "low fat" or "high fiber" can be used only if the foods have met certain criteria by the FDA. For example, a food labeled "low fat" cannot contain more than three grams of fat per serving.

Many people depend on properly labeled foods in order to maintain their health and weight and to prevent deadly reactions. For example, if you are gluten-intolerant, you cannot eat foods that contain any amount of wheat protein. If foods are not labeled properly with every ingredient, you are at risk. Foods that are produced in other countries and shipped to the United States for consumption do not have to meet the same standards, either in purity or in labeling. Some foods produced in the United States are shipped into Mexico for processing to avoid having to follow these requirements; yet the labels say "Grown in the USA," leading people to believe that the food products meet U.S. standards. Some people feel that all foods, regardless of where they are grown or processed, should have to meet the same standards to be sold in the United States. Others believe that following these regulations only increases the cost.

© Vectomart/Shutterstock.com

THINK CRITICALLY

Which side do you agree with and why? How would you assure that pure food standards are met and that labels are accurate for all contents? How important is it that foods labeled "organic" are really organic?

In 1993 the act was modified to require restaurants to comply with health claims made on signs and menus by making nutritional information available upon request. Because of these provisions, consumers are more informed about food products in general and are better able to make choices about menu items based on their true content.

Health Insurance Portability and Accountability Act

The *Health Insurance Portability and Accountability Act (HIPAA)* of 1996 sets rules about who can see your health information. The law applies to doctors, pharmacies, hospitals, health insurance companies, employer group health plans, and Medicare and Medicaid. Protected information includes medical records, conversations, information pertaining to you stored in a computer system, and billing information. Consumers are allowed to have a copy of their health records, have corrections made, know how information is being used, and decide whether to give permission to share this information. Also as a result of HIPAA, Social Security numbers cannot be used as a personal identifier for patients.

Children's Online Privacy Protection Act

The *Children's Online Privacy Protection Act* of 1998 applies to the online collection of personal information from children under 13 years of age. The act details what a website must include in a *privacy policy*, when and how to seek verifiable consent from a parent or guardian, and the responsibilities of the website to protect children's privacy and safety online. Websites that do not comply with the provisions of the act are subject to sanctions levied by the Federal Trade Commission (FTC).

✔ CHECKPOINT

What types of protections are provided by FERPA and HIPAA?

What Is the Consumer Privacy Bill of Rights?

On February 23, 2012, the Obama administration proposed a Consumer Privacy Bill of Rights as part of a comprehensive blueprint for future legislation to protect consumers' privacy. The intent is to give consumers more control over how their personal information is used on the Internet and to set principles for companies that use *personal data*, which is any data that can be linked to a specific individual. Personal data may include data that is linked to a specific computer or other storage device. The proposed bill of rights includes the following basic provisions:

- *Individual control.* Consumers have a right to control what personal data is being collected about them by companies and how it is used.

- *Transparency.* Consumers have a right to easily understandable and accessible information about privacy and security practices used by companies who gather personal data.

- *Respect for context.* Consumers have a right to expect that companies will collect, use, and disclose personal data in ways that are consistent with the context in which the data is provided.

- *Security.* Consumers have a right to secure and responsible handling of personal data to avoid unauthorized access, use, destruction, modification, or improper disclosure of information to others.

- *Access and accuracy.* Consumers have a right to access and correct personal data to avoid risk of adverse consequences if the data is inaccurate.

- *Focused collection.* Consumers have a right to reasonable limits on personal data that companies collect and retain.

- *Accountability.* Consumers have a right to have personal data handled in a manner that assures compliance with standards set forth in the Consumer Privacy Bill of Rights.

The proposal is voluntary, meaning that companies would be able to choose whether or not they want to participate. Companies who choose to participate and who infringe on any of the rights set forth in these guidelines could suffer sanctions by the FTC. The proposal challenged companies to work with consumer privacy advocates and consumer protection enforcement agencies to develop enforceable codes of conduct that would become part of the law.

THINK CRITICALLY

1. Do you think there is a need to tighten and enforce consumer privacy rights in the collection of personal data in this country? Why or why not?

2. What types of penalties would you suggest against companies and others who do not adhere to consumer privacy standards? Explain.

KEY TERMS REVIEW

Match the terms with the definitions. Some terms may not be used.

a. care labels
b. childproof
c. flammability
d. generic drugs
e. prudent layperson
f. recall
g. space-shifting
h. time-shifting

_____ 1. A reasonable, untrained person in a similar situation

_____ 2. Labels that give instructions for cleaning, wash and dry temperatures, and other care needed to preserve the product

_____ 3. A request for consumers to return a defective product to the manufacturer for a refund or repair

_____ 4. Recording video or audio for later viewing or listening

_____ 5. The capacity for catching on fire

_____ 6. Accessing media, such as music or films, stored on one device from another place through another device

_____ 7. Less-expensive medications with the same composition as the equivalent brand-name drugs

CHECK YOUR UNDERSTANDING

L01-1 8. What four rights were added to the Consumer Bill of Rights in 1985?

L01-2 9. How did the Kefauver-Harris Drug Amendment affect the pharmaceutical industry?

APPLY YOUR KNOWLEDGE

L01-2 10. Which consumer protection law has the most significance for you? Describe how you and other consumers have benefited because this law was passed.

THINK CRITICALLY

L01-1 11. Explain the need for the Consumer Bill of Rights. Why do you need these protections? Would you like to see additional rights added to the list? Explain.

L01-1 12. How has technology changed the way we view consumer rights and protection?

The Essential Question _Refer to The Essential Question on p. 612. Consumers have basic rights, such as the right to safety, the right to be informed, the right to choose, and the right to be heard. They also have rights when it comes to flying on airlines, using technology, and receiving medical care. Congress has passed many laws to protect consumers from unsafe products and unfair or deceptive business practices. These laws help ensure that consumers get quality goods and services for their hard-earned money._

The Essential Question *What are some government and private sources of consumer assistance, and how can you contact public officials?*

LEARNING OBJECTIVES

> LO 2-1 List and describe government and private sources of consumer assistance.
> LO 2-2 Explain how to contact public officials to express opinions and file complaints.

KEY TERMS

- USDA, *622*
- NIST, *623*
- FDA, *623*
- CPSC, *624*
- FCC, *624*
- FTC, *624*
- USPIS, *624*
- FAA, *624*
- SEC, *624*
- BBB, *625*
- Consumers Union, *626*
- consumer advocate, *626*

LO 2-1 Sources of Consumer Protection

When you need assistance with a consumer problem, numerous organizations are available to help you. These organizations are found at the federal, state, and local levels and also include private organizations.

Federal Agencies

Many federal government agencies provide information of interest to consumers. Some of these agencies handle consumer complaints, and others direct complaints to agencies or sources that address consumer issues. All of these agencies maintain websites that offer an abundance of helpful information to consumers.

Department of Agriculture

The **USDA** (United States Department of Agriculture) is responsible for developing and executing federal government policy on farming, agriculture, forestry, and food. It works to support the country's agricultural economy; protect and conserve our natural resources; and provide a safe, sufficient, and nutritious food supply for the American people.

Within the USDA, there are a number of agencies that exist to meet various consumer needs regarding the food supply in this country. The *Food Safety and Inspection Service* ensures that the commercial supply of meat, poultry, and processed egg products is safe, wholesome, and correctly labeled and packaged. The *Food and Nutrition Service* provides food assistance programs, such as the Supplemental Nutrition Assistance Program (SNAP, formerly called the Food Stamp Program) and the National School Lunch Program, and information on diets, nutrition, and menu preparation. The *Center for Nutrition Policy and Promotion* develops nutrition research, education, and promotion

© Pan Xunbin/Shutterstock.com

programs for the American public. It developed the MyPlate food guide, which illustrates the five food groups and reminds consumers to eat healthy portions from each group.

National Institute of Standards and Technology

The **NIST** (National Institute of Standards and Technology) is an agency within the U.S. Department of Commerce. One of its missions is to develop and reward standards of excellence in business. NIST sponsors the *Malcolm Baldrige National Quality Award* given each year to U.S. businesses that achieve high standards of quality in their business practices.

NIST also sets uniform standards of weights and measures. The NIST is the reason that you don't have to shop with a tape measure or scale to make sure you get what you pay for. NIST sponsors a network of state and local agencies that set performance standards for measuring devices used to determine the costs and amounts of products sold to consumers. For example, agencies of the NIST network determine the amount of error that is acceptable for a gas pump or grocer's scale and establish testing procedures for enforcing standards.

The NIST also runs one of the world's two atomic clocks, which serves as the source of the nation's official time, and co-invented closed-captioning for people with impaired hearing. NIST research has also contributed to a wide variety of technological developments, including image processing, smoke detectors, and pollution control.

Food and Drug Administration

One of the many agencies within the U.S. Department of Health and Human Services is the **FDA** (Food and Drug Administration). The FDA enforces laws and regulations preventing distribution of mislabeled foods, drugs, cosmetics, and medical devices. The FDA does the following:

- Requires testing and approval of all new drugs
- Tests new and existing products for health and safety standards
- Provides standards and guidelines for poisonous substances
- Sets standards for identification, quality, and volume of food containers
- Establishes guidelines for labels and proper identification of product contents, ingredients, nutrients, and directions for use
- Investigates complaints
- Conducts research and issues reports, guidelines, and warnings about substances found to be dangerous or potentially hazardous to health.

How does the FDA protect consumers?

Consumer Product Safety Commission

The **CPSC** (Consumer Product Safety Commission) protects consumers from unreasonable risk of injury or death from potentially hazardous consumer products. The commission develops and enforces standards for consumer products, bans products that are dangerous, arranges recalls, and conducts research on potential product hazards. In addition, the CPSC offers many publications on safety education.

Federal Communications Commission

The **FCC** (Federal Communications Commission) regulates interstate and international communications by radio, television, wire, satellite, and cable. In addition to educating and informing consumers about telecommunications goods, services, and regulations, the FCC's responsibilities also include issuing operating licenses for radio and TV stations, presiding over legal hearings pertaining to matters involving communications, and maintaining decency standards. The Consumer and Governmental Affairs Bureau develops the FCC's consumer policies and handles consumer questions and complaints.

Federal Trade Commission

The **FTC** (Federal Trade Commission) regulates unfair methods of competition, false or deceptive advertising, deceptive product labeling, and the concealment of the true costs of credit. The FTC is also the federal clearinghouse for complaints of identity theft. The FTC's Bureau of Consumer Protection enforces federal consumer protection laws, helping to enhance consumer confidence. The Bureau also oversees the U.S. National Do Not Call Registry.

United States Postal Inspection Service

The **USPIS** (United States Postal Inspection Service) is a federal law enforcement agency that investigates consumer problems pertaining to illegal use of the mail. The USPIS enforces postal laws, protecting consumers from dangerous articles, fraud, pornography, and identity theft involving the mail.

Federal Aviation Administration

The **FAA** (Federal Aviation Administration) oversees the U.S. commercial aviation industry for the Department of Transportation. It maintains regulations and standards that airline companies, such as United, Delta, and Southwest, must follow in order to transport passengers. The FAA is also responsible for certifying that all commercial aviation aircraft, pilots, companies, and airports meet the standards set forth by federal regulations. The FAA also oversees the nation's air traffic control system, which directs commercial, private, and military aircraft all across the United States.

Securities and Exchange Commission

The main purpose of the **SEC** (Securities and Exchange Commission) is to protect investors and maintain the integrity of the securities markets.

The SEC requires companies to disclose certain financial and other information so that investors can make informed decisions about investment options. The SEC also oversees stock exchanges, brokers, and investment advisers to protect investors in their dealings with securities professionals. The SEC's Office of Investor Education and Advocacy serves investors who have securities-related questions or who have complaints about investment fraud or the mishandling of their investments by securities professionals.

State and Local Assistance

Most states have a consumer protection agency, or the state attorney general may handle consumer complaints. Many county and city governments also have consumer protection offices. Consumer leagues and public-interest research groups are also active at the state and local levels, with newsletters, pamphlets, handbooks, and websites on current consumer issues.

At the local level, consumers have access to legal aid societies, newspaper and broadcast consumer action reporters, and consumer representatives on local utility or licensing boards. Independent consumer groups focusing on specific issues, such as food prices, may operate on the local level as well.

Private Organizations

Not all consumer protection agencies are found at the government level. There are many private organizations for consumers to access when they need to gather information or file complaints.

Better Business Bureau

The **BBB** (Better Business Bureau) is a nonprofit organization focused on creating a more trusting relationship between businesses and consumers. It provides free reports on millions of businesses to help consumers make more informed decisions. The reports contain information about the business, customer reviews, and any complaints filed against the company. These reports are available on the BBB's website.

If consumers are dissatisfied with a business transaction, they can file a complaint with the BBB. Complaints can be filed over the phone, in writing, or by using the BBB's online complaint system. The BBB then acts as an intermediary between consumers and businesses in an attempt to resolve the dispute in a quick and fair manner.

National Consumers League

The *National Consumers League (NCL)* is the nation's oldest nonprofit consumer organization. Initially formed to improve

How can consumers use the services of the BBB?

Assume you are unhappy with the service that you received from a local business. Make up the name of the company and the type of service received. Write a letter of complaint about the business that you would send to the BBB. Be specific in your complaint, giving reasons for your dissatisfaction and asking for a specific remedy. What do you expect as a result of your complaint?

© oculo/Shutterstock.com

working conditions for working-class women, today the NCL represents consumers on marketplace and workplace issues such as child labor, privacy, food safety, and medication information. They also operate Fraud.org (formerly the National Fraud Information Center). This website provides consumers with free information they need to avoid becoming victims of fraud and identity theft. It also has an online fraud report form that consumers can fill out to report telemarketing and online fraud attempts.

Consumer Action

Consumer Action is a national nonprofit advocacy and education organization. Formed in 1971, the organization staffed one of the earliest consumer advice and assistance hotlines, and its picket of British Motors in 1972 established the right of aggrieved consumers to picket businesses. Consumer Action is known for its multilingual consumer education and support in the fields of credit, banking, privacy, insurance, and utilities. It is also known for its Credit Card Survey, an annual survey about credit cards, banks, and lending practices.

Consumers Union

Consumers Union is a nonprofit organization best known as the publisher of *Consumer Reports*, a monthly magazine that publishes reviews, comparisons, and ratings of consumer products and services. To assure that all ratings are unbiased, Consumers Union buys all products it tests and accepts no advertising. In addition to its research and publishing activities, Consumers Union has four advocacy offices that attempt to influence policy that affects consumers.

Consumer Advocates

In addition to working with private organizations, consumers may also seek the support of a consumer advocate—a person who actively promotes consumer causes. Ralph Nader is a well-known consumer advocate. When he finds, through research and investigation, that an injustice or dangerous condition exists, he pursues it on behalf of all consumers. Consumer advocates may file lawsuits against companies to force them to meet safety standards, correct inequitable situations, or properly inform consumers of dangers in the use of their products.

 **CHECKPOINT**

What does the FTC do to help protect consumers?

National elected officials include the President and Vice President and members of Congress. State elected officials include the Governor, secretary of state, treasurer, attorney general, superintendent of public instruction, labor commissioner, and state senators and representatives.

Each court (federal, state, and local) has at least one judge and several clerks of the court to assist in filing and information gathering. County elected officials include the county administrator, district attorney, sheriff, and tax assessor, plus a number of commissioners. Other elected local officials include the mayor, city council members, and city manager.

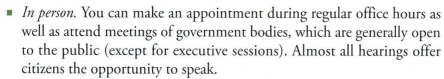

Why is it important to share your views on consumer-related issues with government officials?

In addition, many branches of government now employ communications specialists who are responsible for planning, organizing, and directing public outreach and educational programs. For example, they may develop public service announcements to alert consumers to fraudulent activities.

If you wish to communicate with a public official about a consumer issue, there are several ways to do so.

- *In person.* You can make an appointment during regular office hours as well as attend meetings of government bodies, which are generally open to the public (except for executive sessions). Almost all hearings offer citizens the opportunity to speak.
- *By phone.* Brief phone calls at reasonable hours are generally effective. Your state may supply toll-free numbers for contacting public officials.
- *By e-mail.* Sending an e-mail is the most immediate way to reach a public official. Many public officials have e-mail forms on their official websites that allow constituents (people who live in the areas they represent) to contact them with comments, questions, or concerns. You may also find e-mail addresses of public officials at government websites.
- *By letter.* To be effective, a letter written to the appropriate representative should state clearly the purpose of the letter, identify the proposed legislation or bill with which you have concerns, refer to only one issue, and arrive while the issue is current. Provide reasons for your position on the issue and avoid being emotional. Describe what action you want the public official to take.

 CHECKPOINT

Why would you want to contact an elected official?

Social Work

Social workers help people solve and cope with problems in their everyday lives. They not only strive to improve the lives of individuals but also improve society as a whole.

There are numerous types of social workers, such as child and family social workers, health care social workers, school social workers, and clinical social workers. The type of work they do varies. They often help diagnose and treat mental, behavioral, and emotional issues, including depression and substance abuse.

Most people working in this field work full time and are on call weekends and evenings. Although they work in an office, they also spend time visiting clients.

Employment Outlook

- A faster-than-average rate of employment growth is expected.

Job Titles

- Social worker
- Family therapist
- Psychotherapist

Needed Skills

- A bachelor's degree in social work is required for entry-level social work.
- A master's degree and post-master's degree clinical experience are required for clinical social workers.
- Licensure or certification is required in all states.
- Compassion and interpersonal, listening, and problem-solving skills are necessary.

What's it like to work in . . . *Social Work*

Adam is a child and family social worker for a state human services agency, earning $40,000 yearly. His job duties consist of helping parents find services, such as child care, and apply for benefits, such as food assistance programs. He also intervenes when children are in danger of neglect or abuse. He maintains case files for 12 to 15 clients. During the week, he does home visits as well as observations and clinical reports.

Adam's schedule is varied. Some days he is in the office most of the day, attending meetings and preparing reports; other days he is in the field, gathering information, appearing in court, or doing research. He often has to follow up on case referrals he receives from other state agencies. He meets with clients within 48 hours of receiving a referral.

What About You?

Are you interested in working with people who are in need of emotional and psychological support? Do you like helping others? If so, a career in social work may be for you.

The Career Clusters icons are being used with permission of the: States' Career Clusters Initiative, 2007, www.careerclusters.org

KEY TERMS REVIEW

Match the terms with the definitions. Some terms may not be used.

____ 1. Develops and executes federal government policy on farming, agriculture, forestry, and food

____ 2. A nonprofit organization focused on creating a more trusting relationship between businesses and consumers

____ 3. Oversees the U.S. commercial aviation industry

____ 4. A person who actively promotes consumer causes

____ 5. Enforces laws and regulations preventing distribution of mislabeled foods, drugs, cosmetics, and medical devices

____ 6. Develops and rewards standards of excellence in business

____ 7. Regulates unfair methods of competition, advertising, and product labeling

a. BBB
b. consumer advocate
c. Consumers Union
d. CPSC
e. FAA
f. FCC
g. FDA
h. FTC
i. NIST
j. SEC
k. USDA
l. USPIS

CHECK YOUR UNDERSTANDING

LO2-1 8. What is the purpose of the CPSC?

LO2-1 9. How does the SEC protect investors?

LO2-2 10. What should an effective letter to a public official contain?

APPLY YOUR KNOWLEDGE

LO2-1 11. Select a federal agency that provides consumer protection. Describe what it does for consumers, and list several more things you would like to see the agency do.

THINK CRITICALLY

LO2-1 12. Why is it necessary for the FCC to regulate communications? Do you think this agency is adding value for consumers?

LO2-1 13. How does a consumer advocate help consumers? What issues do you think are important for advocates to understand and work on today?

The Essential Question *Refer to The Essential Question on p. 622. Federal agencies that provide consumer assistance include the USDA, NIST, FDA, CPSC, FCC, FTC, USPIS, FAA, and SEC. Private organizations such as the BBB, NCL, Consumer Action, and Consumers Union also provide assistance. You can contact public officials to express opinions and concerns or file complaints in person or by phone, e-mail, or letter.*

SUMMARY

25.1

- *The Consumer Bill of Rights outlines basic rights that consumers should expect in the marketplace.*

- *Airline passenger rights provide protections to paying passengers on commercial airlines.*

- *The Consumer Technology Bill of Rights outlines permissible reproduction and uses of purchased digital content.*

- *A patients' bill of rights was enacted in 1998 to give patients more control over medical decisions, treatments, and records.*

- *Some laws (such as the Food, Drug, and Cosmetic Act and the Flammable Fabrics Act) set standards for product purity and safety.*

- *Many laws (including the Fair Packaging and Labeling Act and the Nutrition Labeling and Education Act) set rules for product labeling.*

- *Several laws (such as toy safety laws and the Children's Online Privacy Protection Act) are designed to protect children from harm.*

25.2

- *The USDA works to provide a safe, sufficient, and nutritious food supply for the country.*

- *The NIST rewards standards of excellence in business and sets uniform standards of weights and measures.*

- *The FDA approves new drugs, tests products for safety, and sets labeling guidelines.*

- *The CPSC enforces product standards and bans or recalls hazardous products.*

- *The FCC regulates communications by radio, television, wire, satellite, and cable.*

- *The FTC regulates methods of unfair competition, deceptive marketing practices, and concealment of the true costs of credit.*

- *The USPIS investigates problems pertaining to illegal use of the mail.*

- *The FAA oversees the U.S. commercial aviation industry.*

- *The SEC protects investors and maintains the integrity of the securities markets.*

- *Private organizations, such as the BBB and Consumers Union, can assist consumers with incidents of unethical and illegal practices.*

- *If consumers have an issue or a complaint, they can contact public officials in person or by phone, e-mail, or letter.*

APPLY WHAT YOU KNOW

LO1-2   1. Select any garment from your closet. Read the care label. What kinds of information are on the label? How is this information helpful?

LO1-2   2. Identify the law that protects consumers from each of the following abuses:

     a. A box states that it contains 12 ounces of product when it actually contains only 9 ounces.

     b. A doctor tells an employer that an employee has a potentially expensive medical condition. Rather than risk higher health insurance premiums, the employer fires the employee.

     c. A company develops a new "miracle" drug. To get it on the market quickly, the company does not test it sufficiently.

     d. A company develops an effective new cleaning product. However, the chemicals it contains are quite dangerous. To avoid scaring potential customers, the company does not mention the dangers on the label.

LO1-2   3. Look at the label on a food product. List the product and the different types of information found on the label, such as serving size, ingredients, and vitamin and mineral content. Are there ingredients you do not recognize? If so, conduct online research to learn about them. After doing so, what can you conclude about the nutritional value of the food?

LO2-1   4. Visit the Securities and Exchange Commission's website (www.sec.gov). Go to the "About" menu on the homepage and choose "Securities Laws" from the drop-down menu. Select one of the laws listed and briefly summarize how it protects investors.

LO2-1   5. Visit the Better Business Bureau's website (www.bbb.org) and look up the reports on two local businesses. Write a brief summary of the kinds of information that the reports provide about the businesses.

LO2-1   6. Visit the Fraud.org website (www.fraud.org) and answer the following questions:

     a. What services are available to consumers who have complaints?

     b. What is the process of filing a complaint?

MAKE ACADEMIC CONNECTIONS

LO1-1   7. **Communication** Write a bill of rights in an area that concerns you. What rights would you like to have guaranteed to you as a citizen? List the rights on a poster to share with the class. Use one of the bills of rights in Lesson 25.1 as an example.

LO1-2   8. **International Studies** Select another country and research its consumer protection laws. How are they different from laws in the United States?

LO2-1   9. **Social Studies** Prepare a presentation to explain the role of government in consumer protection and why it is important. Use visual examples to explain the societal benefits of governmental consumer protection.

LO2-1   10. **Research** Conduct online research on the Malcolm Baldrige National Quality Award. Write a one-page report explaining the history of the award, its recipients, and its purpose.

Solve Problems and Explore Issues

LO1-2   11. Why should you consider buying generic drugs rather than brand-name drugs? What do you think would happen if drug development companies did not receive patent protection for a number of years before other companies could sell generic equivalents?

LO1-2   12. Why are your rights as protected by FERPA important to you? What could happen if these rights were not protected?

LO2-1   13. List your state and local sources that can provide assistance with a consumer complaint.

LO2-2   14. Check your local newspaper for public notices of hearings by local government groups. List hearings that are scheduled. Which hearings are on issues affecting consumers? How would consumers be affected in each case?

EXTEND YOUR LEARNING

LO2-1   15. **Ethics** Cable companies are essentially monopolies—customers have little, if any, choice in products available to them. Packaged plans and bundles contain features that consumers do not want, yet they have to buy the entire package to get the channels and programs they do want. This bundling raises costs for consumers. Satellite and other providers of similar services have the same bundling plans. To maintain profitability, these communications providers may also charge fees to replace obsolete equipment and repair it or sell costly service contracts. Do you think these business practices are ethical? How can consumers fight back? What can the government do to help protect citizens from these predatory practices?

CHAPTER PROJECT

Each year, state senators and representatives propose new laws and regulations that affect consumers in areas from safety to tax increases. Check recent issues of newspapers, news magazines, or online news sources for reports of proposed new state laws and regulations affecting consumers. Choose an issue that concerns you and investigate it. Prepare a short report describing the law. What is the purpose of the law? Whom would the law benefit and whom might it harm? Who are its proponents and who are its opponents? What would be the cost of the new law to taxpayers? What are the long-term impacts of the law? Then based on your research, prepare a letter or e-mail to the appropriate official with your comments on the proposed law or regulation.

Complete the Guided Decision Making activity for Chapter 25 at **ngl.cengage.com/mypf**.

Dispute Resolution

Consider This...

Jim wanted to paint his apartment. His landlord promised to pay for the paint if Jim provided the labor. Based on this agreement, Jim painted the apartment. However, when he asked the landlord for reimbursement, the landlord refused.

"I've tried everything," Jim told his sister. "I talked to him nicely and reminded him of our verbal agreement. He said that he never made such an agreement and I have nothing in writing to prove it. Then when I moved out of the apartment, he refused to refund my deposit. He said that I painted the apartment without authorization, so he was entitled to keep my deposit. Together the paint and the deposit cost me $900! What can I do to get my money back?"

The Legal System

The Essential Question *What is a three-tiered court system, and what are the steps followed when a lawsuit is filed?*

LEARNING OBJECTIVES

> LO 1-1 Describe the structure of the legal system in the United States.

> LO 1-2 Describe the four phases of a lawsuit.

KEY TERMS

- common law, *634*
- civil case, *634*
- criminal case, *634*
- complaint, *638*
- plaintiff, *638*
- defendant, *638*
- counterclaim, *639*
- discovery, *639*
- deposition, *639*
- verdict, *641*
- judgment, *641*
- appeal, *641*

LO 1-1 Structure of the Legal System

The legal system in the United States is built on several sources of law, including constitutional law, statutory law (laws passed by Congress or state legislature), agency law (laws relating to commercial or contractual dealings), maritime law (laws governing the high seas), and common law. **Common law** is a system of laws based on decisions made in court cases. These decisions set legal *precedents*, which serve as models for deciding similar cases in the future.

At the base of our common law legal system are the courts. *Courts* hold judicial proceedings to hear and decide matters according to the law.

Types of Courts

There are three types of courts—federal, state, and local. Each court is empowered to decide certain types or classes of cases. This power is called *jurisdiction*, which is the legal authority to hear and decide a case. *Trial courts* are said to have *original jurisdiction* because they are the first court to hear a case. *Appellate courts* are said to have *appellate jurisdiction*, or the authority to review the judgment of lower courts.

Types of Cases

Legal matters are classified as either civil or criminal. A **civil case** involves one person who has a dispute with another person or entity. For example, matters such as divorce, estate settlement, or torts (civil violations that result in damages or injuries to others) would be settled in a civil proceeding. A **criminal case** involves a government unit that is

What are the three types of courts in the U.S. judicial system?

© artconcept/Shutterstock.com

© Pan Xunbin/Shutterstock.com

accusing an individual of committing a crime. When a law has been broken, a prosecutor files criminal charges against the accused person. In this country, a person is presumed innocent until proven guilty.

The losing parties may appeal the decision of a civil or criminal court if they believe the court made an error in applying the law. The appellate court reviews decisions of lower courts.

Court Personnel

Our court systems require many people to operate efficiently. Commonly you will find the following participants when a court case is filed:

- The *judge* is the presiding officer in the court and is either elected or appointed. The judge hears testimony from the witnesses and any other evidence presented by the parties of the case, assesses the credibility and arguments of the parties, and then issues rulings based on his or her interpretation of the law and his or her own personal judgment.
- An *attorney* provides legal representation to an individual. Attorneys are usually selected by the parties in the dispute but are sometimes appointed by the court. For example, if you are accused of a crime and cannot afford an attorney, an attorney called a *public defender* will be appointed to help you present your case.
- The *court clerk* enters cases on the court calendar and keeps an accurate record of the proceedings. The clerk also accepts, labels, and safeguards all items of evidence; administers the oath to witnesses and jurors; and sometimes approves bail bonds and computes the costs involved.
- The *court reporter* creates a word-by-word transcription of the trial, usually through the use of a special recording machine called a stenotype machine. These transcriptions are available to each attorney and are used for appeals.
- The *bailiff* maintains order in the courtroom at the instruction of the judge. He or she also is the conduit between the judge and the jury and other members of the court.
- The *jury* is a body of citizens sworn by a court to hear the facts submitted during a trial and to render a verdict. While a judge decides *issues of law*, the jury decides *issues of fact* (guilt or innocence). A juror must be of legal age, a resident, and able to see and hear.

The Three-Tiered Court System

Both the state and the federal levels have a three-tiered court system. It starts with the trial court level. Cases are then appealed to the appellate court level, and finally cases can be appealed to the supreme court level.

The Federal Court System

The authority of federal courts comes directly from the U.S. Constitution and the laws enacted by Congress. The federal courts hear matters that concern the nation as a whole. These matters pertain to constitutional rights, civil rights, interstate commerce, patents and copyrights, federal taxes, currency, and foreign relations. The federal courts may also hear a dispute between citizens of two different states or between U.S. citizens and those of another country, but only if it involves $75,000 or more.

The federal court system is a three-tiered system consisting of the U.S. district courts, U.S. courts of appeal, and U.S. Supreme Court.

U.S. District Courts

The U.S. district courts are the *trial courts* of the federal court system. The United States is currently divided into 94 federal districts, with a court assigned to each. Each district covers a state or a portion of a state. Consequently, some states may be home to more than one federal district court. Every state has at least one U.S. district court. U.S. district courts are staffed by judges who hear cases individually, not as a panel.

Within limits set by Congress and the U.S. Constitution, the district courts have jurisdiction to hear nearly all categories of federal cases, including both civil and criminal matters. Some issues are always considered federal issues, such as bankruptcy and crimes involving interstate commerce. Hijacking, kidnapping, bank robbery, and counterfeiting are all federal crimes and are prosecuted in federal courts. This is called *exclusive jurisdiction* because trial for these issues must take place at a U.S. district court (state courts may not hear these cases).

There are other federal trial courts that have exclusive jurisdiction over certain types of cases. The Court of International Trade addresses cases involving international trade and customs issues. The U.S. Court of Federal Claims has jurisdiction over most monetary claims against the United States in excess of $10,000. The U.S. Tax Court specializes in settling disputes over federal income taxes.

U.S. Courts of Appeal

The 94 judicial districts are organized into 12 regional circuits, each of which has a U.S. court of appeal. Each appellate court has a panel of judges who review final decisions of the district courts within their circuit to determine whether they were correct. The decisions of the courts of appeal can be appealed to the U.S. Supreme Court.

U.S. Supreme Court

The U.S. Supreme Court is the top court of the federal court system and is located in Washington, D.C. There are nine Supreme Court justices, including a *chief justice*. Justices are appointed to their positions for life by the U.S. president. The U.S. Supreme Court is the only federal court expressly established by the U.S. Constitution. Appeals from federal appellate courts and from state supreme courts are considered by the U.S. Supreme Court, which chooses the cases it will hear. Only cases of the greatest importance and national consequence are accepted. Thousands of actions are appealed every year, but the Supreme Court accepts only a small percentage of them.

State and Local Court Systems

The state court systems handle the greatest share of legal matters because the U.S. Constitution sets limits on the federal system. The Tenth Amendment to the Constitution grants each state the sovereign power to enact and enforce state laws.

A state's laws are contained in its state constitution and enacted by its own legislature (statutory law). These laws are binding upon the citizens of the state and must not violate the U.S. Constitution. Each state has the power to run its own court system that will decide issues involving state laws. Each state establishes its own set of court procedures, determines court names, divides areas of responsibility among the various courts, and sets limits of authority among the state courts.

Some issues are tried exclusively in state courts, such as divorce, inheritance, probate, and adoption. Issues that can be heard in either state or federal courts are said to be under *concurrent jurisdiction*. In such cases, the law allows you to choose where to file your case, in either a state or federal court.

Like the federal court system, most state court systems have three tiers. However, some states have only two levels of court. In addition, most states have specialized courts that function at the city or county level.

If a case has concurrent jurisdiction, what does that mean?

State Trial Courts In most states, general *trial courts* have original jurisdiction over both criminal and civil matters. These courts are often called state district courts, circuit courts, superior courts, or courts of common pleas. They hear civil cases involving large sums of money, criminal matters with major penalties, and cases that are appealed from local courts whose decisions are questionable. Judges at this level are usually appointed by the state governor, although some may be elected on state or local ballots.

State Courts of Appeal Most states also have an appellate court level, where trials at the state level can be appealed. A panel of judges renders a decision or refuses to hear the cases, whereupon they may be appealed to the next level.

State Supreme Courts In most states, the highest court is the state supreme court, sometimes called the court of final appeal. Ordinarily, the state supreme court has appellate jurisdiction. The decision of a state supreme court is final, except in cases involving the U.S. Constitution, federal laws, and treaties. These decisions can be appealed from the state supreme court to the U.S. Supreme Court.

Specialized State Courts In every state, there are a number of courts with special jurisdiction at the city or county level. These include municipal courts, county courts, justice-of-the-peace courts, juvenile courts, small claims courts, probate courts, and magistrate courts. They hear minor criminal cases in addition to special legal matters such as traffic violation cases, minor civil disputes, and juvenile cases. At the local level, disputes usually are heard and decided by judges, not by juries.

✔ **CHECKPOINT**

What kinds of cases are heard by the U.S. Supreme Court?

Filing a lawsuit involves many steps, costs, and possible outcomes. You need an attorney who can advise you of your chances of winning your case, explain the laws pertaining to your case, and tell you what you need to do to prepare for trial. The services of a competent attorney aren't cheap. Some attorneys charge a flat fee, but only if the case is relatively simple or routine. Most attorneys charge an hourly rate. Under this arrangement, the attorney gets paid an agreed-upon hourly rate for the hours worked on the case. This could include time spent making phone calls, conducting legal research, consulting with others, and drafting legal documents. Rates can range from $100 an hour to $1,000 an hour or more depending on the location, experience of the lawyer, and nature of the case.

In certain types of lawsuits where a large amount of money is involved, such as automobile accidents and medical malpractice, attorneys often work on a *contingency-fee basis*, which means they receive fees only if you win the case. A typical agreement would provide that you pay one-fourth of your settlement if the case is settled before a lawsuit is filed; one-third if the case goes to trial; and one-half if the case is tried and later appealed. If you lose your case, you do not have to pay the attorney's fee, but you will have to pay expenses your attorney incurred, court costs, and any fines or related expenses you incurred, such as medical costs. You may also be required to pay *compensatory damages* (an amount rightfully owed to a person for harm) or *punitive damages* (a sizable amount designed to discourage the guilty party from acting in the same manner in the future).

All states have a *statute of limitations*, which is a legally defined time limit in which a lawsuit may be filed for various complaints. For example, in many states, personal injury lawsuits must be filed within two years from the date of the injury. A lawsuit filed after the two-year limit will be dismissed.

Generally, a lawsuit involves the following four phases—pleadings, discovery, trial, and appeal. However, parties can stop this process by voluntarily settling at any time.

Pleadings

In the *pleadings* phase, documents are filed with the court. The first document to be filed is the **complaint**, which is a document outlining the issues of the case and the relief (damages) that the plaintiff requests. The **plaintiff** is the person who brings a lawsuit by filing the complaint. A copy of the complaint is *served* (presented) to the defendant named in the lawsuit. The **defendant** is the person against whom the lawsuit is filed. The local sheriff's department or a *process server* may be used to serve the defendant. Because the officials must present the papers to the defendant personally, the serving process may take several days. The defendant then has a specified amount of time in which to *appear* (file a response to the complaint). If the defendant does not appear, the plaintiff will win the case by *default judgment*, whereby the plaintiff is awarded the damages requested in the complaint.

The defendant usually discusses the case with an attorney. Then the defendant's attorney prepares and files an answer to the complaint. The *answer* must

Math Minute

Contingency Fees

Roberto is an attorney who works on a contingency-fee basis. Clients must pay one-fourth of their award if the case is settled before a lawsuit is filed, one-third if the case is settled after the lawsuit is filed but before a trial, and one-half if the case is tried and his client wins. Court costs and other expenses are in addition to the attorneys' fees.

You hire Roberto to represent you in a medical malpractice lawsuit. A trial takes place, and the jury awards you $90,000 in total damages. For your case, Roberto has incurred the following expenses:

Lawsuit filing fees	$ 500
Investigation fees	2,500
Expert witness fees	1,500
Deposition costs	3,000
Miscellaneous copies and phone calls	1,000

You also have medical costs that are outstanding of $11,000.

Based on this information, how much will your attorney receive and how much will you receive?

Solution: Attorney receives: $45,000 contingency fees ($90,000 × ½) + $8,500 attorney expenses = $53,500

Client receives: $90,000 − $64,500 ($53,500 + $11,000 medical costs) = $25,500

address each of the plaintiff's allegations by admitting the allegation, denying it, or pleading a lack of sufficient information to admit or deny the allegation. The defendant may choose to file a **counterclaim**, which is an accusation that the plaintiff is at fault and should pay damages to the defendant. If a counterclaim is filed, the plaintiff then has a set time period in which to file a reply. After the *reply* (admission or denial) is filed, the pleadings phase is finished.

Discovery

Discovery is the process of gathering and sharing evidence in a lawsuit. The purposes of discovery are: (1) to preserve evidence, (2) to eliminate surprise, and (3) to lead to settlement.

In the discovery phase, attorneys gather information, talk to witnesses, prepare legal arguments, take depositions, perform investigations, examine reports, and negotiate with the opposing party. Information not disclosed during discovery cannot be used at trial.

A **deposition** is the sworn statement of a witness that is recorded by a court reporter and put into written form for later use in court. A deposition may also be videotaped. Depositions are used to learn more about the facts of a case and about what the different witnesses contend happened.

In the United States, you can sue anybody for any reason. Of course, that doesn't mean that you will win. The court system is bogged down with millions of cases filed each year. Some of these cases are called *frivolous lawsuits*, which means they have no merit. Frivolous lawsuits are often filed for purposes of harassment or for petty reasons, such as a customer being unsatisfied with a product or a person holding a personal grudge against another citizen. If the court finds the lawsuit to be without merit (frivolous), it can award attorneys' fees to the winning party, which means the person filing the frivolous lawsuit must pay not only his or her own costs but also the legal costs of the winning party. Some people feel this practice is unfair and discourages the poor from filing legitimate lawsuits for fear of losing and having to pay exorbitant costs. Others feel that it is a fair practice to protect those being sued unjustly and to discourage frivolous lawsuits.

THINK CRITICALLY

Which side of the argument do you agree with and why? Do you think that people file lawsuits too quickly in this country?

The discovery phase is carefully administered by the court to determine what evidence will and will not be admitted at trial. Lists of possible witnesses (who will testify at the trial) are entered by both sides of a dispute. Accident reconstruction reports, expert witness opinions, medical records, and other documents are shared and analyzed.

After information gathered by both sides is shared, many cases are settled before going to trial because both parties realize the risk and costs involved in a trial. If the opposing parties can reach a settlement, they sign a formal agreement and the case is resolved. When a settlement cannot be reached, the parties then proceed to the next phase.

Trial

The *trial phase* begins with the setting of a court date. The attorneys representing both sides have a pretrial conference with the judge to plan the trial itself. At the pretrial conference, each party provides to the judge a document, called a *brief*, which outlines the arguments and evidence to be used at trial.

The trial can be either a *bench trial*, where the judge decides the matter, or a *jury trial*, where a group of citizens decides it. If there is a jury trial, the first step is *jury selection*. Citizens have a duty to serve on a jury when called by the court. The court identifies a pool of potential jurors from voting records or motor vehicle registration records. Attorneys for both sides select jurors from the pool and may challenge jurors (have them dismissed) if they believe the jurors are biased. The process of jury selection is called *voir dire*. For a civil case, 6 to 12 people are selected for the jury, while 12 people make up the jury for a criminal case.

The *trial* begins with opening statements from both sides. The plaintiff presents evidence and witnesses; the defendant then does the same. Both sides attempt to prove their claims and to *discredit* evidence and witnesses presented by the other side. In the process of *direct examination*, witnesses are asked questions by the attorney who called them to testify. In *cross-examination*, the same witnesses are asked questions by the opposing party's attorney. This process starts over when the plaintiff "rests" his or her case and the defense case is presented. In deciding civil cases, the burden of proof is called a *preponderance*, or superiority, of the evidence. In other words, one side must convince the jury that its side is more believable. This is sometimes called "clear and convincing evidence." In deciding criminal cases, the burden of proof required by prosecutors is called *beyond a reasonable doubt*. The defense attorneys must prove reasonable doubt of the guilt of the accused; they do not have to prove innocence.

Once all evidence has been presented and witnesses questioned, the attorneys make *closing arguments*. After closing arguments, the judge instructs the jury on the law to be applied to the evidence. The jury then *deliberates*, or carefully considers the arguments of both sides, and reaches a decision, called the **verdict**.

How is the burden of proof required in deciding civil cases different from that required for criminal cases?

Based on the verdict, the court enters a **judgment**, which is the final court ruling that resolves the key issues and establishes the rights and obligations of each party. In a criminal case, the judgment is the ruling of the defendant's guilt or innocence and the consequences of guilt. In a civil case, the judgment usually establishes an amount that the losing party must pay.

Appeal

The final phase begins if the losing party files an appeal. An **appeal** is a request to a higher court to review the decision of a lower court. Appeals are based on errors of law made at the trial court level that led to the verdict. For example, a judge may have failed to admit evidence that should have been admitted or may have granted a motion that should have been denied, and so on. Errors made by the judge in jury instructions can also be the basis of appeal.

Appellate courts may refuse to hear the case, which happens with more than 50 percent of all cases appealed. If heard, the appellate court may *affirm* (agree with the lower court's decision), *reverse* (change the lower court's decision), or *remand* (send the case back for a new trial).

A case heard in a state trial court may be appealed to a court of appeals, after which it may be appealed to the state supreme court. Any matters involving national interests may be appealed to the U.S. Supreme Court, which may or may not choose to hear the case.

 **CHECKPOINT**

Who are the parties to a lawsuit, and which one files a complaint?

Law, Public Safety, Corrections & Security

Court Reporting

Court reporters create verbatim transcripts of legal proceedings, depositions, and other legal events. They play an important role in these proceedings, where an exact record of the spoken word is required.

Court reporters use different methods for recording speech. Most use stenotype machines to record dialogue as it is spoken. Stenotype machines work like keyboards but create words through key combinations rather than single characters. This allows court reporters to keep up with fast-moving dialogue.

Some court reporters use computer-assisted transcription (CAT), which is a type of technology that provides automatic transcription of recorded words. Voice writing allows court reporters to speak into a voice silencer, which is a handheld mask that contains a microphone. Court reporters may also use digital recorders to create an audio or video record rather than a written transcript.

Employment Outlook

- An average rate of employment growth is expected.

Job Titles

- Court reporter
- Court stenographer
- Stenotype operator

Needed Skills

- A certificate or an associate's degree in court reporting from a community college or technical institute is required.
- Certification through the National Court Reporters Association is preferred.
- Ability to concentrate for long periods of time, along with excellent keyboarding and listening skills are required.

What's it like to work in . . . *Court Reporting*

After earning an associate's degree in court reporting and receiving her certification, Laura went to work as a court reporter for her county. She currently earns an annual salary of $45,500.

Laura attends depositions and court hearings for the civil and criminal cases in her county. She records testimony using a stenotype machine and is currently being trained to use CAT technology. She is responsible for ensuring a complete and accurate record of the legal proceedings. After each trial, Laura prepares written transcripts, makes copies, and distributes them to the courts and attorneys. Laura also performs retrieval and storage tasks needed to maintain the court's information systems. Judges and attorneys often rely on Laura to help them find information they need contained in official records.

What About You?

Do you have an interest in the legal system? Are you able to listen carefully and process what you have heard? Would you consider a career in court reporting?

KEY TERMS REVIEW

Match the terms with the definitions. Some terms may not be used.

____ 1. The person who brings a lawsuit by filing a complaint

____ 2. A system of laws based on decisions made in court cases

____ 3. The final court ruling that resolves the key issues and establishes the rights and obligations of each party

____ 4. The decision of the jury

____ 5. A type of court case that involves one person who has a dispute with another person or entity

____ 6. The person against whom a lawsuit is filed

____ 7. The sworn statement of a witness that is recorded by a court reporter and put into written form for later use in court

____ 8. The process of gathering evidence in a lawsuit

a. appeal
b. civil case
c. common law
d. complaint
e. counterclaim
f. criminal case
g. defendant
h. deposition
i. discovery
j. judgment
k. plaintiff
l. verdict

CHECK YOUR UNDERSTANDING

LO1-1 9. How is original jurisdiction different from appellate jurisdiction?

LO1-2 10. What happens during the pleadings phase of a court proceeding?

LO1-2 11. What is an appeal? What forms the basis of an appeal?

APPLY YOUR KNOWLEDGE

LO1-1 12. Describe the structure of the court system in your state. Explain how a lawsuit might progress from the state trial level to the U.S. Supreme Court.

THINK CRITICALLY

LO1-1 13. The judge decides issues of law; the jury decides issues of fact. Explain why this separation of duties is an important part of our legal system.

LO1-2 14. Why would a person who has a personal injury claim against another driver want to enter into a contingency-fee agreement with an attorney?

The Essential Question *Refer to The Essential Question on p. 634. A three-tiered court system consists of trial courts, courts of appeal, and the supreme court. A lawsuit begins with a complaint, which is answered by the defendant. Next is the discovery phase. If the parties cannot reach a settlement during the discovery phase, then there is a trial. The trial concludes with a verdict and judgment. After the trial, the losing party may file an appeal.*

The Essential Question *What self-help remedies are available for consumers when trying to resolve a dispute, and what options are available when they don't work?*

LEARNING OBJECTIVES

› **LO 2-1** Define remedies available to consumers other than individual lawsuits.

› **LO 2-2** Explain alternative dispute resolution (ADR) options.

KEY TERMS

- disputing a charge, *645*
- small claims court, *645*
- class action lawsuit, *646*
- alternative dispute resolution (ADR), *647*
- negotiation, *648*
- mediation, *648*
- arbitration, *649*
- unfair labor practice (ULP), *649*

LO 2-1 Self-Help Remedies

Lawsuits are lengthy, expensive, and emotionally draining. Fortunately, for consumers who buy a defective product or who are unhappy with a product or service, there are other redress options they can pursue.

Informal Discussions

Whenever you have a consumer dispute, you should first try to pursue a settlement with the merchant before deciding to sue. Informal discussions that lead to settlement are much less expensive and easier to achieve than legal remedies.

Contact the retailer, seller, or other party with whom you have the dispute. Describe the situation and your proposed remedy. Listen carefully to the other side, and look for ways to settle the argument so that both sides have their interests met. In many cases, you can resolve the issue without taking further action.

If the informal discussion process does not work, you can proceed to more serious steps, such as withholding payment, returning or refusing merchandise, or disputing a charge.

Withholding Payment

As a consumer, you can withhold payment in a purchase dispute. This assumes

Why should you try to resolve a dispute through informal discussions rather than pursue legal remedies?

you have the merchandise but have not yet paid for it. However, you must put your complaint in writing right away and explain the reason why you are withholding payment on the disputed amount. You cannot have *double remedies*; that is, you cannot expect to keep the merchandise and withhold payment.

Returning or Refusing Merchandise

You can refuse delivery or return merchandise to the seller. Even if the seller refuses to accept it back, you can leave it at the store or other business location. In some cases, you can mail it back or have it delivered back to the business. Be sure to get and keep any receipts or other evidence that the goods were returned. This is proof that you have not benefited from having something for which you are refusing to pay.

Disputing a Charge

If you used credit for a purchase, you can dispute the charge with your credit card company within 60 days of receiving your credit card bill. **Disputing a charge** generally means that you are asking the credit issuer to reverse the charge on your account.

To dispute a charge, you must follow procedures outlined by your credit card issuer. After gathering information and any documentation from you, the credit card issuer will notify the merchant of your dispute. If the merchant responds, the credit card issuer will evaluate the information provided by both sides. If the credit card issuer decides in your favor, a credit is issued to your account from the merchant's account. If the matter is not decided in your favor, you must pay the amount in dispute. If the merchant does not respond, the credit card issuer typically will decide in your favor and issue you a credit from the merchant's account.

By law, your credit card company must get the complaint resolved within two billing cycles or 90 days, whichever comes first. During the investigation, it's important to make payments for other items you've charged on your card. Your credit should not be damaged if you follow the proper procedures for disputing credit charges.

Small Claims Court

If the disputed amount is relatively small, you might consider taking the matter to small claims court. A **small claims court** is a court of limited jurisdiction that resolves cases involving small amounts. Attorneys are typically not allowed; hence, small claims court is often considered the "people's court." There is no jury; a judge decides the matter. Most states set a maximum amount of $2,000 to $5,000 in damages that can be recovered in a small claims court. No formal record is made of the small claims court hearing.

Small claims courts are easy to use. You can file a claim by filling out a form at your county courthouse. Costs of filing a claim are small, typically $50 to $150. To file a claim, you must know the name and address of the person or business with whom you have a problem. You must also know the amount in contention and make a short statement of why you are entitled to the money.

Assume that you purchased a new computer from a local retailer, using cash. After a week's use, the battery no longer holds a charge. You want to return it, but unfortunately you didn't keep the receipt from the merchant. Role play this situation with a classmate who acts as the store manager. What will you say to the manager? What are you willing to accept or do in order to achieve a favorable settlement?

Once you file your claim, a copy of the complaint is served on the defendant. The defendant usually has ten days to appear (from the date he or she is served). If the defendant contests (disagrees with) the claim, the court sets a hearing date. At the hearing, you present your side of the case; the defendant does the same. You may bring in written statements and other evidence as well as witnesses. After hearing arguments from both sides, the judge proclaims a judgment. In most states, plaintiffs cannot appeal the decision, but in some states, the defendant is allowed to appeal.

Unfortunately, winning a judgment is only your first step. The court does nothing on its own to force the defendant to pay the judgment. If the defendant does not voluntarily pay you within 30 days of the filing date of the judgment, you may need to take additional steps to collect your money.

Class Action Lawsuits

A **class action lawsuit** is one in which a large number of people with similar complaints against the same defendant join together to sue. If the plaintiffs win, they split the judgment. Class action lawsuits often involve products that injured many consumers, and the defendant is the product's manufacturer and others in the supply chain (retailers, parts producers, distributors, and so on). Sometimes employees join together to sue their employer for discrimination affecting all of them.

A class action is generally initiated by one or more persons who feel that they, along with a group of other people, have been wronged. A lawyer files suit on behalf of the individual(s) and then files a motion asking the court to formally recognize the case as a class action. If the court grants that motion, the other people who were similarly wronged are notified of the class action and are given an opportunity to participate in the lawsuit as a member of the "class."

In some cases, consumers who cannot afford to pursue legal remedies can convince a consumer protection group to file a lawsuit on their behalf. For example, the American Civil Liberties Union (ACLU) files lawsuits to protect the rights of groups of citizens. The ACLU collects money from donations to pay the costs involved in filing lawsuits.

Governmental Assistance

You may wish to seek help from a federal government agency to stop some objectionable practice and help you get your money back. Many sources of consumer assistance from the federal government were discussed in Chapter 25. In addition, most states have attorney general offices with consumer protection services available to consumers. Websites for state attorney generals often have complaint forms that consumers can fill out. The state office will investigate the complaint and take appropriate action. Figure 26.1 lists many forms of state and federal assistance for consumers.

CHECKPOINT

What are three informal ways to resolve disputes?

LO 2-2 Alternative Dispute Resolution

Alternative dispute resolution (ADR) is a general term covering several formal methods of settling disputes without using the court system. Typical ADR processes include negotiation, mediation, and arbitration. These processes are generally more confidential, less formal, less stressful, and less expensive than taking a case to trial.

FIGURE 26.1 **Government Assistance**

Automobiles	National Highway Traffic Safety Administration
Collection, Credit	State Consumer Protection Division (at your state capital)
Drugs/Foods	Food and Drug Administration
Household	Consumer Product Safety Commission
Investment Fraud	Federal Trade Commission Securities and Exchange Commission
Medical/Dental	State Board of Medical Examiners State Department of Commerce State Board of Dental Examiners State Health Division State Board of Pharmacy
Medicare	Social Security Administration
Misrepresentation/Fraud	State Consumer Protection Division Local District Attorney Local or State Better Business Bureau
Transportation	Surface Transportation Board
Warranties	Federal Trade Commission

State-certified professionals can help you with negotiation, mediation, or arbitration. You can find listings of ADR professionals and ADR resources online by using a search engine. Figure 26.2 lists some ADR resources.

Negotiation

Whenever there is a dispute, negotiation is usually the first step in trying to resolve it. **Negotiation** is a process in which a neutral third person, a *negotiator*, assists two parties in reaching a compromise that is acceptable to both sides. Successful negotiation requires tactful give-and-take. It also requires the parties to be calm and reasonable. However, because strong emotions prohibit parties from talking out the problem rationally, a negotiator is often needed. For example, when getting a divorce, the two parties may be unable to reach an agreement about division of property, visitation for children, and other economic issues. The negotiator guides the discussion and helps the parties recognize what is most important and reach a compromise.

Mediation

When the parties cannot negotiate a settlement, the next level of ADR is called mediation. **Mediation** is a non-binding dispute resolution method in which an independent third person, a *mediator*, helps the parties to reach a voluntary settlement. While mediators may be specialists in certain areas, they do not have to be legal authorities. The mediator generally works with

---

FIGURE 26.2   ADR Resources

- **American Arbitration Association**
  Dispute Resolution Services Worldwide
  Information about ADR, articles, procedures, online services
  www.adr.org

- **American Bar Association**
  Information about ADR choices
  From home page, enter "alternative dispute resolution" in search box
  www.abanet.org

- **CPR International Institute for Conflict Prevention & Resolution**
  Center for Public Resources
  ADR procedures, information, training
  www.cpradr.org

- **Divorce Mediation**
  Getting a divorce mediator; mediating online
  www.divorceinfo.com/mediation.htm

- **Lawyer Referral and Information Service**
  How to find the right attorney, referrals, classification areas
  www.martindale.com

both sides separately, allowing them to speak and state their case. If the parties seem able to do so, the mediator may allow them to speak to each other. The mediator listens and helps both sides sort out what is important and what they would be willing to give up to get it. The mediator proposes a solution and, if the parties agree, prepares a settlement document for the parties to sign.

Arbitration

The highest level of ADR is arbitration. **Arbitration** involves an independent third person, an *arbitrator*, who is a legal authority appointed to help resolve a dispute. Unlike negotiation and mediation, arbitra-

How does arbitration differ from negotiation and mediation?

tion uses strict rules of procedure. Arbitrators have subject matter expertise, which means they have a legal or professional background related to the issue involved. They are often retired judges or attorneys. Arbitrators hear testimony and review evidence.

There are two common types of arbitration: voluntary and binding. With *voluntary arbitration*, the arbitrator listens to both sides and makes a recommendation but cannot impose it. Both parties are free to accept or reject it. The proposed solution often carries weight with both parties, because it is a likely outcome if the parties went to court. Thus, voluntary arbitration often leads to settlement. With *binding arbitration*, the arbitrator makes a decision that is binding on the parties. The parties must agree before arbitration begins that they will accept the decision as final. Once rendered, the arbitrator's decision carries the same legal weight as a ruling by a court.

Labor disputes are often settled with arbitration decisions. Many labor contracts specify that in the event the employee feels that the employer has done something illegal (or against the terms of the labor contract), they will submit to binding arbitration. If the employee works for the state or other contracted employer, the employee can file a complaint called an **unfair labor practice (ULP)** that claims violation of a labor contract and requests an arbitration proceeding. An arbitrator (or panel of arbitrators) is appointed to hear the case, and as agreed before the proceeding begins, the decision of the arbitrator is final and binding. Often arbitration clauses in contracts specify who pays for the arbitration. Both parties could share the cost, or the losing party could be required to pay it all. Arbitration costs can run $15,000 or more.

 **CHECKPOINT**

What is the difference between voluntary and binding arbitration?

How Can You Resolve Online Disputes?

When you buy products online, you are taking a risk. If a product is defective, you often can't return it to a physical store and talk to the manager. However, you do have avenues for redress when shopping on the Internet. Online dispute resolution services include the ability to file a complaint and have an independent online service help you get it resolved. There are numerous online dispute resolution services available for e-consumers.

Filing a complaint with the Better Business Bureau (BBB) is the most popular method consumers use for online transaction disputes. At the BBB's website (www.bbb.org), consumers can use its online complaint system to file complaints against businesses. The BBB then acts as a mediator to try to get both sides to come to a fair resolution.

If you buy from a business that displays a seal of approval from a certification or warranty company, such as WebTrust (www.webtrust.org) or TRUSTe (www.truste.org), you can sometimes find assistance in resolving disputes at these websites. These companies will keep track of complaints, alert members of problems, and monitor disputes to ensure they are resolved satisfactorily and within a reasonable period of time.

For complete alternative dispute resolution (ADR) services similar to those in the traditional brick-and-mortar world, you can go to official ADR sites, such as Cybersettle and eQuibbly. These websites offer arbitration for those who wish to use the service.

If you decide to file a complaint, go to the appropriate website and complete forms that explain the issue. The online merchant should respond, and both of you can continue a dialog until all issues are "on the table." This service is often called *hosted message board* negotiation, and it is a free process for consumers. You post your needs and request for action. The business responds and a conversation follows. You should have specific information, proof of purchase, and other documentation to support your claims. Merchants are willing to participate in the process because they want to retain you as a customer while being treated fairly themselves.

You also have avenues for redress through agencies such as the FTC and your state attorney general's consumer protection division. However, this can be a time-consuming process, and you often receive no financial settlement. Thus, it is wise to shop carefully online and buy only from merchants you know and trust. Doing this will lower your risk of getting into a dispute, and if there is a dispute, it will increase your chances of a successful resolution.

THINK CRITICALLY

1. Have you purchased something online that was of poor quality or wasn't what you ordered? How did you resolve the problem?

2. In what ways is online shopping riskier than shopping in a physical store?

3. Why is it important to look for a seal of approval from a certification or warranty company when shopping online?

KEY TERMS REVIEW

Match the terms with the definitions. Some terms may not be used.

____ 1. Formal methods of settling disputes without using the court system

____ 2. Asking the credit issuer to reverse the charge on your account

____ 3. A complaint filed by an employee claiming violation of a labor contract

____ 4. A lawsuit in which a large number of people with similar complaints against the same defendant join together to sue

____ 5. A non-binding dispute resolution method in which an independent third person helps the parties reach a voluntary settlement

____ 6. The process in which an independent third person who is a legal authority is appointed to help resolve a dispute

____ 7. A court of limited jurisdiction that resolves cases involving small amounts

a. alternative dispute resolution (ADR)
b. arbitration
c. class action lawsuit
d. disputing a charge
e. mediation
f. negotiation
g. small claims court
h. unfair labor practice (ULP)

CHECK YOUR UNDERSTANDING

LO2-1 8. What information do you need to file a claim in small claims court?

LO2-2 9. What is the purpose of alternative dispute resolution?

APPLY YOUR KNOWLEDGE

LO2-1 10. If you were involved in a dispute, what steps would you take before involving third persons or the court? Why?

THINK CRITICALLY

LO2-1 11. Why do people join class action lawsuits? Is this a good idea? Why or why not?

LO2-1 12. Under what circumstances would you consider filing a complaint with a government agency as a means of obtaining redress?

LO2-2 13. Under what circumstances would you seek the assistance of a mediator? Explain the types of situations where people are unable to resolve an issue without help.

The Essential Question *Refer to The Essential Question on p. 644. Self-help remedies for consumer disputes include informal discussions, small claims court, class action lawsuits, and government assistance. When they don't work, there is ADR, which includes negotiation, mediation, and arbitration.*

Assessment

SUMMARY

26.1

- *The U.S. legal system is built on several sources of law, including constitutional law and common law. Common law is based on decisions made in court cases that serve as models for future cases.*

- *Trial courts have original jurisdiction, or the authority to hear cases first. Appellate courts review decisions of lower courts.*

- *A civil case involves one person who has a dispute with another person or entity. A criminal case involves a government unit that is accusing an individual of committing a crime.*

- *Participants in court cases commonly include the judge, attorneys, the court clerk, the court reporter, the bailiff, and the jury.*

- *Federal and most state court systems consist of district trial courts, courts of appeal, and a supreme court.*

- *Generally, a lawsuit involves four phases: pleadings, discovery, trial, and appeal.*

- *With jury trials, jurors are selected from a pool of citizens. The judge instructs the jury on relevant laws. The jury reaches a verdict and the court enters a judgment.*

26.2

- *Consumers can resolve most disputes themselves through informal discussions. If discussions fail, the consumer may withhold payment, return or refuse merchandise, or dispute charges with the credit card company.*

- *Many people use small claims court for relatively small disputed amounts. Attorneys are typically not allowed in small claims court. There is no jury; a judge decides the matter.*

- *A large number of people with similar complaints against the same defendant may join together in a class action lawsuit.*

- *ADR involves settling disputes without using the court system. Typical ADR processes include negotiation, mediation, and arbitration.*

- *A negotiator is a neutral third person that helps two parties reach a compromise. A mediator works with parties separately to reach a non-binding voluntary settlement. Mediators may be specialists in certain areas, but they do not have to be legal authorities.*

- *With voluntary arbitration, the arbitrator, who is a legal authority, makes a recommendation that the parties are free to accept or reject. In binding arbitration, the parties must accept the arbitrator's decision.*

APPLY WHAT YOU KNOW

LO1-1 1. A case that involves a dispute in a city is filed with the circuit court of a county in the same state. After a trial court hears the case, where can it be appealed?

LO1-2 2. After a plaintiff files a lawsuit, explain what happens until a court renders a judgment. What happens if the losing party thinks the court made a "legal" error in the case?

LO2-1 3. As a retail customer, you are dissatisfied with a product you purchased. Explain the self-help remedies and actions to consider in resolving the dispute.

LO2-1 4. Why are small claims courts easy to use and, in some cases, more advantageous than a formal court proceeding?

LO2-2 5. Search the Internet for information about mediators or arbitrators in your state. Write a one-page report describing their qualifications, what they do, how they do it, and how consumers can employ their services.

MAKE ACADEMIC CONNECTIONS

LO1-1 6. **Technology** Enter the keywords "Martindale-Hubbell" in an online search engine and report your findings. Key in other legal terms that you'd like to know more about, such as "real estate law" or "Miranda v. Arizona." You will be able to find many sources of legal information about cases, decisions, and legal matters. Explain how the Internet has changed the way people do research on legal topics.

LO1-1 7. **International Studies** Select one European country and another country in the Middle East or other region where the legal system is very different from the system in the United States. Find information about the structure of their legal system and the basis of their laws. Prepare a one-page report on your findings.

LO1-2 8. **Math** Suppose you file a lawsuit and enter into an agreement with your attorney to pay costs and attorneys' fees of 30 percent of the award. If court costs are $300, investigation fees are $500, and you are awarded a judgment of $30,000, how much will your attorney receive? How much will you receive?

LO1-2 9. **Communication** Write a paper about the legal system and tort law (personal injury claims filed by attorneys). Explain what is meant by "tort reform" and how it could affect large lawsuit damages awarded to victims of torts. Explain how this affects everyone. Cite your sources, including at least one online source.

LO2-1 10. **Social Studies** Conduct online research to learn more about a recent class action lawsuit. Prepare a report on your findings. In the report, provide details on what company was involved in the lawsuit, the issues of the lawsuit, the types of injuries suffered, the outcome (was there a settlement or remedy, and if so, what was it), and any other pertinent information.

SOLVE PROBLEMS AND EXPLORE ISSUES

LO1-2 11. Visit your local law library located at the county courthouse, a public university, or at a law school if there is one in your area. List five types of references available. Look up the statute of limitations for filing lawsuits in your state in the following situations: (a) real property infringement, (b) wrongful death or injury, and (c) civil action where you are the injured party in a contract.

LO1-2 12. Examine a civil lawsuit that has been filed in your county. You can look at records of cases that have been filed in your county, although you may not be given copies free of charge. Read through the case and make notes about the plaintiff, the defendant, the issues, the remedy requested by the plaintiff, and the resolution.

LO2-1 13. Work in groups to determine the appropriate legal remedy for each of the following situations:

    a. The plaintiff was driving his vehicle in a northerly direction when the defendant ran a stop sign going in an easterly direction, causing severe damage to the plaintiff's vehicle and injuries to the plaintiff.

    b. A person has paid money to a telemarketer for a product that was promised but never received.

    c. A local restaurant served food that caused people who ate there on a particular night to get sick. No one died, but several people were very sick for several days, causing high medical bills.

EXTEND YOUR LEARNING

LO1-2 14. **Legal Issues** Juries often award punitive damages to send a message that deters others from committing the same violation. Many people feel that punitive damages in cases such as medical malpractice can have a staggering effect on insurance rates for doctors, thus raising costs for everyone. Do you think that juries should award punitive damages? Should a limit be established on the amount that can be awarded? How would limiting punitive damages by statute affect the judicial system?

CHAPTER PROJECT

Select an ongoing civil or criminal case. Make arrangements to observe the case if it is being tried locally and follow media reports on the case. If it is a high-profile national case, listen to commentaries and other sources critiquing the case in addition to following media reports on the case. Write a two-page report on what you observed, the outcome of the case, and your impression of how the system worked to resolve the issue(s).

Complete the Guided Decision Making activity for Chapter 26 at **ngl.cengage.com/mypf**.

Ralph Nader

Ralph Nader has been a U.S. presidential candidate in four elections. He is most famous, however, for his long career in consumer rights, humanitarianism, and environmentalism.

Nader was born in Winsted, Connecticut, in 1934. He graduated from Princeton University in 1955 and Harvard Law School in 1958. He was a professor at the University of Hartford from 1961 to 1963. In 1964 he moved to Washington, D.C., where he worked for Assistant Secretary of Labor Daniel Patrick Moynihan.

During the 1960s, Nader became a crusader of car safety reform. He advised a U.S. Senate subcommittee on car safety, and in 1965 Nader wrote *Unsafe at Any Speed*, a study that asserted that many American cars were unsafe. Nader's advocacy of car safety and the publicity generated by the publication of *Unsafe of Any Speed* contributed to the passage of the National Traffic and Motor Vehicle Safety Act by Congress in 1966.

During the late 1960s and early 1970s, Nader became America's leading consumer advocate. Many young activists, inspired by Nader's work, joined him on projects. They became known as "Nader's Raiders" and published reports on many subjects, including baby food, insecticides, and mercury poisoning.

Since the 1970s, Nader has been a leader in the antinuclear power and environmental movements. He has also campaigned against what he believes are the dangers of large multinational corporations. During this time, he started a variety of nonprofit organizations such as Public Citizen, the Citizen Advocacy Center, the Disability Rights Center, and the Equal Justice Foundation. In 1999 Nader was recognized for his accomplishments by being named as one of *Time* magazine's 100 most influential Americans of the 20th century.

For over four decades, Ralph Nader has worked to improve the quality of life for Americans. Because of Nader's efforts, we now drive safer cars, breathe better air, drink cleaner water, and work in safer environments.

THINK CRITICALLY

1. How has Ralph Nader made a difference in the lives of consumers today?

2. How did Ralph Nader get into the political arena? How has he used his law background to further his interests?

3. What can you learn from someone like Ralph Nader who has dedicated his life to consumer issues?

Philanthropy and Ethics

Overview

Philanthropy is the act of donating money, goods, time, or effort to support a societal cause, often over an extended period of time. Philanthropists want to leave the world a better place than they found it. Although many philanthropists are wealthy, many people not possessing great wealth also perform philanthropic acts. Everyone has the opportunity to give something back.

Ethics is the study of right versus wrong, good versus bad, just versus unjust. Legal and ethical responsibilities are not the same thing. We can decide to do the moral minimum (do no harm), or we can resolve to do better. At the very least, we should realize that learning leads to knowledge, knowledge leads to wisdom, and wisdom leads to understanding. Only when we realize the need for ethics can we begin the process of learning what will lead us to the desire to do the right thing.

Philanthropy

One reason why philanthropy is important is that it is the primary source of funding for the fine arts; the performing arts; religious, medical, and humanitarian causes; and private (and some public) schools and universities. Many valuable institutions of culture would not continue to exist without the generosity of private philanthropists.

© mangostock/Shutterstock.com

In addition to wealthy individuals, companies, and foundations that have donated vast sums of cash and assets, many nonwealthy people donate substantial portions of their time, effort, and wealth to charitable causes. When you give your time, you are giving the most valuable thing you have. You are sharing more than monetary wealth; you are giving of yourself and sharing that which is most precious of all.

Philanthropy is said to be important because it "feeds the soul of the nation." We are all able to enjoy the richness of culture that results when events are sponsored by those who can afford to pay so that those who cannot afford to pay can experience them as well.

Forms of Philanthropy

Every year, wealthy people give massive amounts of money to various causes. The largest individual bequest was a $31 billion gift from Warren Buffett to the Bill and Melinda Gates Foundation in 2006. Other notable examples include:

- $1 billion from Ted Turner to the United Nations
- $424 million from *Reader's Digest* to the Metropolitan Museum of Art
- $220 million from Nike co-founders Phil and Penny Knight to Oregon Health and Science University
- $200 million from Joan B. Kroc (wife of McDonald's CEO Ray Kroc) to National Public Radio
- $100 million from Facebook co-founder Mark Zuckerberg to Newark Public Schools, the public school system of Newark, New Jersey

While these massive dollar donations grab media attention, there are many other forms of philanthropy that go almost unnoticed in comparison, such as those described below.

- A recent and growing trend in philanthropy is the concept of giving circles. With *giving circles*, a group of individuals who are or who become friends pool their charitable donations and decide together how to use the money to benefit the causes that they care about.
- *Volunteerism* is a very important form of philanthropy. Young people who provide service during their youth reap considerable benefits, not only for those they serve but also in their own character development. When people learn to give early in life, it changes their perspective.
- Many *charitable organizations* exist to support worthy causes. Some of their supporters are wealthy individuals, but most charitable organizations receive the bulk of their funding from many private individuals who give less than $100 each.

Thus, we realize that anyone can be a philanthropist, and anyone can participate in funding societal causes, programs, and needs.

So Many Worthwhile Causes

There are countless charities that you can support. But how do you know which charities are the right ones to receive your money, time, assets, or talents?

After you select the charities that promote the causes you care about, you should do some homework. It is important to check out charities before you donate to make sure those organizations are legitimate, are fiscally sound, use their resources wisely, and are effective. By doing research beforehand, you can be assured that the charity of your choice is what it says it is and is doing what it says it is doing.

There are numerous organizations that evaluate charities. The American Institute of Philanthropy (AIP) publishes a *Charity Rating Guide & Watchdog Report* that provides information and ratings for over 600 charitable organizations. The AIP posts its top-rated charities on its website along with articles and tips to help donors make wise decisions and avoid charity scams. To assess your strengths and weaknesses and make a decision about the type of philanthropist you can be, complete Worksheet 1 (My Philanthropy Plan) provided for you in the *Student Activity Guide* and also presented for reference on the next page.

Ethics and Values

Ethics is the concept of doing the right thing. Being ethical is not the same as following the law. The law does not require us to "do good," but merely to "do no harm." Being ethical is also not the same as doing "whatever society accepts" or following your feelings. Being ethical involves making choices that are based on values. It is a measure of the depth of our character and reveals who we really are.

People base ethical decisions on their personal values and principles, which they develop through individual life experiences. Therefore, since everyone has different experiences, decisions about what is and what is not ethical may vary between individuals. Before making a decision, ask yourself the following three questions:

1. Is this something I will feel good about later?
2. Is this how I would like to be treated by someone else?
3. Would I be proud if my family and friends were to know about it?

Some people apply the legality test to ethics. Consider the following illustration. At the left, taking action is both legal and ethical. Somewhere along the continuum, the choice to take action may remain legal, but since it involves stretching the law or applying it in a way that is not universally accepted, it starts becoming unethical. Thus ethics ends before legality.

Take Action (Yes)	Take Action (Maybe or No)	Take Action (No)
Legal	Technically legal	ILLEGAL
Ethical	UNETHICAL	UNETHICAL

To further explore the issue of ethics, analyze the case studies involving ethics in the marketplace, in the workplace, and on the Internet presented in Worksheets 2, 3, 4, 5, and 6, which are provided for you in the *Student Activity Guide* and also presented for reference on pp. 660–664. In analyzing each case, you must (1) identify the problem, (2) apply relevant knowledge to the solution of the problem, and (3) draw a conclusion or reach a decision based on careful analysis of the problem.

WORKSHEET 1
My Philanthropy Plan

Answer the following questions about yourself and what you can do to help others who are less fortunate than you are. Then make a commitment to give during your lifetime, so that you can help make the world a better place.

1. If you had money to spare, far beyond your wants and needs, how would you choose to spend it? Be specific.

2. What is your favorite charitable organization or cause? Why?

3. What do you consider to be your greatest gift (talent)? How could you use that gift to help others?

4. If you had enough time to spare and didn't need to work for a living, what would you do?

5. Looking back at your life, 100 years after your death, for what would you like to be remembered?

6. List organizations you would like to help and the ways you can help.

WORKSHEET 2
Cutting It Close

Valerie wanted to earn extra money over the summer, so she decided to start a lawn-mowing business in her neighborhood. To advertise her business, she composed a flyer to put in her neighbors' mailboxes. On the flyer, she listed her services: mowing, trimming, and blowing grass clippings off the driveway and sidewalk when she finished. She offered all of these services for one low price.

Several neighbors wanted her service. In fact, more people asked than she had time to serve. Not wanting to pass up the opportunity to earn so much money, Valerie agreed to do the lawns of all who asked. She figured she would find some way to mow them all. Since she was dealing with neighbors, she did not offer any written contracts. They just agreed verbally.

For three weeks, Valerie worked very hard but still could not finish all the lawns she had agreed to mow. She realized, though, that if she didn't trim the lawns, she could mow one additional lawn each weekend, so that's what she decided to do. Valerie reasoned that her mower could cut grass very close to trees and walls, so the trimming didn't really seem necessary. She was giving her customers a very low price, so it was a good deal even without the trimming. Besides, she could now satisfy more customers who otherwise would have to mow their own lawns or take the time to find someone else to do them.

1. Since Valerie and her neighbors did not sign a written contract, is Valerie obligated to perform the services she listed on her flyer? Why or why not?

2. Valerie is 16, so she is a minor. How does this fact affect her legal and ethical obligations to her neighbors?

3. Do you agree with Valerie's reasons for not trimming? Why or why not?

4. Are the benefits she is offering her neighbors worth giving up the trimming service?

5. If you were in Valerie's situation, what would you do? Why?

WORKSHEET 3
I'm Anonymous

Hiroto has met many people online, and he uses several screen names. He visits chat rooms and reads personal ads frequently and sometimes responds to them. He never provides correct information because he doesn't want anyone finding out who he really is. On several occasions, Hiroto made arrangements to meet someone, but often he did not show up as agreed.

As a joke, Hiroto sometimes sends insulting or vaguely threatening e-mail messages to coworkers he doesn't like. He enjoys hearing them talk about the messages at work. Because Hiroto doesn't mean them any real harm, he believes the messages don't hurt anybody. And because he's anonymous, he doesn't think he's taking any risks.

1. Do you think Hiroto is acting appropriately on the Internet? Why or why not?

2. Have you ever acted in similar ways toward people on the Internet? Explain.

3. How would you feel if you received an insulting or threatening e-mail from an anonymous sender?

4. What suggestions would you make to Hiroto about behaving appropriately and staying safe on the Internet?

5. Are there any laws that protect users from actions such as Hiroto's? If so, what are they?

WORKSHEET 4
Something for Nothing

Mahir and Kayla work together at a fast-food restaurant. They are both good workers and have been employed for over a year. Each Christmas, the company they work for has a big party for all employees. Gifts are given away to employees who provide outstanding service during the year.

Mahir and Kayla's manager has worked for the company for over ten years. She discovered a way to falsify information in the computer to her advantage. She gets more than her fair share of gifts while others in the company do not get as much. Mahir and Kayla accidentally discovered this scam. The manager encouraged Mahir and Kayla to participate in the scheme. "You two can get more gifts if you participate. If you try to turn me in, I'll have both of you fired," she said.

1. What is the ethical problem involved in this situation?

2. What are Mahir and Kayla's options?

3. What would you do if you were in this situation? Why?

4. How is this case an example of employee theft in the workplace?

5. Are there employment laws that would protect Mahir and Kayla? If so, what are they?

WORKSHEET 5
It's a Good Deal

When Reynaldo flew to see his relatives last year, he was able to earn enough air miles for a free ticket. The frequent flyer club rules are clear: The ticket is nontransferable.

Reynaldo bought a ticket for a flight across the country but later discovered he couldn't go. A friend of his was planning a similar trip, so Reynaldo offered him the ticket for $100—much cheaper than the cost of a full fare.

When Reynaldo's friend tried to use the ticket, the agent discovered that the ticket belonged to someone else. The airline refused to allow him on the plane without paying the full price for a new ticket. When he told Reynaldo about the problem, Reynaldo said it wasn't his concern.

1. Discuss the issues involved in Reynaldo's dilemma.

2. What's wrong with the owner of a ticket giving or selling it to someone else?

3. Would you participate in this type of a deal? Why or why not?

4. If offered a similar deal, what should you do before accepting it?

WORKSHEET 6
Nobody Got Hurt

Lori bought a new dress to wear for a special occasion. During the course of the evening, she spilled some juice on the dress and was unable to remove all of the stain. The stain was small and not really visible at first glance.

The next day, Lori decided that she would probably never wear the dress again. The dress didn't fit as well as she would have liked, so she decided to get her money back. That afternoon she returned the dress to the store. She claimed the dress was a gift that she didn't like. The store gave her credit for the dress, and Lori bought something else. When asked how she could do something like that, Lori replied, "Why not? Nobody got hurt."

1. Was there anything wrong with what Lori did? Did anybody get hurt? Who?

2. Why do some stores have lenient return policies? Why do some stores have "no return" policies? What store policies would you recommend to avoid this kind of activity?

3. What would you do if you worked in the store and knew what Lori had done?

4. Discuss the ethical principles involved in this case.

20/10 Rule A plan to limit the use of credit to no more than 20 percent of your yearly take-home pay, with payments of no more than 10 percent of monthly take-home pay.

401(k) Plan A defined-contribution plan for employees of companies that operate for a profit.

403(b) Plan A defined-contribution plan for employees of schools, nonprofit organizations, and government units.

Acceleration of Benefits A rider that allows people who have been diagnosed with a serious medical condition that will likely lead to their death in 12 or 24 months (or other specified time period) to collect a portion of their life insurance benefits before death.

Acceptance When a person accepts the terms of an offer.

Adjusted Gross Income Gross income less adjustments.

Adult Foster Care Personal care and services provided for adults in a facility outside of the home when adequate care can no longer be provided.

Agency Bond A bond issued by government agencies and by government-sponsored enterprises.

Alternative Dispute Resolution (ADR) A general term covering several formal methods of settling disputes without using the court system.

Annual Percentage Rate (APR) The cost of credit expressed as a yearly percentage.

Annual Percentage Yield (APY) The actual interest rate an account pays, stated on a yearly basis with the compound interest included.

Annual Report A summary of a corporation's financial results for the year and its prospects for the future.

Annuity A contract in which you make a lump-sum payment or series of payments that earn interest in return for regular disbursements, often after retirement.

Appeal A request to a higher court to review the decision of a lower court.

Appraised Value Home value determined by examining the structure, size, features, and quality as compared to similar homes in the same geographic area.

Appreciation An increase in value.

Arbitration A dispute resolution method that involves an independent third person, an arbitrator, who is a legal authority to help resolve the dispute.

Assessed Value Home value set annually by the city or county in which you live for purposes of computing property taxes owed against your home.

Assets Items of value that a person owns.

Assigned Risk Pool People who are unable to obtain auto insurance due to the high risk they present.

ATM Fee An amount typically charged by an ATM that does not belong to your own bank.

Attractive Nuisance A dangerous place, condition, or object that is particularly attractive to children.

Auction Market A type of securities exchange where buyers enter competitive bids and sellers enter competitive offers at the same time.

Audit An examination of income tax returns by the IRS.

Automatic Deductions Money you have authorized your bank or other organization to move from one account to another at regular intervals.

Bait and Switch An illegal sales technique in which a seller advertises a product with the intention of persuading consumers to buy a more expensive product.

Balanced Fund A mutual fund that seeks both growth and income but attempts to minimize risk by investing in a mixture of stocks and bonds rather than stocks alone.

Bank Reconciliation The process of matching your checkbook register with the bank statement.

Bankruptcy A legal process that relieves debtors of the responsibility of paying their debts or protects them while they try to repay.

Bargaining The process of negotiating an employment contract for union members.

Basic Health Coverage Health insurance coverage that includes medical, hospital, and surgical costs.

Basic Needs The items necessary for maintaining physical life.

BBB A nonprofit organization focused on creating a more trusting relationship between businesses and customers.

Bear Market A prolonged period of falling stock prices and a general feeling of investor pessimism.

Benefits Forms of employer compensation in addition to pay.

Billing Statement An itemized bill showing charges, credits, and payments posted to your account during the billing period.

Blue-Chip Stocks Stocks of large, well-established corporations with a solid record of profitability.

Bond A debt obligation of a corporation or a state or local government.

Bond Default Occurs when a bond issuer cannot meet the interest and/or principal payments.

Bond Fund A group of bonds that have been bundled together and sold in shares to investors.

Bond Listings Extensive tables that contain information about recent trades of bonds.

Bond Rating Tells the investor the risk category that has been assigned to a bond.

Bond Redemption Occurs when a bond is paid off at maturity.

Bonus Incentive pay based on quality of work done, years of service, or a company's sales and profits.

Budget A spending and saving plan based on your expected income and expenses.

Bull Market A prolonged period of rising stock prices and a general feeling of investor optimism.

Bundling Combining services into one package.

Business Plan A formal document that outlines the path a business intends to take to earn and grow revenues.

Callable Bond A bond that the issuer has the right to pay off before its maturity date.

Canceled Check A check that has cleared your account.

Capacity 1. The competence (legal ability) of parties to enter into a contract. 2. The financial ability to repay a loan with present income.

Capital The value of property you possess after deducting your debts.

Capitalism A type of hands-off economic system in which producers and consumers are free to operate and compete in business transactions with minimal, if any, government interference or regulation.

Car Detail A service provided by specialists who clean and polish the exterior, along with cleaning and treating the interior of a car.

Car Registration A license tag fee that must be renewed annually.

Car Title A legal document that establishes ownership of the vehicle.

Car-Buying Service A service that allows you to choose the vehicle features you want and have a professional car buyer handle the price negotiation for you.

Care Labels Labels that give instructions for cleaning, wash and dry temperatures, and other care needed to preserve the product.

Cash Deficit When estimated expenses are greater than estimated income.

Cash Surplus When estimated income is greater than estimated expenses.

Cash Value The savings accumulated in a permanent life insurance policy that you would receive if you canceled your policy.

Cashier's Check A check written by a bank on its own funds.

CC&Rs Rules designed to maintain property values and protect the interests of all property owners.

Certificate of Deposit (CD) A time deposit that earns a fixed rate of interest for a specified length of time.

Certificate of Participation An investment in a pool of mortgages that have been purchased by a government agency or government-sponsored enterprise.

Certified Check A personal check that the bank guarantees or certifies to be good.

Chapter 7 A liquidation form of bankruptcy for individuals that wipes out most debts in exchange for giving up most assets.

Chapter 11 A reorganization form of bankruptcy for businesses that allows them to continue operating under court supervision as they repay their restructured debts.

Chapter 13 A reorganization form of bankruptcy for individuals that allows debtors to keep most of their property and use their income to pay a portion of their debts over three to five years.

Character A responsible attitude toward honoring obligations, often judged on evidence in the person's credit history.

Check Float Writing a check before a deposit has cleared the account.

Checkbook Register A booklet used to record checking account transactions.

Child Support Monthly payments to the custodial parent to help provide food, clothing, and shelter for the children.

Childproof Resistant to tampering by young children.

Civil Case A type of court case that involves one person who has a dispute with another person or entity.

Civil Ceremony A wedding performed by a public official, such as a judge or justice of the peace, rather than a member of the clergy.

Class Action Lawsuit A lawsuit in which a large number of people with similar complaints against the same defendant join together to sue.

Classic Cars Rare cars and older vehicles that are kept in excellent condition that may experience appreciation if valued as collectors' items.

Clearance When a merchant wants to clear out all of the advertised merchandise, but not necessarily at a reduced price.

Closed-End Credit A loan for a specific amount that must be repaid in full, including all finance charges, by a stated due date.

Closing Costs The expenses incurred in transferring ownership from buyer to seller in a real estate transaction.

Co-insurance Clause A provision requiring policyholders to insure their building for a stated percentage of its replacement value in order to receive full reimbursement for a loss.

Co-op A room similar to one in a dormitory at lower cost but with added responsibilities.

COBRA A federal law enacted in 1986 that allows people who leave their job to continue their health insurance under the company plan for a limited period of time.

Codicil A legal document that modifies parts of a will and reaffirms the rest.

Collateral Property pledged to assure repayment of a loan.

Collectible Any physical asset that appreciates in value over time because it is rare or desired by many.

Collective Values Ideals and values that are important to society as a whole.

Collision Coverage Auto insurance that protects your own car against damage from accidents or vehicle overturning.

Commercial Property Land and buildings that produce income through leasing or renting.

Commodities Products that are mined or grown.

Common Law A system of laws based on decisions made in court cases.

Common Stock A type of stock that pays a variable dividend and gives the holder voting rights.

Communist Economic System A type of hands-on economic system in which the government owns and controls most, if not all, of the productive resources of a nation.

Company Advertising Advertising intended to promote the image of a store, company, or retail chain.

Comparison Shopping Checking several places to be sure you are getting the best price for equal quality.

Competition The rivalry among sellers in the same market to win customers.

Complaint A document outlining the issues of the case and the relief (damages) that the plaintiff requests.

Compound Interest Interest paid on the original principal plus accumulated interest.

Comprehensive Coverage Auto insurance that protects you from damage to your car from causes other than collision or vehicle overturning.

Compressed Workweek A work schedule that fits the normal 40-hour workweek into less than five days.

Compression Test A test that detects engine trouble in a car.

Condominium An individually owned unit in an apartment-style complex with shared ownership of common areas.

Consideration Something of value exchanged for something else of value.

Consumer Advocate A person who actively promotes consumer causes.

Consumers Union A nonprofit organization best known as the publisher of *Consumer Reports*, a monthly magazine that publishes reviews, comparisons, and ratings of consumer products and services.

Contingencies Conditions that limit a buyer's liability in case one or more of them are not met.

Contract A legally enforceable agreement between two or more people.

Convertible Bond A corporate bond that can be converted to shares of common stock.

Coordination of Benefits A group health insurance provision that specifies how the insurers will share the cost when more than one policy covers a claim.

Cosigner A person who promises to pay the debt of another person.

Counterclaim An accusation that the plaintiff is at fault and should pay damages to the defendant.

Counteroffer A new offer that changes the original offer.

CPSC An agency that protects consumers from unreasonable risk of injury or death from potentially hazardous consumer products.

Credit The use of someone else's money, borrowed now with the agreement to pay it back later.

Credit Bureau A business that gathers, stores, and sells credit information to other businesses.

Credit Counseling A service to help consumers manage their debt load and credit more wisely.

Credit Freeze A consumer request that requires the credit bureaus to deny all access to a consumer's credit information or files.

Credit History The complete record of your borrowing and repayment performance.

Credit Inquiry A request by a business with a "permissible purpose" to check your credit.

Credit Management Following an individual plan for using credit wisely.

Credit Payment Plan A record of your debts and a strategy for paying them off.

Credit Rating A measure of creditworthiness often identified by a letter grade (A, B, C, D).

Credit Repair The process of reestablishing a good credit rating.

Credit Report A written statement of a consumer's credit history.

Credit Score The total of assigned points based on several factors that tells potential creditors the likelihood that you will repay debt as agreed.

Creditor A person or business that loans money to others.

Creditworthy A determination that you are a good credit risk.

Cremation A process of reducing a body to ashes in a high-temperature oven.

Criminal Case A type of court case that involves a government unit that is accusing an individual of committing a crime.

Custodial Parent The parent with whom the children will live after a divorce.

Custom A long-established practice that takes on the force of an unwritten law.

Data Facts, numbers, or text that can be processed on a computer.

Data Mining The process of gathering and analyzing data from a variety of sources and summarizing it into useful information.

Data Warehousing The management of data storage and retrieval.

Dealer Add-Ons High-priced, high-profit dealer services that add little or no value to an automobile.

Debenture A corporate bond that is based on the general creditworthiness and reputation of the company.

Debit Card A bank card that deducts money from a checking account almost immediately to pay for purchases.

Debt Collector A person or company hired by a creditor to collect the overdue balance on an account.

Debt Consolidation A type of debt relief service in which a finance company loans you money to pay off your debt.

Debt Management Plan A type of debt relief service in which

you make a single monthly payment to a credit counseling organization that distributes the funds to creditors based on a payment schedule.

Debt Settlement Program A type of debt relief service in which a company negotiates with your creditors on your behalf to reduce the amount of debt you owe.

Debtor A person who borrows money from others.

Deception Occurs when false or misleading claims are made about the quality, the price, or the purpose of a particular product.

Deductible The specified amount of a loss that the insured must pay.

Deed The legal document that transfers title of real property from one party to another.

Defendant The person against whom the lawsuit is filed.

Deferred Billing A service available to charge customers whereby purchases are not billed to the customer until much later than the standard billing time.

Defined-Benefit Plan A company-sponsored retirement plan in which employees receive a set monthly amount for life beginning at retirement based on wages earned and number of years of service.

Defined-Contribution Plan A company-sponsored retirement plan in which employees receive a periodic or lump-sum payment based on their account balance and the performance of the investments in their account.

Demand Deposit A type of bank account from which money may be withdrawn at any time.

Deposition The sworn statement of a witness that is recorded by a court reporter and put into written form for later use in court.

Depreciation A decline in the value of property due to normal wear and tear.

Direct Deposit Your net pay is deposited electronically into your bank account.

Direct Investment Buying stock directly from a corporation.

Disability Insurance An insurance plan that makes regular payments to replace income lost when illness or injury prevents the insured from working.

Discharged Debts Previous debts erased by the court during bankruptcy proceedings.

Discovery The process of gathering and sharing evidence in a lawsuit.

Discrimination The act of treating people differently based on prejudice rather than individual merit.

Disposable Income The money you have left to spend or save after taxes and other deductions (required and optional) are taken.

Disputing a Charge Asking the credit issuer to reverse the charge on your account.

Dissolution of Marriage A legal process in which a judge dissolves the bonds of matrimony between two people.

Diversification The spreading of risk among many types of investments.

Dividend Reinvestment The use of dividends previously earned on the stock to buy more shares.

Dividends Money paid to stockholders from the corporation's earnings.

Divorce Decree A final statement of the dissolution decisions.

Dollar-Cost Averaging An investment technique that involves the systematic purchase of an equal dollar amount of the same stock at regular intervals, regardless of the share price.

Dormitory An on-campus building that contains many small rooms that are rented to students.

Double Indemnity A rider that allows the beneficiary to be paid double the face amount of the insurance policy in the event of accidental death.

Down Payment Part of the purchase price paid in cash up front.

Downsizing An economic event whereby jobs are eliminated because company revenues are falling while costs are rising.

Driving Record Includes the number and type of traffic tickets you've received for driving infractions and misdemeanors along with the number of accidents in which you've been involved.

Duplex A building with two separate living units that share a common central wall.

Early Withdrawal Penalty An amount you must pay if you take out any part of your money in a certificate of deposit before the maturity date.

Earnest-Money Offer An offer to buy property accompanied by a deposit.

Earnings Per Share (EPS) A corporation's after-tax earnings (net profit) divided by the number of common stock shares outstanding (shares in the hands of investors).

Economic Risk A risk that may result in gain or loss because of changing economic conditions.

Economy All activities related to the production and distribution of goods and services in a geographic area.

Electronic Funds Transfer (EFT) A computer-based system that enables you to move money from one account to another without writing a check or exchanging cash.

Employee Assistance Plan (EAP) A group benefit that allows employees and their families to seek counseling and other services.

Encryption A code that protects your account name, number, and other information by making it unreadable to others.

Endorsement A written amendment to an insurance policy that reflects changes to it.

Engaged Formally pledged to each other.

Equity The difference between the market value of property and the amount owed on it.

Escrow Account A fund where money is held by your financial institution to pay amounts that will come due during the year.

Escrow Closer An independent person who gathers and verifies information, prepares the closing statement, and makes sure that title passes to the buyer of property.

Estate All that a person owns, less debts owed, at the time of the person's death.

Estate Tax A tax on property transferred from an estate to its heirs.

Estimated Tax The amount of tax you estimate you will owe on income received without withholdings.

Eviction The legal process of removing a tenant from rental property.

Exempt Status Available only to those who know they will not earn enough in one year to owe income tax.

Exempted Property Assets considered necessary for survival that a bankrupt debtor is allowed to keep.

Exemption An amount you may subtract from your income for each person who depends on your income to live.

Experience The knowledge and skills acquired from working in a career field.

FAA An agency that oversees the U.S. commercial aviation industry for the Department of Transportation.

Face Value The amount the bondholder will be repaid at maturity.

Fake Sale A consumer fraud that occurs when a merchant advertises a big sale but keeps the items at regular price or alters the price tags to make them look like a price reduction when there actually is none.

Family Budget A plan that allocates spending, saving, borrowing, and investing of the family's pooled resources to meet future goals.

FCC An agency that regulates interstate and international communications by radio, television, wire, satellite, and cable.

FDA An agency that enforces laws and regulations preventing distribution of mislabeled foods, drugs, cosmetics, and medical devices.

Fiat Money Money that is not backed by gold, but by faith in the general economy and government of the country.

Filing Status Your tax-filing group based on your marital status as of the last day of the tax year.

Finance Charge The total dollar amount of all interest and fees you pay for the use of credit.

Finance Company An organization that makes high-risk consumer loans.

Financial Aid Money in the forms of student loans, grants, or work-study programs that a student may receive to help pay for their education.

Financial Plan A set of goals for spending, saving, and investing the money you receive.

Fixed Expenses Costs that do not change from month to month.

Fixed-Rate Loan A loan for which the interest rate does not change over the life of the loan.

Flammability The capacity for catching on fire.

Flex 125 Plan An employee benefit program that allows employees to set aside money, pretax, to help pay deductibles, copayments, and other health expenses during the year that are not covered by insurance.

Flextime A type of work schedule that allows employees to choose their working hours within a defined time limit.

Follow-up Contact with the employer after the interview but before hiring occurs.

Formal Wedding A wedding that may be held in the afternoon or in the evening, usually at a church or hotel, and participants as well as guests wear formal attire.

FTC An agency that regulates unfair methods of competition, false or deceptive advertising, deceptive product labeling, and the concealment of the true costs of credit.

Full Coverage Liability coverage, collision coverage, comprehensive coverage, personal injury protection (PIP), and uninsured/underinsured motorist coverage purchased together in a single auto insurance policy.

Furnished Rental A rental unit in which the basics—bed, dresser, sofa, chairs, lamps, dining table

and chairs, and essential appliances—are provided.

Futures A contract that obligates the buyer to purchase (or the seller to sell) stock or a commodity for a specified price on a specified date in the future.

Garnishment A legal process that allows part of your paycheck to be withheld for payment of a debt.

Gems Natural, precious stones, such as diamonds, rubies, sapphires, and emeralds.

General Obligation (GO) Bond A municipal bond backed by the power of the issuing state or local government to levy taxes to pay back the debt.

Generic Drugs Medications with the same composition as the equivalent brand-name drugs, but they are generally less expensive.

Gift Tax A tax applied to a gift of money or property.

Global Fund A mutual fund that purchases international stocks and bonds as well as U.S. securities.

Goal A desired end toward which efforts are directed.

Grace Period A timeframe within which you may pay your current balance in full and incur no finance charges.

Grant A form of educational funding that is awarded based on financial need and that does not have to be repaid.

Gross Income All of the taxable income you receive during the year.

Gross Pay The total amount an employee earns before deductions are subtracted.

Group Insurance A type of health insurance in which all those insured have the same coverage and pay a set premium.

Growth and Income Fund A mutual fund whose investment goal is to earn returns from both dividends and capital gains.

Growth Fund A mutual fund whose investment goal is to buy stocks that will increase in value over time.

Growth Stocks Stocks in corporations that reinvest their profits into the business so that it can grow.

Guest Someone you specifically ask to come to your house.

Health Insurance A plan for sharing the risk of high medical costs resulting from injury or illness.

Health Insurance Exchange A marketplace that provides a set of government-regulated and standardized health care plans from which uninsured and underinsured individuals may purchase health insurance policies.

Health Savings Account (HSA) An account used in association with a medical plan that carries a higher annual deductible than typical health plans.

Hedge Any investment or action that helps offset against loss from another investment or action.

Homeowners Insurance Insurance that protects property owners from property and liability risks.

Hospice A nonprofit program consisting of medical and support services provided by a team of professionals and volunteers for those who are dying and for their families.

Hybrid A type of vehicle that uses alternate energy sources, such as natural gas or battery power, in addition to gasoline.

Impulse Buying Buying something without thinking about it and making a conscious decision.

Incentive Pay A form of compensation that encourages employees to strive for higher levels of performance.

Income Fund A mutual fund whose investment goal is to produce current income in the form of interest or dividends.

Income Stocks Stocks in corporations that have a consistent history of paying high dividends to stockholders.

Incontestable Clause A provision of a life insurance policy stating that once the policy has been in effect for a stated period of time, the insurer may no longer question items in the application in order to deny coverage.

Indemnification The process of putting the policyholder back in the same financial condition he or she was in before a loss occurred.

Index Fund A mutual fund that tries to match the performance of a particular index by investing in the companies included in that index.

Individual Retirement Account (IRA) A retirement savings plan that offers tax advantages and allows individuals to set aside a specified amount each year.

Industry Advertising Advertising intended to promote a general product group without regard to where these products are purchased.

Inflation A rise in the general level of prices.

Infomercial A lengthy paid TV advertisement that includes testimonials and product demonstrations.

Informal Wedding A wedding that is usually held during the afternoon and may take place almost anywhere, such as outside or in a home, and no special attire is required for the wedding party or guests.

Information The arrangement of data into useful patterns or relationships.

Inheritance Tax A tax imposed on an heir who inherits property from an estate.

Initial Investing Your first amount set aside for investment purposes only.

Innovations New ideas, products, or services that bring about changes in the way we live.

Inspection Report A written report that details the existing conditions of the house and property.

Insurable Interest Any financial interest in life or property such that, if the life or property were lost or harmed, the insured would suffer financially.

Insurable Risk A pure risk that is faced by a large number of people and for which the amount of the loss can be predicted.

Insurance A method for spreading individual risk among a large group of people to make losses more affordable for all.

Interest Earnings on principal.

Intermediate Goal A goal you wish to accomplish in the next few months or years.

Investing The use of long-term savings to earn a financial return.

Investing Risk The chance that an investment's value will decrease.

Investment-Grade Bond A bond that is considered a high-quality, low-risk bond.

Invoice Price The price the dealer paid for a car.

Involuntary Bankruptcy Bankruptcy that occurs when creditors file a petition with the court asking the court to declare the debtor bankrupt.

Itemized Deductions Expenses you can subtract from adjusted gross income to determine your taxable income.

Itinerary A detailed schedule of events, times, and places.

Job Application A form that asks questions to be sure you are qualified for a job opening.

Job Creation Occurs when the economy is growing (consumer demand is increasing) and new workers are being hired.

Job Interview A face-to-face meeting with a potential employer to discuss a job opening.

Job Rotation A job design in which employees are trained to do more than one specialized task.

Job Sharing A job design in which two people share one full-time position.

Joint Account A checking account opened by two or more people.

Judgment 1. A court order that will allow creditors to collect the debts you have agreed to pay. 2. The final court ruling that resolves the key issues and establishes the rights and obligations of each party.

Junk Bond A bond that has a low rating, or no rating at all.

Keogh Plan A tax-deferred retirement savings plan available to self-employed individuals.

Landlord The owner, or owner's representative, of rental property.

Lease A written agreement that allows a tenant to use property for a set period of time at a set rent payment.

Lemon A car with substantial defects that the manufacturer has been unable to fix after repeated attempts.

Lemon Laws Laws that protect consumers from the consequences of buying a defective car.

Lessee The person who takes possession of the property.

Lessor The landlord or person responsible for the property.

Leverage The use of borrowed money to buy securities.

Liabilities Money or debts owed to others.

Liability Coverage Insurance to protect against claims for bodily injury to another person or damage to another person's property.

Liability Risk The chance of loss that may occur when your errors or actions result in injuries to others or damages to their property.

Life Insurance Insurance that provides funds to the beneficiaries when the insured dies.

Life-Enhancing Wants Items beyond basic needs that add to your quality of life.

Lifelong Learning Actively seeking new knowledge, skills, and experiences that will add to your professional and personal growth throughout your life.

Lifestyle Business A business that provides a good income for the owner and allows him or her more freedom to meet personal needs.

Line of Credit A preestablished amount that can be borrowed on demand with no collateral.

Liquidation When a merchant wants to sell the inventory immediately to turn it into cash.

Liquidity A measure of how quickly you can get your cash without loss of value.

Load The sales fee charged for buying a mutual fund through a broker.

Loan Origination Fee The amount charged by a bank or other lender to process the loan papers.

Loan Shark An unlicensed lender who charges illegally high interest rates.

Lobbying An organized activity by lobbyists (paid activists) to influence public officials to pass laws and make decisions that benefit a profession.

Long-Term Goal A goal you wish to achieve in five or ten years or longer.

Loss Leader An item of merchandise marked down to an unusually low price, sometimes below the store's cost.

Low-Balling A technique whereby a company advertises a product or service at a low price to lure in customers and then attempts to persuade them that they need additional products or services.

Major Medical Coverage Health insurance coverage that provides protection against the catastrophic expenses of a serious injury or illness.

Market Economy A type of economic system where both market forces (based on individual freedoms) and government decisions determine which goods and services are produced and how they are distributed.

Market Value 1. The highest price that a home will bring on the market. 2. The price for which stock is bought and sold in the marketplace.

Maturity Amount How much you will receive (principal plus accrued interest from date of deposit) if you choose to redeem your certificate of deposit.

Maturity Date The date on which an investment becomes due for payment.

Mediation A non-binding dispute resolution method in which an independent third person, a mediator, helps the parties to reach a voluntary settlement.

Minimum Payment The least amount you may pay each month under your credit agreement.

Money Anything that can be used to settle debt.

Money Market Account A type of savings account that offers a more competitive interest rate than a regular savings account.

Money Market Fund A mutual fund that invests in safe, liquid securities, such as Treasury bills and bonds that mature in less than a year.

Monopoly A market with many buyers but only one seller.

Mortgage A loan to purchase real estate.

Multi-Line Discount A decrease in insurance costs that can occur by having more than one type of policy with the same company.

Multi-Policy Discount A decrease in insurance costs that can occur by insuring more than one vehicle with the same company.

Municipal Bond A bond issued by state and local governments.

Mutual Fund The pooling of money from many investors to buy a large selection of securities.

Negotiable An instrument that is legally collectible.

Negotiation A process in which a neutral third person assists two parties in reaching a compromise that is acceptable to both sides.

Net Asset Value (NAV) The market price for a share of a mutual fund.

Net Pay The amount left after all deductions are taken from an employee's gross pay.

Net Worth The difference between assets and liabilities.

NIST An agency within the U.S. Department of Commerce that develops and rewards standards of excellence in business and sets uniform standards of weights and measures.

No-Fault Insurance Auto insurance in which drivers receive reimbursement for their expenses from their own insurer, no matter who caused the accident.

Notarized A process in which a public notary verifies the signature of a person who signs a document.

Notary Public A person who verifies a person's identity, witnesses the person's signature on a legal document, and then "notarizes" the signature as valid.

NSF Fee An overdraft fee assessed when you spend more than you have in your account and don't have overdraft protection.

Odd-Number Pricing The practice of setting prices at uneven amounts rather than whole dollars to make them seem lower.

Offer An invitation to enter into a contract that is made with serious intent by one person to another person.

Open-End Credit A credit arrangement that enables a borrower to use credit up to a stated limit.

Opportunity Cost The value of your next best choice—what you are giving up.

Opt Out Electing not to accept changes to policies.

Option The right, but not the obligation, to buy or sell stock or a commodity for a specified price within a specified time period.

Overbook When an airline sells more reservations than they can fulfill.

Overdraft A check written for more money than your account contains.

Overdraft Protection A bank service that covers checks even if you have insufficient funds in your checking account.

Overinsuring Buying more insurance than is necessary.

Overtime Time worked beyond regular hours.

Oxidize A chemical reaction with the air that causes paint to permanently lose its color and shine.

Paintless Dent Removal A service in which a suction device is attached to your car to remove small dents.

Par Value An assigned dollar value given to each share of stock.

Pawnbroker (or Pawnshop) A legal business that makes high-interest loans based on the value of personal possessions pledged as collateral.

Payroll Savings Plan A plan in which you authorize your employer to make automatic deductions from your paycheck each pay period.

Penny Stocks Low-priced stocks of small companies that have no track record.

Permanent Investments Investment choices that are held for the long run—five or ten years, or longer.

Permanent Life Insurance A life insurance policy that remains in effect for the insured's lifetime and builds a cash value.

Personal Injury Protection (PIP) Auto insurance that pays for medical, hospital, and funeral costs of the insured and his or her family and passengers, regardless of fault.

Personal Preferences Your likes and dislikes.

Personal Property Floater Additional insurance coverage for valuable items not covered by the basic policy.

Personal Risk The chance of loss involving your income and standard of living.

Phishing A scam that uses online pop-up or e-mail messages to deceive you into disclosing personal information.

Pigeon Drop A scam in which a con artist convinces people to give up their money (or personal information) in return for a share of a larger sum of money.

Plaintiff The person who brings a lawsuit by filing the complaint.

Point System A method of evaluation in a credit bureau assigns points based on several factors to compute credit scores for consumers.

Polishing Compound A substance that can smooth out surface scratches, scuffs, and stains.

Ponzi Scheme A fraudulent investment operation in which money collected from new investors is used to pay off earlier investors.

Portability The feature that allows you to continue paying the premiums and convert your group insurance policy to an individual policy when you leave your employer.

Portfolio A collection of investments.

Power of Attorney A legal document authorizing someone to act on your behalf.

Precious Metals Tangible metals that have known and universal value around the world.

Preexisting Condition Any medical condition that a person has before being enrolled in an insurance plan.

Preferred Stock A type of stock that pays a fixed dividend but has no voting rights.

Premium A fee usually paid at regular intervals by the owner of an insurance policy.

Prequalify The process of determining how much money you are qualified to borrow.

Primary Market A market in which investors can buy stocks and bonds when they are first issued by a company.

Prime Rate The interest rate that banks offer to their best business customers.

Principal 1. The amount of money you deposit into a savings account. 2. The amount borrowed on which the borrower pays interest.

Probate The legal process of proving that a deceased person's will is valid and then administering and distributing that person's estate upon death.

Product Advertising Advertising intended to convince consumers to buy a specific good or service.

Profit Sharing A plan that allows employees to share a portion of the company's profits at the end of the corporate year.

Progressive Tax A tax that takes a larger share of one's income as the amount of income grows.

Property Risk The chance of loss or harm to personal or real property.

Property Settlement Agreement A document specifying the division of assets agreed to by both parties of a divorce couple and entered in court for the judge's approval.

Proportional Tax A tax for which the rate stays the same regardless of one's income.

Prospectus A legal document issued by an investment company that provides details about the securities it offers for sale.

Proxy A stockholder's written authorization to transfer his or her voting rights to someone else, usually a company manager.

Prudent Layperson A reasonable, untrained person in a similar position.

Public Corporation A company whose stock is traded openly on stock markets.

Public Goods The goods and services provided by government to its citizens.

Pure Risk A chance of loss with no chance for gain.

Pyramid Scheme A multilevel marketing plan that promises members (distributors) commissions from their own sales and those of other members they recruit.

Rate The percentage of interest you will pay on a loan.

Rate Shopping Looking around for the best interest rate on an auto or mortgage loan.

Reaffirmation An agreement to pay debts that have been legally discharged.

Real Estate Buildings and land.

Real Estate Investment Trust (REIT) A corporation that pools the money of many individuals to invest in a diversified class of properties.

Real Estate Syndicate A group of investors who pool their money to purchase high-priced real estate as a short-term investment.

Rebate Program A type of credit incentive program in which you get back a portion of what you spent in credit purchases over the year.

Recall A request for consumers to return a defective product to the manufacturer for a refund or repair.

Redress A remedy to a problem.

Reference Letter A statement attesting to your character, abilities, and experience, written by someone who can be relied upon to give a sincere report.

References People who have known you for at least a year and can provide information about your skills, character, and achievements.

Regressive Tax A tax that takes a smaller share of one's income as the amount of income grows.

Rent-to-Own Option Renting furniture with an option to buy at a reduced price at the end of the rental period.

Rental Agreement A month-to-month written contract that allows a tenant to leave a rented residence any time as long as he or she gives the required notice.

Rental Inventory A detailed list of current property conditions.

Renters Insurance Insurance that protects renters from property and liability risks.

Renting The process of using another person's property for a fee.

Replacement Value The cost of replacing an item regardless of its actual cash (market) value.

Reservation An advance commitment to receive a service at a specified later date.

Resume A document that describes your work experience, education, abilities, interests, and other information that may be of interest to an employer.

Retraining Learning new and different skills so that an employee can retain the same level of employability.

Revenue Incoming funds to the government collected from individuals and businesses in the form of taxes.

Revenue Bond A municipal bond issued to raise money for a public-works project.

Reverse Mortgage A loan available to homeowners age 62 and older that allows them to convert part of their home equity into income.

Rewards Card A data mining system that gathers and stores information electronically about purchases and grants points (or rewards) that can be redeemed.

Rewards Program A type of credit incentive program in which you earn points, cash back, airline miles, or other special awards that you can redeem at a later date.

Risk Assessment A systematic study of the risks you face.

Risk Assumption The process of accepting the consequences of risk.

Risk Avoidance Lowering your chance for loss by not engaging in the activity that could result in a loss.

Risk Management An organized strategy for controlling financial loss from pure risks.

Risk Reduction Lowering the chance of loss by taking measures to lessen the frequency or severity of losses that may occur.

Risk Shifting Passing risk to another party.

Roth IRA A type of IRA where contributions are taxed, but earnings are not.

Rule of 72 A technique for estimating the number of years required to double your money at a given rate of return.

Safe Deposit Box A place at your bank available to store valuable items or documents.

Safety of Principal A guarantee that you will not lose your savings deposit, even if the bank or other financial institution fails and goes out of business.

Salary A fixed annual amount of gross pay.

Scarcity A basic economic problem in which consumers' wants are unlimited, while the resources for producing the products to satisfy those wants are limited.

Scholarship A cash allowance awarded to a student to help pay education costs.

SEC An agency whose main purpose is to protect investors and maintain the integrity of the securities markets.

Secondary Market A market that is created when stockholders buy and sell previously issued stocks and bonds from one another with the help of brokers.

Secured Bond A bond that is backed by specific assets that serve as security to assure repayment of the debt.

Securities Exchange A marketplace where brokers who are representing investors meet to buy and sell securities.

Security Deposit A refundable amount that a renter pays in advance to protect the property owner against damage or nonpayment.

Self-Assessment Inventory Lists your strong and weak points along with plans for improvement.

Self-Employment Working for yourself

Seller's Acceptance A formal agreement to the terms of the buyer's offer, forming a contract between the parties.

Seller's Counteroffer A rejection of the original offer with a listing of what terms would be acceptable.

Semiformal Wedding A wedding that is usually held during the afternoon or early evening, typically at a church, with less formal wear required of guests.

Seniority The length of time a person has held a job.

Service Credit The providing of a service for which you will pay later.

Service Job A job in which you perform a task or a service for a person or business.

Share Account A savings account representing ownership interest.

Short Selling Selling stock borrowed from a broker that must be replaced at a later time.

Short-Term Goal A goal you expect to reach in a few days or weeks.

Side Business A business where the owner pursues his or her avocation, or secondary occupation, while also working full time for an employer.

Simple Interest Interest computed only on the amount borrowed, without compounding.

Simplified Employee Pension (SEP) Plan A tax-deferred retirement plan available to small businesses.

Small Claims Court A court of limited jurisdiction that resolves cases involving small amounts.

Social Media Forms of electronic communication, such as websites, through which users create online communities to share information.

Socialist Economic System A type of hands-on economic system characterized by a large degree of government control of many of the decisions within the nation.

Space-Shifting Allows media, such as music or films, stored on one device to be accessed from another place through another device.

Special Account A type of checking account that most banks offer to customers who have a small amount of activity in their accounts each month.

Speculative Investing Making bold and high-risk investment choices.

Speculative Risk A risk that may result in either gain or loss.

Spousal Support Money paid by one former spouse to support the other.

Spreadsheet A computer program that organizes data in columns and rows and performs calculations using the data.

Standard Account A type of checking account that usually has a small (or no) monthly service fee and no per-check fee.

Statute of Frauds A law in every state which requires that some contracts must be in writing to be enforceable.

Sticker Price The price shown on the tag in the car's window.

Stock A unit of ownership in a corporation.

Stock Split An increase in the number of outstanding shares of a company's stock.

Stop-Loss Provision An insurance clause that caps or sets a maximum that the insured has to pay out of pocket during any calendar year.

Stop-Payment Order A request that the bank not honor a specific check.

Strategic Investing The careful management of investment alternatives to maximize growth of your portfolio over the next five to ten years.

Studio Apartment An apartment with one large room that serves as the living room, dining area, and bedroom.

Subscribers Businesses that supply information to credit bureaus about their customers' accounts.

Subsidized Loan A form of federal financial aid for which you pay no interest until after you have completed your education, or are no longer enrolled in school.

Sunk Cost An expense that occurred in the past for which money was spent and cannot be recovered.

Systematic Investing Making investments on a regular and planned basis.

Target Market A specific consumer group to which products are designed to appeal.

Tax A payment imposed on a taxpayer by a governmental unit.

Tax Bracket An income range that a tax rate is applied to.

Tax Credit   A reduction of taxes owed.

Tax Evasion   Willful failure to pay taxes.

Tax Liability   The amount of total tax you owe on a year's income.

Tax Shelter   A legal write-off that reduces tax liability.

Taxable Income   The income on which you will pay tax.

Telecommuting   A work model that allows employees to work off-site and remain in contact with their employers through the use of technology.

Temporary Investments   Investment choices that should be re-evaluated within a year or less.

Temporary Life Insurance   A life insurance policy that remains in effect for a specified period of time.

Tenant   A person who rents property.

Time   The period during which the borrower will repay a loan.

Time-Shifting   Recording a video or audio for later viewing or listening.

Title   Legally established ownership to property.

Title Insurance   A policy that protects the buyer from any claims arising from a defective title.

Townhouse   A living space that has two or more levels.

Trade-Off   Getting something in return for giving up something else.

Traditional Economic System   A type of hands-off economic system in which the people decide what decisions will be made and how they will be made.

Traditional IRA   A type of IRA in which you can deduct your contributions each year from your taxable income.

Transcripts   School records that include a listing of courses you have taken along with the credits and grades you've received for them.

Travel Agency   A business that arranges transportation, accommodations, and itineraries for customers.

Trespasser   An unlawful intruder.

Trust   A legal document in which an individual gives someone else control of property, for ultimate distribution to another person.

U

Umbrella Liability Insurance   A supplement to your basic auto and property liability coverage that expands limits and includes additional risks.

Unfair Labor Practice (ULP)   A complaint filed by an employee claiming violation of a labor contract.

Unfurnished Rental   A rental unit that may or may not include basic kitchen appliances, such as a stove and refrigerator, but little else.

Uninsured/Underinsured Motorist Coverage   Auto insurance that pays for your injuries when the other driver is legally liable but unable to pay.

Uninvited Guest   A person presumed to have permission to be on your property.

Union   A group of people who work in the same or similar occupations, organized for the benefit of the employees in those occupations.

Unit Pricing   Tells you how much it costs per ounce or other unit of measure.

Unsubsidized Loan   A form of federal financial aid that starts accruing interest as soon as you use it to pay for tuition or other education costs.

Unused Credit   The remaining credit available to you on current accounts.

Upgrading   Advancing to a higher level of skill to increase your usefulness to an employer.

USDA   An agency responsible for developing and executing federal government policy on farming, agriculture, forestry, and food.

Used Car Rule   A law enforced by the Federal Trade Commission that requires that dealers fully disclose to buyers what is and not covered under warranty for the used vehicle.

USPIS   A federal law enforcement agency that investigates consumer problems pertaining to illegal use of the mail.

Usury Law   A state law that sets a maximum interest rate that may be charged for consumer loans.

V

Values   The principles by which a person lives.

Variable Expenses   Costs that vary in amount and type, depending on the choices you make.

Variable-Rate Loan   A loan for which the interest rate goes up and down with inflation and other economic conditions.

Vehicle Emission Test   A test to verify that a vehicle meets the minimum clean-air standards.

Vehicle Identification Number (VIN)   An alphanumeric number that identifies each vehicle manufactured or sold in the United States.

Venture Business   A business in which the owner wants it to grow into a large company with unlimited growth potential.

Verdict The decision reached by a jury.

Vested The point at which employees have full rights to their retirement accounts.

Voluntary Bankruptcy Bankruptcy that occurs when a debtor files a petition with a federal court asking to be declared bankrupt.

Voluntary Compliance A system in which all citizens prepare and file tax returns on their own.

Wage A fixed hourly rate earned by employees.

Warranty A statement assuring quality and performance of a product or service.

Wealth The accumulation of assets.

Wedding Party The people who are active participants in the wedding ceremony.

Will A legal document that tells how an estate is to be distributed when a person dies.

Work-Study A program that permits students to work at the campus or other college location to earn money.

Zero-Coupon Bond A bond that is sold at a deep discount, makes no interest payments, and is redeemable for its face value at maturity.

Index

Frivolous lawsuits, 640
Front-end load, 458
FTC. *See* Federal Trade
Commission (FTC)
FTC used-car rule, 326
Full coverage, 539
Full-service banks, 117. *See also*
Commercial banks
Full-service brokers, 390, 442
Funerals
costs of, 359–360
letter of instruction, 506
nontraditional, 359
Furnished rental, 279
Future value, 497–499
Futures (investing), 395, 467

Garnishment, 201
Gems, 368, 466
General obligation bond (GO),
438
General power of attorney, 480
Generic Drug Act, 618
Generic drugs, 617
Gift in contemplation of death,
482
Gift registry, 345
Gift taxes, 482
Giving circles, 657
Global fund, 456
Global View
arranged marriages, 346
"career break schemes"
(Australia), 40
credit cards in Thailand, 160
earthquake and tsunamis, 519
the euro, 384
European debt crisis, 444
foreign investing in the United
States, 411
Japanese disposable income, 141
Women's World Banking
(WWB), 119
World Bank financial assistance,
594

Goals
checklist, 25
defined, 24
as influence on spending,
260
intermediate, 25
long-term, 25
short-term, 25
Gold cards, 228
Gold standard, 593
Good credit rating, 188
Good impression, interview,
18–19
Google, 3
Google Plus, 4
Governmental assistance,
646–648
Government and public
administration, careers,
229
Government bonds
agency, 439
municipal, 437–438
savings bonds and treasury
securities, 438–439
tax-exempt, 437, 447
Government health care plans,
555–556
Government National Mortgage
Association (Ginnie Mae),
465
Government-sponsored
enterprises, 439
Government-sponsored retirement
plans, 489–490
Grace period, 165
for bill payments, 188
for credit card payments, 213
Grant, 131
The Graphics Group, 149
Great Recession, and credit,
194
Grievance (unions), 49
Gross income, 65–66, 80
Gross pay, 35
Group budgeting, 282
Group dental and vision
insurance, 41

Group insurance, 40–41, 521,
549–550
Consolidated Omnibus Budget
Reconciliation Act (COBRA),
550
double coverage, 550
flexible benefit plans, 550
Health Insurance Portability
and Accountability Act
(HIPAA), 550
Group life insurance plan, 41,
561–562
Growth and income fund, 454
Growth fund, 454
Growth stocks, 404
Guarantee, 95, 368
Guaranteed insurability riders, 563
Guaranteed-payment checks,
117–118
Guest, 531

Hands-off system, 588
capitalism, 588
others, 588
traditional, 588
Hands-on system, 587–588
communism, 587
socialism, 588
Hatch-Waxman Act, 618
Hazardous Substances Act,
616
Health and medical product
frauds, 600–601
Health care
costs, 578–579
decisions, as element of estate
planning, 506
directive, 505–506
power of attorney, 505
Health insurance
defined, 549
exchanges, 551–552
group, 549–550
group policies, 40–41
individual, 550–551

N

Usury law, 168–169
Utilities
  as homeowner's expense, 303
  installation charges, 281–282
  security deposit on, 278
Utility, 590

V

Vacant land, as investment, 461
Vacation, paid, 40
Vacation homes, 462–463
Vacation pay, 40
Vacation planning
  air travel, 348–350
  at-home preparations, 350
  itineraries, 348
  kind of vacation, 348
  last-minute details, 350–351
  online travel planning, 352
  reservations, 348
Value Line, 389
Values
  collective, 255–256
  and ethics, 658
  as influence on choices, 253
  as influence on spending, 260
  types of, in real estate, 298
Vanguard investments, 457, 471
Variable expenses, 82
Variable life policy, 565
Variable-rate loans, 209, 217
Vehicle costs
  accessories, 332–333
  depreciation, 331
  fuel, 330–331
  maintenance and repairs,
    333–334
  registration and title,
    331–332
  vehicle emission fee, 332
Vehicle emission fee, 332
Vehicle emission test, 322, 332
Vehicle identification number
    (VIN), 321
Venture business, 28

Verdict, 641
Vested, 488
Veterans Administration, 360,
    490
View Points
  adjustable interest rates on
    housing, 302
  on bailouts, 589
  bankruptcy laws, 234
  cell phone use, while driving,
    333
  credit cards marketed to college
    students, 202
  on frivolous lawsuits, 640
  Internet cookies and invasion of
    privacy, 263
  on labeled foods, 619
  mutual funds, 457
  national debt, 438
  permanent life insurance,
    564
  roommate difficulties, 278
  on safe driving, 514
  safety of information stored in
    computer, 97
  schools supported by property
    taxes, 61
Vision insurance, 41, 553
Voir dire, 640
Voluntary arbitration, 649
Voluntary bankruptcy, 232
Voluntary compliance (tax
    payments), 61
Volunteerism, 657

W

Wages, 35. *See also* Pay
  for tax purposes, 65
Waiver of premium riders, 563
Wall Street Journal, 389
Warranties
  on automobiles, 324–326
  defined, 95
  types of, 95
Wealth, defined, 85

Web mining, 4
Websites. *See also* Internet; Social
    media
  keywords, 3
Wedding party, 344
Whole life policy, 565
Wholesome Meat Act, 616
Will, 477, 478
Withholding, of taxes, 37–39
Withholding payment, in
    purchase dispute, 644–645
Women's World Banking
    (WWB), 119
Work environment, 46–47
  telecommuting, 46
Work schedules
  compressed workweek, 47
  flextime, 46
  job rotation, 47
  job sharing, 47
  permanent part-time, 47
  telecommuting, 46
Work-study programs, 131
Workplace safety, 583
World Bank, 594
Wozniak, Steve, 149
Written warranties, 95
WWB. *See* Women's World
    Banking (WWB)

Y

Yahoo!, 3
  finance websites, 457
Yellen, Janet, 571
Yield, 133, 142
YouTube, 4

Z

*0*NET* (DOT), 13
Zero-coupon bond, 436–437
Zoning laws, 303, 463–464
Zuckerberg, Mark, 657